A DOCUMENTARY HISTORY OF AMERICAN LIFE

General Editor: **David Donald,** *The Johns Hopkins University*

Democracy on Trial:

1845–1877

Edited by **ROBERT W. JOHANNSEN**

University of Illinois

Volume 4

A Documentary History of American Life

General Editor: **David Donald**

The Johns Hopkins University

McGRAW-HILL BOOK COMPANY

New York St. Louis San Francisco Toronto London Sydney

Selection 15 is from *Jefferson Davis, Constitutionalist: His Letters. Papers, and Speeches* edited by Dunbar Rowland (Jackson, Miss.: Printed for the Miss. Dept. of Archives & History by J. J. Ives, New York, 1923), IV, pp. 250–280. Reprinted by permission of the Mississippi Department of Archives and History, Jackson, Mississippi.

Selection 29 is reprinted with permission of The Macmillan Company from *The Diary of George Templeton Strong* edited by Allan Nevins and Milton Halsey Thomas. Copyright 1952 by The Macmillan Company.

Selection 38 is from *The Wartime Papers of R. E. Lee* edited by Clifford Dowdey and Louis H. Manarin. Copyright © 1961 by Commonwealth of Virginia. By permission of Little, Brown and Company, publishers.

DEMOCRACY ON TRIAL: 1845–1877

Library of Congress Catalog Card Number 66–14534

1234567890   HD   7321069876

The history of the United States is more a matter of record than is that of any other major world power that has ever existed. The beginnings of our nation are not shrouded in myth or in medieval obscurity, for they can be traced in the precise and explicit directives which the English sovereigns gave their subjects who went to explore or inhabit the New World. At the other end of the time scale, the government of the United States has swiftly moved to declassify and to help publish even the "top secret" papers of World War II and after. For every intervening period the documentary record is voluminous and comprehensive.

A Documentary History of American Life presents an extensive, representative sampling of that vast record. It differs in a number of important ways from the several collections of documents already available to teachers and students. In the first place, it provides the most extensive coverage yet attempted for the entire history of America, from the first expedition of Walter Raleigh through the "Great Society" message to Congress by President Lyndon B. Johnson. The eight volumes of this series, containing approximately 2 million words, afford for the first time a canvas of sufficient size on which to present the panorama of the American past in its full complexity and detail. Moreover, the scope of the series allows the publication of all the significant portions of each document, not merely of selected snippets. Of course, not even a work of this size can include every document relating to American history, but for most students there is abundance here, and each teacher can choose those writings which best fit the needs of his particular courses.

A second major feature of the series is its variety. The seven editors, who have worked closely together during the preparation of these books, agree in rejecting the old notion that a document is necessarily a law, a treaty, or a Supreme Court decision. All these, to be sure, are here present, but so are diary accounts, contemporary letters, essays, poems, and cartoons. All the volumes include documents to illustrate our social, economic, and intellectual, as well as our political and diplomatic, history.

The series is further distinguished by its pedagogical usefulness. Teachers themselves, the seven editors are alert to the problems of college teaching in an age when classes are large and much of the actual instruction must be done by beginning instructors often only a few steps ahead of their pupils. Not just documents are needed, but documents whose relevance is explained and whose implications are explored. For each document, or group of documents, in this series, therefore, there is a full editorial introduction and a brief bibliographical note.

As a result, *A Documentary History of American Life* offers a rich fare to both beginning and advanced students who seek to know our country's history. The editors present these volumes in the profound conviction that only if our citizens understand the past can they intelligently face the future.

The Johns Hopkins University   *David Donald*

PREFACE

Walt Whitman once observed, with reference to the civil conflict then raging in the United States, that "the real war will never get in the books." He was probably right. The proportions of the Civil War are not easily comprehended by a generation removed from it by a century's time. The American people were touched deeply, and scarred, in ways that are difficult to appreciate. Nevertheless, the impact of the war on human beings—their suffering, their disillusion and disappointment, their hopes and aspirations—serves as a continuing challenge to the historian who would reconstruct the past as it was lived. It is hoped that this collection of documents might help to meet this challenge.

The thirty-two-year period covered in this volume opened with expressions of optimism and enthusiasm for the future greatness of Americans and of American democratic institutions. It closed on the same note of hope. The intervening years, however, were tragic years for the American people. Aside from the human suffering, the period witnessed the failure of the very democracy that had been so lavishly extolled. The nation grappled with issues that apparently could not be solved within the democratic process; at least, they were not so solved. The forum of debate and discussion was abandoned in favor of the arbitration of arms. Abraham Lincoln recognized the true significance of the conflict when he said the "issue embraces more than the fate of these United States. It presents to the whole family of man, the question, whether a constitutional republic, or a democracy—a government of the people, by the same people—can, or cannot, maintain its territorial integrity, against its own domestic foes." Democracy, in a very real sense, was on trial.

From out of the tragic holocaust, however, emerged a new and stronger democracy. The naïve enthusiasms of the earlier years gave way to a grim determination to erect an enduring edifice that could demonstrate the worth of human endeavor and the noble tenets of freedom and equality, one that could fulfill the mission which Lincoln so frequently and so eloquently described. Democracy not only had overcome its failure and survived the trial but had also received a renewed commitment from the American people.

The documents which follow have been selected to illustrate in all its facets the travail of Americans between 1845 and 1877. Perhaps they may contribute, in their way, to a further understanding of what Lincoln aptly called America's "great national crisis."

Robert W. Johannsen

CONTENTS

PART **11** The Danger Within

PART **12** Our Fearful Trip Is Done

PART **13** Common Sense and Christian Charity

PART **14** No Inflexible Plan Can Safely Be Prescribed

PART **15** It Is Time That Congress Should Assert Its Sovereignty

PART ONE

Young America

March 4, 1845, was gloomy and rainy in Washington, D.C., as the new President, James Knox Polk, prepared to deliver his Inaugural Address. Shielded from the elements by an umbrella, Polk spurned the arrangements to speak indoors and delivered his address to the people of the United States from the capitol steps. This new young President disclosed, as was the custom, the principles that would guide him in his administration but in doing so he spoke also in glowing terms of the tasks to which the American people had dedicated themselves. The United States, "this Heaven-favored land," he asserted confidently, enjoyed the "most admirable and wisest system of well-regulated self-government among men ever devised by human minds." It was the "noblest structure of human wisdom" wherein burned the fire of liberty, warming and animating "the hearts of happy millions" and inviting "all the nations of the earth to imitate our example." America's people, under the benign influence of their government, were "free to improve their own condition by the legitimate exercise of all their mental and physical powers." They were "permitted collectively and individually to seek their own happiness in their own way." "Who shall assign limits to the achievements of free minds and free hands under the protection of this glorious Union?" he asked.

This was the vision of a youthful America. The nation, like its new President, was yet young—barely three-score-and-ten years old. In its short existence, the United States had enjoyed advantages of growth that were denied to most new nations. Perched on the edge of a vast and untapped wilderness, the nation had room to expand and abundant natural resources to become strong and self-sufficient. Separated from the power struggles of Europe, the United States could develop freely and without serious challenge from rival nations and nationalities (a freedom that was especially evident following the War of 1812). Heterogeneous in the character of its population, newly settled, the nation was free of the bonds of tradition; its people, lacking a common past, found *unity in their hopes for the future. By the 1840s, these hopes for the future had become a broad vision that defied limitation. When President Polk delivered his inaugural lines, he was speaking the sentiments of millions of confident, optimistic Americans.*

This American vision had become a national faith, manifested in many ways. A deep and abiding belief in the superiority of democratic institutions and the conviction that America's future was being guided by a benign destiny inspired a desire for expansion, both ideological and territorial. The phrase "manifest destiny" was employed to describe their responsibility for expansion. Americans felt a high sense of duty, convinced that they had in fact a mission to accomplish in the world since they were, in the high-flown rhetoric of the period, the trustees of humanity. The 1840s were years of great and dramatic territorial expansion as the national flag was firmly planted on the Pacific shores and the United States came closer to the dream of an "ocean-bound republic." Just as important as the extension of its boundaries was the example the nation set for the world to see and to emulate, an example of democratic success and strength unequaled in the history of mankind.

This was a new age of individualism, of opportunity, and of the determination to protect all individuals in the enjoyment of their opportunities. A new concern for the welfare of the individual, coupled with a renewed commitment to the gospel of the Revolutionary fathers, produced a great movement for social change and humanitarian reform. Individual perfection, like national perfection, was within reach; a myriad of reform associations appeared, all seeking the removal of the barriers— social, institutional, political, and religious—which lay in the path. It was a period of bold social experimentation; utopian idealists sought to rearrange society and to guarantee the fullest individual expression through communitarian patterns. Reformers, undaunted by the magnitude of their tasks, attacked liquor, prison conditions, Negro slavery, war, and discrimination against women. Transcendentalists sought to free men's minds, revivalist preachers to free men's souls. Americans of every type and character joined hands in a grand attempt to lead themselves and their neighbors up the rocky and uncertain pathway of human progress.

The vision of "young America" was not all a starry-eyed idealism, but was based on hard realities and the material considerations of national growth as well. Manifest destiny, for example, was stimulated by a desire to carry the nation's flag to the far corners of the American continent, to open up new regions to economic penetration, and to protect a grow-

ing commercial interest. *A need for social reform sprang from the rise of a new industrialism, the growth of a factory system, and all the social problems this produced. The new role of the common man in political life and in governmental administration necessarily resulted in a new concern for the integrity of his personality and individualism. The increased mobility of America's population—immigration from Europe, the rise of the city, and the westward movement—suggested the need for new patterns of social relationships.*

This was young America. Americans were convinced that they, a chosen people, stood on the threshold of true greatness. In the words of one lowly spokesman, the present was but the germ of a still more glorious future. That the future might not hold the glories they envisioned was a prospect they would not seriously entertain. Yet just sixteen years after President Polk gave voice to the faith in America's greatness, the nation lay divided, suffering all the agonies of bloody civil war. The future of democracy itself seemed in doubt.

Ralph Waldo Emerson on the American Character: "The Young American," 1844

Ralph Waldo Emerson (1803–1882), the famous seer of American transcendentalism, was one of the great spokesmen of youthful America whose writings reflect the hopes and aspirations, as well as the confident optimism for the future of man and nation, that characterized American thought during the 1830s and 1840s. Emerson's transcendentalism itself was a means by which man could break the shackles of intellectual conformity and achieve what Emerson repeatedly preached as "self-reliance." The Concord philosopher was strongly concerned with the American national character, its definition and development—a problem with which American thinkers have perennially wrestled. Like many other writers of the period, such as James Fenimore Cooper, Nathaniel Hawthorne, Herman Melville, and Walt Whitman, Emerson called for a distinctive American cultural expression, a truly American national literature, that could reflect national character. The youthful United States, he felt, held a key to the future promise of mankind, being untrammeled by tradition and wholly pliable. Such a promise, he often argued (as in the selection that follows), must be expressed in a genuine national form. America was unique, Americans were unique, American cultural development must be unique and native. It was a literary nationalism to accompany the political and economic nationalism. This cultural milieu resulted in a great flowering of literary activity and achievement in the United States during the 1840s and 1850s, a period frequently referred to as the "American Renaissance."

Emerson's essay, "The Young American," was first delivered as a lecture before the Boston Mercantile Library Association, February 7, 1844. It is reprinted from Dial, *volume 4, April, 1844, pages 484–507. The best edition of Emerson's works is the Centenary Edition, Edward Waldo Emerson (ed.),* The Complete Works of Ralph Waldo Emerson *(1903–1904), twelve volumes; the best biography, Ralph L. Rusk,* The Life of Ralph Waldo Emerson *(1949). For a penetrating discussion and analysis of the movement for a national literature, see Benjamin T. Spencer,* The Quest for Nationality: An American Literary Campaign *(1957).*

It is remarkable, that our people have their intellectual culture from one country, and their duties from another. Our books are European. We were born within the fame and sphere of Shakespeare and Milton, of Bacon, Dryden and Pope; our college text-books are the writings of Butler, Locke, Paley, Blackstone, and Stewart; and our domestic reading has been Clarendon and Hume, Addison and Johnson, Young and Cowper, Edgeworth and Scott, Southey, Coleridge and Wordsworth, and the Edinburgh and Quarterly Reviews. We are sent to a feudal school to learn democracy. A gulf yawns for the young American between his education and his work. We are like the all-accomplished banker's daughter, who, when her education was finished, and her father had become a bankrupt, and she was asked what she could do for him in his sickness and misfortunes,—could she make a shirt, mix bread, scald milk pans? No, but she could waltz, and cut rice-paper, and paint velvet, and transfer drawings, and make satin stitch, and play on the clavicord, and sing German songs, and act charades, and arrange tableaux, and a great many other equally useful and indispensable performances. It has seemed verily so with the education of our young men; the system of thought was the growth of monarchical institutions, whilst those that were flourishing around them were not consecrated to their imagination nor interpreted to their understanding.

This false state of things is newly in a way to be corrected. America is beginning to assert itself to the senses and to the imagination of her children, and Europe is receding in the same degree. This their reaction on education gives a new importance to the internal improvements and to the politics of the country.

There is no American citizen who has not been stimulated to reflection by the facilities now in progress of construction for travel and the transportation of goods in the United States. The alleged effect to augment disproportionately the size of cities, is in a rapid course of fulfilment in this metropolis of New England.

The growth of Boston, never slow, has been so accelerated since the railroads have been opened which join it to Providence, to Albany, and to Portland, that the extreme depression of general trade has not concealed it from the most careless eye. The narrow peninsula, which a few years ago easily held its thirty or forty thousand people, with many pastures and waste lands, not to mention the large private gardens in the midst of the town, has been found too strait when forty are swelled to a hundred thousand. The waste lands have been fenced in and builded over, the private gardens one after the other have become streets. Boston proper consisted of seven hundred and twenty acres of land. Acre after acre has been since won from the sea, and in a short time the antiquary will find it difficult to trace the peninsular topography. Within the last year, the newspapers tell us, from twelve to fifteen hundred buildings of all sorts have been erected, many of them of a rich and durable character. And because each of the new avenues of iron road ramifies like the bough of a tree, the growth of the city proceeds at a geometrical rate. Already a new road is shooting northwest towards the Connecticut and Montreal; and every great line of road that is completed makes cross sections from road to road more practicable, so that the land will presently be mapped in a network of iron.

This rage for road building is beneficent for America, where vast distance is so main a consideration in our domestic politics and trade,

5

inasmuch as the great political promise of the invention is to hold the Union staunch, whose days seemed already numbered by the mere inconvenience of transporting representatives, judges, and officers, across such tedious distances of land and water. Not only is distance annihilated, but when, as now, the locomotive and the steamboat, like enormous shuttles, shoot every day across the thousand various threads of national descent and employment, and bind them fast in one web, an hourly assimilation goes forward, and there is no danger that local peculiarities and hostilities should be preserved.

The new power is hardly less noticeable in its relation to the immigrant population, chiefly to the people of Ireland, as having given employment to hundreds of thousands of the natives of that country, who are continually arriving in every vessel from Great Britain.

In an uneven country the railroad is a fine object in the making. It has introduced a multitude of picturesque traits into our pastoral scenery. The tunneling of mountains, the bridging of streams, the bold mole carried out into a broad silent meadow, silent and unvisited by any but its own neighbors since the planting of the region; the encounter at short distances along the track of gangs of laborers; the energy with which they strain at their tasks; the cries of the overseer or *boss;* the character of the work itself, which so violates and revolutionizes the primal and immemorial forms of nature; the village of shanties, at the edge of beautiful lakes until now the undisturbed haunt of the wild duck, and in the most sequestered nooks of the forest, around which the wives and children of the Irish are seen; the number of foreigners, men and women, whom now the woodsman encounters singly in the forest paths; the blowing of rocks, explosions all day, with the occasional alarm of frightful accident, and the indefinite promise of what the new channel of trade may do and undo for the rural towns, keep the senses and imagination active; and the varied aspects of the enterprise make it the topic of all companies, in cars and boats, and by firesides.

This picture is a little saddened, when too nearly seen, by the wrongs that are done in the contracts that are made with the laborers. Our hospitality to the poor Irishman has not much merit in it. We pay the poor fellow very ill. To work from dark to dark for sixty, or even fifty cents a day, is but pitiful wages for a married man. It is a pittance when paid in cash; but when, as generally happens, through the extreme wants of the one party, met by the shrewdness of the other, he draws his pay in clothes and food, and in other articles of necessity, his case is still worse; he buys everything at disadvantage, and has no adviser or protector. Besides, the labor done is excessive, and the sight of it reminds one of negro-driving. Good farmers and sturdy laborers say that they have never seen so much work got out of a man in a day. Poor fellows! Hear their stories of their exodus from the old country, and their landing in the new, and their fortunes appear as little under their own control as the leaves of the forest around them. As soon as the ship that brought them is anchored, one is whirled off to Albany, one to Ohio, one digs at the levee at New Orleans, and one beside the waterwheels at Lowell, some fetch and carry on the wharves of New York and Boston, some in the woods of Maine. They have too little money, and too little knowledge, to allow them the exercise of much more election of whither to go, or what to do, than the leaf that is blown into this dike or that brook to perish.

And yet their plight is not so grievous as it seems. The escape from the squalid despair of their condition at home, into the unlimited opportunities of their existence here, must be reckoned a gain. The Irish father and mother are very ill paid, and are victims of fraud and private oppression; but their children are instantly received into the schools of the country; they grow up in perfect communication and equality with the native children, and owe to their parents a vigor of constitution which promises them at least an even chance in the competitions of the new generation. Whether it is this confidence that puts a drop of sweetness in their cup, or whether the buoyant spirits natural to the race, it is certain that they seem to have almost a monopoly of the vivacity and good nature in our towns, and contrast broadly, in that particular, with the native people. In the village where I reside, through which a railroad is being built, the charitable ladies, who, moved by the report of the wrongs and distresses of the newly arrived laborers, explored the shanties, with offers of relief, were surprised to find the most civil reception, and the most bounding sportfulness from the oldest to the youngest. Perhaps they may thank these dull shovels as safe vents for peccant humors; and this grim day's work of fifteen or sixteen hours, though deplored by all the humanity of the neighborhood, is a better police than the sheriff and his deputies.

1. But I have abstained too long from speaking of that which led me to this topic,—its importance in creating an American sentiment. An unlooked for consequence of the railroad, is the increased acquaintance it has given the American people with the boundless resources of their own soil. If this invention has reduced England to a third of its size, by bringing people so much near, in this country it has given a new celerity to *time,* or anticipated by fifty years the planting of tracts of land, the choice of water-privileges, the working of mines, and other natural advantages. Railroad iron is a magician's rod, in its power to evoke the sleeping energies of land and water.

The railroad is but one arrow in our quiver, though it has great value as a sort of yard-stick, and surveyor's line. The bountiful continent is ours, state on state, and territory on territory, to the waves of the Pacific sea;

> "Our garden is the immeasurable earth,
> The heaven's blue pillars are Medea's house,"

and new duties, new motives await and cheer us. The task of planting, of surveying, of building upon this immense tract, requires an education and a sentiment commensurate thereto. A consciousness of this fact, is beginning to take the place of the purely trading spirit and education which sprang up whilst all the population lived on the fringe of sea-coast. And even on the coast, prudent men have begun to see that every American should be educated with a view to the values of land. The arts of engineering and of architecture are studied; scientific agriculture is an object of growing attention; the mineral riches are explored; limestone, coal, slate, and iron; and the value of timber-lands is enhanced.

Columbus alleged as a reason for seeking a continent in the West, that the harmony of nature required a great tract of land in the western hemisphere, to balance the known extent of land in the eastern; and it now appears that we must estimate the native values of this immense region to redress the balance of our own judgment, and appreciate the advantages opened to the human race in this country, which is our fortunate home. The land is the appointed remedy for whatever is false and fantastic in our culture. The great continent we inhabit is to be physic and food for our mind, as well as our body. The land, with its tranquillizing, sanative influences, is to repair the errors of a scholastic and traditional education, and bring us into just relations with men and things.

This habit of living in the presence of these invitations of natural wealth is not inoperative; and this habit, combined with the moral sentiment which, in the recent years, has interrogated every institution, and usage, and law, has, very naturally, given a strong direction to the wishes and aims of active young men to withdraw from cities, and cultivate the soil. This inclination has appeared in the most unlooked for quarters, in men supposed to be absorbed in business, and in those connected with the liberal professions. And since the walks of trade were crowded, whilst that of agriculture cannot easily be, inasmuch as the farmer who is not wanted by others, can yet grow his own bread, whilst the manufacturer or the trader who is not wanted, cannot,—this seemed a happy tendency. For, beside all the moral benefit which we may expect from the farmer's profession, when a man enters it from moral causes, this promised the conquering of the soil, plenty, and beyond this, the adorning of the whole continent with every advantage and ornament which labor, ingenuity, and affection for a man's home, could suggest. This great savage country should be furrowed by the plough, and combed by the harrow; these rough Alleganies should know their master; these foaming torrents should be bestridden by proud arches of stone; these wild prairies should be loaded with wheat; the swamps with rice; the hill-tops should pasture innumerable sheep and cattle; the interminable forests should become graceful parks, for use and for delight.

In this country, where land is cheap, and the disposition of the people pacific, every thing invites to the arts of agriculture, of gardening, and domestic architecture. Public gardens, on the scale of such plantations in Europe and Asia, are now unknown to us. There is no feature of the old countries that more agreeably and newly strikes an American, than the beautiful gardens of Europe; such as the Boboli in Florence, the Villa Borghese in Rome, the Villa d'Este in Tivoli: works easily imitated here, and which might well make the land dear to the citizen, and inflame patriotism. It is the fine art which is left for us, now that sculpture, and painting, and religious and civil architecture have become effete, and have passed into second childhood. We have twenty degrees of latitude wherein to choose a seat, and the new modes of travelling enlarge the opportunity of selection, by making it easy to cultivate very distant tracts, and yet remain in strict intercourse with the centres of trade and population. And the whole force of all the arts goes to facilitate the decoration of lands and dwellings. A garden has this advantage, that it makes it indifferent where you live. A well-laid garden makes the face of the country about you of no account; low or high, grand or mean, you have made a beautiful abode worthy of man. If the landscape is pleasing, the garden shows it,—if tame, it excludes it. A little grove, which any farmer can find, or cause to grow near his house, will, in a few years, so fill the eye and mind of the inhabitant, as to make cataracts and chains of mountains quite unnecessary to his scenery; and he is so contented with his alleys, woodlands, orchards, and river, that Niagara, and the Notch of the White Hills, and Nantasket Beach, are superfluities. And yet the selection of a fit houselot has the same advantage over an indifferent one, as the selection to a given employment of a man who has a genius for that work. In the last case, all the culture of years will never make the most painstaking scholar his equal: no more will gardening give the advantage of a happy site to a house in a hole or on a pinnacle. "God Almighty first planted a garden," says Lord Bacon, "and it is the purest of human pleasures. It is the greatest refreshment to the spirits of man, without which, buildings and palaces are but gross handyworks; and a man shall ever see that when ages grow to civility and elegancy, men come to build stately, sooner than to garden finely, as if gardening were the greater perfection." Bacon has followed up this sentiment in his two Essays *on Buildings,* and *on Gardens,* with many pleasing details on the decoration of lands; and Aubrey has given us an engaging account of the manner in which Bacon finished his own manor at Gorhambury. In America, we have hitherto little to boast in this kind. The cities continually drain the country of the best part of its population: the flower of the youth, of both sexes, goes into the towns, and the country is cultivated by a so much inferior class. The land,—travel a whole day together,—looks poverty-stricken, and the buildings plain and poor. In Europe, where society has an aristocratic structure, the land is full of men of the best stock, and the best culture, whose interest and pride it is to remain half the year on their estates, and to fill them with every convenience and ornament. Of course these make model farms, and model architecture, and are a constant education to the eye of the surrounding population. Whatever events in progress shall go to disgust men with cities, and infuse into them the passion for country-life, and country-pleasures, will render a prodigious service to the whole face of this continent, and will further the most poetic of all the occupations of real life, the bringing out by art the native but hidden graces of the landscape.

I look on such improvements, also, as directly tending to endear the land to the inhabitant, and give him whatever is valuable in local attachment. Any relation to the land, the habit of tilling it, or mining it, or even hunting on it, generates the feeling of patriotism. He who keeps shop on it, or he who merely uses it as a support to his desk and ledger, or to his manufactory, values it very little. The vast majority of the people of this country live by the land, and carry its quality in their manners and opinions. We in the Atlantic states, by position, have been commercial, and have, as I said, imbibed easily an European culture. Luckily for us, now that steam has narrowed the Atlantic to a strait, the nervous, rocky West is intruding a new and continental element into the national mind, and we shall yet have an American genius. How much better when the whole land is a garden, and the people have grown up in the bowers of a paradise. Without looking, then, to those extraordinary social influences which are now acting in precisely this direction, but only at what is inevitably doing around us, I think we must regard the *land* as a commanding and increasing power on the American citizen, the sanative and Americanizing influence, which promises to disclose new powers for ages to come.

2. In the second place, the uprise and culmination of the new and anti-feudal power of Commerce, is the political fact of most significance to the American at this hour.

We cannot look on the freedom of this country, in connexion with its youth, without a presentiment that here shall laws and institutions exist on some scale of proportion to the majesty of nature. To men legislating for the vast area betwixt the two oceans, betwixt the snows and the tropics, somewhat of the gravity and grandeur of nature will infuse itself into the code. A heterogenous population crowding on all ships from all corners of the world to the great gates of North America, namely, Boston, New York, and New Orleans, and thence proceeding inward to the prairie and the mountains, and quickly contributing their private thought to the public opinion, their toll to the treasury, and their vote to the election, it cannot be doubted that the legislation of this country should become more catholic and cosmopolitan than that of any other. It seems so easy for America to inspire and express the most expansive and humane spirit; new-born, free, healthful, strong, the land of the laborer, of the democrat, of the philanthropist, of the believer, of the saint, she should speak for the human race. America is the country of the Future. From Washington, its capital city, proverbially 'the city of magnificent distances,' through all its cities, states, and territories, it is a country of beginnings, of projects, of vast designs, and expectations. It has no past: all has an onward and prospective look. And herein is it fitted to receive more readily every generous feature which the wisdom or the fortune of man has yet to impress.

Gentlemen, there is a sublime and friendly Destiny by which the human race is guided,—the race never dying, the individual never spared, —to results affecting masses and ages. Men are narrow and selfish, but the Genius, or Destiny, is not narrow, but beneficent. It is not discovered in their calculated and voluntary activity, but in what befalls, with or without their design. Only what is inevitable interests us, and it turns out that love and good are inevitable, and in the course of things. That Genius has infused itself into nature. It indicates itself by a small excess of good, a small balance in brute facts always favorable to the side of reason. All the facts in any part of nature shall be tabulated, and the results shall indicate the same security and benefit; so slight as to be hardly observable, and yet it is there. The sphere is found flattened at the poles, and swelled at the equator; a form flowing necessarily from the fluid state, yet *the* form, the mathematician assures us, required to prevent the great protuberances of the continent, or even of lesser mountains cast up at any time by earthquakes, from continually deranging the axis of the earth. The census of the population is found to keep an invariable equality in the sexes, with a trifling predominance in favor of the male, as if to counterbalance the necessarily increased exposure of male life in war, navigation, and other accidents. Remark the unceasing effort through-out nature at somewhat better than the actual creatures: *amelioration in nature,* which alone permits and authorizes amelioration in mankind. The population of the world is a conditional population; these are not the best, but the best that could live in the existing state of soils, of gases, animals, and morals: the best that could *yet* live; there shall be a better, please God. This Genius, or Destiny, is of the sternest administration, though rumors exist of its secret tenderness. It may be styled a cruel kindness, serving the whole even to the ruin of the member; a terrible communist, reserving all profits to the community, without dividend to individuals. Its law is, you shall have every thing as a member, nothing to yourself. For Nature is the noblest engineer, yet uses a grinding economy, working up all that is wasted today into tomorrow's creation;— not a superfluous grain of sand, for all the ostentation she makes of expense and public works. It is because Nature thus saves and uses, laboring for the general, that we poor particulars are so crushed and straitened, and find it so hard to live. She flung us out in her plenty, but we cannot shed a hair, or a paring of a nail, but instantly she snatches at the shred, and appropriates it to the general stock. Our condition is like that of the poor wolves: if one of the flock wound himself, or so much as limp, the rest eat him up incontinently.

That serene Power interposes an irresistible check upon the caprices and officiousness of our wills. His charity is not our charity. One of his agents is our will, but that which expresses itself in our will, is stronger than our will. We are very forward to help it, but it will not be accelerated. It resists our meddling, eleemosynary contrivances. We devise sumptuary laws and relief laws, but the principle of population is always reducing wages to the lowest pittance on which human life can be sustained. We legislate against forestalling and monopoly; we would have a common granary for the poor; but the selfishness which stores and hoards the corn for high prices, is the preventive of famine; and the law of self-preservation is surer policy than any legislation can be. We conduct eleemosynary systems, and it turns out that our charity increases pauperism. We inflate our paper currency, we repair commerce with unlimited credit, and are presently visited with unlimited bankruptcy.

It is easy to see that we of the existing generation are conspiring with a beneficence, which, in its working for coming generations, sacrifices the passing one, which infatuates the most selfish men to act against their private interest for the public welfare. We build railroads, we know not for what or for whom; but one thing is very certain, that we who build will receive the very smallest share of benefit therefrom. Immense benefit will accrue; they are essential to the country, but that will be felt not until we are no longer countrymen. We do the like in all matters:—

> "Man's heart the Almighty to the Future set
> By secret and inviolable springs."

We plant trees, we build stone houses, we redeem the waste, we make long prospective laws, we found colleges, hospitals, but for many and remote generations. We should be very much mortified to learn that the little benefit we chanced in our own persons to receive was the utmost they would yield. . . .

We rail at Trade, and the philosopher and lover of man have much harm to say of it; but the historian of the world will see that Trade was the principle of Liberty; that Trade planted America and destroyed Feudalism; that it makes peace and keeps peace, and it will abolish slavery. We complain of the grievous oppression of the poor, and of its building up a new aristocracy on the ruins of the aristocracy it destroyed. But there is this immense difference, that the aristocracy of trade has no permanence, is not entailed, was the result of toil and talent, the result of merit of some kind, and is continually falling, like the waves of the sea, before new claims of the same sort. Trade is an instrument in the hands of that friendly Power which works for us in our own despite. We design it thus and thus; but it turns out otherwise and far better. This beneficent tendency, omnipotent without violence, exists and works. Every observation of history inspires a confidence that we shall not go far wrong; that things mend. That is it. That is the moral of all we learn, that it warrants Hope, HOPE, the prolific mother of reforms. Our part is plainly not to throw ourselves across the track, not to block improvement, and sit till we are stone, but to watch the uprise of successive mornings, and to conspire with the new works of new days. Government has been a fossil; it should be a plant. I conceive that the office of statute law should be to express, and not to impede the mind of mankind. New thoughts, new things. Trade was one instrument, but Trade is also but for a time, and must give way to somewhat broader and better, whose signs are already dawning in the sky.

3. I pass in the third place to speak of the signs of that which is the sequel of trade.

It is in consequence of the revolution in the state of society wrought by trade, that Government in our times is beginning to wear so clumsy and cumbrous an appearance. We have already seen our way to shorter methods. The time is full of good signs. Some of them shall ripen to fruit. All this beneficent socialism is a friendly omen, and the swelling cry of voices for the education of the people, indicates that Government has other offices than those of banker and executioner. Witness the new movements in the civilized world, the Communism of France, Germany, and Switzerland; the Trades' Unions; the English League against the Corn Laws; and the whole *Industrial Statistics,* so called. In Paris, the blouse, the badge of the operative, has begun to make its appearance in the saloons. Witness too the spectacle of three Communities which have within a very short time sprung up within this Commonwealth, beside several others undertaken by citizens of Massachusetts within the territory of other States. These proceeded from a variety of motives, from an impatience of many usages in common life, from a wish for greater freedom than the manners and opinions of society permitted, but in great part from a feeling that the true offices of the State, the State had let fall to the ground; that in the scramble of parties for the public purse, the main duties of government were omitted,—the duty to instruct the ignorant, to supply the poor with work and with good guidance. These communists preferred the agricultural life as the most favorable condition for human culture; but they thought that the farm, as we manage it, did not satisfy the right ambition of man. The farmer, after sacrificing pleasure, taste, freedom, thought, love, to his work, turns out often a bankrupt, like the merchant. This result might well seem astounding. All this drudgery, from cockcrowing to starlight, for all these years, to end in mortgages and the auctioneer's flag, and removing from bad to worse. It is time to have the thing looked into, and with a sifting criticism ascertained who is the fool. It seemed a great deal worse because the farmer is living in the same town with men who pretend to know exactly what he wants. On one side, is agricultural chemistry, coolly exposing the nonsense of our spendthrift agriculture and ruinous expense of manures, and offering, by means of a teaspoonful of artificial guano, to turn a sandbank into corn; and, on the other, the farmer, not only eager for the information, but with bad crops and in debt and bankruptcy, for want of it. Here are Etzlers and countless mechanical projectors, who, with the Fourierists, undoubtingly affirm that the smallest union would make every man rich; —and, on the other side, is this multitude of poor men and women seeking work, and who cannot find enough to pay their board. The science is confident, and surely the poverty is real. If any means could be found to bring these two together!

This was one design of the projectors of the Associations which are now making their first feeble experiments. They were founded in love, and in labor. They proposed, as you know, that all men should take a part in the manual toil, and proposed to amend the condition of men by substituting harmonious, for hostile industry. It was a noble thought of Fourier, which gives a favorable idea of his system, to distinguish in his Phalanx a class as the Sacred Band, by whom whatever duties were disagreeable, and likely to be omitted, were to be assumed.

At least, an economical success seemed certain for the enterprise, and that agricultural association must, sooner or later, fix the price of bread, and drive single farmers into association, in self-defence; as the great commercial and manufacturing companies had already done. The Community is only the continuation of the same movement which made the joint-stock companies for manufactures, mining, insurance, banking, and so forth. It has turned out cheaper to make calico by companies; and it is proposed to plant corn, and to bake bread by companies, and knowing men affirm it will be tried until it is done.

Undoubtedly, abundant mistakes will be made by these first adventurers, which will draw ridicule on their schemes. I think, for example, that they exaggerate the importance of a favorite project of theirs, that of paying talent and labor at one rate, paying all sorts of service at one rate, say ten cents the hour. They have paid it so; but not an instant would a dime remain a dime. In one hand it became an eagle as it fell, and in another hand a copper cent. For, obviously, the whole value of the dime is in knowing what to do with it. One man buys with it a land-title of an Indian, and makes his posterity princes; or buys corn enough to feed the world; or pen, ink, and paper, or a painter's brush, by which he can communicate himself to the human race as if he were fire; and the other buys plums and gooseberries. Money is of no value: it cannot spend itself. All depends on the skill of the spender.

Whether, too, the objection almost universally felt by such women in the community as were mothers, to an associate life, to a common table, and a common nursery, &c., setting a higher value on the private family with poverty, than on an association with wealth, will not prove insuperable, remains to be determined.

But the Communities aimed at a much greater success in securing to all their members an equal, and very thorough education. And the great aims of the movement will not be relinquished, even if these attempts fail, but will be prosecuted by like-minded men in all society, until they succeed.

This is the value of the Communities; not what they have done, but the revolution which they indicate as on the way. Yes, Government must educate the poor man. Look across the country from any hill-side around us, and the landscape seems to crave Government. The actual differences of men must be acknowledged, and met with love and wisdom. These rising grounds which command the champaign below, seem to ask for lords, true lords, *land*-lords, who understand the land and its uses, and the applicabilities of men, and whose government would be what it should; namely, mediation between want and supply. How gladly would each citizen pay a commission for the support and continuation of such good guidance. Goethe said, "no man should be rich but those who understand it:" and certainly the poor are prone to think that very few of the rich understand how to use their advantage to any good purpose; they have not originality, nor even grace in their expenditure. But if this is true of wealth, it is much more true of power; none should be a governor who has not a talent for governing. Now many people have a native skill for carving out business for many hands; a genius for the disposition of affairs; and are never happier than when difficult practical questions which embarrass other men, are to be solved: all lies in light before them: they are in their element. Could any means be contrived to appoint only these! There really seems a progress towards such a state of things, in which this work shall be done by these natural workmen: and this, not certainly through any increased discretion shown by the citizens at elections, but by the gradual contempt into which official government falls, and the increasing disposition of private adventurers to assume its fallen functions. Thus the Post Office is likely to go into disuse before the private transportation shop of Harnden and his competitors. The currency threatens to fall entirely into private hands. Justice is continually administered more and more by private reference, and not by litigation. We have feudal governments in a commercial age. It would be but an easy extension of our commercial system, to pay a private emperor a fee for services, as we pay an architect, or engineer, or a lawyer for advice. If any man has a talent for righting wrong, for administering difficult affairs, for counselling poor farmers how to turn their estates to good husbandry, for combining a hundred private enterprises to a general benefit, let him in the county-town, or in Court-street, put up his sign-board, Mr. Smith, *Governor*, Mr. Johnson, *Working king*.

How can our young men complain of the poverty of things in New England, and not feel that poverty as a demand on their charity to make New England rich? Where is he who seeing a thousand men useless and unhappy, and making the whole region look forlorn by their inaction, and conscious himself of possessing the faculty they want, does not hear his call to go and be their king?

We must have kings, and we must have nobles. Nature is always providing such in every society,—only let us have the real instead of the titular. Let us have our leading and our inspiration from the best. The actual differences in personal power are not to be disputed. In every society some men are born to rule, and some to advise. Let the powers be well directed, directed by love, and they would everywhere be greeted with joy and honor. The chief is the chief all the world over, only not his cap and his plume. It is only their dislike of the pretender, which makes men sometimes unjust to the true and finished man. If society were transparent, the noble would everywhere be gladly received and accredited, and would not be asked for his day's work, but would be felt as benefit, inasmuch as he was noble. That were his duty and stint,—to keep himself pure and purifying, the leaven of his nation. I think I see place and duties for a nobleman in every society; but it is not to drink wine and ride in a fine coach, but to guide and adorn life for the multitude by forethought, by elegant studies, by perseverance, self-devotion, and the remembrance of the humble old friend, by making his life secretly beautiful.

I call upon you, young men, to obey your heart, and be the nobility of this land. In every age of the world, there has been a leading nation, one of a more generous sentiment, whose eminent citizens were willing to stand for the interests of general justice and humanity, at the risk of being called, by the men of the moment, chimerical and fantastic. Which should be that nation but these States? Which should lead that movement, if not New England? Who should lead the leaders, but the Young American? The people, and the world, is now suffering from the want of religion and honor in its public mind. In America, out of doors all seems a market; in doors, an air-tight stove of conventionalism. Every body who comes into our houses savors of these precious habits; the men of the market, the women of the custom. I find no expression in our state papers or legislative debate, in our lyceums or churches, specially in our newspapers, of a high national feeling, no lofty counsels that rightfully stir the blood. I speak of those organs which can be presumed to speak a popular sense. They recommend only conventional virtues, whatever will earn and preserve property; always the capitalist; the college, the church, the hospital, the theatre, the hotel, the road, the ship, of the capitalist,—whatever goes to secure, adorn, enlarge these, is good; what jeopardizes any of these, is damnable. The 'opposition' papers, so-called, are on the same side. They attack the great capitalist, but with the aim to make a capitalist of the poor man. The opposition is between the ins and the outs; between those who have money, and those who wish to have money. . . .

I shall not need to go into an enumeration of our national defects and vices which require this Order of Censors in the state. I might not set down our most proclaimed offences as the worst. It is not often the worst trait that occasions the loudest outcry. Men complain of their suffering, and not of the crime. I fear little from the bad effect of Repudiation; I do not fear that it will spread. Stealing is a suicidal business; you cannot repudiate but once. But the bold face and tardy repentance permitted to this local mischief, reveal a public mind so preoccupied with the love of gain, that the common sentiment of indignation at fraud does not act with its natural force. The more need of a withdrawal from the crowd, and a resort to the fountain of right, by the brave. The timidity of our public opinion, is our disease, or, shall I say, the publicness of opinion, the absence of private opinion. Good-nature is plentiful, but we want justice, with heart of steel, to fight down the proud. The private mind has the access to the totality of goodness and truth, that it may be a balance to a corrupt society; and to stand for the private verdict against popular clamor, is the office of the noble. If a humane measure is propounded in behalf of the slave, or of the Irishman, or the Catholic, or for the succor of the poor, that sentiment, that project, will have the homage of the hero. That is his nobility, his oath of knighthood, to succor the helpless and oppressed; always to throw himself on the side of weakness, of youth, of hope, on the liberal, on the expansive side, never on the defensive, the conserving, the timorous, the lock and bolt system. More than our good will we may not be able to give. We have our own affairs, our own genius, which chains us to our proper work. We cannot give our life to the cause of the debtor, of the slave, or the pauper, as another is doing, but one thing we are bound to, not to blaspheme the sentiment and the work of that man, not to throw stumbling blocks in the way of the abolitionist, the philanthropist, as the organs of influence and opinion are swift to do. It is for us to confide in the beneficent Supreme Power, and not to rely on our money, and on the state because it is the guard of money. At this moment, the terror of old people and of vicious people, is lest the Union of these States be destroyed. As if the Union had any other real basis than the good pleasure of a majority of the citizens to be united. But the wise and just man will always feel that he stands on his own feet; that he imparts strength to the state, not receives security from it; and that if all went down, he and such as he would quite easily combine in a new and better constitution. Every great and memorable community has consisted of formidable individuals, who, like the Roman or the Spartan, lent his own spirit to the state and so made it great. Yet only by the supernatural is a man strong: only by confiding in the Divinity which stirs in us. Nothing is so weak as an egotist. Nothing is mightier than we, when we are vehicles of a truth before which the state and the individual are alike ephemeral.

Gentlemen, the development of our American internal resources, the extension to the utmost of the commercial system, and the appearance of new moral causes which are to modify the state, are giving an aspect of greatness to the Future, which the imagination fears to open. One thing is plain for all men of common sense and common conscience, that here, here in America, is the home of man. After all the deductions which are to be made for our pitiful and most unworthy politics, which stake every gravest national question on the silly die, whether James or whether Jonathan shall sit in the chair and hold the purse, after all the deduction is made for our frivolities and insanities, there still remains an organic simplicity and liberty, which, when it loses its balance redresses itself presently, which offers opportunity to the human mind not known in any other region.

It is true, the public mind wants self-respect. We are full of vanity, of which the most signal proof is our sensitiveness to foreign and especially English censure. One cause of this is our immense reading, and that reading chiefly confined to the productions of the English press. But a more misplaced sensibility than this tenderness to fame on the subject of our country and civil institutions, I cannot recall. Could we not defend and apologize for the sun and rain. Here are we, men of English blood, planted now for five, six, or seven generations on this immense tract in the temperate zone, and so planted at such a conjuncture of time and events, that we have left behind us whatever old and odious establishments the mind of men had outgrown. The unsupportable burdens under which Europe staggers, and almost every month mutters "A Revolution! a Revolution!" we have escaped from as by one bound. No thanks to us; but in the blessed course of events it did happen that this country was not open to the Puritans until they had felt the burden of the feudal system, and until the commercial era in modern Europe had dawned, so that without knowing what they did, they left the whole curse behind, and put the storms of the Atlantic between them and this antiquity. And the felling of the forest, and the settling in so far of the area of this continent, was accomplished under the free spirit of trading communities with a complete success. Not by our right hand, or foresight, or skill, was it done, but by the simple acceptance of the plainest road ever shown men to walk in. It was the human race, under Divine leading, going forth to receive and inhabit their patrimony. And now, if any Englishman, or Frenchman, or Spaniard, or Russian, or German, can find any food for merriment in the spectacle, make him welcome to shake his sides. There never was a people that could better afford to be the subject of a little fun, than we. An honest man may, perhaps, wonder how, with so much to call forth congratulation, our lively visitors should be so merry and critical. Perhaps they have great need of a little holiday and diversion from their domestic cares, like other house-keepers who have a heavy time of it at home and need all the refreshment they can get from kicking up their feet a little now that they have got away on a frolic.

It is also true, that, to imaginative persons in this country, there is somewhat bare and bald in our short history, and unsettled wilderness. They ask, who would live in a new country, that can live in an old? Europe is to our boys and girls, what novels and romances are; and it is not strange they should burn to see the picturesque extremes of an antiquated country. But it is one thing to visit the pyramids, and another to wish to live there. Would they like tithes to the clergy, and sevenths to the government, and horse-guards, and licensed press, and grief when a child is born, and threatening, starved weavers, and a pauperism now constituting one-thirteenth of the population? Instead of the open future expanding here before the eye of every boy to vastness, would they like the closing in of the future to a narrow slit of sky, and that fast contracting to be no future? One thing, for instance, the beauties of aristocracy, we commend to the study of the travelling American. The English, the most conservative people this side of India, are not sensible of the restraint, but an American would seriously resent it. The aristocracy, incorporated by law and education, degrades life for the unprivileged classes. It is a questionable compensation to the embittered feeling of a proud commoner, the reflection that the worthless lord who, by the magic of title, paralyzes his arm, and plucks from him half the graces and rights of a man, is himself also an aspirant excluded with the same ruthlessness from higher circles, since there is no end to the wheels within wheels of this spiral heaven. Something may be pardoned to the spirit of loyalty when it becomes fantastic; and something to the imagination, for the baldest life is symbolic. Philip II. of Spain rated his ambassador for neglecting business of great importance in Italy, whilst he debated some point of honor with the French ambassador; "You have left a business of importance for a ceremony." The ambassador replied, "How? for a ceremony? your majesty's self is but a ceremony." In the East, where the religious sentiment comes in to the support of the aristocracy, and in the Romish church also, there is a grain of sweetness in the tyranny; but in England, the fact seems to me intolerable, what is commonly affirmed, that such is the transcendent honor accorded to wealth and birth, that no man of letters, be his eminence what it may, is received into the best society, except as a lion and a show. It seems to me, that with the lights which are now gleaming in the eyes of all men, residence in that country becomes degradation to any man not employed to revolutionize it. The English have many virtues, many advantages, and the proudest history of the world; but they need all, and more than all the resources of the past to indemnify a heroic gentleman in that country for the mortifications prepared for him by the system of society, and which seem to impose the alternative to resist or to avoid it. That there are mitigations and practical alleviations to this rigor, is not an excuse for the rule. Commanding worth, and personal power must sit crowned in all companies, nor will extraordinary persons be slighted or affronted in any company of civilized men. But the system is an invasion of the sentiment of justice and the native rights of men, which, however decorated, must lessen the value of English citizenship. It is for Englishmen to consider, not for us: we only say, let us live in America, too thankful for our want of feudal institutions. Our houses and towns are like mosses and lichens, so slight and new; but youth is a fault of which we shall daily mend. And really at last all lands are alike. Ours, too, is as old as the Flood, and wants no ornament or privilege which nature could bestow. Here stars, here woods, here hills, here animals, here men abound, and the vast tendencies concur of a new order. If only the men are well employed in conspiring with the designs of the Spirit who led us hither, and is leading us still, we shall quickly enough advance out of all hearing of other's censures, out of all regrets of our own, into a new and more excellent social state than history has recorded.

SELECTION

An Appeal to Manifest Destiny: "Brother Jonathan," 1853

Among the periodicals most devoted to the expression and advancement of America's exuberant nationalism was the United States Magazine and Democratic Review, *published from 1837 to 1859 under a variety of titles (including, for a brief period, the* United States Review*). The* Democratic Review, *as it was commonly called, became a more or less official organ of the Democratic party. The party of Andrew Jackson was regarded as the ideal vehicle for carrying to fruition the great American mission, although expressions of American nationalism were by no means limited to that party. The magazine reflected in its columns the strong sense of destiny that gripped the American people during these years—the idea that America was being guided by an inexorable force that could not be avoided. In fact, it was in the* Democratic Review *that the phrase "manifest destiny" first appeared in print. "Brother Jonathan" was a reaffirmation of the national faith in the 1850s, a period when sectional divisions were beginning to strain the nation's unity. The anonymous writer (probably the editor) stressed the popular notion that the United States was guided by destiny but, unlike other spokesmen, he reminded Americans of some of their weaknesses as well. For a study of the idea of manifest destiny throughout American history, see Albert K. Weinberg,* Manifest Destiny: A Study of Nationalist Expansionism in American History *(1935); a more recent study, focusing more on the 1840s and 1850s, is Frederick Merk's* Manifest Destiny and Mission in American History: A Reinterpretation *(1963). "Brother Jonathan" is reprinted from the* United States Review, *volume 1, May, 1853, pages 433–439.*

Brother Jonathan—though a chip of the old block—has had his habits and character modified by being placed in a different position, and subjected to a new system of discipline from that of the races from whence he sprung. Superficial travellers in America have pronounced the people of the United States to be a heterogeneous medley, without any general features of resemblance or family likeness in habits, manners or character. Never was there a greater blunder. There is no Christian people in the world, of equal numbers, so nearly homogeneous. With a few trifling exceptions, which are not permanent, they all speak one language with a degree of uniformity observed in no other great nation, and their dialect differs much less in the different States than that of England, Scotland and Ireland, or even the adjoining counties of the former. It is the same with all the great continental powers of Europe. In France the old provincial distinctions still remain, in spite of the division into Departments; the inhabitants of the different Provinces or Kingdoms of Spain are indignant at being called Spaniards; Italy is divided into different discordant minor States; Germany comprises nations speaking sixteen different languages; and Russia is half European half Asiatic, half Christian half Pagan, and as the Mississippi boatmen say, a little of the Mussulman. In respect to all the distinctive characteristics that constitute nationality, the United States, though constituting separate sovereignties, at least in regard to their reserved rights, are emphatically one great people, acting in concert in all their foreign relations. Though of an infinite diversity of sects, they are all Christians, believing in one God and one Saviour, and recognising all without exception or preference. Though descended from the most illustrious nations of the world, and having many fathers, whatever trifling differences may prevail among them at first, they in a little time disappear, and the entire mass becomes cemented together by the indissoluble tie of Liberty and Equality. There is no excitement to national jealousies or antipathies where all are equal; and though the Corkonians and Far Downers may occasionally break each other's heads in the indulgence of a national propensity, these distinctions vanish, like spectres at the dawn of day, the moment they begin to feel at home in this world of freedom. The title of American Citizen supersedes all others, and the foreigner, like the lamb in the Fable, chooses for his mother, not the land of his birth, but that of his adoption.

All the great empires of the world have been formed by conquering and incorporating, as far as possible, different nations into one incongruous mass of discordant materials, which being only held together by force, separated into their original identity the moment that force was withdrawn. The wonder is that they lasted so long—not that they did not last longer. The United States, on the contrary, embrace no conquered people —the Indians being removed by purchase—and the late acquisitions from Mexico comprise so small a portion of Spaniards dispersed over an immense surface, that in another generation they will be lost in the deluge of North Americans which will overflow the country. Bound together by a common interest, in one great joint-stock company, the native and the adopted citizen become gradually fused into one mass, in which the former distinctly predominates. Having none of those homebred causes of collision which distracted them at home, and being no longer stimulated by their rulers to dissensions for political purposes, they forget their old traditional antipathies, and come to live together like brothers of one blood and one lineage. The emigrants slide into the great current, just as the tributary streams of the great father of waters enter that mighty river and are lost forever.

In regard to the sectional divisions of East, West, North, and South, with one exception, there is, we think, but little danger to be apprehended, so long as all continue to enjoy an equal degree of prosperity. The dissensions arising from conflicts of interests, often imaginary, may be likened to those which sometimes occur in family circles, occasioning temporary interruptions of harmony that are soon overpowered by the sense of a common interest in matters of a thousand times more consequence to their prosperity and happiness. When not carried to extremes, these differences rather operate to strengthen the confederation by preserving something like an equilibrium in legislation, and preventing one section from establishing a permanent system of policy injurious to another; for though the stronger party may attempt to impose on the weaker, all experience proves that a combined minority is generally an overmatch for a loose majority. The more people, the more likely they are to be divided; but a minority is almost always kept together by a common interest, and a sense of weakness, unless its leaders are corrupted. But in the midst of these bickerings, which are for the most part only little whirlwinds blown up by ambitious pettifogging politicians, there is among all classes in the United States, except a few whose old colonial feelings are not yet extinct, an innate instinctive attachment to the Union, which can only be extinguished by gross and palpable outrages on the interests, feelings, and character of particular classes or sections. This feeling originates in national pride and national patriotism, combined with a conviction, that, except in extreme cases, no advantages that can possibly result from a dissolution of the Union would in any degree compensate for the evils that would follow in its train. The danger is not so much of a separation of the States, as that they may be bribed into a surrender of their most important rights, by grants of land for purposes of improvements, and other legislative boons, and become absorbed in the great vortex of consolidation. We, for our part, are not afraid of a happy people, who, while enjoying their rights, cherish a perfect confidence in their capacity to maintain them. They may grumble a little occasionally. They may threaten a separation, but will never apply for a divorce.

Foreigners accustomed to the dead calm of despotism, which is only at times interrupted by earthquakes and tornadoes, are perpetually confounded by the language of our newspapers during the progress of an electioneering struggle. They believe that every Presidential contest which, in our popular language, "convulses the whole nation," is the prelude to speedy dissolution. When they hear of a great "Waterloo defeat," and of the enemy being routed, horse, foot, and dragoons, and utterly annihilated, they think there is a great civil war raging, and that a bloody battle has been fought between the contending parties. If not this, they are convinced that every man, if not every woman and child in the United States, is so near a state of spontaneous combustion, that a spark or a breath would set them in a flame. When, however, they come to the United States, and see them all quietly engaged in their domestic occupations, and most especially when they witness the cool, dignified composure with which the citizen exercises his sovereignty, they are astonished at the sublime spectacle. If there are occasional exceptions, it is only in our great cities among the lowest rabble, which is sometimes stimulated by the lowest class of pettifogging politicians to a few broken heads and bloody noses. There is but one sectional question that can endanger the Union, and that is of too vital consequence to be treated incidentally. The storm has subsided at present, and we may humbly hope will never be followed by another.

The United States contain, in proportion to their numbers, a greater mass of physical strength and activity than is to be found in any other people; and this arises partly from the rapidity with which they increase, in consequence of which there is always a greater proportion of young men, partly from circumstances we shall presently adduce. In the Western, and indeed throughout all the New States, the men are for the most part in the vigor of life; and there is nowhere to be found that class so numerous in England, whose physical and intellectual qualities have become debilitated by a long series of hereditary monotonous labor in one spot, and at one employment, poorly compensated by a scanty supply of that kind of food which fills the belly without strengthening the members. Throughout by far the greater proportion of the United States, the inhabitants have been accustomed to modes of life, which, while they give full exercise to the body, at the same time call into action the qualities indispensable to the pioneers of a New World. Their course from the beginning required the exercise of courage, hardihood, enterprise, and self-reliance, together with that discernment of spirit and that versatility of talent which accommodates itself to every exigency, and enables men to become their own legislators as well as their own defenders. If they find insuperable difficulties in the way of fortune and distinction in the old settlements, they seek a clearer field and wider space in the new,

mal in nature is a dunce, he certainly stands high in that category, for he copies Europe, and especially England, in everything, especially in its follies, extravagance, and effeminacy. Though free in action, in opinion he is a slave; and though politically independent, he is morally and intellectually still in a state of colonial dependence. Though perpetually boasting of his freedom, he is at the same time adopting the practice and principles of despotism, and applying its maxims to the administration of his government. He sings hosannas to liberty and equality, yet is every day undermining one, and infringing on the rights of the other, by creating monopolies, in the disguise of chartered companies, embodying a vast concentration of wealth, and possessing privileges and immunities in which not one in a thousand of the people can ever partake, and which it is impossible for them to exercise. Jonathan has been so accustomed to think there can be no despotism except under a king, that he has lost sight of the memorable truth, that of all the varieties of government ever instituted, that which makes the name and forms of freedom a cloak for the abuses of power, is the most dangerous to the liberties of mankind. If Jonathan would only think for himself, and resort to his own common sense and experience, instead of making the old superannuated world his looking-glass, we think he would be much more respectable, prosperous and happy. But though such a hale, hearty fellow, he is still tied to the apron-string of his mother, who makes him believe anything she pleases, and while doing him all the sly ill offices in her power, has almost succeeded in persuading him she is the best friend he has in the world. The old lady overwhelms him with all sorts of good books, which, as he gets for almost nothing, he reads with the greater pleasure, and his belief in the Bible is not more implicit than his confidence in the Edinburgh and Quarterly, the London Times, and Blackwood's Magazine. That old Scotch Tory is his oracle. Were it not for our newspapers, and public speakers, Jonathan would never read anything but what is eminently calculated to make him anything but a republican.

Another foible, or fault, of Jonathan, is his propensity to be led away by fanatical excitements. It is true he gets over them pretty soon, but not always before they have done all the mischief possible. While boasting of being of all men in the world the most free from superstition and fanaticism, he is always in a state of spontaneous combustion about some transcendentalism or other, which he pursues with such ardor, that he finally overtakes and treads it under foot. The disease is not exactly chronic with him, but one paroxysm succeeds another so rapidly, that he is never quite well, except at brief intervals. When under the influence of one of these paroxysms, he may be said to require a strait waistcoat, for he is almost as bad as a mad bull in a crockery store, and butts at both law and gospel. If the law stands in the way of jumping over his high ropes, he don't mind it in the least, any more than a constitutional scruple. But we will do him the justice to say that he always comes to himself when it is too late to mend matters. His "sober second thought" is admirable, but like a calm after a storm, which, though very refreshing, cannot lift up the prostrate harvest, or restore the shipwrecked vessels. We would respectfully and affectionately remind him of the old proverb, "Prevention is better than cure," and that there are some evils which cannot be cured, some things which, when done, cannot be undone. It is much better never to run mad, even though we may come to our senses at last.

But the greatest of Brother Jonathan's faults, in our humble opinion, is his horrible craving for money. Not that he is a miser, for he spends as fast as he gets it, and often a great deal faster; but he certainly loves money dearly, and we grieve to say too often, like the sportsman, uses traps and snares to capture his game. We had rather cut off our right thumb than call him a rogue, but he certainly would be none the worse for a little more honesty. The evil spirit of trade possesses him, and he is incessantly digging at the root of all evil, not only in California, but everywhere else. Mercury and Plutus—we mean the Paper Plutus—are his gods, and if on any occasion he gives a variety to his devotion, you will always find him grovelling at the foot of the golden calf. He seems to have no other object in life, no other conception of any enjoyment, but that of making and spending money. He has no other standard of human character, and reverences a worthless millionaire far above a poor man who is only possessed of a thousand good qualities. If you inquire as to the character of a man, he will tell you he is "good," though he may be an exemplary rogue, because he stands high in the money market; or if on the contrary he is a little consumptive in his purse, he is a "poor d—l," beyond all question. It never occurs to him that any man may become rich by persevering in a long life of sordid selfishness; starving his natural appetites to starve again on his acquisition; shutting his heart to all social obligations and human sympathies, and taking advantage of the necessities, credulity, and inexperience of his fellow-creatures. Jonathan should recollect that the possession of wealth is not the proper standard of human character, and that a contemptible rich man is ten times more contemptible than a contemptible poor one, because he is placed above the temptation of those tricks and devices which so often prove too strong for poverty.

This exclusive devotion to money won't do for a free people. You cannot worship God and mammon, nor kneel at the shrine of liberty while groveling at the hoof of the golden calf. He who loves money better than anything else, will sell his conscience and his principles for money, and cannot long retain his freedom, because he is unworthy to be free. We see this exemplified almost continually in whole States and communities sacrificing their political principles to pecuniary considerations, and bartering their rights for grants of lands, for railroads, and other so-called improvements, from which they anticipate additional food to their cupidity. Does Jonathan dream that liberty can take care of herself while he is speculating in railroad stocks, or digging in California, from morning till night? He must think of something else besides gold-dust and loco-motives, and have some other standard of human character, as well as human happiness, or he will go the way of all flesh, and some day or other rattle his golden chains among his fellow-slaves. But we must not be too hard upon Brother Jonathan, who is continually led astray by the example of his old mother, who despises an empty purse and worships millionaires. He is a mighty clever fellow, notwithstanding all his faults, and we earnestly hope will make use of his money for the benefit of his fellow-creatures, not forgetting himself. We should not at all be surprised if he were one day to become wiser and better than the mother that bore him.

The Peculiar Institution

*T**he** exuberant nationalism of "young America" was also, paradoxically, a period of rising sectionalism. Sectional loyalties and alignments mounted in importance, even as the nation's leaders spoke of national unity and of the mission of America in the world. It was this sectionalism that eventually brought disaster to the nation itself, for it presented issues which apparently could not be resolved within the normal framework of democratic government.*

The most divisive and explosive sectional issue in the United States during the mid-century years was the issue of human slavery. Indeed, slavery meant many issues—issues that developed between the North and the South and dramatized the differences in outlook between the two sections. Although these sectional arguments and disagreements took many forms, slavery always remained fundamental and basic. Sectional differences—social, economic, political, and even cultural—could always be traced to the one significant fact that slavery existed in one of the sections and not in the other. Nor was the issue of slavery regarded in any narrow sense. The institution of slavery had become so closely intertwined with the Southern civilization and way of life as to be inseparable from it—or so Southerners thought. In fact, it had become essential to it—the keystone, so to speak, in the arch of Southern civilization.

The commitment of the South to slavery was not always as strong as it became in the mid-nineteenth century. In the late colonial period, and during the early years of the republic, the institution seemed to many observers to be on the decline (although recent research has challenged the conclusion that slavery was becoming increasingly insecure during these years). Not until the invention of the cotton gin and the resultant spread of cotton cultivation during the first decades of the nineteenth century did slavery become an essential factor in Southern life. Its importance as an economic institution was not questioned. As the "cotton kingdom" expanded and as the South became committed to the pattern of staple-crop plantation agriculture it fostered, Southerners were per-

suaded that slavery was vital to their economic prosperity and well-being.

But slavery was more than an economic institution to the Southerner. It was also, in his mind, a necessary social institution—necessary as a means of social control and of public safety, as well as a base on which to erect a social structure. The slaves, in the words of a South Carolina Senator in 1858, constituted the "very mud-sill of society" that was prerequisite to "that other class which leads progress, civilization, and refinement." Slavery served the South also as a source for political power; the institution must be strengthened and expanded, it was thought, so that the section's role in the nation might be strengthened and expanded. Additional slave states would mean more Southern power in the national councils.

Such considerations produced an evolution in Southern thinking about slavery. At first regarded as an evil (many emancipation societies existed in the South in the early years of the century), slavery soon became a necessary evil. By the mid-century, the institution was viewed as a positive good, "the most safe and stable basis for free institutions in the world," according to John C. Calhoun, the South's greatest spokesman and defender. Yet the Southern attitude toward slavery remained ambivalent. Doubts, fears, and anxieties pervaded Southern society. An elaborate system of laws was developed to provide a rigid control over the slave population, and the fear of slave uprising was always present. As this transition in Southern thinking was effected, the Southern mind became less receptive to any suggestion of reform of the social and economic structure. Steps were actually taken to erect what one writer has called an "intellectual blockade" against ideas that would threaten the status quo. Many Southerners shut their eyes and their ears to the humanitarian movements that were sweeping the Western world, seeking refuge instead in a naive romanticism that heightened their isolation and their conservatism. Southern cultural expression was itself enlisted in the cause of justifying slavery to the world. Novelists, poets, scientists, and preachers of the Gospel joined in soothing the Southern conscience by their vindication of the "peculiar institution" they thought so vital.

The deepening commitment of the Southerner (both slaveholder and nonslaveholder) to slavery in the face of a rising tide of resentment throughout the Western world, and the dangerous isolationism and stubborn conservatism which this commitment promoted could only have tragic consequences—tragic to the nation as well as to the South.

SELECTION

A Novelist Describes "Southern Life as It Is": Mrs. Mary Eastman's "Aunt Phillis's Cabin," 1852

The publication in 1852 of Harriet Beecher Stowe's Uncle Tom's Cabin, *a milestone in the Northern antislavery movement, inspired a flurry of Southern publications defending slavery. In just a few years, a score or more "anti-Tom" novels were published by Southern writers who sought to "correct" the Northern woman's portrayal of slavery. They were determined to describe "Southern life as it is." Mrs. Mary Henderson Eastman (1818–1880), the wife of an Army officer and the author of books and poems on Indians and Indian legends, was one who responded to Mrs. Stowe's attack. Her reply, appropriately titled* Aunt Phillis's Cabin, *pictured slave life as little short of idyllic. True or not, it was the picture of slavery many Southerners had come to accept. Mrs. Eastman's book was said to have sold over 18,000 copies within the first few weeks of its publication, although it never reached the heights of popularity enjoyed by its Northern counterpart. In the selection that follows (Philadelphia: Lippincott, 1852) pages 112–118, Mrs. Eastman emphasized some of the favorite themes of slavery's defenders—the kindness of the slaveholder toward his slave, the deep attachment of the slave to his owner, and the simple carefree life of the slave and his family.*

There are three excellent studies of Southern antebellum thought: two by Clement Eaton, The Growth of Southern Civilization, 1790–1860 *(1961) and* The Mind of the Old South *(1964); and William R. Taylor's* Cavalier and Yankee: The Old South and American National Character *(1961).*

Phillis was at her ironing early in the morning, for she liked to hurry it over before the heat of the day. Her cabin doors were open, and her flowers, which had been watered by a slight rain that fell about daybreak, looked fresh and beautiful. Her house could be hardly called a cabin, for it was very much superior to the others on the plantation, though they were all comfortable. Phillis was regarded by the Weston family as the most valuable servant they owned—and, apart from her services, there were strong reasons why they were attached to her. She had nursed Mrs. Weston in her last illness, and as her death occurred immediately after Arthur's birth, she nourished him as her own child, and loved him quite as well. Her comfort and wishes were always objects of the greatest consideration to the family, and this was proved whenever occasion allowed. Her neatly white-washed cottage was enclosed by a wooden fence in good condition—her little garden laid out with great taste, if we except the rows of stiffly-trimmed box which Phillis took pride in. A large willow tree shaded one side of it; and on the other, gaudy sunflowers reared their heads, and the white and Persian lilacs, contrasted with them. All kinds of small flowers and roses adorned the front of the house, and you might as well have sought for a diamond over the whole place, as a weed. The back of the lot was arranged for the accommodation of her pigs and chickens; and two enormous peacocks, that were fond of sunning themselves by the front door, were the handsomest ornaments about the place.

The room in which Phillis ironed, was not encumbered with much furniture. Her ironing-table occupied a large part of its centre, and in the ample fireplace was blazing a fire great enough to cook a repast for a moderate number of giants. Behind the back door stood a common pine bedstead, with an enormous bed upon it. How any bedstead held such a bed was remarkable; for Phillis believed there was a virtue in feathers even in the hottest weather, and she would rather have gone to roost on the nearest tree than to have slept on anything else. The quilt was of a domestic blue and white, her own manufacture, and the cases to the pillows were very white and smooth. A little, common trundle bedstead was underneath, and on it was the bedding which was used for the younger children at night. The older ones slept in the servants' wing in the house, Phillis making use of two enormous chests, which were Bacchus's, and her wardrobes, for sleeping purposes for a couple more. To the right of the bed, was the small chest of drawers, over which was suspended Bacchus's many-sided piece of shaving glass, and underneath it a pine box containing his shaving weapons. Several chairs, in a disabled state, found places about the room, and Phillis's clothes-horse stood with open arms, ready to receive the white and well-ironed linen that was destined to hang upon it. On each side of the fireplace was a small dresser, with plates and jars of all sizes and varieties, and over each were suspended some branches of trees, inviting the flies to rest upon them. There was no cooking done in this room, there being a small shed for that purpose, back of the house; not a spot of grease dimmed the whiteness of the floors, and order reigned supreme, marvellous to relate! where a descendant of Afric's daughters presided.

Lydia had gone as usual to Miss Janet, and several of the other children were busy about the yard, feeding the chickens, sweeping up, and employed in various ways; the only one who ever felt inclined to be lazy, and who was in body and mind the counterpart of his father, being seated on the door step, declaring he had a pain in his foot.

The adjoining room was the place in which Phillis's soul delighted, the door of it being at all times locked, and the key lost in the depths of her capacious pocket. From this place of retirement it emerged when any of the family honored her with their company, especially when attended by visitors; and after their departure, traces of their feet were carefully sought with keen and anxious eyes, and quickly obliterated with broom and duster.

This, her sanctum sanctorum, was a roomy apartment with three windows, each shaded by white cotton curtains. On the floor was a home-made carpet; no hand was employed in its manufacture save its owner's, from the time she commenced tearing the rags in strips, to the final blow given to the last tack that confined it to the floor. A very high post bedstead, over which were suspended white cotton curtains, gave an air of grandeur to one side of the room. No one had slept in it for ten years, though it was made with faultless precision. The quilt over it contained pieces of every calico and gingham dress that had been worn in the Weston family since the Revolution, and in the centre had been transferred from a remnant of curtain calico, an eagle with outstretched wings. The pillow cases were finished off with tape trimming, Alice's work, at Cousin Janet's suggestion. Over an old fashioned-mahogany bureau hung an oval looking glass, which was carefully covered from the flies. An easy chair stood by the window at the foot of the bed, which had, like most of the other ancient looking pieces of furniture, occupied a conspicuous place in Mr. Weston's house. Six chairs planted with unyielding stiffness against the walls seemed to grow out of the carpet; and the very high fender enclosed a pair of andirons that any body with tolerable eyesight could have seen their faces in.

Over the mantel piece were suspended two pictures. One was a likeness of Mr. Weston, cut in paper over a black surface, with both hands behind him, and his right foot foremost; the other was a picture of the Shepherds in Pilgrim's Progress, gazing through a spy-glass at the Celestial city. Alice's first sampler, framed in a black frame, hung on one side of the room, and over it was a small sword which used to swing by Arthur's side, when receiving lessons in military science from Bacchus, who, in his own opinion, was another Bonaparte. Into this room Phillis's children gazed with wondering eyes; and those among the plantation servants who had been honored with a sight of it, declared it superior, in every respect, to their master's drawing room; holding in especial reverence a small table, covered with white, which supported the weight of Phillis's family Bible, where were registered in Arthur's and Alice's handwriting, the births of all her twelve descendants, as well as the ceremony which united her to their illustrious father.

Phillis was ironing away with a good heart, when she was interrupted by a summons to attend her master in the library. She obeyed it with very little delay, and found Mr. Weston seated in his arm-chair, looking over a note which he held in his hand.

"Come in, Phillis," he said, in a kind but grave manner. "I want to speak with you for a few moments; and as I have always found you truthful, I have no doubt you will be perfectly so on the present occasion."

"What is it, master?" Phillis said, respectfully.

"I received a note, yesterday, from Mr. Dawson, about his servant Jim, who ran away three weeks ago. He charges me with having permitted my servants to shelter him for the night, on my plantation; having certain information, that he was seen leaving it the morning after the severe storm we had about that time. If you know any thing of it, Phillis, I require you to tell it to me; I hardly think any of the other servants had opportunities of doing so, and yet I cannot believe that you would so far forgot yourself as to do what is not only wrong, but calculated to involve me in serious difficulties with my neighbors."

"I hope you will not be angry with me, master?" said Phillis, "but I can't tell a lie; I let Jim stay in my room that night, and I've been mightily troubled about it; I was afeard you would be angry with me, if you heard of it, and yet, master, I could not help it when it happened."

"Could not help it! Phillis," said Mr. Weston. "What do you mean by that? Why did you not inform me of it, that I might have sent him off?"

"I couldn't find it in my heart, sir," said Phillis, the tears coming in her fine eyes. "The poor creature come in when the storm was at its worst. I had no candle lit, for the lightning was so bright that I hadn't no call for any other light. Bacchus was out in it all, and I was thinking he would be brought in dead drunk, or dead in earnest, when all at once Jim burst open the door, and asked me to let him stay there. I know'd he had run away, and at first I told him to go off, and not be gitting me into trouble; but, master, while I was sending him off such a streak of lightning come in, and such a crash of thunder, that I thought the Almighty had heard me turn him out, and would call me to account for it, when Jim and me should stand before him at the Judgment Day. I told Jim he had better go back to his master, that he wouldn't have any comfort, always hiding himself, and afeard to show his face, but he declared he would die first; and so as I couldn't persuade him to go home agin, I couldn't help myself, for I thought it would be a sin and shame, to turn a beast out in such a storm as that. As soon as the day began to break, and before, too, I woke him up, and told him never to come to my cabin again, no matter what happened. And so, master, I've told you the whole truth, and I am sure you couldn't have turned the poor wretch out to perish in that storm, no matter what would have come of it after."

Phillis had gained confidence as she proceeded, and Mr. Weston heard her without interruption.

"I can hardly blame you," he then said, "for what you have done; but, Phillis, it must never be repeated. Jim is a great rascal, and if I were his master I would be glad to be rid of him, but my plantation must not shelter runaway slaves. I am responsible for what my servants do. I should be inclined to hold other gentlemen responsible for the conduct of theirs. The laws of Virginia require the rights of the master to be respected, and though I shan't make a constable of myself, still I will not allow any such thing to be repeated. Did Bacchus know it?"

"No, indeed, sir; he hates Jim, and no good, may be, would have come of his knowing it; besides, he was asleep long after Jim went off, and there was too much whiskey in him to depend on what he'd have to say."

"That will do, Phillis; and see that such a thing never happens again," said Mr. Weston.

Phillis went back to her ironing, assured her master was not angry with her. Yet she sighed as she thought of his saying, "see that such a thing never happens again." "If it had been a clear night," she thought within herself, "he shouldn't have stayed there. But it was the Lord himself that sent the storm, and I can't see that he never sends another. Anyway its done, and can't be helped;" and Phillis busied herself with her work and her children.

I have not given Phillis's cottage as a specimen of the cabins of the negroes of the South. It is described from the house of a favorite servant. Yet are their cabins generally, healthy and airy. Interest, as well as a wish for the comfort and happiness of the slave, dictates an attention to his wants and feelings. "Slavery," says Voltaire, "is as ancient as war; war as human nature." It is to be wished that *truth* had some such intimate connection with human nature. Who, for instance, could read without an indignant thought, the following description from the pen of Mrs. Stowe: "They (their cabins) were rude shells, destitute of any pieces of furniture, except a heap of straw, foul with dirt, spread confusedly over the floor." "The small village was alive with no inviting sounds; hoarse, guttural voices, contending at the handmills, where their morsel of hard corn was yet to be ground into meal to fit it for the cake that was to constitute their only supper." But such statements need no denial; the very appearance of the slaves themselves show their want of truth. Look at their sound and healthy limbs, hear the odd, but sweet and musical song that arrests the traveler as he goes on his way; listen to the ready jest which is ever on his lips, and see if the slavery which God has permitted in all ages to exist, is as is here described; and judge if our fair Southern land is tenanted by such fiends as they are represented to be, by those who are trying to make still worse the condition of a mass of God's creatures, born to a life of toil, but comparative freedom from care. If it be His will that men should be born free and equal, that will is not revealed in the Bible from the time of the patriarchs to the present day. There are directions there for the master and the slave. When the period of emancipation advances, other signs of the times will herald it, besides the uncalled-for interference, and the gross misrepresentations, of the men and women of the North.

Sidney Smith said of a man, who was a great talker, that a few flashes of silence would make a great improvement in him. So of the Abolition cause, a few flashes of truth would make it decidedly more respectable.

SELECTION

A Defense of the Peculiar Institution: George Fitzhugh on Negro Slavery, 1854

Northern attacks on slavery and the growing importance of the slavery issue to national politics brought the Southern defense of slavery to a new level of militancy during the 1850s. Writers of imaginative literature, like Mrs. Eastman, were joined by scholars, men of letters, and students of Southern society —George Frederick Holmes, William J. Grayson, Edmund Ruffin, to name only a few—and scientists like Josiah Nott. Perhaps the greatest apologist for slavery during this decade was the Virginian George Fitzhugh (1806–1881). As a contributing editor to two Richmond newspapers, an author of books and pamphlets, and a public speaker, Fitzhugh developed a strong and elaborate social justification for slavery, while at the same time delivering a savage indictment against industrial society. His two books, Sociology for the South; or, The Failure of Free Society *(1854) and* Cannibals All! or Slaves without Masters *(1857), emphasized the advantages of slavery for Southern white and Negro alike, while depicting the insecurity and exploitation of the Northern industrial worker. In a statement that had a particular impact on Northern thinking, Fitzhugh suggested that slavery might someday be adopted by the North for the white workingman and predicted that the nation must soon become either all slave or all free. A comprehensive survey of proslavery argu-*

ments is in William S. Jenkins, Pro-Slavery Thought in the Old South *(1935); for Fitzhugh, see Harvey Wish,* George Fitzhugh, Propagandist of the Old South *(1943), and C. Vann Woodward's introduction to the John Harvard Library edition of* Cannibals All! *(1960) Fitzhugh's "Defense" is reprinted from* Sociology for the South; or, The Failure of Free Society *(Richmond, Va.: A. Morris, 1854), pages 82–95.*

We have already stated that we should not attempt to introduce any new theories of government and of society, but merely try to justify old ones, so far as we could deduce such theories from ancient and almost universal practices. Now it has been the practice in all countries and in all ages, in some degree, to accommodate the amount and character of government control to the wants, intelligence, and moral capacities of the nations or individuals to be governed. A highly moral and intellectual people, like the free citizens of ancient Athens, are best governed by a democracy. For a less moral and intellectual one, a limited and constitutional monarchy will answer. For a people either very ignorant or very wicked, nothing short of military despotism will suffice. So among individuals, the most moral and well-informed members of society require no other government than law. They are capable of reading and understanding the law, and have sufficient self-control and virtuous disposition to obey it. Children cannot be governed by mere law; first, because they do not understand it, and secondly, because they are so much under the influence of impulse, passion and appetite, that they want sufficient self-control to be deterred or governed by the distant and doubtful penalties of the law. They must be constantly controlled by parents or guardians, whose will and orders shall stand in the place of law for them. Very wicked men must be put into penitentiaries; lunatics into asylums, and the most wild of them into straight jackets, just as the most wicked of the sane are manacled with irons; and idiots must have committees to govern and take care of them. Now, it is clear the Athenian democracy would not suit a negro nation, nor will the government of mere law suffice for the individual negro. He is but a grown up child, and must be governed as a child, not as a lunatic or criminal. The master occupies towards him the place of parent or guardian. We shall not dwell on this view, for no one will differ with us who thinks as we do of the negro's capacity, and we might argue till dooms-day, in vain, with those who have a high opinion of the negro's moral and intellectual capacity.

Secondly. The negro is improvident; will not lay up in summer for the wants of winter; will not accumulate in youth for the exigencies of age. He would become an insufferable burden to society. Society has the right to prevent this, and can only do so by subjecting him to domestic slavery.

In the last place, the negro race is inferior to the white race, and living in their midst, they would be far outstripped or outwitted in the chase of free competition. Gradual but certain extermination would be their fate. We presume the maddest abolitionist does not think the negro's providence of habits and money-making capacity at all to compare to those of the whites. This defect of character would alone justify enslaving him, if he is to remain here. In Africa or the West Indies, he would become idolatrous, savage and cannibal, or be devoured by savages and cannibals. At the North he would freeze or starve.

We would remind those who deprecate and sympathize with negro slavery, that his slavery here relieves him from a far more cruel slavery in Africa, or from idolatry and cannibalism, and every brutal vice and crime that can disgrace humanity; and that it christianizes, protects, supports and civilizes him; that it governs him far better than free laborers at the North are governed. There, wife murder has become a mere holiday pastime; and where so many wives are murdered, almost all must be brutally treated. Nay, more: men who kill their wives or treat them brutally, must be ready for all kinds of crime, and the calendar of crime at the North proves the inference to be correct. Negroes never kill their wives. If it be objected that legally they have no wives, then we reply, that in an experience of more than forty years, we never yet heard of a negro man killing a negro woman. Our negroes are not only better off as to physical comfort than free laborers, but their moral condition is better.

But abolish negro slavery, and how much of slavery still remains. Soldiers and sailors in Europe enlist for life; here, for five years. Are they not slaves who have not only sold their liberties, but their lives also? And they are worse treated than domestic slaves. No domestic affection and self-interest extend their ægis over them. No kind mistress, like a guardian angel, provides for them in health, tends them in sickness, and soothes their dying pillow. Wellington at Waterloo was a slave. He was bound to obey, or would, like admiral Byng, have been shot for gross misconduct, and might not, like a common laborer, quit his work at any moment. He had sold his liberty, and might not resign without the consent of his master, the king. The common laborer may quit his work at any moment, whatever his contract; declare that liberty is an inalienable right, and leave his employer to redress by a useless suit for damages. The highest and most honorable position on earth was that of the slave Wellington; the lowest, that of the free man who cleaned his boots and fed his hounds. The African cannibal, caught, christianized and enslaved, is as much elevated by slavery as was Wellington. The kind of slavery is adapted to the men enslaved. Wives and apprentices are slaves; not in theory only, but often in fact. Children are slaves to their parents, guardians and teachers. Imprisoned culprits are slaves. Lunatics and idiots are slaves also. Three-fourths of free society are slaves, no better treated, when their wants and capacities are estimated, than negro slaves. The masters in free society, or slave society, if they perform properly their duties, have more cares and less liberty than the slaves themselves. "In the sweat of thy face shalt thou earn thy bread!" made all men slaves, and such all *good men* continue to be.

Negro slavery would be changed immediately to some form of peonage, serfdom or villienage, if the negroes were sufficiently intelligent and provident to manage a farm. No one would have the labor and trouble of management, if his negroes would pay in hires and rents one-half what free tenants pay in rent in Europe. Every negro in the South would be soon liberated, if he would take liberty on the terms that white tenants hold it. The fact that he cannot enjoy liberty on such terms, seems conclusive that he is only fit to be a slave.

But for the assaults of the abolitionists, much would have been done ere this to regulate and improve Southern slavery. Our negro mechanics do not work so hard, have many more privileges and holidays, and are better fed and clothed than field hands, and are yet more valuable to their masters. The slaves of the South are cheated of their rights by the purchase of Northern manufactures which they could produce. Besides, if we would employ our slaves in the coarser processes of the mechanic arts and manufactures, such as brick making, getting and hewing timber for ships and houses, iron mining and smelting, coal mining, grading railroads and plank roads, in the manufacture of cotton, tobacco, &c., we would find a vent in new employments for their increase, more humane and more profitable than the vent afforded by new states and territories. The nice and finishing processes of manufactures and mechanics should be reserved for the whites, who only are fitted for them, and thus, by diversifying pursuits and cutting off dependence on the North, we might benefit and advance the interests of our whole population. Exclusive agriculture has depressed and impoverished the South. We will not here dilate on this topic, because we intend to make it the subject of a separate essay. Free trade doctrines, not slavery, have made the South agricultural and dependent, giving her a sparse and ignorant population, ruined her cities, and expelled her people.

Would the abolitionists approve of a system of society that set white children free, and remitted them at the age of fourteen, males and females, to all the rights, both as to person and property, which belong to adults? Would it be criminal or praiseworthy to do so? Criminal, of course. Now, are the average of negroes equal in information, in native intelligence, in prudence of providence, to well-informed white children of fourteen? We who have lived with them for forty years, think not. The competition of the world would be too much for the children. They would be cheated out of their property and debased in their morals. Yet they would meet every where with sympathizing friends of their own color, ready to aid, advise and assist them. The negro would be exposed to the same competition and greater temptations, with no greater ability to contend with them, with these additional difficulties. He would be welcome nowhere; meet with thousands of enemies and no friends. If he went North, the white laborers would kick him and cuff him, and drive him out of employment. If he went to Africa, the savages would cook him and eat him. If he went to the West Indies, they would not let him in, or if they did, they would soon make of him a savage and idolater.

We have a further question to ask. If it be right and incumbent to subject children to the authority of parents and guardians, and idiots and lunatics to committees, would it not be equally right and incumbent to give the free negroes masters, until at least they arrive at years of discretion, which very few ever did or will attain? What is the difference between the authority of a parent and of a master? Neither pay wages, and each is entitled to the services of those subject to him. The father may not sell his child forever, but may hire him out till he is twenty-one. The free negro's master may also be restrained from selling. Let him stand in *loco parentis,* and call him papa instead of master. Look closely into slavery, and you will see nothing so hideous in it; or if you do, you will find plenty of it at home in its most hideous form.

The earliest civilization of which history gives account is that of Egypt. The negro was always in contact with that civilization. For four thousand years he has had opportunities of becoming civilized. Like the wild horse, he must be caught, tamed and domesticated. When his subjugation ceases he again runs wild, like the cattle on the Pampas of the South, or the horses on the prairies of the West. His condition in the West Indies proves this.

It is a common remark, that the grand and lasting architectural structures of antiquity were the results of slavery. The mighty and continued association of labor requisite to their construction, when mechanic art was so little advanced, and labor-saving processes unknown, could only have been brought about by a despotic authority, like that of the master over his slaves. It is, however, very remarkable, that whilst in taste and artistic skill the world seems to have been retrograding ever since the decay and abolition of feudalism, in mechanical invention and in great utilitarian operations requiring the wielding of immense capital and much labor, its progress has been unexampled. Is it because capital is more despotic in its authority over free laborers than Roman masters and feudal lords were over their slaves and vassals?

Free society has continued long enough to justify the attempt to generalize its phenomena, and calculate its moral and intellectual influences. It is obvious that, in whatever is purely utilitarian and material, it incites invention and stimulates industry. Benjamin Franklin, as a man and a philosopher, is the best exponent of the working of the system. His sentiments and his philosophy are low, selfish, atheistic and material. They tend directly to make man a mere "featherless biped," well-fed, well-clothed and comfortable, but regardless of his soul as "the beasts that perish."

Since the Reformation the world has as regularly been retrograding in whatever belongs to the departments of genius, taste and art, as it has been progressing in physical science and its application to mechanical construction. . . . There is not a poet, an orator, a sculptor, or painter in the world. The tedious elaboration necessary to all the productions of high art would be ridiculed in this money-making, utilitarian, charlatan age. Nothing now but what is gaudy and costly excites admiration. The public taste is debased.

But far the worst feature of modern civilization, which is the civilization of free society, remains to be exposed. Whilst labor-saving processes have probably lessened by one half, in the last century, the amount of work needed for comfortable support, the free laborer is compelled by capital and competition to work more than he ever did before, and is less comfortable. The organization of society cheats him of his earnings, and those earnings go to swell the vulgar pomp and pageantry of the ignorant millionaires, who are the only great of the present day. These reflections might seem, at first view, to have little connexion with negro slavery; but it is well for us of the South not to be deceived by the tinsel glare and glitter of free society, and to employ ourselves in doing our duty at home, and studying the past, rather than in insidious rivalry of the expensive pleasures and pursuits of men whose sentiments and whose aims are low, sensual and grovelling.

Human progress, consisting in moral and intellectual improvement, and there being no agreed and conventional standard weights or measures of moral and intellectual qualities and quantities, the question of progress can never be accurately decided. We maintain that man has not improved, because in all save the mechanic arts he reverts to the distant past for models to imitate, and he never imitates what he can excel.

We need never have white slaves in the South, because we have black ones. Our citizens, like those of Rome and Athens, are a privileged class. We should train and educate them to deserve the privileges and to per-form the duties which society confers on them. Instead, by a low demagoguism depressing their self-respect by discourses on the equality of man, we had better excite their pride by reminding them that they do not fulfil the menial offices which white men do in other countries. Society does not feel the burden of providing for the few helpless paupers in the South. And we should recollect that here we have but half the people to educate, for half are negroes; whilst at the North they profess to educate all. It is in our power to spike this last gun of the abolitionists. We should educate all the poor. The abolitionists say that it is one of the necessary consequences of slavery that the poor are neglected. It was not so in Athens, and in Rome, and should not be so in the South. If we had less trade with and less dependence on the North, all our poor might be profitably and honorably employed in trades, professions and manufactures. Then we should have a rich and denser population. Yet we but marshal her in the way that she was going. The South is already aware of the necessity of a new policy, and has begun to act on it. Every day more and more is done for education, the mechanic arts, manufactures and internal improvements. We will soon be independent of the North.

We deem this peculiar question of negro slavery of very little im-portance. The issue is made throughout the world on the general subject of slavery in the abstract. The argument has commenced. One set of ideas will govern and control after awhile the civilized world. Slavery will every where be abolished, or every where be re-instituted. We think the opponents of practical, existing slavery, are estopped by their own admission; nay, that unconsciously, as socialists, they are the defenders and propagandists of slavery, and have furnished the only sound argu-ments on which its defence and justification can be rested. We have intro-duced the subject of negro slavery to afford us a better opportunity to disclaim the purpose of reducing the white man any where to the condi-tion of negro slaves here. It would be very unwise and unscientific to govern white men as you would negroes. Every shade and variety of slavery has existed in the world. In some cases there has been much of legal regulation, much restraint of the master's authority; in others, none at all. The character of slavery necessary to protect the whites in Europe should be much milder than negro slavery, for slavery is only needed to protect the white man, whilst it is more necessary for the government of the negro even than for his protection. But even negro slavery should not be outlawed. We might and should have laws in Virginia, as in Louisiana, to make the master subject to presentment by the grand jury and to punishment, for any inhuman or improper treatment or neglect of his slave.

We abhor the doctrine of the "Types of Mankind;" first, because it is at war with scripture, which teaches us that the whole human race is descended from a common parentage; and, secondly, because it encourages and incites brutal masters to treat negroes, not as weak, ignorant and dependent brethren, but as wicked beasts, without the pale of humanity. The Southerner is the negro's friend, his only friend. Let no intermeddling abolitionist, no refined philosophy, dissolve this friendship.

SELECTION

A Former Slave Speaks Out against Slavery: Frederick Douglass on the Treatment of Slaves, 1855

Frederick Douglass (1817?–1895) was born to slavery near Easton, Maryland, the son of a white father and a Negro slave mother. As a youth, he was sent to Baltimore as a house servant, learning to read and write and developing his first notions of freedom. Later he learned the trade of a ship's caulker and was allowed to hire his own time. After one unsuccessful attempt, for which he was returned to the plantation as a field hand for a time, Douglass was able in 1838 to escape his bondage. He very quickly came to the attention of Northern abolitionists and before long was employed as an agent of the Massachusetts Anti Slavery Society. He remained active in the cause of abolition throughout the pre-Civil War period and became widely known throughout the country for his writing and lecturing on behalf of the crusade against slavery. In 1845, he published his Narrative of the Life of Frederick Douglass, *a small volume that was later expanded to* My Bondage and My Freedom *(from which the following selection is taken). Douglass became the most influential free Negro in the North and one of the most controversial agitators for Negro freedom. His account of slave conditions, written to advance the abolitionist movement, differs greatly from the rosy hues painted by slavery's apologists. The final, expanded version of Douglass' autobiography appeared as* The Life and Times of Frederick Douglass *(1881). Douglass' writings have been collected in Philip S. Foner,* The Life and Writings of Frederick Douglass *(1950–1955), four volumes; for a biography of Douglass, see Benjamin Quarles,* Frederick Douglass *(1948). A recent, scholarly study of slavery is in Kenneth M. Stampp,* The Peculiar Institution: Slavery in the Ante-Bellum South *(1956). The extract quoted below is reprinted from* My Bondage and My Freedom *(New York: Miller, Orton & Mulligan, 1855), pages 89–106.*

. . . Why am I a slave? Why are some people slaves, and others masters? Was there ever a time when this was not so? How did the relation commence? These were the perplexing questions which began now to claim

my thoughts, and to exercise the weak powers of my mind, for I was still but a child, and knew less than children of the same age in the free states. As my questions concerning these things were only put to children a little older, and little better informed than myself, I was not rapid in reaching a solid footing. By some means I learned from these inquiries, that *"God, up in the sky,"* made every body; and that he made *white* people to be masters and mistresses, and *black* people to be slaves. This did not satisfy me, nor lessen my interest in the subject. I was told, too, that God was good, and that He knew what was best for me, and best for everybody. This was less satisfactory than the first statement; because it came, point blank, against all my notions of goodness. It was not good to let old master cut the flesh off Esther, and make her cry so. Besides, how did people know that God made black people to be slaves? Did they go up in the sky and learn it? or, did He come down and tell them so? All was dark here. It was some relief to my hard notions of the goodness of God, that, although he made white men to be slaveholders, he did not make them to be *bad* slaveholders, and that, in due time, he would punish the bad slave-holders; that he would, when they died, send them to the bad place, where they would be "burnt up." Nevertheless, I could not reconcile the relation of slavery with my crude notions of goodness.

Then, too, I found that there were puzzling exceptions to this theory of slavery on both sides, and in the middle. I knew of blacks who were *not* slaves; I knew of whites who were *not* slaveholders; and I knew of persons who were *nearly* white, who were slaves. *Color,* therefore, was a very unsatisfactory basis for slavery.

Once, however, engaged in the inquiry, I was not very long in finding out the true solution of the matter. It was not *color,* but *crime,* not *God,* but *man,* that afforded the true explanation of the existence of slavery; nor was I long in finding out another important truth, viz: what man can make, man can unmake. The appalling darkness faded away, and I was master of the subject. There were slaves here, direct from Guinea; and there were many who could say that their fathers and mothers were stolen from Africa—forced from their homes, and compelled to serve as slaves. This, to me, was knowledge; but it was a kind of knowledge which filled me with a burning hatred of slavery, increased my suffering, and left me without the means of breaking away from my bondage. Yet it was knowl-edge quite worth possessing. I could not have been more than seven or eight years old, when I began to make this subject my study. It was with me in the woods and fields; along the shore of the river, and wherever my boyish wanderings led me; and though I was, at that time, quite ignorant of the existence of the free states, I distinctly remember being, *even then,* most strongly impressed with the idea of being a freeman some day. This cheering assurance was an inborn dream of my human nature—a constant menace to slavery—and one which all the powers of slavery were unable to silence or extinguish.

Up to the time of the brutal flogging of my Aunt Esther—for she was my own aunt—and the horrid plight in which I had seen my cousin from Tuckahoe, who had been so badly beaten by the cruel Mr. Plummer, my attention had not been called, especially, to the gross features of slavery. I had, of course, heard of whippings, and of savage *rencontres* between overseers and slaves, but I had always been out of the way at the times and places of their occurrence. My plays and sports, most of the time, took me from the corn and tobacco fields, where the great body of the hands were at work, and where scenes of cruelty were enacted and witnessed. But, after the whipping of Aunt Esther, I saw many cases of the same shocking nature, not only in my master's house, but on Col. Lloyd's plantation. One of the first which I saw, and which greatly agitated me, was the whipping of a woman belonging to Col. Lloyd, named Nelly. The offense alleged against Nelly, was one of the commonest and most indefinite in the whole catalogue of offenses usually laid to the charge of slaves, viz: "impudence." This may mean almost anything, or nothing at all, just according to the caprice of the master or overseer, at the moment. But, whatever it is, or is not, if it gets the name of "impudence," the party charged with it is sure of a flogging. This offense may be committed in various ways; in the tone of an answer; in answering at all; in not answering; in the expression of countenance; in the motion of the head; in the gait, manner and bearing of the slave. In the case under consideration, I can easily believe that, according to all slaveholding standards, here was a genuine instance of impudence. In Nelly there were all the necessary conditions for committing the offense. She was a bright mulatto, the recognized wife of a favorite "hand" on board Col. Lloyd's sloop, and the mother of five sprightly children. She was a vigorous and spirited woman, and one of the most likely, on the plantation, to be guilty of impudence. My attention was called to the scene, by the noise, curses and screams that proceeded from it; and, on going a little in that direction, I came upon the parties engaged in the skirmish. Mr. Sevier, the overseer, had hold of Nelly, when I caught sight of them; he was endeavoring to drag her toward a tree, which endeavor Nelly was sternly resisting; but to no purpose, except to retard the progress of the overseer's plans. Nelly—as I have said—was the mother of five children; three of them were present, and though quite small, (from seven to ten years old, I should think,) they gallantly came to their mother's defense, and gave the overseer an excellent pelting with stones. One of the little fellows ran up, seized the overseer by the leg and bit him; but the monster was too busily engaged with Nelly, to pay any attention to the assaults of the children. There were numerous bloody marks on Mr. Sevier's face, when I first saw him, and they increased as the struggle went on. The imprints of Nelly's fingers were visible, and I was glad to see them. Amidst the wild screams of the children—*"Let my mammy go"*—*"let my mammy go"*—there escaped, from between the teeth of the bullet-headed overseer, a few bitter curses, mingled with threats, that "he would teach the d—d b—h how to give a white man impudence." There is no doubt that Nelly felt herself superior, in some respects, to the slaves around her. She was a wife and a mother; her husband was a valued and favorite slave. Besides, he was one of the first hands on board of the sloop, and the sloop hands—since they had to represent the plantation abroad—were generally treated tenderly. The overseer never was allowed to whip Harry; why then should he be allowed to whip Harry's wife? Thoughts of this kind, no doubt, influenced her; but, for whatever reason, she nobly resisted, and, unlike most of the slaves, seemed determined to make her whipping cost Mr. Sevier as much as possible. The blood on his (and her) face, attested her skill, as well as her courage and dexterity in using her nails. Maddened by her resistance, I expected to see Mr. Sevier level her to the ground by a stunning blow; but no; like a savage bull-dog—which he resembled both in temper and appearance—he maintained his grip, and steadily dragged his victim toward the tree, disregarding alike her blows, and the cries of the children for their mother's release. He would, doubtless, have knocked her down with his hickory stick, but that such act might have cost him his place. It is often deemed advisable to knock a *man* slave down, in order to tie him, but it is considered cowardly and inexcusable, in an overseer, thus to deal with a *woman*. He is expected to tie her up, and to give her what is called, in southern parlance, a "genteel flogging," without any very great outlay of strength or skill. I watched, with palpitating interest, the course of the preliminary struggle, and was saddened by every new advantage gained over her by the ruffian. There were times when she seemed likely to get the better of the brute, but he finally overpowered her, and succeeded in getting his rope around her arms, and in firmly tying her to the tree, at which he had been aiming. This done, and Nelly was at the mercy of his merciless lash; and now, what followed, I have no heart to describe. The cowardly creature made good his every threat; and wielded the lash with all the hot zest of furious revenge. The cries of the woman, while undergoing the terrible infliction, were mingled with those of the children, sounds which I hope the reader may never be called upon to hear. When Nelly was untied, her back was covered with blood. The red stripes were all over her shoulders. She was whipped—severely whipped; but she was not subdued, for she continued to denounce the overseer, and to call him every vile name. He had bruised her flesh, but had left her invincible spirit undaunted. Such floggings are seldom repeated by the same overseer. They prefer to whip those who are most easily whipped. The old doctrine that submission is the best cure for outrage and wrong, does not hold good on the slave plantation. He is whipped oftenest, who is whipped easiest; and that slave who has the courage to stand up for himself against the overseer, although he may have many hard stripes at the first, becomes, in the end, a freeman, even though he sustain the formal relation of a slave. "You can shoot me but you can't whip me," said a slave to Rigby Hopkins; and the result was that he was neither whipped nor shot. If the latter had been his fate, it would have been less deplorable than the living and lingering death to which cowardly and slavish souls are subjected. I do not know that Mr. Sevier ever undertook to whip Nelly again. He probably never did, for it was not long after his attempt to subdue her, that he was taken sick, and died. The wretched man died as he had lived, unrepentant; and it was said—with how much truth I know not—that in the very last hours of his life, his ruling passion showed itself, and that when wrestling with death, he was uttering horrid oaths, and flourishing the cowskin, as though he was tearing the flesh off some helpless slave. One thing is certain, that when he was in health, it was enough to chill the blood, and to stiffen the hair of an ordinary man, to hear Mr. Sevier talk. Nature, or his cruel habits, had given to his face an expression of unusual savageness, even for a slave-driver. Tobacco and rage had worn his teeth short, and nearly every sentence that escaped their compressed grating, was commenced or concluded with some outburst of profanity. His presence made the field alike the field of blood, and of blasphemy. Hated for his cruelty, despised for his cowardice, his death was deplored by no one outside his own house—if indeed it was deplored there; it was regarded by the slaves as a merciful interposition of Providence. Never went there a man to the grave loaded with heavier curses. Mr. Sevier's place was promptly taken by a Mr. Hopkins, and the change was quite a relief, he being a very different man. He was, in all respects, a better man than his predecessor; as good as any man can be, and yet be an overseer. His course was characterized by no extraordinary cruelty; and when he whipped a slave, as he sometimes did, he seemed to take no especial pleasure in it, but, on the contrary, acted as though he felt it to be a mean business. Mr. Hopkins stayed but a short time; his place— much to the regret of the slaves generally—was taken by a Mr. Gore, of whom more will be said hereafter. It is enough, for the present, to say, that he was no improvement on Mr. Sevier, except that he was less noisy and less profane.

I have already referred to the business-like aspect of Col. Lloyd's plantation. This business-like appearance was much increased on the two days at the end of each month, when the slaves from the different farms came to get their monthly allowance of meal and meat. These were gala days for the slaves, and there was much rivalry among them as to *who* should be elected to go up to the great house farm for the allowance, and, indeed, to attend to any business at this, (for them,) the capital. The beauty and grandeur of the place, its numerous slave population, and the fact that Harry, Peter and Jake—the sailors of the sloop—almost always kept, privately, little trinkets which they bought at Baltimore, to sell, made it a privilege to come to the great house farm. Being selected, too, for this office, was deemed a high honor. It was taken as a proof of confidence and favor; but, probably, the chief motive of the competitors for the place, was, a desire to break the dull monotony of the field, and to get beyond the overseer's eye and lash. Once on the road with an ox team, and seated on the tongue of his cart, with no overseer to look after him, the slave was comparatively free; and, if thoughtful, he had time to think. Slaves are generally expected to sing as well as to work. A silent slave is not liked by masters or overseers. *"Make a noise,"* *"make a noise,"* and *"bear a hand,"* are the words usually addressed to the slaves when there is silence amongst them. This may account for the almost constant singing heard in the southern states. There was, generally, more or less singing among the teamsters, as it was one means of letting the overseer know where they were, and that they were moving on with the work. But, on allowance day, those who visited the great house farm were peculiarly excited and noisy. While on their way, they would make the dense old woods, for miles around, reverberate with their wild notes. These were not always merry because they were wild. On the contrary, they were mostly of a plaintive cast, and told a tale of grief and sorrow. In the most boisterous outbursts of rapturous sentiment, there was ever a tinge of deep melancholy. I have never heard any songs like those anywhere since I left slavery, except when in Ireland. There I heard the same *wailing notes*, and was much affected by them. It was during the famine of 1845–6. . . .

The remark is not unfrequently made, that slaves are the most contented and happy laborers in the world. They dance and sing, and make all manner of joyful noises—so they do; but it is a great mistake to suppose them happy because they sing. The songs of the slave represent the sorrows, rather than the joys, of his heart; and he is relieved by them, only as an aching heart is relieved by its tears. Such is the constitution of the human mind, that, when pressed to extremes, it often avails itself of the most opposite methods. Extremes meet in mind as in matter. When the slaves on board of the "Pearl" were overtaken, arrested, and carried to prison— their hopes for freedom blasted—as they marched in chains they sang, and found (as Emily Edmunson tells us) a melancholy relief in singing. The singing of a man cast away on a desolate island, might be as appropriately considered an evidence of his contentment and happiness, as the singing of a slave. Sorrow and desolation have their songs, as well as joy and peace. Slaves sing more to *make* themselves happy, than to express their happiness.

It is the boast of slaveholders, that their slaves enjoy more of the physical comforts of life than the peasantry of any country in the world. My experience contradicts this. The men and the women slaves on Col. Lloyd's farm, received, as their monthly allowance of food, eight pounds of pickled pork, or their equivalent in fish. The pork was often tainted, and the fish was of the poorest quality—herrings, which would bring very little if offered for sale in any northern market. With their pork or fish, they had one bushel of Indian meal—unbolted—of which quite fifteen per cent was fit only to feed pigs. With this, one pint of salt was given; and this was the entire monthly allowance of a full grown slave, working constantly in the open field, from morning until night, every day in the month except Sunday, and living on a fraction more than a quarter of a pound of meat per day, and less than a peck of corn-meal per week. There is no kind of work that a man can do which requires a better supply of food to prevent physical exhaustion, than the field-work of a slave. So much for the slave's allowance of food; now for his raiment. The yearly allowance of clothing for the slaves on this plantation, consisted of two tow-linen shirts—such linen as the coarsest crash towels are made of; one pair of trowsers of the same material, for summer, and a pair of trowsers and a jacket of woolen, most slazily put together, for winter; one pair of yarn stockings, and one pair of shoes of the coarsest description. The slave's entire apparel could not have cost more than eight dollars per year. The allowance of food and clothing for the little children, was committed to their mothers, or to the older slave-women having the care of them. Children who were unable to work in the field, had neither shoes, stockings, jackets nor trowsers given them. Their clothing consisted of two coarse tow-linen shirts—already described—per year; and when these failed them, as they often did, they went naked until the next allowance day. Flocks of little children from five to ten years old, might be seen on Col. Lloyd's plantation, as destitute of clothing as any little heathen on the west coast of Africa; and this, not merely during the summer months, but during the frosty weather of March. The little girls were no better off than the boys; all were nearly in a state of nudity.

As to beds to sleep on, they were known to none of the field hands;

nothing but a coarse blanket—not so good as those used in the north to cover horses—was given them, and this only to the men and women. The children stuck themselves in holes and corners, about the quarters; often in the corner of the huge chimneys, with their feet in the ashes to keep them warm. The want of beds, however, was not considered a very great privation. Time to sleep was of far greater importance, for, when the day's work is done, most of the slaves have their washing, mending and cooking to do; and, having few or none of the ordinary facilities for doing such things, very many of their sleeping hours are consumed in necessary preparations for the duties of the coming day.

The sleeping apartments—if they may be called such—have little regard to comfort or decency. Old and young, male and female, married and single, drop down upon the common clay floor, each covering up with his or her blanket,—the only protection they have from cold or exposure. The night, however, is shortened at both ends. The slaves work often as long as they can see, and are late in cooking and mending for the coming day; and, at the first gray streak of morning, they are summoned to the field by the driver's horn.

More slaves are whipped for oversleeping than for any other fault. Neither age nor sex finds any favor. The overseer stands at the quarter door, armed with stick and cowskin, ready to whip any who may be a few minutes behind time. When the horn is blown, there is a rush for the door, and the hindermost one is sure to get a blow from the overseer. Young mothers who worked in the field, were allowed an hour, about ten o'clock in the morning, to go home to nurse their children. Sometimes they were compelled to take their children with them, and to leave them in the corner of the fences, to prevent loss of time in nursing them. The overseer generally rides about the field on horseback. A cowskin and a hickory stick are his constant companions. The cowskin is a kind of whip seldom seen in the northern states. It is made entirely of untanned, but dried, ox hide, and is about as hard as a piece of well-seasoned live oak. It is made of various sizes, but the usual length is about three feet. The part held in the hand is nearly an inch in thickness; and, from the extreme end of the butt or handle, the cowskin tapers its whole length to a point. This makes it quite elastic and springy. A blow with it, on the hardest back, will gash the flesh, and make the blood start. Cowskins are painted red, blue and green, and are the favorite slave whip. I think this whip worse than the "cat-o'-nine-tails." It condenses the whole strength of the arm to a single point, and comes with a spring that makes the air whistle. It is a terrible instrument, and is so handy, that the overseer can always have it on his person, and ready for use. The temptation to use it is over strong; and an overseer can, if disposed, always have cause for using it. With him, it is literally a word and a blow, and, in most cases, the blow comes first.

As a general rule, slaves do not come to the quarters for either breakfast or dinner, but take their "ash cake" with them, and eat it in the field. This was so on the home plantation; probably, because the distance from the quarter to the field, was sometimes two, and even three miles.

The dinner of the slaves consisted of a huge piece of ash cake, and a small piece of pork, or two salt herrings. Not having ovens, nor any suitable cooking utensils, the slaves mixed their meal with a little water, to such thickness that a spoon would stand erect in it; and, after the wood had burned away to coals and ashes, they would place the dough between oak leaves and lay it carefully in the ashes, completely covering it; hence, the bread is called ash cake. The surface of this peculiar bread is covered with ashes, to the depth of a sixteenth part of an inch, and the ashes, certainly, do not make it very grateful to the teeth, nor render it very palatable. The bran, or coarse part of the meal, is baked with the fine, and bright scales run through the bread. This bread, with its ashes and bran, would disgust and choke a northern man, but it is quite liked by the slaves. They eat it with avidity, and are more concerned about the quantity than about the quality. They are far too scantily provided for, and are worked too steadily, to be much concerned for the quality of their food. The few minutes allowed them at dinner time, after partaking of their coarse repast, are variously spent. Some lie down on the "turning row," and go to sleep; others draw together, and talk; and others are at work with needle and thread, mending their tattered garments. Sometimes you may hear a wild, hoarse laugh arise from a circle, and often a song. Soon, however, the overseer comes dashing through the field. *"Tumble up! Tumble up,* and to *work, work,"* is the cry; and, now, from twelve o'clock (mid-day) till dark, the human cattle are in motion, wielding their clumsy hoes; hurried on by no hope of reward, no sense of gratitude, no love of children, no prospect of bettering their condition; nothing, save the dread and terror of the slave-driver's lash. So goes one day, and so comes and goes another.

But, let us now leave the rough usage of the field, where vulgar coarseness and brutal cruelty spread themselves and flourish, rank as weeds in the tropics; where a vile wretch, in the shape of a man, rides, walks, or struts about, dealing blows, and leaving gashes on broken-spirited men and helpless women, for thirty dollars per month—a business so horrible, hardening, and disgraceful, that, rather than engage in it, a decent man would blow his own brains out—and let the reader view with me the equally wicked, but less repulsive aspects of slave life; where pride and pomp roll luxuriously at ease; where the toil of a thousand men supports a single family in easy idleness and sin. This is the great house; it is the home of the LLOYDS! Some idea of its splendor has already been given— and, it is here that we shall find that height of luxury which is the opposite of that depth of poverty and physical wretchedness that we have just now been contemplating. But, there is this difference in the two extremes; viz: that in the case of the slave, the miseries and hardships of his lot are imposed by others, and, in the master's case, they are imposed by himself. The slave is a subject, subjected by others; the slaveholder is a subject, but he is the author of his own subjection. There is more truth in the saying, that slavery is a greater evil to the master than to the slave, than many, who utter it, suppose. The self-executing laws of eternal justice follow close on the heels of the evil-doer here, as well as elsewhere; making escape from all its penalties impossible. But, let others philosophize; it is my province here to relate and describe; only allowing myself a word or two, occasionally, to assist the reader in the proper understanding of the facts narrated.

SELECTION **6**

J. D. B. DeBow Emphasizes the Importance of Slavery to the Nonslaveholder, 1860

James D. B. DeBow (1820–1867) was one of the most influential spokesmen for Southern interests in the antebellum period. Born in Charleston, he later moved to New Orleans, where he established DeBow's Review. *The first number appeared in January, 1846. As editor of* DeBow's Review, *Debow effectively served Southern interests, principally economic, and his editorials were widely read throughout the United States. A strong admirer of John C. Calhoun, he gradually became an outspoken and radical partisan for Southern rights. In December, 1860, only two weeks before South Carolina would become the first Southern state to secede, DeBow wrote a letter (the selection which follows) in which he analyzed the central role played by slavery in Southern social and economic life and noted the strong stake held by the nonslaveholder in the perpetuation of the institution. Like many of his contemporaries, DeBow concluded that the establishment of a Southern nation was the only sure refuge from the storm of Northern aggression. For a study of DeBow and his influence, see Ottis C. Skipper,* J. D. B. DeBow: Magazinist of the Old South *(1958). The extract from "The Non-Slaveholders of the South," is reprinted from DeBow et al.,* The Interest in Slavery of the Southern Non-Slaveholder, The Right of Peaceful Secession, Slavery in the Bible *(Charleston, S.C.: Evans & Cogswell, 1860), pages 3–12.*

Nashville, Dec. 5, 1860.

My dear Sir:—Whilst in Charleston recently, I adverted, in conversation with you, to some considerations affecting the question of slavery in its application to the several classes of population at the South and especially to the non-slaveholding class, who, I maintained, were even more deeply interested than any other in the maintainance of our institutions, and in the success of the movement now inaugurated, for the entire social, industrial and political independence of the South. At your request, I promised to elaborate and commit to writing the points of that conversation, which I now proceed to do, in the hope that I may thus be enabled to give some feeble aid to a cause which is worthy of the Sydneys, Hampdens and Patrick Henrys, of earlier times.

When in charge of the national census office, several years since, I found that it had been stated by an abolition Senator from his seat, that the number of slaveholders at the South did not exceed 150,000. Convinced that it was a gross misrepresentation of the facts, I caused a careful examination of the returns to be made, which fixed the actual number at 347,255, and communicated the information, by note, to Senator Cass, who read it in the Senate. I first called attention to the fact that the number embraced slaveholding families, and that to arrive at the actual number of slaveholders, it would be necessary to multiply by the proportion of persons, which the census showed to a family. When this was done, the number was swelled to about 2,000,000.

Since these results were made public, I have had reason to think, that the separation of the schedules of the slave and the free, was calculated to lead to omissions of the single properties, and that on this account it would be safe to put the number of families at 375,000, and the number of actual slaveholders at about two million and a quarter.

Assuming the published returns, however, to be correct, it will appear that one-half of the population of South Carolina, Mississippi, and Louisiana, excluding the cities, are slaveholders, and that one-third of the population of the entire South are similarly circumstanced. The average number of slaves is nine to each slave-holding family, and one-half of the whole number of such holders are in possession of less than five slaves.

It will thus appear that the slaveholders of the South, so far from constituting numerically an insignificant portion of its people, as has been malignantly alleged, make up an aggregate, greater in relative proportion than the holders of any other species of property whatever, in any part of the world; and that of no other property can it be said, with equal truthfulness, that it is an interest of the whole community. Whilst every other family in the States I have specially referred to, are slaveholders, but one family in every three and a half families in Maine, New Hampshire, Massachusetts and Connecticut, are holders of agricultural land; and, in European States, the proportion is almost indefinitely less. The proportion which the slaveholders of the South, bear to the entire population is greater than that of the owners of land or houses, agricultural stock, State, bank, or other corporation securities anywhere else. No political economist will deny this. Nor is that all. Even in the States which are among the largest slaveholding, South Carolina, Georgia and Tennessee, the land proprietors outnumber nearly two to one, in relative proportion, the owners of the same property in Maine, Massachusetts and Connecticut, and if the average number of slaves held by each family throughout the South be but nine, and if one-half of the whole number of slaveholders own under five slaves, it will be seen how preposterous is the allegation of our enemies, that the slaveholding class is an organized wealthy aristocracy. *The poor men of the South are the holders of one to five slaves, and it would be equally consistent with truth and justice, to say that they represent, in reality, its slaveholding interest.*

The fact being conceded that there is a very large class of persons in the slaveholding States, who have no direct ownership in slaves; it may be well asked, upon what principle a greater antagonism can be presumed between them and their fellow-citizens, than exists among the larger class of non-landholders in the free States and the landed interest there? If a conflict of interest exists in one instance, it does in the other, and if patriotism and public spirit are to be measured upon so low a standard, the social fabric at the North is in far greater danger of dissolution than it is here.

Though I protest against the false and degrading standard, to which Northern orators and statesmen have reduced the measure of patriotism, which is to be expected from a free and enlightened people, and in the name of the non-slaveholders of the South, fling back the insolent charge that they are only bound to their country by its "loaves and fishes," and would be found derelict in honor and principle and public virtue in proportion as they are needy in circumstances; I think it but easy to show that the interest of the poorest non-slaveholder among us, is to make common cause with, and die in the last trenches in defence of, the slave property of his more favored neighbor.

The non-slaveholders of the South may be classed as either such as desire and are incapable of purchasing slaves, or such as have the means to purchase and do not because of the absence of the motive, preferring to hire or employ cheaper white labor. A class conscientiously objecting to the ownership of slave-property, does not exist at the South, for all such scruples have long since been silenced by the profound and unanswerable arguments to which Yankee controversy has driven our statesmen, popular orators and clergy. Upon the sure testimony of God's Holy Book, and upon the principles of universal polity, they have defended and justified the institution. The exceptions which embrace recent importations into Virginia, and into some of the Southern cities from the free States of the North, and some of the crazy, socialistic Germans in Texas, are too un-important to affect the truth of the proposition.

The non-slaveholders are either urban or rural, including among the former the merchants, traders, mechanics, laborers and other classes in the towns and cities; and among the latter, the tillers of the soil in sections where slave property either could, or could not be profitably employed.

As the *competition of free labor with slave labor* is the gist of the argument used by the opponents of slavery, and as it is upon this that they rely in support of a future social *conflict* in our midst, it clear that in cases where the competition cannot possibly exist, the argument, whatever weight it might otherwise have, must fall to the ground.

Now, from what can such competition be argued in our cities? Are not all the interests of the merchant and those whom he employs of necessity upon the side of the slaveholder? The products which he buys, the commodities which he sells, the profits which he realizes, the hopes of future fortune which sustain him; all spring from this source, and from no other. The cities, towns and villages of the South, are but so many agencies for converting the products of slave labor into the products of other labor obtained from abroad, and as in every other agency the interest of the agent is, that the principal shall have as much as possible to sell, and be enabled as much as possible to buy. In the absence of every other source of wealth at the South, its mercantile interests are so interwoven with those of slave labor as to be almost identical. What is true of the merchant is true of the clerk, the drayman, or the laborer whom he employs—the mechanic who builds his houses, the lawyer who argues his causes, the physician who heals, the teacher, the preacher, etc., etc. If the poor mechanic could have ever complained of the competition, in the cities, of slave labor with his, that cause or complaint in the enormous increase of value of slave property has failed, since such increase has been exhausting the cities and towns of slave labor, or making it so valuable that he can work in competition with it and receive a rate of remuneration greatly higher than in any of the non-slaveholding towns or cities at the

North. In proof of this, it is only necessary to advert to the example of the City of Charleston, which has a larger proportion of slaves than any other at the South, where the first flag of Southern independence was unfurled, and where the entire people, with one voice, rich and poor, merchant, mechanic and laborer, stand nobly together. Another illustration may be found in the city of New York, almost as dependent upon Southern slavery as Charleston itself, which records a majority of nearly thirty thousand votes against the further progress of abolitionism.

As the competition does not exist in the cities it is equally certain that it does not exist in those sections of the South, which are employed upon the cultivation of commodities, in which slave labor could not be used, and that there exists no conflict there except in the before stated cases of Virginia and Texas, and some of the counties of Missouri, Maryland and Kentucky. These exceptions are, however, too unimportant to affect the great question of slavery in fifteen States of the South, and are so kept in check as to be incapable of effecting any mischief even in the communities referred to. It would be the baldest absurdity to suppose that the poor farmers of South Carolina, North Carolina and Tennessee, who grow corn, wheat, bacon and hogs and horses, are brought into any sort of competition with the slaves of these or other States, who, while they consume these commodities, produce but little or none of them.

The competition and conflict, if such exist at the South, between slave labor and free labor, is reduced to the single case of such labor being employed side by side, in the production of the same commodities and could be felt only in the cane, cotton, tobacco and rice fields, where almost the entire agricultural slave labor is exhausted. Now, any one cognizant of the actual facts, will admit that the free labor which is employed upon these crops, disconnected from and in actual independence of the slaveholder, is a very insignificant item in the account, and whether in accord or in conflict would affect nothing the permanency and security of the institution. It is a competition from which the non-slaveholder cheerfully retires when the occasion offers, his physical organization refusing to endure that exposure to tropical suns and fatal miasmas which alone are the condition of profitable culture and any attempt to reverse the laws which God has ordained, is attended with disease and death. Of this the poor white foreign laborer upon our river swamps and in our southern cities, especially in Mobile and New Orleans, and upon the public works of the South, is a daily witness.

Having then followed out, step by step, and seen to what amounts the so much paraded competition and conflict between the non-slaveholding and slaveholding interests of the South; I will proceed to present several general considerations which must be found powerful enough to influence the non-slaveholders, if the claims of patriotism were inadequate, to resist any attempt to overthrow the institutions and industry of the section to which they belong.

1. *The non-slaveholder of the South is assured that the remuneration afforded by his labor, over and above the expense of living, is larger than that which is afforded by the same labor in the free States.* To be convinced of this he has only to compare the value of labor in the Southern cities with those of the North, and to take note annually of the large number of laborers who are represented to be out of employment there, and who

migrate to our shores, as well as to other sections. No white laborer in return has been forced to leave our midst or remain without employment.
Such as have left, have immigrated from States where slavery was less
productive. Those who come among us are enabled soon to retire to their
homes with a handsome competency. The statement is nearly as true for
the agricultural as for other interests, as the statistics will show. . . .

2. *The non-slaveholders, as a class, are not reduced by the necessity of
our condition, as is the case in the free States, to find employment in
crowded cities and come into competition in close and sickly workshops
and factories, with remorseless and untiring machinery.* They have but
to compare their condition in this particular with the mining and manufacturing operatives of the North and Europe, to be thankful that God has
reserved them for a better fate. Tender women, aged men, delicate children, toil and labor there from early dawn until after candle light, from
one year to another, for a miserable pittance, scarcely above the starvation
point and without hope of amelioration. The records of British free labor
have long exhibited this and those of our own manufacturing States are
rapidly reaching it and would have reached it long ago, but for the excessive bounties which in the way of tariffs have been paid to it, without an
equivalent by the slaveholding and non-slaveholding laborer of the South.
Let this tariff cease to be paid for a single year and the truth of what is
stated will be abundantly shown.

3. *The non-slaveholder is not subjected to that competition with foreign
pauper labor, which has degraded the free labor of the North and demoralized it to an extent which perhaps can never be estimated.* From
whatever cause, it has happened, whether from climate, the nature of our
products or of our labor, the South has been enabled to maintain a more
homogeneous population and show a less admixture of races than the
North. This the statistics show. . . .

Our people partake of the true American character, and are mainly the
descendants of those who fought the battles of the Revolution, and who
understand and appreciate the nature and inestimable value of the liberty
which it brought. Adhering to the simple truths of the Gospel and the
faith of their fathers, they have not run hither and thither in search of all
the absurd and degrading isms which have sprung up in the rank soil of
infidelity. They are not Mormons or Spiritualists, they are not Owenites,
Fourierites, Agrarians, Socialists, Free-lovers or Millerites. They are not
for breaking down all the forms of society and of religion and re-construct-
ing them; but prefer law, order and existing institutions to the chaos
which radicalism involves. The competition between native and foreign
labor in the Northern States, has already begotten rivalry and heart-
burning, and riots; and lead to the formation of political parties there
which have been marked by a degree of hostility and proscription to which
the present age has not afforded another parallel. At the South we have
known none of this, except in two or three of the larger cities, where the
relations of slavery and freedom scarcely exist at all. The foreigners that
are among us at the South are of a select class, and from education and
example approximate very nearly to the native standard.

4. *The non-slaveholder of the South preserves the status of the white
man, and is not regarded as an inferior or a dependant.* He is not told that
the Declaration of Independence, when it says that all men are born free

and equal, refers to the negro equally with himself. It is not proposed to him that the free negro's vote shall weigh equally with his own at the ballot-box, and that the little children of both colors shall be mixed in the classes and benches of the school-house, and embrace each other filially in its outside sports. It never occurs to him, that a white man could be degraded enough to boast in a public assembly, as was recently done in New York, of having actually slept with a negro. And his patriotic ire would crush with a blow the free negro who would dare, in his presence, as is done in the free States, to characterize the father of the country as a "scoundrel." No white man at the South serves another as a body servant, to clean his boots, wait on his table, and perform the menial services of his household. His blood revolts against this, and his necessities never drive him to it. He is a companion and an equal. When in the employ of the slaveholder, or in intercourse with him, he enters his hall, and has a seat at his table. If a distinction exists, it is only that which education and refinement may give, and this is so courteously exhibited as scarcely to strike attention. The poor white laborer at the North is at the bottom of the social ladder, whilst his brother here has ascended several steps and can look down upon those who are beneath him, at an infinite remove.

5. *The non-slaveholder knows that as soon as his savings will admit, he can become a slaveholder, and thus relieve his wife from the necessities of the kitchen and the laundry, and his children from the labors of the field.* This, with ordinary frugality, can, in general, be accomplished in a few years, and is a process continually going on. Perhaps twice the number of poor men at the South own a slave to what owned a slave ten years ago. The universal disposition is to purchase. It is the first use for savings, and the negro purchased is the last possession to be parted with. If a woman, her children become heir-looms and make the nucleus of an estate. It is within my knowledge, that a plantation of fifty or sixty persons has been established, from the descendants of a single female, in the course of the lifetime of the original purchaser.

6. *The large slaveholders and proprietors of the South begin life in great part as non-slaveholders.* It is the nature of property to change hands. Luxury, liberality, extravagance, depreciated land, low prices, debt, distribution among children, are continually breaking up estates. All over the new States of the Southwest enormous estates are in the hands of men who began life as overseers or city clerks, traders or merchants. Often the overseer marries the widow. Cheap lands, abundant harvests, high prices, give the poor man soon a negro. His ten bales of cotton bring him another, and second crop increases his purchases, and so he goes on opening land and adding labor until in a few years his draft for $20,000 upon his merchant becomes a very marketable commodity.

7. *But should such fortune not be in reserve for the non-slaveholder, he will understand that by honesty and industry it may be realized to his children.* More than one generation of poverty in a family is scarcely to be expected at the South, and is against the general experience. It is more unusual here for poverty than wealth to be preserved through several generations in the same family.

8. *The sons of the non-slaveholder are and have always been among the*

leading and ruling spirits of the South; in industry as well as in politics.
Every man's experience in his own neighborhood will evince this. He has
but to task his memory. In this class are the McDuffies, Langdon Cheves,
Andrew Jacksons, Henry Clays, and Rusks, of the past; the Hammonds,
Yanceys, Orrs, Memmingers, Benjamins, Stephens, Soules, Browns of
Mississippi, Simms, Porters, Magraths, Aikens, Maunsel Whites, and an
innumerable host of the present; and what is to be noted, these men have
not been made demagogues for that reason, as in other quarters, but are
among the most conservative among us. Nowhere else in the world have
intelligence and virtue disconnected from ancestral estates, the same opportunities for advancement, and nowhere else is their triumph more
speedy and signal.

9. *Without the institution of slavery, the great staple products of the
South would cease to be grown, and the immense annual results, which
are distributed among every class of the community, and which give life
to every branch of industry; would cease.* The world furnishes no instances
of these products being grown upon a large scale by free labor. The English
now acknowledge their failure in the East Indies. Brazil, whose slave
population nearly equals our own, is the only South American State which
has prospered. Cuba, by her slave labor, showers wealth upon old Spain,
whilst the British West India Colonies have now ceased to be a source
of revenue, and from opulence have been, by emancipation, reduced to
beggary. St. Domingo shared the same fate, and the poor whites have been
massacred equally with the rich. . . .

10. *If emancipation be brought about as will undoubtedly be the case,
unless the encroachments of the fanatical majorities of the North are resisted now the slaveholders, in the main, will escape the degrading equality which must result, by emigration, for which they would have the means,
by disposing of their personal chattels: whilst the non-slaveholders, without these resources, would be compelled to remain and endure the degradation.* This is a startling consideration. In Northern communities, where the
free negro is one in a hundred of the total population, he is recognized and
acknowledged often as a pest, and in many cases even his presence is
prohibited by law. What would be the case in many of our States, where
every other inhabitant is a negro, or in many of our communities, as for
example the parishes around and about Charleston, and in the vicinity of
New Orleans where there are from twenty to one hundred negroes to each
white inhabitant? Low as would this class of people sink by emancipation
in idleness, superstition and vice, the white man compelled to live among
them, would by the power exerted over him, sink even lower, unless as is
to be supposed he would prefer to suffer death instead.

In conclusion, my dear sir, I must apologize to the non-slaveholders of
the South, of which class, I was myself until very recently a member, for
having deigned to notice at all the infamous libels which the common
enemies of the South have circulated against them, and which our every-
day experience refutes; but the occasion seemed a fitting one to place
them truly and rightly before the world. This I have endeavored faithfully
to do. They fully understand the momentous questions which now agitate
the land in all their relations. They perceive the inevitable drift of Northern aggression, and know that if necessity impel to it, as I verily believe

Lecturers traveled widely throughout the North, pamphlets were distributed, petitions and memorials were presented to Congress. Through the American Anti-Slavery Society, founded in 1833, abolitionism delivered an impact that was unprecedented even during this period of reform ferment. It became clear to some, however, that moral persuasion was not enough. Direct political action, it was thought, would accomplish the abolitionist's goals more quickly and more effectively. Political abolition, dating from 1840 when the Liberty party entered the presidential competition, drove a wedge into abolitionist ranks. Some, like Theodore Dwight Weld and James Gillespie Birney, saw in political action new channels for their energies; others, like William Lloyd Garrison and Wendell Phillips, preferred to remain outside the political arena. With the rise of political abolition and the resultant split, the coherence of the movement was destroyed. Political action, as its supporters soon discovered, frequently necessitated a dilution of goals. The Liberty, Free Soil, and Republican parties, to which abolitionists gave their support, never offered clear-cut abolitionist platforms.

The decade of the 1850s was an auspicious one for the antislavery crusade. Although abolitionists had lost much of their former fiery and revolutionary character, they succeeded in popularizing their goals beyond their earlier dreams. The decade opened with the passage of the Fugitive Slave Act, a concession to the South that served to crystallize Northern sentiment behind the antislavery movement. Personal liberty laws extending constitutional protection to runaways were passed by some Northern states to thwart the act's enforcement, and a series of violent outbreaks resulted as outraged citizens in Northern cities sought to prevent the return of fugitive slaves to their bondage. Most significant, however, was the publication of Harriet Beecher Stowe's Uncle Tom's Cabin in 1852, an appeal that carried the antislavery cause into the homes of countless people who had never before thought strongly about the evils of slavery. The decade closed with the ill-fated attempt of John Brown to lead the slaves out of their bondage, an event that aroused fears and alarms in the South and brought the ultimate success of the abolition movement closer to realization.

The abolition crusade, like the other humanitarian reform efforts of the pre-Civil War decades, had its roots in the belief in the innate worth of the human personality and in the conviction that man could indeed be made perfect. Slavery was a gigantic obstacle to the achievement of the perfection to which Americans aspired. It negated the natural rights tra-

dition which gave birth to the American nation itself, and contradicted the promise of the Declaration of Independence. The abolitionists were men of humanity who strove mightily to bring freedom to a large enslaved class. Theirs was a moral crusade, attended by all the fervor and zeal that springs from convictions of moral right. Although the abolition of slavery was eventually achieved by constitutional amendment, its price was great. By interjecting questions of morality into political discussion in the 1850s, the abolitionists helped to raise politics to a new plane where compromise (the essence of politics) was well-nigh impossible. Militant abolitionism, one might argue, closed all avenues to the achievement of emancipation except that of civil war.

A New England Poet Advances the Cause of Abolition: John Greenleaf Whittier's "Anti-Slavery Poems"

John Greenleaf Whittier (1807–1892), one of New England's great literary figures, was also one of abolitionism's strongest supporters. As early as 1826, he became acquainted with William Lloyd Garrison, and by 1833 was persuaded by him to join the antislavery crusade. Whittier, however, became increasingly critical of Garrison's approach to abolitionist reform and eventually broke with Garrison altogether. For example, unlike Garrison, he supported direct political action, running for Congress in 1842 on the Liberty party ticket. He served the antislavery cause as editor of the Pennsylvania Freeman *and his poems, which exhibited the fervor and militancy of the movement, did much to publicize abolition. The following poems were written at various times during the forties and fifties: "Paean" to express the joy of the antislavery crusaders at Martin Van Buren's defection from the Democratic party in 1848 and the organization of the Free Soil party; "A Sabbath Scene" and "The Rendition" in reaction against the Fugitive Slave Act of 1850 and the successful attempt to return Anthony Burns, a fugitive slave in Boston, to slavery; and "A Word for the Hour" expressing the view of some abolitionists that the Southern slave states should be allowed to leave the Union peaceably in 1860–1861. They are reprinted from* Anti-Slavery Poems, Songs of Labor & Reform *(London: Macmillan, 1889), pages 140–148, 159–163, 170–171, 218–219. An excellent, comprehensive study of the abolitionist movement is Louis Filler,* The Crusade against Slavery, 1830–1860 *(1960). The standard edition of Whittier's writings is* The Complete Writings of John Greenleaf Whittier *(1892), seven volumes; for a biography of Whittier, see John A. Pollard,* John Greenleaf Whittier: Friend of Man *(1949).*

Paean

Now, joy and thanks forevermore!
   The dreary night has wellnigh passed,
The slumbers of the North are o'er,
   The Giant stands erect at last!

More than we hoped in that dark time
   When, faint with watching, few and worn,
We saw no welcome day-star climb
   The cold gray pathway of the morn!

O weary hours! O night of years!
   What storms our darkling pathway swept,
Where, beating back our thronging fears,
   By Faith alone our march we kept.

How jeered the scoffing crowd behind,
   How mocked before the tyrant train,
As, one by one, the true and kind
   Fell fainting in our path of pain!

They died, their brave hearts breaking slow,
   But, self-forgetful to the last,
In words of cheer and bugle blow
   Their breath upon the darkness passed.

A mighty host, on either hand,
   Stood waiting for the dawn of day
To crush like reeds our feeble band;
   The morn has come, and where are they?

Troop after troop their line forsakes;
   With peace-white banners waving free,
And from our own the glad shout breaks,
   Of Freedom and Fraternity!

Like mist before the growing light,
   The hostile cohorts melt away;
Our frowning foemen of the night
   Are brothers at the dawn of day!

As unto these repentant ones
   We open wide our toil-worn ranks,
Along our line a murmur runs
   Of song, and praise, and grateful thanks.

Sound for the onset! Blast on blast!
   Till Slavery's minions cower and quail;
One charge of fire shall drive them fast
   Like chaff before our Northern gale!

O prisoners in your house of pain,
   Dumb, toiling millions, bound and sold,
Look! stretched o'er Southern vale and plain,
   The Lord's delivering hand behold!

Above the tyrant's pride of power,
   His iron gates and guarded wall,
The bolts which shattered Shinar's tower
   Hang, smoking, for a fiercer fall.

Awake! awake! my Fatherland!
  It is thy Northern light that shines;
This stirring march of Freedom's band
  The storm-song of thy mountain pines.

Wake, dwellers where the day expires!
  And hear, in winds that sweep your lakes
And fan your prairies' roaring fires,
  The signal-call that Freedom makes!

A Sabbath Scene

Scarce had the solemn Sabbath-bell
  Ceased quivering in the steeple,
Scarce had the parson to his desk
  Walked stately through his people,

When down the summer-shaded street
  A wasted female figure,
With dusky brow and naked feet,
  Came rushing wild and eager.

She saw the white spire through the trees,
  She heard the sweet hymn swelling:
O pitying Christ! a refuge give
  That poor one in Thy dwelling!

Like a scared fawn before the hounds,
  Right up the aisle she glided,
While close behind her, whip in hand,
  A lank-haired hunter strided.

She raised a keen and bitter cry,
  To Heaven and Earth appealing;
Were manhood's generous pulses dead?
  Had woman's heart no feeling?

A score of stout hands rose between
  The hunter and the flying:
Age clenched his staff, and maiden eyes
  Flashed tearful, yet defying.

"Who dares profane this house and day?"
  Cried out the angry pastor.
"Why, bless your soul, the wench's a slave,
  And I'm her lord and master!

"I've law and gospel on my side,
  And who shall dare refuse me?"
Down came the parson, bowing low,
  "My good sir, pray excuse me!

"Of course I know your right divine
  To own and work and whip her;
Quick, deacon, throw that Polyglott
  Before the wench, and trip her!"

Plump dropped the holy tome, and o'er
  Its sacred pages stumbling,
Bound hand and foot, a slave once more,
  The hapless wretch lay trembling.

I saw the parson tie the knots,
  The while his flock addressing,
The Scriptural claims of slavery
  With text on text impressing.

"Although," said he, "on Sabbath day
  All secular occupations
Are deadly sins, we must fulfil
  Our moral obligations:

"And this commends itself as one
  To every conscience tender;
As Paul sent back Onesimus,
  My Christian friends, we send her!"

Shriek rose on shriek,—the Sabbath air
  Her wild cries tore asunder;
I listened, with hushed breath, to hear
  God answering with his thunder!

All still! the very altar's cloth
  Had smothered down her shrieking,
And, dumb, she turned from face to face,
  For human pity seeking!

I saw her dragged along the aisle,
  Her shackles harshly clanking;
I heard the parson, over all,
  The Lord devoutly thanking!

My brain took fire: "Is this," I cried,
  "The end of prayer and preaching?
Then down with pulpit, down with priest,
  And give us Nature's teaching!

"Foul shame and scorn be on ye all
  Who turn the good to evil,
And steal the Bible from the Lord,
  To give it to the Devil!

"Than garbled text or parchment law
   I own a statute higher;
And God is true, though every book
   And every man's a liar!"

Just then I felt the deacon's hand
   In wrath my coat-tail seize on;
I heard the priest cry, "Infidel!"
   The lawyer mutter, "Treason!"

I started up,—where now were church,
   Slave, master, priest, and people?
I only heard the supper-bell,
   Instead of clanging steeple.

But, on the open window's sill,
   O'er which the white blooms drifted,
The pages of a good old Book
   The wind of summer lifted,

And flower and vine, like angel wings
   Around the Holy Mother,
Waved softly there, as if God's truth
   And Mercy kissed each other.

And freely from the cherry-bough
   Above the casement swinging,
With golden bosom to the sun,
   The oriole was singing.

As bird and flower made plain of old
   The lesson of the Teacher,
So now I heard the written Word
   Interpreted by Nature!

For to my ear methought the breeze
   Bore Freedom's blessed word on;
Thus saith the Lord: Break every yoke,
   Undo the heavy burden!

The Rendition

I heard the train's shrill whistle call,
   I saw an earnest look beseech,
   And rather by that look than speech
My neighbor told me all.

And, as I thought of Liberty
   Marched handcuffed down that sworded street,
   The solid earth beneath my feet
Reeled fluid as the sea.

I felt a sense of bitter loss,—
   Shame, tearless grief, and stifling wrath,
   And loathing fear, as if my path
A serpent stretched across.

All love of home, all pride of place,
   All generous confidence and trust,
   Sank smothering in that deep disgust
And anguish of disgrace.

Down on my native hills of June,
   And home's green quiet, hiding all,
   Fell sudden darkness like the fall
Of midnight upon noon!

And Law, an unloosed maniac, strong,
   Blood-drunken, through the blackness trod,
   Hoarse-shouting in the ear of God
The blasphemy of wrong.

"O Mother, from thy memories proud,
   Thy old renown, dear Commonwealth,
   Lend this dead air a breeze of health,
And smite with stars this cloud.

"Mother of Freedom, wise and brave,
   Rise awful in thy strength," I said;
   Ah me! I spake but to the dead;
I stood upon her grave!

A Word for the Hour

The firmament breaks up. In black eclipse
Light after light goes out. One evil star,
Luridly glaring through the smoke of war,
As in the dream of the Apocalypse,
Drags others down. Let us not weakly weep
Nor rashly threaten. Give us grace to keep
Our faith and patience; wherefore should we leap
On one hand into fratricidal fight,
Or, on the other, yield eternal right,
Frame lies of law, and good and ill confound?
What fear we? Safe on freedom's vantage-ground
Our feet are planted: let us there remain
In unrevengeful calm, no means untried
Which truth can sanction, no just claim denied,
The sad spectators of a suicide!
They break the links of Union: shall we light
The fires of hell to weld anew the chain
On that red anvil where each blow is pain?

Draw we not even now a freer breath,
As from our shoulders falls a load of death
Loathsome as that the Tuscan's victim bore
When keen with life to a dead horror bound?
Why take we up the accursed thing again?
Pity, forgive, but urge them back no more
Who, drunk with passion, flaunt disunion's rag
With its vile reptile-blazon. Let us press
The golden cluster on our brave old flag
In closer union, and, if numbering less,
Brighter shall shine the stars which still remain.

SELECTION

Harriet Beecher Stowe's Indictment of Slavery: "Uncle Tom's Cabin," 1852

Harriet Beecher Stowe (1811–1896) was moved to write her classic fictional indictment of slavery by the passage of the Fugitive Slave Act of 1850. Born in Connecticut, the daughter of Lyman Beecher, a clergyman, she moved to Cincinnati in 1832 when her father accepted the presidency of Lane Theological Seminary. Four years later she married Calvin Stowe, one of the professors at the seminary. Mrs. Stowe lived in Cincinnati for eighteen years, during which time she came into contact with fugitive slaves. In 1850, she moved to Brunswick, Maine, when her husband joined the faculty of Bowdoin College. Uncle Tom's Cabin was first serialized in the abolitionist publication, the National Era, in 1851. The following year, it was published as a book and proved to be an immediate best seller. Although fictional, her account of slavery was based to a large degree on fact. In 1853, she published the Key to Uncle Tom's Cabin, containing documentation for many of her descriptions of slavery. Mrs. Stowe, inexperienced as a writer, intended to appeal to moderate thinking individuals in both North and South (above all to Southerners), hoping to demonstrate some of the tragic consequences of slavery. Instead, her book was received with protest and resentment in the South; in the North, it proved invaluable to the antislavery movement, publicizing the cause and recruiting converts. Although Mrs. Stowe was not wholly accepted by abolitionists, they received her book with enthusiasm. The significance of Uncle Tom's Cabin to the abolitionist crusade was appreciated by Abraham Lincoln when he addressed her years later as "the little woman who wrote the book that made this great war." For recent studies of Mrs. Stowe, see Edmond Wilson's Patriotic Gore: Studies in the Literature of the American Civil War (1962), pages 3–58; Edward Wagenknecht, Harriet Beecher Stowe: The Known and the Unknown (1965); and Forrest Wilson, Crusader in Crinoline: The Life of Harriet Beecher Stowe

(1941). A recent edition of Uncle Tom's Cabin *contains a fine introduction by* Kenneth S. Lynn *(1962). The extract reprinted here is taken from* Uncle Tom's Cabin: or, Life among the Lowly *(Boston: John P. Jewett & Co., 1852), volume 1, pages 172–194.*

Select Incident of Lawful Trade

Mr. Haley and Tom jogged onward in their wagon, each, for a time, absorbed in his own reflections. Now, the reflections of two men sitting side by side are a curious thing,—seated on the same seat, having the same eyes, ears, hands and organs of all sorts, and having pass before their eyes the same objects,—it is wonderful what a variety we shall find in these same reflections!

As, for example, Mr. Haley: he thought first of Tom's length, and breadth, and height, and what he would sell for, if he was kept fat and in good case till he got him into market. He thought of how he should make out his gang; he thought of the respective market value of certain suppositious men and women and children who were to compose it, and other kindred topics of the business; then he thought of himself, and how humane he was, that whereas other men chained their "niggers" hand and foot both, he only put fetters on the feet, and left Tom the use of his hands, as long as he behaved well; and he sighed to think how ungrateful human nature was, so that there was even room to doubt whether Tom appreciated his mercies. He had been taken in so by "niggers" whom he had favored; but still he was astonished to consider how good natured he yet remained!

As to Tom, he was thinking over some words of an unfashionable old book, which kept running through his head again and again, as follows: "We have here no continuing city, but we seek one to come; wherefore God himself is not ashamed to be called our God; for he hath prepared for us a city." These words of an ancient volume, got up principally by "ignorant and unlearned men," have, through all time, kept up, somehow, a strange sort of power over the minds of poor, simple fellows, like Tom. They stir up the soul from its depths, and rouse, as with trumpet call, courage, energy, and enthusiasm, where before was only the blackness of despair.

Mr. Haley pulled out of his pocket sundry newspapers, and began looking over their advertisements, with absorbed interest. He was not a remarkably fluent reader, and was in the habit of reading in a sort of recitative half-aloud, by way of calling in his ears to verify the deductions of his eyes. In this tone he slowly recited the following paragraph:

> Executor's Sale,—Negroes!—Agreeably to order of court, will be sold, on Tuesday, February 20, before the Court-house door, in the town of Washington, Kentucky, the following negroes: Hagar, aged 60; John, aged 30; Ben, aged 21; Saul, aged 25; Albert, aged 14. Sold for the benefit of the creditors and heirs of the estate of Jesse Blutchford, Esq.
>
> SAMUEL MORRIS,
THOMAS FLINT,
Executors.

"This yer I must look at," said he to Tom, for want of somebody else to talk to.

"Ye see, I'm going to get up a prime gang to take down with ye, Tom; it'll make it sociable and pleasant like,—good company will, ye know. We must drive right to Washington first and foremost, and then I'll clap you into jail, while I does the business."

Tom received this agreeable intelligence quite meekly; simply wondering, in his own heart, how many of these doomed men had wives and children, and whether they would feel as he did about leaving them. It is to be confessed, too, that the naïve, off-hand information that he was to be thrown into jail by no means produced an agreeable impression on a poor fellow who had always prided himself on a strictly honest and upright course of life. Yes, Tom, we must confess it, was rather proud of his honesty, poor fellow,—not having very much else to be proud of;—if he had belonged to some of the higher walks of society, he, perhaps, would never have been reduced to such straits. However, the day wore on, and the evening saw Haley and Tom comfortably accommodated in Washington,—the one in a tavern, and the other in a jail.

About eleven o'clock the next day, a mixed throng was gathered around the court-house steps,—smoking, chewing, spitting, swearing, and conversing, according to their respective tastes and turns,—waiting for the auction to commence. The men and women to be sold sat in a group apart, talking in a low tone to each other. The woman who had been advertised by the name of Hagar was a regular African in feature and figure. She might have been sixty, but was older than that by hard work and disease, was partially blind, and somewhat crippled with rheumatism. By her side stood her only remaining son, Albert, a bright-looking little fellow of fourteen years. The boy was the only survivor of a large family, who had been successively sold away from her to a southern market. The mother held on to him with both her shaking hands, and eyed with intense trepidation every one who walked up to examine him.

"Don't be feard, Aunt Hagar," said the oldest of the men, "I spoke to Mas'r Thomas 'bout it, and he thought he might manage to sell you in a lot both together."

"Dey needn't call me worn out yet," said she, lifting her shaking hands. "I can cook yet, and scrub, and scour,—I'm wuth a buying, if I do come cheap;—tell em dat ar,—you *tell* em," she added, earnestly.

Haley here forced his way into the group, walked up to the old man, pulled his mouth open and looked in, felt of his teeth, made him stand and straighten himself, bend his back, and perform various evolutions to show his muscles; and then passed on to the next, and put him through the same trial. Walking up last to the boy, he felt of his arms, straightened his hands, and looked at his fingers, and made him jump, to show his agility.

"He an't gwine to be sold widout me!" said the old woman, with passionate eagerness; "he and I goes in a lot together; I's rail strong yet, Mas'r, and can do heaps o' work,—heaps on it, Mas'r."

"On plantation?" said Haley, with a contemptuous glance. "Likely story!" and, as if satisfied with his examination, he walked out and looked, and stood with his hands in his pocket, his cigar in his mouth, and his hat cocked on one side, ready for action.

"What think of 'em?" said a man who had been following Haley's examination, as if to make up his own mind from it.

"Wal," said Haley, spitting, "I shall put in, I think, for the youngerly ones and the boy."

"They want to sell the boy and the old woman together," said the man.

"Find it a tight pull;—why, she's an old rack o' bones,—not worth her salt."

"You wouldn't, then?" said the man.

"Anybody'd be a fool 't would. She's half blind, crooked with rheumatis, and foolish to boot."

"Some buys up these yer old critturs, and ses there's a sight more wear in 'em than a body'd think," said the man, reflectively.

"No go, 't all," said Haley; "wouldn't take her for a present,—fact,—I've *seen*, now."

"Wal, 't is kinder pity, now, not to buy her with her son,—her heart seems so sot on him,—s'pose they fling her in cheap."

"Them that's got money to spend that ar way, it's all well enough. I shall bid off on that ar boy for a plantation-hand;—wouldn't be bothered with her, no way,—not if they'd give her to me," said Haley.

"She'll take on desp't," said the man.

"Nat'lly, she will," said the trader, coolly.

The conversation was here interrupted by a busy hum in the audience; and the auctioneer, a short, bustling, important fellow, elbowed his way into the crowd. The old woman drew in her breath, and caught instinctively at her son.

"Keep close to yer mammy, Albert,—close,—dey'll put us up togedder," she said.

"O, mammy, I'm feard they won't," said the boy.

"Dey must, child; I can't live, no ways, if they don't," said the old creature, vehemently.

The stentorian tones of the auctioneer, calling out to clear the way, now announced that the sale was about to commence. A place was cleared, and the bidding began. The different men on the list were soon knocked off at prices which showed a pretty brisk demand in the market; two of them fell to Haley.

"Come, now, young un," said the auctioneer, giving the boy a touch with his hammer, "be up and show your springs, now."

"Put us two up togedder, togedder,—do please, Mas'r," said the old woman, holding fast to her boy.

"Be off," said the man, gruffly, pushing her hands away; "you come last. Now, darkey, spring;" and, with the word, he pushed the boy toward the block, while a deep, heavy groan rose behind him. The boy paused, and looked back; but there was no time to stay, and, dashing the tears from his large, bright eyes, he was up in a moment.

His fine figure, alert limbs, and bright face, raised an instant competition, and half a dozen bids simultaneously met the ear of the auctioneer. Anxious, half-frightened, he looked from side to side, as he heard the clatter of contending bids,—now here, now there,—till the hammer fell. Haley had got him. He was pushed from the block toward his new master, but stopped one moment, and looked back, when his poor old mother, trembling in every limb, held out her shaking hands toward him.

"Buy me too, Mas'r, for de dear Lord's sake!—buy me,—I shall die if you don't!"

"You'll die if I do, that's the kink of it," said Haley,—"no!" And he turned on his heel.

The bidding for the poor old creature was summary. The man who had addressed Haley, and who seemed not destitute of compassion, bought her for a trifle, and the spectators began to disperse.

The poor victims of the sale, who had been brought up in one place together for years, gathered round the despairing old mother, whose agony was pitiful to see.

"Couldn't dey leave me one? Mas'r allers said I should have one,—he did," she repeated over and over, in heartbroken tones.

"Trust in the Lord, Aunt Hagar," said the oldest of the men, sorrowfully.

"What good will it do?" said she, sobbing passionately.

"Mother, mother,—don't! don't!" said the boy. "They say you's got a good master."

"I don't care,—I don't care. O, Albert! oh, my boy! you's my last baby. Lord, how ken I?"

"Come, take her off, can't some of ye?" said Haley, dryly; "don't do no good for her to go on that ar way."

The old men of the company, partly by persuasion and partly by force, loosed the poor creature's last despairing hold, and, as they led her off to her new master's wagon, strove to comfort her.

"Now!" said Haley, pushing his three purchases together, and producing a bundle of handcuffs, which he proceeded to put on their wrists; and fastening each handcuff to a long chain, he drove them before him to the jail.

A few days saw Haley, with his possessions, safely deposited on one of the Ohio boats. It was the commencement of his gang, to be augmented, as the boat moved on, by various other merchandise of the same kind, which he, or his agent, had stored for him in various points along shore.

The La Belle Rivière, as brave and beautiful a boat as ever walked the waters of her namesake river, was floating gayly down the stream, under a brilliant sky, the stripes and stars of free America waving and fluttering over head; the guards crowded with well-dressed ladies and gentlemen walking and enjoying the delightful day. All was full of life, buoyant and rejoicing;—all but Haley's gang, who were stored, with other freight, on the lower deck, and who, somehow, did not seem to appreciate their various privileges, as they sat in a knot, talking to each other in low tones.

"Boys," said Haley, coming up, briskly, "I hope you keep up good heart, and are cheerful. Now, no sulks, ye see; keep stiff upper lip, boys; do well by me, and I'll do well by you."

The boys addressed responded the invariable "Yes, Mas'r," for ages the watchword of poor Africa; but it's to be owned they did not look particularly cheerful; they had their various little prejudices in favor of wives, mothers, sisters, and children, seen for the last time,—and though "they that wasted them required of them mirth," it was not instantly forthcoming.

"I've got a wife," spoke out the article enumerated as "John, aged

thirty," and he laid his chained hand on Tom's knee,—"and she don't
know a word about this, poor girl!"

"Where does she live?" said Tom.

"In a tavern a piece down here," said John; "I wish, now, I *could* see
her once more in this world," he added.

Poor John! It *was* rather natural; and the tears that fell, as he spoke,
came as naturally as if he had been a white man. Tom drew a long breath
from a sore heart, and tried in his poor way, to comfort him.

And over head, in the cabin, sat fathers and mothers, husbands and
wives; and merry, dancing children moved round among them, like so
many little butterflies, and everything was going on quite easy and comfortable.

"O, mamma," said a boy, who had just come up from below, "there's
a negro trader on board, and he's brought four or five slaves down there."

"Poor creatures!" said the mother, in a tone between grief and indignation.

"What's that?" said another lady.

"Some poor slaves below," said the mother.

"And they've got chains on," said the boy.

"What a shame to our country that such sights are to be seen!" said
another lady.

"O, there's a great deal to be said on both sides of the subject," said a
genteel woman, who sat at her state-room door sewing, while her little
girl and boy were playing round her. "I've been south, and I must say I
think the negroes are better off than they would be to be free."

"In some respects, some of them are well off, I grant," said the lady
to whose remark she had answered. "The most dreadful part of slavery,
to my mind, is its outrages on the feelings and affections,—the separating
of families, for example."

"'That *is* a bad thing, certainly," said the other lady, holding up a baby's
dress she had just completed, and looking intently on its trimmings; "but
then, I fancy, it don't occur often."

"O, it does," said the first lady, eagerly; "I've lived many years in Kentucky and Virginia both, and I've seen enough to make any one's heart
sick. Suppose, ma'am, your two children, there, should be taken from you,
and sold?"

"We can't reason from our feelings to those of this class of persons,"
said the other lady, sorting out some worsteds on her lap.

"Indeed, ma'am, you can know nothing of them, if you say so," answered
the first lady, warmly. "I was born and brought up among them. I know
they *do* feel, just as keenly, even more so, perhaps,—as we do."

The lady said "Indeed!" yawned, and looked out the cabin window, and
finally repeated, for a finale, the remark with which she had begun,—
"After all, I think they are better off than they would be to be free."

"It's undoubtedly the intention of Providence that the African race
should be servants,—kept in a low condition," said a grave-looking gentleman in black, a clergyman, seated by the cabin door. " 'Cursed be Canaan;
a servant of servants shall he be,' the scripture says."

"I say, stranger, is that ar what that text means?" said a tall man,
standing by.

"Undoubtedly. It pleased Providence, for some inscrutable reason, to doom the race to bondage, ages ago; and we must not set up our opinion against that."

"Well, then, we'll all go ahead and buy up niggers," said the man, "if that's the way of Providence,—won't we, Squire?" said he, turning to Haley, who had been standing, with his hands in his pockets, by the stove, and intently listening to the conversation.

"Yes," continued the tall man, "we must all be resigned to the decrees of Providence. Niggers must be sold, and trucked round, and kept under; it's what they's made for. 'Pears like this yer view's quite refreshing, an't it, stranger?" said he to Haley.

"I never thought on't," said Haley. "I couldn't have said as much, myself; I ha'nt no larning. I took up the trade just to make a living; if 'tan't right, I calculated to 'pent on't in time, *ye* know."

"And now you'll save yerself the trouble, won't ye?" said the tall man. "See what 'tis, now, to know scripture. If ye'd only studied yer Bible, like this yer good man, ye might have know'd it before, and saved ye a heap o' trouble. Ye could jist have said, 'Cussed be'—what's his name?— 'and 't would all have come right.'" And the stranger, who was no other than the honest drover whom we introduced to our readers in the Kentucky tavern, sat down, and began smoking, with a curious smile on his long, dry face.

A tall, slender young man, with a face expressive of great feeling and intelligence, here broke in, and repeated the words, "'All things whatsoever ye would that men should do unto you, do ye even so unto them.' I suppose," he added, "*that* is scripture, as much as 'Cursed be Canaan.'"

"Wal, it seems quite *as* plain a text, stranger," said John the drover, "to poor fellows like us, now;" and John smoked on like a volcano.

The young man paused, looked as if he was going to say more, when suddenly the boat stopped, and the company made the usual steamboat rush, to see where they were landing.

"Both them ar chaps parsons?" said John to one of the men, as they were going out.

The man nodded.

As the boat stopped, a black woman came running wildly up the plank, darted into the crowd, flew up to where the slave gang sat, and threw her arms round that unfortunate piece of merchandise before enumerated— "John, aged thirty," and with sobs and tears bemoaned him as her husband.

But what needs tell the story, told too oft,—every day told,—of heartstrings rent and broken,—the weak broken and torn for the profit and convenience of the strong! It needs not to be told;—every day is telling it,—telling it, too, in the ear of One who is not deaf, though he be long silent.

The young man who had spoken for the cause of humanity and God before stood with folded arms, looking on this scene. He turned, and Haley was standing at his side. "My friend," he said, speaking with thick utterance, "how can you, how dare you, carry on a trade like this? Look at those poor creatures! Here I am, rejoicing in my heart that I am going home to my wife and child; and the same bell which is a signal to carry me onward towards them will part this poor man and his wife forever. Depend upon it, God will bring you into judgment for this."

The trader turned away in silence.

"I say, now," said the drover, touching his elbow, "there's differences in parsons, an't there? 'Cussed be Canaan' don't seem to go down with this 'un, does it?"

Haley gave an uneasy growl.

"And that ar an't the worst on't," said John; "mabbe it won't go down with the Lord, neither, when ye come to settle with Him, one o' these days, as all on us must, I reckon."

Haley walked reflectively to the other end of the boat.

"If I make pretty handsomely on one or two next gangs," he thought, "I reckon I'll stop off this yer; it's really getting dangerous." And he took out his pocket-book, and began adding over his accounts,—a process which many gentlemen besides Mr. Haley have found a specific for an uneasy conscience.

The boat swept proudly away from the shore, and all went on merrily, as before. Men talked, and loafed, and read, and smoked. Women sewed, and children played, and the boat passed on her way.

One day, when she lay to for a while at a small town in Kentucky, Haley went up into the place on a little matter of business.

Tom, whose fetters did not prevent his taking a moderate circuit, had drawn near the side of the boat, and stood listlessly gazing over the railings. After a time, he saw the trader returning, with an alert step, in company with a colored woman, bearing in her arms a young child. She was dressed quite respectably, and a colored man followed her, bringing along a small trunk. The woman came cheerfully onward, talking, as she came, with the man who bore her trunk, and so passed up the plank into the boat. The bell rung, the steamer whizzed, the engine groaned and coughed, and away swept the boat down the river.

The woman walked forward among the boxes and bales of the lower deck, and, sitting down, busied herself with chirruping to her baby.

Haley made a turn or two about the boat, and then, coming up, seated himself near her, and began saying something to her in an indifferent undertone.

Tom soon noticed a heavy cloud passing over the woman's brow; and that she answered rapidly, and with great vehemence.

"I don't believe it,—I won't believe it!" he heard her say. "You're jist a foolin with me."

"If you won't believe it, look here!" said the man, drawing out a paper; "this yer's the bill of sale, and there's your master's name to it; and I paid down good solid cash for it, too, I can tell you,—so, now!"

"I don't believe Mas'r would cheat me so; it can't be true!" said the woman, with increasing agitation.

"You can ask any of these men here, that can read writing. Here!" he said, to a man that was passing by, "jist read this yer, won't you! This yer gal won't believe me, when I tell her what 'tis."

"Why, it's a bill of sale, signed by John Fosdick," said the man, "making over to you the girl Lucy and her child. It's all straight enough, for aught I see."

The woman's passionate exclamations collected a crowd around her, and the trader briefly explained to them the cause of the agitation.

"He told me that I was going down to Louisville, to hire out as cook to the same tavern where my husband works,—that's what Mas'r told me, his own self; and I can't believe he'd lie to me," said the woman.

"But he has sold you, my poor woman, there's no doubt about it," said a good-natured looking man, who had been examining the papers; "he has done it, and no mistake."

"Then it's no account talking," said the woman, suddenly growing quite calm; and, clasping her child tighter in her arms, she sat down on her box, turned her back round, and gazed listlessly into the river.

"Going to take it easy, after all!" said the trader. "Gal's got grit, I see."

The woman looked calm, as the boat went on; and a beautiful soft summer breeze passed like a compassionate spirit over her head,—the gentle breeze, that never inquires whether the brow is dusky or fair that it fans. And she saw sunshine sparkling on the water, in golden ripples, and heard gay voices, full of ease and pleasure, talking around her everywhere; but her heart lay as if a great stone had fallen on it. Her baby raised himself up against her, and stroked her cheeks with his little hands; and, springing up and down, crowing and chatting, seemed determined to arouse her. She strained him suddenly and tightly in her arms, and slowly one tear after another fell on his wondering, unconscious face; and gradually she seemed, and little by little, to grow calmer, and busied herself with tending and nursing him.

The child, a boy of ten months, was uncommonly large and strong of his age, and very vigorous in his limbs. Never, for a moment, still, he kept his mother constantly busy in holding him, and guarding his springing activity.

"That's a fine chap!" said a man, suddenly stopping opposite to him, with his hands in his pockets. "How old is he?"

"Ten months and a half," said the mother.

The man whistled to the boy, and offered him part of a stick of candy, which he eagerly grabbed at, and very soon had it in a baby's general depository, to wit, his mouth.

"Rum fellow!" said the man. "Knows what's what!" and he whistled, and walked on. When he had got to the other side of the boat, he came across Haley, who was smoking on top of a pile of boxes.

The stranger produced a match, and lighted a cigar, saying, as he did so,

"Decentish kind o' wench you've got round there, stranger."

"Why, I reckon she *is* tol'able fair," said Haley, blowing the smoke out of his mouth.

"Taking her down south?" said the man.

Haley nodded, and smoked on.

"Plantation hand?" said the man.

"Wal," said Haley, "I'm fillin' out an order for a plantation, and I think I shall put her in. They told me she was a good cook; and they can use her for that, or set her at the cotton-picking. She's got the right fingers for that; I looked at 'em. Sell well, either way;" and Haley resumed his cigar.

"They won't want the young'un on a plantation," said the man.

"I shall sell him, first chance I find," said Haley, lighting another cigar.

"S'pose you'd be selling him tol'able cheap," said the stranger, mounting the pile of boxes, and sitting down comfortably.

"Don't know 'bout that," said Haley; "he's a pretty smart young'un,—straight, fat, strong; flesh as hard as a brick!"

"Very true, but then there's all the bother and expense of raisin'."

"Nonsense!" said Haley; "they is raised as easy as any kind of critter there is going; they an't a bit more trouble than pups. This yer chap will be running all round, in a month."

"I've got a good place for raisin', and I thought of takin' in a little more stock," said the man. "One cook lost a young'un last week,—got drownded in a wash-tub, while she was a hangin' out clothes,—and I reckon it would be well enough to set her to raisin' this yer."

Haley and the stranger smoked a while in silence, neither seeming willing to broach the test question of the interview. At last the man resumed:

"You wouldn't think of wantin' more than ten dollars for that ar chap, seeing you *must* get him off yer hand, any how?"

Haley shook his head, and spit impressively.

"That won't do, no ways," he said, and began his smoking again.

"Well, stranger, what will you take?"

"Well, now," said Haley, "I *could* raise that ar chap myself, or get him raised; he's oncommon likely and healthy, and he'd fetch a hundred dollars, six months hence; and, in a year or two, he'd bring two hundred, if I had him in the right spot;—so I shan't take a cent less nor fifty for him now."

"O, stranger! that's rediculous, altogether," said the man.

"Fact!" said Haley, with a decisive nod of his head.

"I'll give thirty for him," said the stranger, "but not a cent more."

"Now, I'll tell ye what I will do," said Haley, spitting again, with renewed decision. "I'll split the difference, and say forty five; and that's the most I will do."

"Well, agreed!" said the man, after an interval.

"Done!" said Haley. "Where do you land?"

"At Louisville," said the man.

"Louisville," said Haley. "Very fair, we get there about dusk. Chap will be asleep,—all fair,—get him off quietly, and no screaming,—happens beautiful,—I like to do everything quietly,—I hates all kind of agitation and fluster." And so, after a transfer of certain bills had passed from the man's pocket-book to the trader's, he resumed his cigar.

It was a bright, tranquil evening when the boat stopped at the wharf at Louisville. The woman had been sitting with her baby in her arms, now wrapped in a heavy sleep. When she heard the name of the place called out, she hastily laid the child down in a little cradle formed by the hollow among the boxes, first carefully spreading under it her cloak; and then she sprung to the side of the boat, in hopes that, among the various hotel-waiters who thronged the wharf, she might see her husband. In this hope, she pressed forward to the front rails, and, stretching far over them, strained her eyes intently on the moving heads on the shore, and the crowd pressed in between her and the child.

"Now's your time," said Haley, taking the sleeping child up, and handing him to the stranger. "Don't wake him up, and set him to crying, now; it would make a devil of a fuss with the gal." The man took the bundle carefully, and was soon lost in the crowd that went up the wharf.

When the boat, creaking, and groaning, and puffing, had loosed from the wharf, and was beginning slowly to strain herself along, the woman returned to her old seat. The trader was sitting there,—the child was gone!

"Why, why,—where?" she began, in bewildered surprise.

"Lucy," said the trader, "your child's gone; you may as well know it first as last. You see, I know'd you couldn't take him down south; and I got a chance to sell him to a first-rate family, that'll raise him better than you can."

The trader had arrived at that stage of Christian and political perfection which has been recommended by some preachers and politicians of the north, lately, in which he had completely overcome every humane weakness and prejudice. His heart was exactly where yours, sir, and mine could be brought, with proper effort and cultivation. The wild look of anguish and utter despair that the woman cast on him might have disturbed one less practised; but he was used to it. He had seen that same look hundreds of times. You can get used to such things, too, my friend; and it is the great object of recent efforts to make our whole northern community used to them, for the glory of the Union. So the trader only regarded the mortal anguish which he saw working in those dark features, those clenched hands, and suffocating breathings, as necessary incidents of the trade, and merely calculated whether she was going to scream, and get up a commotion on the boat; for, like other supporters of our peculiar institution, he decidedly disliked agitation.

But the woman did not scream. The shot had passed too straight and direct through the heart, for cry or tear.

Dizzily she sat down. Her slack hands fell lifeless by her side. Her eyes looked straight forward, but she saw nothing. All the noise and hum of the boat, the groaning of the machinery, mingled dreamily to her bewildered ear; and the poor, dumb-stricken heart had neither cry nor tear to show for its utter misery. She was quite calm.

The trader, who, considering his advantages, was almost as humane as some of our politicians, seemed to feel called on to administer such consolation as the case admitted of.

"I know this yer comes kinder hard, at first, Lucy," said he; "but such a smart, sensible gal as you are, won't give way to it. You see it's *necessary*, and can't be helped!"

"O! don't, Mas'r, don't!" said the woman, with a voice like one that is smothering.

"You're a smart wench, Lucy," he persisted; "I mean to do well by ye, and get ye a nice place down river; and you'll soon get another husband, —such a likely gal as you—"

"O! Mas'r, if you *only* won't talk to me now," said the woman, in a voice of such quick and living anguish that the trader felt that there was something at present in the case beyond his style of operation. He got up, and the woman turned away, and buried her head in her cloak.

The trader walked up and down for a time, and occasionally stopped and looked at her.

"Takes it hard, rather," he soliloquized, "but quiet, tho';—let her sweat a while; she'll come right, by and by!"

Tom had watched the whole transaction from first to last, and had a perfect understanding of its results. To him, it looked like something unutterably horrible and cruel, because, poor, ignorant black soul! he had not learned to generalize, and to take enlarged views. If he had only been instructed by certain ministers of Christianity, he might have thought better of it, and seen in it an every-day incident of a lawful trade; a trade which is the vital support of an institution which an American divine tells us has *"no evils but such as are inseparable from any other relations in social and domestic life."* But Tom, as we see, being a poor, ignorant fellow, whose reading had been confined entirely to the New Testament, could not comfort and solace himself with views like these. His very soul bled within him for what seemed to him the *wrongs* of the poor suffering thing that lay like a crushed reed on the boxes; the feeling, living, bleeding, yet immortal *thing*, which American state law coolly classes with the bundles, and bales, and boxes, among which she is lying.

Tom drew near, and tried to say something; but she only groaned. Honestly, and with tears running down his own cheeks, he spoke of a heart of love in the skies, of a pitying Jesus, and an eternal home; but the ear was deaf with anguish, and the palsied heart could not feel.

Night came on,—night calm, unmoved, and glorious, shining down with her innumerable and solemn angel eyes, twinkling, beautiful, but silent. There was no speech nor language, no pitying voice or helping hand, from that distant sky. One after another, the voices of business or pleasure died away; all on the boat were sleeping, and the ripples at the prow were thinly heard. Tom stretched himself out on a box, and there, as he lay, he heard, ever and anon, a smothered sob or cry from the prostrate creature,—"O! what shall I do? O Lord! O good Lord, do help me!" and so, ever and anon, until the murmur died away in silence.

At midnight, Tom waked, with a sudden start. Something black passed quickly by him to the side of the boat, and he heard a splash in the water. No one else saw or heard anything. He raised his head,—the woman's place was vacant! He got up, and sought about him in vain. The poor bleeding heart was still, at last, and the river rippled and dimpled just as brightly as if it had not closed above it.

Patience! patience! ye whose hearts swell indignant at wrongs like these. Not one throb of anguish, not one tear of the oppressed, is forgotten by the Man of Sorrows, the Lord of Glory. In his patient, generous bosom he bears the anguish of a world. Bear thou, like him, in patience, and labor in love; for sure as he is God, "the year of his redeemed *shall* come."

The trader waked up bright and early, and came out to see to his live stock. It was now his turn to look about in perplexity.

"Where alive is that gal?" he said to Tom.

Tom, who had learned the wisdom of keeping counsel, did not feel called on to state his observations and suspicions, but said he did not know.

"She surely couldn't have got off in the night at any of the landings, for I was awake, and on the look-out, whenever the boat stopped. I never trust these yer things to other folks."

This speech was addressed to Tom quite confidentially, as if it was something that would be specially interesting to him. Tom made no answer.

The trader searched the boat from stem to stern, among boxes, bales and barrels, around the machinery, by the chimneys, in vain.

"Now, I say, Tom, be fair about this yer," he said, when, after a fruitless search, he came where Tom was standing. "You know something about it, now. Don't tell me,—I know you do. I saw the gal stretched out here about ten o'clock, and ag'in at twelve, and ag'in between one and two; and then at four she was gone, and you was a sleeping right there all the time. Now, you know something,—you can't help it."

"Well, Mas'r," said Tom, "towards morning something brushed by me, and I kinder half woke; and then I hearn a great splash, and then I clare woke up, and the gal was gone. That's all I know on't."

The trader was not shocked nor amazed; because, as we said before, he was used to a great many things that you are not used to. Even the awful presence of Death struck no solemn chill upon him. He had seen Death many times,—met him in the way of trade, and got acquainted with him, —and he only thought of him as a hard customer, that embarrassed his property operations very unfairly; and so he only swore that the gal was a baggage, and that he was devilish unlucky, and that, if things went on in this way, he should not make a cent on the trip. In short, he seemed to consider himself an ill-used man, decidedly; but there was no help for it, as the woman had escaped into a state which *never will* give up a fugitive,—not even at the demand of the whole glorious Union. The trader, therefore, sat discontentedly down, with his little account-book, and put down the missing body and soul under the head of *losses!*

"He's a shocking creature, isn't he,—this trader? so unfeeling! It's dreadful, really!"

"O, but nobody thinks anything of these traders! They are universally despised,—never received into any decent society."

But who, sir, makes the trader? Who is most to blame? The enlightened, cultivated, intelligent man, who supports the system of which the trader is the inevitable result, or the poor trader himself? You make the public sentiment that calls for his trade, that debauches and depraves him, till he feels no shame in it; and in what are you better than he?

Are you educated and he ignorant, you high and he low, you refined and he coarse, you talented and he simple?

In the day of a future Judgment, these very considerations may make it more tolerable for him than for you.

In concluding these little incidents of lawful trade, we must beg the world not to think that American legislators are entirely destitute of humanity, as might, perhaps, be unfairly inferred from the great efforts made in our national body to protect and perpetuate this species of traffic.

Who does not know how our great men are outdoing themselves, in declaiming against the *foreign* slave-trade. There are a perfect host of Clarksons and Wilberforces risen up among us on that subject, most edifying to hear and behold. Trading negroes from Africa, dear reader, is so horrid! It is not to be thought of! But trading them from Kentucky,— that's quite another thing!

SELECTION

An Abolitionist Leader Defines His Program:
William Lloyd Garrison's "Anti-Slavery Platform"

William Lloyd Garrison (1805–1879) stands deservedly as the founder of militant abolitionism. Born in Newburyport, Massachusetts, he was apprenticed to a printer at an early age and later served as editor of various New England papers. In 1829, he undertook the cause of total and immediate freedom for Negro slaves; three years later, the New England Anti-Slavery Society was organized under his auspices. For over three decades, he remained the movement's principal driving force. A man of genuine humanitarian impulses and a single-minded devotion to the goal of freedom for the nation's slaves, Garrison always found himself at the center of controversy. His strong emotional appeal, his pacificism, and his disapproval of political action brought splits within the abolitionist ranks and many of his early followers eventually broke with him. Through the columns of his newspaper, the Liberator *(first published in 1831), he kept the repulsive aspects of slavery before the public eye. He denounced the United States government and, on one occasion, publicly burned a copy of the Constitution for its toleration of slavery. His methods won for him a dedicated following among the abolitionists and served to keep his movement in the spotlight, but they also subjected him to the abuse and violence of Northern critics. By the 1850s, he had the satisfaction of witnessing a growing acceptance of his goals in the North. The selection that follows, written and published earlier, was reprinted in 1852 in a collection of Garrison's writings:* Selections from the Writings and Speeches of William Lloyd Garrison *(Boston: R. F. Wallcut, 1852), pages 317–324. Two recent biographies of Garrison have appeared: Walter M. Merrill,* Against Wind and Tide: A Biography of Wm. Lloyd Garrison *(1963) and John L. Thomas,* The Liberator, William Lloyd Garrison: A Biography *(1963). A valuable shorter work is Russel B. Nye's* William Lloyd Garrison and the Humanitarian Reformers *(1955).*

It is the strength and glory of the Anti-Slavery cause, that its principles are so simple and elementary, and yet so vital to freedom, morality and religion, as to commend themselves to the understandings and consciences of men of every sect and party, every creed and persuasion, every caste and color. They are self-evident truths—fixed stars in the moral firmament—blazing suns in the great universe of mind, dispensing light and heat over the whole surface of humanity, and around which all social and moral affinities revolve in harmony. They are to be denied, only as the existence of a God, or the immortality of the soul, is denied. Unlike human theories, they can never lead astray; unlike human devices, they can never be made subservient to ambition or selfishness. When Jesus gave this rule of action to a Jewish lawyer, who interrogated him, "Thou shalt love thy neighbor as thyself," and illustrated its meaning by the case of the man fallen among thieves, aided by one with whom he was at mortal variance because of sectarian and national antipathies, the Great Teacher evidently intended to inculcate this among other truths, that all men are bound to rally upon the broad ground of a common humanity, to succor the distressed, without reference to the caste, the creed, the country, or the name of the sufferer;—or, in other words, that when a victim of robbers lies weltering in his blood, he only is "neighbor to him," who pours wine and oil into his wounds, forgetful of all other considerations; while he who passes by on the other side does but act the priest and the Levite. We repeat it, therefore, that it is the strength and glory of the Anti-Slavery cause, that men of all sects not only ought to unite, but are united in one common phalanx, to break every yoke, and let the oppressed go free. Why should it not be so? It is a reproach to the name of Christianity, that while its professors, however widely differing in their religious or political sentiments, eagerly associate together for the purpose of MONEY-GETTING—to establish banks, build railroads, dig canals, and erect manufactories— they are slow, almost reluctant, to give each other the right hand of fellowship in carrying on an enterprise of mercy. When they themselves are thirsty, they ask not who it is that proffers them a cup of cold water; when they are oppressed, they care not who it is that breaks their fetters; when they are threatened with death, they demand not in a cavilling spirit, who it is that comes to their rescue. When the mother country attempted to bind the chains of civil despotism upon the limbs of our fathers, how ineffectual would have been their struggle for emancipation, if they had stood aloof from each other on account of sectarian or political disagreements, and refused to coöperate *en masse* for a common object, to effect a common deliverance! Would the war have been finished in seven years? Would it not have been ended, disastrously, in less than seven months? If each religious sect, if each political party, had resolved to prosecute the war *per se*, in an invidious and antagonistical form, would England have lost the brightest gem that was ever set in her regal crown? Never. And what were they styled, who, in those "times that tried men's souls," for any pretext whatever, refused to stand shoulder to shoulder in breasting the tide of British despotism? Tories—traitors to their country—the enemies of liberty. Why were they bound to forget their creeds and their names, and to throw themselves, as one man, into "the imminent deadly breach," for the preservation of their liberty? First, because it was a common good which was to be secured; secondly, because it was a common ground to be occupied by all who were not willing to wear the yoke of bondage; thirdly, because disunion would have been inevitable defeat; and lastly, and for the all-conclusive reason, that all sects and parties in England, the government, the people, were united together for the subjugation of the colonies, and nothing but a similar union of the people of the colonies could have procured their independence.

The moral conflict now waging against American slavery is, in many of its aspects, a parallel case. Its object, like the love of God, consults the happiness of all men: it is a common one, in which all sects and all parties have an equal, the deepest interest. The ground on which it is fought is a common one, broad enough to contain all who would occupy it. Disunion in the ranks is defeat—no true friend to the cause will seek to foment it. Those who refuse to enlist, because they are not agreed upon other and minor points with the gallant band who are struggling against the opposing hosts of despotism—what are they? Are they the friends of emancipation? No. What are they? Neutrals? Neutrality in such a struggle is the abhorrence of God, and active rebellion against his government. The Moloch of slavery finds worshippers and defenders among all classes of society throughout the land; and it is to be remarked—it is a fact too alarming and too important to be forgotten, that, wherever they are, at the East or West, the North or South—whatever the party they espouse, or to whatever denomination they belong, their sympathies, feelings, interests, opinions, blend together like the drops of the ocean, to sink the victims of oppression beyond the fathom line of humanity. Their language is one; their shibboleth the same; their grand hailing sign of distress the same; their grip and knock the same. In their spirit, they are alike; in their purpose, identical; in their fellowship, undivided. Upon almost every other subject, they differ wide as the poles asunder; but upon the duty of paying homage to the bloody idol set up in our land, their agreement is perfect. Are the children of this world to be always wiser than the children of light? If Episcopalians, Methodists, Baptists, Presbyterians, Unitarians, &c. &c., are joined hand to hand, and heart to heart, in earnest defence of slavery; if they associate together, plot together, co-operate together, to uphold that execrable system; shall not, may not, cannot members of the same religious persuasions, who desire the utter extirpation of slavery, and will not bow down to the image of Baal, nor pass through the fire to Moloch, be as united, as forgetful of their other variances, as ready to act in concert? If the friends and the opponents of the national administration are found in the same phalanx, fighting in defence of the worst oppressors; shall they not also be found leagued together for the rescue of the oppressed? When the standard of HUMANITY is unfurled to the breeze, in the sunshine of heaven, who that is created in the image of God, who that is human, will not rally under its folds? Let us suppose a case. In the progress of the revolutionary struggle, there were many dark periods, when the cause of liberty seemed to be at its last gasp; when its champions began to fear, that the night of despotism must inevitably settle over the land, with no hope that there would ever be another dawn of Freedom's day. Let us suppose, that, in the darkest hour, when Washington and his barefooted followers, in the midst of winter, were retreating before their victorious enemy, and tracking their snowy path with blood, some of them had suddenly thrown down their arms, and declared that they could no longer be associated with men whose religious or political creed differed from their own, or who refused to subscribe to any creed. Suppose they had attempted to seduce others from the cause, by inflaming their suspicions and alienating their affections, by artful appeals and slanderous representations. Suppose they had tried to cut off the supplies which were sent to enable the tried and faithful few to carry on the war, until victory perched upon their standard, or the last drop of blood had oozed from their veins. And suppose that these factious individuals had boasted of their patriotism, and professed that they were actuated by love of country, and gave as one reason for their mutinous conduct, that, in withdrawing themselves from the army, they believed they should be able to do more execution, inasmuch as a large portion of the enemy coincided with them in religious profession, and would certainly be more willing to be shot down or taken captive by them, than by those who held to a different creed. What would have been thought, what said of conduct like this? Would not the whole world, civilized and savage, have cried out, "Shame! shame!" But suppose, in addition to all this, that they had eulogized the conduct of those tories, who had refused to join the little patriotic army, as "men who had a quick sense of propriety, and were not willing to be identified with their movements;" whose hearts bled for the oppressed colonists, but who were beaten off from active exertion in their behalf, in consequence of the character and measures of those who were carrying on the war. Suppose they had declared, that their feelings had often been exceedingly pained by the abuse which was heaped upon tory ministers and other excellent tory Christians, who did not feel prepared to enter fully into the efforts of the revolutionists. Suppose, further, they had carried on a secret correspondence with the disaffected in various parts of the land, as well as made their appeals to them in public, urging them to come forward in a body, take the cause into their own hands, and carry it on in a manner to suit themselves. Suppose, finally, that, in view of this mutiny, shouts should be heard in all the enemy's camps, rending the very heavens with their exultation. In what light would the conduct of those disorganizers have appeared to the friends of American liberty throughout the world? As dictated by a superior regard, a more holy concern for the success of the Right? Impossible. Nay, they would have been viewed, despite all their flaming professions of attachment to the cause, as recreant to it.

This supposition will serve to illustrate a similar defection which has taken place in the Anti-Slavery ranks, in this Commonwealth, and in other parts of the country, during the past year, through clerical chicanery and the spirit of sectarian narrowness; yet pretending to be animated by the deepest solicitude for the integrity and welfare of our great movement.

Whilst we should watchfully see to it, that nothing of human passion, or personal hatred, or sectarian bitterness, or party policy, enters into our feelings in assailing the execrable system of American slavery, and in rebuking the transcendent wickedness of American slaveholders, we should be equally on our guard not to give heed to the suggestions of a false charity, or to dilute the pure word of liberty. Let our single purpose be— regardless whom it may please or offend among men—to speak the truth of God in its simplicity and power—not to conceal danger, or gild over crime, or screen the wrong-doer. It is not light that is needed on this subject, so much as a heart of flesh. While the chains of millions of our enslaved countrymen are clanking in our ears, and their cries are piercing the heavens, and we know that their bodies and spirits (which are God's) are daily sold under the hammer of the auctioneer as household goods or working cattle, we need no nice adjustment of abstractions, no metaphysical reasonings, to convince us that such scenes are dreadful, and such practices impious. All the nobility of our manhood, all that is nature within us, all the instincts and faculties of our souls, settle the question instantly. With the indignation that fired the bosom of a Brougham, each of us exclaims—"Tell me not of rights! talk not of the property of the planter in his slaves! I deny the right, I acknowledge not the property! The principles, the feelings of our nature rise in rebellion against it. Be the appeal made to the understanding or the heart, the sentence is the same that rejects it." O, the odious inconsistency of the American people! When the iron heel of Turkish despotism was planted upon the necks of the Greeks; when the Autocrat of Russia was sending his barbarian hordes to conquer the unconquerable Poles; when the incensed populace of Paris contended for the space of three days with the National Guards, and drove Charles the Tenth from his throne; when the news of the passage of the Stamp Act, and the tax on tea, by the mother country, was received by our fathers, and insurrections for liberty broke out in all parts of the colonies; when, at a subsequent period, the tidings came that American citizens had been captured by the Algerines, and were pining in bondage; when, at a still later period, the rights of American seamen ceased to be respected by Great Britain, and some six or seven thousand were said to have been impressed; on each and on all of those memorable occasions, no denunciation against the oppressors was regarded as too strong, no impeachment of motives too sweeping, no agitation too great, no zeal too burning, no sacrifice too dear, no peril too imminent to be encountered. O, no! Then weakness became strength; prudence, noble daring; moderation, impetuosity; caution, a generous disdain of consequences; charity, righteous indignation! Then the cold blood philosophy, congealed by icy frigidness, was changed into the warm fluid of patriotic life; then the abstractions of metaphysics became practical realities, affecting life, liberty, and the pursuit of happiness; then halting expediency was transformed into high, immutable, eternal principle. Then the man, who, at such a crisis, had dared to mock the agony of men's minds, and to insult their understandings, by giving them grave and severe homilies upon the duty of being cautious, and prudent, and charitable, and upon the propriety of exercising moderation and being dumb—such a man would have been doomed and treated as recreant to God and liberty. Then the land trembled as Freedom went forth to battle. Then words, however huge, expostulations, however earnest, petitions, however importunate, assertions of rights, however bold and uncompromising in language, were deemed wholly inadequate to such a crisis. Paving-stones in the streets were taken up, and hurled at the heads of the myrmidons of tyranny; human blood was poured out like water, and the dead bodies of the friends and foes of liberty were piled up in hecatombs round about. Then the press spoke out in thunder-tones—the public halls and churches rang with the shouts of victory, or resounded with heart-stirring appeals to arms; and even "ministers of the gospel" felt that, in a strife for the rights of man, carnal weapons were not less efficacious than spiritual weapons, and hence it is recorded that some of them carried loaded muskets into the pulpit on the Sabbath day. Now, we do not say that all this conduct was justifiable—God forbid! We have not so learned duty. But, in the name of justice and mercy, we protest against being condemned for our zeal or language, our principles or measures, by the men who eulogize such deeds and such excitements as we have just recited. The only lesson they can teach us is, that our zeal is tame, our sensibility obtuse, our language weak, our self-sacrifice nothing, compared to the wrongs to be redressed, the evils to be overcome.

SELECTION **10**

An Abolitionist Martyr Goes to His Death:
John Brown's Last Words, 1859

One abolitionist who was not content to rely on moral persuasion or on the slow workings of the political process was John Brown (1800–1859), an almost legendary figure in the annals of the antislavery movement. Passionate and sincere, Brown's approach to the abolitionist's goal was that of a fanatic. He first came to notice in Kansas in 1856 when he led a small group of zealots in the murder of several proslavery settlers. Imbued with the notion that he had been divinely selected to lead the slaves out of their bondage, by violence if necessary, he made plans for an armed slave insurrection, for which he received financial support from many prominent abolitionists. Brown's raid on the Federal arsenal at Harpers Ferry, Virginia, in October, 1859, was the result. Captured, he was tried and executed in December. The raid, coming on the eve of a crucial presidential election year, did much to polarize the sectional conflict and destroy the influence of moderate counsel. Its significance for the abolitionist movement, as C. Vann Woodward has pointed out, was a significance of means—the end of nonviolence for the achievement of abolition. In his final statement, Brown predicted that freedom for the slave could not be secured "but with Blood." The following extracts are reprinted from F. B. |Sanborn| (ed.), The Life and Letters of John Brown, Liberator of Kansas and Martyr of Virginia *(Boston: Roberts Brothers, 1891), pages 584–585, 620. Woodward's analysis of Brown's raid is in "John Brown's Private War," in* The Burden of Southern History *(1960). A sympathetic biography of Brown is Oswald Garrison Villard's* John Brown, 1800–1859: A Biography Fifty Years After *(1910).*

FINAL ADDRESS TO THE COURT, NOVEMBER 2, 1859

I have, may it please the Court, a few words to say.

In the first place, I deny everything but what I have all along admitted: of a design on my part to free slaves. I intended certainly to have made a clean thing of that matter, as I did last winter, when I went into Missouri and there took slaves without the snapping of a gun on either side, moving them through the country, and finally leaving them in Canada. I designed to have done the same thing again on a larger scale. That was all I intended. I never did intend murder, or treason, or the destruction of property, or to excite or incite slaves to rebellion, or to make insurrection.

I have another objection, and that is that it is unjust that I should suffer such a penalty. Had I interfered in the manner which I admit, and which I admit has been fairly proved—for I admire the truthfulness and candor of the greater portion of the witnesses who have testified in this case—had I so interfered in behalf of the rich, the powerful, the intelligent, the so-called great, or in behalf of any of their friends, either father, mother, brother, sister, wife or children, or any of that class, and suffered and sacrificed what I have in this interference, it would have been all right. Every man in this Court would have deemed it an act worthy of reward rather than punishment.

This Court acknowledges, too, as I suppose, the validity of the law of God. I see a book kissed, which I suppose to be the Bible, or at least the New Testament, which teaches me that all things whatsoever I would that men should do to me, I should do even so to them. It teaches me, further, to remember them that are in bonds as bound with them. I endeavored to act up to that instruction. I say I am yet too young to understand that God is any respecter of persons. I believe that to have interfered as I have done, as I have always freely admitted I have done, in behalf of His despised poor, I did no wrong, but right. Now, if it is deemed necessary that I should forfeit my life for the furtherance of the ends of justice, and mingle my blood further with the blood of my children and with the blood of millions in this slave country whose rights are disregarded by wicked, cruel, and unjust enactments, I say, let it be done.

Let me say one word further. I feel entirely satisfied with the treatment I have received on my trial. Considering all the circumstances, it has been more generous than I expected. But I feel no consciousness of guilt. I have stated from the first what was my intention, and what was not. I never had any design against the liberty of any person, nor any disposition to commit treason or incite slaves to rebel or make any general insurrection. I never encouraged any man to do so, but always discouraged any idea of that kind.

Let me say, also, in regard to the statements made by some of those who were connected with me, I hear it has been stated by some of them that I have induced them to join me. But the contrary is true. I do not say this to injure them, but as regretting their weakness. Not one but joined me of his own accord, and the greater part at their own expense. A number of them I never saw, and never had a word of conversation with, till the day they came to me, and that was for the purpose I have stated.

Now, I have done.

FINAL MESSAGE, DECEMBER 2, 1859

I John Brown am now quite *certain* that the crimes of this *guilty land: will never be purged away;* but with Blood. I had *as I now think: vainly* flattered myself that without *very much* bloodshed; it might be done.

PART FOUR

The Question of Federal Control of Slavery in the Territories

The dominant political issue of the fifteen years preceding the Civil War was not the moral question of slavery, as defined by Southern apologists or by Northern abolitionists, but rather the question of slavery in the territories. It was not that the American people were so directly or narrowly concerned with the fate of the Western territories; rather the question of slavery in the territories was, to many Northerners and Southerners, the political expression or manifestation of a more fundamental disagreement over slavery itself. The territories provided a test of strength between the sections that was closely related to the deeper sectional differences. It was doubted whether the moral question could be settled within the existing framework of government and politics; however, there were few doubts that the territories could be dealt with through normal political processes. In one fashion, then, slavery in the territories became symbolic of the deeper conflict. To Northern critics of slavery, the territories were the first area of attack in a larger crusade against slavery in the South. To the Southerners, the territories became the first line of defense for their "peculiar institution" or, more significantly, for Southern civilization itself.

The issue sprang from a growing relationship between slavery and national expansion, and became complicated by the whole role of slavery in the South and in the nation. For political as well as economic reasons, Southerners thought that slavery must expand in order to survive. Actually the issue was an old one, dating from the earliest years of the republic. The first real crisis over slavery in the territories, however, came in 1819–1820, with Missouri's desire to enter the Union as a slave state. The issue was settled at that time by the Missouri Compromise, with the establishment of an arbitrary line—36°30′ north latitude—that would separate free from slave territory in the Louisiana Purchase area. The Missouri Compromise line was reaffirmed when Texas was admitted to the Union in 1845 and when Oregon Territory was created in 1848. This solution was *obvious for both Texas and Oregon; the former already had a sizable slave population, the latter was considered ill-adapted to slave labor. Less obvious was whether slavery should be allowed in the territory acquired from Mexico as a result of the Mexican War.*

Early in the war with Mexico, Northerners made it clear that the Missouri Compromise solution would be unacceptable in the new lands secured from the nation's Southern neighbor. The Wilmot Proviso, first introduced in Congress in 1846, declared in fact that slavery should be forever prohibited from these lands, a policy the South could not accept. Although it never passed Congress, the Wilmot Proviso sparked a debate not only over slavery in the territories but also over the broader constitutional question of the power of the Federal government, through Congress, to regulate the internal affairs of the territories. Three positions were expressed during the discussion in the late 1840s; these same positions persisted, with some modification, until the recourse to arms in 1861. Many Northerners supported the principle of the Wilmot Proviso, arguing that Congress not only held the power but also the obligation to keep slavery out of the new territories. Most Southerners took an opposite stand, maintaining that citizens of all states had an equal right to emigrate to the territories with their property, meaning simply that slaves could be taken to, and held in, the new territories acquired from Mexico. A third position was advanced as a compromise between the two extremes. The question of slavery in the territories, the supporters of this view stated, could only be settled by the people who lived in the territories—a principle that became known as "popular sovereignty."

A crisis was averted by the Compromise of 1850, an attempt to settle the territorial issue as well as other points of difference between the two sections. California was admitted to the Union as a free state and the two territories of Utah and New Mexico were established. In each case it was the principle of popular sovereignty that prevailed. By the early 1850s, then, two formulae, mutually inconsistent, had been utilized to settle the question of slavery in the territories—an arbitrary line separating free from slave territory for the old Louisiana Purchase, and popular sovereignty for the lands in the Mexican cession. Which of these would prevail was determined in 1854 when Stephen A. Douglas, Senator from Illinois, introduced his famous Kansas-Nebraska Act, repealing the Missouri Compromise and affirming popular sovereignty as the basis for territorial organization.

For the next four years, the issue of slavery in the territories became principally the issue of slavery in Kansas Territory. Confusion and chaos reigned in that troubled area as the forces of slavery extension and the forces of slavery restriction vied for political supremacy. By the middle of the decade, the issue was without doubt the dominant political question in the nation. Parties rose and fell, sectional differences became more sharply focused, and reasonable discussion more rare. In 1857, the Supreme Court entered the fray when a majority of the justices handed down the Dred Scott decision, a distinct victory for the Southern point of view in the contest. Yet this Southern triumph was not to last long. The very next year, Kansas was lost to slavery and the South, as Kansans turned their backs on the proslave Lecompton constitution, a document which would have admitted Kansas as a slave state. Later in the same year, Douglas, debating Abraham Lincoln at Freeport, Illinois, counseled the territories on how they might still exercise their popular sovereignty despite the Supreme Court decision.

Although no further territories existed after 1858 in which the slavery question had not been settled, the debate over slavery within the territories raged on. The discussion attained a new level of abstraction and became further divorced from reality, lending credence to James G. Blaine's often-quoted statement that the quarrel involved an imaginary Negro in an impossible place. There were few slaves in the territories and but few people in either North or South who seriously believed that the territories were physically adapted to slavery. By the end of the 1850s, however, this issue of slavery in the territories had acquired wider meaning; it had become symbolic of slavery's role in the South and the South's role in the nation. The moral implications of slavery were invoked, and with the elevation of slavery in the territories to the high level of principle, emotions were raised and compromise became difficult. The election of 1860 was the final showdown. The three positions that had developed during the debates over the Wilmot Proviso were now repeated in virtually their same form. Only the South had reached a new extreme. Southerners and Northern Republicans now stood together in favor of Federal control of slavery in the territories, the former desiring slavery's protection and the latter arguing that it must not be allowed to exist. In the middle stood the adherents of popular sovereignty. The election of 1860 did not settle the issue, if indeed it would have been possible to settle it.

Stephen A. Douglas Implements Popular Sovereignty:
The Kansas-Nebraska Act, 1854

In January, 1854, Stephen A. Douglas, Senator from Illinois and Chairman of the Senate Committee on Territories, introduced the Kansas-Nebraska Act into the United States Senate. The act created two new territories out of the unorganized portions of the old Louisiana Purchase, an area that had been set aside as a permanent Indian frontier not many years before. The acquisition of new lands on the Pacific in the 1840s meant that this Indian frontier lay in the center of the nation, athwart the lines of communication and transportation to the Pacific Coast. Pressures for the organization of the area mounted, and Douglas's bill was the result. But the Kansas-Nebraska Act did more than create two additional territories. It also repealed the Missouri Compromise and provided for popular sovereignty; the people of Kansas and Nebraska Territories were to determine the slavery question for themselves, without interference from the national government. The act thus became a milestone in the quarrel over slavery in the territories and, in terms of its consequences, one of the most significant measures of the sectional conflict. A storm of protest in the North followed its passage. The new anti-Nebraska, or Republican, party was called into existence to lead the opposition to popular sovereignty and the possible extension of slavery. In Kansas itself, four years of turmoil and bloodshed— "Bleeding Kansas"—were ushered in as Northerners and Southerners sought control over the territorial government. The controversial section of the Kansas-Nebraska Act follows. The act has long been the subject of conflicting interpretations by historians, many of whom have been concerned primarily with Douglas's motives in sponsoring the legislation. For a good summary of these interpretations, see Roy F. Nichols, "The Kansas-Nebraska Act: A Century of Historiography," Mississippi Valley Historical Review, *volume 43, September, 1956, pages 187–212. For a biography of Douglas, see George Fort Milton,* The Eve of Conflict: Stephen A. Douglas and the Needless War *(1934); Douglas's letters have been collected in Robert W. Johannsen (ed.),* The Letters of Stephen A. Douglas *(1961). The text of the act is reprinted from* U.S. Statutes at Large, *volume 10, page 289.*

Sec. 32. And be it further enacted, . . . That the Constitution, and all laws of the United States which are not locally inapplicable, shall have the same force and effect within the said Territory of Kansas as elsewhere within the United States, except the eighth section of the act preparatory to the admission of Missouri into the Union, approved March sixth, eighteen hundred and twenty, which, being inconsistent with the principle of non-intervention by Congress with slavery in the States and Territories, as recognized by the legislation of eighteen hundred and fifty, commonly called the Compromise Measures, is hereby declared inoperative and void; it being the true intent and meaning of this act not to legislate slavery into any Territory or State, nor to exclude it therefrom, but to leave the people thereof perfectly free to form and regulate their domestic institutions in their own way, subject only to the Constitution of the United States: *Provided,* That nothing herein contained shall be construed to revive or put in force any law or regulation which may have existed prior to the act of sixth of March, eighteen hundred and twenty, either protecting, establishing, prohibiting, or abolishing slavery. . . .

SELECTION **12**

The Supreme Court Rules on Slavery in the Territories: "Dred Scott v. Sandford," 1857

On March 6, 1857, two days after James Buchanan was inaugurated as President of the United States, the Supreme Court entered the sectional contest when it handed down its decision in the case Dred Scott v. Sanford *(misspelled Sandford in the original report). Scott was the Negro slave of an Army officer who, upon his owner's death, sued for his freedom on the ground that his temporary residence at the Rock Island Arsenal, Illinois (a free state), and at Fort Snelling (in Federal territory made free by the Missouri Compromise) released him from bondage. The case, first argued in 1846, continued in both Missouri state courts and Federal courts until it finally reached the nation's highest tribunal. The Dred Scott case included nine separate opinions (one from each judge), but that of Chief Justice Roger B. Taney is generally regarded as reflecting the majority decision. Taney, a Maryland slaveowner, had served in the Cabinet of Andrew Jackson as Attorney General and Secretary of the Treasury. His role in the bank war brought him national fame. In 1836, he was appointed by Jackson to the Supreme Court as Chief Justice—a post he held until his death in 1864. In his decision, Taney declared that Scott was not a citizen of Missouri and therefore had not been entitled to sue in its courts. More significantly, the court ruled that the Missouri Compromise, forbidding slavery north of 36°30′ in the national territories, was unconstitutional. Congress, Taney maintained, had no power to prohibit slavery in a Federal territory; by extension, this power also could not be exercised by a territorial legislature. In the Dred Scott decision, therefore, the Supreme Court struck at both the slavery restriction platform of the Republican party and the popular*

*sovereignty doctrine of Stephen A. Douglas. The decision was a triumph for the
South in the struggle over the issue of slavery in the territories. A fine and
comprehensive discussion of the case is in Vincent C. Hopkins,* Dred Scott's
Case *(1951). The case itself is reprinted from the* United States Reports,
19 Howard, pages 399–454.

r. Chief Justice Taney delivered the opinion of the court. . . .
There are two leading questions presented by the record:

1. Had the Circuit Court of the United States jurisdiction to hear and determine the case between these parties? And
2. If it had jurisdiction, is the judgment it has given erroneous or not?

The plaintiff in error, who was also the plaintiff in the court below, was,
with his wife and children, held as slaves by the defendant, in the State
of Missouri; and he brought this action in the Circuit Court of the United
States for that district, to assert the title of himself and his family to
freedom.

The declaration is in the form usually adopted in that State to try
questions of this description, and contains the averment necessary to give
the court jurisdiction; that he and the defendant are citizens of different
States; that is, that he is a citizen of Missouri, and the defendant a citizen
of New York.

The defendant pleaded in abatement to the jurisdiction of the court,
that the plaintiff was not a citizen of the State of Missouri, as alleged in
his declaration, being a negro of African descent, whose ancestors were of
pure African blood, and who were brought into this country and sold as
slaves. . . .

Before we speak of the pleas in bar, it will be proper to dispose of the
questions which have arisen on the plea in abatement.

That plea denies the right of the plaintiff to sue in a court of the United
States, for the reasons therein stated.

If the question raised by it is legally before us, and the court should
be of opinion that the facts stated in it disqualify the plaintiff from becoming a citizen, in the sense in which that word is used in the Constitution of the United States, then the judgment of the Circuit Court is
erroneous, and must be reversed. . . .

The question is simply this: Can a negro, whose ancestors were imported into this country, and sold as slaves, become a member of the
political community formed and brought into existence by the Constitution of the United States, and as such become entitled to all the rights,
and privileges, and immunities, guarantied by that instrument to the
citizen? One of which rights is the privilege of suing in a court of the
United States in the cases specified in the Constitution.

It will be observed, that the plea applies to that class of persons only
whose ancestors were negroes of the African race, and imported into this
country, and sold and held as slaves. The only matter in issue before the
court, therefore, is, whether the descendants of such slaves, when they
shall be emancipated, or who are born of parents who had become free

before their birth, are citizens of a State, in the sense in which the word citizen is used in the Constitution of the United States. And this being the only matter in dispute on the pleadings, the court must be understood as speaking in this opinion of that class only, that is, of those persons who are the descendants of Africans who were imported into this country, and sold as slaves. . . .

The words "people of the United States" and "citizens" are synonymous terms, and mean the same thing. They both describe the political body who, according to our republican institutions, form the sovereignty, and who hold the power and conduct the Government through their representatives. They are what we familiarly call the "sovereign people," and every citizen is one of this people, and a constituent member of this sovereignty. The question before us is, whether the class of persons described in the plea in abatement compose a portion of this people, and are constituent members of this sovereignty? We think they are not, and that they are not included, and were not intended to be included, under the word "citizens" in the Constitution, and can therefore claim none of the rights and privileges which that instrument provides for and secures to citizens of the United States. On the contrary, they were at that time considered as a subordinate and inferior class of beings, who had been subjugated by the dominant race, and, whether emancipated or not, yet remained subject to their authority, and had no rights or privileges but such as those who held the power and the Government might choose to grant them.

It is not the province of the court to decide upon the justice or injustice, the policy or impolicy, of these laws. The decision of that question belonged to the political or law-making power; to those who formed the sovereignty and framed the Constitution. The duty of the court is, to interpret the instrument they have framed, with the best lights we can obtain on the subject, and to administer it as we find it, according to its true intent and meaning when it was adopted.

In discussing this question, we must not confound the rights of citizenship which a State may confer within its own limits, and the rights of citizenship as a member of the Union. It does not by any means follow, because he has all the rights and privileges of a citizen of a State, that he must be a citizen of the United States. He may have all of the rights and privileges of the citizen of a State, and yet not be entitled to the rights and privileges of a citizen in any other State. For, previous to the adoption of the Constitution of the United States, every State had the undoubted right to confer on whomsoever it pleased the character of citizen, and to endow him with all its rights. But this character of course was confined to the boundaries of the State, and gave him no rights or privileges in other States beyond those secured to him by the laws of nations and the comity of States. Nor have the several States surrendered the power of conferring these rights and privileges by adopting the Constitution of the United States. Each State may still confer them upon an alien, or any one it thinks proper, or upon any class or description of persons; yet he would not be a citizen in the sense in which that word is used in the Constitution of the United States, nor entitled to sue as such in one of its courts, nor to the privileges and immunities of a citizen in the other States. The rights which he would acquire would be restricted to the State which gave them. . . .

It is very clear, therefore, that no State can, by any act or law of its own, passed since the adoption of the Constitution, introduce a new member into the political community created by the Constitution of the United States. It cannot make him a member of this community by making him a member of its own. And for the same reason it cannot introduce any person, or description of persons, who were not intended to be embraced in this new political family, which the Constitution brought into existence, but were intended to be excluded from it.

The question then arises, whether the provisions of the Constitution, in relation to the personal rights and privileges to which the citizen of a State should be entitled, embraced the negro African race, at that time in this country, or who might afterwards be imported, who had then or should afterwards be made free in any State; and to put it in the power of a single State to make him a citizen of the United States, and endue him with the full rights of citizenship in every other State without their consent? Does the Constitution of the United States act upon him whenever he shall be made free under the laws of a State, and raised there to the rank of a citizen, and immediately clothe him with all the privileges of a citizen in every other State, and in its own courts?

The court think the affirmative of these propositions cannot be maintained. And if it cannot, the plaintiff in error could not be a citizen of the State of Missouri, within the meaning of the Constitution of the United States, and, consequently, was not entitled to sue in its courts.

It is true, every person, and every class and description of persons, who were at the time of the adoption of the Constitution recognised as citizens in the several States, became also citizens of this new political body; but none other; it was formed by them, and for them and their posterity, but for no one else. And the personal rights and privileges guarantied to citizens of this new sovereignty were intended to embrace those only who were then members of the several State communities, or who should afterwards by birthright or otherwise become members, according to the provisions of the Constitution and the principles on which it was founded. It was the union of those who were at that time members of distinct and separate political communities into one political family, whose power, for certain specified purposes, was to extend over the whole territory of the United States. And it gave to each citizen rights and privileges outside of his State which he did not before possess, and placed him in every other State upon a perfect equality with its own citizens as to rights of person and rights of property; it made him a citizen of the United States.

It becomes necessary, therefore, to determine who were citizens of the several States when the Constitution was adopted. And in order to do this, we must recur to the Governments and institutions of the thirteen colonies, when they separated from Great Britain and formed new sovereignties, and took their places in the family of independent nations. We must inquire who, at that time, were recognised as the people or citizens of a State, whose rights and liberties had been outraged by the English Government; and who declared their independence, and assumed the powers of Government to defend their rights by force of arms.

In the opinion of the court, the legislation and histories of the times, and the language used in the Declaration of Independence, show, that neither the class of persons who had been imported as slaves, nor their descendants, whether they had become free or not, were then acknowledged as a part of the people, nor intended to be included in the general words used in that memorable instrument.

It is difficult at this day to realize the state of public opinion in relation to that unfortunate race, which prevailed in the civilized and enlightened portions of the world at the time of the Declaration of Independence, and when the Constitution of the United States was framed and adopted. But the public history of every European nation displays it in a manner too plain to be mistaken.

They had for more than a century before been regarded as beings of an inferior order, and altogether unfit to associate with the white race, either in social or political relations; and so far inferior, that they had no rights which the white man was bound to respect; and that the negro might justly and lawfully be reduced to slavery for his benefit. He was bought and sold, and treated as an ordinary article of merchandise and traffic, whenever a profit could be made by it. This opinion was at that time fixed and universal in the civilized portion of the white race. It was regarded as an axiom in morals as well as in politics, which no one thought of disputing, or supposed to be open to dispute; and men in every grade and position in society daily and habitually acted upon it in their private pursuits, as well as in matters of public concern, without doubting for a moment the correctness of this opinion. . . .

The language of the Declaration of Independence is . . . conclusive:
It begins by declaring that,

> When in the course of human events it becomes necessary for one people to dissolve the political bands which have connected them with another, and to assume among the powers of the earth the separate and equal station to which the laws of nature and nature's God entitle them, a decent respect for the opinions of mankind requires that they should declare the causes which impel them to the separation.

It then proceeds to say:

> We hold these truths to be self-evident: that all men are created equal; that they are endowed by their Creator with certain unalienable rights; that among them is life, liberty, and the pursuit of happiness; that to secure these rights, Governments are instituted, deriving their just powers from the consent of the governed.

The general words above quoted would seem to embrace the whole human family, and if they were used in a similar instrument at this day would be so understood. But it is too clear for dispute, that the enslaved African race were not intended to be included, and formed no part of the people who framed and adopted this declaration; for if the language, as understood in that day, would embrace them, the conduct of the distinguished men who framed the Declaration of Independence would have been utterly and flagrantly inconsistent with the principles they asserted; and instead of the sympathy of mankind, to which they so confidently appealed, they would have deserved and received universal rebuke and reprobation. . . .

This state of public opinion had undergone no change when the Con-

stitution was adopted, as is equally evident from its provisions and language. . . .

. . . there are two clauses in the Constitution which point directly and
specifically to the negro race as a separate class of persons, and show
clearly that they were not regarded as a portion of the people or citizens
of the Government then formed.

One of these clauses reserves to each of the thirteen States the right to
import slaves until the year 1808, if it thinks proper. And the importation
which it thus sanctions was unquestionably of persons of the race of which
we are speaking, as the traffic in slaves in the United States had always
been confined to them. And by the other provision the States pledge themselves to each other to maintain the right of property of the master, by
delivering up to him any slave who may have escaped from his service,
and be found within their respective territories. By the first above-men-
tioned clause, therefore, the right to purchase and hold this property is
directly sanctioned and authorized for twenty years by the people who
framed the Constitution. And by the second, they pledge themselves to
maintain and uphold the right of the master in the manner specified, as
long as the Government they then formed should endure. And these two
provisions show, conclusively, that neither the description of persons
therein referred to, nor their descendants, were embraced in any of the
other provisions of the Constitution; for certainly these two clauses were
not intended to confer on them or their posterity the blessings of liberty,
or any of the personal rights so carefully provided for the citizen. . . .

The legislation of the States . . . shows, in a manner not to be mistaken,
the inferior and subject condition of that race at the time the Constitution
was adopted, and long afterwards, throughout the thirteen States by which
that instrument was framed; and it is hardly consistent with the respect
due to these States, to suppose that they regarded at that time, as fellow-
citizens and members of the sovereignty, a class of beings whom they had
thus stigmatized; whom, as we are bound, out of respect to the State
sovereignties, to assume they had deemed it just and necessary thus to
stigmatize, and upon whom they had impressed such deep and enduring
marks of inferiority and degradation; or, that when they met in convention
to form the Constitution, they looked upon them as a portion of their
constituents, or designed to include them in the provisions so carefully
inserted for the security and protection of the liberties and rights of their
citizens. It cannot be supposed that they intended to secure to them rights,
and privileges, and rank, in the new political body throughout the Union,
which every one of them denied within the limits of its own dominion.
More especially, it cannot be believed that the large slaveholding States
regarded them as included in the word citizens, or would have consented
to a Constitution which might compel them to receive them in that character from another State. For if they were so received, and entitled to the
privileges and immunities of citizens, it would exempt them from the
operation of the special laws and from the police regulations which they
considered to be necessary for their own safety. It would give to persons
of the negro race, who were recognised as citizens in any one State of the
Union, the right to enter every other State whenever they pleased, singly
or in companies, without pass or passport, and without obstruction, to
sojourn there as long as they pleased, to go where they pleased at every

hour of the day or night without molestation, unless they committed some violation of law for which a white man would be punished; and it would give them the full liberty of speech in public and in private upon all subjects upon which its own citizens might speak; to hold public meetings upon political affairs, and to keep and carry arms wherever they went. And all of this would be done in the face of the subject race of the same color, both free and slaves, and inevitably producing discontent and insubordination among them, and endangering the peace and safety of the State. . . .

. . . it is said that a person may be a citizen, and entitled to that character, although he does not possess all the rights which may belong to other citizens; as, for example, the right to vote, or to hold particular offices; and that yet, when he goes into another State, he is entitled to be recognised there as a citizen, although the State may measure his rights by the rights which it allows to persons of a like character or class resident in the State, and refuse to him the full rights of citizenship.

This argument overlooks the language of the provision in the Constitution of which we are speaking.

Undoubtedly, a person may be a citizen, that is, a member of the community who form the sovereignty, although he exercises no share of the political power, and is incapacitated from holding particular offices. Women and minors, who form a part of the political family, cannot vote; and when a property qualification is required to vote or hold a particular office, those who have not the necessary qualification cannot vote or hold the office, yet they are citizens.

So, too, a person may be entitled to vote by the law of the State, who is not a citizen even of the State itself. And in some of the States of the Union foreigners not naturalized are allowed to vote. And the State may give the right to free negroes and mulattoes, but that does not make them citizens of the State, and still less of the United States. And the provision in the Constitution giving privileges and immunities in other States, does not apply to them.

Neither does it apply to a person who, being the citizen of a State, migrates to another State. For then he becomes subject to the laws of the State in which he lives, and he is no longer a citizen of the State from which he removed. And the State in which he resides may then, unquestionably, determine his *status* or condition, and place him among the class of persons who are not recognised as citizens, but belong to an inferior and subject race; and may deny him the privileges and immunities enjoyed by its citizens.

But so far as mere rights of person are concerned, the provision in question is confined to citizens of a State who are temporarily in another State without taking up their residence there. It gives them no political rights in the State, as to voting or holding office, or in any other respect. For a citizen of one State has no right to participate in the government of another. But if he ranks as a citizen in the State to which he belongs, within the meaning of the Constitution of the United States, then, whenever he goes into another State, the Constitution clothes him, as to the rights of person, with all the privileges and immunities which belong to citizens of the State. And if persons of the African race are citizens of a State, and of the United States, they would be entitled to all of these privileges and immunities in every State, and the State could not restrict them; for they would hold these privileges and immunities under the paramount authority of the Federal Government, and its courts would be bound to maintain and enforce them, the Constitution and laws of the State to the contrary notwithstanding. . . .

No one, we presume, supposes that any change in public opinion or feeling, in relation to this unfortunate race, in the civilized nations of Europe or in this country, should induce the court to give to the words of the Constitution a more liberal construction in their favor than they were intended to bear when the instrument was framed and adopted. Such an argument would be altogether inadmissible in any tribunal called on to interpret it. If any of its provisions are deemed unjust, there is a mode prescribed in the instrument itself by which it may be amended; but while it remains unaltered, it must be construed now as it was understood at the time of its adoption. It is not only the same in words, but the same in meaning, and delegates the same powers to the Government, and reserves and secures the same rights and privileges to the citizen; and as long as it continues to exist in its present form, it speaks not only in the same words, but with the same meaning and intent with which it spoke when it came from the hands of its framers, and was voted on and adopted by the people of the United States. Any other rule of construction would abrogate the judicial character of this court, and make it the mere reflex of the popular opinion or passion of the day. This court was not created by the Constitution for such purposes. Higher and graver trusts have been confided to it, and it must not falter in the path of duty. . . .

And upon a full and careful consideration of the subject, the court is of opinion, that, upon the facts stated in the plea in abatement, Dred Scott was not a citizen of Missouri within the meaning of the Constitution of the United States, and not entitled as such to sue in its courts; and, consequently, that the Circuit Court had no jurisdiction of the case, and that the judgment on the plea in abatement is erroneous. . . .

We proceed . . . to inquire whether the facts relied on by the plaintiff entitled him to his freedom. . . .

In considering this part of the controversy, two questions arise: 1. Was he, together with his family, free in Missouri by reason of the stay in the territory of the United States hereinbefore mentioned? And 2. If they were not, is Scott himself free by reason of his removal to Rock Island, in the State of Illinois, as stated in the above admissions?

We proceed to examine the first question.

The act of Congress, upon which the plaintiff relies, declares that slavery and involuntary servitude, except as a punishment for crime, shall be forever prohibited in all that part of the territory ceded by France, under the name of Louisiana, which lies north of thirty-six degrees thirty minutes north latitude, and not included within the limits of Missouri. And the difficulty which meets us at the threshold of this part of the inquiry is, whether Congress was authorized to pass this law under any of the powers granted to it by the Constitution; for if the authority is not given by that instrument, it is the duty of this court to declare it void and inoperative, and incapable of conferring freedom upon any one who is held as a slave under the laws of any one of the States.

The counsel for the plaintiff has laid much stress upon that article in the Constitution which confers on Congress the power "to dispose of and make all needful rules and regulations respecting the territory or other property belonging to the United States;" but, in the judgment of the court, that provision has no bearing on the present controversy, and the power there given, whatever it may be, is confined, and was intended to be confined, to the territory which at that time belonged to, or was claimed by, the United States, and was within their boundaries as settled by the treaty with Great Britain, and can have no influence upon a territory afterwards acquired from a foreign Government. It was a special provision for a known and particular territory, and to meet a present emergency, and nothing more. . . .

We do not mean . . . to question the power of Congress in this respect. The power to expand the territory of the United States by the admission of new States is plainly given; and in the construction of this power by all the departments of the Government, it has been held to authorize the acquisition of territory, not fit for admission at the time, but to be admitted as soon as its population and situation would entitle it to admission. It is acquired to become a State, and not to be held as a colony and governed by Congress with absolute authority; and as the propriety of admitting a new State is committed to the sound discretion of Congress, the power to acquire territory for that purpose, to be held by the United States until it is in a suitable condition to become a State upon an equal footing with the other States, must rest upon the same discretion. It is a question for the political department of the Government, and not the judicial; and whatever the political department of the Government shall recognise as within the limits of the United States, the judicial department is also bound to recognise, and to administer in it the laws of the United States, so far as they apply, and to maintain in the Territory the authority and rights of the Government, and also the personal rights and rights of property of individual citizens, as secured by the Constitution. All we mean to say on this point is, that, as there is no express regulation in the Constitution defining the power which the General Government may exercise over the person or property of a citizen in a Territory thus acquired, the court must necessarily look to the provisions and principles of the Constitution, and its distribution of powers, for the rules and principles by which its decision must be governed.

Taking this rule to guide us, it may be safely assumed that citizens of the United States who migrate to a Territory belonging to the people of the United States, cannot be ruled as mere colonists, dependent upon the will of the General Government, and to be governed by any laws it may think proper to impose. The principle upon which our Governments rest, and upon which alone they continue to exist, is the union of States, sovereign and independent within their own limits in their internal and domestic concerns, and bound together as one people by a General Government, possessing certain enumerated and restricted powers, delegated to it by the people of the several States, and exercising supreme authority within the scope of the powers granted to it, throughout the dominion of the United States. A power, therefore, in the General Government to obtain and hold colonies and dependent territories, over which they might legislate without restriction, would be inconsistent with its own existence in its present form. Whatever it acquires it acquires for the benefit of the people of the several States who created it. It is their trustee acting for them, and charged with the duty of promoting the interests of the whole people of the Union in the exercise of the powers specifically granted. . . .

But the power of Congress over the person or property of a citizen can never be a mere discretionary power under our Constitution and form of Government. The powers of the Government and the rights and privileges of the citizen are regulated and plainly defined by the Constitution itself. And when the Territory becomes a part of the United States, the Federal Government enters into possession in the character impressed upon it by those who created it. It enters upon it with its powers over the citizen strictly defined, and limited by the Constitution, from which it derives its own existence, and by virtue of which alone it continues to exist and act as a Government and sovereignty. It has no power of any kind beyond it; and it cannot, when it enters a Territory of the United States, put off its character, and assume discretionary or despotic powers which the Constitution has denied to it. It cannot create for itself a new character separated from the citizens of the United States, and the duties it owes them under the provisions of the Constitution. The Territory being a part of the United States, the Government and the citizen both enter it under the authority of the Constitution, with their respective rights defined and marked out; and the Federal Government can exercise no power over his person or property, beyond what that instrument confers, nor lawfully deny any right which it has reserved. . . .

Thus the rights of property are united with the rights of person, and placed on the same ground by the fifth amendment to the Constitution, which provides that no person shall be deprived of life, liberty, and property, without due process of law. And an act of Congress which deprives a citizen of the United States of his liberty or property, merely because he came himself or brought his property into a particular Territory of the United States, and who had committed no offense against the laws, could hardly be dignified with the name of due process of law. . . .

The powers over person and property of which we speak are not only not granted to Congress, but are in express terms denied, and they are forbidden to exercise them. And this prohibition is not confined to the States, but the words are general, and extend to the whole territory over which the Constitution gives it power to legislate, including those portions of it remaining under Territorial Government, as well as that covered by States. It is a total absence of power everywhere within the dominion of the United States, and places the citizens of a Territory, so far as these rights are concerned, on the same footing with citizens of the States, and guards them as firmly and plainly against any inroads which the General Government might attempt, under the plea of implied or incidental powers. And if Congress itself cannot do this—if it is beyond the powers conferred on the Federal Government—it will be admitted, we presume, that it could not authorize a Territorial Government to exercise them. It could confer no power on any local Government, established by its authority, to violate the provisions of the Constitution. . . .

Now, as we have already said in an earlier part of this opinion, upon a different point, the right of property in a slave is distinctly and expressly affirmed in the Constitution. The right to traffic in it, like an ordinary article of merchandise and property, was guarantied to the citizens of the United States, in every State that might desire it, for twenty years.

And the Government in express terms is pledged to protect it in all future time, if the slave escapes from his owner. This is done in plain words—too plain to be misunderstood. And no word can be found in the Constitution which gives Congress a greater power over slave property, or which entitles property of that kind to less protection than property of any other description. The only power conferred is the power coupled with the duty of guarding and protecting the owner in his rights.

Upon these considerations, it is the opinion of the court that the act of Congress which prohibited a citizen from holding and owning property of this kind in the territory of the United States north of the line therein mentioned, is not warranted by the Constitution, and is therefore void; and that neither Dred Scott himself, nor any of his family, were made free by being carried into this territory; even if they had been carried there by the owner, with the intention of becoming a permanent resident. . . .

As Scott was a slave when taken into the State of Illinois by his owner, and was there held as such, and brought back in that character, his *status*, as free or slave, depended on the laws of Missouri, and not of Illinois. . . .

Upon the whole, therefore, it is the judgment of this court, that it appears by the record before us that the plaintiff in error is not a citizen of Missouri, in the sense in which that word is used in the Constitution; and that the Circuit Court of the United States, for that reason, had no jurisdiction in the case, and could give no judgment in it. Its judgment for the defendant must, consequently, be reversed, and a mandate issued, directing the suit to be dismissed for want of jurisdiction.

SELECTION

Self-government for the Territories: Stephen A. Douglas's Debate with Lincoln, October 15, 1858

Stephen A. Douglas (1813–1861), Senator from Illinois, was the leading proponent of popular sovereignty during the 1850s. He believed that only by allowing the people in the territories to settle the question of slavery for themselves, without interference from Congress, could the Democratic party be maintained as a national party and the Union be preserved. To him, slavery was a domestic issue, of significance primarily to those who must be directly affected by it. He regarded slavery, as he said, as an issue of practical politics, not a moral question. Only by so doing, he was convinced, could the nation be saved from destruction. Douglas fought hard throughout the decade on behalf of popular sovereignty. His record, from the Compromise of 1850 to his campaigns for the Presidency in 1860, was a consistent one. His position, however, came to displease both the Northern antislavery enthusiasts and the Southern slavery extensionists, and he ended the decade fighting for his political life against both groups. In 1858, Douglas met Abraham Lincoln in seven joint debates as he sought reelection to the United States Senate. The debates allowed him to develop his position and to answer his critics, both Northern and Southern. He resisted Lincoln's attempt to introduce the moral question of slavery, and sought to keep the arguments on the pragmatic level he regarded as so important to national political stability. Douglas won his reelection, but the real significance of the debates was not apparent until two years later. A provocative interpretation of the Lincoln-Douglas debates is in Harry V. Jaffa, Crisis of the House Divided: An Interpretation of the Issues in the Lincoln-Douglas Debates *(1959). The extract below is reprinted from Stephen A. Douglas, "Rejoinder: Seventh Joint Debate, Alton, October 15, 1858," Roy P. Basler et al. (eds.),* The Collected Works of Abraham Lincoln *(New Brunswick: Rutgers, 1953), 9 volumes, volume 3, pages 318–325.*

Mr. Lincoln has concluded his remarks by saying that there is not such an Abolitionist as I am in all America. (Laughter.) If he could make the Abolitionists of Illinois believe that, he would not have much show for the Senate. (Great laughter and applause.) Let him make the Abolitionists believe the truth of that statement and his political back is broken. (Renewed laughter.)

His first criticism upon me is the expression of his hope that the war of the administration will be prosecuted against me and the Democratic party of his State with vigor. He wants that war prosecuted with vigor; I have no doubt of it. His hopes of success, and the hopes of his party depend solely upon it. They have no chance of destroying the Democracy of this State except by the aid of federal patronage. ("That's a fact," "good," and cheers.) He has all the federal office-holders here as his allies, ("That's so,") running separate tickets against the Democracy to divide the party although the leaders all intend to vote directly the Abolition ticket, and only leave the green-horns to vote this separate ticket who refuse to go into the Abolition camp. (Laughter and cheers.) There is something really refreshing in the thought that Mr. Lincoln is in favor of prosecuting one war vigorously. (Roars of laughter.) It is the first war I ever knew him to be in favor of prosecuting. (Renewed laughter.) It is the first war that I ever knew him to believe to be just or constitutional. (Laughter and cheers.) When the Mexican war [was] being waged, and the American army was surrounded by the enemy in Mexico, he thought that war was unconstitutional, unnecessary and unjust. ("That's so," "you've got him," "he voted against it," &c.) He thought it was not commenced on the right *spot*. (Laughter.)

When I made an incidental allusion of that kind in the joint discussion over at Charleston some weeks ago, Lincoln, in replying, said that I, Douglas, had charged him with voting against supplies for the Mexican war, and then he reared up, full length, and swore that he never voted against the supplies—that it was a slander—and caught hold of Ficklin, who sat on the stand, and said, "Here, Ficklin, tell the people that it is a lie." (Laughter and cheers.) Well, Ficklin, who had served in Congress with him, stood up and told them all that he recollected about it. It was that when George Ashmun, of Massachusetts, brought forward a resolution declaring the war unconstitutional, unnecessary, and unjust, that Lincoln had voted for it. "Yes," said Lincoln, "I did." Thus he confessed that he voted that the war was wrong, that our country was in the wrong, and consequently that the Mexicans were in the right; but charged that I had slandered him by saying that he voted against the supplies. I never charged him with voting against the supplies in my life, because I knew that he was not in Congress when they were voted. (Tremendous shouts of laughter.) The war was commenced on the 13th day of May, 1846, and on that day we appropriated in Congress ten millions of dollars and fifty thousand men to prosecute it. During the same session we voted more men and more money, and at the next session we voted more men and more money, so that by the time Mr. Lincoln entered Congress we had enough men and enough money to carry on the war, and had no occasion to vote any more. (Laughter and cheers.) When he got into the House, being opposed to the war, and not being able to stop the supplies, because they had all gone forward, all he could do was to follow the lead of Corwin, and prove that the war was not begun on the right spot, and that it was unconstitutional, unnecessary, and wrong. Remember, too, that this he did after the war had been begun. It is one thing to be opposed to the declaration of a war, another and very different thing to take sides with the enemy against your own country after the war has been commenced. ("Good," and cheers.) Our army was in Mexico at the time, many battles had been fought; our citizens, who were defending the honor of their country's flag, were surrounded by the daggers, the guns and the poison of the enemy. Then it was that Corwin made his speech in which he declared that the American soldiers ought to be welcomed by the Mexicans with bloody hands and hospitable graves; then it was that Ashmun and Lincoln voted in the House of Representatives that the war was unconstitutional and unjust; and Ashmun's resolution, Corwin's speech, and Lincoln's vote were sent to Mexico and read at the head of the Mexican army, to prove to them that there was a Mexican party in the Congress of the United States who were doing all in their power to aid them. ("That's the truth," "Lincoln's a traitor," etc.) That a man who takes sides with the common enemy against his own country in time of war should rejoice in a war being made on me now, is very natural. (Immense applause.) And in my opinion, no other kind of a man would rejoice in it. ("That's true," "hurrah for Douglas," and cheers.)

Mr. Lincoln has told you a great deal to day about his being an old line Clay Whig ("He never was.") Bear in mind that there are a great many old Clay Whigs down in this region. It is more agreeable, therefore, for him to talk about the old Clay Whig party than it is for him to talk Abolitionism. We did not hear much about the old Clay Whig party up in the Abolition districts. How much of an old line Henry Clay Whig was he? Have you read Gen. Singleton's speech at Jacksonville? (Yes, yes, and cheers.) You know that Gen. Singleton was, for twenty-five years, the confidential friend of Henry Clay in Illinois, and he testified that in 1847, when the constitutional convention of this State was in session, the Whig members were invited to a Whig caucus at the house of Mr. Lincoln's brother-in-law, where Mr. Lincoln proposed to throw Henry Clay overboard and take up Gen. Taylor in his place, giving, as his reason, that if the Whigs did not take up Gen. Taylor the Democrats would. (Cheers and laughter.) Singleton testifies that Lincoln, in that speech, urged, as another reason for throwing Henry Clay overboard, that the Whigs had fought long enough for principle and ought to begin to fight for success. Singleton also testifies that Lincoln's speech did have the effect of cutting Clay's throat, and that he, Singleton, and others withdrew from the caucus in indignation. He further states that when they got to Philadelphia to attend the national convention of the Whig party, that Lincoln was there, the bitter and deadly enemy of Clay, and that he tried to keep him (Singleton) out of the convention because he insisted on voting for Clay, and Lincoln was determined to have Taylor. (Laughter and applause.) Singleton says that Lincoln rejoiced with very great joy when he found the mangled remains of the murdered Whig statesman lying cold before him. Now, Mr. Lincoln tells you that he is an old line Clay Whig! (Laughter and cheers.) Gen. Singleton testifies to the facts I have narrated in a public speech which has been printed and circulated broadcast over the State for weeks, yet not a lisp have we heard from Mr. Lincoln on the subject, except that he is an old Clay Whig.

What part of Henry Clay's policy did Lincoln ever advocate? He was in Congress in 1848–9 when the Wilmot proviso warfare disturbed the peace and harmony of the country until it shook the foundation of the republic from its centre to its circumference. It was that agitation that brought Clay forth from his retirement at Ashland again to occupy his seat in the Senate of the United States, to see if he could not, by his great wisdom and experience, and the renown of his name, do something to restore peace and quiet to a disturbed country. Who got up that sectional strife that Clay had to be called upon to quell? I have heard Lincoln boast that he voted forty-two times for the Wilmot proviso, and that he would have voted as many times more if he could. (Laughter.) Lincoln is the man, in connection with Seward, Chase, Giddings, and other Abolitionists, who got up that strife that I helped Clay to put down. (Tremendous applause.) Henry Clay came back to the Senate in 1849, and saw that he must do something to restore peace to the country. The Union Whigs and the Union Democrats welcomed him the moment he arrived, as the man for the occasion. We believed that he, of all men on earth, had been preserved by Divine Providence to guide us out of our difficulties, and we Democrats rallied under Clay then, as you Whigs in nullification time rallied under the banner of old Jackson, forgetting party when the country was in danger, in order that we might have a country first, and parties afterwards. ("Three cheers for Douglas.")

And this reminds me that Mr. Lincoln told you that the slavery question was the only thing that ever disturbed the peace and harmony of the Union. Did not nullification once raise its head and disturb the peace of this Union in 1832? Was that the slavery question, Mr. Lincoln? Did not disunion raise its monster head during the last war with Great Britain? Was that the slavery question, Mr. Lincoln? The peace of this country has been disturbed three times, once during the war with Great Britain, once on the tariff question, and once on the slavery question. ("Three cheers for Douglas.") His argument, therefore, that slavery is the only question that has ever created dissension in the Union falls to the ground. It is true that agitators are enabled now to use this slavery question for the purpose of sectional strife. ("That's so.") He admits that in regard to all things else, the principle that I advocate, making each State and territory free to decide for itself ought to prevail. He instances the cranberry laws, and the oyster laws, and he might have gone through the whole list with the same effect. I say that all these laws are local and domestic, and that local and domestic concerns should be left to each State and each territory to manage for itself. If agitators would acquiesce in that principle, there never would be any danger to the peace and harmony of this Union. ("That's so," and cheers.)

Mr. Lincoln tries to avoid the main issue by attacking the truth of my proposition, that our fathers made this government divided into free and slave States, recognizing the right of each to decide all its local questions for itself. Did they not thus make it? It is true that they did not establish slavery in any of the States, or abolish it in any of them; but finding thirteen States twelve of which were slave and one free, they agreed to form a government uniting them together, as they stood divided into free and slave States, and to guarantee forever to each State the right to do as it pleased on the slavery question. (Cheers.) Having thus made the government, and conferred this right upon each State forever, I assert that this government can exist as they made it, divided into free and slave States, if any one State chooses to retain slavery. (Cheers.) He says that he looks forward to a time when slavery shall be abolished every-where. I look forward to a time when each State shall be allowed to do as it pleases. If it chooses to keep slavery forever, it is not my business, but its own; if it chooses to abolish slavery, it is its own business—not mine. I care more for the great principle of self-government, the right of the people to rule, than I do for all the negroes in Christendom. (Cheers.) I would not endanger the perpetuity of this Union. I would not blot out the great inalienable rights of the white men for all the negroes that ever existed. (Renewed applause.) Hence, I say, let us maintain this govern-ment on the principles that our fathers made it, recognizing the right of each State to keep slavery as long as its people determine, or to abolish it when they please. (Cheers.) But Mr. Lincoln says that when our fathers made this government they did not look forward to the state of things now existing; and therefore he thinks the doctrine was wrong; and he quotes Brooks, of South Carolina, to prove that our fathers then thought that probably slavery would be abolished, by each State acting for itself before this time. Suppose they did; suppose they did not foresee what has occurred,—does that change the principles of our government? They did not probably foresee the telegraph that transmits intelligence by lightning, nor did they foresee the railroads that now form the bonds of union be-tween the different States, or the thousand mechanical inventions that have elevated mankind. But do these things change the principles of the government? Our fathers, I say, made this government on the principle of the right of each State to do as it pleases in its own domestic affairs, subject to the constitution, and allowed the people of each to apply to every new change of circumstance such remedy as they may see fit to improve their condition. This right they have for all time to come. (Cheers.)

Mr. Lincoln went on to tell you that he does not at all desire to inter-fere with slavery in the States where it exists, nor does his party. I ex-pected him to say that down here. (Laughter.) Let me ask him then how he is going to put slavery in the course of ultimate extinction everywhere, if he does not intend to interfere with it in the States where it exists? (Renewed laughter.) He says that he will prohibit it in all territories, and the inference is then that unless they make free States out of them he will keep them out of the Union; for, mark you, he did not say whether or not he would vote to admit Kansas with slavery or not, as her people might apply; (he forgot that as usual, &c;) he did not say whether or not he was in favor of bringing the territories now in existence into the Union on the principle of Clay's compromise measures on the slavery question. I told you that he would not. (Give it to him, he deserves it, &c.) His idea is that he will prohibit slavery in all the territories, and thus force them all to become free States, surrounding the slave States with a cordon of free States, and hemming them in, keeping the slaves confined to their present limits whilst they go on multiplying until the soil on which they live will no longer feed them, and he will thus be able to put slavery in a course of ultimate extinction by starvation. (Cheers.) He will extinguish slavery in the Southern States as the French general exterminated the Algerines when he smoked them out. He is going to extinguish slavery by surrounding the slave States, hemming in the slaves, and starving them out of existence as you smoke a fox out of his hole. And he intends to do that in the name of humanity and Christianity, in order that we may get rid of the terrible crime and sin entailed upon our fathers of holding slaves. (Laughter and cheers.) Mr. Lincoln makes out that line of policy, and appeals to the moral sense of justice, and to the Christian feeling of the community to sustain him. He says that any man who holds to the contrary doctrine is in the position of the king who claimed to govern by divine right. Let us examine for a moment and see what principle it was that overthrew the divine right of George the Third to govern us. Did not these colonies rebel because the British parliament had no right to pass laws concerning our property and domestic and private institutions without our consent? We demanded that the British government should not pass such laws unless they gave us representation in the body passing them,—and this the British government insisting on doing,—we went to war, on the principle that the home government should not control and govern distant colonies without giving them a representation. Now, Mr. Lincoln proposes to govern the territories without giving the people a representation, and calls on Congress to pass laws controlling their property and domestic concerns without their consent and against their will. Thus, he asserts for his party the identical principle asserted by George III. and the tories of the Revolution. (Cheers.)

I ask you to look into these things, and then to tell me whether the democracy or the abolitionists are right. I hold that the people of a territory, like those of a State, (I use the language of Mr. Buchanan in his letter of acceptance,) have the right to decide for themselves whether slavery shall or shall not exist within their limits. ("That's the idea," "Hurrah for Douglas.") The point upon which Chief Justice Taney expresses his opinion is simply this, that slaves being property, stand on an equal footing with other property, and consequently that the owner has the same right to carry that property into a territory that he has any other, subject to the same conditions. Suppose that one of your merchants was to take fifty or one hundred thousand dollars worth of liquors to

Kansas. He has a right to go there under that decision, but when he gets there he finds the Maine liquor law in force, and what can he do with his property after he gets it there? He cannot sell it, he cannot use it, it is subject to the local law, and that law is against him, and the best thing he can do with it is to bring it back into Missouri or Illinois and sell it. If you take negroes to Kansas, as Col. Jeff. Davis said in his Bangor speech, from which I have quoted to-day, you must take them there subject to the local law. If the people want the institution of slavery they will protect and encourage it; but if they do not want it they will withhold that protection, and the absence of local legislation protecting slavery excludes it as completely as a positive prohibition. ("That's so," and cheers.) You slaveholders of Missouri might as well understand what you know practically, that you cannot carry slavery where the people do not want it. ("That's so.") All you have a right to ask is that the people shall do as they please; if they want slavery let them have it; if they do not want it, allow them to refuse to encourage it.

My friends, if, as I have said before, we will only live up to this great fundamental principle there will be peace between the North and the South. Mr. Lincoln admits that under the constitution on all domestic questions, except slavery, we ought not to interfere with the people of each State. What right have we to interfere with slavery any more than we have to interfere with any other question. He says that this slavery question is now the bone of contention. Why? Simply because agitators have combined in all the free States to make war upon it. Suppose the agitators in the States should combine in one-half of the Union to make war upon the railroad system of the other half? They would thus be driven to the same sectional strife. Suppose one section makes war upon any other peculiar institution of the opposite section, and the same strife is produced. The only remedy and safety is that we shall stand by the constitution as our fathers made it, obey the laws as they are passed, while they stand the proper test and sustain the decisions of the Supreme Court and the constituted authorities.

SELECTION

Abraham Lincoln Speaks for the Republican Party:
Address at Cooper Institute, February 27, 1860

Abraham Lincoln (1809–1865) was, by 1860, widely recognized as a spokesman for the Republican party. A man of limited political experience, he had been aroused by the Kansas-Nebraska Act in 1854 and from that time on played an increasingly important role in both state and national politics. His debates with

*Douglas in 1858 brought him nationwide recognition; for the next two years he
was much in demand as a political speaker. On February 27, 1860, Lincoln
delivered one of the significant addresses of his career at Cooper Institute in
New York, presenting his party's position on the broader sectional questions
of the day and answering Douglas's claims on behalf of popular sovereignty. To
Lincoln, slavery was a moral wrong, a monstrous evil. Like all such evils, he felt
that slavery should be placed in a state of "ultimate extinction," that is, it
should not be allowed to expand out of the states in which it existed. For
Lincoln, as for most Republicans, the moral question of slavery and the issue
of slavery in the territories were merged. Slavery negated the natural-rights
doctrine and the dictum that all men are created equal; it contradicted the
democratic and humanitarian goals of the reform movements of the early nineteenth century. As important to Lincoln was the realization that slavery
dimmed the effectiveness of the great American experiment in democracy. The
national government, he thought, had an obligation and responsibility to see
that this evil did not spread to new territories.*

   The text of this address is reprinted from Roy P. Basler et al. (eds.), The
Collected Works of Abraham Lincoln *(New Brunswick: Rutgers, 1953), 9 vol-
umes, volume 3, pages 522–550. A very good analysis of the pre-Presidential
Lincoln is in Don E. Fehrenbacher's* Prelude to Greatness: Lincoln in the
1850s *(1962). A fine biography of Lincoln is that by Benjamin P. Thomas,*
Abraham Lincoln *(1952).*

Mr. President and Fellow-Citizens of New York:—The facts with
which I shall deal this evening are mainly old and familiar; nor
is there anything new in the general use I shall make of them. If there shall
be any novelty, it will be in the mode of presenting the facts, and the
inferences and observations following that presentation.

   In his speech last autumn, at Columbus, Ohio, as reported in "The
New-York Times," Senator Douglas said:

> *Our fathers, when they framed the Government under which we live,
> understood this question just as well, and even better, than we do now.*

   I fully indorse this, and I adopt it as a text for this discourse. I so adopt
it because it furnishes a precise and an agreed starting point for a discussion between Republicans and that wing of the Democracy headed by
Senator Douglas. It simply leaves the inquiry:

> *What was the understanding those fathers had of the question men-
> tioned?*

   What is the frame of Government under which we live?

   The answer must be: "The Constitution of the United States." That
Constitution consists of the original, framed in 1787, (and under which
the present government first went into operation,) and twelve subsequently
framed amendments, the first ten of which were framed in 1789.

   Who were our fathers that framed the Constitution? I suppose the
"thirty-nine" who signed the original instrument may be fairly called our

fathers who framed that part of the present Government. It is almost exactly true to say they framed it, and it is altogether true to say they fairly represented the opinion and sentiment of the whole nation at that time. Their names, being familiar to nearly all, and accessible to quite all, need not now be repeated.

I take these "thirty-nine" for the present, as being "our fathers who framed the Government under which we live."

What is the question which, according to the text, those fathers understood "just as well, and even better than we do now?"

It is this: Does the proper division of local from federal authority, or anything in the Constitution, forbid *our Federal Government* to control as to slavery in *our Federal Territories?*

Upon this, Senator Douglas holds the affirmative, and Republicans the negative. This affirmation and denial form an issue; and this issue—this question—is precisely what the text declares our fathers understood "better than we."

Let us now inquire whether the "thirty-nine," or any of them, ever acted upon this question; and if they did, how they acted upon it—how they expressed that better understanding?

In 1784, three years before the Constitution—the United States then owning the Northwestern Territory, and no other, the Congress of the Confederation had before them the question of prohibiting slavery in that Territory; and four of the "thirty-nine," who afterward framed the Constitution, were in that Congress, and voted on that question. Of these, Roger Sherman, Thomas Mifflin, and Hugh Williamson voted for the prohibition, thus showing that, in their understanding, no line dividing local from federal authority, nor anything else, properly forbade the Federal Government to control as to slavery in federal territory. The other of the four—James M'Henry—voted against the prohibition, showing that, for some cause, he thought it improper to vote for it.

In 1787, still before the Constitution, but while the Convention was in session framing it, and while the Northwestern Territory still was the only territory owned by the United States, the same question of prohibiting slavery in the territory again came before the Congress of the Confederation; and two more of the "thirty-nine" who afterward signed the Constitution, were in that Congress, and voted on the question. They were William Blount and William Few; and they both voted for the prohibition—thus showing that, in their understanding, no line dividing local from federal authority, nor anything else, properly forbade the Federal Government to control as to slavery in federal territory. This time the prohibition became a law, being part of what is now well known as the Ordinance of '87.

The question of federal control of slavery in the territories, seems not to have been directly before the Convention which framed the original Constitution; and hence it is not recorded that the "thirty-nine," or any of them, while engaged on that instrument, expressed any opinion of that precise question.

In 1789, by the first Congress which sat under the Constitution, an act was passed to enforce the Ordinance of '87, including the prohibition of slavery in the Northwestern Territory. The bill for this act was reported by one of the "thirty-nine," Thomas Fitzsimmons, then a member of the

House of Representatives from Pennsylvania. It went through all its stages without a word of opposition, and finally passed both branches without yeas and nays, which is equivalent to an unanimous passage. In this Congress there were sixteen of the thirty-nine fathers who framed the original Constitution. They were John Langdon, Nicholas Gilman, Wm. S. Johnson, Roger Sherman, Robert Morris, Thos. Fitzsimmons, William Few, Abraham Baldwin, Rufus King, William Paterson, George Clymer, Richard Bassett, George Read, Pierce Butler, Daniel Carroll, James Madison.

This shows that, in their understanding, no line dividing local from federal authority, nor anything in the Constitution, properly forbade Congress to prohibit slavery in the federal territory; else both their fidelity to correct principle, and their oath to support the Constitution, would have constrained them to oppose the prohibition.

Again, George Washington, another of the "thirty-nine," was then President of the United States, and, as such, approved and signed the bill; thus completing its validity as a law, and thus showing that, in his understanding, no line dividing local from federal authority, nor anything in the Constitution, forbade the Federal Government, to control as to slavery in federal territory.

No great while after the adoption of the original Constitution, North Carolina ceded to the Federal Government the country now constituting the State of Tennessee; and a few years later Georgia ceded that which now constitutes the States of Mississippi and Alabama. In both deeds of cession it was made a condition by the ceding States that the Federal Government should not prohibit slavery in the ceded country. Besides this, slavery was then actually in the ceded country. Under these circumstances, Congress, on taking charge of these countries, did not absolutely prohibit slavery within them. But they did interfere with it—take control of it—even there, to a certain extent. In 1798, Congress organized the Territory of Mississippi. In the act of organization, they prohibited the bringing of slaves into the Territory, from any place without the United States, by fine, and giving freedom to slaves so brought. This act passed both branches of Congress without yeas and nays. In that Congress were three of the "thirty-nine" who framed the original Constitution. They were John Langdon, George Read and Abraham Baldwin. They all, probably, voted for it. Certainly they would have placed their opposition to it upon record, if, in their understanding, any line dividing local from federal authority, or anything in the Constitution, properly forbade the Federal Government to control as to slavery in federal territory.

In 1803, the Federal Government purchased the Louisiana country. Our former territorial acquisitions came from certain of our own States; but this Louisiana country was acquired from a foreign nation. In 1804, Congress gave a territorial organization to that part of it which now constitutes the State of Louisiana. New Orleans, lying within that part, was an old and comparatively large city. There were other considerable towns and settlements, and slavery was extensively and thoroughly intermingled with the people. Congress did not, in the Territorial Act, prohibit slavery; but they did interfere with it—take control of it—in a more marked and extensive way than they did in the case of Mississippi. The substance of the provision therein made, in relation to slaves, was:

First. That no slave should be imported into the territory from foreign parts.

Second. That no slave should be carried into it who had been imported into the United States since the first day of May, 1798.

Third. That no slave should be carried into it, except by the owner, and for his own use as a settler; the penalty in all the cases being a fine upon the violator of the law, and freedom to the slave.

This act also was passed without yeas and nays. In the Congress which passed it, there were two of the "thirty-nine." They were Abraham Baldwin and Jonathan Dayton. As stated in the case of Mississippi, it is probable they both voted for it. They would not have allowed it to pass without recording their opposition to it, if, in their understanding, it violated either the line properly dividing local from federal authority, or any provision of the Constitution.

In 1819–20, came and passed the Missouri question. Many votes were taken, by yeas and nays, in both branches of Congress, upon the various phases of the general question. Two of the "thirty-nine"—Rufus King and Charles Pinckney—were members of that Congress. Mr. King steadily voted for slavery prohibition and against all compromises, while Mr. Pinckney as steadily voted against slavery prohibition and against all compromises. By this, Mr. King showed that, in his understanding, no line dividing local from federal authority, nor anything in the Constitution, was violated by Congress prohibiting slavery in federal territory; while Mr. Pinckney, by his votes, showed that, in his understanding, there was some sufficient reason for opposing such prohibition in that case.

The cases I have mentioned are the only acts of the "thirty-nine," or of any of them, upon the direct issue, which I have been able to discover.

To enumerate the persons who thus acted, as being four in 1784, two in 1787, seventeen in 1789, three in 1798, two in 1804, and two in 1819–20—there would be thirty of them. But this would be counting John Langdom, Roger Sherman, William Few, Rufus King, and George Read, each twice, and Abraham Baldwin, three times. The true number of those of the "thirty-nine" whom I have shown to have acted upon the question, which, by the text, they understood better than we, is twenty-three, leaving sixteen not shown to have acted upon it in any way.

Here, then, we have twenty-three out of our thirty-nine fathers "who framed the Government under which we live," who have, upon their official responsibility and their corporal oaths, acted upon the very question which the text affirms they "understood just as well, and even better than we do now;" and twenty-one of them—a clear majority of the whole "thirty nine"—so acting upon it as to make them guilty of gross political impropriety and wilful perjury, if, in their understanding, any proper division between local and federal authority, or anything in the Constitution they had made themselves, and sworn to support, forbade the Federal Government to control as to slavery in the federal territories. Thus the twenty-one acted; and, as actions speak louder than words, so actions, under such responsibility, speak still louder.

Two of the twenty-three voted against Congressional prohibition of slavery in the federal territories, in the instances in which they acted upon the question. But for what reasons they so voted is not known. They may have done so because they thought a proper division of local from federal authority, or some provision or principle of the Constitution, stood in the way; or they may, without any such question, have voted against the prohibition, on what appeared to them to be sufficient grounds of expediency. No one who has sworn to support the Constitution, can conscientiously vote for what he understands to be an unconstitutional measure, however expedient he may think it; but one may and ought to vote against a measure which he deems constitutional, if, at the same time, he deems it inexpedient. It, therefore, would be unsafe to set down even the two who voted against the prohibition, as having done so because, in their understanding, any proper division of local from federal authority, or anything in the Constitution, forbade the Federal Government to control as to slavery in federal territory.

The remaining sixteen of the "thirty-nine," so far as I have discovered, have left no record of their understanding upon the direct question of federal control of slavery in the federal territories. But there is much reason to believe that their understanding upon that question would not have appeared different from that of their twenty-three compeers, had it been manifested at all.

For the purpose of adhering rigidly to the text, I have purposely omitted whatever understanding may have been manifested by any person, however distinguished, other than the thirty-nine fathers who framed the original Constitution; and, for the same reason, I have also omitted whatever understanding may have been manifested by any of the "thirty-nine" even, on any other phase of the general question of slavery. If we should look into their acts and declarations on those other phases, as the foreign slave trade, and the morality and policy of slavery generally, it would appear to us that on the direct question of federal control of slavery in Federal territories, the sixteen, if they had acted at all, would probably have acted just as the twenty-three did. Among that sixteen were several of the most noted anti-slavery men of those times—as Dr. Franklin, Alexander Hamilton and Gouverneur Morris—while there was not one now known to have been otherwise, unless it may be John Rutledge, of South Carolina.

The sum of the whole is, that of our thirty-nine fathers who framed the original Constitution, twenty-one—a clear majority of the whole—certainly understood that no proper division of local from federal authority, nor any part of the Constitution, forbade the Federal Government to control slavery in the federal territories; while all the rest probably had the same understanding. Such, unquestionably, was the understanding of our fathers who framed the original Constitution; and the text affirms that they understood the question "better than we."

But, so far, I have been considering the understanding of the question manifested by the framers of the original Constitution. In and by the original instrument, a mode was provided for amending it; and, as I have already stated, the present frame of "the Government under which we live" consists of that original, and twelve amendatory articles framed and adopted since. Those who now insist that federal control of slavery in federal territories violates the Constitution, point us to the provisions which they suppose it thus violates; and, as I understand, they all fix upon provisions in these amendatory articles, and not in the original instrument.

The Supreme Court, in the Dred Scott case, plant themselves upon the fifth amendment, which provides that no person shall be deprived of "life, liberty or property without due process of law;" while Senator Douglas and his peculiar adherents plant themselves upon the tenth amendment, providing that "the powers not delegated to the United States by the Constitution," "are reserved to the States respectively, or to the people."

Now, it so happens that these amendments were framed by the first Congress which sat under the Constitution—the identical Congress which passed the act already mentioned, enforcing the prohibition of slavery in the Northwestern Territory. Not only was it the same Congress, but they were the identical, same individual men who, at the same session, and at the same time within the session, had under consideration, and in progress toward maturity, these Constitutional amendments, and this act prohibiting slavery in all the territory the nation then owned. The Constitutional amendments were introduced before, and passed after the act enforcing the Ordinance of '87; so that, during the whole pendency of the act to enforce the Ordinance, the Constitutional amendments were also pending.

The seventy-six members of that Congress, including sixteen of the framers of the original Constitution, as before stated, were preeminently our fathers who framed that part of "the Government under which we live," which is now claimed as forbidding the Federal Government to control slavery in the federal territories.

Is it not a little presumptuous in any one at this day to affirm that the two things which that Congress deliberately framed, and carried to maturity at the same time, are absolutely inconsistent with each other? And does not such affirmation become impudently absurd when coupled with the other affirmation from the same mouth, that those who did the two things, alleged to be inconsistent, understood whether they really were inconsistent better than we—better than he who affirms that they are inconsistent?

It is surely safe to assume that the thirty-nine framers of the original Constitution, and the seventy-six members of the Congress which framed the amendments thereto, taken together, do certainly include those who may be fairly called "our fathers who framed the Government under which we live." And so assuming, I defy any man to show that any one of them ever, in his whole life, declared that, in his understanding, any proper division of local from federal authority, or any part of the Constitution, forbade the Federal Government to control as to slavery in the federal territories. I go a step further. I defy any one to show that any living man in the whole world ever did, prior to the beginning of the present century, (and I might almost say prior to the beginning of the last half of the present century,) declare that, in his understanding, any proper division of local from federal authority, or any part of the Constitution, forbade the Federal Government to control as to slavery in the federal territories. To those who now so declare, I give, not only "our fathers who framed the Government under which we live," but with them all other living men within the century in which it was framed, among whom to search, and they shall not be able to find the evidence of a single man agreeing with them.

Now, and here, let me guard a little against being misunderstood. I do not mean to say we are bound to follow implicitly in whatever our fathers did. To do so, would be to discard all the lights of current experience—to reject all progress—all improvement. What I do say is, that if we would supplant the opinions and policy of our fathers in any case, we should do so upon evidence so conclusive, and argument so clear, that even their great authority, fairly considered and weighed, cannot stand; and most surely not in a case whereof we ourselves declare they understood the question better than we.

If any man at this day sincerely believes that a proper division of local from federal authority, or any part of the Constitution, forbids the Federal Government to control as to slavery in the federal territories, he is right to say so, and to enforce his position by all truthful evidence and fair argument which he can. But he has no right to mislead others, who have less access to history, and less leisure to study it, into the false belief that "our fathers, who framed the Government under which we live," were of the same opinion—thus substituting falsehood and deception for truthful evidence and fair argument. If any man at this day sincerely believes "our fathers who framed the Government under which we live," used and applied principles, in other cases, which ought to have led them to understand that a proper division of local from federal authority or some part of the Constitution, forbids the Federal Government to control as to slavery in the federal territories, he is right to say so. But he should, at the same time, brave the responsibility of declaring that, in his opinion, he understands their principles better than they did themselves; and especially should he not shirk that responsibility by asserting that they "understood the question just as well, and even better, than we do now."

But enough! *Let all who believe that "our fathers, who framed the Government under which we live, understood this question just as well, and even better, than we do now," speak as they spoke, and act as they acted upon it. This is all Republicans ask—all Republicans desire—in relation to slavery. As those fathers marked it, so let it be again marked, as an evil not to be extended, but to be tolerated and protected only because of and so far as its actual presence among us makes that toleration and protection a necessity. Let all the guaranties those fathers gave it, be, not grudgingly, but fully and fairly maintained.* For this Republicans contend, and with this, so far as I know or believe, they will be content.

And now, if they would listen—as I suppose they will not—I would address a few words to the Southern people.

I would say to them:—You consider yourselves a reasonable and a just people; and I consider that in the general qualities of reason and justice you are not inferior to any other people. Still, when you speak of us Republicans, you do so only to denounce us as reptiles, or, at the best, as no better than outlaws. You will grant a hearing to pirates or murderers, but nothing like it to "Black Republicans." In all your contentions with one another, each of you deems an unconditional condemnation of "Black Republicanism" as the first thing to be attended to. Indeed, such condemnation of us seems to be an indispensable prerequisite—license, so to speak—among you to be admitted or permitted to speak at all. Now, can you, or not, be prevailed upon to pause and to consider whether this is quite just to us, or even to yourselves? Bring forward your charges and specifications, and then be patient long enough to hear us deny or justify.

You say we are sectional. We deny it. That makes an issue; and the burden of proof is upon you. You produce your proof; and what is it? Why, that our party has no existence in your section—gets no votes in your section. The fact is substantially true; but does it prove the issue? If it does, then in case we should, without change of principle, begin to get votes in your section, we should thereby cease to be sectional. You cannot escape this conclusion; and yet, are you willing to abide by it? If you are, you will probably soon find that we have ceased to be sectional, for we shall get votes in your section this very year. You will then begin to discover, as the truth plainly is, that your proof does not touch the issue. The fact that we get no votes in your section, is a fact of your making, and not of ours. And if there be fault in that fact, that fault is primarily yours, and remains so until you show that we repel you by some wrong principle or practice. If we do repel you by any wrong principle or practice, the fault is ours; but this brings you to where you ought to have started—to a discussion of the right or wrong of our principle. If our principle, put in practice, would wrong your section for the benefit of ours, or for any other object, then our principle, and we with it, are sectional, and are justly opposed and denounced as such. Meet us, then, on the question of whether our principle, put in practice, would wrong your section; and so meet us as if it were possible that something may be said on our side. Do you accept the challenge? No! Then you really believe that the principle which "our fathers who framed the Government under which we live" thought so clearly right as to adopt it, and indorse it again and again, upon their official oaths, is in fact so clearly wrong as to demand your condemnation without a moment's consideration.

Some of you delight to flaunt in our faces the warning against sectional parties given by Washington in his Farewell Address. Less than eight years before Washington gave that warning, he had, as President of the United States, approved and signed an act of Congress, enforcing the prohibition of slavery in the Northwestern Territory, which act embodied the policy of the Government upon that subject up to and at the very moment he penned that warning; and about one year after he penned it, he wrote La Fayette that he considered that prohibition a wise measure, expressing in the same connection his hope that we should at some time have a confederacy of free States.

Bearing this in mind, and seeing that sectionalism has since arisen upon this same subject, is that warning a weapon in your hands against us, or in our hands against you? Could Washington himself speak, would he cast the blame of that sectionalism upon us, who sustain his policy, or upon you who repudiate it? We respect that warning of Washington, and we commend it to you, together with his example pointing to the right application of it.

But you say you are conservative—eminently conservative—while we are revolutionary, destructive, or something of the sort. What is conservatism? Is it not adherence to the old and tried, against the new and untried? We stick to, contend for, the identical old policy on the point in controversy which was adopted by "our fathers who framed the Government under which we live;" while you with one accord reject, and scout, and spit upon that old policy, and insist upon substituting something new. True, you disagree among yourselves as to what that substitute shall be. You are divided on new propositions and plans, but you are unanimous in rejecting and denouncing the old policy of the fathers. Some of you are for reviving the foreign slave trade; some for a Congressional Slave-Code for the Territories; some for Congress forbidding the Territories to prohibit Slavery within their limits; some for maintaining Slavery in the Territories through the judiciary; some for the "gur-reat pur-rinciple" that "if one man would enslave another, no third man should object," fantastically called "Popular Sovereignty;" but never a man among you in favor of federal prohibition of slavery in federal territories, according to the practice of "our fathers who framed the Government under which we live." Not one of all your various plans can show a precedent or an advocate in the century within which our Government originated. Consider, then, whether your claim of conservatism for yourselves, and your charge of destructiveness against us, are based on the most clear and stable foundations.

Again, you say we have made the slavery question more prominent than it formerly was. We deny it. We admit that it is more prominent, but we deny that we made it so. It was not we, but you, who discarded the old policy of the fathers. We resisted, and still resist, your innovation; and thence comes the greater prominence of the question. Would you have that question reduced to its former proportions? Go back to that old policy. What has been will be again, under the same conditions. If you would have the peace of the old times, readopt the precepts and policy of the old times.

You charge that we stir up insurrections among your slaves. We deny it; and what is your proof? Harper's Ferry! John Brown!! John Brown was no Republican; and you have failed to implicate a single Republican in his Harper's Ferry enterprise. If any member of our party is guilty in that matter, you know it or you do not know it. If you do know it, you are inexcusable for not designating the man and proving the fact. If you do not know it, you are inexcusable for asserting it, and especially for persisting in the assertion after you have tried and failed to make the proof. You need not be told that persisting in a charge which one does not know to be true, is simply malicious slander.

Some of you admit that no Republican designedly aided or encouraged the Harper's Ferry affair; but still insist that our doctrines and declarations necessarily lead to such results. We do not believe it. We know we hold to no doctrine, and make no declaration, which were not held to and made by "our fathers who framed the Government under which we live." You never dealt fairly by us in relation to this affair. When it occurred, some important State elections were near at hand, and you were in evident glee with the belief that, by charging the blame upon us, you could get an advantage of us in those elections. The elections came, and your expectations were not quite fulfilled. Every Republican man knew that, as to himself at least, your charge was a slander, and he was not much inclined by it to cast his vote in your favor. Republican doctrines and declarations are accompanied with a continual protest against any interference whatever with your slaves, or with you about your slaves. Surely, this does not encourage them to revolt. True, we do, in common with "our fathers, who framed the Government under which we live," declare our belief that slavery is wrong; but the slaves do not hear us declare even this. For anything we say or do, the slaves would scarcely know there is a Republican party. I believe they would not, in fact, generally know it but for your misrepresentation's of us, in their hearing. In your political contests among yourselves, each faction charges the other with sympathy with Black Republicanism; and then, to give point to the charge, defines Black Republicanism to simply be insurrection, blood and thunder among the slaves.

Slave insurrections are no more common now than they were before the Republican party was organized. What induced the Southampton insurrection, twenty-eight years ago, in which, at least, three times as many lives were lost as at Harper's Ferry? You can scarcely stretch your very elastic fancy to the conclusion that Southampton was "got up by Black Republicanism." In the present state of things in the United States, I do not think a general, or even a very extensive slave insurrection, is possible. The indispensable concert of action cannot be attained. The slaves have no means of rapid communication; nor can incendiary freemen, black or white, supply it. The explosive materials are everywhere in parcels; but there neither are, nor can be supplied, the indispensable connecting trains.

Much is said by Southern people about the affection of slaves for their masters and mistresses; and a part of it, at least, is true. A plot for an uprising could scarcely be devised and communicated to twenty individuals before some one of them, to save the life of a favorite master or mistress, would divulge it. This is the rule; and the slave revolution in Hayti was not an exception to it, but a case occurring under peculiar circumstances. The gunpowder plot of British history, though not connected with slaves, was more in point. In that case, only about twenty were admitted to the secret; and yet one of them, in his anxiety to save a friend, betrayed the plot to that friend, and, by consequence, averted the calamity. Occasional poisonings from the kitchen, and open or stealthy assassinations in the field, and local revolts extending to a score or so, will continue to occur as the natural results of slavery; but no general insurrection of slaves, as I think, can happen in this country for a long time. Whoever much fears, or much hopes for such an event, will be alike disappointed.

In the language of Mr. Jefferson, uttered many years ago, "It is still in our power to direct the process of emancipation, and deportation, peaceably, and in such slow degrees, as that the evil will wear off insensibly; and their places be, *pari passu*, filled up by free white laborers. If, on the contrary, it is left to force itself on, human nature must shudder at the prospect held up."

Mr. Jefferson did not mean to say, nor do I, that the power of emancipation is in the Federal Government. He spoke of Virginia; and, as to the power of emancipation, I speak of the slaveholding States only. The Federal Government, however, as we insist, has the power of restraining the extension of the institution—the power to insure that a slave insurrection shall never occur on any American soil which is now free from slavery.

John Brown's effort was peculiar. It was not a slave insurrection. It was an attempt by white men to get up a revolt among slaves, in which the slaves refused to participate. In fact, it was so absurd that the slaves, with all their ignorance, saw plainly enough it could not succeed. That affair, in its philosophy, corresponds with the many attempts, related in history, at the assassination of kings and emperors. An enthusiast broods over the oppression of a people till he fancies himself commissioned by Heaven to liberate them. He ventures the attempt, which ends in little else than his own execution. Orsini's attempt on Louis Napoleon, and John Brown's attempt at Harper's Ferry were, in their philosophy, precisely the same. The eagerness to cast blame on old England in the one case, and on New England in the other, does not disprove the sameness of the two things.

And how much would it avail you, if you could, by the use of John Brown, Helper's Book, and the like, break up the Republican organization? Human action can be modified to some extent, but human nature cannot be changed. There is a judgment and a feeling against slavery in this nation, which cast at least a million and a half of votes. You cannot destroy that judgment and feeling—that sentiment—by breaking up the political organization which rallies around it. You can scarcely scatter and disperse an army which has been formed into order in the face of your heaviest fire; but if you could, how much would you gain by forcing the sentiment which created it out of the peaceful channel of the ballot-box, into some other channel? What would that other channel probably be? Would the number of John Browns be lessened or enlarged by the operation?

But you will break up the Union rather than submit to a denial of your Constitutional rights.

That has a somewhat reckless sound; but it would be palliated, if not fully justified, were we proposing, by the mere force of numbers, to deprive you of some right, plainly written down in the Constitution. But we are proposing no such thing.

When you make these declarations, you have a specific and well-understood allusion to an assumed Constitutional right of yours, to take slaves into the federal territories, and to hold them there as property. But no such right is specifically written in the Constitution. That instrument is literally silent about any such right. We, on the contrary, deny that such a right has any existence in the Constitution, even by implication.

Your purpose, then, plainly stated, is, that you will destroy the Government, unless you be allowed to construe and enforce the Constitution as you please, on all points in dispute between you and us. You will rule or ruin in all events.

This, plainly stated, is your language. Perhaps you will say the Supreme Court has decided the disputed Constitutional question in your favor. Not quite so. But waiving the lawyer's distinction between dictum and decision, the Court have decided the question for you in a sort of way. The Court have substantially said, it is your Constitutional right to take slaves into the federal territories, and to hold them there as property. When I say the decision was made in a sort of way, I mean it was made in a divided Court, by a bare majority of the Judges, and they not quite agreeing with one another in the reasons for making it; that it is so made as that its avowed supporters disagree with one another about its meaning, and that it was mainly based upon a mistaken statement of fact—the statement in the opinion that "the right of property in a slave is distinctly and expressly affirmed in the Constitution."

An inspection of the Constitution will show that the right of property in a slave is not "*distinctly* and *expressly* affirmed" in it. Bear in mind, the Judges do not pledge their judicial opinion that such right is *impliedly* affirmed in the Constitution; but they pledge their veracity that it is "*distinctly* and *expressly*" affirmed there—"distinctly," that is, not mingled with anything else—"expressly," that is, in words meaning just that, without the aid of any inference, and susceptible of no other meaning.

If they had only pledged their judicial opinion that such right is affirmed in the instrument by implication, it would be open to others to show that neither the word "slave" nor "slavery" is to be found in the Constitution, nor the word "property" even, in any connection with language alluding to the things slave, or slavery, and that wherever in that instrument the slave is alluded to, he is called a "person;"—and wherever his master's legal right in relation to him is alluded to, it is spoken of as "service or labor which may be due,"—as a debt payable in service or labor. Also, it would be open to show, by contemporaneous history, that this mode of alluding to slaves and slavery, instead of speaking of them, was employed on purpose to exclude from the Constitution the idea that there could be property in man.

To show all this, is easy and certain.

When this obvious mistake of the Judges shall be brought to their notice, is it not reasonable to expect that they will withdraw the mistaken statement, and reconsider the conclusion based upon it?

And then it is to be remembered that "our fathers, who framed the Government under which we live"—the men who made the Constitution decided this same Constitutional question in our favor, long ago—decided it without division among themselves, when making the decision; without division among themselves about the meaning of it after it was made, and, so far as any evidence is left, without basing it upon any mistaken statement of facts.

Under all these circumstances, do you really feel yourselves justified to break up this Government, unless such a court decision as yours is, shall be at once submitted to as a conclusive and final rule of political action? But you will not abide the election of a Republican President! In that supposed event, you say, you will destroy the Union; and then, you say the great crime of having destroyed it will be upon us! That is cool. A highwayman holds a pistol to my ear, and mutters through his teeth, "Stand and deliver, or I shall kill you, and then you will be a murderer!"

To be sure, what the robber demanded of me—my money—was my own; and I had a clear right to keep it; but it was no more my own than my vote is my own; and the threat of death to me, to extort my money, and the threat of destruction to the Union, to extort my vote, can scarcely be distinguished in principle.

A few words now to Republicans. *It is exceedingly desirable that all parts of this great Confederacy shall be at peace, and in harmony, one with another. Let us Republicans do our part to have it so. Even though much provoked, let us do nothing through passion and ill temper. Even though the southern people will not so much as listen to us, let us calmly consider their demands, and yield to them if, in our deliberate view of our duty, we possibly can.* Judging by all they say and do, and by the subject and nature of their controversy with us, let us determine, if we can, what will satisfy them.

Will they be satisfied if the Territories be unconditionally surrendered to them? We know they will not. In all their present complaints against us, the Territories are scarcely mentioned. Invasions and insurrections are the rage now. Will it satisfy them, if, in the future, we have nothing to do with invasions and insurrections? We know it will not. We so know, because we know we never had anything to do with invasions and insurrections; and yet this total abstaining does not exempt us from the charge and the denunciation.

The question recurs, what will satisfy them? Simply this: We must not only let them alone, but we must, somehow, convince them that we do let them alone. This, we know by experience, is no easy task. We have been so trying to convince them from the very beginning of our organization, but with no success. In all our platforms and speeches we have constantly protested our purpose to let them alone; but this has had no tendency to convince them. Alike unavailing to convince them, is the fact that they have never detected a man of us in any attempt to disturb them.

These natural, and apparently adequate means all failing, what will convince them? This, and this only: cease to call slavery *wrong*, and join them in calling it *right*. And this must be done thoroughly—done in *acts* as well as in *words*. Silence will not be tolerated—we must place ourselves avowedly with them. Senator Douglas's new sedition law must be enacted and enforced, suppressing all declarations that slavery is wrong, whether made in politics, in presses, in pulpits, or in private. We must arrest and return their fugitive slaves with greedy pleasure. We must pull down our Free State constitutions. The whole atmosphere must be disinfected from all taint of opposition to slavery, before they will cease to believe that all their troubles proceed from us.

I am quite aware they do not state their case precisely in this way. Most of them would probably say to us, "Let us alone, *do* nothing to us, and *say* what you please about slavery." But we do let them alone—have never disturbed them—so that, after all, it is what we say, which dissatisfies them. They will continue to accuse us of doing, until we cease saying.

I am also aware they have not, as yet, in terms, demanded the overthrow of our Free-State Constitutions. Yet those Constitutions declare the wrong of slavery, with more solemn emphasis, than do all other sayings against it; and when all these other sayings shall have been silenced, the overthrow of these Constitutions will be demanded, and nothing be left to resist the demand. It is nothing to the contrary, that they do not demand the whole of this just now. Demanding what they do, and for the reason they do, they can voluntarily stop nowhere short of this consummation. Holding, as they do, that slavery is morally right, and socially elevating, they cannot cease to demand a full national recognition of it, as a legal right, and a social blessing.

Nor can we justifiably withhold this, on any ground save our conviction that slavery is wrong. If slavery is right, all words, acts, laws, and constitutions against it, are themselves wrong, and should be silenced, and swept away. If it is right, we cannot justly object to its nationality—its universality; if it is wrong, they cannot justly insist upon its extension—its enlargement. All they ask, we could readily grant, if we thought slavery right; all we ask, they could as readily grant, if they thought it wrong. Their thinking it right, and our thinking it wrong, is the precise fact upon which depends the whole controversy. Thinking it right, as they do, they are not to blame for desiring its full recognition, as being right; but, thinking it wrong, as we do, can we yield to them? Can we cast our votes with their view, and against our own? In view of our moral, social, and political responsibilities, can we do this?

Wrong as we think slavery is, we can yet afford to let it alone where it is, because that much is due to the necessity arising from its actual presence in the nation; but can we, while our votes will prevent it, allow it to spread into the National Territories, and to overrun us here in these Free States? If our sense of duty forbids this, then let us stand by our duty, fearlessly and effectively. Let us be diverted by none of those sophistical contrivances wherewith we are so industriously plied and be-labored—contrivances such as groping for some middle ground between the right and the wrong, vain as the search for a man who should be neither a living man nor a dead man—such as a policy of "don't care" on a question about which all true men do care—such as Union appeals be-seeching true Union men to yield to Disunionists, reversing the divine rule, and calling, not the sinners, but the righteous to repentance—such as invocations to Washington, imploring men to unsay what Washington said, and undo what Washington did.

Neither let us be slandered from our duty by false accusations against us, nor frightened from it by menaces of destruction to the Government nor of dungeons to ourselves. LET US HAVE FAITH THAT RIGHT MAKES MIGHT, AND IN THAT FAITH, LET US, TO THE END, DARE TO DO OUR DUTY AS WE UNDERSTAND IT.

SELECTION

A Slave Code for the Territories: Jefferson Davis's Senate Speech, May 8, 1860

Jefferson Davis (1808–1889) presented the position of the South on the issue of slavery in the territories during the important election year of 1860. Douglas had developed his doctrine of popular sovereignty in an article in Harper's Magazine *in September, 1859; Lincoln had responded with the Republican view in his Cooper Institute address; Davis now completed the exposition with his statement of the Southern stand on the issue. Davis, a veteran of the Mexican War, former Cabinet member and United States Senator from Mississippi, had become the champion of Southern interests in Congress, inheriting the mantle formerly worn by John C. Calhoun. Early in 1860, he introduced a series of resolutions into the Senate in which he formulated, among other things, the Southern demand for Federal protection of slavery in the territories. Later in May, 1860, he elaborated these resolutions in a formal speech (the selection that follows). This Southern position had evolved from Calhoun's earlier concern for the equal rights of Southerners in the territories, although the slave code proposition itself had been anticipated as early as 1848 in the "Alabama Platform" of William L. Yancey. Davis's resolutions were presented in 1860 virtually in the form of an ultimatum to both the Democratic party and the North—a clear expression of the only platform on which the South would agree to stand, although not all Southerners accepted this extreme position. The speech given below is taken from Dunbar Rowland (ed.), Jefferson Davis, Constitutionalist: His Letters, Papers and Speeches (Jackson, Miss.: Mississippi Department of Archives and History, 1923), 10 volumes, volume 4, pages 252–280. Reprinted by permission of the Mississippi Department of Archives and History, Jackson, Mississippi. A valuable study of the slave code proposal in the context of Southern constitutional arguments is Arthur Bestor's "State Sovereignty and Slavery: A Reinterpretation of Proslavery Constitutional Doctrine, 1846–1860," Journal of the Illinois State Historical Society (Summer, 1961), volume 54, pages 117–180. For a biography of Davis, see Hudson Strode, Jefferson Davis (1955–1964), three volumes.*

Mr. President, among the many blessings for which we are indebted to our ancestry, is that of transmitting to us a written Constitution; a fixed standard to which, in the progress of events, every case may be referred, and by which it may be measured. But for this, the wise men who formed our Government dared not have hoped for its perpetuity; for they saw floating down the tide of time wreck after wreck, marking the short life of every Republic which had preceded them. With this, however, to check, to restrain, and to direct their posterity, they might reasonably hope the Government they founded should last forever; that it should secure the great purposes for which it was ordained and established; that it would be the shield of their posterity equally in every part of the country, and equally in all time to time. It was this which mainly distinguished the formation of our Government from those confederacies or republics which had preceded it; and this is the best foundation for our hope to-day. The resolutions which have been read, and which I had the honor to present to the Senate, are little more than the announcement of what I hold to be the clearly-expressed declarations of the Constitution itself. To that fixed standard it is sought, at this time, when we are drifting far from the initial point, and when clouds and darkness hover over us, to bring back the Government, and to test our condition to-day by the rules which our fathers laid down for us in the beginning.

The differences which exist between different portions of the country, the rivalries and the jealousies of to-day, though differing in degree, are exactly of the nature of those which preceded the formation of the Constitution. Our fathers were aware of the different interests of the navigating and planting States, as they were then regarded. They sought to compose those difficulties, and by compensating advantages given by one to the other, to form a Government equal and just in its operation; and which, like the gentle showers of heaven, should fall twice blessed, blessing him that gives and him that receives. This beneficial action and reaction between the different interests of the country constituted the bond of union and the motive of its formation. They constitute it to-day, if we are sufficiently wise to appreciate our interests, and sufficiently faithful to observe our trust. Indeed, with the extension of territory, with the multiplication of interests, with the varieties, increasing from time to time, of the products of this great country, the bonds which bind the Union together should have increased. Rationally considered, they have increased, because the free trade which was established in the beginning has now become more valuable to the people of the United States than their trade with all the rest of the world.

I do not propose to argue questions of natural rights and inherent powers; I plant my reliance upon the Constitution; that Constitution which you have all sworn to support; that Constitution which you have solemnly pledged yourself to maintain while you hold the seat you now occupy in the Senate; to which you are bound in its spirit and in its letter, not grudgingly, but willingly, to render your obedience and support as long as you hold office under the Federal Government. When the tempter entered the garden of Eden and induced our common mother to offend against the law which God had given to her through Adam, he was the first teacher of that "higher law" which sets the will of the individual above the solemn rule which he is bound, as a part of every community, to observe. From the effect of the introduction of that teaching of the higher law in the garden of Eden, and the fall consequent upon it, came sin into the world; and from sin came death and banishment and subjugation, as the punishments of sin; the loss of life, unfettered liberty, and perfect happiness followed from that first great law which was given by God to fallen man.

Why, then, shall we talk about natural rights? Who is to define them? Where is the judge that is to sit over the court to try natural rights? What is the era at which you will fix the date by which you will determine the breadth, the length, and the depth of those called the rights of nature? Shall it be after the fall, when the earth was covered with thorns, and man had to earn his bread in the sweat of his brow? or shall it be when there was equality between the sexes, when he lived in the garden, when all his wants were supplied, and when thorns and thistles were unknown on the face of the earth? Shall it be then? Shall it be after the flood, when, for the first sin committed after the waters retired from the face of the earth, the doom of slavery was fixed upon the mongrel descendants of Ham? If after the flood, and after that decree, how idle is all this prating about natural rights as standing above the obligations of civil government? The Constitution is the law supreme to every American. It is the plighted faith of our fathers; it is the hope of our posterity. I say, then, I come not to argue questions outside of or above the Constitution, but to plead the cause of right of law and order under the Constitution, and to plead it to those who have sworn to abide by that obligation.

One of the fruitful sources, as I hold it, of the errors which prevail in our country, is the theory that this is a Government of one people; that the Government of the United States was formed by a mass. The Government of the United States is a compact between the sovereign members who formed it; and if there be one feature common to all the colonies planted upon the shores of America, it is desire for community independence. It was for this the Puritan, the Huguenot, the Catholic, the Quaker, the Protestant left the land of their nativity, and guided by the shadows thrown by the fires of European persecution, they sought and found the American refuge of civil and religious freedom. Whilst they existed as separate and distinct colonies they were not forbearing towards each other. They oppressed opposite religions. They did not come here with the enlarged idea of no established religion. The Puritans drove out the Quakers; the Church of England men drove out the Catholics. Persecution reigned through the colonies, except, perhaps, that of the Catholic colony of Maryland; but the rule was, persecution. Therefore I say the common idea, and the only common idea, was community independence—the right of each independent people to do as they pleased in their domestic affairs.

The Declaration of Independence was made by the colonies, each for itself. The recognition of their independence was not for the colonies united, but for each of the colonies which had maintained its independence; and so when the Constitution was formed, the delegates were not elected by the people *en masse,* but they came from each one of the States; and when the Constitution was formed, it was referred, not to the people *en masse,* but to the States severally, and severally by them ratified and approved. But if there be anything which enforces this idea more than another, it is the unequal dates at which it received this approval. From first to last, nearly two years and a half elapsed; and the Government went into operation something like a year, I believe more than a year, before the last ratification was made. Is it, then, contended that, by this ratification and adoption of the Constitution, the States surrendered that sovereignty which they had previously gained? Can it be that men who braved the perils of the ocean, the privations of the wilderness, who fought the war of the Revolution, in the hour of their success, when all was sunshine and peace around them, came voluntarily forward to lay down that community independence for which they had suffered so much and so long? Reason forbids it; but if reason did not furnish a sufficient answer, the action of the States themselves forbids it. . . .

I spoke, however, Mr. President, but a moment ago, of the difference of policies, products, population, constituting the great motive for the union. It indeed was its necessity. Had all the people been alike—had their institutions all been the same—there would have been no interest to bring them together; there would have been no cause or necessity for any restraint being imposed upon them. It was the fact that they differed which rendered it necessary to have some law governing their intercourse. It was the fact that their products were opposite—that their pursuits were various—that rendered it the great interest of the people that they should have free trade existing among each other; that free trade which Franklin characterized as being between the States such as existed between the counties of England.

Since that era, however, a fiber then unknown in the United States, and the production of which is dependent upon the domestic institution of African slavery, has come to be cultivated in such amounts, to enter so into the wearing apparel of the world, so greatly to add to the comfort of the poor that it may be said to-day that that little fiber, cotton, wraps the commercial world and binds it to the United States in bonds to keep the peace with us which no Government dare break. It has built up the northern States. It is their great manufacturing interest to-day. It supports their shipping abroad. It enables them to purchase in the market of China, when the high premium to be paid on the milled dollar would otherwise exclude them from that market. These are a part of the blessings resulting from that increase and variety of product which could not have existed if we had all been alike; which would have been lost to-day unless free trade between the United States was still preserved. . . .

The great principle which lay at the foundation of this fixed standard, the Constitution of the United States, was the equality of rights between the States. This was essential; it was necessary; it was a step which had to be taken first, before any progress could be made. It was the essential requisite of the very idea of sovereignty in the State; of a compact voluntarily entered into between sovereigns; and it is that equality of right under the Constitution on which we now insist. But more, when the States united they transferred their forts, their armament, their ships, and their right to maintain armies and navies, to the Federal Government. It was the disarmament of the States, under the operation of a league which made the warlike operations, the powers of defense, common to them all. Then, with this equality of the States, with this disarmament of the States, if there had been nothing in the Constitution to express it, I say the protection of every constitutional right would follow as a necessary incident, and could not be denied by any one who could understand and would admit the true theory of such a Government.

We claim protection, first, because it is our right; secondly, because it is the duty of the General Government; and thirdly, because we have entered into a compact together, which deprives each State of the power of using all the means which it might employ for its own defense. This is the general theory of the right of protection. What is the exception to it? Is there an exception? If so, who made it? Does the Constitution discriminate between different kinds of property? Did the Constitution attempt to assimilate the institutions of the different States confederated together? Was there a single State in this Union that would have been so unfaithful to the principles which had prompted them in their colonial position, and which had prompted them at a still earlier period, to seek and try the temptations of the wilderness—is there one which would have consented to allow the Federal Government to control or to discriminate between her institutions and those of her confederate States?

But if it be contended that this is argument, and that you need authority, I will draw it from the fountain; from the spring before it had been polluted; from the debates in the formation of the Constitution; from the views of those who at least it will be admitted understood what they were doing. . . .

Here, as will be observed, everywhere was recognized and admitted the doctrine of community independence and State equality—no interference with the institutions of a State; no interference even prospectively save and except with their consent; and thus it followed that at one time it was proposed to except, from the power to prohibit the further introduction of Africans, those States which insisted upon retaining the power; and finally it was agreed that a date should be fixed beyond which, probably, none of them desired to retain it. These were States acting in their sovereign capacity; they possessed power to do as they pleased; and that was the view which they took of it. I ask, then, how are we, their descendants, those holding under their authority, to assume a power which they refused to admit, upon principles eternal and lying at the foundation of the Constitution itself?

If, then, there be no such distinction or discrimination; if protection be the duty (and who will deny it) with which this Government is charged, and for which the States pay taxes, because of which they surrendered their armies and their navies; if general protection be the general duty, I ask, in the name of reason and constitutional right—I ask you to point me to authority by which a discrimination is made between slave property and any other. Yet this is the question now fraught with evil to our country. It is this which has raised the hurricane threatening to sweep our political institutions before it. This is the dark spot which some already begin to fear may blot out the constellation of the Union from the political firmament of mankind. Does it not become us, then, calmly to consider it, justly to weigh it; to hold it in balances from which the dust has been blown, in order that we may see where truth, right and the obligations of the Constitution require us to go? . . .

From the postulates which I have laid down result the fourth and fifth resolutions. They are the two which I expect to be opposed. They contain the assertion of the equality of rights of all the people of the United States in the Territories, and they declare the obligation of the Congress to see these rights protected. I admit that the United States may acquire eminent domain. I admit that the United States may have sovereignty over territory; otherwise the sovereign jurisdiction which we obtained by conquest or treaty would not pass to us. I deny that their agent, the Federal Government, under the existing Constitution, can have eminent domain; I deny that it can have sovereignty. I consider it as the mere agent of the States—an agent of limited power; and that it can do nothing save that which the Constitution empowers it to perform; and that, though the treaty or the deed of cession may direct or control, it cannot enlarge or expand the powers of the Congress; that it is not sovereign in any essential particular. It has functions to perform, and those functions I propose now to consider.

The power of Congress over the Territories—a subject not well-defined in the Constitution of the United States—has been drawn from various sources by different advocates of that power. One has found it in the grant of power to dispose of the territory and other public property. That is to say, because the agent was authorized to sell a particular thing, or to dispose of it by grant or barter, therefore he has sovereign power over that and all else which the principal constituting him an agent may hereafter acquire! The property, besides the land, consisted of forts, of ships, of armaments, and other things which had belonged to the States in their separate capacity, and were turned over to the Government of the Confederation, and transferred to the Government of the United States, and of this, together with the land so transferred, the Federal Government had the power to dispose; and of territory thereafter acquired, of arms thereafter made or purchased, of forts thereafter constructed, or custom-houses, or docks, or lights, or buoys; of all these, of course, it had power to dispose. It had the power to create them; it must, of necessity, have had the power to dispose of them. It was only necessary to confer the power to dispose of those things which the Federal Government did not create, of those things which came to it from the States, and over which they might signify their will for its control.

I look upon it as the mere power to dispose of, for considerations and objects defined in the trust, the land held by the United States, none of which then was within the limits of the States, and the other public property which the United States received from the States after the formation of the Union. I do not agree with those who say the Government has no power to establish a temporary and civil government within a Territory. I stand half way between the extremes of squatter sovereignty and of congressional sovereignty. I hold that the Congress has power to establish a civil government; that it derives it from the grants of the Constitution— not the one which is referred to; and I hold that that power is limited and restrained, first by the Constitution itself, and then by every rule of popular liberty and sound discretion, to the narrowest limits which the necessities of the case require. The Congress has power to defend the territory, to repel invasion, to suppress insurrection; the Congress has power to see the laws executed. For this, it may have a civil magistracy—territorial courts. It has the power to establish a Federal judiciary. To that Federal judiciary, from these local courts, may come up to be decided questions with regard to the laws of the United States, and the Constitution of the United States. These, combined, give power to establish a temporary government sufficient, perhaps, for the simple wants of the inhabitants of a Territory, until they shall acquire the population, until they shall have the resources and the interests which justify them in becoming a State. . . .

Thus we find the Supreme Court sustaining the proposition that the Federal Government has power to establish a temporary civil government within the limits of a Territory; but that it can enact no law which will endure beyond the temporary purposes for which such government was established. In other cases the decisions of the court run in the same line; and in 1855 the then Attorney General . . . foretold what must have been the decision of the Supreme Court on the Missouri compromise, anticipating the decision subsequently made in the case of Dred Scott; that decision for which the venerable justices have been so often and so violently arraigned. . . .

It was not long after this official opinion of the Attorney General before the case arose on which the decision was made which has so agitated the country. Fortunate, indeed, was it for the public peace that land and religion had been decided—those questions on which men might reason had been the foundation of judicial decision—before that which drives all reason, it seems, from the mind of man, came to be presented: the question whether Cuffee should be kept in his normal condition or not; the question whether the Congress of the United States could decide what might or might not be property in a Territory. The case being that of an officer of the Army sent into a Territory to perform his public duty, having taken with him his negro slave. The court, however, in giving their decision in this case—or their opinion, if it suits gentlemen better—have gone into the question with such clearness, such precision, and such amplitude, that it will relieve me from the necessity of arguing it any further to make a reference to some sentences contained in that opinion. And here let me say, I cannot see how those who agreed on a former occasion that the constitutional right of the slaveholder to take his property into the Territory—the constitutional power of the Congress and the constitutional power of the Territory to legislate upon that subject—should be a judicial question, can now attempt to escape the operation of an opinion which covers the exact political question which it was known beforehand the court would be called upon to decide. Decided in strictness of technical language it was known it could not be. Hundreds, thousands, a vast variety of cases may arise, and centuries elapse, and leave that court, if our Union still exists, deciding questions in relation to that character of property in the Territories; but the great and fundamental idea was that, after thirty years of angry controversy, dividing the people and paralyzing the arm of the Federal Government, some umpire should be sought which would compose the difficulty and set it upon a footing to leave us in future to proceed in peace; and that umpire was selected which the Constitution had provided to decide questions of law. . . .

Here, then, Mr. President, I say the umpire selected as the referee in the controversy has decided that neither the Congress nor its agent, the territorial government, has the power to invade or impair the right of property within the limits of a Territory. I will not inquire whether it be technically a decision or not. It was obligatory on those who selected the umpire and agreed to abide by the award.

It is well known to those who have been associated with me in the two Houses of Congress that, from the commencement of the question, I have been the determined opponent of what is called squatter sovereignty. I never gave it countenance, and I am now least of all disposed to give it quarter. In 1848 it made its appearance for good purposes. . . . At the first blush, I believed it to be a fallacy—a fallacy fraught with mischief; that it escaped an issue which was upon us which it was our duty to meet; that it escaped it by a side path, which led to greater danger. I thought it a fallacy which would surely be exploded. I doubted then, and still more for some time afterwards, when held to a dread responsibility for the position which I occupied—I doubted whether I should live to see that fallacy exploded. It has been more speedily and, to the country, more injuriously, than I anticipated. In the meantime, what has been its operation? Let Kansas speak—the first great field on which the trial was made. What was then the consequence? The Federal Government withdrawing control, leaving the contending sections, excited to the highest point upon this question, each to send forth its army, Kansas became the battle field, and Kansas the cry which well nigh led to civil war. This was the first fruit. More deadly than the fatal upas, its effect was not limited to the mere spot of ground on which the dew fell from its leaves, but it spread throughout the United States; it kindled all which had been collected for years of inflammable material. It was owing to the strength of our Government and the good sense of the quiet masses of the people that it did not wrap our country in one widespread conflagration.

What right had Congress then, or what right has it now, to abdicate any power conferred upon it as trustee of the States? What right had Congress then, or has it now, to shrink from the performance of a duty because the mere counters spread on the table may be swept off, when they have not answered the purposes for which they were placed? What is it to you or me, or any one, when we weigh our own continuation in place against the great interests of which we are conservators; against the welfare of the country, and the liberty of our posterity to the remotest ages? What is it, I say, which can be counted in the balance on our side against the performance of that duty which is imposed upon us? If any one believes Congress has not the constitutional power, he acts conscientiously in insisting upon Congress not usurping it. If any one believes that the squatters upon the lands of the United States within a Territory are invested with sovereignty, having won it by some of those processes unknown to history, without grant or without revolution, without money and without price, he adhering to the theory may pursue it to its conclusion. To the first class, those who claim sovereign power over the Territories for Congress, I say, lay your hand upon the Constitution, and find there the warrant of your authority. Of the second, those of whom I have last spoken, I ask, in the Constitution, reason, right, or justice, what is there to sustain your theory? . . .

But again, sir, nothing seems to me more illogical than the argument that this power is acquired by a grant from the Congress, connected with the other argument that Congress have not got the power to do the act themselves; that is to say, that the recipient takes more than the giver possessed; that a Territorial Legislature can do anything which a State Legislature can do, and that "subject to the Constitution" means merely the restraints imposed upon both. This is confounding the whole theory and the history of our Government. The States were the grantors; they made the compact; they gave the Federal agent its powers; they inhibited themselves from doing certain things, and all else they retained to themselves. This Federal agent got just so much as the States chose to give, no more. It could do nothing save by warrant of the authority of the grant made by the States. Therefore its powers are not comparable to the powers of the State Legislature, because one is the creature of grant, and the other the exponent of sovereign power. The Supreme Court have covered the whole ground of the relation of the Congress to the Territorial Legislatures—the agent of the States and the agent of the Congress—and the restrictions put upon the one are those put upon the other, in language so clear as to render it needless further to labor the subject.

In 1850, following the promulgation of this notion of squatter sovereignty, we had the idea of non-intervention introduced into the Senate of the United States, and it is strange to me how that idea has expanded. It seems to have been more malleable than gold, to have been hammered out to an extent that covers boundless regions undiscovered by those who proclaimed the doctrine. Non-intervention then meant, as the debates show, that Congress should neither prohibit nor establish slavery in the Territories. That I hold to now. Will any one suppose that Congress then meant by non-intervention that Congress should legislate in no regard in respect to property in slaves? Why, sir, the very acts which they passed at the time refute it. There is the fugitive slave law, and that abomination of laws which assumed to confiscate the property of a citizen who should attempt to bring it into this District with intent to remove it to sell it at some other time and at some other place. Congress acted then upon the subject, acted beyond the limit of its authority as I believed, confidently believed; and if ever that act comes before the Supreme Court, I feel satisfied that they will declare it null and void. Are we to understand that those men, thus acting at the very moment, intended by non-intervention to deny and repudiate the laws they were then creating? . . .

By what species of legerdemain this doctrine of non-intervention has come to extend to a paralysis of the Government on the whole subject, to exclude the Congress from any kind of legislation whatever, I am at a loss to conceive. Certain it is, it was not the theory of that period, and it was not contended for in all the controversies we had then. I had no faith in it then; I considered it an evasion; I held that the duty of Congress ought to be performed; that the issue was before us, and ought to be met, the sooner the better; that truth would prevail if presented to the people; borne down to-day, it would rise up to-morrow; and I stood then on the same general plea which I am making now. The Senator from Illinois [Mr. Douglas] and myself differed at that time, as I presume we do now. We differed radically then. He opposed every proposition which I made, voting against propositions to give power to a Territorial Legislature to protect slave property which should be taken there; to remove the obstruction of the Mexican laws; voting for a proposition to exclude the conclusion that slavery might be taken there; voting for the proposition expressly to prohibit its introduction; voting for the proposition to keep in force the laws of Mexico which prohibited it. Some of these votes, it is but just to him I should say, I think he gave perforce of his instructions; but others of them, I think it is equally fair to suppose, were outside of the limits of any instructions which could have been given before the fact.

In 1854, advancing in this same general line of thought, the Congress, in enacting territorial bills, left out a provision which had before been usually contained in them, requiring the Legislature of the Territory to submit its laws to the Congress of the United States. It has been sometimes assumed that this was the recognition of the power of the Territorial Legislature to exercise plenary legislation, as might that of a State. . . .

But did this omission of the obligation to send here the laws of the Territories work this grant of power to the Territorial Legislature? Certainly not; it could not; and that it did not, is evinced by the fact that at a subsequent period, the organic act was revised because the legislation of the Territory of Kansas was offensive to the Congress of the United States. Congress could not abdicate its authority; it could not abandon its trust; and when it omitted the requirement that the laws should be sent back, it created a casus which required it to act without the official records being laid before it, as they would have been if the obligation had existed. That was all the difference. It was not enforcing upon the agent the obligation to send the information. It left Congress, as to its power, just where it was. I find myself physically unable to go as fully into the subject as I intended, and therefore, omitting a reference to those acts, suffice it to say, that here was the recognition of the obligation of Congress to interpose against a Territorial Legislature for the protection of personal right. That is what we ask of Congress now. I am not disposed to ask this Congress to go into speculative legislation. I am not one of those who would willingly see this Congress enact a code to be applied to all Territories and for all time to come. I only ask that cases, as they arise, may be met according to the exigency. I ask that when personal and property rights in the Territories are not protected, then the Congress, by existing laws and governmental machinery, shall intervene and provide such means as will secure in each case, as far as may be, an adequate remedy. I ask no slave code, nor horse code, nor machine code. I ask that the Territorial Legislature be made to understand beforehand that the Congress of the United States does not concede to them the power to interfere with the rights of person or property guaranteed by the Constitution, and that it will apply the remedy, if the Territorial Legislature should so far forget its duty, so far transcend its power, as to commit that violation of right. That is the announcement of the fifth resolution. . . .

These are the general views which I entertain of our right of protection and the duty of the Government. They are those which are entertained by the constituency I have the honor to represent, whose delegation has recently announced those principles at Charleston. I honor them, and I approve their conduct. I think their bearing was worthy of the mother State which sent them there; and I doubt not she will receive them with joy and gratitude. They have asserted and vindicated her equality of right. By that asserted equality of right I doubt not she will stand. For weal or for woe, for prosperity or adversity, for the preservation of the great blessings which we enjoy, or the trial of a new and separate condition, I trust Mississippi never will surrender the smallest atom of the sovereignty, independence, and equality, to which she was born, to avoid any danger or any sacrifice to which she may thereby be exposed.

The sixth resolution of the series declares at what time a State may form a constitution and decide upon her domestic institutions. I deny this right to the territorial condition because the Territory belongs in common to the States. Every citizen of the United States as a joint owner of that Territory has a right to go into it with any property which he may possess. These territorial inhabitants require municipal law, police, and government. They should have it, but it should be restricted to their own necessities. They have no right within their municipal power to attempt to decide the rights of the people of the States. They have no right to exclude any citizen of the United States from coming and equally enjoying this common possession; it is for the purpose of preserving order, giving protection to rights of person and property, that a municipal territorial government should be instituted. . . .

We have had agitation, changing in its form, and gathering intensity, for the last forty years. It was first for political power, and directed against new States; now it has assumed a social form, is all-prevailing, and has reached the point of revolution and civil war. For it was only last fall that an overt act was committed by men who were sustained by arms and money, raised by extensive combination among the non-slaveholding States, to carry treasonable war against the State of Virginia, because now as before the Revolution, and ever since she held the African in bondage. This is part of the history and marks the necessity of the times. It warns us to stop and reflect, to go back to the original standard, to measure our acts by the obligation of our fathers, by the pledges they made one to the other, to see whether we are conforming to our plighted faith, and to ask seriously, solemnly, looking each other inquiringly in the face, what we should do to save our country.

This agitation being at first one of sectional pride for political power, has at last degenerated or grown up to (as you please) a trade. There are men who habitually set aside a portion of money which they are annually to apply to what are called "charitable purposes;" that is to say, so far as I understand it, to support some vagrant lecturer, whose purpose is agitation and mischief wherever he goes. This constitutes, therefore, a trade; a class of people are thus employed, employed for mischief, for incendiary purposes, perhaps not always understood by those who furnish the money; but such is the effect; such is the result of their action; and in this state of the case I call upon the Senate to affirm the great principles on which our institutions rest. In no spirit of crimination have I stated the reasons why I present it. For these reasons, I call upon them now to restrain the growth of evil passion, and to bring back the public sense as far as in them lies, by earnest and united effort, if it may be, to crown our country with peace, and start it once more in its primal channel on a career of progressive prosperity and justice.

The majority section cannot be struggling for additional power in order to preserve their rights. If any of them ever believed in what is called southern aggression, they know now they have the majority in the representative districts and in the electoral college. They cannot, therefore, fear an invasion of their rights. . . . We have made no war against you. We have asked no discrimination in our favor. We claim to have but the Constitution fairly and equally administered. To consent to less than this, would be to sink in the scale of manhood; would be to make our posterity so degraded that they would curse this generation for robbing them of the rights their revolutionary fathers bequeathed them.

Is this expected? Yet it is for the assertion of such thoughts, such intents as these, that we of the South are arraigned as threatening and attempting to menace the North. I understand the artful dodge which induces the use of that word "menace." No portion of our people are subject to fear, nor are they to be intimidated by threats. They all have much of that sentiment which feels a pride in peril's hour; and therefore it is that our demand of equal rights, our assertion of the determination never to surrender them, has been tortured into a menace to those with whom we have ever sought to live in peace. It is not a threat, but a warning; and that warning is given in the spirit of fraternity. When we say to those who have a common destiny, a common interest with us, "stop ere your tread is on an empire's dust," it is not to destroy, but to avoid the dread alternative; we call you to the sober reckoning of the account before you. It would be idle to expect us to be satisfied with mere declarations that the only purpose is to prevent slaves being taken into the Territories. . . . How can they prate philanthropy to us who hold in bondage a race of men who never were free; who for thousands of years have occupied the condition they did in the American colonies, and do now in the southern States, and who live in a quietude and happiness which she might be well employed in bestowing on the suffering peasantry of England and her colonial dependencies of the East.

Among the great purposes declared in the preamble of the Constitution is one to provide for the general welfare. Provision for the general welfare implies general fraternity. This Union was not expected to be held together by coercion; the power of force as a means was denied. They sought, however, to bind it perpetually together with that which was stronger than triple bars of brass and steel—the ceaseless current of kind offices, renewing and renewed in an eternal flow, and gathering volume and velocity as it rolled. It was a function intended not for the injury of any. It declared its purpose to be the benefit of all. Concessions which were made between the different States in the convention prove the motive. Each gave to the other what was necessary to it; what each could afford to spare. Young as a nation, our triumphs under this system have had no parallel in human history. We have tamed a wilderness; we have spanned a continent. We have built up a granary that secures the commercial world against the fear of famine. Higher than all this, we have achieved a moral triumph. We have received, by hundreds of thousands, a constant tide of immigrants—energetic if not well educated, fleeing, some from want, some from oppression, some from the penalties of violated law—received them into our society; and by the gentle suasion of a Government which exhibits no force, by removing want and giving employment, they have subsided into peaceful citizens, and have increased the wealth and power of our country.

If, then, this temple so blessed, and to the roof of which we were about to look to see it extended over the continent, giving a protecting arm to infant republics that need it—if this temple is tottering on its pillars, what, I ask, can be a higher or nobler duty for the Senate to perform than to rush to its pillars and uphold them, or be crushed in the attempt? We have tampered with a question which has grown in magnitude by each year's delay. It requires to be plainly met; the truth to be told. The patriotism and the sound sense of the people, whenever the Federal Government from its high places of authority shall proclaim the truth in unequivocal language, will, in my firm belief, receive and approve it. But so long as we deal like the Delphic oracle in words of double meaning, so long as we attempt to escape from responsibility, and exhibit our fear to declare the truth by the fact that we do not act upon it, we must expect speculative theory to occupy the mind of the public, and error to increase as time rolls on. But if the sad fate should be ours, for this most minute cause, to destroy our Government, the historian who shall attempt philosophically to examine the question will, after he has put on his microscopic glasses and discovered it, be compelled to cry out, veritably so the unseen insect in the course of time destroys the mighty oak. Now, I believe—may I not say I believe if not, then I hope—there is yet time, by the full explicit declaration of the truth, to disabuse the popular mind, to arouse the popular heart, to expose the danger from lurking treason and ill-concealed hostility; to rally a virtuous people to their country's rescue, who circling closer and deeper, as the storm gathers fury, around the ark of their father's covenant, will place it in security, there happily to remain a sign of fraternity, justice, and equality, to our remotest posterity.

PART FIVE

The Momentous Issue of Civil War

*he moral question of slavery and the issue of slavery in the terri-
tories were, to many Americans, symptomatic of deeper and more
fundamental differences between the North and the South. They were not
merely surface questions but had roots that went deep into the very com-
position of civilization itself. At stake in the struggle was not simply the
question of slavery or freedom for a few million Southern Negroes nor
the status of slavery in several Western territories. At stake were two ways
of life, two differing civilizations even, which were apparently incompatible. It might be argued that the institution of slavery was at the core
of the disagreement, but in fact slavery had become so much a part of
Southern life that the whole fabric of civilization in the South seemed to be
identified with slavery's fate.*

*Coexistence between these two ways of life was, in the view of those who
were committed to the extreme Northern and Southern positions, not possible nor even desirable. Northern abolitionists had repeatedly called for
the dissolution of the Union and the separation of the free states from the
slave states. Secession had been threatened with increasing frequency by
Southern hotheads and fire-eaters ever since the crisis over slavery in the
Mexican cession. People in both camps were convinced (had, in fact, convinced themselves) that the nation could not long remain divided between
a free and a slaveholding society. George Fitzhugh, the Virginia defender
of slavery, was one of the first to predict that the United States would
someday become either all free or all slave. The idea was picked up and
further developed by Abraham Lincoln when, speaking for Illinois Republicans in 1858, he asserted, "I believe this government cannot endure
permanently half slave and half free. . . . It will become all one thing, or
all the other." Lincoln ruled out any third alternative; coexistence, to
him, was simply not possible. Later during the same year, William H.
Seward, New York's prominent Republican Senator, followed the same
theme, arguing that "opposing and enduring forces" did in fact add up to
an "irrepressible conflict."*

The question of the inevitability of the Civil War is one which has inspired a great deal of speculation, not always fruitful. Whether the war was inevitable or not, the fact remains that there were influential people in the 1850s who believed that conflict between North and South was unavoidable. By their very statements and influence, they did much to make it so.

Contributing to the notion of inevitability was the rise of a romantic Southern nationalism during the last decades of peace before the Civil War. Men like Robert Barnwell Rhett, Charleston's fiery newspaper editor, and Alabama's William Lowndes Yancey, the "Prince of Fire-eaters," saw in the South not simply a well-delineated section of the Union but a nation in its own right. They argued for the secession of the slave states and the erection of a Southern nation with increasing effect during the 1850s. Southerners became convinced that they held all the necessary ingredients for an independent national existence—a social structure that was unique in the Union, a cultural and economic homogeneity, and (to some, most important of all) a resource that could, with proper use, bring the rest of the world to its knees. "Cotton is king," boasted South Carolina's Senator James H. Hammond in 1858. No power on earth, he declared, would dare make war upon cotton. Referring to the extent of the slaveholding area, he asked, "Is not that territory enough to make an empire that shall rule the world?" The Southern mind, already defensive in its attitude, was turned inward upon itself by such boasts. Differences between the South and the rest of the nation were magnified and exaggerated; the isolation of Southerners deepened. "We are, I fear," wrote a Southern professor, "within a few years of disunion & perhaps of civil war; and all because neither side knows the other."

From out of this Southern nationalism came an emphasis on states' rights, the immediate justification for a separation from the rest of the United States. The sequence of events in the late 1850s, culminating in the election of Abraham Lincoln to the Presidency in 1860, persuaded Southerners that their destiny, and safety, lay outside the Union. Invoking the Constitution and reciting long-standing grievances against Northern perversions of constitutional government and the rights of sovereign states, seven Deep South states, led by South Carolina, severed their ties with the United States—the first step in the realization of the dream of Southern nationhood. For the new Republican President, as well as for most Northerners, such a development was intolerable. The South had thrown down the gauntlet and the challenge could not be ignored.

William H. Seward Warns of an Irrepressible Conflict:
Speech at Rochester, N.Y., October 25, 1858

William H. Seward (1801–1872) was in 1858 a leader of the new Republican party and that party's most prominent contender for the presidential nomination in 1860. A former Whig governor of New York, he had been elected to the United States Senate in 1849 and served continuously until 1861, when he was appointed Secretary of State in the Cabinet of Abraham Lincoln. Seward, although leaning toward a conservative policy in the sectional conflict, was nevertheless a man of strong and genuine antislavery convictions. His statement in 1850 that there was a "higher law" than the Constitution which would affect slavery had aroused Southern animosity and gave an impression of Seward's radicalism that was not entirely warranted. In 1858, he again achieved notoriety when he expressed a growing Northern interpretation of the sectional struggle in a significant speech in Rochester, New York. His views followed a pattern already established by others, including Lincoln several months before: the North and the South possessed two radically different, antagonistic, and incompatible systems; either freedom or slavery must soon become universal; conflict between the sections (between "opposing and enduring forces") was irrepressible, compromise vain and ephemeral. Seward's statements were delivered a few weeks before election day and were designed to promote the fortunes of the Republican party. It was not clear, however, that Republican victory would in any way reduce the intensity of the conflict. Seward regarded the rise of Republicanism as part of a "revolution"; political victory would merely bring this revolution closer to its ultimate consummation. How the revolution's goals could be secured, short of violence, however, Seward did not say. There is no recent biography of Seward nor is there a suitable study of the idea of "irrepressible conflict," which, by 1858, had gained popularity and support in both North and South. An important study which places this idea in a larger context of events leading to the eventual explosion is Avery Craven, The Coming of the Civil War *(1942; rev. ed., 1957). For a biography of Seward, see Frederic Bancroft,* The Life of William H. Seward *(1900), two volumes. Seward's speech is reprinted from George E. Baker (ed.),* The Works of William H. Seward *(New York. Redfield, 1853 1884 [volume 5, Boston: Houghton Mifflin]), volume 4, pages 289–302.*

he unmistakable outbreaks of zeal which occur all around me, show that you are earnest men—and such a man am I. Let us therefore, at least for a time, pass by all secondary and collateral questions, whether of a personal or of a general nature, and consider the main subject of the present canvass. The democratic party—or, to speak more accurately, the party which wears that attractive name—is in possession of the federal government. The republicans propose to dislodge that party, and dismiss it from its high trust.

The main subject, then, is, whether the democratic party deserves to retain the confidence of the American people. In attempting to prove it unworthy, I think that I am not actuated by prejudices against that party, or by prepossessions in favor of its adversary; for I have learned, by some experience, that virtue and patriotism, vice and selfishness, are found in all parties, and that they differ less in their motives than in the policies they pursue.

Our country is a theatre, which exhibits, in full operation, two radically different political systems; the one resting on the basis of servile or slave labor, the other on the basis of voluntary labor of freemen.

The laborers who are enslaved are all negroes, or persons more or less purely of African derivation. But this is only accidental. The principle of the system is, that labor in every society, by whomsoever performed, is necessarily unintellectual, groveling and base; and that the laborer, equally for his own good and for the welfare of the state, ought to be enslaved. The white laboring man, whether native or foreigner, is not enslaved, only because he cannot, as yet, be reduced to bondage.

You need not be told now that the slave system is the older of the two, and that once it was universal.

The emancipation of our own ancestors, Caucasians and Europeans as they were, hardly dates beyond a period of five hundred years. The great melioration of human society which modern times exhibit, is mainly due to the incomplete substitution of the system of voluntary labor for the old one of servile labor, which has already taken place. This African slave system is one which, in its origin and in its growth, has been altogether foreign from the habits of the races which colonized these states, and established civilization here. It was introduced on this new continent as an engine of conquest, and for the establishment of monarchical power, by the Portuguese and the Spaniards, and was rapidly extended by them all over South America, Central America, Louisiana and Mexico. Its legitimate fruits are seen in the poverty, imbecility, and anarchy, which now pervade all Portuguese and Spanish America. The free-labor system is of German extraction, and it was established in our country by emigrants from Sweden, Holland, Germany, Great Britain and Ireland.

We justly ascribe to its influences the strength, wealth, greatness, intelligence, and freedom, which the whole American people now enjoy. One of the chief elements of the value of human life is freedom in the pursuit of happiness. The slave system is not only intolerable, unjust, and inhuman, towards the laborer, whom, only because he is a laborer, it loads down with chains and converts into merchandise, but is scarcely less severe upon the freeman, to whom, only because he is a laborer from necessity, it denies facilities for employment, and whom it expels from the community because it cannot enslave and convert him into merchandise also. It is necessarily improvident and ruinous, because, as a general truth, communities prosper and flourish or droop and decline in just the degree that they practise or neglect to practise the primary duties of justice and humanity. The free-labor system conforms to the divine law of equality, which is written in the hearts and consciences of man, and therefore is always and everywhere beneficent.

The slave system is one of constant danger, distrust, suspicion, and watchfulness. It debases those whose toil alone can produce wealth and resources for defense, to the lowest degree of which human nature is capable, to guard against mutiny and insurrection, and thus wastes energies which otherwise might be employed in national development and aggrandizement.

The free-labor system educates all alike, and by opening all the fields of industrial employment, and all the departments of authority, to the unchecked and equal rivalry of all classes of men, at once secures universal contentment, and brings into the highest possible activity all the physical, moral and social energies of the whole state. In states where the slave system prevails, the masters, directly or indirectly, secure all political power, and constitute a ruling aristocracy. In states where the free-labor system prevails, universal suffrage necessarily obtains, and the state inevitably becomes, sooner or later, a republic or democracy.

Russia yet maintains slavery, and is a despotism. Most of the other European states have abolished slavery, and adopted the system of free labor. It was the antagonistic political tendencies of the two systems which the first Napoleon was contemplating when he predicted that Europe would ultimately be either all Cossack or all republican. Never did human sagacity utter a more pregnant truth. The two systems are at once perceived to be incongruous. But they are more than incongruous—they are incompatible. They never have permanently existed together in one country, and they never can. It would be easy to demonstrate this impossibility, from the irreconcilable contrast between their great principles and characteristics. But the experience of mankind has conclusively established it. Slavery, as I have already intimated, existed in every state in Europe. Free labor has supplanted it everywhere except in Russia and Turkey. State necessities developed in modern times, are now obliging even those two nations to encourage and employ free labor; and already, despotic as they are, we find them engaged in abolishing slavery. In the United States, slavery came into collision with free labor at the close of the last century, and fell before it in New England, New York, New Jersey and Pennsylvania, but triumphed over it effectually, and excluded it for a period yet undetermined, from Virginia, the Carolinas and Georgia. Indeed, so incompatible are the two systems, that every new state which is organized within our ever extending domain makes its first political act a choice of the one and the exclusion of the other, even at the cost of civil war, if necessary. The slave states, without law, at the last national election, successfully forbade, within their own limits, even the casting of votes for a candidate for president of the United States supposed to be favorable to the establishment of the free-labor system in new states.

Hitherto, the two systems have existed in different states, but side by side within the American Union. This has happened because the Union is a confederation of states. But in another aspect the United States constitute only one nation. Increase of population, which is filling the states out to their very borders, together with a new and extended net-work of railroads and other avenues, and an internal commerce which daily becomes more intimate, is rapidly bringing the states into a higher and more perfect social unity or consolidation. Thus, these antagonistic systems are continually coming into closer contact, and collision results.

Shall I tell you what this collision means? They who think that it is accidental, unnecessary, the work of interested or fanatical agitators, and therefore ephemeral, mistake the case altogether. It is an irrepressible conflict between opposing and enduring forces, and it means that the United States must and will, sooner or later, become either entirely a slave-holding nation, or entirely a free-labor nation. Either the cotton and rice-fields of South Carolina and the sugar plantations of Louisiana will ultimately be tilled by free labor, and Charleston and New Orleans become marts for legitimate merchandise alone, or else the rye-fields and wheat-fields of Massachusetts and New York must again be surrendered by their farmers to slave culture and to the production of slaves, and Boston and New York become once more markets for trade in the bodies and souls of men. It is the failure to apprehend this great truth that induces so many unsuccessful attempts at final compromise between the slave and free states, and it is the existence of this great fact that renders all such pretended compromises, when made, vain and ephemeral. Startling as this saying may appear to you, fellow citizens, it is by no means an original or even a moderate one. Our forefathers knew it to be true, and unanimously acted upon it when they framed the constitution of the United States. They regarded the existence of the servile system in so many of the states with sorrow and shame, which they openly confessed, and they looked upon the collision between them, which was then just revealing itself, and which we are now accustomed to deplore, with favor and hope. They knew that either the one or the other system must exclusively prevail.

Unlike too many of those who in modern time invoke their authority, they had a choice between the two. They preferred the system of free labor, and they determined to organize the government, and so to direct its activity, that that system should surely and certainly prevail. For this purpose, and no other, they based the whole structure of government broadly on the principle that all men are created equal, and therefore free—little dreaming that, within the short period of one hundred years, their descendants would bear to be told by any orator, however popular, that the utterance of that principle was merely a rhetorical rhapsody; or by any judge, however venerated, that it was attended by mental reservations, which rendered it hypocritical and false. By the ordinance of 1787, they dedicated all of the national domain not yet polluted by slavery to free labor immediately, thenceforth and forever; while by the new constitution and laws they invited foreign free labor from all lands under the sun, and interdicted the importation of African slave labor, at all times, in all places, and under all circumstances whatsoever. It is true that they necessarily and wisely modified this policy of freedom, by leaving it to the several states, affected as they were by differing circumstances, to abolish slavery in their own way and at their own pleasure, instead of confiding that duty to congress; and that they secured to the slave states, while yet retaining the system of slavery, a three-fifths representation of slaves in the federal government, until they should find themselves able to relinquish it with safety. But the very nature of these modifications fortifies my position that the fathers knew that the two systems could not endure within the Union, and expected that within a short period slavery would disappear forever. Moreover, in order that these modifications might not altogether defeat their grand design of a republic maintaining universal equality, they provided that two-thirds of the states might amend the constitution.

It remains to say on this point only one word, to guard against misapprehension. If these states are to again become universally slaveholding, I do not pretend to say with what violations of the constitution that end shall be accomplished. On the other hand, while I do confidently believe and hope that my country will yet become a land of universal freedom, I do not expect that it will be made so otherwise than through the action of the several states coöperating with the federal government, and all acting in strict conformity with their respective constitutions.

The strife and contentions concerning slavery, which gently-disposed persons so habitually deprecate, are nothing more than the ripening of the conflict which the fathers themselves not only thus regarded with favor, but which they may be said to have instituted.

It is not to be denied, however, that thus far the course of that contest has not been according to their humane anticipations and wishes. In the field of federal politics, slavery, deriving unlooked-for advantages from commercial changes, and energies unforeseen from the facilities of combination between members of the slaveholding class and between that class and other property classes, early rallied, and has at length made a stand, not merely to retain its original defensive position, but to extend its sway throughout the whole Union. It is certain that the slaveholding class of American citizens indulge this high ambition, and that they derive encouragement for it from the rapid and effective political successes which they have already obtained. The plan of operation is this: By continued appliances of patronage and threats of disunion, they will keep a majority favorable to these designs in the senate, where each state has an equal representation. Through that majority they will defeat, as they best can, the admission of free states and secure the admission of slave states. Under the protection of the judiciary, they will, on the principle of the Dred Scott case, carry slavery into all the territories of the United States now existing and hereafter to be organized. By the action of the president and the senate, using the treaty-making power, they will annex foreign slaveholding states. In a favorable conjuncture they will induce congress to repeal the act of 1808, which prohibits the foreign slave trade, and so they will import from Africa, at the cost of only twenty dollars a head, slaves enough to fill up the interior of the continent. Thus relatively increasing the number of slave states, they will allow no amendment to the constitution prejudicial to their interest; and so, having permanently established their power, they expect the federal judiciary to nullify all state laws which shall interfere with internal or foreign commerce in slaves. When the free states shall be sufficiently demoralized to tolerate these designs, they reasonably conclude that slavery will be accepted by those states themselves. I shall not stop to show how speedy or how complete would be the ruin which the accomplishment of these slaveholding schemes would bring upon the country. For one, I should not remain in the country to test the sad experiment. Having spent my manhood, though not my whole life, in a free state, no aristocracy of any kind, much less an aristocracy of slaveholders, shall ever make the laws of the land in which I shall be content to live. Having seen the society around me universally engaged in agriculture, manufactures and trade, which were innocent and beneficent, I shall never be a denizen of a state where men and women are reared as cattle, and bought and sold as merchandise. When that evil day shall come, and all further effort at resistance shall be impossible, then, if there shall be no better hope for redemption than I can now foresee, I shall say with Franklin, while looking abroad over the whole earth for a new and more congenial home, "Where liberty dwells, there is my country."

You will tell me that these fears are extravagant and chimerical. I answer, they are so; but they are so only because the designs of the slave-holders must and can be defeated. But it is only the possibility of defeat that renders them so. They cannot be defeated by inactivity. There is no escape from them, compatible with non-resistance. How, then, and in what way, shall the necessary resistance be made. There is only one way. The democratic party must be permanently dislodged from the government. The reason is, that the democratic party is inextricably committed to the designs of the slaveholders, which I have described. Let me be well understood. I do not charge that the democratic candidates for public office now before the people are pledged to—much less that the democratic masses who support them really adopt—those atrocious and dangerous designs. Candidates may, and generally do, mean to act justly, wisely and patriotically, when they shall be elected; but they become the ministers and servants, not the dictators, of the power which elects them. The policy which a party shall pursue at a future period is only gradually developed, depending on the occurrence of events never fully foreknown. The motives of men, whether acting as electors or in any other capacity, are generally pure. Nevertheless, it is not more true that "hell is paved with good intentions," than it is that earth is covered with wrecks resulting from innocent and amiable motives.

The very constitution of the democratic party commits it to execute all the designs of the slaveholders, whatever they may be. It is not a party of the whole Union, of all the free states and of all the slave states; nor yet is it a party of the free states in the north and in the northwest; but it is a sectional and local party, having practically its seat within the slave states, and counting its constituency chiefly and almost exclusively there. Of all its representatives in congress and in the electoral colleges, two-thirds uniformly come from these states. Its great element of strength lies in the vote of the slaveholders, augmented by the representation of three-fifths of the slaves. Deprive the democratic party of this strength, and it would be a helpless and hopeless minority, incapable of continued organization. The democratic party, being thus local and sectional, acquires new strength from the admission of every new slave state, and loses relatively by the admission of every new free state into the Union.

A party is in one sense a joint stock association, in which those who contribute most direct the action and management of the concern. The slaveholders contributing in an overwhelming proportion to the capital strength of the democratic party, they necessarily dictate and prescribe its policy. The inevitable caucus system enables them to do so with a show of fairness and justice. If it were possible to conceive for a moment that the democratic party should disobey the behests of the slaveholders, we should then see a withdrawal of the slaveholders, which would leave the party to perish. The portion of the party which is found in the free states is a mere appendage, convenient to modify its sectional character, without impairing its sectional constitution, and is less effective in regulating its movement than the nebulous tail of the comet is in determining the appointed though apparently eccentric course of the fiery sphere from which it emanates.

To expect the democratic party to resist slavery and favor freedom, is as unreasonable as to look for protestant missionaries to the catholic propaganda of Rome. The history of the democratic party commits it to the policy of slavery. It has been the democratic party, and no other agency, which has carried that policy up to its present alarming culmination. . . .

It has no policy, state or federal, for finance, or trade, or manufacture, or commerce, or education, or internal improvements, or for the protection or even the security of civil or religious liberty. It is positive and uncompromising in the interest of slavery—negative, compromising, and vacillating, in regard to everything else. It boasts its love of equality, and wastes its strength, and even its life, in fortifying the only aristocracy known in the land. It professes fraternity, and, so often as slavery requires, allies itself with proscription. It magnifies itself for conquests in foreign lands, but it sends the national eagle forth always with chains, and not the olive branch, in his fangs.

This dark record shows you, fellow citizens, what I was unwilling to announce at an earlier stage of this argument, that of the whole nefarious schedule of slaveholding designs which I have submitted to you, the democratic party has left only one yet to be consummated—the abrogation of the law which forbids the African slave trade.

Now, I know very well that the democratic party has, at every stage of these proceedings, disavowed the motive and the policy of fortifying and extending slavery, and has excused them on entirely different and more plausible grounds. But the inconsistency and frivolity of these pleas prove still more conclusively the guilt I charge upon that party It must, indeed, try to excuse such guilt before mankind, and even to the consciences of its own adherents. There is an instinctive abhorrence of slavery, and an inborn and inhering love of freedom in the human heart, which render palliation of such gross misconduct indispensable. It disfranchised the free African on the ground of a fear that, if left to enjoy the right of suffrage, he might seduce the free white citizens into amalgamation with his wronged and despised race. The democratic party condemned and deposed John Quincy Adams, because he expended twelve millions a year, while it justifies his favored successor in spending seventy, eighty and even one hundred millions, a year. It denies emancipation in the District of Columbia, even with compensation to masters and the consent of the people, on the ground of an implied constitutional inhibition, although the constitution expressly confers upon congress sovereign legislative power in that district, and although the democratic party is tenacious of the principle of strict construction. It violated the express provisions of the constitution in suppressing petition and debate on the subject of slavery, through fear of disturbance of the public harmony, although it claims that the electors have a right to instruct their representatives, and even demand their resignation in cases of contumacy. It extended slavery over Texas, and connived at the attempt to spread it across the Mexican territories, even to the shores of the Pacific ocean, under a plea of enlarging the area of freedom. It abrogated the Mexican slave law and the Missouri compromise prohibition of slavery in Kansas, not to open the new territories to slavery, but to try therein the new and fascinating theories of non-intervention and popular sovereignty; and, finally, it overthrew both these new and elegant systems by the English Lecompton bill and the Dred Scott decision, on the ground that the free states ought not to enter the Union without a population equal to the representative basis of one member of congress, although slave states might come in without inspection as to their numbers.

Will any member of the democratic party now here claim that the authorities chosen by the suffrages of the party transcended their partisan platforms, and so misrepresented the party in the various transactions, I have recited? Then I ask him to name one democratic statesman or legislator, from Van Buren to Walker, who, either timidly or cautiously like them, or boldly and defiantly like Douglas, ever refused to execute a behest of the slaveholders and was not therefore, and for no other cause, immediately denounced, and deposed from his trust, and repudiated by the democratic party for that contumacy.

I think, fellow citizens, that I have shown you that it is high time for the friends of freedom to rush to the rescue of the constitution, and that their very first duty is to dismiss the democratic party from the administration of the government.

Why shall it not be done? All agree that it ought to be done. What, then, shall prevent its being done? Nothing but timidity or division of the opponents of the democratic party.

Some of these opponents start one objection, and some another. Let us notice these objections briefly. One class say that they cannot trust the republican party; that it has not avowed its hostility to slavery boldly enough, or its affection for freedom earnestly enough.

I ask, in reply, is there any other party which can be more safely trusted? Every one knows that it is the republican party, or none, that shall displace the democratic party. But I answer, further, that the character and fidelity of any party are determined, necessarily, not by its pledges, programmes, and platforms, but by the public exigencies, and the temper of the people when they call it into activity. Subserviency to slavery is a law written not only on the forehead of the democratic party, but also in its very soul—so resistance to slavery, and devotion to freedom, the popular elements now actively working for the republican party among the people, must and will be the resources for its ever-renewing strength and constant invigoration.

Others cannot support the republican party, because it has not sufficiently exposed its platform, and determined what it will do, and what it will not do, when triumphant. It may prove too progressive for some, and too conservative for others. As if any party ever foresaw so clearly the course of future events as to plan a universal scheme of future action, adapted to all possible emergencies. Who would ever have joined even the whig party of the revolution, if it had been obliged to answer, in 1775, whether it would declare for independence in 1776, and for this noble federal constitution of ours in 1787, and not a year earlier or later? The people will be as wise next year, and even ten years hence, as we are now. They will oblige the republican party to act as the public welfare and the interests of justice and humanity shall require, through all the stages of its career, whether of trial or triumph.

Others will not venture an effort, because they fear that the Union would not endure the change. Will such objectors tell me how long a constitution can bear a strain directly along the fibres of which it is composed? This is a constitution of freedom. It is being converted into a constitution of slavery. It is a republican constitution. It is being made an aristocratic one. Others wish to wait until some collateral questions concerning temperance, or the exercise of the elective franchise are properly settled. Let me ask all such persons, whether time enough has not been wasted on these points already, without gaining any other than this single advantage, namely, the discovery that only one thing can be effectually done at one time, and that the one thing which must and will be done at any one time is just that thing which is most urgent, and will no longer admit of postponement or delay. Finally, we are told by faint-hearted men that they despond; the democratic party, they say is unconquerable, and the dominion of slavery is consequently inevitable. I reply that the complete and universal dominion of slavery would be intolerable enough, when it should have come, after the last possible effort to escape should have been made. There would then be left to us the consoling reflection of fidelity to duty.

But I reply further, that I know—few, I think, know better than I—the resources and energies of the democratic party, which is identical with the slave power. I do ample prestige to its traditional popularity. I know, further—few, I think, know better than I—the difficulties and disadvantages of organizing a new political force, like the republican party, and the obstacles it must encounter in laboring without prestige and without patronage. But, understanding all this, I know that the democratic party must go down, and that the republican party must rise into its place. The democratic party derived its strength, originally, from its adoption of the principles of equal and exact justice to all men. So long as it practised this principle faithfully, it was invulnerable. It became vulnerable when it renounced the principle, and since that time it has maintained itself, not by virtue of its own strength, or even of its traditional merits, but because there as yet had appeared in the political field no other party that had the conscience and the courage to take up, and avow, and practice the life-inspiring principle which the democratic party had surrendered. At last, the republican party has appeared. It avows, now, as the republican party of 1800 did, in one word, its faith and its works, "Equal and exact justice to all men." Even when it first entered the field, only half organized, it struck a blow which only just failed to secure complete and triumphant victory. In this, its second campaign, it has already won advantages which render that triumph now both easy and certain.

The secret of its assured success lies in that very characteristic which, in the mouth of scoffers, constitutes its great and lasting imbecility and reproach. It lies in the fact that it is a party of one idea; but that idea is a noble one—an idea that fills and expands all generous souls; the idea of equality—the equality of all men before human tribunals and human laws, as they all are equal before the Divine tribunal and Divine laws.

I know, and you know, that a revolution has begun. I know, and all the world knows, that revolutions never go backward. Twenty senators and a hundred representatives proclaim boldly in congress to-day sentiments and opinions and principles of freedom which hardly so many men, even in this free state, dared to utter in their own homes twenty years ago. While the government of the United States, under the conduct of the democratic party, has been all that time surrendering one plain and castle after another to slavery, the people of the United States have been no less steadily and perseveringly gathering together the forces with which to recover back again all the fields and all the castles which have been lost, and to confound and overthrow, by one decisive blow, the betrayers of the constitution and freedom forever.

SELECTION

A Southern Fire-eater Proposes a Southern Nation: Robert Barnwell Rhett's Speech at Grahamville, S.C., July 4, 1859

The South Carolinian Robert Barnwell Rhett (1800–1876) was one of the key figures in the Southern movement for independence. Editor of the outspoken Charleston Mercury, *Rhett served for twelve years in the national House of Representatives, 1837–1849, and sat in the United States Senate in 1850–1852 as the successor of John C. Calhoun. He was, as one historian has written, one of those who "cannot be ignored in any attempt to understand how civil strife came to the United States." Since the late 1830s, Rhett had argued the desirability of Southern independence. Like Seward and other Northerners, he recognized the North and the South as two different civilizations. Although he did not use the exact wording, he too described an "irrepressible conflict" between the two sections. Rhett's solution to the conflict was Southern independence. The South must, to insure its own continued existence, govern itself outside the Union. "Let it be, that I am a Traitor," he once said, "The word has no terrors for me." An open and avowed disunionist, Rhett intensified his campaign for Southern independence in the late 1850s, along with such compatriots as William Lowndes Yancey of Alabama and Virginia's Edmund Ruffin. In a Fourth of July Address in 1859 (the following selection), Rhett urged the people of the South to unite in their opposition to Northern aggression. The election of 1860 would be the final showdown between the sections. Defeat for the South, he argued, should signify the end of the Union and the establishment of an independent Southern nation. The text of his speech is reprinted from the* Charleston Mercury, *July 7, 1859. A sound biographical study of Rhett is Laura A. White's* Robert Barnwell Rhett: Father of Secession *(1931); for a study of the Southern movement for nationalism and independence in the 1850s, see Avery Craven,* The Growth of Southern Nationalism, 1848–1861 *(1953). The concept of Southern nationalism, in the context of Southern cultural life and expression, has been receiving an increased amount of attention from historians. A useful work is Rollin G. Osterweis,* Romanticism and Nationalism in the Old South *(1949).*

ellow-citizens: I come, at your request, to communicate my views of public affairs. In doing so I recognize at once a right and a duty —a right on your part to know my opinions, and a duty on my part to put them before you. I served in the House of Representatives and Senate of the United States at fourteen sessions of Congress. During this period I was at one time alone amongst the public men of South Carolina; and at other times I have been in a minority in the State. Yet for this whole term you gave me all you had to bestow. More grateful than the loud acclaims of triumph, you ever accorded to me your sympathy, your confidence, your support. Time has gone on working out its mighty changes. The great actors with whom I once played on the stage of life's drama are now heard no more. CALHOUN, MCDUFFIE, HAYNE, HAMILTON, TAYLOR, MILLER, TURNBULL, with whom I counselled upon first entrance into public life, have passed hence to their last account. They died without seeing the consummation of their anxious labors. The peace and safety of the South had not been assured. They have left us still an inheritance of difficulty and danger. But they have also left us a precious legacy of their brave examples. They stood forth the intrepid defenders of the rights and honor of their section. That equality of State and section for which they contended and which they disdained to surrender, has, in our hands, practically fallen to the earth. You, it is true, have done all in your power to avert this result. If we must now struggle, feebler in comparison, on lower ground and with a weaker moral power, against an increasing northern predominance and audacity, it has been in spite of the political protest of the old Seventh Congressional District of South Carolina. Ready in '32— ready in '44—ready in '50—ready, I trust, always, you stand in the South the living embodiment of the high spirit of resistance to the aggressions and encroachments of the North. You are the only people in the United States who, at a regular election ordered by a State, have elected representatives to a Southern Congress, with a view to a Southern Confederacy, and I am the honored representative you chose in that election.

In the Senate of the United States I propounded and advocated before the world the dissolution of the present Union and the creation of another Confederacy amongst the southern States. I was not ignorant of the state of public feeling at that time. I knew that such a policy was exceedingly distasteful to the greater portion of the people of the United States; and to none more so than to the political abolitionists—the SEWARDS, CHASES and SUMNERS of the North. The continuance of the present Union, they all know, is absolutely necessary to their policy of sectional rule and aggrandizement. To dissolve it is to snatch from them their prey and to seal their political execution. Events with which you are acquainted made it incumbent on me, in my opinion, to leave public life seven years ago. If I misapprehended the true state of things, I was hardly fit to direct them; and if I correctly understood them, it would not be difficult to bear patiently that fate which awaits every man who is before his times. So I retired voluntarily from public life, and left events which I could not control to the guidance of others deemed wiser than myself. You know the result. Instead of our having peace, never since the foundation of the government have the agitations concerning slavery been more fierce and unintermitted than within the last seven years. . . .

Gentlemen: In order that we may comprehend the true condition of the southern States in the Union, it is necessary to understand the nature of the government by which it exists and the motives which established it. If the views entertained by the northern people of the constitution are correct, nothing was easier than to establish the government of the United States. It is a consolidated democracy; and every one of the thirteen colonies furnished an example for its easy construction. Throwing off the authority of the parent country, there stood thirteen States, with all the great instrumentalities of free government inherited from our English ancestors. They had representation—the partition of powers between the executive, legislative and judicial departments of government—trial by jury—the *habeas corpus* act—the independence of the judiciary, and the toleration of all religions. Cast all the States into one—make of them one people—and there was a precedent in every colony for a grand consolidated representative democracy in which a majority should rule. Nothing was easier than to set up such a government. But it is a notorious fact that the formation of the Constitution of the United States was a most difficult enterprise. The convention which framed it sat for months; more than once it came to a dead stand from an impossibility of agreement. Something, therefore, besides a consolidated democracy must have been required. What, then, was the great motive for establishing the union of the States as it exists under the constitution, and the great difficulty in establishing it? The answer to this question may show us our true condition and the source of all our discontents and dangers.

The great leading motive for the union of the States under a constitution, was the fear of foreign powers. The States were too weak to stand alone. It required all their united power to achieve their independence, and this power was equally necessary to protect and insure it. If the States, in 1790, had had the wealth and population they now possess, no such constitution as that of the United States would ever have been adopted. The question was, how could we be so united as to *be one people,* in relation to foreign nations for self-protection—and yet, in relation to one another, be separate, distinct and independent States. Here was the difficulty in making the constitution. The statesmen of that day had been taught hard thinking by hard fighting. They had not thrown off the British yoke to submit to its being imposed by any of the American States on others. They knew perfectly well the dissimilarity of the States in climate, pursuits of industry and institutions. Some were necessarily commercial, others manufacturing, and others agricultural. Some could grow the great tropical productions, on which the commerce of the world has always lived. Others could hardly grow their bread. Some could be cultivated only by African slaves; others were best adapted to the labor of the Caucasian race. African slavery was, therefore, an evil to some and to others a blessing. It was, therefore, the grand design of the constitution to reserve to each State and section the exclusive control of every interest which was peculiar to it, and to impart to a general government power only over these interests which were common to all the States and sections, with the view of obtaining thereby protection from foreign nations. By such a constitution only would the people of the several States be protected, and yet free. To have given power to a general government over sectional interests, amongst such incongruous peoples, would have been the establishment of a despotism, unless the section having such interests was the majority—and then it would be superfluous and useless. Representation would not protect the minority section, because the ruling representatives would not be elected by the minority or responsible to them. And if the majority or ruling section have interests or passions antagonistic to the interests or institutions of the minority section, the government would not only be an arbitrary despotism but an oppressive tyranny. The framers of the Constitution of the United States thoroughly understood these principles. They designed the Government of the United States to be in conformity therewith. They established a free government, not a despotism—a confederated republic, with very limited powers—not a consolidated democracy with all powers.

Whilst the great cause which produced the Union—the fear of foreign nations—continued, the constitution, in the main, fulfilled the purposes of its creation, and the people of the States lived in peace with each other. One event, however, did endanger the continuance of the Union; and that event showed clearly how any sectional oppression, real or imaginary, in the operation of the government, would occasion its overthrow. The war of 1812 was produced by northern interests. It was an effort on the part of the government to protect them from the aggressions of foreign nations. Our ships belonging to the North were searched and plundered. Our sailors, citizens of the North, were impressed on the high seas. The war which ensued was undertaken to redress these wrongs. Yet when it bore hardly on the commercial interests of the northern people, they speedily mediated a dissolution of the Union. In fact, nothing but the peace of 1813, at the time it took place, prevented such a result. If the war had lasted eighteen months longer, the Union would have been dissolved by the secession of northern States. This war demonstrated, nevertheless, our ability to protect ourselves from foreign nations. The apprehensions which drove us together into a Union no longer existed, and the northern people turned to the internal operations of the government. They now sought by its instrumentality to make the South tributary to their enrichment and their power. The limitations and checks of the constitution formed a barrier to their designs. It was necessary to sweep them away. The government must be made a consolidated democracy by which their power as a majority may be omnipotent. The Supreme Court of the United States, by its decisions in favor of the Alien and Sedition laws and a Bank of the United States, laid the foundation for that latitudinous construction of the Constitution of the United States by which its limitations were virtually abrogated. The dogma was boldly avowed that the constitution was made by the people of the United States as *one people,* and conferred all powers on the General Government, limited only by "the general welfare." The Tariff of 1816, and the rejection of Missouri from the Union on account of her constitution tolerating slavery, showed the two great points on which they could best, and intended, to build up a consolidated democracy for the predominance of the North over the South.

Gentlemen: the highest statesmanship never looks to the present merely. The great future, in which a nation is to live for ages, can only be reached beneficently by a policy laid deep in the nature of things, and suitable to the capacity and character of a people. Louis XIV said, "after me the deluge." He spoke the policy of his dynasty, which only lasted for a brief season, and then was extinguished by flight or the scaffold. The greater part of rulers are but providers for the day. To allay a present discontent— to postpone a difficulty—and to cast upon a burdened future troubles too great for their ability to master successfully—is their common, but feeble and selfish policy. The true statesman will look to remedy, not merely to patch up the ills of the body politic. He strives to settle discontents, not increase them, by yielding to unjust and menacing pretensions. He knows that to submit to aggression is to encourage it; to endure wrong is to invite the repetition of it. The only firm basis of peace amongst a free or intelligent people, is to meet wrong and conquer injustice. It is to build the national policy on the eternal principles of truth and right. When the northern people first developed, by the rejection of Missouri from the Union on account of slavery, their design of excluding the people of the South from the common territories, there was a way to peace—the only way. The rights of the South and the integrity of the constitution ought to have been maintained at all hazards. The contest would then have ended in one of three ways. The rights of the South would have been conceded; the constitution would have been amended; or the Union would have been dissolved. There was not at that time the least danger of the northern people breaking up the Union for any such aggressive pretensions. They understood too well the value of the South to them in the Union. They would not have given it up for the gratification of a slavery fanaticism, which would have been defeated by the very act of disunion. We would have had permanent power by one of the two first alternatives. But the evil genius of concession ruled our counsels. On the very eve of victory the leaders of the South surrendered our rights in a compromise. They yielded to Congress the power of excluding us from our territories. A temporary peace was obtained by the overthrow of the constitution and the sectional triumph of the North over the South on the vital matter of slavery. . . .

And now where are we? What is really the nature of the general government under which we live? The sectional majority from the North grows stronger and more resolute every day. They have the power of controlling the legislation of Congress. They failed in controlling the executive, also, in the late Presidential election, but by a few votes. They expect confidently to succeed at the next Presidential election. Having mastered these two great departments of the government, they openly declare their determination to command the third—the Judiciary of the United States— and to sweep away every obstacle to their sectional domination and the consolidation of the government. Their measures of legislative policy are increased tariffs, by which a greater tribute shall be wrung from the South for the benefit of their manufacturers; internal improvements and national railroads, by which the treasury shall be exhausted, to the benefit of the North, where the public money is chiefly spent, and by which, at the same time, higher tariffs seem justified; land for the landless, by which the northern and emigrant population shall take all the common territories and make free States of them, and by which, at the same time again, the treasury be deprived of the revenue that should result from the sales of our public lands, that higher tariffs may seem further justified; squatter sovereignty, with no protection to slave property by the legislation of Congress in our territories, and, as a consequence, no more slave States; and, finally, as declared by their acknowledged leader, the abolition of slavery itself throughout the southern States. Such are their measures of policy. And the end these are designed to accomplish is a consolidated democracy, limitless in its power. The North is to rule the South.

Now, my friends, whether such a policy is consistent with the Constitution of the United States or not, is of no sort of consequence. If it is, then the constitution establishes a sectional despotism over the South. And if it is not, then the constitution is abolished by the North, the only power which can maintain it. The South, being a minority, is powerless to enforce its terms by legislation; and if she submits to its abrogation by the North, she accepts a naked despotism.

For one, I boldly declare, that if the oppressive measures meditated by the North were not meditated—if, in the spirit of a marvellous magnanimity and equity, they were disposed to leave us practically an unoppressive government—I would, as a freeman, disdain to accept of it. Liberty does not consist in the mere absence of oppression, but in the right and security to be free. It never yet existed by forbearance from those in power. If it did, it can have no safe guarantee for its continuance. We of the South, of all the people inhabiting the earth's surface, must rule ourselves. We must have a free government. To be a free government to us, we must be able to control it. It must be our government, and not the government of others, by which we are ruled, either beneficently or tyrannically. Whether a despotism consists of one man or of twenty millions, in no way, and at no time ought it to be endured. But the northern people do not leave us room to suppose that in assuming a despotism over us, they intend it to be beneficently harmless in its operation. Ambition and rapacity are stamped upon their policy. Any one acquainted with the history of this country cannot fail to perceive how, step by step, for nearly a half century, they have steadily advanced to its consummation; and as they have advanced, broader and deeper views open on their policy. They themselves may scarcely know the extremes to which they will be carried. A people who once enter upon the path of unrighteous aggrandizement, can never tell what injustice—what crimes—what horrors—they may be ready ultimately to perpetrate. One measure leads to another. Resistance must be suppressed. Violence comes. Blood is shed, and a blood-thirsty spirit is apt to rule their counsels amidst the fury of the passions. Shall we of the South trust our rights and institutions to the forbearance, or justice, or charity of the northern people—when they themselves, by their highest official representatives, declare their determination to blot them out?

The greatest deceivers in the world are often ourselves, of ourselves Men realize with difficulty the full potency of evils which are against them. Even when admitted as possible, their occurrence, it is hoped, may not be certain—or something in the future may transpire to defeat their effects. Thus they will often drift on, passive and uneasy, until they suddenly find themselves amidst the breakers of revolution. The wisdom rightly to understand and bravely and firmly to meet the perils of our condition, is the property of the few only. It seems wonderful, after all the experience we have had of the people of the North, that there should be a man in the

South so misguided or ignorant as to put any confidence in their forbearance or equity. Yet there are such men even in Congress. In the imbecility of an abandoned self-protection, we hear them say: "We know that the sceptre of power is departed from the South; but we will trust in the faith and magnanimity of the North; we will trust to their interest, for it is not to their interest to abolish slavery in the South; their commerce is too much promoted, and their necessities too well supplied"! Is magnanimity a very noted characteristic of nations, especially towards those whom they have long hated as rivals and enemies? Is interest the infallible guide to the policy of nations in this world of ignorance and passion, misrule and blood? Was France governed by interest when she expelled the Huguenots from her bosom, and abolished slavery in Hayti? Was England, when she forced on us the revolution of 1776, and ordained emancipation in Jamaica? Do not all men act from motives of interest? Yet look at the fatuity, the infidelity and misery which blacken the world. Are not men—weak, passionate, lustful men—the rulers of nations?—and when were they ever ruled by a consistent regard to their best and highest interests? How full of mistakes and follies have been the councils of the wisest nation! Yet we of the South are to trust our rights, our liberties and institutions, to the conscience and faith of a people who, in all their national dealings with us, have exhibited the most faithless selfishness, fanaticism and ambition. What are such counsels but the weak refuge of a helpless, foregone submission? Eight millions of white men, with four millions of slaves, are too rich a prey to be given up to the control of any other people. They are too mighty in their strength to trust any other people to shape their destinies. They must be independent and free in the high station for which they are designed amongst the great nations of the earth.

Fellow-citizens: a free government is a most solemn trust, as well as a great boon. Covered all over as the world is by despotisms which minister to the luxury and power of the free, a government which exists for all it protects, and is professedly based on justice to all, should be maintained with the sternest fidelity. It is not for ourselves alone—for us who are now here for a few brief years—nor for our posterity alone. These are few, when compared with the multitudes who crowd the world. And not only for us and them, but for all races capable of civil liberty, and for all ages, we should maintain our institutions. We especially in the South have a great problem to work out in the politics of the world. Confusion reigns even amongst its most enlightened thinkers and rulers. The capacity of the races of men—the rights of the people and the duties of government, are matters of doubt. Some maintain that all races are equal; and all, therefore, are capable of civil liberty. Others contend that no people—not even the people of the United States—are fit for a free and just government; and in proof they point to the contests and injustice which prevails between the sections of the Union, to support the affirmative. Others, again, in view of the failure of these States to be just to each other, maintain that the only proper object of government is order and protection. Liberty, self-government by the people, is an impossibility. It is for us to throw light on this scepticism and confusion. It is for us to demonstrate that all the races of men are not equal, but that the Caucasian and the African may be benignedly combined in one society—the one slave, the other free. It is for us to prove that we of the South at least are fit for a free government, by enforcing it in the Union: and if this is impracticable, then by establishing it apart for ourselves. It is for us to show that order and protection are not incompatible with free institutions, and that we, being capable of understanding and appreciating them, can hold fast to what has been gained for the cause of liberty, by so much toil, and suffering, and blood. Every civilized nation of the world, with the hostages for peace which our productions take from them, must wish us prosperity; whilst the Republics of old—the light and glory of ancient times—with slave institutions similar to our own, stand forth as examples to guide us to a glorious independence.

There seems to be an irrepressible desire amongst all nations to extend their limits and their power. *Expansion is their law.* The lust for plunder or fame which stimulated an ALEXANDER and a GENGHIS KHAN, has long since given way to a system of colonial incorporation. By this means more barbarous peoples are civilized and improved, and the more civilized nations have become, the more intense seems to be their desire for expansion. At this moment the greatest conquerors are the most civilized nations of the world. France seeks expansion in Algeria and Egypt, Russia in Turkey and Upper Asia, the United States over this continent, and Great Britain all over the world. The restless energy which knowledge and civilization imparts, will not be satisfied with limits, but spreads abroad its eager enterprise and dominion. It is the destiny of human nature; and the Almighty may have imparted this desire for expansion to nations, in order that civilization and his true religion may be extended. The Caucasian race is not only to be the masters but the spiritual pastors of the world. As the Jews extirpated the heathen nations around them by God's command, so the weaker races may be destined to perish or to fall beneath the subjection and tutelage of the superior races of the world.

With no people on the earth is this policy of expansion more necessary than with the people of the southern States. By the combination of the labor of the Caucasian and the African, the richest portions of the world can alone be cultivated. Have all their lavish beauty and fertility been created only to be wastes—the home of wild beasts or wilder men? And shall we, in whose hands have been deposited the labor and power by which they can be made instrumental to man's necessities and the most important and glorious portions of the earth, abandon the high mission imposed upon us, and leave them to a savage sterility? If we do, it may be with us in this as in other perversions of the proper nature of things. That which would have been our strength may become our weakness. Pent up and confined within compulsory limits, the labor of the two races may become valueless, and the proportions between them possibly be so disturbed as to lead to insurrections—northern intervention and final emancipation. This certainly is the benevolent end contemplated by our northern brethren in seeking to prevent the expansion of the South. Shall we submit to be single amongst all civilized peoples in the world, in our inability to expand? Shall we bow down to so hostile a policy? I answer—no! If in all other things our union with the North was unexceptionable, I would break it on this one pretension alone. Expansion shall be the law of the South, as of the North. We are of the dominant Caucasian race, and will perform our part in civilizing the world, and bringing into beneficent subjection and cultivation its most productive regions of sun and beauty. The broad expanse of the tropics on this continent lies stretching for thirty degrees on both sides of the Equator for our civil conquest and possession. Shall we not occupy it? Shall not Japhet and Ham go out together and take their portion of the inheritance of the earth? Let the North colonize the colder regions, where the white man can labor advantageously in the fields for the productions of nature. We, with the African, will possess the rest. Nor need we ask them, or any other people, to make good our title.

"If these things are so, why should we have any anxieties about the perpetuity of African slavery in the South? It is of God, and cannot be over thrown." We hear such an argument for inaction and submission to northern interference every day. Institutions may be everlasting; yet may they be changed or abolished in different ages and different localities. Political liberty may never die out in the world, yet does it not leave a people, who become unworthy of it by their indifference, ignorance or corruption? If liberty may be lost to a people, why not slavery? And have we not on this continent proofs enough that slavery may be abolished amongst a people? What advantage—what blessing is there of God's bestowment that man has not abused and lost? From Paradise to his last destiny, what is the history of the human family, individually or collectively, but a history of advantages neglected—benefits despised—blessings abused and forfeited? The man who talks of any blessing or institution being eternal amongst a people, is a shallow neophyte in morals and a charlatan in politics. He is ignorant of the Bible. He sets aside experience and history, and builds his policy on the loose sands of his own weak conceits or weaker resolutions. We all know that to preserve our personal integrity and virtue, requires continual watchfulness, stern self-denial, and often the most courageous suffering. Is it not the same with nations, which are but the aggregate of individuals, with the same morals and motives for their governance? If you would have a free government, you must make it so. If you would have it continue to be free, you must watch and labor for it. If you would maintain your institutions, with a world prejudiced or in arms against them, you must erect a barrier of glittering steel, or of more effulgent courage and energy for their protection. The man who talks of his rights, as a reason for his inactivity—or of the nature of things as a justification of his submission to their perversion and destruction—is as faithless to himself as to others. He is unfit to be the custodiary of any rights, or a minister in carrying out the glorious order of events designed for the human happiness and power. In the fierce struggle of this licentious world, there is but one instrumentality by which, in a government like ours, of conflicting interests and passions, the eternal proclivity to oppression and despotism can be averted. It is not in vain appeals for justice. It is not in a vainer submission to wrong. It is not in an august argumentation, by which we call up unaided Nature herself to substantiate our rights, that our salvation can be secured. We must act. We must resist.

Gentlemen, we have before us now, raging on the continent of Europe, a bloody contest for the independence of nationalities. The world's space is too large for its occupation by one organization of peoples. The variety of languages on the earth show the design of the Almighty in throwing its inhabitants into many political associations. An undefined repulsive antagonism between nations, as much as any attractive local sympathy, seems to be necessary to keep up their separation. It is useless to reason about the benefits conferred by the conquerors or masters of a civilized people. They are foreigners, and in that word is hatred. Austria contends that her rule in Italy has been most beneficial for the people. Justice is enforced, property protected, and advancing prosperity and affluence attest her fidelity to the trust committed to her in 1815 by her allies. But is Italy satisfied? Again and again has she tried to expel the Austrian from that beautiful land of bright sun and brighter memories. And now, from her furthest confines where an Austrian has not trod, her people gather in mustering lines to achieve the independence of Italy. There is not a generous heart in all Christendom which does not sympathize with the Italian and bid him God's speed, as he rushes to the battle for his native land. Let Italy be for Italy, is the voice of humanity, although potentates may again cut up the map of Europe with their swords. And was it not so with Scotland, when for ages she resisted an amalgamation with England? And was it not—is it not so with Poland? Even now the heart of the Pole yearns for the tempestuous and capricious despotism of his nobles in olden times rather than the steady and more advantageous rule of Russian domination. Are the people of Ireland to this day content with her identification with England? The people of England and Ireland, Russia and Poland, Austria and Italy, are not more distinct and antagonist in their characteristics, pursuits and institutions—their sympathies and views —than the people of our Northern and Southern States. A common struggle for independence, and a sense of weakness, threw them together under one government. Disagreement and contention have marked their union from its commencement, until at length all sympathy between the two great sections of the Union seems to be lost. They look upon each other as enemies to be overcome, rather than friends to be supported. The bond of union— the Constitution—is broken. How long will a Union without a constitution —without confidence, without heart—endure? I know full well how powerful are the prejudices which exist amongst every people in favor of their government—be it what it may. A distinguished philosopher has said that "man is a bundle of prejudices." All governments have their bigots and fanatics. It is human. The double-headed Eagle of Austria, at this moment, probably excites as wide an enthusiasm as the younger emblem of that imperial bird over the stars and stripes. The greater part of mankind have no time to consider the nature of their government; and if they have, they are unable to comprehend its operations. They therefore fall back, in supporting it, to an unreasoning faith. At this moment, after ages of oppressive error, how confused and absurd are the ideas of many called to the responsible position of legislators, as to the nature of taxation by duties or imports! If there is anything which a free people should understand, it is the nature and extent of the tax they pay to support their government. What man in his senses can suppose it to be just or politic for a government to take from a citizen for its support, *one dollar for itself and two for another citizen*. Yet this is exactly what we, who boast that our system of government is based on the most righteous equality, have submitted to for generations. The citizen who pays these indirect taxes does not understand it. Many do not know that they pay any taxes at all to the general government. Even the order, the protection they receive from the government of the States, they attribute to the general government. We know the general government only by its taxation, and even its taxation is so insidious as to be unperceived to many. Yet our prosperity and peace—the result of our State governments and of our magnificent staples—are attributed to the operations of the Government of the United States. Is it surprising, under such circumstances, that Union devotees and fanatics should spring up everywhere to paralyze our counsels? They do not reflect that our prosperity, if it did arise exclusively from the beneficent action of the general government, is no more a criterion of liberty in a people than of virtue in an individual. Brazil, and Cuba and Japan are refluent of prosperity. Are they free? The best government in the world, so far as protection to the person and property are concerned between man and man, is probably the imperial government of France. Are the French free? Liberty is justice. It can dwell neither with the oppressor nor with the submissively oppressed. The curse of wrong to others strips the wrong-doer of that purity which can alone make him a righteous repeller of tyranny; and submission to oppression degrades its victims, and fills the heart with compromising fears and base compliances, and reasoning subterfuges, instead of the truthful aspirations and stern resolutions of the high spirit of liberty. Is it surprising that superstition should thus become substituted for patriotism, and faith for reasoning; and that after a few years of misrule, the oppressed become habituated to their condition? First we endure, and then, in the imbecility of custom or fears of change, admire and love a despotic government. The first step in the broad road to ruin and dishonor, with nations as with individuals, is often decisive of their destiny. How thoroughly did our great ancestors understand this truth, when they fought their great battles for liberty! They did not allow the hand of oppression to rest on them, much less to press them.

Delay is the canker of great enterprises. There may be wisdom in delay when delay leads to action. I can understand the importance of time for preparation, although the necessity for preparation is usually our folly. But I cannot understand how a bare, naked submission to unconstitutional misrule for thirty years can be anything else but a base and wicked imbecility. Two generations have passed away since I reached the years of manhood. I found, when I entered into life, the whole South inflamed on the vital matter of unconstitutional taxation. We had before us the very question which occasioned the resistance of our fathers to British misgovernment, and their glorious example in the independence they achieved rather than endure it. Yet we submitted to the principle of unjust and unconstitutional taxation imposed upon us by the North, and we have borne it to this day. One submission soon produced its natural fruit of renewed interference and aggression on the institution of slavery. We have borne that too; until at length, to be persecuted and harassed alternately on one or the other of these vital matters, seems to be the law of our political existence in the Union. Yet we still have men, not actually in mockery, warning us against haste, and entreating caution in our measures. Can it be unreasonable at any time to be free, and to cast off a pragmatical and vulgar tyranny? Is not a whole life of endurance of unconstitutional oppression, enough for freedom—enough for any wisdom in delay—too much for safety or honor? How long shall we stand the resistless and despised victims of northern fanaticism and rapacity? How long shall we cry "wait!"—whilst the North advances in power and insolence, and each successive year brings her nearer to the consummation of her policy of dominion over us, and over this continent? Shall we wait until the expedient of JOHN QUINCY ADAMS for emancipating our slaves shall be enforced? He declared that the general government, by the treaty-making power, could constitutionally abolish slavery in the South. Insurrections may be produced, and then the general government, having a right to interpose her military power, as the condition of peace may, by treaty ordain emancipation. Whether by this, or the more direct way of congressional legislation, providing for "the general welfare," who doubts that in the day when the northern people possess the power, and *will* it, emancipation will be a law of Congress? Shall we wait for this blissful consummation—when the fires of insurrection will light up our homes and the North shall stand by to watch and guard the conflagration? Such things will probably never be, because the South will not await their fearful coming, but will anticipate them. When will she anticipate them and act out her redemption? When will her mighty heart beat free in the enjoyment of her rights, safe under the shield of her own protection; and, casting off the incubus of ignorance and error and fear, which now like a fool toad sits upon her bosom, rise up and command the liberation and independence of the South?

There are premonitions of changes in the moral as in the physical world. The mutterings of the political tempest, which the next presidential election must produce, already breaks upon the ear. The proud robbers whom we have raised up to power and place in the North, by our continual submissions, still insist, in defiance of the decisions of the Supreme Court of the United States, in denying our rights, and in affirming their right to defeat them in our territories. It has been in vain that those in the North who respect the constitution and the rights of the South have proclaimed, from time to time, that the South would resist and the Union be dissolved We have justified the contempt of our enemies, not the good opinion of our friends. The South has not resisted. The Union is not dissolved; and our aggressors, triumphing in our submission, hold place and power for our harassment, and their exaltation and aggrandizement. Those are thus raised to official dignity who are worthy, in themselves, of neither influence nor consideration. They are fitting representatives of the meaner passions of the people—avarice, ambition, fanaticism, jealousy, hate; whilst those who would represent the nobler virtues of the North are subsidized or driven from public life. To submit to the encroachment of this vulgar crew of plunderers and fanatics, is a degradation no other free people than the people of the South ever endured; but to submit to their *rule* will be the desperation of a weak and conquered race—conquered without a fight. Shall this be the doom of the South in the next presidential election? Let us go into the contest it must occasion, as if it will bear to future generations our justification or our shame. Frankness and truth are due to all men; but especially must it be due *from the South to the South*. Let us place before the world fully and fairly the rights which we claim under the constitution, denied by our confederates of the North. Not to assert them in the face of the denial of them by the master section of the Union, is basely to abandon them. Fully and fairly exposed, undimmed by equivocations, unpolluted by hypocrisies, with a candidate fully and fairly representing them, let us meet the contest of the next presidential election. And let us meet it unitedly. The North in the last fall elections—democrats with black republicans—united to exclude us from the enjoyment of our rights in our territories. We have no other alternative, if we would be faithful to ourselves, than to unite for their vindication. The prospects are cheering that the South will harmonize more than she has ever done on this great question. Our frontier States, from present indications, will not be much behind the central States of the South in their fidelity to our rights and institutions. And above all, let no question not immediately connected with the aggressions of the North divide us into parties against each other. This will be fatal to all resistance or redress. Our first great duty is to place the South above or beyond the power of the North. First make our property safe under our own control before we divide as to measures for its increase and extension. After our safety is accomplished it will be time enough for the South to determine on measures most expedient to promote her agricultural interests or advance her general prosperity. By a policy thus marked by union, the result cannot be doubtful. If our rights are victorious in the next presidential election, we may consider it as a kind augury of a more auspicious future. If they are overthrown, let this election be the last contest between the North and the South; and the long, weary night of our dishonor and humiliation be dispersed at last, by the glorious spring day of a Southern confederacy.

Gentlemen: RAWLINS LOWNDES declared in our State Convention, assembled to consider the Constitution of the United States, that the only epitaph he desired to be placed upon his tomb was, that he opposed to the last the adoption of the Constitution of the United States by South Carolina. The sagacity of this distinguished patriot stands vindicated by the events which surround us. Should the public regard, after I am gone, ever reach my humble services, let it be remembered that after twenty years of earnest effort to preserve the Union, by keeping it within the limitations of the Constitution, and arresting its fatal tendency to despotism, I turned at last to the salvation of my native land—the South—and in my latter years did all I could to dissolve her connection with the North, and to establish for her a Southern confederacy.

SELECTION

A Southern State Justifies Secession: South Carolina's "Declaration of the Immediate Causes," 1860

Abraham Lincoln was elected President in November, 1860, and about six weeks later, on December 20, South Carolina seceded from the Union. Robert Barnwell Rhett was an influential member of the secession convention; with the passage of the secession ordinance, his long-sought goal became a reality. Christopher Memminger, a reluctant secessionist who had joined the movement only after Lincoln's election, was selected to draw up a declaration of the causes that justified the state's action (the document that follows). Unlike Rhett, Memminger did not dwell on the broad considerations of Southern nationality and the necessity for self-government, but rather emphasized more recent and more specific causes—the failure of the North to enforce the Fugitive Slave Law, the election of a minority President, and the threat this election posed to slavery—finding the ultimate justification for secession in the Declaration of Independence and the Constitution. Although South Carolina acted alone, other Southern states soon followed her example. Within two months, Mississippi, Florida, Alabama, Georgia, Louisiana and Texas had approved secession ordinances and had withdrawn from the Union. The stand-ard account of the secession movement is Dwight L. Dumond's The Secession Movement, 1860–1861 *(1931); with specific reference to South Carolina, Harold S. Schultz,* Nationalism and Sectionalism in South Carolina, 1852–1860: A Study of the Movement for Southern Independence *(1950) provides important background. A fine recent study of the Southern secession conventions is Ralph A. Wooster,* The Secession Conventions of the South *(1962).*

The text below is reprinted from the Declaration of the Immediate Causes Which Induce and Justify the Secession of South Carolina from the Federal Union *(Charleston, S.C.: Evans and Cogswell, 1860).*

The People of the State of South Carolina, in Convention assembled, on the 26th day of April, A. D., 1852, declared that the frequent violations of the Constitution of the United States, by the Federal Govern-ment, and its encroachments upon the reserved rights of the States, fully justified this State in then withdrawing from the Federal Union; but in deference to the opinions and wishes of the other slaveholding States, she forbore at that time to exercise this right. Since that time, these encroach-ments have continued to increase, and further forbearance ceases to be a virtue.

And now the State of South Carolina having resumed her separate and equal place among nations, deems it due to herself, to the remaining United States of America, and to the nations of the world, that she should declare the immediate causes which have led to this act.

In the year 1765, that portion of the British Empire embracing Great Britain, undertook to make laws for the government of that portion com-posed of the thirteen American Colonies. A struggle for the right of self-government ensued, which resulted, on the 4th July, 1776, in a Declaration by the Colonies, "that they are, and of right ought to be, FREE AND INDE-PENDENT STATES; and that, as free and independent States, they have full power to levy war, conclude peace, contract alliances, establish commerce, and to do all other acts and things which independent States may of right do."

They further solemnly declared that whenever any "form of govern-ment becomes destructive of the ends for which it was established, it is the right of the people to alter or abolish it, and to institute a new govern-ment." Deeming the Government of Great Britain to have become destructive of these ends, they declared that the Colonies "are absolved from all allegiance to the British Crown, and that all political connection between them and the State of Great Britain is, and ought to be, totally dissolved."

In pursuance of this Declaration of Independence, each of the thirteen States proceeded to exercise its separate sovereignty; adopted for itself a Constitution, and appointed officers for the administration of government in all its departments—Legislative, Executive and Judicial. For purposes of defence, they united their arms and their counsels; and, in 1778, they entered into a league known as the Articles of Confederation, whereby they agreed to entrust the administration of their external relations to a common agent, known as the Congress of the United States, expressly declaring, in the first article, "that each State retains its sovereignty, freedom and independence, and every power, jurisdiction and right which is not, by this Confederation, expressly delegated to the United States in Congress assembled."

Under this Confederation the War of the Revolution was carried on, and on the 3d September, 1783, the contest ended, and a definitive Treaty was signed by Great Britain, in which she acknowledged the Independence of the Colonies in the following terms:

> *Article 1.*—His Britannic Majesty acknowledges the said United States, viz: New Hampshire, Massachusetts Bay, Rhode Island and Providence Plantations, Connecticut, New York, New Jersey, Pennsylvania, Delaware, Maryland, Virginia, North Carolina, South Carolina and Georgia, to be FREE, SOVEREIGN AND INDEPENDENT STATES; that he treats them as such; and for himself, his heirs and successors, relinquishes all claims to the government, propriety and territorial rights of the same and every part thereof.

Thus were established the two great principles asserted by the Colonies, namely: the right of a State to govern itself; and the right of a people to abolish a Government when it becomes destructive of the ends for which it was instituted. And concurrent with the establishment of these principles, was the fact, that each Colony became and was recognized by the mother Country as a FREE, SOVEREIGN AND INDEPENDENT STATE.

In 1787, Deputies were appointed by the States to revise the Articles of Confederation, and on 17th September, 1787, these Deputies recommended, for the adoption of the States, the Articles of Union, known as the Constitution of the United States.

The parties to whom this Constitution was submitted, were the several sovereign States; they were to agree or disagree, and when nine of them agreed, the compact was to take effect among those concurring; and the General Government, as the common agent, was then to be invested with their authority.

If only nine of the thirteen States had concurred, the other four would have remained as they then were—separate, sovereign States, independent of any of the provisions of the Constitution. In fact, two of the States did not accede to the Constitution until long after it had gone into operation among the other eleven; and during that interval, they each exercised the functions of an independent nation.

By this Constitution, certain duties were imposed upon the several States, and the exercise of certain of their powers were restrained, which necessarily implied their continued existence as sovereign States. But, to remove all doubt, an amendment was added, which declared that the powers not delegated to the United States by the Constitution, nor prohibited by it to the States, are reserved to the States, respectively, or to the people. On 23d May, 1788, South Carolina, by a Convention of her people, passed an Ordinance assenting to this Constitution, and afterwards altered her own Constitution, to conform herself to the obligations she had undertaken.

Thus was established, by compact between the States, a Government, with defined objects and powers, limited to the express words of the grant. This limitation left the whole remaining mass of power subject to the clause reserving it to the States or to the people, and rendered unnecessary any specification of reserved rights.

We hold that the Government thus established is subject to the two great principles asserted in the Declaration of Independence; and we hold further, that the mode of its formation subjects it to a third fundamental principle, namely: the law of compact. We maintain that in every compact between two or more parties, the obligation is mutual; that the failure of one of the contracting parties to perform a material part of the agreement, entirely releases the obligation of the other; and that where no arbiter is provided, each party is remitted to his own judgment to determine the fact of failure, with all its consequences.

In the present case, that fact is established with certainty. We assert, that fourteen of the States have deliberately refused for years past to fulfil their constitutional obligations, and we refer to their own Statutes for the proof.

The Constitution of the United States, in its 4th Article, provides as follows:

> No person held to service or labor in one State, under the laws thereof, escaping into another shall, in consequence of any law or regulation therein, be discharged from such service or labor, but shall be delivered up, on claim of the party to whom such service or labor may be due.

This stipulation was so material to the compact, that without it that compact would not have been made. The greater number of the contracting parties held slaves, and they had previously evinced their estimate of the value of such a stipulation by making it a condition in the Ordinance for the government of the territory ceded by Virginia, which now composes the States north of the Ohio river.

The same article of the Constitution stipulates also for rendition by the several States of fugitives from justice from the other States.

The General Government, as the common agent, passed laws to carry into effect these stipulations of the States. For many years these laws were executed. But an increasing hostility on the part of the non-slaveholding States to the Institution of Slavery has led to a disregard of their obligations, and the laws of the General Government have ceased to effect the objects of the Constitution. The States of Maine, New Hampshire, Vermont, Massachusetts, Connecticut, Rhode Island, New York, Pennsylvania, Illinois, Indiana, Michigan, Wisconsin and Iowa, have enacted laws which either nullify the Acts of Congress or render useless any attempt to execute them. In many of these States the fugitive is discharged from the service or labor claimed, and in none of them has the State Government complied with the stipulation made in the Constitution. The State of New Jersey, at an early day, passed a law in conformity with her constitutional obligation; but the current of anti-slavery feeling has led her more recently to enact laws which render inoperative the remedies provided by her own law and by the laws of Congress. In the State of New York even the right of transit for a slave has been denied by her tribunals; and the States of Ohio and Iowa have refused to surrender to justice fugitives charged with murder, and with inciting servile insurrection in the State of Virginia. Thus the constitutional compact has been deliberately broken and disregarded by the non-slaveholding States, and the consequence follows that South Carolina is released from her obligation.

The ends for which this Constitution was framed are declared by itself to be "to form a more perfect union, establish justice, insure domestic tranquility, provide for the common defence, promote the general welfare, and secure the blessings of liberty to ourselves and our posterity."

These ends it endeavored to accomplish by a Federal Government, in which each State was recognized as an equal, and had separate control over its own institutions. The right of property in slaves was recognized by giving to free persons distinct political rights, by giving them the right to represent, and burthening them with direct taxes for three-fifths of their slaves; by authorizing the importation of slaves for twenty years; and by stipulating for the rendition of fugitives from labor.

We affirm that these ends for which this Government was instituted have been defeated, and the Government itself has been made destructive of them by the action of the non-slaveholding States. Those States have assumed the right of deciding upon the propriety of our domestic institutions; and have denied the rights of property established in fifteen of the States and recognized by the Constitution; they have denounced as sinful the institution of Slavery; they have permitted the open establishment among them of societies, whose avowed object is to disturb the peace and to eloign the property of the citizens of other States. They have encouraged and assisted thousands of our slaves to leave their homes; and those who remain, have been incited by emissaries, books and pictures to servile insurrection.

For twenty-five years this agitation has been steadily increasing, until it has now secured to its aid the power of the Common Government. Observing the *forms* of the Constitution, a sectional party has found within that article establishing the Executive Department, the means of subverting the Constitution itself. A geographical line has been drawn across the Union, and all the States north of that line have united in the election of a man to the high office of President of the United States whose opinions and purposes are hostile to slavery. He is to be entrusted with the administration of the Common Government, because he has declared that that "Government cannot endure permanently half slave, half free," and that the public mind must rest in the belief that Slavery is in the course of ultimate extinction.

This sectional combination for the subversion of the Constitution, has been aided in some of the States by elevating to citizenship persons, who, by the Supreme Law of the land, are incapable of becoming citizens; and their votes have been used to inaugurate a new policy, hostile to the South, and destructive to its peace and safety.

On the 4th of March next, this party will take possession of the Government. It has announced, that the South shall be excluded from the common Territory; that the Judicial Tribunals shall be made sectional, and that a war must be waged against slavery until it shall cease throughout the United States.

The Guaranties of the Constitution will then no longer exist; the equal rights of the States will be lost. The slaveholding States will no longer have the power of self-government, or self-protection, and the Federal Government will have become their enemy.

Sectional interest and animosity will deepen the irritation, and all hope of remedy is rendered vain, by the fact that public opinion at the North has invested a great political error with the sanctions of a more erroneous religious belief.

We, therefore, the people of South Carolina, by our delegates, in Convention assembled appealing to the Supreme Judge of the world for the rectitude of our intentions, have solemnly declared that the Union heretofore existing between this State and the other States of North America, is dissolved, and that the State of South Carolina has resumed her position among the nations of the world, as a separate and independent State; with full power to levy war, conclude peace, contract alliances, establish commerce, and to do all other acts and things which independent States may of right do.

SELECTION

The Response of the North: Abraham Lincoln's First Inaugural Address, March 4, 1861

The winter months of 1860–1861—from the election of Lincoln in November to his inauguration the following March—were tense and exciting ones for the American people. Seven Southern states seceded from the Union and formed an independent Southern confederacy during this period. President Buchanan, about to leave office, was careful not to commit the nation to any policy that might result in hostilities between the seceded states and the national government, although his opposition toward the Southern movement stiffened. Lincoln was conspicuously silent during the secession crisis. In Congress, supporters of compromise were feverishly trying to find a basis for an amicable settlement of the sectional difficulties. Compromise did not succeed, however, partly because Republicans (advised by Lincoln) steadfastly refused to support any overture to the South, partly because Southerners themselves felt that the struggle had gone far beyond the point at which compromise would be feasible, partly also because no compromise was ever proposed that really attacked the heart of the sectional differences. Lincoln's Inaugural Address on March 4, 1861, was eagerly awaited as the first statement of policy of the new administration. Its moderate and conciliatory tone was widely recognized throughout most of the nation, but Southern secessionists branded it as a declaration of war against the South. It was a masterful statement of the President's obligations and responsibilities as he saw them; the burden of opening hostilities was placed squarely on the South.

Lincoln's First Inaugural Address is reprinted from Roy P. Basler et al. *(eds.),* The Collected Works of Abraham Lincoln *(New Brunswick: Rutgers, 1953), 9 volumes, volume 4, pages 262–271. For an illuminating study of the role of Republicans during the secession crisis, see David M. Potter,* Lincoln and His Party in the Secession Crisis *(1942; new ed., 1962); for Northern reactions generally, see Kenneth M. Stampp,* And the War Came: The North and the Secession Crisis, 1860–1861 *(1950). A valuable and informative synthesis of American history during these crisis years is in Allan Nevins,* The Emergence of Lincoln *(1950), two volumes.*

Fellow citizens of the United States:

In compliance with a custom as old as the government itself, I appear before you to address you briefly, and to take, in your presence, the oath prescribed by the Constitution of the United States, to be taken by the President "before he enters on the execution of his office."

I do not consider it necessary, at present, for me to discuss those matters of administration about which there is no special anxiety, or excitement.

Apprehension seems to exist among the people of the Southern States, that by the accession of a Republican Administration, their property, and their peace, and personal security, are to be endangered. There has never been any reasonable cause for such apprehension. Indeed, the most ample evidence to the contrary has all the while existed, and been open to their inspection. It is found in nearly all the published speeches of him who now addresses you. I do but quote from one of those speeches when I declare that "I have no purpose, directly or indirectly, to interfere with the institution of slavery in the States where it exists. I believe I have no lawful right to do so, and I have no inclination to do so." Those who nominated and elected me did so with full knowledge that I had made this, and many similar declarations, and had never recanted them. And more than this, they placed in the platform, for my acceptance, and as a law to themselves, and to me, the clear and emphatic resolution which I now read:

> *Resolved,* That the maintenance inviolate of the rights of the States, and especially the right of each State to order and control its own domestic institutions according to its own judgment exclusively, is essential to that balance of power on which the perfection and endurance of our political fabric depend; and we denounce the lawless invasion by armed force of the soil of any State or Territory, no matter under what pretext, as among the gravest of crimes.

I now reiterate these sentiments: and in doing so, I only press upon the public attention the most conclusive evidence of which the case is susceptible, that the property, peace and security of no section are to be in anywise endangered by the now incoming Administration. I add too, that all the protection which, consistently with the Constitution and the laws, can be given, will be cheerfully given to all the States when lawfully demanded, for whatever cause—as cheerfully to one section, as to another.

There is much controversy about the delivering up of fugitives from service or labor. The clause I now read is as plainly written in the Constitution as any other of its provisions:

> No person held to service or labor in one State, under the laws thereof, escaping into another, shall, in consequence of any law or regulation therein, be discharged from such service or labor, but shall be delivered up on claim of the party to whom such service or labor may be due.

It is scarcely questioned that this provision was intended by those who made it, for the reclaiming of what we call fugitive slaves; and the intention of the law-giver is the law. All members of Congress swear their support to the whole Constitution—to this provision as much as to any other. To the proposition, then, that slaves whose cases come within the terms of this clause, "shall be delivered up," their oaths are unanimous. Now, if they would make the effort in good temper, could they not, with nearly equal unanimity, frame and pass a law, by means of which to keep good that unanimous oath?

There is some difference of opinion whether this clause should be enforced by national or by state authority; but surely that difference is not a very material one. If the slave is to be surrendered, it can be of but little consequence to him, or to others, by which authority it is done. And should any one, in any case, be content that his oath shall go unkept, on a merely unsubstantial controversy as to *how* it shall be kept?

Again, in any law upon this subject, ought not all the safeguards of liberty known in civilized and humane jurisprudence to be introduced, so that a free man be not, in any case, surrendered as a slave? And might it not be well, at the same time, to provide by law for the enforcement of that clause in the Constitution which guaranties that "The citizens of each State shall be entitled to all privileges and immunities of citizens in the several States?"

I take the official oath to-day, with no mental reservations, and with no purpose to construe the Constitution or laws, by any hypercritical rules. And while I do not choose now to specify particular acts of Congress as proper to be enforced, I do suggest, that it will be much safer for all, both in official and private stations, to conform to, and abide by, all those acts which stand unrepealed, than to violate any of them, trusting to find impunity in having them held to be unconstitutional.

It is seventy-two years since the first inauguration of a President under our national Constitution. During that period fifteen different and greatly distinguished citizens, have, in succession, administered the executive branch of the government. They have conducted it through many perils; and, generally, with great success. Yet, with all this scope for precedent, I now enter upon the same task for the brief constitutional term of four years, under great and peculiar difficulty. A disruption of the Federal Union heretofore only menaced, is now formidably attempted.

I hold, that in contemplation of universal law, and of the Constitution, the Union of these States is perpetual. Perpetuity is implied, if not expressed, in the fundamental law of all national governments. It is safe to assert that no government proper, ever had a provision in its organic law for its own termination. Continue to execute all the express provisions of our national Constitution, and the Union will endure forever—it being impossible to destroy it, except by some action not provided for in the instrument itself.

Again, if the United States be not a government proper, but an association of States in the nature of contract merely, can it, as a contract, be peaceably unmade, by less than all the parties who made it? One party to a contract may violate it—break it, so to speak; but does it not require all to lawfully rescind it?

Descending from these general principles, we find the proposition that, in legal contemplation, the Union is perpetual, confirmed by the history of the Union itself. The Union is much older than the Constitution. It was formed in fact, by the Articles of Association in 1774. It was matured and continued by the Declaration of Independence in 1776. It was further matured and the faith of all the then thirteen States expressly plighted and engaged that it should be perpetual, by the Articles of Confederation in 1778. And finally, in 1787, one of the declared objects for ordaining and establishing the Constitution, was *"to form a more perfect union."*

But if destruction of the Union, by one, or by a part only, of the States, be lawfully possible, the Union is *less* perfect than before the Constitution, having lost the vital element of perpetuity.

It follows from these views that no State, upon its own mere motion, can lawfully get out of the Union,—that *resolves* and *ordinances* to that effect are legally void; and that acts of violence, within any State or States, against the authority of the United States, are insurrectionary or revolutionary, according to circumstances.

I therefore consider that, in view of the Constitution and the laws, the Union is unbroken; and, to the extent of my ability, I shall take care, as the Constitution itself expressly enjoins upon me, that the laws of the Union be faithfully executed in all the States. Doing this I deem to be only a simple duty on my part; and I shall perform it, so far as practicable, unless my rightful masters, the American people, shall withhold the requisite means, or, in some authoritative manner, direct the contrary. I trust this will not be regarded as a menace, but only as the declared purpose of the Union that it *will* constitutionally defend, and maintain itself.

In doing this there needs to be no bloodshed or violence; and there shall be none, unless it be forced upon the national authority. The power confided to me, will be used to hold, occupy, and possess the property, and places belonging to the government, and to collect the duties and imposts; but beyond what may be necessary for these objects, there will be no invasion—no using of force against, or among the people anywhere. Where hostility to the United States, in any interior locality, shall be so great and so universal, as to prevent competent resident citizens from holding the Federal offices, there will be no attempt to force obnoxious strangers among the people for that object. While the strict legal right may exist in the government to enforce the exercise of these offices, the attempt to do so would be so irritating, and so nearly impracticable with all, that I deem it better to forego, for the time, the uses of such offices.

The mails, unless repelled, will continue to be furnished in all parts of the Union. So far as possible, the people everywhere shall have that sense of perfect security which is most favorable to calm thought and reflection. The course here indicated will be followed, unless current events, and experience, shall show a modification, or change, to be proper; and in every case and exigency, my best discretion will be exercised, according to circumstances actually existing, and with a view and a hope of a peaceful solution of the national troubles, and the restoration of fraternal sympathies and affections.

That there are persons in one section, or another who seek to destroy the Union at all events, and are glad of any pretext to do it, I will neither affirm or deny; but if there be such, I need address no word to them. To those, however, who really love the Union, may I not speak?

Before entering upon so grave a matter as the destruction of our national fabric, with all its benefits, its memories, and its hopes, would it not be wise to ascertain precisely why we do it? Will you hazard so desperate a step, while there is any possibility that any portion of the ills you fly from, have no real existence? Will you, while the certain ills you fly to, are greater than all the real ones you fly from? Will you risk the commission of so fearful a mistake?

All profess to be content in the Union, if all constitutional rights can be maintained. Is it true, then, that any right, plainly written in the Constitution, has been denied? I think not. Happily the human mind is so constituted, that no party can reach to the audacity of doing this. Think, if you can, of a single instance in which a plainly written provision of the Constitution has ever been denied. If, by the mere force of numbers, a majority should deprive a minority of any clearly written constitutional right, it might, in a moral point of view, justify revolution—certainly would, if such right were a vital one. But such is not our case. All the vital rights of minorities, and of individuals, are so plainly assured to them, by affirmations and negations, guaranties and prohibitions, in the Constitution, that controversies never arise concerning them. But no organic law can ever be framed with a provision specifically applicable to every question which may occur in practical administration. No foresight can anticipate, nor any document of reasonable length contain express provisions for all possible questions. Shall fugitives from labor be surrendered by national or by State authority? The Constitution does not expressly say. *May* Congress prohibit slavery in the territories? The Constitution does not expressly say. *Must* Congress protect slavery in the territories? The Constitution does not expressly say.

From questions of this class spring all our constitutional controversies, and we divide upon them into majorities and minorities. If the minority will not acquiesce, the majority must, or the government must cease. There is no other alternative; for continuing the government, is acquiescence on one side or the other. If a minority, in such case, will secede rather than acquiesce, they make a precedent which, in turn, will divide and ruin them; for a minority of their own will secede from them, whenever a majority refuses to be controlled by such minority. For instance, why may not any portion of a new confederacy, a year or two hence, arbitrarily secede again, precisely as portions of the present Union now claim to secede from it. All who cherish disunion sentiments, are now being educated to the exact temper of doing this. Is there such perfect identity of interests among the States to compose a new Union, as to produce harmony only; and prevent renewed secession?

Plainly, the central idea of secession, is the essence of anarchy. A majority, held in restraint by constitutional checks, and limitations, and always changing easily, with deliberate changes of popular opinions and sentiments, is the only true sovereign of a free people. Whoever rejects it, does, of necessity, fly to anarchy or to despotism. Unanimity is impossible; the rule of a minority, as a permanent arrangement, is wholly inadmissable; so that, rejecting the majority principle, anarchy, or despotism in some form, is all that is left.

I do not forget the position assumed by some, that constitutional questions are to be decided by the Supreme Court; nor do I deny that such decisions must be binding in any case, upon the parties to a suit, as to the object of that suit, while they are also entitled to very high respect and consideration, in all parallel cases, by all other departments of the government. And while it is obviously possible that such decision may be erroneous in any given case, still the evil effect following it, being limited to that particular case, with the chance that it may be over-ruled, and never become a precedent for other cases, can better be borne than could the evils of a different practice. At the same time the candid citizen must confess that if the policy of the government, upon vital questions, affecting the whole people, is to be irrevocably fixed by decisions of the Supreme Court, the instant they are made, in ordinary litigation between parties, in personal actions, the people will have ceased, to be their own rulers, having, to that extent, practically resigned their government, into the hands of that eminent tribunal. Nor is there, in this view, any assault upon the court, or the judges. It is a duty, from which they may not shrink, to decide cases properly brought before them; and it is no fault of theirs, if others seek to turn their decisions to political purposes.

One section of our country believes slavery is *right*, and ought to be extended, while the other believes it is *wrong*, and ought not to be extended. This is the only substantial dispute. The fugitive slave clause of the Constitution, and the law for the suppression of the foreign slave trade, are each as well enforced, perhaps, as any law can ever be in a community where the moral sense of the people imperfectly supports the law itself. The great body of the people abide by the dry legal obligation in both cases, and a few break over in each. This, I think, cannot be perfectly cured; and it would be worse in both cases *after* the separation of the sections, than before. The foreign slave trade, now imperfectly suppressed, would be ultimately revived without restriction, in one section; while fugitive slaves, now only partially surrendered, would not be surrendered at all, by the other.

Physically speaking, we cannot separate. We cannot remove our respective sections from each other, nor build an impassable wall between them. A husband and wife may be divorced, and go out of the presence, and beyond the reach of each other; but the different parts of our country cannot do this. They cannot but remain face to face; and intercourse, either amicable or hostile, must continue between them. Is it possible then to make that intercourse more advantageous, or more satisfactory, *after* separation than *before?* Can aliens make treaties easier than friends can make laws? Can treaties be more faithfully enforced between aliens, than laws can among friends? Suppose you go to war, you cannot fight always; and when, after much loss on both sides, and no gain on either, you cease fighting, the identical old questions, as to terms of intercourse, are again upon you.

This country, with its institutions, belongs to the people who inhabit it. Whenever they shall grow weary of the existing government, they can exercise their *constitutional* right of amending it, or their *revolutionary* right to dismember, or overthrow it. I can not be ignorant of the fact that many worthy, and patriotic citizens are desirous of having the national constitution amended. While I make no recommendation of amendments, I fully recognize the rightful authority of the people over the whole subject, to be exercised in either of the modes prescribed in the instrument itself; and I should, under existing circumstances, favor, rather than oppose, a fair opportunity being afforded the people to act upon it.

I will venture to add that, to me, the convention mode seems preferable, in that it allows amendments to originate with the people themselves, instead of only permitting them to take, or reject, propositions, originated by others, not especially chosen for the purpose, and which might not be precisely such, as they would wish to either accept or refuse. I understand a proposed amendment to the Constitution—which amendment, however, I have not seen, has passed Congress, to the effect that the federal government, shall never interfere with the domestic institutions of the States, including that of persons held to service. To avoid misconstruction of what I have said, I depart from my purpose not to speak of particular amendments, so far as to say that, holding such a provision to now be implied constitutional law, I have no objection to its being made express, and irrevocable.

The Chief Magistrate derives all his authority from the people, and they have conferred none upon him to fix terms for the separation of the States. The people themselves can do this also if they choose; but the executive, as such, has nothing to do with it. His duty is to administer the present government, as it came to his hands, and to transmit it, unimpaired by him, to his successor.

Why should there not be a patient confidence in the ultimate justice of the people? Is there any better, or equal hope, in the world? In our present differences, is either party without faith of being in the right? If the Almighty Ruler of nations, with his eternal truth and justice, be on your side of the North, or on yours of the South, that truth, and that justice, will surely prevail, by the judgment of this great tribunal, the American people.

By the frame of the government under which we live, this same people have wisely given their public servants but little power for mischief; and have, with equal wisdom, provided for the return of that little to their own hands at very short intervals.

While the people retain their virtue, and vigilance, no administration, by any extreme of wickedness or folly, can very seriously injure the government, in the short space of four years.

My countrymen, one and all, think calmly and *well,* upon this whole subject. Nothing valuable can be lost by taking time. If there be an object to *hurry* any of you, in hot haste, to a step which you would never take *deliberately,* that object will be frustrated by taking time; but no good object can be frustrated by it. Such of you as are now dissatisfied, still have the old Constitution unimpaired, and, on the sensitive point, the laws of your own framing under it; while the new administration will have no immediate power, if it would, to change either. If it were admitted that you who are dissatisfied, hold the right side in the dispute, there still is no single good reason for precipitate action. Intelligence, patriotism, Christianity, and a firm reliance on Him, who has never yet forsaken this favored land, are still competent to adjust, in the best way, all our present difficulty.

In *your* hands, my dissatisfied fellow countrymen, and not in *mine,* is the momentous issue of civil war. The government will not assail *you.* You can have no conflict, without being yourselves the aggressors. *You* have no oath registered in Heaven to destroy the government, while *I* shall have the most solemn one to "preserve, protect and defend" it.

I am loath to close. We are not enemies, but friends. We must not be enemies. Though passion may have strained, it must not break our bonds of affection. The mystic chords of memory, stretching from every battle-field, and patriot grave, to every living heart and hearthstone, all over this broad land, will yet swell the chorus of the Union, when again touched, as surely they will be, by the better angels of our nature.

We the People of the Confederate States

On February 4, 1861, delegates from six seceded Southern states *(Texas had not yet formally withdrawn from the Union)* met at Montgomery, Alabama's capital city. They were earnest, dedicated men, well known nationally, enthusiastic for an independent South, and devoted to their task of establishing a Southern nation. The delegates faced three difficult responsibilities. Their first job was to draft a provisional constitution for the new nation and to sit as a constitutional convention for the permanent constitution. Secondly, executive officers—a President and a Vice President—had to be selected to lead the nation until elections could be held throughout the South. Finally, the convention delegates would serve as a provisional Congress, legislating for the Confederate States of America until a permanent Congress could be elected in accord with the new constitution. There was an air of urgency throughout the deliberations. Abraham Lincoln would be inaugurated President of the United States on March 4 and there was widespread feeling that the new Southern nation should be a fait accompli by that time. The Montgomery Convention represented the culmination of many years of agitation by Southern nationalists; as secession became a reality Southern leaders tolerated no delay in organizing the Confederacy.

The "founding fathers" of the Confederate States were men of talent and experience. They were also, by and large, men who had been devoted to the Constitution of the United States, men who regarded their independence movement as springing in large part from deep constitutional conflicts. The majority of the delegates were conservative in thought and attitude and the new nation would reflect this conservatism. The radical fire-eaters who had borne the brunt of the Southern nationalist movement and who had done so much to marshal support and enthusiasm for secession were either absent from the Montgomery meeting or exercised small influence on its deliberations. The new nation would involve little break with the past; there was to be a smooth, almost indiscernible, transition. It was to be simply a "transfer of rulership," and in no sense a revolution.

The conservative character of the nationalism at Montgomery, in striking contrast to the fiery, flamboyant speeches that had accompanied secession, was manifested in the manner in which the delegates undertook to discharge their threefold function.

Some of the delegates preferred to adopt the Constitution of the United States as their own; it had been the North, they argued, that had perverted constitutional government, not the South. Their very presence in Montgomery was the result of Northern perfidy toward the Constitution and of Northern betrayal of the sacred compact into which all the states had voluntarily entered. In two days, a provisional constitution had been drawn up and a committee appointed to draft a permanent document. Within five weeks, the permanent constitution of the Confederacy was completed. The final draft bore a marked resemblance to the Constitution under which the delegates had lately lived. Changes were introduced to "perfect" the old document and to guard against the kind of ambiguous interpretation they felt to be one of the old Constitution's major shortcomings. For President of the new nation, the convention selected Mississippi's Jefferson Davis, after an unsuccessful attempt to award the highest office to a Georgian. Davis, a distinguished Southern leader with an exemplary record of government service, both civil and military, represented the convention's ascendant conservatism. His choice made the movement more palatable to many Southerners, especially to those in states which had not yet seceded, and was in effect an announcement to the world that the Southern people were not engaged in a radical and revolutionary activity. As if to compound this conservatism, the delegates selected Alexander H. Stephens, Georgia's outspoken opponent of secession, as Vice President, an unusual and unwise selection as later events would prove.

Davis and Stephens were provisional officers and the convention a provisional Congress; each would serve only until national elections could be held for a permanent government. In the meantime, the administrative structure of the Confederacy was erected, offices were provided for and filled, and the new government set in motion.

Although the Montgomery delegates were moved by what one writer has called a "mania for unanimity," the stresses and strains that were to prove so crucial to the Confederacy in the following years were first revealed in the discussions that attended the birth of the Southern nation. The gulf between the radical fire-eaters and the conservative leadership was made dramatically apparent, especially to those zealots who had risked all in the cause of Southern independence earlier. The doctrine of states' rights—the bogey of the Confederacy—reared its head as soon as the delegates debated the relative merits of centralized authority and state power.

The fathers of the Confederacy, however, accomplished their purpose. Their new government was erected and operating by the time Lincoln took his oath of office in March. The task had been achieved so quickly and so smoothly that many in the South confidently believed they would be allowed to pursue their own national destiny unmolested by the North. Little was said and even less done to stay their course. A new nation had been built—hastily built, to be sure, but the consequences of this haste were not at this point apparent. A new power had come into being, a new flag unfurled for all the world to see.

The Constitution of the Confederate States of America

The permanent constitution of the Confederate States was adopted unanimously by the Montgomery Convention on March 11, 1861, displacing the provisional constitution under which the convention had been acting. Regarded as "one of the most interesting documents of fundamental law in America," the new constitution reflected the conservative character of the Southern national movement. Based to a large extent on the United Sates Constitution, from which it copied both principle and language, the document also included certain innovations designed to make its authority more explicit and to improve governmental administration generally. Although state sovereignty was recognized, the constitution clearly established a nation with centralized authority; significantly, no mention was made of a right of secession. Slavery in the territories, an issue between North and South earlier, was afforded positive protection. Each of the Confederate States ratified the constitution, but in no state was it submitted to the people.

The text of the constitution is reprinted from Constitution of the Confederate States of America *(Richmond, Va.: Wyatt M. Elliott, 1861). For a good discussion of Confederate constitution-making and of the permanent constitution itself, see Charles Robert Lee's* The Confederate Constitutions *(1963).*

We, the people of the Confederate States, each State acting in its sovereign and independent character, in order to form a permanent Federal Government, establish justice, insure domestic tranquility, and secure the blessings of liberty to ourselves and our posterity—invoking the favor and guidance of Almighty God—do ordain and establish this Constitution for the Confederate States of America.

Article I

Section I
All legislative powers herein delegated shall be vested in a Congress of the Confederate States, which shall consist of a Senate and House of Representatives.

Section II
1. The House of Representatives shall be composed of members chosen every second year by the people of the several States; and the electors in each State shall be citizens of the Confederate States, and have the qualifications requisite for electors of the most numerous branch of the State Legislature; but no person of foreign birth, not a citizen of the Confederate States, shall be allowed to vote for any officer, civil or political, State or Federal.

2. No person shall be a representative, who shall not have attained the age of twenty-five years, and be a citizen of the Confederate States, and who shall not, when elected, be an inhabitant of that State in which he shall be chosen.

3. Representatives and direct taxes shall be apportioned among the several States, which may be included within this Confederacy, according to their respective numbers, which shall be determined by adding to the whole number of free persons, including those bound to service for a term of years, and excluding Indians not taxed, three fifths of all slaves. The actual enumeration shall be made within three years after the first meeting of the Congress of the Confederate States, and within every subsequent term of ten years, in such manner as they shall, by law, direct. The number of representatives shall not exceed one for every fifty thousand, but each State shall have at least one representative; and until such enumeration shall be made, the State of South Carolina shall be entitled to choose six—the State of Georgia ten—the State of Alabama nine—the State of Florida two—the State of Mississippi seven—the State of Louisiana six— and the State of Texas six.

4. When vacancies happen in the representation from any State, the Executive authority thereof shall issue writs of election to fill such vacancies.

5. The House of Representatives shall choose their Speaker and other officers; and shall have the sole power of impeachment; except that any judicial or other federal officer resident and acting solely within the limits of any State, may be impeached by a vote of two-thirds of both branches of the Legislature thereof.

Section III

1. The Senate of the Confederate States shall be composed of two Senators from each State, chosen for six years by the Legislature thereof, at the regular session next immediately preceding the commencement of the term of service; and each Senator shall have one vote.

2. Immediately after they shall be assembled, in consequence of the first election, they shall be divided as equally as may be into three classes. The seats of the Senators of the first class shall be vacated at the expiration of the second year; of the second class at the expiration of the fourth year, and of the third class at the expiration of the sixth year; so that one-third may be chosen every second year; and if vacancies happen by resignation or otherwise, during the recess of the Legislature of any State, the Executive thereof may make temporary appointments until the next meeting of the Legislature, which shall then fill such vacancies.

3. No person shall be a Senator who shall not have attained the age of thirty years, and be a citizen of the Confederate States; and who shall not, when elected, be an inhabitant of the State for which he shall be chosen.

4. The Vice President of the Confederate States shall be President of the Senate, but shall have no vote, unless they be equally divided.

5. The Senate shall choose their other officers; and also a President *pro tempore* in the absence of the Vice President, or when he shall exercise the office of President of the Confederate States.

6. The Senate shall have the sole power to try all impeachments. When sitting for that purpose, they shall be on oath or affirmation. When the President of the Confederate States is tried the Chief Justice shall preside; and no person shall be convicted without the concurrence of two-thirds of the members present.

7. Judgment in cases of impeachment shall not extend further than to removal from office, and disqualification to hold and enjoy any office of honor, trust or profit, under the Confederate States; but the party convicted shall, nevertheless, be liable and subject to indictment, trial, judgment and punishment according to law.

Section IV

1. The times, places and manner of holding elections for Senators and Representatives, shall be prescribed in each State by the Legislature thereof, subject to the provisions of this Constitution; but the Congress may, at any time, by law, make or alter such regulations, except as to the times and places of choosing Senators.

2. The Congress shall assemble at least once in every year; and such meeting shall be on the first Monday in December, unless they shall, by law, appoint a different day.

Section V

1. Each House shall be the judge of the elections, returns and qualifications of its own members, and a majority of each shall constitute a quorum to do business; but a smaller number may adjourn from day to day, and may be authorized to compel the attendance of absent members, in such manner and under such penalties as each House may provide.

2. Each House may determine the rules of its proceedings, punish its members for disorderly behavior, and, with the concurrence of two-thirds of the whole number, expel a member.

3. Each House shall keep a journal of its proceedings, and from time to time publish the same, excepting such parts as may in their judgment require secrecy; and the yeas and nays of the members of either House, on any question, shall, at the desire of one-fifth of those present, be entered on the journal.

4. Neither House, during the session of Congress, shall, without the consent of the other, adjourn for more than three days, nor to any other place than that in which the two Houses shall be sitting.

Section VI

1. The Senators and Representatives shall receive a compensation for their services, to be ascertained by law, and paid out of the treasury of the Confederate States. They shall, in all cases, except treason, felony, and breach of the peace, be privileged from arrest during their attendance at the session of their respective Houses, and in going to and returning

from the same; and for any speech or debate in either House, they shall not be questioned in any other place.

2. No Senator or Representative shall, during the time for which he was elected, be appointed to any civil office under the authority of the Confederate States, which shall have been created, or the emoluments whereof shall have been increased during such time; and no person holding any office under the Confederate States shall be a member of either House during his continuance in office. But Congress may, by law, grant to the principal officer in each of the Executive Departments a seat upon the floor of either House, with the privilege of discussing any measures appertaining to his department.

Section VII

1. All bills for raising revenue shall originate in the House of Representatives; but the Senate may propose or concur with amendments as on other bills.

2. Every bill which shall have passed both Houses, shall, before it becomes a law, be presented to the President of the Confederate States; if he approve, he shall sign it; but if not, he shall return it with his objections to that House in which it shall have originated, who shall enter the objections at large on their journal, and proceed to reconsider it. If, after such reconsideration, two-thirds of that House shall agree to pass the bill, it shall be sent, together with the objections, to the other House, by which it shall likewise be reconsidered, and if approved by two-thirds of that House, it shall become a law. But in all such cases, the votes of both Houses shall be determined by yeas and nays, and the names of the persons voting for and against the bill shall be entered on the journal of each House respectively. If any bill shall not be returned by the President within ten days (Sundays excepted) after it shall have been presented to him, the same shall be a law, in like manner as if he had signed it, unless the Congress, by their adjournment, prevent its return; in which case it shall not be a law. The President may approve any appropriation and disapprove any other appropriation in the same bill. In such case he shall, in signing the bill, designate the appropriations disapproved; and shall return a copy of such appropriations, with his objections, to the House in which the bill shall have originated; and the same proceedings shall then be had as in case of other bills disapproved by the President.

3. Every order, resolution or vote, to which the concurrence of both Houses may be necessary (except on a question of adjournment) shall be presented to the President of the Confederate States, and before the same shall take effect, shall be approved by him; or being disapproved by him, shall be re-passed by two-thirds of both Houses according to the rules and limitations prescribed in case of a bill.

Section VIII

The Congress shall have power—

1. To lay and collect taxes, duties, imposts, and excises, for revenue necessary to pay the debts, provide for the common defence, and carry on the Government of the Confederate States; but no bounties shall be granted from the treasury; nor shall any duties or taxes on importations

from foreign nations be laid to promote or foster any branch of industry; and all duties, imposts, and excises shall be uniform throughout the Confederate States:

2. To borrow money on the credit of the Confederate States:

3. To regulate commerce with foreign nations, and among the several States, and with the Indian tribes; but neither this, nor any other clause contained in the Constitution, shall ever be construed to delegate the power to Congress to appropriate money for any internal improvement intended to facilitate commerce; except for the purpose of furnishing lights, beacons, and buoys, and other aids to navigation upon the coasts, and the improvement of harbors and the removing of obstructions in river navigation, in all which cases, such duties shall be laid on the navigation facilitated thereby, as may be necessary to pay the costs and expenses thereof:

4. To establish uniform laws of naturalization, and uniform laws on the subject of bankruptcies, throughout the Confederate States, but no law of Congress shall discharge any debt contracted before the passage of the same:

5. To coin money, regulate the value thereof and of foreign coin, and fix the standard of weights and measures:

6. To provide for the punishment of counterfeiting the securities and current coin of the Confederate States:

7. To establish post offices and post routes; but the expenses of the Post Office Department, after the first day of March in the year of our Lord eighteen hundred and sixty three, shall be paid out of its own revenues:

8. To promote the progress of science and useful arts, by securing for limited times to authors and inventors the exclusive right to their respective writings and discoveries:

9. To constitute tribunals inferior to the Supreme Court:

10. To define and punish piracies and felonies committed on the high seas, and offences against the law of nations:

11. To declare war, grant letters of marque and reprisal, and make rules concerning captures on land and water:

12. To raise and support armies; but no appropriation of money to that use shall be for a longer term than two years:

13. To provide and maintain a navy:

14. To make rules for the government and regulation of the land and naval forces:

15. To provide for calling forth the militia to execute the laws of the Confederate States, suppress insurrections, and repel invasions:

16. To provide for organizing, arming, and disciplining the militia, and for governing such part of them as may be employed in the service of the Confederate States; reserving to the States, respectively, the appointment of the officers, and the authority of training the militia according to the discipline prescribed by Congress:

17. To exercise exclusive legislation, in all cases whatsoever, over such district (not exceeding ten miles square) as may, by cession of one or more States and the acceptance of Congress, become the seat of the Government of the Confederate States; and to exercise like authority over all places purchased by the consent of the Legislature of the State in which the same shall be, for the erection of forts, magazines, arsenals, dock-yards, and other needful buildings: and

18. To make all laws which shall be necessary and proper for carrying into execution the foregoing powers, and all other powers vested by this Constitution in the Government of the Confederate States, or in any department or officer thereof.

Section IX

1. The importation of negroes of the African race, from any foreign country, other than the slaveholding States or Territories of the United States of America, is hereby forbidden; and Congress is required to pass such laws as shall effectually prevent the same.

2. Congress shall also have power to prohibit the introduction of slaves from any State not a member of, or Territory not belonging to, this Confederacy.

3. The privilege of the writ of habeas corpus shall not be suspended, unless when in cases of rebellion or invasion the public safety may require it.

4. No bill of attainder, *ex post facto* law, or law denying or impairing the right of property in negro slaves shall be passed.

5. No capitation or other direct tax shall be laid, unless in proportion to the census or enumeration hereinbefore directed to be taken.

6. No tax or duty shall be laid on articles exported from any State, except by a vote of two-thirds of both Houses.

7 No preference shall be given by any regulation of commerce or revenue to the ports of one State over those of another.

8. No money shall be drawn from the treasury, but in consequence of appropriations made by law; and a regular statement and account of the receipts and expenditures of all public money shall be published from time to time.

9. Congress shall appropriate no money from the treasury except by a vote of two-thirds of both Houses, taken by yeas and nays, unless it be asked and estimated for by some one of the heads of Department, and submitted to Congress by the President; or for the purpose of paying its own expenses and contingencies; or for the payment of claims against the Confederate States, the justice of which shall have been judicially declared by a tribunal for the investigation of claims against the Government, which it is hereby made the duty of Congress to establish.

10. All bills appropriating money shall specify in federal currency the exact amount of each appropriation and the purposes for which it is made; and Congress shall grant no extra compensation to any public contractor, officer, agent or servant, after such contract shall have been made or such service rendered.

11. No title of nobility shall be granted by the Confederate States; and no person holding any office of profit or trust under them, shall, without the consent of the Congress, accept of any present, emolument, office or title of any kind whatever from any king, prince or foreign State.

12. Congress shall make no law respecting an establishment of religion, or prohibiting the free exercise thereof; or abridging the freedom of speech, or of the press; or the right of the people peaceably to assemble and petition the government for a redress of grievances.

13. A well regulated militia being necessary to the security of a free State, the right of the people to keep and bear arms shall not be infringed.

14. No soldier shall, in time of peace, be quartered in any house without the consent of the owner; nor in time of war, but in a manner to be prescribed by law.

15. The right of the people to be secure in their persons, houses, papers, and effects against unreasonable searches and seizures, shall not be violated; and no warrants shall issue but upon probable cause, supported by oath or affirmation, and particularly describing the place to be searched, and the persons or things to be seized.

16. No person shall be held to answer for a capital or otherwise infamous crime, unless on a presentment or indictment of a grand jury, except in cases arising in the land or naval forces, or in the militia, when in actual service, in time of war or public danger; nor shall any person be subject, for the same offence, to be twice put in jeopardy of life or limb; nor be compelled, in any criminal case, to be a witness against himself; nor be deprived of life, liberty, or property, without due process of law; nor shall private property be taken for public use, without just compensation.

17. In all criminal prosecutions the accused shall enjoy the right to a speedy and public trial, by an impartial jury of the State and district wherein the crime shall have been committed, which district shall have been previously ascertained by law, and to be informed of the nature and cause of the accusation; to be confronted with the witnesses against him; to have compulsory process for obtaining witnesses in his favor; and to have the assistance of counsel for his defence.

18. In suits at common law, where the value in controversy shall exceed twenty dollars, the right of trial by jury shall be preserved; and no fact so tried by a jury shall be otherwise reexamined in any court of the Confederacy, than according to the rules of the common law.

19. Excessive bail shall not be required, nor excessive fines imposed, nor cruel and unusual punishments inflicted.

20. Every law, or resolution having the force of law, shall relate to but one subject, and that shall be expressed in the title.

Section X

1. No State shall enter into any treaty, alliance or confederation; grant letters of marque and reprisal; coin money; make anything but gold and silver coin a tender in payment of debts; pass any bill of attainder, or *ex post facto* law, or law impairing the obligation of contracts; or grant any title of nobility.

2. No State shall, without the consent of the Congress, lay any imposts or duties on imports or exports, except what may be absolutely necessary for executing its inspection laws; and the net produce of all duties and imposts, laid by any State on imports or exports, shall be for the use of the treasury of the Confederate States; and all such laws shall be subject to the revision and control of Congress.

3. No State shall, without the consent of Congress, lay any duty on tonnage, except on sea-going vessels, for the improvement of its rivers and harbors navigated by the said vessels; but such duties shall not conflict with any treaties of the Confederate States with foreign nations; and any surplus revenue thus derived, shall, after making such improvement, be paid into the common treasury; nor shall any State keep troops or ships

of war in time of peace, enter into any agreement or compact with another State, or with a foreign power, or engage in war, unless actually invaded, or in such imminent danger as will not admit of delay. But when any river divides or flows through two or more States, they may enter into compacts with each other to improve the navigation thereof.

Article II

Section I

1. The executive power shall be vested in a President of the Confederate States of America. He and the Vice President shall hold their offices for the term of six years; but the President shall not be reëligible. The President and Vice President shall be elected as follows:

2. Each State shall appoint, in such manner as the Legislature thereof may direct, a number of electors equal to the whole number of Senators and Representatives to which the State may be entitled in the Congress; but no Senator or Representative, or person holding an office of trust or profit under the Confederate State, shall be appointed an elector.

3. The electors shall meet in their respective States and vote by ballot for President and Vice President, one of whom, at least, shall not be an inhabitant of the same State with themselves; they shall name in their ballots the person voted for as President, and in distinct ballots the person voted for as Vice President, and they shall make distinct lists of all persons voted for as President, and of all persons voted for as Vice President, and of the number of votes for each, which lists they shall sign and certify, and transmit, sealed, to the seat of the Government of the Confederate States, directed to the President of the Senate; the President of the Senate shall, in the presence of the Senate and House of Representatives, open all the certificates, and the votes shall then be counted; the person having the greatest number of votes for President shall be the President, if such number be a majority of the whole number of electors appointed; and if no person have such majority, then, from the persons having the highest numbers, not exceeding three, on the list of those voted for as President, the House of Representatives shall choose immediately, by ballot, the President. But in choosing the President, the votes shall be taken by States, the representation from each State having one vote; a quorum for this purpose shall consist of a member or members from two-thirds of the States, and a majority of all the States shall be necessary to a choice. And if the House of Representatives shall not choose a President, whenever the right of choice shall devolve upon them, before the fourth day of March next following, then the Vice President shall act as President, as in case of the death, or other constitutional disability of the President.

4. The person having the greatest number of votes as Vice President, shall be the Vice President, if such number be a majority of the whole number of electors appointed; and if no person have a majority, then, from the two highest numbers on the list the Senate shall choose the Vice President; a quorum for the purpose shall consist of two-thirds of the whole number of Senators, and a majority of the whole number shall be necessary to a choice.

5. But no person constitutionally ineligible to the office of President shall be eligible to that of Vice President of the Confederate States.

6. The Congress may determine the time of choosing the electors, and the day on which they shall give their votes; which day shall be the same throughout the Confederate States.

7. No person except a natural-born citizen of the Confederate States, or a citizen thereof, at the time of the adoption of this Constitution, or a citizen thereof born in the United States prior to the 20th of December, 1860, shall be eligible to the office of President; neither shall any person be eligible to that office who shall not have attained the age of thirty-five years, and been fourteen years a resident within the limits of the Confederate States, as they may exist at the time of his election.

8. In case of the removal of the President from office, or of his death, resignation, or inability to discharge the powers and duties of the said office, the same shall devolve on the Vice President; and the Congress may, by law, provide for the case of removal, death, resignation, or inability both of the President and Vice President, declaring what officer shall then act as President, and such officer shall act accordingly until the disability be removed or a President shall be elected.

9. The President shall, at stated times, receive for his services a compensation, which shall neither be increased nor diminished during the period for which he shall have been elected; and he shall not receive within that period any other emolument from the Confederate States, or any of them.

10. Before he enters on the execution of his office, he shall take the following oath or affirmation:

"I do solemnly swear (or affirm) that I will faithfully execute the office of President of the Confederate States, and will to the best of my ability, preserve, protect and defend the Constitution thereof."

Section II

1. The President shall be commander-in-chief of the army and navy of the Confederate States, and of the militia of the several States, when called into the actual service of the Confederate States; he may require the opinion, in writing, of the principal officer in each of the Executive Departments, upon any subject relating to the duties of their respective offices; and he shall have power to grant reprieves and pardons for offences against the Confederate States, except in cases of impeachment.

2. He shall have power, by and with the advice and consent of the Senate, to make treaties, provided two-thirds of the Senators present concur; and he shall nominate, and by and with the advice and consent of the Senate, shall appoint ambassadors, other public ministers and consuls, Judges of the Supreme Court, and all other officers of the Confederate States, whose appointments are not herein otherwise provided for, and which shall be established by law; but the Congress may, by law, vest the appointment of such inferior officers, as they think proper, in the President alone, in the courts of law or in the heads of Departments.

3. The principal officer in each of the Executive Departments, and all persons connected with the diplomatic service, may be removed from office at the pleasure of the President. All other civil officers of the Executive Department may be removed at any time by the President, or other ap-

pointing power, when their services are unnecessary, or for dishonesty, incapacity, inefficiency, misconduct, or neglect of duty; and when so removed, the removal shall be reported to the Senate, together with the reasons therefor.

4. The President shall have power to fill all vacancies that may happen during the recess of the Senate, by granting commissions which shall expire at the end of their next session; but no person rejected by the Senate shall be re-appointed to the same office during their ensuing recess.

Section III

1. The President shall, from time to time, give to the Congress information of the state of the Confederacy, and recommend to their consideration such measures as he shall judge necessary and expedient; he may, on extraordinary occasions, convene both Houses or either of them; and in case of disagreement between them, with respect to the time of adjournment, he may adjourn them to such time as he shall think proper; he shall receive ambassadors and other public ministers; he shall take care that the laws be faithfully executed, and shall commission all the officers of the Confederate States.

Section IV

1. The President, Vice President, and all civil officers of the Confederate States, shall be removed from office on impeachment for, and conviction of, treason, bribery, or other high crimes and misdemeanors.

Article III

Section I

1. The judicial power of the Confederate States shall be vested in one Supreme Court and in such Inferior Courts as the Congress may from time to time ordain and establish. The judges, both of the Supreme and Inferior Courts, shall hold their offices during good behavior, and shall, at stated times, receive for their services a compensation, which shall not be diminished during their continuance in office.

Section II

1. The judicial power shall extend to all cases arising under this Constitution, the laws of the Confederate States, and treaties made or which shall be made under their authority; to all cases affecting ambassadors, other public ministers and consuls; to all cases of admiralty and maritime jurisdiction; to controversies to which the Confederate States shall be a party; to controversies between two or more States; between a State and citizen of another State where the State is plaintiff; between citizens claiming lands under grants of different States, and between a State or the citizens thereof, and foreign States, citizens or subjects; but no State shall be sued by a citizen or subject of any foreign State.

2. In all cases affecting ambassadors, other public ministers and consuls, and those in which a State shall be a party, the Supreme Court shall have original jurisdiction. In all the other cases beforementioned the Supreme Court shall have appellate jurisdiction, both as to law and fact, with such exceptions and under such regulations, as the Congress shall make.

3. The trial of all crimes, except in cases of impeachment, shall be by jury, and such trials shall be held in the State where the said crimes shall have been committed; but when not committed within any State, the trial shall be at such place or places as the Congress may, by law, have directed.

Section III

1. Treason against the Confederate States shall consist only in levying war against them, or in adhering to their enemies, giving them aid and comfort. No person shall be convicted of treason unless on the testimony of two witnesses to the same overt act, or on confession in open court.

2. The Congress shall have power to declare the punishment of treason, but no attainder of treason shall work corruption of blood, or forfeiture, except during the life of the person attainted.

Article IV

Section I

1. Full faith and credit shall be given in each State to the public acts, records and judicial proceedings of every other State. And the Congress may, by general laws, prescribe the manner in which such acts, records, and proceedings shall be proved, and the effect thereof.

Section II

1. The citizens of each State shall be entitled to all the privileges and immunities of citizens in the several States, and shall have the right of transit and sojourn in any State of this Confederacy, with their slaves and other property; and the right of property in said slaves shall not be thereby impaired.

2. A person charged in any State with treason, felony, or other crime against the laws of such State, who shall flee from justice, and be found in another State, shall, on demand of the Executive authority of the State from which he fled, be delivered up to be removed to the State having jurisdiction of the crime.

3. No slave or other person held to service or labor in any State or Territory of the Confederate States, under the laws thereof, escaping or lawfully carried into another, shall, in consequence of any law or regulation therein, be discharged from such service or labor; but shall be delivered up on claim of the party to whom such slave belongs, or to whom such service or labor may be due.

Section III

1. Other States may be admitted into this Confederacy by a vote of two-thirds of the whole House of Representatives, and two-thirds of the Senate, the Senate voting by States; but no new State shall be formed or erected within the jurisdiction of any other State; nor any State be formed by the junction of two or more States, or parts of States, without the consent of the Legislatures of the States concerned as well as of the Congress.

2. The Congress shall have power to dispose of and make all needful

rules and regulations concerning the property of the Confederate States, including the lands thereof.

3. The Confederate States may acquire new territory; and Congress shall have power to legislate and provide governments for the inhabitants of all territory belonging to the Confederate States, lying without the limits of the several States; and may permit them, at such times, and in such manner as it may by law provide, to form States to be admitted into the Confederacy. In all such territory, the institution of negro slavery as it now exists in the Confederate States, shall be recognized and protected by Congress, and by the territorial government; and the inhabitants of the several Confederate States and Territories, shall have the right to take to such territory any slaves, lawfully held by them in any of the States or Territories of the Confederate States.

4. The Confederate States shall guaranty to every State that now is or hereafter may become a member of this Confederacy, a republican form of government, and shall protect each of them against invasion; and on application of the Legislature (or of the Executive when the Legislature is not in session) against domestic violence.

Article V

Section I

1. Upon the demand of any three States, legally assembled in their several conventions, the Congress shall summon a convention of all the States, to take into consideration such amendments to the Constitution as the said States shall concur in suggesting at the time when the said demand is made: and should any of the proposed amendments to the Constitution be agreed on by the said convention—voting by States—and the same be ratified by the Legislatures of two thirds of the several States, or by conventions in two-thirds thereof—as the one or the other mode of ratification may be proposed by the general convention, they shall thenceforward form a part of this Constitution. But no State shall, without its consent, be deprived of its equal representation in the Senate.

Article VI

1. The Government established by this Constitution is the successor of the Provisional Government of the Confederate States of America, and all the laws passed by the latter shall continue in force until the same shall be repealed or modified; and all the officers appointed by the same shall remain in office until their successors are appointed and qualified, or the offices abolished.

2. All debts contracted and engagements entered into before the adoption of this Constitution shall be as valid against the Confederate States under this Constitution as under the Provisional Government.

3. This Constitution, and the laws of the Confederate States, made in pursuance thereof, and all treaties made, or which shall be made under the authority of the Confederate States, shall be the supreme law of the

land; and the judges in every State shall be bound thereby, anything in the constitution or laws of any State to the contrary notwithstanding.

4. The Senators and Representatives before mentioned, and the members of the several State legislatures, and all executive and judicial officers, both of the Confederate States and of the several States, shall be bound by oath or affirmation, to support this Constitution; but no religious test shall ever be required as a qualification to any office or public trust under the Confederate States.

5. The enumeration, in the Constitution, of certain rights, shall not be construed to deny or disparage others retained by the people of the several States.

6. The powers not delegated to the Confederate States by the Constitution, nor prohibited by it to the States are reserved to the States, respectively, or to the people thereof.

Article VII

1. The ratification of the conventions of five States shall be sufficient for the establishment of this Constitution between the States so ratifying the same.

2. When five States shall have ratified this Constitution, in the manner before specified, the Congress under the Provisional Constitution, shall prescribe the time for holding the election of President and Vice President; and, for the meeting of the Electoral College; and, for counting the votes, and inaugurating the President. They shall, also, prescribe the time for holding the first election of members of Congress under this Constitution, and the time for assembling the same. Until the assembling of such Congress, the Congress under the Provisional Constitution shall continue to exercise the legislative powers granted them; not extending beyond the time limited by the Constitution of the Provisional Government.

SELECTION

A New President of a New Nation: Jefferson Davis's Inaugural Address, February 18, 1861

Nine days after his election as Provisional President of the Confederate States of America, Jefferson Davis delivered his Inaugural Address from the portico of the Alabama capitol in Montgomery. Davis had expressed some reservations regarding secession as a proper policy for the South in 1860–1861; his choice for the Presidency, an office he accepted without enthusiasm, was an indication of

the conservative nature of the Montgomery Convention. His Inaugural Address
demonstrated even further the conservatism of the new nation. He stressed the
continuity between the old United States and the new Confederate States.
Only the constituent parts had been changed, he noted, not the system of
government. He portrayed the movement as a popular one and, while he hoped
for peace, he declared a firm resolve to appeal to arms for the achievement and
preservation of Southern independence if necessary. Expressing the general
hope of the Southern nation-builders, he dedicated himself to the difficult tasks
that lay ahead. For general discussions of the organization of the Confederacy,
see the appropriate sections of E. Merton Coulter, The Confederate States of
America, 1861–1865 *(1950) and the shorter, but highly valuable, work by*
Clement Eaton, A History of the Southern Confederacy *(1954). See also*
Hudson Strode, Jefferson Davis *(1955–1964), volume 2,* Confederate President.
The Text of Davis's Inaugural Address is reprinted from James D. Richardson
(ed.), A Compilation of the Messages and Papers of the Confederacy *(Nash-*
ville, Tenn.: United States Publishing Company, 1906), 2 volumes, volume 1,
pages 32–36.

Gentlemen *of the Congress of the Confederate States of America,*
Friends, and Fellow-citizens: Called to the difficult and responsible
station of Chief Magistrate of the Provisional Government which you have
instituted, I approach the discharge of the duties assigned to me with
humble distrust of my abilities, but with a sustaining confidence in the
wisdom of those who are to guide and aid me in the administration of
public affairs, and an abiding faith in the virtue and patriotism of the
people. Looking forward to the speedy establishment of a permanent government to take the place of this, which by its greater moral and physical
power will be better able to combat with many difficulties that arise from
the conflicting interests of separate nations, I enter upon the duties of the
office to which I have been chosen with the hope that the beginning of our
career, as a Confederacy, may not be obstructed by hostile opposition to
our enjoyment of the separate existence and independence we have asserted, and which, with the blessing of Providence, we intend to maintain.

Our present political position has been achieved in a manner unprecedented in the history of nations. It illustrates the American idea that
governments rest on the consent of the governed, and that it is the right
of the people to alter or abolish them at will whenever they become destructive of the ends for which they were established. The declared purpose of the compact of the Union from which we have withdrawn was to
"establish justice, insure domestic tranquility, provide for the common
defense, promote the general welfare, and secure the blessings of liberty
to ourselves and our posterity;" and when, in the judgment of the sovereign States composing this Confederacy, it has been perverted from the
purposes for which it was ordained, and ceased to answer the ends for
which it was established, a peaceful appeal to the ballot box declared that,
so far as they are concerned, the Government created by that compact
should cease to exist. In this they merely asserted the right which the
Declaration of Independence of July 4, 1776, defined to be "inalienable."
Of the time and occasion of its exercise they as sovereigns were the final

judges, each for itself. The impartial and enlightened verdict of mankind will vindicate the rectitude of our conduct; and He who knows the hearts of men will judge of the sincerity with which we have labored to preserve the Government of our fathers in its spirit.

The right solemnly proclaimed at the birth of the United States, and which has been solemnly affirmed and reaffirmed in the Bills of Rights of the States subsequently admitted into the Union of 1789, undeniably recognizes in the people the power to resume the authority delegated for the purposes of government. Thus the sovereign States here represented have proceeded to form this Confederacy; and it is by abuse of language that their act has been denominated a revolution. They formed a new alliance, but within each State its government has remained; so that the rights of person and property have not been disturbed. The agent through which they communicated with foreign nations is changed, but this does not necessarily interrupt their international relations. Sustained by the consciousness that the transition from the former Union to the present Confederacy has not proceeded from a disregard on our part of just obligations, or any failure to perform every constitutional duty, moved by no interest or passion to invade the rights of others, anxious to cultivate peace and commerce with all nations, if we may not hope to avoid war, we may at least expect that posterity will acquit us of having needlessly engaged in it. Doubly justified by the absence of wrong on our part, and by wanton aggression on the part of others, there can be no cause to doubt that the courage and patriotism of the people of the Confederate States will be found equal to any measure of defense which their honor and security may require.

An agricultural people, whose chief interest is the export of commodities required in every manufacturing country, our true policy is peace, and the freest trade which our necessities will permit. It is alike our interest and that of all those to whom we would sell, and from whom we would buy, that there should be the fewest practicable restrictions upon the interchange of these commodities. There can, however, be but little rivalry between ours and any manufacturing or navigating community, such as the Northeastern States of the American Union. It must follow, therefore, that mutual interest will invite to good will and kind offices on both parts. If, however, passion or lust of dominion should cloud the judgment or inflame the ambition of those States, we must prepare to meet the emergency and maintain, by the final arbitrament of the sword, the position which we have assumed among the nations of the earth.

We have entered upon the career of independence, and it must be inflexibly pursued. Through many years of controversy with our late associates of the Northern States, we have vainly endeavored to secure tranquility and obtain respect for the rights to which we were entitled. As a necessity, not a choice, we have resorted to the remedy of separation, and henceforth our energies must be directed to the conduct of our own affairs, and the perpetuity of the Confederacy which we have formed. If a just perception of mutual interest shall permit us peaceably to pursue our separate political career, my most earnest desire will have been fulfilled. But if this be denied to us, and the integrity of our territory and jurisdiction be assailed, it will but remain for us with firm resolve to appeal to arms and invoke the blessing of Providence on a just cause.

As a consequence of our new condition and relations, and with a view to meet anticipated wants, it will be necessary to provide for the speedy and efficient organization of branches of the Executive department having special charge of foreign intercourse, finance, military affairs, and the postal service. For purposes of defense, the Confederate States may, under ordinary circumstances, rely mainly upon the militia; but it is deemed advisable, in the present condition of affairs, that there should be a well-instructed and disciplined army, more numerous than would usually be required on a peace establishment. I also suggest that, for the protection of our harbors and commerce on the high seas, a navy adapted to those objects will be required. But this, as well as other subjects appropriate to our necessities, have doubtless engaged the attention of Congress.

With a Constitution differing only from that of our fathers in so far as it is explanatory of their well-known intent, freed from sectional conflicts, which have interfered with the pursuit of the general welfare, it is not unreasonable to expect that States from which we have recently parted may seek to unite their fortunes to ours under the Government which we have instituted. For this your Constitution makes adequate provision; but beyond this, if I mistake not the judgment and will of the people, a reunion with the States from which we have separated is neither practicable nor desirable. To increase the power, develop the resources, and promote the happiness of the Confederacy, it is requisite that there should be so much of homogeneity that the welfare of every portion shall be the aim of the whole. When this does not exist, antagonisms are engendered which must and should result in separation.

Actuated solely by the desire to preserve our own rights, and promote our own welfare, the separation by the Confederate States has been marked by no aggression upon others, and followed by no domestic convulsion. Our industrial pursuits have received no check, the cultivation of our fields has progressed as heretofore, and, even should we be involved in war, there would be no considerable diminution in the production of the staples which have constituted our exports, and in which the commercial world has an interest scarcely less than our own. This common interest of the producer and consumer can only be interrupted by exterior force which would obstruct the transmission of our staples to foreign markets—a course of conduct which would be as unjust, as it would be detrimental, to manufacturing and commercial interests abroad.

Should reason guide the action of the Government from which we have separated, a policy so detrimental to the civilized world, the Northern States included, could not be dictated by even the strongest desire to inflict injury upon us; but, if the contrary should prove true, a terrible responsibility will rest upon it, and the suffering of millions will bear testimony to the folly and wickedness of our aggressors. In the meantime there will remain to us, besides the ordinary means before suggested, the well-known resources for retaliation upon the commerce of an enemy.

Experience in public stations, of subordinate grade to this which your kindness has conferred, has taught me that toil and care and disappointment are the price of official elevation. You will see many errors to forgive, many deficiencies to tolerate; but you shall not find in me either want of zeal or fidelity to the cause that is to me the highest in hope, and of most enduring affection. Your generosity has bestowed upon me an undeserved distinction, one which I neither sought nor desired. Upon the continuance of that sentiment, and upon your wisdom and patriotism, I rely to direct and support me in the performance of the duties required at my hands.

We have changed the constituent parts, but not the system of government. The Constitution framed by our fathers is that of these Confederate States. In their exposition of it, and in the judicial construction it has received, we have a light which reveals its true meaning.

Thus instructed as to the true meaning and just interpretation of that instrument, and ever remembering that all offices are but trusts held for the people, and that powers delegated are to be strictly construed, I will hope by due diligence in the performance of my duties, though I may disappoint your expectations, yet to retain, when retiring, something of the good will and confidence which welcome my entrance into office.

It is joyous in the midst of perilous times to look around upon a people united in heart, where one purpose of high resolve animates and actuates the whole; where the sacrifices to be made are not weighed in the balance against honor and right and liberty and equality. Obstacles may retard, but they cannot long prevent, the progress of a movement sanctified by its justice and sustained by a virtuous people. Reverently let us invoke the God of our fathers to guide and protect us in our efforts to perpetuate the principles which by his blessing they were able to vindicate, establish, and transmit to their posterity. With the continuance of his favor ever gratefully acknowledged, we may hopefully look forward to success, to peace, and to prosperity.

PART SEVEN

A People's Contest

*T*he guns of Charleston harbor shattered Southern hopes that their movement for independence would be a peaceful one. The long and anxious months of indecision and suspense were now over. Ever since the election of Lincoln, an air of uncertainty had hung over the land. The fate of two nations hung in the balance as men groped for a way out of their difficulties. Would the United States, under its new presidential leadership, allow the South to depart in peace and without challenge? Would the new Confederate States be able to pursue its independent course without the distraction of a Northern coercive policy? Both questions were conclusively and negatively answered in Charleston harbor during the early morning hours of April 12, 1861.

The firing on Fort Sumter aroused Northerners and Southerners to a high state of patriotic fervor. Both nations enjoyed a unity hardly matched again during the entire war. Excitement ran high. Abraham Lincoln, in his first official act after Sumter's surrender, called for volunteers to put down the "rebellion" and summoned Congress into a special session. Leaders representing all political stripes pledged their support to the government in the crisis. Men eagerly flocked to the colors, in greater numbers than could be received by the armed forces. Davis and the Southern leadership now girded themselves for the ordeal that faced their young nation. The most significant result of the firing on Fort Sumter and of Lincoln's call for volunteer troops was the secession of the states of the upper South. Unwilling to join in the campaign against their sister states, Virginia, North Carolina, Tennessee, and Arkansas responded indignantly and resentfully to Lincoln's call and immediately joined the Confederacy. Not sharing the nationalistic impulse of the lower South, these states became a part of an enlarged and strengthened Confederate States through their unwillingness to endorse Lincoln's "coercive" policy. Accompanying the excitement in both nations was a deep sense of relief. The tension of the secession winter had been broken; a definite and unambiguous policy had been invoked. War was now a reality.

The coming of war brought with it some disturbing questions. What had caused the conflict? What had become of the "American dream"? How did the American people (who not long before had been lauding their nation's glorious destiny) now suddenly find themselves battling for the very life of that nation? What was the true nature and character of the conflict now commencing? With the opening of hostilities Americans on both sides of the Mason-Dixon line began asking themselves these questions, desperately seeking answers to the most perplexing problem they had ever encountered. Nor was this soul-searching unique to the Civil War generation. Americans for over a century have been asking the same questions and seeking the same answers.

Each side found a unity in a common interpretation of the coming of conflict. To Northerners, the war was an unjustified rebellion against constitutional government. Without legitimate excuse, the nation had been sundered and national authority attacked. Responsibility for the disaster was attached to a small conspiratorial group of aggressive and diabolical Southern leaders. A plot to destroy the Union in order to perpetuate the Southern "slavocracy" was pieced together and traced deep in the nation's past. To Southerners, on the other hand, the war was a crusade for national self-determination, a justifiable protest against an overbearing and oppressive Northern majority. Swayed by an unscrupulous band of fanatical agitators, Northern leaders had ignored and even perverted constitutional guarantees. Through the election of Lincoln, the Northern populace had signaled its determination to undermine constitutional government even further, and to destroy the civilization of the South. Southerners had no alternative but to invoke the high principle of self-government and to resist Northern aggression with all the resources they could command.

In a sense, the two Presidents, Lincoln and Davis, were the first official historians of the coming of Civil War. Each sought explanations for the tragedy that now befell the American people. For each, the true character of the conflict transcended the events that gave it immediate cause. Each side was fighting for the right. To Davis as well as Lincoln, the war that followed Sumter's bombardment was "a people's contest."

Jefferson Davis on the Coming of the Civil War:
Message to the Confederate Congress, April 29, 1861

Two weeks after Lincoln issued his proclamation calling for troops, President Jefferson Davis addressed a special session of the Confederate Congress. Lincoln's proclamation was regarded as a declaration of war against the Confederacy. Little time was lost by the Southern President in summoning the lawmakers and in urging them to make all necessary preparations for the struggle that now faced the Southern people. Davis, however, also took occasion to review relations with the United States and to present "in a succinct statement" a discussion of the events that had finally resulted in the clash of arms. His message was the first official Southern statement of the causes of the Civil War. Although he borrowed from the arguments of the radicals in tracing the history of the conflict between the North and South, he emphasized the conservative character of the Confederate independence movement. States' rights and the right of secession were strongly acknowledged, and almost the entire justification for Southern action was placed on a constitutional argument. The North was held responsible not only for the long sectional conflict but also for the events that led immediately to the outbreak of hostilities.

The message is reprinted from James D. Richardson (ed.), A Compilation of the Messages and Papers of the Confederacy (Nashville, Tenn.: United States Publishing Company, 1906), 2 volumes, volume 1, pages 63–82. For an excellent discussion of the evolutionary development of the interpretations of the causes of the Civil War during the past century, including the statements made by both Davis and Lincoln early in the war, see Thomas J. Pressly, Americans Interpret Their Civil War (1954).

Montgomery, April 29, 1861

Gentlemen of the Congress: It is my pleasing duty to announce to you that the Constitution framed for the establishment of a permanent Government for the Confederate States has been ratified by conventions in each of those States to which it was referred. To inaugurate the Government in its full proportions and upon its own substantial basis of the popular will, it only remains that elections should be held for the designation of the officers to administer it. There is every reason to believe that at no distant day other States, identified in political principles and community of interests with those which you represent, will join this Confederacy, giving to its typical constellation increased splendor, to its Government of free, equal, and sovereign States a wider sphere of usefulness, and to the friends of constitutional liberty a greater security for its harmonious and perpetual existence. It was not, however, for the purpose of making this announcement that I have deemed it my duty to convoke you at an earlier day than that fixed by yourselves for your meeting. The declaration of war made

191

against this Confederacy by Abraham Lincoln, the President of the United States, in his proclamation issued on the 15th day of the present month, rendered it necessary, in my judgment, that you should convene at the earliest practicable moment to devise the measures necessary for the defense of the country. The occasion is indeed an extraordinary one. It justifies me in a brief review of the relations heretofore existing between us and the States which now unite in warfare against us and in a succinct statement of the events which have resulted in this warfare, to the end that mankind may pass intelligent and impartial judgment on its motives and objects. During the war waged against Great Britain by her colonies on this continent a common danger impelled them to a close alliance and to the formation of a Confederation, by the terms of which the colonies, styling themselves States, entered *"severally* into a firm league of friendship with each other for their common defense, the security of their liberties, and their mutual and general welfare, binding themselves to assist each other against all force offered to or attacks made upon them, or any of them, on account of religion, sovereignty, trade, or any other pretense whatever." In order to guard against any misconstruction of their compact, the several States made explicit declaration in a distinct article—that *"each* State *retains its* sovereignty, freedom, and independence, and every power, jurisdiction, and right which is not by this Confederation *expressly delegated* to the United States in Congress assembled."

Under this contract of alliance, the war of the Revolution was successfully waged, and resulted in the treaty of peace with Great Britain in 1783, by the terms of which the several States were *each by name* recognized to be independent. The Articles of Confederation contained a clause whereby all alterations were prohibited unless confirmed by the Legislatures of *every State* after being agreed to by the Congress; and in obedience to this provision, under the resolution of Congress of the 21st of February, 1787, the several States appointed delegates who attended a convention "for the *sole and express purpose* of revising the Articles of Confederation and reporting to Congress and the several Legislatures such alterations and provisions therein as shall, when agreed to in Congress *and confirmed by the States,* render the Federal Constitution adequate to the exigencies of Government and the preservation of the Union." It was by the delegates chosen by the *several States* under the resolution just quoted that the Constitution of the United States was framed in 1787 and submitted to the *several States* for ratification, as shown by the seventh article, which is in these words: "The ratification of the *conventions of nine States* shall be sufficient for the establishment of this Constitution *between the States* so ratifying the same." I have italicized certain words in the quotations just made for the purpose of attracting attention to the singular and marked caution with which the States endeavored in every possible form to exclude the idea that the separate and independent sovereignty of each State was merged into one common government and nation, and the earnest desire they evinced to impress on the Constitution its true character—that of a *compact between* independent States. The Constitution of 1787, having, however, omitted the clause already recited from the Articles of Confederation, which provided in explicit terms that each State *retained* its sovereignty and independence, some alarm was felt in the States, when invited to ratify the Constitution, lest this omission should be construed into an abandonment of their cherished principle, and they refused to be satisfied until amendments were added to the Constitution placing beyond any pretense of doubt the reservation by the States of all their sovereign rights and powers not expressly delegated to the United States by the Constitution.

Strange, indeed, must it appear to the impartial observer, but it is none the less true that all these carefully worded clauses proved unavailing to prevent the rise and growth in the Northern States of a political school which has persistently claimed that the government thus formed was not a compact *between* States, but was in effect a national government, set up *above* and *over* the States. An organization created by the States to secure the blessings of liberty and independence against *foreign* aggression, has been gradually perverted into a machine for their control in their *domestic* affairs. The *creature* has been exalted above its *creators;* the *principals* have been made subordinate to the *agent* appointed by themselves. The people of the Southern States, whose almost exclusive occupation was agriculture, early perceived a tendency in the Northern States to render the common government subservient to their own purposes by imposing burdens on commerce as a protection to their manufacturing and shipping interests. Long and angry controversies grew out of these attempts, often successful, to benefit one section of the country at the expense of the other. And the danger of disruption arising from this cause was enhanced by the fact that the Northern population was increasing, by immigration and other causes, in a greater ratio than the population of the South. By degrees, as the Northern States gained preponderance in the National Congress, self-interest taught their people to yield ready assent to any plausible advocacy of their right as a majority to govern the minority without control. They learned to listen with impatience to the suggestion of any constitutional impediment to the exercise of their will, and so utterly have the principles of the Constitution been corrupted in the Northern mind that, in the inaugural address delivered by President Lincoln in March last, he asserts as an axiom, which he plainly deems to be undeniable, that the theory of the Constitution requires that in all cases the majority shall govern; and in another memorable instance the same Chief Magistrate did not hesitate to liken the relations between a State and the United States to those which exist between a county and the State in which it is situated and by which it was created. This is the lamentable and fundamental error on which rests the policy that has culminated in his declaration of war against these Confederate States. In addition to the long-continued and deep-seated resentment felt by the Southern States at the persistent abuse of the powers they had delegated to the Congress, for the purpose of enriching the manufacturing and shipping classes of the North at the expense of the South, there has existed for nearly half a century another subject of discord, involving interests of such transcendent magnitude as at all times to create the apprehension in the minds of many devoted lovers of the Union that its permanence was impossible. When the several States delegated certain powers to the United States Congress, a large portion of the laboring population consisted of African slaves imported into the colonies by the mother country. In twelve out of the thirteen States negro slavery existed, and the right of property in slaves was protected by law. This property was recognized in the Constitution, and provision was made against its loss by the escape of the slave. The increase in the number of slaves by further importation from Africa was also secured by a clause forbidding Congress to prohibit the slave trade anterior to a certain date, and in no clause can there be found any delegation of power to the Congress authorizing it in any manner to legislate to the prejudice, detriment, or discouragement of the owners of that species of property, or excluding it from the protection of the Government.

The climate and soil of the Northern States soon proved unpropitious to the continuance of slave labor, whilst the converse was the case at the South. Under the unrestricted free intercourse between the two sections, the Northern States consulted their own interests by selling their slaves to the South and prohibiting slavery within their limits. The South were willing purchasers of a property suitable to their wants, and paid the price of the acquisition without harboring a suspicion that their quiet possession was to be disturbed by those who were inhibited not only by want of constitutional authority, but by good faith as vendors, from disquieting a title emanating from themselves. As soon, however, as the Northern States that prohibited African slavery within their limits had reached a number sufficient to give their representation a controlling voice in the Congress, a persistent and organized system of hostile measures against the rights of the owners of slaves in the Southern States was inaugurated and gradually extended. A continuous series of measures was devised and prosecuted for the purpose of rendering insecure the tenure of property in slaves. Fanatitical organizations, supplied with money by voluntary subscriptions, were assiduously engaged in exciting amongst the slaves a spirit of discontent and revolt; means were furnished for their escape from their owners, and agents secretly employed to entice them to abscond; the constitutional provision for their rendition to their owners was first evaded, then openly denounced as a violation of conscientious obligation and religious duty; men were taught that it was a merit to elude, disobey, and violently oppose the execution of the laws enacted to secure the performance of the promise contained in the constitutional compact; owners of slaves were mobbed and even murdered in open day solely for applying to a magistrate for the arrest of a fugitive slave; the dogmas of these voluntary organizations soon obtained control of the Legislatures of many of the Northern States, and laws were passed providing for the punishment, by ruinous fines and long-continued imprisonment in jails and penitentiaries, of citizens of the Southern States who should dare to ask aid of the officers of the law for the recovery of their property. Emboldened by success, the theater of agitation and aggression against the clearly expressed constitutional rights of the Southern States was transferred to the Congress; Senators and Representatives were sent to the common councils of the nation, whose chief title to this distinction consisted in the display of a spirit of ultra fanaticism, and whose business was not "to promote the general welfare or insure domestic tranquility," but to awaken the bitterest hatred against the citizens of sister States by violent denunciation of their institutions; the transaction of public affairs was impeded by repeated efforts to usurp powers not delegated by the Constitution, for the purpose of impairing the security of property in slaves, and reducing those States which held slaves to a condition of inferiority. Finally a great party was organized for the purpose of obtaining the administration of the Government, with the avowed object of using its power for the total exclusion of the slave States from all participation in the benefits of the public domain acquired by all the States in common, whether by conquest or purchase; of surrounding them entirely by States in which slavery should be prohibited; of thus rendering the property in slaves so insecure as to be comparatively worthless, and thereby annihilating in effect property worth thousands of millions of dollars. This party, thus organized, succeeded in the month of November last in the election of its candidate for the Presidency of the United States.

In the meantime, under the mild and genial climate of the Southern States and the increasing care and attention for the well-being and comfort of the laboring class, dictated alike by interest and humanity, the African slaves had augmented in number from about 600,000, at the date of the adoption of the constitutional compact, to upward of 4,000,000. In moral and social condition they had been elevated from brutal savages into docile, intelligent, and civilized agricultural laborers, and supplied not only with bodily comforts but with careful religious instruction. Under the supervision of a superior race their labor had been so directed as not only to allow a gradual and marked amelioration of their own condition, but to convert hundreds of thousand of square miles of the wilderness into cultivated lands covered with a prosperous people; towns and cities had sprung into existence, and had rapidly increased in wealth and population under the social system of the South; the white population of the Southern slaveholding States had augmented from about 1,250,000 at the date of the adoption of the Constitution to more than 8,500,000 in 1860; and the productions of the South in cotton, rice, sugar, and tobacco, for the full development and continuance of which the labor of African slaves was and is indispensable, had swollen to an amount which formed nearly three-fourths of the exports of the whole United States and had become absolutely necessary to the wants of civilized man. With interests of such overwhelming magnitude imperiled, the people of the Southern States were driven by the conduct of the North to the adoption of some course of action to avert the danger with which they were openly menaced. With this view the Legislatures of the several States invited the people to select delegates to conventions to be held for the purpose of determining for themselves what measures were best adapted to meet so alarming a crisis in their history. Here it may be proper to observe that from a period as early as 1798 there had existed in *all* of the States of the Union a party almost uninterruptedly in the majority based upon the creed that each State was, in the last resort, the sole judge as well of its wrongs as of the mode and measure of redress. Indeed, it is obvious that under the law of nations this principle is an axiom as applied to the relations of independent sovereign States, such as those which had united themselves under the constitutional compact. The Democratic party of the United States repeated, in its successful canvass in 1856, the declaration made in numerous previous political contests, that it would "faithfully abide by and uphold the principles laid down in the Kentucky and Virginia resolutions of 1798, and in the report of Mr. Madison to the Virginia Legislature in 1799; and that it adopts those principles as constituting one of the main foundations of its political creed." The principles thus emphatically announced embrace that to which I have already adverted—the right of each State to judge of and redress the wrongs of which it complains. These principles were maintained by overwhelming majorities of the people of all the States of the Union at different elections, especially in the elections of Mr. Jefferson in 1805, Mr. Madison in 1809, and Mr. Pierce in 1852. In the exercise of a right so ancient, so well-established, and so necessary for self-preservation, the people of the Confederate States, in their conventions, determined that the wrongs which they had suffered and the evils with which they were menaced required that they should revoke the delegation of powers to the Federal Government which they had ratified in their several conventions. They consequently passed ordinances resuming all their rights as sovereign and independent States and dissolved their connection with the other States of the Union.

Having done this, they proceeded to form a new compact amongst themselves by new articles of confederation, which have been also ratified by the conventions of the several States with an approach to unanimity far exceeding that of the conventions which adopted the Constitution of 1787. They have organized their new Government in all its departments; the functions of the executive, legislative, and judicial magistrates are performed in accordance with the will of the people, as displayed not merely in a cheerful acquiescence, but in the enthusiastic support of the Government thus established by themselves; and but for the interference of the Government of the United States in this legitimate exercise of the right of a people to self-government, peace, happiness, and prosperity would now smile on our land. That peace is ardently desired by this Government and people has been manifested in every possible form. Scarce had you assembled in February last when, prior even to the inauguration of the Chief Magistrate you had elected, you passed a resolution expressive of your desire for the appointment of commissioners to be sent to the Government of the United States "for the purpose of negotiating friendly relations between that Government and the Confederate States of America, and for the settlement of all questions of disagreement between the two Governments upon principles of right, justice, equity, and good faith." It was my pleasure as well as my duty to coöperate with you in this work of peace. Indeed, in my address to you on taking the oath of office, and before receiving from you the communication of this resolution, I had said "as a necessity, not a choice, we have resorted to the remedy of separation, and henceforth our energies must be directed to the conduct of our own affairs and the perpetuity of the Confederacy which we have formed. If a just perception of mutual interests shall permit us peaceably to pursue our separate political career, my most earnest desire will have been fulfilled." It was in furtherance of these accordant views of the Congress and the Executive that I made choice of three discreet, able, and distinguished citizens, who repaired to Washington. Aided by their cordial cooperation and that of the Secretary of State, every effort compatible with self-respect and the dignity of the Confederacy was exhausted before I allowed myself to yield to the conviction that the Government of the United States was determined to attempt the conquest of this people and that our cherished hopes of peace were unattainable.

On the arrival of our commissioners in Washington on the 5th of March they postponed, at the suggestion of a friendly intermediary, doing more than giving informal notice of their arrival. This was done with a view to afford time to the President, who had just been inaugurated, for the discharge of other pressing official duties in the organization of his Administration before engaging his attention in the object of their mission. It was not until the 12th of the month that they officially addressed the Secretary of State, informing him of the purpose of their arrival, and stating, in the language of their instructions, their wish "to make to the Government of the United States overtures for the opening of negotiations, assuring the Government of the United States that the President, Congress, and people of the Confederate States earnestly desire a peaceful solution of these great questions; that it is neither their interest nor their wish to make any demand which is not founded on strictest justice, nor do any act to injure their late confederates."

To this communication no formal reply was received until the 8th of April. During the interval the commissioners had consented to waive all questions of form. With the firm resolve to avoid war if possible, they went so far even as to hold during that long period unofficial intercourse through an intermediary, whose high position and character inspired the hope of success, and through whom constant assurances were received from the Government of the United States of peaceful intentions; of the determination to evacuate Fort Sumter; and further, that no measure changing the existing status prejudicially to the Confederate States, especially at Fort Pickens, was in contemplation, but that in the event of any change of intension on the subject, notice would be given to the commissioners. The crooked paths of diplomacy can scarcely furnish an example so wanting in courtesy, in candor, and directness as was the course of the United States Government toward our commissioners in Washington. . . .

Early in April the attention of the whole country, as well as that of our commissioners, was attracted to extraordinary preparations for an extensive military and naval expedition in New York and other Northern ports. These preparations commenced in secrecy, for an expedition whose destination was concealed, only became known when nearly completed, and on the 5th, 6th, and 7th of April transports and vessels of war with troops, munitions, and military supplies sailed from Northern ports bound southward. Alarmed by so extraordinary a demonstration, the commissioners requested the delivery of an answer to their official communication of the 12th of March, and thereupon received on the 8th of April a reply, dated on the 15th of the previous month, from which it appears that during the whole interval, whilst the commissioners were receiving assurances calculated to inspire hope of the success of their mission, the Secretary of State and the President of the United States had already determined to hold no intercourse with them whatever; to refuse even to listen to any proposals they had to make, and had profited by the delay created by their own assurances in order to prepare secretly the means for effective hostile operations. That these assurances were given has been virtually confessed by the Government of the United States by its sending a messenger to Charleston to give notice of its purpose to use force if opposed in its intention of supplying Fort Sumter. No more striking proof of the absence of good faith in the conduct of the Government of the United States toward this Confederacy can be required than is contained in the circumstances which accompanied this notice. According to the usual course of navigation the vessels composing the expedition designed for the relief of Fort Sumter might be expected to reach Charleston Harbor on the 9th of April. Yet, with our commissioners actually in Washington, detained under assurances that notice should be given of any military movement, the notice was not addressed to *them,* but a messenger was sent to Charleston to give the notice to the Governor of South Carolina, and the notice was so given at a late hour on the 8th of April, the eve of the very day on which the fleet might be expected to arrive.

That this maneuver failed in its purpose was not the fault of those who contrived it. A heavy tempest delayed the arrival of the expedition and gave time to the commander of our forces at Charleston to ask and receive the instructions of this Government. Even then, under all the provocation incident to the contemptuous refusal to listen to our commissioners, and the tortuous course of the Government of the United States, I was sincerely anxious to avoid the effusion of blood, and directed a proposal to be made to the commander of Fort Sumter, who had avowed himself to be nearly out of provisions, that we would abstain from directing our fire on Fort Sumter if he would promise not to open fire on our forces unless first attacked. This proposal was refused and the conclusion was reached that the design of the United States was to place the besieging force at Charleston between the simultaneous fire of the fleet and the fort. There remained, therefore, no alternative but to direct that the fort should at once be reduced. This order was executed by General Beauregard with the skill and success which were naturally to be expected from the well-known character of that gallant officer; and although the bombardment lasted but thirty-three hours our flag did not wave over its battered walls until after the appearance of the hostile fleet off Charleston. Fortunately, not a life was lost on our side, and we were gratified in being spared the necessity of a useless effusion of blood, by the prudent caution of the officers who commanded the fleet in abstaining from the evidently futile effort to enter the harbor for the relief of Major Anderson. . . .

Scarcely had the President of the United States received intelligence of the failure of the scheme which he had devised for the reënforcement of Fort Sumter, when he issued the declaration of war against this Confederacy which has prompted me to convoke you. In this extraordinary production that high functionary affects total ignorance of the existence of an independent Government, which, possessing the entire and enthusiastic devotion of its people, is exercising its functions without question over seven sovereign States, over more than 5,000,000 of people, and over a territory whose area exceeds half a million of square miles. He terms sovereign States "combinations too powerful to be suppressed by the ordinary course of judicial proceedings or by the powers vested in the marshals by law." He calls for an army of 75,000 men to act as a *posse comitatus* in aid of the process of the courts of justice in States where no courts exist whose mandates and decrees are not cheerfully obeyed and respected by a willing people. He avows that "the *first* service to be assigned to the forces called out" will be not to execute the process of courts, but to capture forts and strongholds situated within the admitted limits of this Confederacy and garrisoned by its troops; and declares that "this effort" is intended "to maintain the perpetuity of popular government."

He concludes by commanding "the persons composing the combinations aforesaid"—to wit, the 5,000,000 of inhabitants of these States—"to retire peaceably to their respective abodes within twenty days." Apparently contradictory as are the terms of this singular document, one point is unmistakably evident. The President of the United States called for an army of 75,000 men, whose *first* service was to be to capture our forts. It was a plain declaration of war which I was not at liberty to disregard because of my knowledge that under the Constitution of the United States the President was usurping a power granted exclusively to the Congress. He is the sole organ of communication between that country and foreign powers. The law of nations did not permit me to question the authority of the Executive of a foreign nation to declare war against this Confederacy. Although I might have refrained from taking active measures for our defense, if the States of the Union had all imitated the action of Virginia, North Carolina, Arkansas, Kentucky, Tennessee, and Missouri, by denouncing the call for troops as an unconstitutional usurpation of power to which they refused to respond, I was not at liberty to disregard the fact that many of the States seemed quite content to submit to the exercise of the power assumed by the President of the United States, and were actively engaged in levying troops to be used for the purpose indicated in the proclamation. Deprived of the aid of Congress at the moment, I was under the necessity of confining my action to a call on the States for volunteers for the common defense, in accordance with the authority you had confided to me before your adjournment. I deemed it proper, further, to issue proclamation inviting application from persons disposed to aid our defense in private armed vessels on the high seas, to the end that preparations might be made for the immediate issue of letters of marque and reprisal which you alone, under the Constitution, have power to grant. I entertain no doubt you will concur with me in the opinion that in the absence of a fleet of public vessels it will be eminently expedient to supply their place by private armed vessels, so happily styled by the publicists of the United States "the militia of the sea," and so often and justly relied on by them as an efficient and admirable instrument of defensive warfare. I earnestly recommend the immediate passage of a law authorizing me to accept the numerous proposals already received. I cannot close this review of the acts of the Government of the United States without referring to a proclamation issued by their President, under date of the 19th instant, in which, after declaring that an insurrection has broken out in this Confederacy against the Government of the United States, he announces a blockade of all the ports of these States, and threatens to punish as pirates all persons who shall molest any vessel of the United States under letters of marque issued by this Government. Notwithstanding the authenticity of this proclamation you will concur with me that it is hard to believe it could have emanated from a President of the United States. Its announcement of a mere paper blockade is so manifestly a violation of the law of nations that it would seem incredible that it could have been issued by authority; but conceding this to be the case so far as the Executive is concerned, it will be difficult to satisfy the people of these States that their late confederates will sanction its declarations— will determine to ignore the usages of civilized nations, and will inaugurate a war of extermination on both sides by treating as pirates open enemies acting under the authority of commissions issued by an organized government. If such proclamation was issued, it could only have been published under the sudden influence of passion, and we may rest assured mankind will be spared the horrors of the conflict it seems to invite. . . .

In conclusion, I congratulate you on the fact that in every portion of our country there has been exhibited the most patriotic devotion to our common cause. Transportation companies have freely tendered the use of their lines for troops and supplies. The presidents of the railroads of the Confederacy, in company with others who control lines of communication with States that we hope soon to greet as sisters, assembled in convention in this city, and not only reduced largely the rates heretofore demanded for mail service and conveyance of troops and munitions, but voluntarily proffered to receive their compensation, at these reduced rates, in the bonds of the Confederacy, for the purpose of leaving all the resources of the Government at its disposal for the common defense. Requisitions for troops have been met with such alacrity that the numbers tendering their services have in every instance greatly exceeded the demand. Men of the highest official and social position are serving as volunteers in the ranks. The gravity of age and the zeal of youth rival each other in the desire to be foremost for the public defense; and though at no other point than the one heretofore noticed have they been stimulated by the excitement incident to actual engagement and the hope of distinction for individual achievement, they have borne what for new troops is the most severe ordeal—patient toil and constant vigil, and all the exposure and discomfort of active service, with a resolution and fortitude such as to command approbation and justify the highest expectation of their conduct when active valor shall be required in place of steady endurance. A people thus united and resolved cannot shrink from any sacrifice which they may be called on to make, nor can there be a reasonable doubt of their final success, however long and severe may be the test of their determination to maintain their birthright of freedom and equality as a trust which it is their first duty to transmit undiminished to their posterity. A bounteous Providence cheers us with the promise of abundant crops. The fields of grain which will within a few weeks be ready for the sickle give assurance of the amplest supply of food for man; whilst the corn, cotton, and other staple productions of our soil afford abundant proof that up to this period the season has been propitious. We feel that our cause is just and holy; we protest solemnly in the face of mankind that we desire peace at any sacrifice save that of honor and independence; we seek no conquest, no aggrandizement, no concession of any kind from the States with which we were lately confederated; all we ask is to be let alone; that those who never held power over us shall not now attempt our subjugation by arms. This we will, this we must, resist to the direst extremity. The moment that this pretension is abandoned the sword will drop from our grasp, and we shall be ready to enter into treaties of amity and commerce that cannot but be mutually beneficial. So long as this pretension is maintained, with a firm reliance on that Divine Power which covers with its protection the just cause, we will continue to struggle for our inherent right to freedom, independence, and self-government.

SELECTION **23**

Abraham Lincoln on the Coming of the Civil War:
Message to Congress in Special Session, July 4, 1861

The Congress of the United States was summoned into special session by President Lincoln in his proclamation of April 15, 1861. The special session, he declared, would convene on July 4—a date undoubtedly selected for its symbolic importance. As was the case with President Davis, President Lincoln felt obliged, in his message opening the session, to review the events that had culminated in the commencement of hostilities, including the tortuous course that finally resulted in the decision to reinforce Fort Sumter. The burden of aggression, the responsibility for opening the war, was placed squarely on the South. Like Davis, Lincoln also reviewed the larger question of the nature and character of the conflict, as well as the question of its fundamental causes. The message was an official statement of the Northern interpretation. Unlike Davis, Lincoln placed the struggle in the larger context of "the whole family of man," arguing that the fate of democratic government in the world would depend on the ability of the United States to overpower its domestic foes. The struggle, Lincoln was confident, could be a short and decisive one, and he asked Congress to make adequate preparations to guarantee such a result.

The text of the message is reprinted from Roy P. Basler et al. (eds.), The Collected Works of Abraham Lincoln (New Brunswick: Rutgers, 1953), 9 volumes, volume 4, pages 421–441. For a discussion of Lincoln's message in the context of early wartime interpretations of the causes of the war, see the work by Pressly cited previously. Historians have differed in their interpretations of the steps leading to the bombardment of Fort Sumter. See Charles W. Ramsdell, "Lincoln and Fort Sumter," Journal of Southern History, volume 3, August, 1937, pages 259–288; Kenneth M. Stampp, "Lincoln and the Strategy of Defense in the Crisis of 1861," Journal of Southern History, volume 11, August, 1945, pages 297–323; James G. Randall, "Lincoln's Sumter Dilemma," in Lincoln: The Liberal Statesman (1947), pages 88–117; and Richard N. Current, Lincoln and the First Shot (1963).

Fellow-citizens of the Senate and House of Representatives:

Having been convened on an extraordinary occasion, as authorized by the Constitution, your attention is not called to any ordinary subject of legislation.

At the beginning of the present Presidential term, four months ago, the functions of the Federal Government were found to be generally suspended within the several States of South Carolina, Georgia, Alabama, Mississippi, Louisiana, and Florida, excepting only those of the Post Office Department.

Within these States, all the Forts, Arsenals, Dock-yards, Customhouses, and the like, including the movable and stationary property in, and about them, had been seized, and were held in open hostility to this Government, excepting only Forts Pickens, Taylor, and Jefferson, on, and near the Florida coast, and Fort Sumter, in Charleston harbor, South Carolina. The Forts thus seized had been put in improved condition; new ones had been built; and armed forces had been organized, and were organizing, all avowedly with the same hostile purpose.

The Forts remaining in the possession of the Federal government, in, and near, these States, were either besieged or menaced by warlike preparations; and especially Fort Sumter was nearly surrounded by well-protected hostile batteries, with guns equal in quality to the best of its own, and outnumbering the latter as perhaps ten to one. A disproportionate share, of the Federal muskets and rifles, had somehow found their way into these States, and had been seized, to be used against the government. Accumulations of the public revenue, lying within them had been seized for the same object. The Navy was scattered in distant seas; leaving but a very small part of it within the immediate reach of the government. Officers of the Federal Army and Navy, had resigned in great numbers; and, of those resigning, a large proportion had taken up arms against the government. Simultaneously, and in connection, with all this, the purpose to sever the Federal Union, was openly avowed. In accordance with this purpose, an ordinance had been adopted in each of these States, declaring the States, respectively, to be separated from the National Union. A formula for instituting a combined government of these states had been promulgated; and this illegal organization, in the character of confederate States was already invoking recognition, aid, and intervention, from Foreign Powers.

Finding this condition of things, and believing it to be an imperative duty upon the incoming Executive, to prevent, if possible, the consummation of such attempt to destroy the Federal Union, a choice of means to that end became indispensable. This choice was made; and was declared in the Inaugural address. The policy chosen looked to the exhaustion of all peaceful measures, before a resort to any stronger ones. It sought only to hold the public places and property, not already wrested from the Government, and to collect the revenue; relying for the rest, on time, discussion, and the ballot-box. It promised a continuance of the mails, at government expense, to the very people who were resisting the government; and it gave repeated pledges against any disturbance to any of the people, or any of their rights. Of all that which a president might constitutionally, and justifiably, do in such a case, everything was foreborne, without which, it was believed possible to keep the government on foot.

On the 5th of March, (the present incumbent's first full day in office) a letter of Major Anderson, commanding at Fort Sumter, written on the 28th of February, and received at the War Department on the 4th of March, was, by that Department, placed in his hands. This letter expressed the professional opinion of the writer, that re-inforcements could not be thrown into that Fort within the time for his relief, rendered necessary by the limited supply of provisions, and with a view of holding possession of the same, with a force of less than twenty thousand good, and well-disciplined men. This opinion was concurred in by all the officers

of his command; and their *memoranda* on the subject, were made enclosures of Major Anderson's letter. The whole was immediately laid
before Lieutenant General Scott, who at once concurred with Major Anderson in opinion. On reflection, however, he took full time, consulting with
other officers, both of the Army and the Navy; and, at the end of four
days, came reluctantly, but decidedly, to the same conclusion as before.
He also stated at the same time that no such sufficient force was then at
the control of the Government, or could be raised, and brought to the
ground, within the time when the provisions in the Fort would be exhausted. In a purely military point of view, this reduced the duty of the
administration, in the case, to the mere matter of getting the garrison
safely out of the Fort.

It was believed, however, that to so abandon that position, under the
circumstances, would be utterly ruinous; that the *necessity* under which
it was to be done, would not be fully understood—that, by many, it would
be construed as a part of a *voluntary* policy—that, at home, it would
discourage the friends of the Union, embolden its adversaries, and go far
to insure to the latter, a recognition abroad—that, in fact, it would be our
national destruction consummated. This could not be allowed. Starvation
was not yet upon the garrison; and ere it would be reached, *Fort Pickens*
might be reinforced. This last, would be a clear indication of *policy,* and
would better enable the country to accept the evacuation of Fort Sumter,
as a military *necessity*. An order was at once directed to be sent for the
landing of the troops from the Steamship Brooklyn, into Fort Pickens.
This order could not go by land, but must take the longer, and slower
route by sea. The first return news from the order was received just one
week before the fall of Fort Sumter. The news itself was, that the officer
commanding the Sabine, to which vessel the troops had been transferred
from the Brooklyn, acting upon some *quasi* armistice of the late administration, (and of the existence of which the present administration, up to
the time the order was despatched, had only too vague and uncertain
rumors, to fix attention) had refused to land the troops. To now re-inforce
Fort Pickens, before a crisis would be reached at Fort Sumter was impossible—rendered so by the near exhaustion of provisions in the latter-
named Fort. In precaution against such a conjuncture, the government
had, a few days before, commenced preparing an expedition, as well
adapted as might be, to relieve Fort Sumter, which expedition was intended to be ultimately used, or not, according to circumstances. The
strongest anticipated case, for using it, was now presented; and it was
resolved to send it forward. As had been intended, in this contingency, it
was also resolved to notify the Governor of South Carolina, that he might
expect an attempt would be made to provision the Fort; and that, if the
attempt should not be resisted, there would be no effort to throw in men,
arms, or ammunition, without further notice, or in case of an attack upon
the Fort. This notice was accordingly given; whereupon the Fort was attacked, and bombarded to its fall, without even awaiting the arrival of the
provisioning expedition.

It is thus seen that the assault upon, and reduction of, Fort Sumter,
was, in no sense, a matter of self defence on the part of the assailants.
They well knew that the garrison in the Fort could, by no possibility,
commit aggression upon them. They knew—they were expressly notified—

that the giving of bread to the few brave and hungry men of the garrison, was all which would on that occasion be attempted, unless themselves, by resisting so much, should provoke more. They knew that this Government desired to keep the garrison in the Fort, not to assail them, but merely to maintain visible possession, and thus to preserve the Union from actual, and immediate dissolution—trusting, as herein-before stated, to time, discussion, and the ballot-box, for final adjustment; and they assailed, and reduced the Fort, for precisely the reverse object—to drive out the visible authority of the Federal Union, and thus force it to immediate dissolution.

That this was their object, the Executive well understood; and having said to them in the inaugural address, "You can have no conflict without being yourselves the aggressors," he took pains, not only to keep this declaration good, but also to keep the case so free from the power of ingenious sophistry, as that the world should not be able to misunderstand it. By the affair at Fort Sumter, with its surrounding circumstances, that point was reached. Then, and thereby, the assailants of the Government, began the conflict of arms, without a gun in sight, or in expectancy, to return their fire, save only the few in the Fort, sent to that harbor, years before, for their own protection, and still ready to give that protection, in whatever was lawful. In this act, discarding all else, they have forced upon the country, the distinct issue: "Immediate dissolution, or blood."

And this issue embraces more than the fate of these United States. It presents to the whole family of man, the question, whether a constitutional republic, or a democracy—a government of the people, by the same people —can, or cannot, maintain its territorial integrity, against its own domestic foes. It presents the question, whether discontented individuals, too few in numbers to control administration, according to organic law, in any case, can always, upon the pretences made in this case, or on any other pretences, or arbitrarily, without any pretence, break up their Government, and thus practically put an end to free government upon the earth. It forces us to ask: "Is there, in all republics, this inherent, and fatal weakness?" "Must a government, of necessity, be too *strong* for the liberties of its own people, or too *weak* to maintain its own existence?"

So viewing the issue, no choice was left but to call out the war power of the Government; and so to resist force, employed for its destruction, by force, for its preservation.

The call was made; and the response of the country was most gratifying; surpassing, in unanimity and spirit, the most sanguine expectation. Yet none of the States commonly called Slave-states, except Delaware, gave a Regiment through regular State organization. A few regiments have been organized within some others of those states, by individual enterprise, and received into the government service. Of course the seceded States, so called, (and to which Texas had been joined about the time of the inauguration,) gave no troops to the cause of the Union. The border States, so called, were not uniform in their actions; some of them being almost *for* the Union, while in others—as Virginia, North Carolina, Tennessee, and Arkansas—the Union sentiment was nearly repressed, and silenced. The course taken in Virginia was the most remarkable—perhaps the most important. A convention, elected by the people of that State, to consider this very question of disrupting the Federal Union, was in session at the capital of Virginia when Fort Sumter fell. To this body the people had chosen a large majority of *professed* Union men. Almost immediately after the fall of Sumter, many members of that majority went over to the original disunion minority, and, with them, adopted an ordinance for withdrawing the State from the Union. Whether this change was wrought by their great approval of the assault upon Sumter, or their great resentment at the government's resistance to that assault, is not definitely known. Although they submitted the ordinance, for ratification, to a vote of the people, to be taken on a day then somewhat more than a month distant, the convention, and the Legislature, (which was also in session at the same time and place) with leading men of the State, not members of either, immediately commenced acting, as if the State were already out of the Union. They pushed military preparations vigorously forward all over the state. They seized the United States Armory at Harper's Ferry, and the Navyyard at Gosport, near Norfolk. They received—perhaps invited—into their state, large bodies of troops, with their warlike appointments, from the so-called seceded States. They formally entered into a treaty of temporary alliance, and co-operation with the so-called "Confederate States," and sent members to their Congress at Montgomery. And, finally, they permitted the insurrectionary government to be transferred to their capital at Richmond.

The people of Virginia have thus allowed this giant insurrection to make its nest within her borders; and this government has no choice left but to deal with it, *where* it finds it. And it has the less regret, as the loyal citizens have, in due form, claimed its protection. Those loyal citizens, this government is bound to recognize, and protect, as being Virginia.

In the border States, so called—in fact, the middle states—there are those who favor a policy which they call "armed neutrality"—that is, an arming of those states to prevent the Union forces passing one way, or the disunion, the other, over their soil. This would be disunion completed. Figuratively speaking, it would be the building of an impassable wall along the line of separation. And yet, not quite an impassable one; for, under the guise of neutrality, it would tie the hands of the Union men, and freely pass supplies from among them, to the insurrectionists, which it could not do as an open enemy. At a stroke, it would take all the trouble off the hands of secession, except only what proceeds from the external blockade. It would do for the disunionists that which, of all things, they most desire feed them well, and give them disunion without a struggle of their own. It recognizes no fidelity to the Constitution, no obligation to maintain the Union; and while very many who have favored it are, doubtless, loyal citizens, it is, nevertheless, treason in effect.

Recurring to the action of the government, it may be stated that, at first, a call was made for seventy-five thousand militia; and rapidly following this, a proclamation was issued for closing the ports of the insurrectionary districts by proceedings in the nature of Blockade. So far all was believed to be strictly legal. At this point the insurrectionists announced their purpose to enter upon the practice of privateering.

Other calls were made for volunteers, to serve three years, unless sooner discharged; and also for large additions to the regular Army and Navy. These measures, whether strictly legal or not, were ventured upon, under what appeared to be a popular demand, and a public necessity; trusting, then as now, that Congress would readily ratify them. It is believed that nothing has been done beyond the constitutional competency of Congress.

Soon after the first call for militia, it was considered a duty to authorize the Commanding General, in proper cases, according to his discretion, to suspend the privilege of the writ of habeas corpus; or, in other words, to arrest, and detain, without resort to the ordinary processes and forms of law, such individuals as he might deem dangerous to the public safety. This authority has purposely been exercised but very sparingly. Nevertheless, the legality and propriety of what has been done under it, are questioned; and the attention of the country has been called to the proposition that one who is sworn to "take care that the laws be faithfully executed," should not himself violate them. Of course some consideration was given to the questions of power, and propriety, before this matter was acted upon. The whole of the laws which were required to be faithfully executed, were being resisted, and failing of execution, in nearly one-third of the States. Must they be allowed to finally fail of execution, even had it been perfectly clear, that by the use of the means necessary to their execution, some single law, made in such extreme tenderness of the citizen's liberty, that practically, it relieves more of the guilty, than of the innocent, should, to a very limited extent, be violated? To state the question more directly, are all the laws, *but one,* to go unexecuted, and the government itself go to pieces, lest that one be violated? Even in such a case, would not the official oath be broken, if the government should be overthrown, when it was believed that disregarding the single law, would tend to preserve it? But it was not believed that this question was presented. It was not believed that any law was violated. The provision of the Constitution that "The privilege of the writ of habeas corpus, shall not be suspended unless when, in cases of rebellion or invasion, the public safety may require it," is equivalent to a provision—is a provision—that such privilege may be suspended when, in cases of rebellion, or invasion, the public safety *does* require it. It was decided that we have a case of rebellion, and that the public safety does require the qualified suspension of the privilege of the writ which was authorized to be made. Now it is insisted that Congress, and not the Executive, is vested with this power. But the Constitution itself, is silent as to which, or who, is to exercise the power; and as the provision was plainly made for a dangerous emergency, it cannot be believed the framers of the instrument intended, that in every case, the danger should run its course, until Congress could be called together; the very assembling of which might be prevented, as was intended in this case, by the rebellion.

No more extended argument is now offered; as an opinion, at some length, will probably be presented by the Attorney General. Whether there shall be any legislation upon the subject, and if any, what, is submitted entirely to the better judgment of Congress.

The forbearance of this government had been so extraordinary, and so long continued, as to lead some foreign nations to shape their action as if they supposed the early destruction of our national Union was probable. While this, on discovery, gave the Executive some concern, he is now happy to say that the sovereignty, and rights of the United States, are now everywhere practically respected by foreign powers; and a general sympathy with the country is manifested throughout the world. . . .

It is now recommended that you give the legal means for making this contest a short, and a decisive one; that you place at the control of the government, for the work, at least four hundred thousand men, and four hundred millions of dollars. That number of men is about one tenth of those of proper ages within the regions where, apparently, *all* are willing to engage; and the sum is less than a twentythird part of the money value owned by the men who seem ready to devote the whole. A debt of six hundred millions of dollars *now,* is a less sum per head, than was the debt of our revolution, when we came out of that struggle; and the money value in the country now, bears even a greater proportion to what it was *then,* than does the population. Surely each man has as strong a motive *now,* to *preserve* our liberties, as each had *then,* to *establish* them.

A right result, at this time, will be worth more to the world, than ten times the men, and ten times the money. The evidence reaching us from the country, leaves no doubt, that the material for the work is abundant; and that it needs only the hand of legislation to give it legal sanction, and the hand of the Executive to give it practical shape and efficiency. One of the greatest perplexities of the government, is to avoid receiving troops faster than it can provide for them. In a word, the people will save their government, if the government itself, will do its part, only indifferently well.

It might seem, at first thought, to be of little difference whether the present movement at the South be called "secession" or "rebellion." The movers, however, well understand the difference. At the beginning, they knew they could never raise their treason to any respectable magnitude, by any name which implies *violation* of law. They knew their people possessed as much of moral sense, as much of devotion to law and order, and as much pride in, and reverence for, the history, and government, of their common country, as any other civilized, and patriotic people. They knew they could make no advancement directly in the teeth of these strong and noble sentiments. Accordingly they commenced by an insidious debauching of the public mind. They invented an ingenious sophism, which, if conceded, was followed by perfectly logical steps, through all the incidents, to the complete destruction of the Union. The sophism itself is, that any state of the Union may, *consistently* with the national Constitution, and therefore *lawfully,* and *peacefully,* withdraw from the Union, without the consent of the Union, or of any other state. The little disguise that the supposed right is to be exercised only for just cause, themselves to be the sole judge of its justice, is too thin to merit any notice.

With rebellion thus sugar-coated, they have been drugging the public mind of their section for more than thirty years; and, until at length, they have brought many good men to a willingness to take up arms against the government the day *after* some assemblage of men have enacted the farcical pretence of taking their State out of the Union, who could have been brought to no such thing the day *before.*

This sophism derives much—perhaps the whole—of its currency, from the assumption, that there is some omnipotent, and sacred supremacy, pertaining to a *State*—to each State of our Federal Union. Our States have neither more, nor less power, than that reserved to them, in the Union, by the Constitution—no one of them ever having been a State *out* of the Union. The original ones passed into the Union even *before* they cast off their British colonial dependence; and the new ones each came into the Union directly from a condition of dependence, excepting Texas. And even Texas, in its temporary independence, was never designated a State. The new ones only took the designation of States, on coming into the Union, while that name was first adopted for the old ones, in, and by, the Declaration of Independence. Therein the "United Colonies" were declared to be "Free and Independent States"; but, even then, the object plainly was not to declare their independence of *one another,* or of the *Union;* but directly the contrary, as their mutual pledge, and their mutual action, before, at the time, and afterwards, abundantly show. The express plighting of faith, by each and all of the original thirteen, in the Articles of Confederation, two years later, that the Union shall be perpetual, is most conclusive. Having never been States, either in substance, or in name, *outside* of the Union, whence this magical omnipotence of "State rights," asserting a claim of power to lawfully destroy the Union itself? Much is said about the "sovereignty" of the States; but the word, even, is not in the national Constitution; nor, as is believed, in any of the State constitutions. What is a "sovereignty," in the political sense of the term? Would it be far wrong to define it "A political community, without a political superior"? Tested by this, no one of our States, except Texas, ever was a sovereignty. And even Texas gave up the character on coming into the Union; by which act, she acknowledged the Constitution of the United States, and the laws and treaties of the United States made in pursuance of the Constitution, to be, for her, the supreme law of the land. The States have their *status* IN the Union, and they have no other *legal status.* If they break from this, they can only do so against law, and by revolution. The Union, and not themselves separately, procured their independence, and their liberty. By conquest, or purchase, the Union gave each of them, whatever of independence, and liberty, it has. The Union is older than any of the States; and, in fact, it created them as States. Originally, some dependent colonies made the Union; and, in turn, the Union threw off their old dependence, for them, and made them States, such as they are. Not one of them ever had a State constitution, independent of the Union. Of course, it is not forgotten that all the new States framed their constitutions, before they entered the Union; nevertheless, dependent upon, and preparatory to, coming into the Union.

Unquestionably the States have the powers, and rights, reserved to them in, and by the National Constitution; but among these, surely, are not included all conceivable powers, however mischievous, or destructive; but, at most, such only, as were known in the world, at the time, as governmental powers; and certainly, a power to destroy the government itself, had never been known as a governmental—as a merely administrative power. This relative matter of National power, and State rights, as a principle, is no other than the principle of *generality,* and *locality.* Whatever concerns the whole, should be confided to the whole—to the general government; while, whatever concerns *only* the State, should be left exclusively, to the State. This is all there is of original principle about it.

Whether the National Constitution, in defining boundaries between the two, has applied the principle with exact accuracy, is not to be questioned. We are all bound by that defining, without question.

What is now combatted, is the position that secession is *consistent* with the Constitution—is *lawful,* and *peaceful.* It is not contended that there is any express law for it; and nothing should ever be implied as law, which leads to unjust, or absurd consequences. The nation purchased, with money, the countries out of which several of these States were formed. Is it just that they shall go off without leave, and without refunding? The nation paid very large sums, (in the aggregate, I believe, nearly a hundred millions) to relieve Florida of the aboriginal tribes. Is it just that she shall now be off without consent, or without making any return? The nation is now in debt for money applied to the benefit of these so-called seceding States, in common with the rest. Is it just, either that creditors shall go unpaid, or the remaining States pay the whole? A part of the present national debt was contracted to pay the old debts of Texas. Is it just that she shall leave, and pay no part of this herself?

Again, if one State may secede, so may another; and when all shall have seceded, none is left to pay the debts. Is this quite just to creditors? Did we notify them of this sage view of ours, when we borrowed their money? If we now recognize this doctrine, by allowing the seceders to go in peace, it is difficult to see what we can do, if others choose to go, or to extort terms upon which they will promise to remain.

The seceders insist that our Constitution admits of secession. They have assumed to make a National Constitution of their own, in which, of necessity, they have either *discarded*, or *retained*, the right of secession, as they insist, it exists in ours. If they have discarded it, they thereby admit that, on principle, it ought not to be in ours. If they have retained it, by their own construction of ours they show that to be consistent they must secede from one another, whenever they shall find it the easiest way of settling their debts, or effecting any other selfish, or unjust object. The principle itself is one of disintegration, and upon which no government can possibly endure.

If all the States, save one, should assert the power to *drive* that one out of the Union, it is presumed the whole class of seceder politicians would at once deny the power, and denounce the act as the greatest outrage upon State rights. But suppose that precisely the same act, instead of being called "driving the one out," should be called "the seceding of the others from that one," it would be exactly what the seceders claim to do; unless, indeed, they make the point, that the one, because it is a minority, may rightfully do, what the others, because they are a majority, may not rightfully do. These politicians are subtle, and profound, on the rights of minorities. They are not partial to that power which made the Constitution, and speaks from the preamble, calling itself "We, the People."

It may well be questioned whether there is, to-day, a majority of the legally qualified voters of any State, except perhaps South Carolina, in favor of disunion. There is much reason to believe that the Union men are the majority in many, if not in every other one, of the so-called seceded States. The contrary has not been demonstrated in any one of them. It is ventured to affirm this, even of Virginia and Tennessee; for the result of an election, held in military camps, where the bayonets are all on one side of the question voted upon, can scarcely be considered as demonstrating popular sentiment. At such an election, all that large class who are, at once, *for* the Union, and *against* coercion, would be coerced to vote against the Union.

It may be affirmed, without extravagance, that the free institutions we enjoy, have developed the powers, and improved the condition, of our whole people, beyond any example in the world. Of this we now have a striking, and an impressive illustration. So large an army as the government has now on foot, was never before known, without a soldier in it, but who had taken his place there, of his own free choice. But more than this: there are many single Regiments whose members, one and another, possess full practical knowledge of all the arts, sciences, professions, and whatever else, whether useful or elegant, is known in the world; and there is scarcely one, from which there could not be selected, a President, a Cabinet, a Congress, and perhaps a Court, abundantly competent to administer the government itself. Nor do I say this is not true, also, in the army of our late friends, now adversaries, in this contest; but if it is, so much better the reason why the government, which has conferred such benefits on both them and us, should not be broken up. Whoever, in any section, proposes to abandon such a government, would do well to consider, in deference to what principle it is, that he does it—what better he is likely to get in its stead—whether the substitute will give, or be intended to give, so much of good to the people. There are some foreshadowings on this subject. Our adversaries have adopted some Declarations of Independence; in which, unlike the good old one, penned by Jefferson, they omit the words "all men are created equal." Why? They have adopted a temporary national constitution, in the preamble of which, unlike our good old one, signed by Washington, they omit "We, the People," and substitute "We, the deputies of the sovereign and independent States." Why? Why this deliberate pressing out of view, the rights of men, and the authority of the people?

This is essentially a People's contest. On the side of the Union, it is a struggle for maintaining in the world, that form, and substance of government, whose leading object is, to elevate the condition of men—to lift artificial weights from all shoulders—to clear the paths of laudable pursuit for all—to afford all, an unfettered start, and a fair chance, in the race of life. Yielding to partial, and temporary departures, from necessity, this is the leading object of the government for whose existence we contend.

I am most happy to believe that the plain people understand, and appreciate this. It is worthy of note, that while in this, the government's hour of trial, large numbers of those in the Army and Navy, who have been favored with the offices, have resigned, and proved false to the hand which had pampered them, not one common soldier, or common sailor is known to have deserted his flag.

Great honor is due to those officers who remain true, despite the example of their treacherous associates; but the greatest honor, and most important fact of all, is the unanimous firmness of the common soldiers, and common sailors. To the last man, so far as known, they have successfully resisted the traitorous efforts of those, whose commands, but an hour before, they obeyed as absolute law. This is the patriotic instinct of the plain people. They understand, without an argument, that destroying the government, which was made by Washington, means no good to them.

Our popular government has often been called an experiment. Two points in it, our people have already settled—the successful *establishing*, and the successful *administering* of it. One still remains—its successful *maintenance* against a formidable [internal] attempt to overthrow it. It is now for them to demonstrate to the world, that those who can fairly carry an election, can also suppress a rebellion—that ballots are the rightful, and peaceful, successors of bullets; and that when ballots have fairly, and constitutionally, decided, there can be no successful appeal, back to bullets; that there can be no successful appeal, except to ballots themselves, at succeeding elections. Such will be a great lesson of peace; teaching men that what they cannot take by an election, neither can they take it by a war—teaching all, the folly of being the beginners of a war.

Lest there be some uneasiness in the minds of candid men, as to what is to be the course of the government, towards the Southern States, *after* the rebellion shall have been suppressed, the Executive deems it proper to say, it will be his purpose then, as ever, to be guided by the Constitution, and the laws; and that he probably will have no different understanding of the powers, and duties of the Federal government, relatively to the rights of the States, and the people, under the Constitution, than that expressed in the inaugural address.

He desires to preserve the government, that it may be administered for all, as it was administered by the men who made it. Loyal citizens everywhere, have the right to claim this of their government; and the government has no right to withhold, or neglect it. It is not perceived that, in giving it, there is any coercion, any conquest, or any subjugation, in any just sense of those terms.

The Constitution provides, and all the States have accepted the provision, that "The United States shall guarantee to every State in this Union a republican form of government." But, if a State may lawfully go out of the Union, having done so, it may also discard the republican form of government; so that to prevent its going out, is an indispensable *means*, to the *end*, of maintaining the guaranty mentioned; and when an end is lawful and obligatory, the indispensable means to it, are also lawful, and obligatory.

It was with the deepest regret that the Executive found the duty of employing the war-power, in defence of the government, forced upon him. He could but perform this duty, or surrender the existence of the government. No compromise, by public servants, could, in this case, be a cure; not that compromises are not often proper, but that no popular government can long survive a marked precedent, that those who carry an election, can only save the government from immediate destruction, by giving up the main point, upon which the people gave the election. The people themselves, and not their servants, can safely reverse their own deliberate decisions. As a private citizen, the Executive could not have consented that these institutions shall perish; much less could he, in betrayal of so vast, and so sacred a trust, as these free people had confided to him. He felt that he had no moral right to shrink; nor even to count the chances of his own life, in what might follow. In full view of his great responsibility, he has, so far, done what he has deemed his duty. You will now, according to your own judgment, perform yours. He sincerely hopes that your views, and your action, may so accord with his, as to assure all faithful citizens, who have been disturbed in their rights, of a certain, and speedy restoration to them, under the Constitution, and the laws.

And having thus chosen our course, without guile, and with pure purpose, let us renew our trust in God, and go forward without fear, and with manly hearts.

PART EIGHT

A Place among the Nations of the World

A significant aspect of the Confederacy's struggle for independence was its effort to secure recognition and assistance from abroad. Equally important was the determination of the United States to prevent such a development. The competition between the two nations on the diplomatic front seemed at times as important as their clash on the military front, and its outcome was sometimes just as uncertain. Both countries recognized the importance of the attitudes of foreign governments and peoples toward the Civil War.

The Confederacy had by far the more difficult task. To her new and inexperienced government fell the job of persuading foreign nations that the Southern people had built and indeed deserved an independent government. She had to demonstrate that her movement toward independence had been justified and, more important, that she could maintain this independence against the military challenge of the North. Her struggle could not be represented as a "civil war" but must be convincingly portrayed as a war between two independent powers. The first diplomatic efforts of the Confederacy were aimed at the United States, when commissioners sought in Washington early in 1861 to establish friendly relations with the United States. Their failure was the South's first diplomatic setback and made more difficult the establishment of relations with other foreign countries.

Diplomatic recognition was the paramount object of Southern diplomats, but it was only one of the Confederacy's goals; military assistance and financial support remained additional and important aims of Southern representatives abroad. In seeking to realize these goals, the Confederacy enjoyed certain advantages. The emphasis on constitutional arguments for secession, and the ennobling appeal to the high end of self-government and independence, enhanced the Confederate cause in foreign capitals. It was, William H. Russell of the London Times pointed out, a conflict between independence and empire. The fact that the South was also defending slavery was at first of little importance in the diplomatic struggle, since Lincoln himself had refused to place Northern war aims on an antislavery basis. *The conservative character of the independence movement satisfied Europeans that this was no radical revolution. The obvious economic advantages of an independent South—a low tariff policy and a direct trade between the Southern ports and Europe, for example—appealed to certain European classes. Finally, there was the South's trump card. Withhold cotton, said South Carolina's Senator Hammond in 1858, and all Europe will topple headlong. The Confederacy's control of the cotton supply would surely bring Europe into the fray on the side of Southern independence. Or so Southerners confidently expected.*

There was a dimmer side to the Confederacy's diplomatic efforts. Southern diplomacy had, of necessity, to be aggressive in character; Southern diplomats had to be persuasive. Recognition by the world's powers of a new member in the family of nations was a difficult goal under the best of circumstances. Unfortunately, the calibre of Southern diplomatic representatives was often insufficiently high to achieve this task. With a dearth of experienced diplomats, Davis had to appoint individuals who, in many cases, were ill-suited to the work they sought to accomplish. Access to foreign capitals was difficult. There were no easy diplomatic channels already in existence which could be utilized. The Union naval blockade of the Southern coastline compounded the difficulty of communications. In the last analysis, Southerners expected too much of cotton, and the failure of "King Cotton" was one of the greatest blows to Confederate diplomacy.

While Southern efforts to secure foreign recognition faced formidable and even insuperable difficulties, Northern diplomacy enjoyed certain built-in advantages. The United States relied on a long tradition of cordial diplomatic relations with other nations; Northern diplomats had merely to seek the preservation of this status quo. *Control of the sea insured easy communications with foreign governments. In marked contrast to his Southern counterpart, Lincoln could and did rely on men of high calibre and ability (although William H. Seward, it is true, aroused no little suspicion among European leaders). Charles Francis Adams, Lincoln's choice for Minister to Great Britain, was clearly one of the best appointments the President made. The task of these emissaries was a negative one—to keep Europe from intervening in the conflict and so assisting the Southern cause. The Northern argument that the war was in fact nothing more than a rebellion or insurrection (although belied by Lincoln's own proclamation of the blockade) proved to be an increasingly persuasive one. As soon as the slavery question was introduced as a war aim in the fall of 1862, the force of world humanitarian opinion was brought to the support of the Union. The economic wealth and military potential of the United States instilled a note of caution in the reactions of foreign governments to the warring groups.*

Even so, the South came perilously close to achieving its diplomatic goals. Northern military reverses in the East during the first two years of the war provided telling support to the Southern insistence that independence could be maintained. With the turning of the military tide and the introduction of the slavery question this Southern advantage was lost. By 1863, victory on the diplomatic front had been won by the United States.

Robert Toombs Instructs the First Confederate Commissioners Abroad, March 16, 1861

Six weeks after the organization of the Confederate States, but before the opening of hostilities at Fort Sumter, Robert Toombs (1810–1885), the Georgian who served as the South's first Secretary of State, issued instructions to the first Confederate commissioners assigned to Europe. Theirs was the task of justifying the Southern withdrawal from the Union and of persuading Great Britain, France, Russia, and Belgium that the Confederacy should be admitted "into the family of independent nations." Toombs emphasized the several reasons why he was confident the Confederacy would maintain its independence, not overlooking a veiled threat of what might befall the British realm if the Southern cotton supply should suddenly fail. However, the delegation of commissioners was not noted for its diplomatic experience and prowess. William L. Yancey had been the leader of the fire-eaters, outspoken in his advocacy of a revolutionary break with the United States; Pierre A. Rost had been a Louisiana judge; and A. Dudley Mann, although he had had some minor diplomatic experience, proved temperamentally ill-suited to the task. In spite of the high hopes expressed by Toombs, the trio's efforts failed.

The best and most complete discussion of Confederate diplomacy is in Frank L. Owsley's King Cotton Diplomacy: Foreign Relations of the Confederate States of America *(rev., Harriet C. Owsley, 2d ed., 1959). The text of the Toombs passage is reprinted from* Official Records of the Union and Confederate Navies in the War of the Rebellion *(Washington: Government Printing Office, 1922), series 2, volume 3, pages 191–195.*

Department of State,
Montgomery, March 16, 1861.

Gentlemen: You have been appointed by the President, by and with the advice and consent of Congress, special commissioners to Europe. Herewith you will receive your commissions as such to Great Britain, France, Russia, and Belgium, together with the usual letters of credence and introduction, accrediting and empowering you to represent the Confederate States near the Governments of those countries.

In view of the importance of the mission with which you are charged, it is desirable that you should proceed to London with all dispatch consistent with your convenience and enter upon the discharge of your duties.

As shortly after your arrival at that city as you may deem judicious, you will seek an interview with Her Britannic Majesty's principal secretary for foreign affairs and communicate to him the object which you are deputed to accomplish.

You will inform him that the several Commonwealths composing the Confederate States of America have, by act of their people in convention assembled, severed their connection with the United States, have re-assumed the powers which they delegated to the Federal Government for certain specified purposes under the compact known as the Constitution of the United States, and have formed an independent government, perfect in all its branches, and endowed with every attribute of sovereignty and power necessary to entitle them to assume a place among the nations of the world.

Although it will not be necessary to enter into a detailed statement of the reasons which impelled the people of the Confederate States to dissolve their union with the United States, it may be well to allude to some of the more prominent of the causes which produced that result in order to show that the step was not taken hastily or passionately, but after long, patient, and mature deliberation, when the people became convinced that their honor, social and material welfare demanded separation as the best means by which those vital interests could be preserved.

You can point with force to the efforts which have been persistently made by the manufacturing States of the North to compel the agricultural interests of the South, out of the proceeds of their industry, to pay bounties to Northern manufacturers in the shape of high-protective duties on foreign imports. Since the year 1828, whenever they had the power, the manufacturing Northern States, disregarding the obligations of our compact, in violation of the principles of justice and fair dealing, and in contempt of all remonstrance and entreaty, have carried this policy to great extremes, to the serious detriment of the industry and enterprise of the South.

This policy, the injustice of which is strikingly illustrated by the high-protective tariff just adopted by the Government at Washington, furnishes a strong additional vindication of the wisdom of action of the Confederate States, especially in the estimation of those countries whose commercial interests, like those of Great Britain, are diametrically opposed to protective tariffs.

When, however, in addition to this system, by which millions were annually extorted from our people to foster Northern monopolies, the attempt was made to overthrow the constitutional barriers by which our property, our social system, and our right to control our own institutions were protected, separation from associates who recognized no law but self-interests and the power of numerical superiority became a necessity dictated by the instincts of self-preservation.

You will not fail to explain that in withdrawing from the United States the Confederate States have not violated any obligation of allegiance. They have merely exercised the sovereignty which they have possessed since their separation from Great Britain, and jealously guarded, by revoking the authority which, for defined purposes and within defined limits, they had voluntarily delegated to the General Government, and by reassuming themselves the exercise of the authority so delegated.

In consummating this act of separation, no public or private interest has suffered the least shock or detriment. No right has been impaired, no obligation has been forfeited. Everywhere in the Confederate States order and respect for individual and collective rights have been scrupulously observed.

The Confederate States, therefore, present themselves for admission into the family of independent nations and ask for that acknowledgment and friendly recognition which are due to every people capable of self-government and possessed of the power to maintain their independence.

The Confederate States have a well-organized Government, instituted by the free will of their citizens in the active exercise of all the functions of sovereignty, and are capable of defending themselves.

The Constitution which their Congress have just unanimously adopted (a copy of which, duly authenticated by this department, you will hand to her Britannic Majesty's secretary of foreign affairs) is the best proof which you can afford of the wisdom, moderation, and justice which have guided their counsels.

One of the Confederate States (Alabama) has already, by an almost unanimous vote of her convention, ratified that instrument, and, doubtless, long before you reach your destination all the other States of the Confederacy will have accepted it with equal unanimity as their fundamental law. It is the confident expectation of the President and people of the Confederate States that the enlightened Government of Great Britain will speedily acknowledge our independence and welcome us among the nations of the world.

The recent course which the British Government pursued in relation to the recognition of the right of the Italian people to change their form of government and choose their own rulers encourages this Government to hope that they will pursue a similar policy in regard to the Confederate States. Reasons no less grave and valid than those which actuated the people of Sicily and Naples to cast off a government not of their choice, and detrimental to their interests, have impelled the people of the Confederate States to dissolve the compact with the United States, which, diverted from the just and beneficent purposes of its founders, had become dangerous to their peace, prosperity, and interest. Representations may, however, be made to the British Government by the Government at Washington that our existence as an independent country will be of but temporary duration, and that we can be induced by certain concessions to reenter the Union from which we recently severed our connection.

If an impression of this kind has been or shall be made upon the British ministry, you will leave no exertions unemployed for its definitive removal. I need not assure that neither the Government nor the citizens of the Confederate States of America regard such an occurrence as within the range of possibility. Our experience of the past, our hopes of the future, unite us cordially in a resolute purpose not again to identify our political fortunes with the Northern States. If we were not secure in our rights and property under such an instrument as the Constitution of the United States, we see no reasonable prospect of securing them by additional guaranties. You will, therefore, steadily maintain in your intercourse with foreign functionaries and otherwise that in every contingency the Confederate States are resolute in their purpose to preserve and perpetuate their national independence. The Confederate States assume this position in the firm conviction that thus alone can they secure their future happiness and tranquility, and that they have the moral and physical strength to hold and cause their position to be respected. Against the only power which is at all likely to question our independence and disturb our peace—the United States— we possess abundant means for successful defense. In the first place, we are in a condition now to bring into the field 100,000 well-armed troops, and should they be required this number could be increased almost to the extent of our arms-bearing population. Secondly, should the United States, actuated by lust of dominion, numerical superiority, or the fancied possession of a right to compel our allegiance to them, determine to invade our soil or otherwise assail us, they would have to contend not only against the 5,000,000 people of the Confederate States but against the 8,000,000 also who inhabit the eight other States allied to us by community of institutions and interest and by geographical position, and who, although they have not as yet resolved to sever their connection with the United States, would do so immediately and join us in arms the moment the first gun was fired against us by order of the Government of the United States. The resolutions of the popular conventions of those States amply attest the accuracy of this calculation. Thirdly, you are aware that in most, if not all, of the Northern States large and influential portions of the population have manifested the most determined opposition to any attempt to force us to reunite ourselves to our late confederates.

Fourthly, you will remember that the Government of the United States is at this time wholly destitute of the power and the means to commence an aggressive war. The legislative branch of the Government has refused, by omitting to make the necessary provisions for that purpose, to arm the Executive with any authority to make war. It is needless also to point out in what condition the United States would be placed were they to be entirely cut off from our custom for their manufactures, and our two hundred and fifty millions of produce for their commerce and exchanges.

This combination of powerful inducements to preserve peace on the part of the United States, together with the large material strength and resources which we possess, render it apparent to every observer that we have no unusual reasons to fear war.

As soon as you shall be received officially by Great Britain you will propose to negotiate a treaty of friendship, commerce, and navigation, and you are accordingly furnished herewith with full powers for that purpose. The principal aim of the Confederate States in their policy with foreign Governments is peace and commerce. It will be their constant care to employ every means consistent with honor to maintain the one and extend the other. In their traffic with foreign countries they intend to act upon that wise maxim of political economy, "Buy where you can buy cheapest and sell where you can sell dearest." Import duties for mere revenue purposes, so moderate as to closely approximate free trade, will render their market peculiarly accessible to the manufactories of Europe, while their liberal navigation system will present valuable attractions to countries largely engaged in that enterprising pursuit.

It must be borne in mind that nearly one-half of all the Atlantic coast and the whole of the Mexican Gulf coast, lately within the boundaries of the United States, is at present within the boundaries of the Confederate States.

The Confederate States produce nearly nineteen-twentieths of all the cotton grown in the States which recently constituted the United States. There is no extravagance in the assertion that the gross amount of the annual yield of the manufactories of Great Britain from the cotton of the Confederate States reaches $600,000,000. The British ministry will comprehend fully the condition to which the British realm would be reduced if the supply of our staple should suddenly fail or even be considerably diminished. A delicate allusion to the probability of such an occurrence might not be unkindly received by the minister of foreign affairs, an occurrence, I will add, that is inevitable if this country shall be involved in protracted hostilities with the North. The President feels no hesitation in authorizing you to enter into such stipulations as in your judgment will be most advantageous to this country, subject, of course, to his approval and that of the coordinate branch of the treaty-making power.

You are further to express to the British minister the willingness of this Government to assume the obligations of the treaties concluded between the United States and Great Britain and now in force. The only exception is in reference to the clause of the treaty of Washington, known as the Ashburton treaty, which obliges the United States to maintain a naval force on the coast of Africa for the suppression of the African slave trade. It is not in our power to comply with this obligation. We have prohibited the African slave trade, and intend in good faith to prevent it in our country. But we are not prepared at this time to aid the rest of the world in promoting that object.

When the object of your mission to London is accomplished you will proceed to Paris, and thence to Brussels, St. Petersburg, and such other places as the President may hereafter direct. The arguments which you will use with Great Britain to induce her to establish relations with the Confederate States may be employed with France and the other countries to which you are accredited. With each of these countries you will propose to negotiate treaties of friendship, commerce, and navigation similar to that which you will propose to Great Britain, subject to the same reservations as to ratifications here.

You will correspond, as frequently as occasion may require, with this Department, transmitting your dispatches by such conveyances as you may deem the most safe and expeditious.

I remain, gentlemen, very respectfully, yours,

R. TOOMBS.

WILLIAM L. YANCEY, PIERRE A. ROST, A. DUDLEY MANN, Esquires.

SELECTION **25**

William H. Seward Defines the Union and the War: Letter to William L. Dayton, June 17, 1861

Northern diplomatic efforts were directed by William H. Seward, Lincoln's
choice for Secretary of State. Seward's task was not only to win support for
the Union cause among foreign, primarily European, nations but also to prevent
the Confederacy from achieving its goal of recognition. To assist him in these
tasks, he had the benefit of able and experienced individuals. Charles Francis
Adams was sent to represent the United States in London, and William L.
Dayton, of New Jersey and the Republican party's first Vice-Presidential
candidate, became Minister to France. From the beginning, France leaned
toward the Confederacy. While its leaders urged recognition and intervention,
they were reluctant to make such a move until England had done so first. On
May 13, 1861, Great Britain recognized Southern belligerency with a declara-
tion of neutrality. Issued in response to Lincoln's blockade proclamation, the
declaration was soon copied by France, Spain, Netherlands and Brazil—a blow
to the North and a gesture toward the Confederate cause. Seward countered
with a denial that war existed between the North and the South; the clash of
arms was merely an insurrection or insurgency. Diplomatic relations between
the United States and foreign nations, he argued, would remain unchanged by
the Union's attempts to suppress the insurrection. For diplomatic purposes, the
Union was unbroken—"the United States are one whole undivided nation,
especially so far as foreign nations are concerned." Donaldson Jordan and
Edwin J. Pratt, Europe and the American Civil War *(1931), describe European*
reactions generally to the Civil War, while Ephraim D. Adams's Great Britain
and the American Civil War (1925) two volumes, is best on Anglo-American
relations. A good analysis of the problems facing Northern diplomats is in
Norman A. Graebner, "Northern Diplomacy and European Neutrality," David
Donald (ed.), Why the North Won the Civil War *(1960), pages 49–75.*
Seward's letter is reprinted from George E. Baker (ed.), The Works *of William*
H. Seward (New York: Redfield, 1853–1884 [volume 5, Boston: Houghton
Mifflin]), volume 5, pages 268–276.

June 17, 1861.—Every instruction which this government has given
to its representatives abroad, since the recent change of administration took place, has expressed our profound anxiety lest the disloyal
citizens who are engaged in an attempt to overthrow the Union should obtain aid and assistance from foreign nations, either in the form of a recognition of their pretended sovereignty, or in some other and more qualified or
guarded manner. Every instruction has expressed our full belief that,
without such aid or assistance, the insurrection would speedily come to an
end, while any advantage that it could derive from such aid or assistance
could serve no other purpose than to protract the existing struggle and

aggravate the evils it is inflicting on our own country and on foreign and friendly nations. Every instruction bears evidence of an earnest solicitude to avoid even an appearance of menace or of want of comity towards foreign powers; but at the same time it has emphatically announced, as is now seen to have been necessary, our purpose not to allow any one of them to expect to remain in friendship with us if it should, with whatever motive, practically render such aid or assistance to the insurgents. We have intended not to leave it doubtful that a concession of sovereignty to the insurgents, though it should be indirect or unofficial, or though it should be qualified so as to concede only belligerent or other partial rights, would be regarded as inconsistent with the relations due to us by friendly nations. Nor has it been left at all uncertain that we shall, in every event, insist that these United States must be considered and dealt with now, as heretofore, by such nations as exclusively sovereign for all purposes whatsoever within the territories over which the Constitution has been extended. On the other hand, we have not, at any time, been unmindful of the peculiar circumstances which might excite apprehensions on the part of commercial nations for the safety of their subjects and their property in the conflicts which might occur upon sea as well as on land between the forces of the United States and those of the insurgents.

The United States have never disclaimed the employment of letters of marque as a means of maritime war. The insurgents early announced their intention to commission privateers. We knew that friendly nations would be anxious for guarantees of safety from injury by that form of depredation upon the national commerce. We knew also that such nations would desire to be informed whether their flags should be regarded as protecting goods, not contraband of war, of disloyal citizens, found under them, and whether the goods, not contraband, of subjects of such nations would be safe from confiscation when found in vessels of disloyal citizens of the United States. This administration, free from some of the complications of those which had preceded it, promptly took up the negotiations relating to the declaration of the Congress of Paris, just at the point where they had been suspended by President Buchanan. We found it just and humane in itself so far as it goes, and that it had only failed to be accepted by the United States because foreign nations had refused to accept an additional principle proposed by this government, yet more just and humane than any which it does contain, namely, that the property of private citizens, not contraband, should be exempted from confiscation in maritime war. While still willing and desirous to have that further principle incorporated in the law of nations, we nevertheless instructed you, and all our representatives in foreign countries, to waive it, if necessary, and to stipulate, subject to the concurrence of the Senate of the United States, our adhesion to the declaration of the Congress of Paris as a whole and unmodified. This was done so early as the 25th day of April last, long before the date of the instructions which Mr. Mercier proposed to submit to us. We have ever since that time been waiting for the responses of foreign powers to this high and liberal demonstration on our part. We have, however, received no decisive answers on the subject from those powers.

It was under these circumstances that on the fifteenth day of June instant, the minister from France and the minister from Great Britain, having previously requested an interview, were received by me. Each of them announced that he was charged by his government to read a despatch to me and to give me a copy if I should desire it. I answered that, owing to the peculiar circumstances of the times, I could not consent to an official reading or delivery of these papers without first knowing their characters and objects. They confidentially and with entire frankness put the despatches into my hands for an informal preliminary examination. Having thus become possessed of their characters, I replied to those ministers that I could not allow them to be officially communicated to this government. They will doubtless mention this answer to their respective states. I give you now the reasons of this government for pursuing this course in regard to the despatch from France, that you may communicate them to the French government, if you shall find it necessary or expedient. Some time ago we learned through our legation at St. Petersburg that an understanding had been effected between the governments of Great Britain and France that they should take one and the same course on the subject of the political disturbances in this country, including the possible recognition of the insurgents. At a later period this understanding was distinctly avowed by Mr. Thouvenel to Mr. Sanford, who had been informally introduced by me to the French Minister for Foreign Affairs, and by Lord John Russell to Mr. Dallas, our late minister in London. The avowal in each case preceded the arrival of our newly appointed ministers in Europe, with their instructions for the discharge of their respective missions.

On receiving their avowals I immediately instructed yourself and Mr. Adams "that although we might have expected a different course on the part of these two great powers, yet, as the fact that an understanding existed between them did not certainly imply an unfriendly spirit, we should not complain of it, but that it must be understood by the French and British governments that we shall deal hereafter, as heretofore, in this case, as in all others, with each power separately, and that the agreement for concerted action between them would not at all influence the course we should pursue." The concert thus avowed has been carried out. The ministers came to me together; the instructions they proposed to me differ in form, but are counterparts in effect.

Adhering to our previous decision, which before this time has doubtless been made known to the government of France, we do not make this concert, under the circumstances, a reason for declining to hear the instruction with which Mr. Mercier is charged. That paper does not expressly deny the sovereignty of the United States of America, but it does assume, inconsistently with that sovereignty, that the United States are not altogether and for all purposes one sovereign power, but that this nation consists of two parties, of which this government is one. France purposes to take cognizance of both parties as belligerents, and for some purposes to hold communication with each. The instruction would advise us indeed that we must not be surprised if France shall address herself to a government which she says is to be installed at Montgomery, for certain explanations. This intimation is conclusive in determining this government not to allow the instruction to be read to it.

The United States, rightly jealous, as we think, of their sovereignty, cannot suffer themselves to debate any abridgment of that sovereignty with France or with any other nation. Much less can it consent that France shall announce to it a conclusion of her own against that sovereignty, which conclusion France has adopted without any previous conference with the United States on the subject. This government insists that the

United States are one whole undivided nation, especially so far as foreign nations are concerned, and that France is, by the law of nations and by treaties, not a neutral power between two imaginary parties here, but a friend of the United States.

In the spirit of this understanding of the case, we are not only not wishing to seek or to give offence to France, but, on the contrary, we desire to preserve peace and friendship with that great power, as with all other nations. We do not feel at liberty to think, and do not think, that France intended any want of consideration towards the United States in directing that the instruction in question should be read to us. Outside of that paper we have abundant evidence of the good feeling and good wishes of the Emperor, and even his anxious solicitude for the same consummation which is the supreme object of our own desires and labors, namely, the preservation of the American Union in its full and absolute integrity.

Doubtless the proceeding has been the result of inadvertence. We feel ourselves at liberty to think that it would not have occurred if we had been so fortunate as to have been heard through you in the consultations of the French government. We think we can easily see how the inadvertence has occurred. France seems to have mistaken a mere casual and ephemeral insurrection here, such as is incidental in the experience of all nations, because all nations are merely human societies, such as have sometimes happened in the history of France herself, for a war which has flagrantly separated this nation into two coëxisting political powers which are contending in arms against each other after the separation.

It is erroneous, so far as foreign nations are concerned, to suppose that any war exists in the United States. Certainly there cannot be two belligerent powers where there is no war. There is here, as there has always been, one political power, namely, the United States of America, competent to make war and peace, and conduct commerce and alliances with all foreign nations. There is none other, either in fact, or recognized by foreign nations. There is, indeed, an armed sedition seeking to overthrow the government, and the government is employing military and naval forces to repress it. But these facts do not constitute a war presenting two belligerent powers, and modifying the national character, rights, and responsibilities, or the characters, rights, and responsibilities of foreign nations. It is true that insurrection may ripen into revolution, and that revolution thus ripened may extinguish a previously existing state, or divide it into one or more independent states, and that if such states continue their strife after such division, then there exists a state of war affecting the characters, rights, and duties of all parties concerned. But this only happens when the revolution has run its successful course.

The French government says, in the instruction which has been tendered to us, that certain facts which it assumes confer upon the insurgents of this country, in the eyes of foreign powers, all the appearances of a government *de facto*, wherefore, whatever may be its regrets, the French government must consider the two contending parties as employing the forces at their disposal in conformity with the laws of war.

This statement assumes not only that the law of nations entitles any insurrectionary faction, when it establishes a *de facto* government, to be treated as a belligerent, but also that the fact of the attainment of this status is to be determined by the appearance of it in the eyes of foreign nations. If we should concede both of these positions, we should still insist that the existence of a *de facto* government, entitled to belligerent rights, is not established in the present case. We have already heard from most of the foreign nations. There are only two which seem so to construe appearances, and France is one of them. Are the judgments of these two to outweigh those of all other nations? Doubtless each nation may judge and act for itself, but it certainly cannot expect the United States to accept its decision upon a question vital to their national existence. The United States will not refine upon the question when and how new nations are born out of existing nations. They are well aware that the rights of the states involve their duties and their destinies, and they hold those rights to be absolute as against all foreign nations. These rights do not at all depend on the appearances which their condition may assume in the eyes of foreign nations, whether strangers, neutrals, friends, or even allies. The United States will maintain and defend their sovereignty throughout the bounds of the Republic, and they deem all other nations bound to respect that sovereignty until, if ever, Providence shall consent that it shall be successfully overthrown. Any system of public law or national morality that conflicts with this would resolve society, first in this hemisphere and then in the other, into anarchy and chaos.

This government is sensible of the importance of the step it takes in declining to hear the communication the tender of which has drawn out these explanations. It believes, however, that it need not disturb the good relations which have so long and so happily subsisted between the United States and France. The paper, as understood, while implying a disposition on the part of France to accord belligerent rights to the insurgents, does not name, specify, or even indicate one such belligerent right. On the other hand, the rights which it asserts that France expects, as a neutral, from the United States, as a belligerent, are even less than this government, on the 25th of April, instructed you to concede and guaranty to her by treaty, as a friend. On that day we offered to her our adhesion to the declaration of Paris, which contains four propositions, namely: 1st. That privateering shall be abolished. 2d. That a neutral flag covers enemy's goods not contraband of war. 3d. That goods of a neutral, not contraband, shall not be confiscated, though found in an enemy's vessel. 4th. That blockades, in order to be lawful, must be maintained by competent force. We have always, when at war, conceded the last three of these rights to neutrals; *a fortiori,* we could not when at peace deny them to friendly nations. The first-named concession was proposed on the grounds already mentioned. We are still ready to guarantee these rights, by convention with France, whenever she shall authorize either you or her minister here to enter into convention. There is no reservation or difficulty about their application in the present case. We hold all the citizens of the United States, loyal or disloyal, alike included by the law of nations and treaties; and we hold ourselves bound by the same obligations to see, so far as may be in our power, that all our citizens, whether maintaining this government or engaged in overthrowing it, respect those rights in favor of France and of every other friendly nation. In any case, not only shall we allow no privateer or national vessel to violate the rights of friendly nations as I have thus described them, but we shall also employ all our naval force to prevent the insurgents from violating them, just as much as we do to prevent them from violating the laws of our own country.

What, then, does France claim of us that we do not accord to her?

Nothing. What do we refuse to France by declining to receive the communication sent to us through the hands of Mr. Mercier? Nothing but the privilege of telling us that we are at war, when we maintain we are at peace, and that she is a neutral, when we prefer to recognize her as a friend.

Of course, it is understood that on this occasion we reserve, as on all others, our right to suppress the insurrection by naval as well as by military power, and for that purpose to close such of our ports as have fallen or may fall into the hands of the insurgents, either directly or in the more lenient and equitable form of a blockade, which for the present we have adopted. It is thus seen that there is no practical subject of difference between the two governments. The United States will hope that France will not think it necessary to adhere to and practise upon the speculation concerning the condition of our internal affairs which she has proposed to communicate to us. But however this may be, the United States will not anticipate any occasion for a change of the relations which, with scarcely any interruption, have existed between the two nations for three quarters of a century, and have been very instrumental in promoting, not merely the prosperity and greatness of each state, but the cause of civil and religious liberty and free institutions throughout the world.

This government understands equally the interest of friendly nations and its own in the present emergency. If they shall not interfere, the attempt at revolution here will cease without inflicting serious evils upon foreign nations. All that they can do by any interference, with a view to modify our action, will only serve to prolong the present unpleasant condition of things, and possibly to produce results that would be as universally calamitous as they would be irretrievable.

The case, as it now stands, is the simple, ordinary one that has happened at all times and in all countries. A discontented domestic faction seeks foreign intervention to overthrow the Constitution and the liberties of its own country. Such intervention, if yielded, is ultimately disastrous to the cause it is designed to aid. Every uncorrupted nation, in its deliberate moments, prefers its own integrity, even with unbearable evils, to division through the power or influence of any foreign state. This is so in France. It is not less so in this country. Down deep in the heart of the American people—deeper than the love of trade, or of freedom—deeper than the attachment to any local or sectional interest, or partizan pride or individual ambition—deeper than any other sentiment—is that one out of which the Constitution of this Union arose, namely, American independence—independence of all foreign control, alliance, or influence. Next above it lies the conviction that neither peace, nor safety, nor public liberty, nor prosperity, nor greatness, nor empire, can be attained here with the sacrifice of the unity of the people of North America. Those who, in a frenzy of passion, are building expectations on other principles do not know what they are doing. Whenever one part of this Union shall be found assuming bonds of dependence or of fraternity towards any foreign people, to the exclusion of the sympathies of their native land, then, even if not before, that spirit will be reawakened which brought the states of this Republic into existence, and which will preserve them united until the common destiny which it opened to them shall be fully and completely realized.

PART NINE

A Glimpse of War's Hell-scenes

he Civil War was a time of unparalleled sacrifice and suffering. The true ugliness of war was brought home to the American people and very few emerged from the conflict unscathed. The conflict involved human beings and because of this the real story of the war must be told in human terms. But precisely because it is a human story, Walt Whitman's famous adage that "the real war will never get in the books" is perhaps correct. The countless instances of heroism, of unmitigated terror, of sacrifice and hurt, of disillusion and weariness will forever remain undocumented. One can only try, through the available records, to appreciate the impact the war had on those Americans who found themselves caught in the maelstrom. Although the war has been romanticized by succeeding generations, there was little romance in the conflict. The blood, filth, fright, and confusion of the battlefield should not be forgotten, just as the suffering, both psychological and material, of those who were left at home must be ever kept in mind. War is never pretty and the Civil War was uglier than most.

It is difficult to estimate with any degree of certainty the number of men who served in the Union and Confederate Armies during the war. Records were inadequately kept or nonexistent. An intelligent guess places the figure at slightly more than 1,500,000 for the North and just over 1,000,000 for the South, the latter being about one-fifth the total white population of the Confederacy. In excess of 618,000 of these young men (or about one out of every four soldiers) lost their lives in the conflict— 360,222 fatalities on the Union side and 258,000 on the Confederate side. Of this total, only some 204,000 (110,070 Union, 94,000 Confederate) were battle casualties. Almost two-thirds of the lives that were lost were lost because of disease and sickness, testimony to the crude and primitive medical facilities as well as to the small attention paid to health standards in the army camps. Many of those who escaped death, whether of battle wounds or disease, found themselves prisoners of the enemy. Such cold and impersonal statistics, however, can hardly convey an appreciation of the human cost of the war.

Behind the lines, North and South, life was profoundly influenced by the course of the war. Social, economic, and even political conditions were closely tied to the fluctuating fortunes of the military forces. For the Confederate States, the best years were the first. Entering the war economically strong and politically united, Southerners enjoyed high morale, confident in their expectation that independence would be for them a continuing reality. The first two years of the war were also years of military victory for the Southern armies. One historian has described the last months of 1862 as the Golden Age of the Confederacy. As the war continued, however, the South became weaker and less able to carry on the fight. The blockade, cutting off the South from its customary sources of supply and creating serious shortages, combined with the inflationary policy of the Confederate government to produce a growing chaos in economic life. As the situation became worse, the Southern people gradually lost faith in their own cause; their will to continue the war lessened. Political disunity weakened the government in its attempt to prosecute the conflict with vigor. The invading Northern armies brought the sufferings of war directly to the Southern people, and many parts of the Southern countryside were ravaged by the contending hosts.

By contrast, the North grew stronger as the conflict continued. The nadir of Northern fortunes appeared early in the war. Economic hard times followed the disruption of the Union with its severance of North-South commercial ties, and the Union Armies suffered one humiliating defeat after another, especially in the East. Opposition to the Lincoln administration reflected a general war-weariness, and movements supporting a negotiated peace with the Confederacy gained support. The war, however, brought prosperity and strength to the North, while it brought only weakness and disintegration to the South. A land of cities and countryside, of factories and farms, the United States was able to develop its full economic potential in spite of the distractions the war encouraged. War contracts, and the increased demand for manufactured items, produced an industrial expansion that was unmatched up to this time. The needs of the armed forces and of foreign customers stimulated a comparable agricultural growth. Most important, with the advent of good times came the will and determination to fight on to ultimate victory. The year 1863 was in some ways a turning point for the North; while the war would last for two more bloody years, there seemed little doubt among Northerners after that time that their cause would be victorious in the end.

"An Inkling of This War": From Walt Whitman's "Specimen Days"

Walt Whitman (1819–1892), the famous poet, was one of the most sensitive observers of the Civil War, and his descriptions of conditions at the front and behind the lines are among the best ever recorded. In 1862, he volunteered as a male nurse. For the duration of the conflict, he ministered to both Union and Confederate wounded in field hospitals at the front lines and in military hospitals in and around Washington, D.C. In his jottings during the war (later collected in the book from which the following selection was taken), and in his war poetry, published later as Drum Taps, *Whitman caught the quality of the suffering of those who participated in the war, many of whom ultimately paid the supreme sacrifice. For Whitman, the war was a national tragedy; like Lincoln, he believed that its true meaning transcended the question of union or disunion. The cause of freedom and equality everywhere depended upon its outcome. Whitman's prose writings about the Civil War have been collected and edited by Walter Lowenfels in* Walt Whitman's Civil War *(1960), an excellent account of the human side to the conflict. For the best military study of the conflict, although limited to the Northern side, see Bruce Catton's exciting and moving trilogy,* Mr. Lincoln's Army *(1951);* Glory Road: The Bloody Route from Fredericksburg to Gettysburg *(1952); and* A Stillness at Appomattox *(1953). Bell Wiley has written of the common soldier, North and South, in* The Life of Johnny Reb: The Common Soldier of the Confederacy *(1943) and* The Life of Billy Yank: The Common Soldier of the Union *(1952).*

The text of the extract below is reprinted from Walt Whitman, Specimen Days & Collect *(Philadelphia: Rees Welsh & Co., 1882–1883), pages 20–06, 57.*

Down at the Front

Falmouth, Va., opposite Fredericksburgh, December 21, 1862.—Begin my visits among the camp hospitals in the army of the Potomac. Spend a good part of the day in a large brick mansion on the banks of the Rappahannock, used as a hospital since the battle—seems to have receiv'd only the worst cases. Out doors, at the foot of a tree, within ten yards of the front of the house, I notice a heap of amputated feet, legs, arms, hands, &c., a full load for a one-horse cart. Several dead bodies lie near, each cover'd with its brown woolen blanket. In the door-yard, towards the river, are fresh graves, mostly of officers, their names on pieces of barrel-staves or broken boards, stuck in the dirt. (Most of these bodies were subsequently taken up and transported north to their friends.) The large mansion is quite crowded upstairs and down, everything impromptu, no system, all bad enough, but I have no doubt the best that can be done; all the wounds pretty bad, some frightful, the men in their old clothes, unclean and bloody. Some of the wounded are rebel soldiers and officers, prisoners. One, a Mississippian, a captain, hit badly in leg, I talk'd with some time; he ask'd me for papers, which I gave him. (I saw him three months afterward in Washington, with his leg amputated, doing well.) I went through the rooms, down stairs and up. Some of the men were dying. I had nothing to give at that visit, but wrote a few letters to folks home, mothers, &c. Also talk'd to three or four, who seem'd most susceptible to it, and needing it.

After First Fredericksburg

December 23 to 31.—The results of the late battle are exhibited everywhere about here in thousands of cases, (hundreds die every day,) in the camp, brigade, and division hospitals. These are merely tents, and sometimes very poor ones, the wounded lying on the ground, lucky if their blankets are spread on layers of pine or hemlock twigs, or small leaves. No cots; seldom even a mattress. It is pretty cold. The ground is frozen hard, and there is occasional snow. I go around from one case to another. I do not see that I do much good to these wounded and dying; but I cannot leave them. Once in a while some youngster holds on to me convulsively, and I do what I can for him; at any rate, stop with him and sit near him for hours, if he wishes it.

Besides the hospitals, I also go occasionally on long tours through the camps, talking with the men, &c. Sometimes at night among the groups around the fires, in their shebang enclosures of bushes. These are curious shows, full of characters and groups. I soon get acquainted anywhere in camp, with officers or men, and am always well used. Sometimes I go down on picket with the regiments I know best. As to rations, the army here at present seems to be tolerably well supplied, and the men have enough, such as it is, mainly salt pork and hard tack. Most of the regiments lodge in the flimsy little shelter-tents. A few have built themselves huts of logs and mud, with fire-places.

Back to Washington

January, '63.—Left camp at Falmouth, with some wounded, a few days since, and came here by Aquia creek railroad, and so on government steamer up the Potomac. Many wounded were with us on the cars and boat. The cars were just common platform ones. The railroad journey of ten or twelve miles was made mostly before sunrise. The soldiers guarding the road came out from their tents or shebangs of bushes with rumpled hair and half-awake look. Those on duty were walking their posts, some on banks over us, others down far below the level of the track. I saw large cavalry camps off the road. At Aquia creek landing were numbers of wounded going north. While I waited some three hours, I went around among them. Several wanted word sent home to parents, brothers, wives, &c., which I did for them, (by mail the next day from Washington.) On the boat I had my hands full. One poor fellow died going up.

I am now remaining in and around Washington, daily visiting the hospitals. Am much in Patent-office, Eighth street, H street, Armory-square, and others. Am now able to do a little good, having money, (as almoner of others home,) and getting experience. To-day, Sunday afternoon and till nine in the evening, visited Campbell hospital; attended specially to one case in ward I, very sick with pleurisy and typhoid fever, young man, farmer's son, D. F. Russell, company E, 60th New York, downhearted and feeble; a long time before he would take any interest; wrote a letter home to his mother, in Malone, Franklin county, N. Y., at his request; gave him some fruit and one or two other gifts; envelop'd and directed his letter, &c. Then went thoroughly through ward 6, observ'd every case in the ward, without, I think, missing one; gave perhaps from twenty to thirty persons, each one some little gift, such as oranges, apples, sweet crackers, figs, &c.

Thursday, Jan. 21.—Devoted the main part of the day to Armory-square hospital; went pretty thoroughly through wards F, G, H, and I; some fifty cases in each ward. In ward F supplied the men throughout with writing paper and stamp'd envelope each; distributed in small portions, to proper subjects, a large jar of first-rate preserv'd berries, which had been donated to me by a lady—her own cooking. Found several cases I thought good subjects for small sums of money, which I furnish'd. (The wounded men often come up broke, and it helps their spirits to have even the small sum I give them.) My paper and envelopes all gone, but distributed a good lot of amusing reading matter; also, as I thought judicious, tobacco, oranges, apples, &c. Interesting cases in ward I; Charles Miller, bed 19, company D, 53d Pennsylvania, is only sixteen years of age, very bright, courageous boy, left leg amputated below the knee; next bed to him, another young lad very sick; gave each appropriate gifts. In the bed above, also, amputation of the left leg; gave him a little jar of raspberries; bed I, this ward, gave a small sum; also to a soldier on crutches, sitting on his bed near . . . . (I am more and more surprised at the very great proportion of youngsters from fifteen to twenty-one in the army. I afterwards found a still greater proportion among the southerners.)

Evening, same day, went to see D. F. R., before alluded to; found him remarkably changed for the better; up and dress'd quite a triumph; he afterwards got well, and went back to his regiment. Distributed in the wards a quantity of note-paper, and forty or fifty stamp'd envelopes, of which I had recruited my stock, and the men were much in need. . . .

Hospital Scenes and Persons

Letter Writing. When eligible, I encourage the men to write, and myself, when called upon, write all sorts of letters for them, (including love letters, very tender ones.) Almost as I reel off these memoranda, I write for a new patient to his wife. M. de F., of the 17th Connecticut, company H, has just come up (February 17th) from Windmill point, and is received in ward II, Armory square. He is an intelligent looking man, has a foreign accent, black-eyed and hair'd, a Hebraic appearance. Wants a telegraphic message sent to his wife, New Canaan, Conn. I agree to send the message—but to make things sure I also sit down and write the wife a letter, and despatch it to the postoffice immediately, as he fears she will come on, and he does not wish her to, as he will surely get well.

Saturday, January 30th.—Afternoon, visited Campbell hospital. Scene of cleaning up the ward, and giving the men all clean clothes—through the ward (6) the patients dressing or being dress'd—the naked upper half of the bodies—the good-humor and fun—the shirts, drawers, sheets of beds, &c., and the general fixing up for Sunday. Gave J. L. 50 cents.

Wednesday, February 4th.—Visited Armory-square hospital, went pretty thoroughly through wards E and D. Supplied paper and envelopes to all who wish'd—as usual, found plenty of men who needed those articles. Wrote letters. Saw and talk'd with two or three members of the Brooklyn 14th regt. A poor fellow in ward D, with a fearful wound in a fearful condition, was having some loose splinters of bone taken from the neighborhood of the wound. The operation was long, and one of great pain—yet, after it was well commenced, the soldier bore it in silence. He sat up, propp'd—was much wasted—had lain a long time quiet in one position (not for days only but weeks,) a bloodless, brown-skinn'd face, with eyes full of determination—belong'd to a New York regiment. There was an unusual cluster of surgeons, medical cadets, nurses, &c., around his bed— I thought the whole thing was done with tenderness, and done well. In one case, the wife sat by the side of her husband, his sickness typhoid fever, pretty bad. In another, by the side of her son, a mother—she told me she had seven children, and this was the youngest. (A fine, kind, healthy, gentle mother, good-looking, not very old, with a cap on her head, and dress'd like home—what a charm it gave to the whole ward.) I liked the woman nurse in ward E—I noticed how she sat a long time by a poor fellow who just had, that morning, in addition to his other sickness, bad hemorrhage—she gently assisted him, reliev'd him of the blood, holding a cloth to his mouth, as he coughed it up—he was so weak he could only just turn his head over on the pillow.

One young New York man, with a bright, handsome face, had been lying several months from a most disagreeable wound, receiv'd at Bull Run. A bullet had shot him right through the bladder, hitting him front, low in the belly, and coming out back. He had suffer'd much—the water came out of the wound, by slow but steady quantities, for many weeks—so that he lay almost constantly in a sort of puddle—and there were other disagreeable circumstances. He was of good heart, however. At present comparatively comfortable, had a bad throat, was delighted with a stick of horehound candy I gave him, with one or two other trifles.

Patent-office Hospital

February 23.—I must not let the great hospital at the Patent-office pass away without some mention. A few weeks ago the vast area of the second story of that noblest of Washington buildings was crowded close with rows of sick, badly wounded and dying soldiers. They were placed in three very large apartments. I went there many times. It was a strange, solemn, and, with all its features of suffering and death, a sort of fascinating sight. I go sometimes at night to soothe and relieve particular cases. Two of the immense apartments are fill'd with high and ponderous glass cases, crowded with models in miniature of every kind of utensil, machine or invention, it ever enter'd into the mind of man to conceive; and with curiosities and foreign presents. Between these cases are lateral openings, perhaps eight feet wide and quite deep, and in these were placed the sick, besides a great long double row of them up and down through the middle of the hall. Many of them were very bad cases, wounds and amputations. Then there was a gallery running above the hall in which there were beds also. It was, indeed, a curious scene, especially at night when lit up. The glass cases, the beds, the forms lying there, the gallery above, and the marble pavement under foot—the suffering, and the fortitude to bear it in various degrees—occasionally, from some, the groan that could not be repress'd—sometimes a poor fellow dying, with emaciated face and glassy eye, the nurse by his side, the doctor also there, but no friend, no relative— such were the sights but lately in the Patent-office. . . .

An Army Hospital Ward

Let me specialize a visit I made to the collection of barrack-like one-story edifices, Campbell hospital, out on the flats, at the end of the then horse railway route, on Seventh street. There is a long building appropriated to each ward. Let us go into ward 6. It contains to-day, I should judge, eighty or a hundred patients, half sick, half wounded. The edifice is nothing but boards, well whitewash'd inside, and the usual slender-framed iron bed- steads, narrow and plain. You walk down the central passage, with a row on either side, their feet towards you, and their heads to the wall. There are fires in large stoves, and the prevailing white of the walls is reliev'd by some ornaments, stars, circles, &c., made of evergreens. The view of the whole edifice and occupants can be taken at once, for there is no partition. You may hear groans or other sounds of unendurable suffering from two or three of the cots, but in the main there is quiet—almost a painful absence of demonstration; but the pallid face, the dull'd eye, and the moisture on the lip, are demonstration enough. Most of these sick or hurt are evidently young fellows from the country, farmers' sons, and such like. Look at the fine large frames, the bright and broad countenances, and the many yet lingering proofs of strong constitution and physique. Look at the patient and mute manner of our American wounded as they lie in such a sad collection; representatives from all New England, and from New York, and New Jersey, and Pennsylvania—indeed from all the States and all the cities—largely from the west. Most of them are entirely with- out friends or acquaintances here—no familiar face, and hardly a word of judicious sympathy or cheer, through their sometimes long and tedious sickness, or the pangs of aggravated wounds. . . .

The Wounded from Chancellorsville

May, '63.—As I write this, the wounded have begun to arrive from Hooker's command from bloody Chancellorsville. I was down among the first arrivals. The men in charge told me the bad cases were yet to come. If that is so I pity them, for these are bad enough. You ought to see the scene of the wounded arriving at the landing here at the foot of Sixth street, at night. Two boat loads came about half-past seven last night. A little after eight it rain'd a long and violent shower. The pale, helpless soldiers had been debark'd, and lay around on the wharf and neighborhood anywhere. The rain was, probably, grateful to them; at any rate they were exposed to it. The few torches light up the spectacle. All around—on the wharf, on the ground, out on side places—the men are lying on blankets, old quilts, &c., with bloody rags bound round heads, arms, and legs. The attendants are few, and at night few outsiders also—only a few hard-work'd transportation men and drivers. (The wounded are getting to be common, and people grow callous.) The men, whatever their condition, lie there, and patiently wait till their turn comes to be taken up. Near by, the ambulances are now arriving in clusters, and one after another is call'd to back up and take its load. Extreme cases are sent off on stretchers. The men generally make little or no ado, whatever their sufferings. A few groans that cannot be suppress'd, and occasionally a scream of pain as they lift a man into the ambulance. To-day, as I write, hundreds more are expected, and to-morrow and the next day more, and so on for many days. Quite often they arrive at the rate of 1000 a day.

A Night Battle, over a Week Since

May 12.—There was part of the late battle at Chancellorsville, (second Fredericksburg,) a little over a week ago, Saturday, Saturday night and Sunday, under Gen. Joe Hooker, I would like to give just a glimpse of—(a moment's look in a terrible storm at sea—of which a few suggestions are enough, and full details impossible.) The fighting had been very hot during the day, and after an intermission the latter part, was resumed at night, and kept up with furious energy till 3 o'clock in the morning. That after-noon (Saturday) an attack sudden and strong by Stonewall Jackson had gain'd a great advantage to the southern army, and broken our lines, entering us like a wedge, and leaving things in that position at dark. But Hooker at 11 at night made a desperate push, drove the secesh forces back, restored his original lines, and resumed his plans. This night scrim-mage was very exciting, and afforded countless strange and fearful pictures. The fighting had been general both at Chancellorsville and northeast at Fredericksburgh. (We hear of some poor fighting, episodes, skedaddling on our part. I think not of it. I think of the fierce bravery, the general rule.) One corps, the 6th, Sedgewick's, fights four dashing and bloody battles in thirty-six hours, retreating in great jeopardy, losing largely but maintaining itself, fighting with the sternest desperation under all circum-stances, getting over the Rappahannock only by the skin of its teeth, yet getting over. It lost many, many brave men, yet it took vengeance, ample vengeance.

But it was the tug of Saturday evening, and through the night and Sunday morning, I wanted to make a special note of. It was largely in the woods, and quite a general engagement. The night was very pleasant, at times the moon shining out full and clear, all Nature so calm in itself, the early summer grass so rich, and foliage of the trees—yet there the battle raging, and many good fellows lying helpless, with new accessions to them, and every minute amid the rattle of muskets and crash of cannon, (for there was an artillery contest too,) the red life-blood oozing out from heads or trunks or limbs upon that green and dew-cool grass. Patches of

the woods take fire, and several of the wounded, unable to move, are consumed—quite large spaces are swept over, burning the dead also—some of
the men have their hair and beards singed—some, burns on their faces
and hands—others holes burnt in their clothing. The flashes of fire from
the cannon, the quick flaring flames and smoke, and the immense roar—
the musketry so general, the light nearly bright enough for each side to see
the other—the crashing, tramping of men—the yelling—close quarters—
we hear the secesh yells—our men cheer loudly back, especially if Hooker
is in sight—hand to hand conflicts, each side stands up to it, brave, de-
termin'd as demons, they often charge upon us—a thousand deeds are done
worth to write newer greater poems on—and still the woods on fire—still
many are not only scorch'd—too many, unable to move, are burn'd to
death.

  Then the camps of the wounded—O heavens, what scene is this?—is this
indeed *humanity*—these butchers' shambles? There are several of them.
There they lie, in the largest, in an open space in the woods, from 200 to
300 poor fellows—the groans and screams—the odor of blood, mixed with
the fresh scent of the night, the grass, the trees—that slaughter-house! O
well is it their mothers, their sisters cannot see them—cannot conceive,
and never conceiv'd, these things. One man is shot by a shell, both in the
arm and leg—both are amputated—there lie the rejected members. Some
have their legs blown off—some bullets through the breast—some inde-
scribably horrid wounds in the face or head, all mutilated, sickening, torn,
gouged out—some in the abdomen—some mere boys—many rebels, badly
hurt—they take their regular turns with the rest, just the same as any—
the surgeons use them just the same. Such is the camp of the wounded—
such a fragment, a reflection afar off of the bloody scene—while over all
the clear, large moon comes out at times softly, quietly shining. Amid the
woods, that scene of flitting souls—amid the crack and crash and yelling
sounds—the impalpable perfume of the woods—and yet the pungent,
stifling smoke—the radiance of the moon, looking from heaven at intervals
so placid—the sky so heavenly—the clear-obscure up there, those buoyant
upper oceans—a few large placid stars beyond, coming silently and
languidly out, and then disappearing—the melancholy, draperied night
above, around. And there, upon the roads, the fields, and in those woods,
that contest, never one more desperate in any age or land—both parties
now in force—masses—no fancy battle, no semi-play, but fierce and savage
demons fighting there—courage and scorn of death the rule, exceptions
almost none.

  What history, I say, can ever give—for who can know—the mad, de-
termin'd tussle of the armies, in all their separate large and little squads—
as this—each steep'd from crown to toe in desperate, mortal purports?
Who know the conflict, hand-to-hand—the many conflicts in the dark,
those shadowy-tangled, flashing-moonbeam'd woods—the writhing groups
and squads—the cries, the din, the cracking guns and pistols—the distant
cannon—the cheers and calls and threats and awful music of the oaths—
the indescribable mix—the officers' orders, persuasions, encouragements—
the devils fully rous'd in human hearts—the strong shout, *Charge, men,*
charge—the flash of the naked sword, and rolling flame and smoke? And
still the broken, clear and clouded heaven—and still again the moonlight
pouring silvery soft its radiant patches over all. Who paint the scene, the

sudden partial panic of the afternoon, at dusk? Who paint the irrepressible advance of the second division of the Third corps, under Hooker himself, suddenly order'd up—those rapid-filing phantoms through the woods? Who show what moves there in the shadows, fluid and firm—to save, (and it did save,) the army's name, perhaps the nation? as there the veterans hold the field. (Brave Berry falls not yet—but death has mark'd him— soon he falls.)

Unnamed Remains the Bravest Soldier

Of scenes like these, I say, who writes—whoe'er can write the story? Of many a score—aye, thousands, north and south, of unwrit heroes, unknown heroisms, incredible, impromptu, first-class desperations—who tells? No history ever—no poem sings, no music sounds, those bravest men of all—those deeds. No formal general's report, nor book in the library, nor column in the paper, embalms the bravest, north or south, east or west. Unnamed, unknown, remain, and still remain, the bravest soldiers. Our manliest—our boys—our hardy darlings; no picture gives them. Likely, the typic one of them (standing, no doubt, for hundreds, thousands,) crawls aside to some bush-clump, or ferny tuft, on receiving his death-shot—there sheltering a little while, soaking roots, grass and soil, with red blood—the battle advances, retreats, flits from the scene, sweeps by—and there, haply with pain and suffering (yet less, far less, than is supposed,) the last lethargy winds like a serpent round him—the eyes glaze in death—none recks—perhaps the burial-squads, in truce, a week afterwards, search not the secluded spot—and there, at last, the Bravest Soldier crumbles in mother earth, unburied and unknown. . . .

Multiply the above by scores, aye hundreds—verify it in all the forms that different circumstances, individuals, places, could afford—light it with every lurid passion, the wolf's, the lion's lapping thirst for blood—the passionate, boiling volcanoes of human revenge for comrades, brothers slain—with the light of burning farms, and heaps of smutting, smouldering black embers—and in the human heart everywhere black, worse embers— and you have an inkling of this war.

SELECTION

A Confederate Officer in a Northern Prison Camp: Horace Carpenter's "Plain Living at Johnson's Island"

From the beginning of the war, both the Northern and Southern armies took prisoners of war, an action which belied the North's frequent assertion that this was an insurrection and not a war between belligerent powers. Prison camps were provided by both sides to receive the men who were taken. Efforts to provide a workable system of exchange proved fruitless, and the number of prisoners increased steadily throughout the war, crowding the usually inadequate facilities established to house them. Some were paroled on the battlefields, but most were sent to camps behind the lines. Although many lurid and gruesome tales have been told about the treatment of prisoners of war, it seems clear that each side cared for its prisoners as well as it was able under the existing circumstances. Obviously, Union prisoners in Confederate camps often suffered more than their counterparts in the North, especially later in the war, but Southern soldiers and civilians generally were also worse off than people in the North. The lot of the prisoner was a hard one wherever he was, whether shivering before Lake Michigan's icy blasts at Camp Douglas in Chicago or enduring the mosquito-infested field at Andersonville, Georgia. Housing and sanitation facilities were frequently inadequate, and fatalities among prisoners ran high on both sides. Horace Carpenter of St. Helena Parish, Louisiana, a captain in the Confederate army who was captured in 1863 at Port Hudson, spent sixteen months as a prisoner of war at Johnson's Island, in Lake Erie, and later wrote of his experience in "Plain Living at Johnson's Island," Century, volume 41, March, 1891, pages 709–715, from which this extract is reprinted. An authoritative and dispassionate study of the treatment of Civil War prisoners is in William B. Hesseltine, Civil War Prisons: A Study in War Psychology *(1930).*

. . . Johnson's Island is situated about three miles north of Sandusky, Ohio, in Lake Erie, and was the place selected by the United States Government for the custody and storage of Confederate officers, and it was well adapted to its purpose. Notwithstanding frequent attempts, I cannot remember a single instance of a prisoner who escaped.

The prison was situated on the west end of the island, the prison officers' quarters on the outside, together with the inclosure containing the prison buildings, occupying most of the available space. With the interior I became painfully familiar, but outside the walls was an unknown country, as my outings were extremely limited as to frequency. As a matter of fact few of us went out—such as did go staid out. The buildings for the use of the prisoners were 13 in number (an unlucky number), forming two rows facing each other and separated by a street about 150 feet in width, which formed a campus or parade ground. The first winter of our stay it served as a baseball park, and was also the battlefield for snowball fights in which every private engaged was an officer. These buildings were called "blocks" and were numbered from west to east, the odd numbers being on the south side. They stood six in each row, Block 13 occupying the middle space between Nos. 11 and 12. Block 8 was in use as the prison hospital. The blocks were two stories in height, and there was no marked difference in their construction except that about four of the upper blocks were subdivided into smaller rooms which afforded greater privacy to their occupants. It seems that when the prison was first opened it was used as a mixed or general prison, and these upper blocks were assigned to the officers, who were not allowed to mingle with the enlisted men, the line of separation being marked by stakes, but latterly it was used as an officers' prison only. With this exception each block contained three rooms on the upper and two on the lower floor, the middle room upstairs being much the smallest. They were the ordinary frame houses, weather-boarded but unsealed on the inside, and it can be readily noted that while they were well enough in summer,—except towards the last, when overcrowded,— they offered but slight protection against the rigors of a Northern winter. They were better, however, than outdoors, as they protected us from wind and rain. The sinks were situated in the rear of the buildings, one for each block, and but two or at most three men were allowed to visit them at one and the same time, and this notwithstanding that the blocks contained on an average over two hundred and fifty men each.

It was the severity of the winters that told so heavily on us. Many were from the extreme South, and some had never seen a fall of snow. Coming from New Orleans, and wearing such clothing as was adapted to its climate in the month of September, the first day of January, 1864, was a revelation. On that day the thermometer marked twenty-five degrees below zero, and the writer was not more warmly clad than when now on a summer's night in that same city he writes these lines. So intense was the cold that the sentries were taken from the walls and the ice king kept watch and ward for Uncle Sam. The big gate could have been left open and few of the prisoners would have taken the chance of escape in view of almost certain death. The entire winters were bitter cold, and from our exposed position I am satisfied that the cold was much more intense than on the mainland.

Occasional gales would now and then sweep across the island, testing the strength of our buildings, and it was during one of these that two officers took refuge in a dry well as affording the greatest protection against the storm. One of these, on being asked by the other to offer up a prayer for their preservation, replied that he was acquainted only with the Lord's Prayer, and there was nothing in that to cover the emergency.

Around and forming the inclosure was a board fence about twelve feet high, lighted at night by lanterns which told tales on such prowling "Rebs" as violated the prison regulations. On the south the lower portion of this fence was formed of upright stakes with narrow spaces between, which permitted a view of the bay; the rest was planked solid, while on the out- side ran a gallery on which the sentinels walked their rounds, showing hip high above the parapet. The whole inclosure was technically called the "Bull Pen," and was invariably spoken of as such. A guard-house, sutler's shop, and some few other buildings were scattered here and there on the grounds. The south fence lay within a few yards of the bay, from which source we drew our supply of water in winter, cutting a hole in the thick ice for that purpose.

The bay was guarded by the United States steamer *Michigan,* which, when the season permitted, lay within a few hundred yards of the shore. Other steamers, loaded with excursionists, would occasionally run close in, prompted by curiosity, and taunt us with their shouts and jeers. Their favorite pastime was, or seemed to be, the singing of patriotic songs, which was admissible, and I could find no reasonable cause of complaint as to the sopranos and contraltos, but when basso-profondos and barytones musically expressed their intention to "rally round the flag," I thought of thousands of Northern men already engaged in that occupation far to the front, who, if not so vocalistic, were at least equally patriotic.

I was assigned to Block 11, Room 3, and was advised at once to study "Pierson's Ten Commandments." The first eight of this decalogue, with the exception of No. 6, referred to matters of police and fatigue duty only, but the rest were of a different character and were well worth committing to memory in order to avoid serious accidents. They were as follows:

Order No. 6.—All persons will be required to remain in their own quarters after retreat (sundown), except when they have occasion to visit the sinks; lights will be extinguished at "taps" (10 P.M.), and no fires will be allowed after that time.

Order No. 9.—No prisoner will be allowed to loiter between the buildings and the north and west fences, and they will be permitted north of the buildings only when passing to and from the sinks; nor will they approach the fences anywhere else nearer than thirty feet, as the line is marked out by the stakes.

Order No. 10.—Guards and sentinels will be required to fire on all who violate the above orders. Prisoners will therefore bear them carefully in mind and be governed by them; to forget under such circumstances is inexcusable, and may prove fatal.

By order of Lieut.-Col. William S. Pierson.

B. W. Wells, *Lieut. and Post Adjutant.*

Thirty feet from the fence was the "dead-line" referred to in Order No. 9. It consisted of stakes driven into the ground, about twenty-five or thirty feet apart, and as they stood unconnected by either rope or railing it will be readily understood that the intervening space was necessarily an imaginary line. On the north side the sinks were situated in the rear of the buildings, about ten feet from the fence, and consequently they lay twenty feet within the dead-line. It was on this side of the inclosure that Captain J. D. Meadows of the 1st Alabama Regiment was shot by the guard on Post 13 and severely wounded.

I have read articles in which the terrible dead-line was held up and denounced as brutal and inhuman, but I doubt if there existed an inclosed military prison North or South that did not possess this distinctive feature. Its use was to prevent prisoners crowding against the fence, and I do not remember that we regarded it in any other light than a very necessary precaution. We knew that the sentinel was required to shoot without warning the prisoner who crossed that line, and we felt that most of them were willing to do so; hence, if we violated Order No. 9 we were liable to be killed under Order No. 10. The matter rested entirely with ourselves. We had to bear evils of a far more serious nature over which we had no control, and such trifles as dead-lines worried us but little.

At the time I was at Johnson's Island there were about 2500 officers in confinement, and the quarters were well crowded. The sleeping arrangements consisted of bunks in tiers of three, each furnished with the usual army bedtick stuffed with straw, and far superior to the earth and ditch which had been our beds for months previous to our capture. The crowded condition of the prison necessitated that two men should occupy each bunk, which had the redeeming feature in winter that the occupants were sheltered by two blankets instead of one.

It was an evil genius that selected my bunk, for it lay just under the roof, and sometimes the snow, finding its way in, would cover me with a wet blanket. I have a vivid recollection of the result in the form of an attack of lumbago that sent my forehead to my knees and put it beyond my power to assume the position of a soldier for many days. With the thermometer well down in the tube, scantiest of bedclothing, and no fire, you can well imagine what portion of "tired nature's sweet restorer" fell to our lot. Under the circumstances it is not strange that pulmonary and rheumatic complaints should have prevailed to a great extent. I know one man who is now, after the lapse of twenty-five years, chained to his chair hopelessly crippled, a souvenir of his imprisonment.

Rations of wood were brought in daily, and to each mess was delivered an ax and a bucksaw. These were collected and taken out each night, and should any mess fail to return them no wood was brought in until the missing tools were given up. This happened once during my stay, but private enterprise, looking to the escape of a few, had to give way to the public weal, and the ax and saw "showed up." Details from the mess were made each day for police and fatigue duty, and the most fatiguing duty, as I remember it, was sawing wood; not that there was so much to saw, but the most of us were not used to it. Shortly after reveille a non-commissioned officer and guard entered the room and we were mustered for roll-call. Sometimes the guard would bring us the newspaper, giving double-leaded information, oft-times revised and corrected in subsequent issues. After roll-call we were free to kill the monotony of confinement as best we could, all parts of the inclosure being for our use except the north side and beyond the dead-line. "Retreat" sent us to our quarters, and, knowing the penalty, we were strict observers of this rule. It was for an alleged violation of this rule that Lieutenant Gibson of the 11th Arkansas lost his life. He was visiting some friends in a neighboring block, and hearing "retreat" sounded he started to his room, and was about to enter when the sentinel ordered him back to his quarters. He endeavored to explain that he was then going into his room, but the explanation was evidently unsatisfactory. The sentinel fired and killed him.

The only antidote to the terrible ennui of prison life was occupation, and very few were without employment of some kind. In fact, during the latter part of our stay it was an infallible sign of surrender when the men became listless and no longer cared for the things which had heretofore been either their work or their recreation. Work-benches sprang up in every available spot; rings were made of gutta-percha buttons; rulers and oyster shells were transformed into charms, rings, and breast-pins, equal in artistic design and execution to the best specimens of professional handiwork. In one instance, with nothing better than the wood-pile on which to draw for material, one of the men fashioned a violin; and a four-bladed penknife, complete in all its parts, attested the skill of one of my messmates. Articles manufactured by the prisoners were in demand and found a ready sale, the medium of traffic being the prison officials, who sold them on the outside, returning the proceeds to the manufacturer, who was enabled to better his condition until such time as money lost its purchasing power. I do not remember that a visitor was ever allowed inside the prison walls, but I do recall that a wife once obtained permission to visit the island, and, standing on the outside of the "pen," was allowed to look at her husband as he stood on the landing of the stairs of Block 2. I do not think the termination of the war would have been delayed five seconds had they taken him under guard to the wife or allowed her to enter the prison.

Books and newspapers were admitted after due examination, and with many of us formed our sole refuge. Classes were opened, old studies resumed or new ones begun. A first-class minstrel band known as the "Rebellonians" gave entertainments from time to time and played to crowded houses. All the popular airs of the day were conscripted and the words rewritten to express our peculiar views of the situation. The dramatic element had its innings, and I think that Peeler's "Battle of Gettysburg" had the unprecedented run of three weeks, at one performance per week. We never succeeded in putting on a first-class ballet. These performances took place in the afternoon, for, as before stated, the guards had very pronounced views as to our being absent from quarters after retreat.

All letters to and from the prisoners were opened and examined by our jailers, and, if found in order, were stamped with "Examined" and the initials of the man who had read the letter and passed it. Our correspondence was limited only as to the number per diem, space, expression of political sentiment, and ability to pay postage. With these exceptions there were no restrictions. We were allowed to write on one side of a half-sheet of paper, and our correspondents were subjected to the same rule. I have received notifications that letters addressed to me were held because they violated this rule, and have been instructed to inform the writers accordingly. To be placed on the black-list meant stoppage of our mail, and in order to realize the severity of the punishment you must put yourself in the position of a prisoner with letters your only communication with the outside world. It must have been from this cause that I acquired a terse, jerky style that has clung to me ever since. Sentimentally, "cleanliness is indeed next to godliness", practically, it is conducive to health and comfort, and we tried to enforce its unwritten laws. When a "fresh fish" was assigned to our room he was initiated by being required to take a bath and to boil his clothes, long experience in army matters having proven that this was the only way of getting rid of that energetic little pest known as the *Pediculus vestimenti*—it was one of the species crawling on a lady's bonnet-string that suggested an ode to the poet Burns.

As our clothing gradually grew worse, soap and water seemed to lose their powers, and we resorted to dyeing such garments as needed renovation, using for that purpose a liquid dye. You simply emptied the vial into a pot of boiling water, immersed the garment to be operated on, and *voilà!* One of my mess was a Lieutenant Blank, who knew some things very well, and he, wishing to improve the appearance of an old flannel shirt, sought out the hospital steward who sold the liquid and put the question, "What is it you fellows dye with here?" The steward, supposing that he had some inquisitive statistician on his hands, answered that they died of different things, but thought that pneumonia had the call just then. "Well," said B., "give me a two-bit bottle." Of course the story leaked out, and the lieutenant ran the gantlet. Some mornings afterward B. mounted a chair and made a speech. In crude but unmistakable words, and with a depth of meaning in their utterance, he announced that the next man who said "pneumonia" in his hearing would have him to whip. Most of us, knowing the difficulty of the undertaking, were so much on our guard that we did not dare to cough or to give in any manner the least suggestion of a pulmonary complaint, lest we should have cause to regret our indiscretion.

Retreat found us in our quarters, and at 10 P.M. "taps" extinguished our lights. I have heard that for a violation of this rule the guards would often fire into the block. Believing this to be true, I can vouch for its having happened at least once during my stay. It was during the evening that we gathered around the stove or the long table and discussed matters of interest,—the war, the absorbing question of exchange,—swapped yarns, some of the number being exceptionally good *raconteurs,* or listened while some "Truthful James" taxed our credulity to the verge of courtesy. And here, lest I forget it, I desire to apologize in behalf of our stove. I have known it, when doing its best, fail to melt the frost on the window-panes less than eight feet distant.

"Taps" sent us to our bunks, except such night-owls as grouped together and conversed in undertones. Sometimes a voice would start in song, another and another would join, and though neither voices nor execution were of a high order, the wet eyelids of many a homesick "Reb" would pay tribute to "Home, Sweet Home," or "Only Waiting." It was at night, alone with our thoughts, that we carried the heaviest load, when fancy bridged the distance that separated us from the homes that had been silent to us for many months.

I do not know how nostalgia ranks as a separate and specific disease, but I do know that it handicaps a man terribly in his struggle for life. Later on, during my convalescence in the hospital, one of my command lay near me, and I could hear him murmur to himself, "I shall never see home again"; and, steadily sinking, Lieutenant Starns turned his face to the wall and died.

During the earlier portion of our stay we constantly looked forward to exchange, and it was this hope that served in a great measure to mitigate the ills of our prison life. The "grape-vine" spoke to us of little else. The main feature of this prison telegraph was its complete unreliability. As I remember, it was never correct, even by accident; but it sang songs of exchange and release, and, while feeling the notes to be false, we yet liked the music and hoped it true. It was towards the fall of 1864 that I began to give up all hope of exchange, and could see no prospect of release save the close of the war, or death. I looked the matter squarely in the face, and could see no rational reason why the North should either desire or consent to an exchange. The Southern army, unable to recruit its losses, was being depleted; for every man killed, wounded, or missing made a permanent vacancy. With grim humor it was said that our conscript officers had been ordered to take every man not over two weeks dead. Why, then, should the North make the mistake of recruiting the Southern army with fifty thousand veteran soldiers, and they with experience enough of prison life to justify extra exertions in avoiding a second visit? I could then see no reason for it; and though I have since read much concerning the reasons for a non-exchange, I am satisfied that the above is about the correct solution of the problem.

Were I to write only the experience of the first four months of our imprisonment, I could have little to say in the way of complaint aside from the ills which necessarily attend confinement and form a part of every prisoner's lot. It was not heaven, but as yet it did not represent the other extreme. Our treatment by the officers of Hoffman's Battalion was, as far as I know, courteous enough; and as to the enlisted men who guarded us, my principal objection, aside from their propensity to shoot, lay in the fact that most of them could not address us as "Rebels" without qualifying the term with the adjective "damned."

Our food was abundant, owing to our ability to purchase from the post sutler and the hucksters who came into the prison daily, besides which many were in receipt of supplies from friends and relatives in the North, and hence were entirely independent of the prison rations and fed on dainties not found on the prison *menu*. The men looked well and strong, and in marked contrast with their appearance later on. Just when the change took place I do not remember, but it came suddenly. I connect it in some way with the spring of 1864. We bade a final adieu to sutler and purveyors of every kind, and realized that a limited ration would hereafter be our only supply; that we must content ourselves as best we could with such quantity as the Government saw fit to give. Money could buy nothing in the way of food; and speaking for myself I reached at last that stage when, were it in my power, I would have bartered gold for bread, ounce for ounce. We were forbidden to write for food, and it was only by strategy that, if written, such letters reached their destination. It sometimes happened that the post surgeon would allow such packages as reached the island to be delivered to their owners. He evidently had a professional dislike to sickness and suffering. The vital question with us was the victuals question. As to the daily ration, I remember that it consisted of a loaf of bread and a small piece of fresh meat. Its actual weight I do not remember, if I ever knew; I do know that it was insufficient to satisfy the cravings of hunger, and left us each day with a little less life and strength with which to fight the battle of the day to follow. I heard that our surgeons (Confederate) formulated a protest in which they asserted that the quantity of food furnished each man was not more than sufficient to sustain life. Coffee was unknown, and I remember on several occasions far apart receiving two potatoes and an onion. If these were given medicinally the dose was homeopathic, and it was certainly scurvy treatment. As the months passed on a marked change was noticeable in the appearance of the men. They became depressed and listless, and unsuspected traits of disposition cropped to the surface. The parade-ground was dotted with gaunt, cadaverous men, with a far-away look in their eyes and with hunger and privation showing in every line of their emaciated bodies. It was believed by many among us that this mode of treatment was enforced as a retaliatory measure, and this belief certainly received strong support when, looking across the bay, we saw a city whose waste alone would have supplied our wants. I have seen a hungry "Reb" plunge his hand into the swill-barrel of some mess, and, letting the water drain through his fingers, greedily devour what chance had given him—if anything. Speaking for myself, and well aware of what I state, I assert that for months I was not free from the cravings of hunger. One-half of my loaf and the meat portion of my ration was eaten for dinner. I supped on the remaining piece of bread, and breakfasted with "Duke Humphrey." I sometimes dreamed of food, but cannot remember in my dreams ever to have eaten it, becoming, as it were, a sort of Johnson's Island Tantalus.

When we arrived on the island the rats were so numerous that they were common sights on the parade-ground. Later on they disappeared. Many of the prisoners ate them. If asked if I myself have ever eaten one I answer no, because to cook a rat properly (like Mrs. Glasse's hare) you must first catch him. I have sat half frozen in our mess kitchen armed with a stick, spiked with a nail, but was never fortunate enough to secure the game. A dog would have served the purpose better, but the chances were that some hungry "Reb" would have eaten the dog.

One of the Northern illustrated papers published a picture of one of the Belle Isle prisoners which certainly showed an extreme state of emaciation. Some of the mess suggested that I compete with him, kindly offering to back the Confederate entry. I think they would have won their bets; for, though regretting that I must acknowledge the fact, I am confident that I was the worse-looking specimen of the two. I had entered the prison weighing over 140 pounds, and then weighed less than 100. To a demonstrator of anatomy I would have been invaluable as a living osteological text-book. The prolonged confinement had told severely on us, and the men could not but yield to its depressing influence. There was little to vary the dreary monotony that made each day the repetition of the day before and the type of the day to follow. This alone would have been sufficient, but when scant food and cold were thrown into the scale it is little wonder that both mind and body should yield under the constant strain. Many of us were far into the second winter of our confinement, and with all hope of release gone we had nothing left—only to wait for the end, whatever that end might be; and it was weary waiting. It was generally known among us that some mitigation of our condition would be afforded such as took the oath of allegiance, and as this meant increased food and better clothing some few availed themselves of the offer. But one case came under my notice—that of a member of the mess; he, I presume, could not help it, as it was with him simply a question of endurance, and he gave up. It was said of him that he froze up early in the first November and did not thaw out until the following June. The prospect of a repetition was too much for him.

It is small wonder, then, that many found their way into the prison hospital (then managed by Confederate physicians, prisoners like ourselves), and thence to the prison graveyard. Thanks to the generosity of a Louisiana officer (Colonel J. O. Nixon, I think), who furnished the lumber, headboards were placed at the graves of our dead, and as very many of these were carved in our room I have some personal knowledge as to their being numerous, though I cannot speak with certainty as to the actual number of deaths or the percentage of mortality. I would here state incidentally that the only occasion on which I passed beyond the limits of the inclosure was when, with two or three others, I assisted in placing these boards in the graveyard. . . .

SELECTION

Behind the Lines in the Confederacy: A Richmond Woman's Wartime Observations

The war fell heavily on the Southern people. Not only did they have to bear the want and deprivation that developed in the Confederacy after the first years, but they also had to live under the growing threat of Northern military invasion. The burdens of carrying on the daily routine of life at home were borne most weightily by Southern women. With a very large proportion of the men in the armed forces, the women had to assume increasing social and economic responsibilities in the wartorn South. Many women kept diaries and recorded their observations, providing graphic accounts of the impact of the war upon Southern life. One of the best of these is that of Mrs. S. A. B. Putnam, a resident of the Confederate capital, whose book reflects the rise and fall of Southern hopes. The exigencies of war, the effectiveness of the blockade, and the loss of agricultural production resulted in critical shortages in the South; a damaging inflation drove already rising prices even higher. Suffering was acute for many, especially those in families who depended upon the meagre pay allowed a Confederate soldier. The hard times were blamed on speculators, "extortionists," blockade-runners, and others who seemed to be profiting from the war; but the problem was deeper and more complicated. Some Southern women expressed their dissatisfaction with the deteriorating conditions by turning to violence, as in the bread riots of Salisbury, North Carolina, and of Richmond, in the spring of 1863. Frequent appeals were made to local and state governments and to the Confederate government itself for relief, but the few gestures made toward the establishment of relief programs proved ineffective. Voluntary agencies undertook relief work but with no better success. As living conditions worsened, the will to continue the struggle weakened. Large numbers of Southerners became disenchanted with their cause. The wartime plight of Southern civilians was enhanced by the destruction and suffering that often accompanied the Northern armies as they penetrated deeper into Southern territory. The burning of Columbia, South Carolina, and of Richmond (described in the following selection) were two such incidents that became indelibly stamped on the Southern mind.

The impact of the war on the Confederate home front is the subject of Bell Wiley, The Plain People of the Confederacy (1943) and Charles W. Ramsdell, Behind the Lines in the Southern Confederacy (1944). Perhaps the best known diary of a Southern woman is Mary Boykin Chesnut's Diary from Dixie (1949). Other useful and informative firsthand accounts by Southern women are Kate Stone, Brokenburn: The Journal of Kate Stone, 1861–1868 (1955); Emma LeConte, When the World Ended: The Diary of Emma LeConte (1957); and Sarah M. Dawson, A Confederate Girl's Diary (1960). The text of Mrs. Putnam's observations is reprinted from Richmond during the War: Four Years of Personal Observation (New York: G. W. Carleton & Co., 1867), pages 208–211, 362–369.

. . . in the Spring of this year, (1863,) a most disgraceful riot, to which, in order to conceal the real designs of the lawless mob engaged in it, was given the name of the "bread riot."

The rioters were represented in a heterogeneous crowd of Dutch, Irish, and free negroes—of men, women, and children—armed with pistols, knives, hammers, hatchets, axes, and every other weapon which could be made useful in their defence, or might subserve their designs in breaking into stores for the purpose of thieving. More impudent and defiant robberies were never committed, than disgraced, in the open light of day, on a bright morning in spring, the city of Richmond. The cry for bread with which this violence commenced was soon subdued, and instead of articles of food, the rioters directed their efforts to stores containing dry-goods, shoes, etc. Women were seen bending under loads of sole-leather, or dragging after them heavy cavalry boots, brandishing their huge knives, and swearing, though apparently well fed, that they were dying from starvation—yet it was difficult to imagine how they could masticate or digest the edibles under the weight of which they were bending. Men carried immense loads of cotton cloth, woolen goods, and other articles, and but few were seen to attack the stores where flour, groceries, and other provisions were kept.

This disgraceful mob was put to flight by the military. Cannon were planted in the street, and the order to disperse or be fired upon drove the rioters from the commercial portion of the city to the Capitol Square, where they menaced the Governor, until, by the continued threatenings of the State Guards and the efforts of the police in arresting the ringleaders, a stop was put to these lawless and violent proceedings.

It cannot be denied that *want of bread* was at this time too fatally true, but the sufferers for food were not to be found in this mob of vicious men and lawless víragoes who, inhabiting quarters of the city where reigned riot and depravity, when followed to their homes after this demonstration, were discovered to be well supplied with articles of food. Some of them were the keepers of stores, to which they purposed adding the stock stolen in their raid on wholesale houses.

This demonstration was made use of by the disaffected in our midst, and by our enemies abroad, for the misrepresentation and exaggeration of our real condition. In a little while the papers of the North published the most startling and highly colored accounts of the starving situation of the inhabitants of Richmond. By the prompt preventive measures brought into requisition this riot was effectually silenced, and no demonstration of the kind was afterwards made during the war.

The real sufferers were not of the class who would engage in acts of violence to obtain bread, but included the most worthy and highly cultivated of our citizens, who, by the suspension of the ordinary branches of business, and the extreme inflation in the prices of provisions, were often reduced to abject suffering; and helpless refugees, who, driven from comfortable homes, were compelled to seek relief in the crowded city, at the time insufficiently furnished with the means of living for the resident population, and altogether inadequate to the increased numbers thrown daily into it by the progress of events. How great their necessities must have been can be imagined from the fact that many of our women, reared in the utmost ease, delicacy and refinement, were compelled to dispose of all articles of taste and former luxury, and frequently necessary articles of clothing, to meet the everyday demands of life.

These miseries and inconveniences were submitted to in no fault-finding spirit; and although the poverty of the masses increased from day, to-day there is no doubt that the sympathies of the people were unfalteringly with the revolution in all its phases. Our sufferings were severe, and the uncomplaining temper in which they were borne was surely no evidence that there was in the Southern masses a disposition of craven submission, but rather of heroic devotion to a cause which brought into exercise the sublime power "to suffer and be strong." While our enemies in their country were fattening upon all the comforts of life, faring sumptuously every day, clothing themselves in rich garments, and enjoying all that could make existence desirable, they made merry over the miseries endured by the South, and laughed at the self-abnegation of a people who surrendered luxuries and comforts without a murmur for the cause of the revolution.

Our churches were stripped of their cushions, which furnished beds for the hospitals. Private houses were denuded of pillows to place under the heads of the sick. Carpets and curtains were cut up for blankets for the soldiers, and many a poor woman yielded up her couch to the invalid and suffering. Many times the dinner was taken from the table and distributed to soldiers in their march through our streets, when perhaps there was nothing in the larder with which to prepare another for the self-sacrificing family which had so generously disposed of the principal meal of the day. The generosity of our people was unstinted, and became more and more beautifully manifest as our poverty increased. A disposition was evinced to withhold nothing of ease or luxury which might in any way benefit a cause that called forth the most earnest devotion of patriotism. . . .

The morning of the 2d of April, 1865, dawned brightly over the capital of the Southern Confederacy. A soft haze rested over the city, but above that, the sun shone with the warm pleasant radiance of early spring. The sky was cloudless. No sound disturbed the stillness of the Sabbath morn, save the subdued murmur of the river, and the cheerful music of the church bells. The long familiar tumult of war broke not upon the sacred calmness of the day. Around the War Department, and the Post Office, news gatherers were assembled for the latest tidings, but nothing was bruited that deterred the masses from seeking their accustomed places in the temples of the living God. At St. Paul's church the usual congregation was in attendance. President Davis occupied his pew.

It was again the regular monthly return for the celebration of the sacra ment of the Lord's Supper. The services were progressing as usual, no agitation nor disturbance withdrew the thoughts from holy contemplation, when a messenger was observed to make his way up the aisle, and to place in the hands of the President a sealed package. Mr. Davis arose, and was noticed to walk rather unsteadily out of the church. An uneasy whisper ran through the congregation, and intuitively they seemed possessed of the dreadful secret of the sealed dispatch—the unhappy condition of General Lee's army and the necessity for evacuating Richmond. The dispatch stated that this was inevitable unless his lines could be reformed before eight o'clock that evening.

At the Second Presbyterian Church, Dr. Hoge, who had received information of the dire calamity impending over us, told his congregation of our situation, and the probability that never again would they meet there for worship, and in the thrilling eloquence of which he is so truly the master, bade them farewell.

The direful tidings spread with the swiftness of electricity. From lip to lip, from men, women, children and servants, the news was bandied, but many received it at first, as only a "Sunday sensation rumor." Friend looked into the face of friend to meet only an expression of incredulity; but later in the day, as the truth, stark and appalling, confronted us, the answering look was that of stony, calm despair. Late in the afternoon the signs of evacuation became obvious to even the most incredulous. Wagons were driven furiously through the streets, to the different departments, where they received as freight, the archives of the government, and carried them to the Danville Depot, to be there conveyed away by railroad.

Thousands of the citizens determined to evacuate the city with the government. Vehicles commanded any price in any currency possessed by the individual desiring to escape from the doomed capital. The streets were filled with excited crowds hurrying to the different avenues for transportation, intermingled with porters carrying huge loads, and wagons piled up with incongruous heaps of baggage, of all sorts and descriptions. The banks were all open, and depositors were busily and anxiously collecting their specie deposits, and directors were as busily engaged in getting off their bullion. Millions of dollars of paper money, both State and Confederate, were carried to the Capitol Square and buried.

Night came on, but with it no sleep for human eyes in Richmond. Confusion worse confounded reigned, and grim terror spread in wild contagion. The City Council met, and ordered the destruction of all spirituous liquors, fearing lest, in the excitement, there would be temptation to drink, and thus render our situation still more terrible. In the gutters ran a stream of whiskey, and its fumes filled and impregnated the air. After night-fall Richmond was ruled by the mob. In the principal business section of the city they surged in one black mass from store to store, breaking them open. robbing them, and in some instances (it is said) applying the torch to them.

In the alarm and terror, the guards of the State Penitentiary fled from their posts, and numbers of the lawless and desperate villains incarcerated there, for crimes of every grade and hue, after setting fire to the workshops, made good the opportunity for escape, and donning garments stolen wherever they could get them, in exchange for their prison livery, roamed over the city like fierce, ferocious beasts. No human tongue, no pen, however gifted, can give an adequate description of the events of that awful night.

While these fearful scenes were being enacted on the streets, in-doors there was scarcely less excitement and confusion. Into every house terror penetrated. Ladies were busily engaged in collecting and secreting all the valuables possessed by them, together with cherished correspondence, yet they found time and presence of mind to prepare a few comforts for friends forced to depart with the army or the government. Few tears were shed; there was no time for weakness or sentiment. The grief was too deep, the agony too terrible to find vent through the ordinary channels of distress. Fathers, husbands, brothers and friends clasped their loved ones to their bosoms in convulsive and agonized embraces, and bade an adieu, oh, how heart-rending! perhaps, thought many of them, forever.

At midnight the train on the Danville Railroad bore off the officers of the Government, and at the same hour many persons made their escape on the canal packets, and fled in the direction of Lynchburg.

But a still more terrible element was destined to appear and add to the horrors of the scene. From some authority—it seems uncertain what—an order had been issued to fire the four principal tobacco warehouses. They were so situated as to jeopardize the entire commercial portion of Richmond. At a late hour of the night, Mayor Mayo had dispatched, by a committee of citizens, a remonstrance against this reckless military order. But in the mad excitement of the moment the protest was unheeded. The torch was applied, and the helpless citizens were left to witness the destruction of their property. The rams in the James River were blown up. The "Richmond," the "Virginia" No. 2 and the "Beaufort" were all scattered in fiery fragments to the four winds of heaven. The noise of these explosions, which occurred as the first grey streaks of dawn broke over Richmond, was like that of a hundred cannon at one time. The very foundations of the city were shaken; windows were shattered more than two miles from where these gun-boats were exploded, and the frightened inhabitants imagined that the place was being furiously bombarded. The "Patrick Henry," a receiving-ship, was scuttled, and all the shipping at the wharves was fired except the flag-of-truce steamer "Allison."

As the sun rose on Richmond, such a spectacle was presented as can never be forgotten by those who witnessed it. To speed destruction, some malicious and foolish individuals had cut the hose in the city. The fire was progressing with fearful rapidity. The roaring, the hissing, and the crackling of the flames were heard above the shouting and confusion of the immense crowd of plunderers who were moving amid the dense smoke like demons, pushing, rioting and swaying with their burdens to make a passage to the open air. From the lower portion of the city, near the river, dense black clouds of smoke arose as a pall of crapo to hide the ravages of the devouring flames, which lifted their red tongues and leaped from building to building as if possessed of demoniac instinct, and intent upon wholesale destruction. All the railroad bridges, and Mayo's Bridge, that crossed the James River and connected with Manchester, on the opposite side, were in flames.

The most remarkable scenes, however, were said to have occurred at the commissary depot. Hundreds of Government wagons were loaded with bacon, flour and whiskey, and driven off in hot haste to join the retreating army. In a dense throng around the depot stood hundreds of men, women and children, black and white, provided with anything in which they could carry away provisions, awaiting the opening of the doors to rush in and help themselves. A cascade of whiskey streamed from the windows. About sunrise the doors were thrown open to the populace, and with a rush that seemed almost sufficient to bear off the building itself, they soon swept away all that remained of the Confederate commissariat of Richmond.

By this time the flames had been applied to or had reached the arsenal, in which several hundred car loads of loaded shell were left. At every moment the most terrific explosions were sending forth their awful reverberations, and gave us the idea of a general bombardment. All the horrors of the final conflagration, when the earth shall be wrapped in flames and melt with fervent heat, were, it seemed to us, prefigured in our capital.

At an early hour in the morning, the Mayor of the city, to whom it had been resigned by the military commander, proceeded to the lines of the enemy and surrendered it to General Godfrey Weitzel, who had been left by General Ord, when he withdrew one-half of his division to the lines investing Petersburg, to receive the surrender of Richmond.

As early as eight o'clock in the morning, while the mob held possession of Main Street, and were busily helping themselves to the contents of the dry goods stores and other shops in that portion of the city, and while a few of our cavalry were still to be seen here and there in the upper portions, a cry was raised: "The Yankees! The Yankees are coming!" Major A. H. Stevens, of the Fourth Massachusetts Cavalry, and Major E. E. Graves, of his staff, with forty cavalry, rode steadily into the city, proceeded directly to the Capital, and planted once more the "Stars and Stripes"—the ensign of our subjugation—on that ancient edifice. As its folds were given to the breeze, while still we heard the roaring, hissing, crackling flames, the explosions of the shells and the shouting of the multitude, the strains of an old, familiar tune floated upon the air—a tune that, in days gone by, was wont to awaken a thrill of patriotism. But now only the most bitter and crushing recollections awoke within us, as upon our quickened hearing fell the strains of "The Star Spangled Banner." For us it was a requiem for buried hopes.

As the day advanced, Weitzel's troops poured through the city. Long lines of negro cavalry swept by the Exchange Hotel, brandishing their swords and uttering savage cheers, replied to by the shouts of those of their own color, who were trudging along under loads of plunder, laughing and exulting over the prizes they had secured from the wreck of the stores, rather than rejoicing at the more precious prize of freedom which had been won for them. On passed the colored troops, singing, "John Brown's body is mouldering in the grave," etc.

By one o'clock in the day, the confusion reached its height. As soon as the Federal troops reached the city they were set to work by the officers to arrest the progress of the fire. By this time a wind had risen from the south, and seemed likely to carry the surging flames all over the northwestern portion of the city. The most strenuous efforts were made to prevent this, and the grateful thanks of the people of Richmond are due to General Weitzel and other officers for their energetic measures to save the city from entire destruction.

The Capitol Square now presented a novel appearance. On the south, east, and west of its lower half, it was bounded by burning buildings. The flames bursting from the windows, and rising from the roofs, were proclaiming in one wild roar their work of destruction. Myriads of sparks, borne upward by the current of hot air, were brightening and breaking in the dense smoke above. On the sward of the Square, fresh with the emerald green of early spring, thousands of wretched creatures, who had been driven from their dwellings by the devouring flames, were congregated. Fathers and mothers, and weeping, frightened children sought this open space for a breath of fresh air. But here, even, it was almost as hot as a furnace. Intermingled with these miserable beings were the Federal troops in their garish uniform, representing almost every nation on the continent of Europe, and thousands of the *Corps d'Afrique*. All along on the north side of the Square were tethered the horses of the Federal cavalry, while, dotted about, were seen the white tents of the sutlers, in which there were temptingly displayed canned fruits and meats, crackers, cheese, etc.

The roaring, crackling and hissing of the flames, the bursting of shells at the Confederate Arsenal, the sounds of instruments of martial music, the neighing of the horses, the shoutings of the multitude, in which could be distinctly distinguished the coarse, wild voices of the negroes, gave an idea of all the horrors of Pandemonium. Above all this scene of terror, hung a black shroud of smoke through which the sun shone with a lurid angry glare like an immense ball of blood that emitted sullen rays of light, as if loth to shine over a scene so appalling.

Remembering the unhappy fate of the citizens of Columbia and other cities of the South, and momentarily expecting pillage, and other evils incidental to the sacking of a city, great numbers of ladies sought the proper military authorities and were furnished with safeguards for the protection of themselves and their homes. These were willingly and generously furnished, and no scene of violence is remembered to have been committed by the troops which occupied Richmond.

Throughout the entire day, those who had enriched themselves by plundering the stores were busy in conveying off their goods. Laughing and jesting negroes tugged along with every conceivable description of merchandise, and many an astute shopkeeper from questionable quarters of Richmond thus added greatly to his former stock.

The sun had set upon this terrible day before the awful reverberations of exploding shells at the arsenal ceased to be heard over Richmond. The evening came on. A deathlike quiet pervaded the late heaving and tumultuous city, broken only by the murmuring waters of the river. Night drew her sable mantle over the mutilated remains of our beautiful capital, and we looked, and bolted, and barred our doors; but sleep had fled our eyelids. All night long we kept a fearful vigil, and listened with beating heart and quickened ears for the faintest sound that might indicate the development of other and more terrible phases of horror. But from all these we were mercifully and providentially spared. . . .

SELECTION

Victory in Battle and Disorder at Home: George Templeton Strong on Gettysburg and the New York Draft Riots, 1863

The summer of 1863 was in many ways a turning point of the war. The Union Army not long before had suffered a disastrous defeat at Chancellorsville, repeating a pattern that had become all too familiar to Northerners. Emboldened by his success, Robert E. Lee embarked upon a second invasion of the

North, less than a year after his first attempt had been turned back at Antietam. By late June, Lee's forces had crossed the Potomac and were marching across Maryland into Southern Pennsylvania. Contact was made with the Union Army outside the small town of Gettysburg, and a bloody three-day battle ensued. The Battle of Gettysburg is probably the best known and most closely studied military engagement of the war. Although both armies suffered crippling blows, Lee abandoned his invasion and withdrew into Virginia. More than any other engagement, the results of the battle persuaded Northerners that victory would ultimately be theirs. George Templeton Strong (1820–1875), a New York attorney and executive of the United States Sanitary Commission (the Civil War counterpart of the modern Red Cross), carefully recorded his reactions to Gettysburg in his voluminous and incisive diary. Celebration of the victory, however, was quickly cut short. A few days after the battle, New York City witnessed three days of serious and bloody rioting, as local citizens demonstrated against the enforcement of the recently passed national conscription law. The draft riots were reflective of the city's general Southern sympathy as well as of the conservative peace views held by many of its leaders. Troops were rushed from Gettysburg to quell the disturbance. By mid-August, conscription in the city was peacefully resumed. The riots were not an isolated occurrence; similar disorders were experienced in other cities. The reaction against conscription was symptomatic of a deeper hostility expressed by Northern conservative elements against certain measures of the Lincoln administration.

Life behind the lines in the North has not attracted the attention of historians to the same extent as life in the Confederacy. A useful, but outdated, summary is in Emerson D. Fite, Social and Industrial Conditions in the North during the Civil War *(1910). Allan Nevins is at work on a study that promises to fill the gap, two volumes of which have been published:* The War for the Union: The Improvised War, 1861–1862 *(1959) and* The War for the Union: War becomes Revolution, 1862–1863 *(1960). The second volume carries the story only to the eve of Gettysburg.*

The extract printed below is from Allan Nevins and Milton Halsey Thomas (eds.), The Diary of George Templeton Strong *(New York: Macmillan, 1952), 4 volumes, volume 3, pages 326–339, reprinted by permission of Macmillan and Company.*

. . . *June 29,* [1863] *Monday.* The hardly credible news that Hooker is relieved and General Meade is in command!!! A change of generals when a great decisive battle seems all but actually begun, and may well be delivered before the new commander is comfortably settled in his saddle! God help us! . . .

People far better pleased with the change of commanders than I expected to find them. Clitz, dining with Henry Fearing at West Point yesterday and, of course, knowing nothing of this change, said that Meade was sure to come out "at the top of the pile" before the war was over. . . .

July 1. At the Union League Club tonight I found a large assemblage; also, sundry telegrams confirming what the newspapers tell us, that Meade is advancing and that Lee has paused and is calling in his scattered columns and concentrating either for battle or for a retreat with his wagon loads of plunder. Harrisburg breathes more freely, and the Pennsylvania militia is mustering in considerable (numerical) force. Much good they would do, to be sure, in combat with Lee's desperadoes, cunning sharp-shooters, and stark, hard-riding moss-troopers.

July 3.   Half-past nine of a muggy morning. We can scarcely fail to have most weighty news before night.

There was a battle at or near Gettysburg on the first, resulting appar-ently in our favor. We lost a valuable officer in General Reynolds. Fight probably renewed yesterday, but no information on that point. There are no official reports; an unpleasant indication, but the government has main-tained the most resolute silence as to all army movements during this campaign. . . .

Evening. No definite news at all. We were told by the bulletin boards at noon that Vicksburg had surrendered, and I believed the story till about one in the afternoon, when it turned out not entirely authentic. Never mind. Do not the *Times, Tribune, Post* and *Commercial* daily certify that the "fall" of Vicksburg is "only a question of time," as distinguished from one of eternity?

July 4, Saturday.   A cloudy, muggy, sultry Fourth. Awake nearly all last night, tormented by headache and wakened out of each successive catnap by pyrotechnic racket. At or soon after daylight, Calvary Church bells began clanging, and cannon firing "a national salute" in Union Square. I arose bilious, headachy, backachy, sour, and savage. Read morn-ing papers. Their news from Meade's army was fragmentary and vague but hopeful. Spent the morning watching over Johnny and Temple, and Johnny's friend, Master Lewis French, firing off no end of crackers, little and big, "columbiads" included. What an infernal noise they make!

At half-past five appeared Walter Cutting with news from the army up to eight last night. There was fighting on the afternoon of the second, renewed yesterday, when the rebels attacked Meade's left centre in great force and were twice repulsed with severe loss. Our cavalry was operating on their flank. Both armies seem to have held their original position. *Gratias agimus Tibi.* This can hardly turn out to have been worse than a drawn battle, and that to an invading aggressive army is equivalent to defeat, as we have good reason to know. Defeat and failure in this desper-ate undertaking is a serious matter to the woman-floggers. . . .

It would seem that General Daniel Sickles has lost a leg. Wadsworth is wounded. Poor General Barlow (Mrs. Arabella Barlow née Griffith's husband) severely wounded again and probably a prisoner.

July 5.   A memorable day, even should its glorious news prove but half true. Tidings from Gettysburg have been arriving in fragmentary instalments, but with a steady crescendo toward complete, overwhelming victory. If we can believe what we hear, Lee is smitten hip and thigh, and his invincible "Army of Northern Virginia" shattered and destroyed. But I am skeptical, especially as to news of victory, and expect to find large deductions from our alleged success in tomorrow morning's newspapers. There has been a great battle in which we are, on the whole, victorious. The woman-floggers are badly repulsed and retreating, with more or less loss of prisoners, guns, and matériel. So much seems certain, and that is enough to thank God for most devoutly, far better than we dared hope a week ago. This may have been one of the great decisive battles of history.

It has been a day of quiet rain. Ellie went to Trinity Church with the children. I stayed at home, read, and lay in wait for extras. An extra *Herald* came at noon, another an hour or two later. Both encouraging. At six P.M. appeared Dr. Bellows with a telegram from Olmsted at Philadelphia as follows, to wit: "Private advices tend to confirm report of capture of over fifteen thousand prisoners and one hundred guns. Lee retreating. Pleasanton holds Potomac fords." Olmsted is wary, shrewd, and never sanguine. This despatch was not sent without strong evidence to support it. I carried it down at once to Union League Club and saw it posted on our bulletin board to the intense delectation of a half-dozen people who were hanging about the premises hungering for news. . . .

At suppertime, ten P.M., a *Tribune* extra. News of victory continued. "Prisoners and guns taken"; x plus y prisoners arrived at Baltimore and "acres of cars" laden with prisoners blocked on the railroad. Lee retreating toward Williamsport. Official despatch from General French to General Halleck announcing capture of pontoon train at Williamsport. Significant. The Potomac fords are full just now. Just suppose Meade should bag Lee and his horde of traitors as Burgoyne and Cornwallis were bagged near a century ago. Imagine it! But there is no such luck now.

At half-past eleven, in rushed the exuberant Colonel Frank Howe with a budget of telegrams. Lee utterly routed and disorganized, with loss of thirty thousand prisoners (!) and all his artillery. Details of capture of three or four blockade-running Britishers at Mobile and Charleston I omit as comparatively uninteresting. Now to bed and then for the morning papers. We may be fearfully disillusionated even yet.

July 6. Mugginess continues. Morning papers give us little additional light, if any. Evening papers do. I regret to see no official statement of guns captured. But an extra *Herald* despatch dated at noon today gives us a splendidly colored picture of Lee's retreat and tells how teamsters and artillery men are cutting their traces and riding off for life on their draft-mules; how even Couch's militia regiments are following up the defeated army and bagging whole brigades; and how there is general panic, rout, and *sauve qui peut*. All of which is pleasant to read, but probably fictitious. So is a telegram, no doubt, that I find at Union League Club tonight: "All Lee's artillery captured and thirty thousand prisoners." I take it Lee is badly whipped, but will get across the Potomac with the bulk of his army more or less demoralized. . . .

The results of this victory are priceless. Philadelphia, Baltimore, and Washington are safe. Defeat would have seriously injured all three. The rebels are hunted out of the North, their best army is routed, and the charm of Robert Lee's invincibility broken. The Army of the Potomac has at last found a general that can handle it, and it has stood nobly up to its terrible work in spite of its long disheartening list of hard-fought failures, and in spite of the McClellan influence on its officers.

Government is strengthened four-fold at home and abroad. Gold one hundred and thirty-eight today, and government securities rising. Copperheads are palsied and dumb for the moment at least. S. L. M. Barlow &

Co., who are making a catspaw of poor, confiding McClellan and using his unaccountable popularity to stir up disaffection, have lost half their power of mischief. People will soon be cackling, gabbling and gobbling and braying about "George G." as they have been about "George B." George B. is brave, honest, and true, but he has no eye for men, no insight into human character. So he has unconsciously allowed his old friends of days before the war (a long time ago) to use him for their own ends. And as they happen to be Breckinridge Democrats—Constitutional Conservatives—sympathizers and Dirt-Eaters, they have so played him off against the government that he has been for six months past well worth any two rebel generals to the rebel cause. But even their impudence can hardly clamor for his restoration to chief command of the army of Gettysburg. (N.B. I might not object to see him in Halleck's shoes.)

People downtown very jolly today. "This ends the Rebellion." So I was told a dozen times. My cheerful and agreeable but deluded friends, there must be battles by the score before that outbreak from the depths of original sin is "ended." But there does seem to be some kind of obscure Union movement in benighted old North Carolina. Wiseacres profess to know all about it. "Highest authority," "not at liberty to state," and so on, "but I knew it was all arranged with the government through General Foster a week ago" that if General Lee were well licked, North Carolina would secede at once and return to her anxious and heartbroken family. I am not sure I like the prospect. The Returning Prodigal will be represented by a batch of Congressmen swaggering through the corridors of the Capitol with pockets full of revolvers and mouths full of brag and tobacco, ready to play the old Southern game over again. They will fall on their kind old Uncle Sam's neck, of course, and do their best to break it the first time their chivalric sensibilities are stimulated into action, and Uncle Sam will kill the fatted calf and appoint these magnanimous beings Cabinet officers and chairmen of committees on the army. I trust he may not mistake himself for the fatted animal in the pardonable extravagance of his generosity, and so commit national suicide. . . .

July 11, Saturday. The Commission has spent near twenty thousand dollars this week and received as much. It is doing an immense business around Gettysburg. Olmsted reports our losses there inside seven thousand and Bellows twenty thousand!!!

From negative evidence it appears that Lee's retreat was no rout. He shews a firm front at Williamsport and Hagerstown, seeking to recross the Potomac now in high freshet. Meade is at his heels, and another great battle is expected. Olmsted thinks it will be more severe than the last.

I observe that the Richmond papers are in an orgasm of brag and bluster and bloodthirstiness beyond all historical precedent even in their chivalric columns. That's an encouraging sign. Another is the unusual number of stragglers and deserters from Lee's army. Rebel generals, even when defeated, have heretofore kept their men well in hand.

July 12. Despatches in morning papers, though severally worthless, give one the impression when taken collectively that Lee is getting safely across the Potomac and back to Old Virginny's shore, bag and baggage, guns, plunder and all. Whereupon the able editors begin to denounce

Meade, their last new Napoleon, as incapable and outgeneralled. . . . People forget that an army of fifty thousand and upward cannot be bagged bodily unless its general be a Mack or a Dupont. But I shall be disappointed if the rebels get home without a clawing.

Draft has begun here and was in progress in Boston last week. *Demos* takes it good-naturedly thus far, but we shall have trouble before we are through. The critical time will be when defaulting conscripts are haled out of their houses, as many will be. That soulless politician, Seymour, will make mischief if he dare. So will F'nandy Wood, Brooks, Marble, and other reptiles. May they only bring their traitorous necks within the cincture of a legal halter! This draft will be the *experimentum crucis* to decide whether we have a government among us.

July 13, Monday.   A notable day. Stopped at the Sanitary Commission office on my way downtown to endorse a lot of checks that had accumulated during my absence, and heard there of rioting in the upper part of the city. As Charley is at Newport and Bidwell in Berkshire County, I went to Wall Street nevertheless; but the rumors grew more and more unpleasant, so I left it at once and took a Third Avenue car for uptown. At the Park were groups and small crowds in more or less excitement (which found relief afterwards, I hear, in hunting down and maltreating sundry unoffending niggers), but there was nothing to indicate serious trouble. The crowded car went slowly on its way, with its perspiring passengers, for the weather was still of this deadly muggy sort with a muddy sky and lifeless air. At Thirteenth Street the track was blocked by a long line of stationary cars that stretched indefinitely up the Avenue, and I took to the sidewalk. Above Twentieth Street all shops were closed, and many people standing and staring or strolling uptown, not riotously disposed but eager and curious. Here and there a rough could be heard damning the draft. No policemen to be seen anywhere. Reached the seat of war at last, Forty-sixth Street and Third Avenue. Three houses on the Avenue and two or three on the street were burned down: engines playing on the ruins—more energetically, I'm told, than they did when their efforts would have been useful.

The crowd seemed just what one commonly sees at any fire, but its nucleus of riot was concealed by an outside layer of ordinary peaceable lookers-on. Was told they had beat off a squad of police and another of "regulars" (probably the Twelfth Militia). At last, it opened and out streamed a posse of perhaps five hundred, certainly less than one thousand, of the lowest Irish day laborers. The rabble was perfectly homogeneous. Every brute in the drove was pure Celtic—hod-carrier or loafer. They were unarmed. A few carried pieces of fence-paling and the like. They turned off west into Forty-fifth Street and gradually collected in front of two three-story dwelling houses on Lexington Avenue, just below that street, that stand alone together on a nearly vacant block. Nobody could tell why these houses were singled out. Some said a drafting officer lived in one of them, others that a damaged policeman had taken refuge there. The mob was in no hurry; they had no need to be; there was no one to molest them or make them afraid. The beastly ruffians were masters of the situation and of the city. After a while sporadic paving-stones began to fly at the windows, ladies and children emerged from the rear and had a rather hard scramble over a high board fence, and then scudded off across the open, Heaven knows whither. Then men and small boys appeared at rear windows and began smashing the sashes and the blinds and shied out light articles, such as books and crockery, and dropped chairs and mirrors into the back yard; the rear fence was demolished and loafers were seen marching off with portable articles of furniture. And at last a light smoke began to float out of the windows and I came away. I could endure the disgraceful, sickening sight no longer, and what could I *do?*

The fury of the low Irish women in that region was noteworthy. Stalwart young vixens and withered old hags were swarming everywhere, all cursing the "bloody draft" and egging on their men to mischief.

Omnibussed down to No. 823, where is news that the Colored Half Orphan Asylum on Fifth Avenue, just above the reservoir, is burned. *"Tribune* office to be burned tonight." Railroad rails torn up, telegraph wires cut, and so on. If a quarter one hears be true, this is an organized insurrection in the interest of the rebellion and Jefferson Davis rules New York today.

Attended to business. Then with Wolcott Gibbs to dinner at Maison Dorée. During our symposium, there was an alarm of a coming mob, and we went to the window to see. The "mob" was moving down Fourteenth Street and consisted of just thirty-four lousy, blackguardly Irishmen with a tail of small boys. Whither they went, I cannot say, nor can I guess what mischief the handful of *canaille* chose to do. A dozen policemen would have been more than a match for the whole crew, but there were no policemen in sight.

Walked uptown with Wolcott Gibbs. Large fire on Broadway and Twenty-eighth Street. Signs of another to the east, said to be on Second Avenue. Stopped awhile at Gibb's in Twenty-ninth Street, where was madame, frightened nearly to death, and then to St Nicholas Hotel to see the mayor and General Wool. We found a lot of people with them. There were John Jay and George W. Blunt and Colonel Howe and John Austin Stevens, Jr., all urging strong measures. But the substantial and weighty and influential men were not represented; out of town, I suppose. Their absence emboldened Gibbs and myself to make pressure for instant action, but it was vain. We begged that martial law might be declared. Opdyke said that was Wool's business, and Wool said it was Opdyke's, and neither would act. "Then, Mr. Mayor, issue a proclamation calling on all loyal and law-abiding citizens to enroll themselves as a volunteer force for defense of life and property." "Why," quoth Opdyke, "that is *civil war at once.*" Long talk with Colonel Cram, Wool's chief of staff, who professes to believe that everything is as it should be and sufficient force on the ground to prevent further mischief. Don't believe it. Neither Opdyke nor General Wool is nearly equal to this crisis. Came off disgusted. Went to Union League Club awhile. No comfort there. Much talk, but no one ready to do anything whatever, not even to telegraph to Washington.

We telegraphed, two or three of us, from General Wool's rooms, to the President, begging that troops be sent on and stringent measures taken. The great misfortune is that nearly all our militia regiments have been despatched to Pennsylvania. All the military force I have seen or heard

of today were in Fifth Avenue at about seven P.M. There were two or
three feeble companies of infantry, a couple of howitzers, and a squadron
or two of unhappy-looking "dragoons."

These wretched rioters have been plundering freely, I hear. Their outbreak will either destroy the city or damage the Copperhead cause fatally.
Could we but catch the scoundrels who have stirred them up, what a
blessing it would be! God knows what tonight or tomorrow may bring
forth. We may be thankful that it is now (quarter past twelve) raining
briskly. Mobs have no taste for the effusion of cold water. I'm thankful,
moreover, that Ellie and the children are out of town. I sent Johnny off
to Cornwall this afternoon in charge of John the waiter.

July 14. Eleven P.M. Fire bells clanking, as they have clanked at intervals through the evening. Plenty of rumors throughout the day and
evening, but nothing very precise or authentic. There have been sundry
collisions between the rabble and the authorities, civil and military. Mob
fired upon. It generally runs, but on one occasion appears to have rallied,
charged the police and militia, and forced them back in disorder. The
people are waking up, and by tomorrow there will be adequate organization to protect property and life. Many details come in of yesterday's
brutal, cowardly ruffianism and plunder. Shops were cleaned out and a
black man hanged in Carmine Street, for no offense but that of Nigritude.
Opdyke's house again attacked this morning by a roaming handful of
Irish blackguards. Two or three gentlemen who chanced to be passing
saved it from sack by a vigorous charge and dispersed the popular uprising (as the *Herald, World,* and *News* call it), with their walking
sticks and their fists.

Walked uptown perforce, for no cars and few omnibi were running.
They are suppressed by threats of burning railroad and omnibus stables,
the drivers being wanted to reinforce the mob. Tiffany's shop, Ball &
Black's, and a few other Broadway establishments are closed. (Here I
am interrupted by report of a fire near at hand, and a great glare on the
houses across the Park. Sally forth, and find the Eighteenth Ward station
house, Twenty-second Street, near First Avenue, in full blaze. A splendid
blaze it made, but I did not venture below Second Avenue, finding myself
in a crowd of Celtic spectators disgorged by the circumjacent tenement
houses. They were exulting over the damage to "them bloody police," and
so on. I thought discretion the better part of curiosity. Distance lent
enchantment to that view.)

At 823 with Bellows four to six; then home. At eight to Union League
Club. Rumor it's to be attacked tonight. Some say there is to be great
mischief tonight and that the rabble is getting the upper hand. Home at
ten and sent for by Dudley Field, Jr., to confer about an expected attack
on his house and his father's, which adjoin each other in this street just
below Lexington Avenue. He has a party there with muskets and talks
of fearful trouble before morning, but he is always a blower and a very
poor devil. Fire bells again at twelve-fifteen. No light of conflagration is
visible.

Bellows's report from Gettysburg and from Meade's headquarters very
interesting. Thinks highly of Meade. Thinks the battle around Williamsport will be tolerably evenly matched, Lee having been decidedly beaten

a week ago, but not at all demoralized. But there's a despatch at the Union League Club tonight that Lee has moved his whole army safely across, except his rear guard, which we captured.

A good deal of yelling to the eastward just now. The Fields and their near neighbour, Colonel Frank Howe, are as likely to be attacked by this traitor-guided mob as any people I know. If they *are,* we shall see trouble in this quarter, and Gramercy Park will acquire historical associations. O, how tired I am! But I feel reluctant to go to bed. I believe I dozed off a minute or two. There came something like two reports of artillery, perhaps only falling walls. There go two jolly Celts along the street, singing a genuine Celtic howl, something about "Tim O'Laggerty," with a refrain of pure Erse. Long live the sovereigns of New York, Brian Boroo *redivivus* and multiplied. Paddy has left his Egypt—Connaught—and reigns in this promised land of milk and honey and perfect freedom. Hurrah, there goes a strong squad of police marching eastward down this street, followed by a company of infantry with gleaming bayonets. One A.M. Fire bells again, southeastward, "Swinging slow with sullen roar." Now they are silent, and I shall go to bed, at least for a season. . . .

PART TEN

A New Birth of Freedom

In his Inaugural Address in March, 1861, President Lincoln stated his conviction that the United States was one and inseparable, and announced his resolve to maintain the Union against the challenge of Southern secession and independence. Following the surrender of Fort Sumter, Lincoln's resolution became the war aim of the North: to preserve the Union and insure the return of the seceded states. During the frightening, tense days after the defeat of the Union Army at Bull Run in July, 1861, Congress officially sanctioned this war aim. In a resolution submitted by Kentucky's John J. Crittenden, Congress declared that the war was being fought "to defend and maintain the supremacy of the Constitution, and to preserve the Union with all the dignity, equality, and rights of the several States unimpaired." In other words, the purpose of the North was simply to restore the status quo as it existed before the conflict began, nothing more, nothing less. With this statement of the war aim, President Lincoln fully concurred.

It soon became apparent, however, that such a statement was highly unrealistic, for the status quo to be restored held within it the very forces of conflict and disunion that had caused the war. Obviously, the North must go beyond mere preservation of the Union. That slavery should become the target of Northern war purposes was natural. Not only the abolitionists but also antislavery men of all types and persuasions had come to believe that the institution of slavery was at the root of the nation's difficulties. To abolish slavery would be to rid the nation of a continuing source of conflict and friction. The exigencies of the war itself encouraged an attack on slavery. Early in the war, Negro slaves penetrated the Union lines and local commanders found themselves in the awkward situation either of returning the slaves to their Confederate masters (as the Fugitive Slave Law demanded) or holding them. Benjamin Butler established a precedent when he declared such slaves to be "contraband of war" and therefore free of their bondage. A confiscation act passed by Congress in August, 1861, sought to meet this problem when it declared that slaves used for hostile military purposes were subject to confiscation and, by implication, entitled to their freedom. President Lincoln, mindful of the need to keep the border slave states in the Union, resisted this trend toward the acceptance of abolition as a war aim. In his message to Congress in December, 1861, he reiterated his conviction that the integrity of the Union should remain the primary object of the struggle. "We should not be in haste," he said, "to determine that radical and extreme measures, which may reach the loyal as well as the disloyal, are indispensable."

However, Lincoln, too, soon recognized that slavery must be a casualty of the war. He gave deep and serious thought to the question. His position on slavery was, and always had been, conservative, and it was this general outlook that now molded his stand. Lincoln was convinced that the emancipation of slaves could only legitimately be carried out by the states. He felt, in addition, that emancipation should be gradual and compensated; that is, that the slaveowners should be compensated for their loss of property. Finally, he never quite relinquished his notion that freed slaves could (and should) be colonized outside the United States. In 1862, he made successive appeals to the border slave states, urging them to take the lead in adopting state emancipation programs. In December, 1862, he presented to Congress a proposal for constitutional amendments that would provide gradual, compensated emancipation over a period of thirty-seven years (till 1900) in order, he said, to spare "both races from the evils of sudden derangement." Congress, he hoped, would also appropriate money for the colonization of free Negroes outside the United States. None of his plans was favorably received.

Meanwhile, Congress had been busy. An attempt to reaffirm the Crittenden resolution in December, 1861, was defeated. Later, slavery was abolished in the District of Columbia, with compensation to slaveholders, and in the territories, without compensation. In July, one of the most important and least known acts committing the nation to a policy of abolition was passed—the Second Confiscation Act. In a significant, but often overlooked clause, the act provided that "all slaves of persons who shall hereafter be engaged in rebellion against the Government of the United States, or who shall in any way give aid thereto . . . shall be forever free." This act was far-reaching and extreme and, perhaps for these reasons, Lincoln disliked it. He made no attempt to enforce it.

Congress's actions, however, were very soon overshadowed by Lincoln's own dramatic gesture toward a policy of emancipation. Unrelenting pressure from the Radical Republicans, and a growing fear that the struggle on the diplomatic front might be lost, persuaded the President to issue the Emancipation Proclamation—the preliminary announcement in September, 1862, and the proclamation itself the following January. Still, Lincoln insisted that the proclamation did not represent a shift in general policy on his part; it was justified solely on grounds of military necessity. Actually, the Emancipation Proclamation did not go as far as Congress had gone in the Second Confiscation Act. That Lincoln had not moved so far toward an unqualified abolition position as some people thought (or hoped) was soon demonstrated by the fact that his proposal to Congress for gradual, compensated emancipation was delivered after the preliminary announcement of the Emancipation Proclamation.

Nonetheless, by 1863, in spite of Lincoln's protestations, the war had become revolution and the "radical and extreme measures" Lincoln had warned against were soon reality. It was Congress that freed the slaves, not Lincoln. Antislavery men concluded that a policy of abolition could only be secured through a constitutional amendment, not through the kind of piecemeal, halfhearted process that seemed to be developing. The Thirteenth Amendment to the Constitution was introduced and debated in 1864 but was not finally passed until January, 1865. Its ratification was completed by the following December.

Thus the abolition of slavery became a primary aim of the war and one of the war's greatest results. Freedom for Negro slaves, however, was not achieved out of any deep national commitment to humanitarianism or racial equality, but rather because of the widespread awareness that to preserve the Union with slavery intact was simply out of the question. For many, including Lincoln, emancipation was justified on military grounds, as a means of shortening the war. Only to a few did abolition represent the fruition of a long and dedicated struggle to a humanitarian purpose.

Lincoln Appeals to the Border States for Compensated Emancipation, 1862

President Lincoln, from the beginning of the conflict, had been concerned lest the border slave states throw in their lot with their sister slave states to the south. Before hostilities began, he was reported to have expressed a willingness to trade the evacuation of Fort Sumter for the disbanding of Virginia's secession convention. He hoped, he once said, to have God on his side; but he knew he had to have Kentucky. He was reluctant to countenance any program of emancipation that would penalize the loyal slave states as well as punish the disloyal ones. Lincoln was also convinced that emancipation was a matter for state action. During the 1850s he believed that the restriction of slavery to the states in which it existed would lead to the institution's "ultimate extinction." If a policy of emancipation were to be adopted, however, he felt that it must be voluntary, gradual, and with compensation to the slaveowners who would be deprived of their property. In March, 1862, he sent a message to Congress in which he proposed a resolution that would pledge the cooperation of the United States to any state which might adopt a gradual, compensated emancipation program. Such a resolution was passed the following month, but nothing was ever done to implement it. The following July, Lincoln summoned the representatives and senators of the loyal border slave states to the White House and sought to persuade them to initiate a compensated emancipation program in their own states. The text of the letter that follows is reprinted from Roy P. Basler et al. (eds.), The Collected Works of Abraham Lincoln (New Brunswick: Rutgers, 1953), 9 volumes, volume 5, pages 317–319. Lincoln reiterated once again his support for the colonization of the slaves so freed; but his proposal was rejected. A majority of the group replied that such a policy would only stiffen the resistance of the seceded states and stimulate a spirit of secession in the border states. For the role of the border states during the Civil War, see Edward C. Smith, The Borderland in the Civil War (1927). Lincoln's program for gradual, compensated emancipation is analyzed in James G. Randall, Constitutional Problems under Lincoln (rev. ed., 1951) and in Randall's Lincoln the President: Springfield to Gettysburg (1945), two volumes.

entlemen. After the adjournment of Congress, now very near, I shall have no opportunity of seeing you for several months. Believing that you of the border-states hold more power for good than any other equal number of members, I feel it a duty which I can not justifiably waive, to make this appeal to you. I intend no reproach or complaint when I assure you that in my opinion, if you all had voted for the resolution in the gradual emancipation message of last March, the war would now be substantially ended. And the plan therein proposed is yet one of the most potent, and swift means of ending it. Let the states which are in rebellion see, definitely and certainly, that, in no event, will the states you represent ever join their proposed Confederacy, and they can not, much longer maintain the contest. But you can not divest them of their hope to ultimately have you with them so long as you show a determination to perpetuate the institution within your own states. Beat them at elections, as you have overwhelmingly done, and, nothing daunted, they still claim you as their own. You and I know what the lever of their power is. Break that lever before their faces, and they can shake you no more forever.

Most of you have treated me with kindness and consideration; and I trust you will not now think I improperly touch what is exclusively your own, when, for the sake of the whole country I ask "Can you, for your states, do better than to take the course I urge? ["] Discarding *punctillio,* and maxims adapted to more manageable times, and looking only to the unprecedentedly stern facts of our case, can you do better in any possible event? You prefer that the constitutional relation of the states to the nation shall be practically restored, without disturbance of the institution; and if this were done, my whole duty, in this respect, under the constitution, and my oath of office, would be performed. But it is not done, and we are trying to accomplish it by war. The incidents of the war can not be avoided. If the war continue long, as it must, if the object be not sooner attained, the institution in your states will be extinguished by mere friction and abrasion—by the mere incidents of the war. It will be gone, and you will have nothing valuable in lieu of it. Much of its value is gone already. How much better for you, and for your people, to take the step which, at once, shortens the war, and secures substantial compensation for that which is sure to be wholly lost in any other event. How much better to thus save the money which else we sink forever in the war. How much better to do it while we can, lest the war ere long render us pecuniarily unable to do it. How much better for you, as seller, and the nation as buyer, to sell out, and buy out, that without which the war could never have been, than to sink both the thing to be sold, and the price of it, in cutting one another's throats.

I do not speak of emancipation *at once,* but of a *decision* at once to emancipate *gradually.* Room in South America for colonization, can be obtained cheaply, and in abundance; and when numbers shall be large enough to be company and encouragement for one another, the freed people will not be so reluctant to go.

I am pressed with a difficulty not yet mentioned—one which threatens division among those who, united are none too strong. An instance of it is known to you. Gen. Hunter is an honest man. He was, and I hope, still is, my friend. I valued him none the less for his agreeing with me in the general wish that all men everywhere, could be free. He proclaimed all men free within certain states, and I repudiated the proclamation. He expected more good, and less harm from the measure, than I could believe would follow. Yet in repudiating it, I gave dissatisfaction, if not offence, to many whose support the country can not afford to lose. And this is not the end of it. The pressure, in this direction, is still upon me, and is increasing. By conceding what I now ask, you can relieve me, and much more, can relieve the country, in this important point. Upon these considerations I have again begged your attention to the message of March last. Before leaving the Capital, consider and discuss it among yourselves. You are patriots and statesmen; and, as such, I pray you, consider this proposition; and, at the least, commend it to the consideration of your states and people. As you would perpetuate popular government for the best people in the world, I beseech you that you do in no wise omit this. Our common country is in great peril, demanding the loftiest views, and boldest action to bring it speedy relief. Once relieved, its form of government is saved to the world; its beloved history, and cherished memories, are vindicated; and it's happy future fully assured, and rendered inconceivably grand. To you, more than to any others, the privilege is given, to assure that happiness, and swell that grandeur, and to link your own names therewith forever.

SELECTION

"Forever Free": Lincoln's Preliminary Emancipation Proclamation, 1862

In his letter to the border state representatives (the preceding document), Lincoln wrote of the increasing pressure to which he was subjected by the partisans of an emancipation policy. The military struggle was going badly; the course of international relations seemed uncertain. Tactics had to be changed, he later recalled, or the game would be lost. On July 22, 1862, President Lincoln first discussed his plans to issue the Emancipation Proclamation with the members of his Cabinet. A draft was drawn; but, on the advice of Secretary of State Seward, it was withheld until Northern arms might experience a military victory. Antietam, although not a clear victory, provided the opportunity. On September 22, Lincoln issued the preliminary Emancipation Proclamation; the final proclamation was to be announced on the following January 1. Lincoln justified the statement on the ground of military expediency. It was, to him, clearly a war measure which he sincerely hoped might cause the South to end its rebellion sooner. It represented no important shift either in Lincoln's attitude toward Northern war aims or in the direction of Northern antislavery legislation. Lincoln palliated its effect by citing in his proclamation a portion of the Second Confiscation Act (passed the previous July), and by alluding once again to his preference for gradual, compensated emancipation and colonization. Although it did not go as far as Congress's Second Confiscation Act, the Emancipation Proclamation has

completely overshadowed all other steps that were taken toward the develop-
ment of emancipation as a war aim. On January 1, the final proclamation was
announced, designating those states or parts of states which were to be
affected by it. Since the slaves were freed only where United States authority
could not reach, it is safe to assume that the Emancipation Proclamation did
not, at the time of its issuance, free a single slave. The proclamation did,
however, contribute to the rather slow conversion of the goals of the conflict
to a revolutionary purpose.

The text of the preliminary Emancipation Proclamation is taken from
Roy P. Basler et al. (eds.), The Collected Works of Abraham Lincoln *(New*
Brunswick: Rutgers, 1953), 9 volumes, volume 5, pages 433–436. John Hope
Franklin has written the only complete history of the proclamation in his The
Emancipation Proclamation (1963). The works by James G. Randall cited above
are also useful.

I, Abraham Lincoln, President of the United States of America, and , Commander-in-chief of the Army and Navy thereof, do hereby proclaim and declare that hereafter, as heretofore, the war will be prosecuted for the object of practically restoring the constitutional relation between the United States, and each of the states, and the people thereof, in which states that relation is, or may be suspended, or disturbed.

That it is my purpose, upon the next meeting of Congress to again recommend the adoption of a practical measure tendering pecuniary aid to the free acceptance or rejection of all slave-states, so called, the people whereof may not then be in rebellion against the United States, and which states, may then have voluntarily adopted, or thereafter may voluntarily adopt, immediate, or gradual abolishment of slavery within their respective limits; and that the effort to colonize persons of African descent, with their consent, upon this continent, or elsewhere, with the previously obtained consent of the Governments existing there, will be continued.

That on the first day of January in the year of our Lord, one thousand eight hundred and sixty-three, all persons held as slaves within any state, or designated part of a state, the people whereof shall then be in rebellion against the United States shall be then, thenceforward, and forever free; and the executive government of the United States, including the military and naval authority thereof, will recognize and maintain the freedom of such persons, and will do no act or acts to repress such persons, or any of them, in any efforts they may make for their actual freedom.

That the executive will, on the first day of January aforesaid, by proclamation, designate the States, and parts of states, if any, in which the people thereof respectively, shall then be in rebellion against the United States; and the fact that any state, or the people thereof shall, on that day be, in good faith represented in the Congress of the United States, by members chosen thereto, at elections wherein a majority of the qualified voters of such state shall have participated, shall, in the absence of strong countervailing testimony, be deemed conclusive evidence that such state and the people thereof, are not then in rebellion against the United States.

That attention is hereby called to an act of Congress entitled "An act to make an additional Article of War" approved March 13, 1862, and which act is in the words and figure following:

Be it enacted by the Senate and House of Representatives of the United States of America in Congress assembled, That hereafter the following shall be promulgated as an additional article of war for the government of the army of the United States, and shall be obeyed and observed as such:

Article—. All officers or persons in the military or naval service of the United States are prohibited from employing any of the forces under their respective commands for the purpose of returning fugitives from service or labor, who may have escaped from any persons to whom such service or labor is claimed to be due, and any officer who shall be found guilty by a court-martial of violating this article shall be dismissed from the service.

Sec. 2.   And be it further enacted, That this act shall take effect from and after its passage.

Also to the ninth and tenth sections of an act entitled "An Act to suppress Insurrection, to punish Treason and Rebellion, to seize and confiscate property of rebels, and for other purposes," approved July 17, 1862, and which sections are in the words and figures following:

Sec. 9.   And be it further enacted, That all slaves of persons who shall hereafter be engaged in rebellion against the government of the United States, or who shall in any way give aid or comfort thereto, escaping from such persons and taking refuge within the lines of the army; and all slaves captured from such persons or deserted by them and coming under the control of the government of the United States; and all slaves of such persons found *on* (or) being within any place occupied by rebel forces and afterwards occupied by the forces of the United States, shall be deemed captives of war, and shall be forever free of their servitude and not again held as slaves.

Sec. 10.   And be it further enacted, That no slave escaping into any State, Territory, or the District of Columbia, from any other State, shall be delivered up, or in any way impeded or hindered of his liberty, except for crime, or some offence against the laws, unless the person claiming said fugitive shall first make oath that the person to whom the labor or service of such fugitive is alleged to be due is his lawful owner, and has not borne arms against the United States in the present rebellion, nor in any way given aid and comfort thereto; and no person engaged in the military or naval service of the United States shall, under any pretence whatever, assume to decide on the validity of the claim of any person to the service or labor of any other person, or surrender up any such person to the claimant, on pain of being dismissed from the service.

And I do hereby enjoin upon and order all persons engaged in the military and naval service of the United States to observe, obey, and enforce, within their respective spheres of service, the act, and sections above recited.

And the executive will in due time recommend that all citizens of the United States who shall have remained loyal thereto throughout the rebellion, shall (upon the restoration of the constitutional relations between the United States, and their respective states, and people, if that relation shall have been suspended or disturbed) be compensated for all losses by acts of the United States, including the loss of slaves. . . .

SELECTION **32**

The Gettysburg Address, 1863

On November 19, 1863, a cemetery on the battlefield of Gettysburg was dedicated. Edward Everett, the well-known New England orator, delivered the principal dedicatory address, a long and tedious discourse on the Union, the war, and the battle which had so recently raged on that very ground. Abraham Lincoln, whose presence on the program had been an afterthought, followed Everett. By contrast, his remarks were almost shockingly brief. His address, however, is one of the finest examples of prose writing in the English language. A tender and touching tribute to those who gave their lives at Gettysburg, it was a reaffirmation of the freedom and democracy to which Lincoln and the nation were dedicated. The President's remarks were popularly and well received; even Everett complimented him on coming nearer to the "central idea of the occasion" in two minutes than he, Everett, had done in two hours. Much has been written about the Gettysburg Address, reprinted here from Roy P. Basler et al. (eds.), The Collected Works of Abraham Lincoln *(New Brunswick: Rutgers, 1953), 9 volumes, volume 7, page 23. But most accounts have been concerned with the more superficial, external circumstances of the occasion. Among the better works is F. Lauriston Bullard, "A Few Appropriate Remarks":* Lincoln's Gettysburg Address *(1944). A fine summary of the occasion appears in Randall,* Lincoln the President, *volume 2, pages 303–320.*

Four score and seven years ago our fathers brought forth on this continent, a new nation, conceived in Liberty, and dedicated to the proposition that all men are created equal.

Now we are engaged in a great civil war, testing whether that nation, or any nation so conceived and so dedicated, can long endure. We are met on a great battle-field of that war. We have come to dedicate a portion of that field, as a final resting place for those who here gave their lives that that nation might live. It is altogether fitting and proper that we should do this.

But, in a larger sense, we can not dedicate—we can not consecrate—we can not hallow—this ground. The brave men, living and dead, who struggled here, have consecrated it, far above our poor power to add or detract. The world will little note, nor long remember what we say here, but it can never forget what they did here. It is for us the living, rather, to be dedicated here to the unfinished work which they who fought here have thus far so nobly advanced. It is rather for us to be here dedicated to the great task remaining before us—that from these honored dead we take increased devotion to that cause for which they gave the last full measure of devotion—that we here highly resolve that these dead shall not have died in vain—that this nation, under God, shall have a new birth of freedom—and that government of the people, by the people, for the people, shall not perish from the earth.

SELECTION **33**

Emancipation by Constitutional Amendment: Lyman Trumbull on the Thirteenth Amendment, 1864

Although the nation had become committed to the abolition of slavery as a war aim, no clear-cut policy emerged to implement this goal. Rather the North's emancipation program was a patchwork quilt of military decrees, congressional resolutions and legislation, state actions, and presidential procla-mations. By 1864, the need for uniting these expressions in a single statement of policy was recognized. Lincoln himself had frequently expressed his doubts about the constitutionality of presidential or congressional emancipation, doubts that were shared by many others. It was clear that a constitutional amendment was not only desirable but also necessary. Early in 1864, Lyman Trumbull (1813–1896), Senator from Illinois, reported the proposed Thirteenth Amendment to the Constitution from the Senate Judiciary Committee. The amendment was briefly and simply stated: "Neither slavery nor involuntary servitude, except as a punishment for crime whereof the party shall have been duly convicted, shall exist within the United States, or any place subject to their jurisdiction." In his speech supporting the amendment on March 28 (the selection that follows), Trumbull reviewed the various actions taken on behalf of a policy of emancipation, and the necessity, as he saw it, for dealing with the question in a constitutional amendment. Not all members of Congress were so persuaded. While the Senate passed the amendment, the House of Representatives proved unable to secure the required majority. The measure was revived in the following Congress and finally, on January 31, 1865, re-ceived the necessary support. The Thirteenth Amendment was ratified by the required number of states (including eight former members of the Con-federacy) and was declared adopted by the following December. With the adoption of the amendment, the revolution which the war had bred had been consummated. It was, wrote James G. Randall, "the first example of the use of the amending process to accomplish a specific reform on a nation-wide scale." There is no full-scale study of the Thirteenth Amendment. The consti-tutional aspects of emancipation have been ably treated in Randall's Constitu-tional Problems under Lincoln, *cited above. Trumbull's speech is taken from the* Congressional Globe, *Thirty-eighth Congress, first session, pages 1313–1314.*

Mr. President, as the organ of the Committee on the Judiciary which has reported this resolution to the Senate, I desire to present briefly some of the considerations which induced me, at least, to give it my support. It is a proposition so to amend the Constitution of the United States as forever to prohibit slavery within its jurisdiction, and authorize the Congress of the United States to pass such laws as may be necessary to carry this provision into effect.

Without stopping to inquire into all the causes of our troubles, and of the distress, desolation, and death which have grown out of this atrocious rebellion, I suppose it will be generally admitted that they sprung from slavery. If a large political party in the North attribute these troubles to the impertinent interference of northern philanthropists and fanatics with an institution in the southern States with which they had no right to interfere, I reply, if there had been no such institution there could have been no such alleged impertinent interference; if there had been no slavery in the South, there could have been no abolitionists in the North to interfere with it. If, upon the other hand, it be said that this rebellion grows out of the attempt on the part of those in the interest of slavery to govern this country so as to perpetuate and increase the slaveholding power, and failing in this that they have endeavored to overthrow the Government and set up an empire of their own, founded upon slavery as its chief cornerstone, I reply, if there had been no slavery there could have been no such foundation on which to build. If the freedom of speech and of the press, so dear to freemen everywhere, and especially cherished in this time of war by a large party in the North who are now opposed to interfering with slavery, has been denied us all our lives in one half the States of the Union, it was by reason of slavery.

If these Halls have resounded from our earliest recollections with the strifes and contests of sections, ending sometimes in blood, it was slavery which almost always occasioned them. No superficial observer, even, of our history North or South, or of any party, can doubt that slavery lies at the bottom of our present troubles. Our fathers who made the Constitution regarded it as an evil, and looked forward to its early extinction. They felt the inconsistency of their position, while proclaming the equal rights of all to life, liberty, and happiness, they denied liberty, happiness, and life itself to a whole race, except in subordination to them. It was impossible, in the nature of things, that a Government based on such antagonistic principles could permanently and peacefully endure, nor did its founders expect it would. They looked forward to the not distant, nor as they supposed uncertain period when slavery should be abolished, and the Government become in fact, what they made it in name, one securing the blessings of liberty to all. The history of the last seventy years has proved that the founders of the Republic were mistaken in their expectations; and slavery, so far from gradually disappearing as they had anticipated, had so strengthened itself that in 1860 its advocates demanded the control of the nation in its interests, failing in which they attempted its overthrow. This attempt brought into hostile collision the slaveholding aristocracy, who made the right to live by the toil of others the chief article of their faith, and the free laboring masses of the North, who believed in the right of every man to eat the bread his own hands had earned.

In the earlier stages of the war there was an indisposition on the part of the executive authority to interfere with slavery at all. For a long time slaves who escaped from their rebel owners and came within our lines were driven back. Congress, however, at an early day took action upon this subject, and at the very first session which met after the rebellion broke out, the special session of July, 1861, a law was passed declaring free all slaves who were permitted by their masters to take any part in the rebellion. Under the provisions of that act, had it been efficiently executed, a great many slaves must necessarily have obtained their freedom. The constitutionality of the act would seem to be clear. I do not suppose that even my honorable friend from Kentucky [Mr. DAVIS] would deny the proposition that if we captured a slave engaged, by consent of his master, in constructing rebel works and fortifications, we might set him free.

That act, however, has not been executed. So far as I am advised not a single slave has been set at liberty under it. Subsequently, at the regular session of Congress which convened in December, 1861, an act of a more comprehensive character was passed—a law providing for the freedom of all slaves who should come within the lines of our armies, who should be deserted by their masters, or who should be found in regions of country which had been occupied by rebel troops and afterwards came within our possession, and who belonged to rebel masters. It is under the provisions of this law that most of the slaves made free have been emancipated. This act also authorized the President of the United States to organize and employ as many persons of African descent as he should think proper to aid in the suppression of the rebellion. But it was a long time before this law was put in operation. Although it was an act called for by the public sentiment of the country, and although it was the duty of those charged with the execution of the laws to see that it was faithfully executed, it was more than a year after its enactment before any considerable number of persons of African descent were organized and armed; and even at this day a much smaller number are in the service than would have been by an efficient execution of the law. It was not until after the passage of this act that our officers, especially in the West, ceased to expel slaves who came within the lines of our Army; and so persistently was this practice persevered in that Congress had to interfere by positive enactment, and declare that any officer of the Army or Navy who aided in restoring a slave to his master should be dismissed from the public service, before it could be stopped.

But, sir, had these laws, all of them, been efficiently executed they would not wholly have extirpated slavery. They were only aimed at the slaves of rebels. Congress never undertook to free the slaves of loyal men; no act has ever passed for that purpose.

At a later period, the President by proclamation undertook to free the slaves in certain localities. Notice of this proclamation was given in September, 1862, and it was to become effective in January, 1863. Unlike the acts of Congress, which undertook to free the slaves of rebels only, and of such as came under our control, the President's proclamation excepted from its provisions the regions of country subject to our authority, and declared free the slaves only who were in regions of country from which the authority of the United States was expelled, enjoining upon the persons proposed to be made free to abstain from all violence unless in necessary self-defense, and recommending them in all cases, when allowed, to labor faithfully for reasonable wages.

The force and effect of this proclamation are understood very differently by its advocates and opponents. The former insist that it is and was within the constitutional power of the President, as Commander-in-Chief, to issue such a proclamation; that it is the noblest act of his life or the age; and that by virtue of its provisions all slaves within the localities designated become *ipso facto* free; while others declare that it was issued without competent authority, and has not and cannot effect the emancipation of a single slave. These latter insist that the most the President could do, as commander of the armies of the United States, would be, in the absence of legislation, to seize and free the slaves which came within the control of the Army; that the power exercised by a commander-in-chief, as such, must be a power exercised in fact, and that beyond his lines where his armies cannot go his orders are mere *brutum fulmen,* and can neither work a forfeiture of property nor freedom of slaves; that the power of Frémont and Hunter, commanders-in-chief for a certain time in their departments, who assumed to free the slaves within their respective commands, was just as effective within the boundaries of their commands as that of the Commander-in-Chief of all the departments, who as commander could not draw to himself any of his presidential powers; and that neither had or could have any force except within the lines and where the Army actually had the power to execute the order; that to that extent the previous acts of Congress would free the slaves of rebels, and if the President's proclamation had any effect it would only be to free the slaves of loyal men, for which the laws of the land did not provide. I will not undertake to say which of these opinions is correct, nor is it necessary for my purposes to decide. It is enough for me to show that any and all these laws and proclamations, giving to each the largest effect claimed by its friends, are ineffectual to the destruction of slavery. The laws of Congress if faithfully executed would leave remaining the slaves belonging to loyal masters, which, considering how many are held by children and females not engaged in the rebellion, would be no inconsiderable number, and the President's proclamation excepts from its provisions all of Delaware, Maryland, Kentucky, Tennessee, Missouri, and a good portion of Louisiana and Virginia—almost half the slave States.

If then we are to get rid of the institution, we must have some more efficient way of doing it than by the proclamations that have been issued or the acts of Congress which have been passed.

Some, however, say that we may pass an act of Congress to abolish slavery altogether, and petitions are sent to Congress asking it to pass such a law. I am as anxious to get rid of slavery as any person; but has Congress authority to pass a law abolishing slavery everywhere, freeing the slaves of the loyal, the slaves of the friends of the Government as well as the slaves of the disloyal and of the enemies of the Government? Why, sir, it has been an admitted axiom from the foundation of this Government, among all parties, that Congress had no authority to interfere with slavery in the States where it existed. But it is said this was in a time of peace, and we are now at war, and Congress has authority to carry on war, and in carrying on war we may free the slaves. Why so? Because it is necessary; for no other reason. If we can do it by act of Congress it must be because it is a necessity to the prosecution of the war. We have authority to put down the enemies of the country; we have the right to slay them in battle; we have authority to confiscate their property; but, mark you, does that give any authority to slay the friends of the country, to confiscate the property of the friends of the country, or to free the slaves of the friends of the country?

But it is said that freeing slaves would aid us in raising troops; that slaves are unwilling to volunteer and enter the public service unless other slaves are made free, and that we could raise troops better, sooner, and have a more efficient army if slavery were declared abolished. Suppose that were so, is it a necessity? Can we not raise an army without doing this? Has not the Congress of the United States unlimited authority to provide for the raising of armies by draft, by force to put any and every man capable of bearing arms into its service? Have we not already passed a law compelling men to enter the service of the Government in its defense and for the putting down this rebellion? Then there is no necessity to free the slaves in order to raise an army.

But it is a convenience, perhaps some will say. Sir, it is not because a measure would be convenient that Congress has authority to adopt it. The measure must be appropriate and needful to carry into effect some granted power, or we have no authority to adopt it. I can imagine a thousand things that would aid us to raise troops which no one would contend Congress had authority to do. We now find that it is costing us a large sum of money to carry on this war. There are apprehensions in some quarters that the finances of the country will not be sufficient to prosecute it to the end. A measure that would enable us to carry on the war cheaper would certainly be one in aid of this war power. In consequence of the prosperity which prevails in the country, wages at this time are very high. Men are unwilling to enlist without large bounties and large pay, because they get high wages at home. Suppose we introduce a bill that no man shall be paid in any manufacturing establishment, at any mechanic art, or for his daily labor, more than ten cents a day, and we visit with penalties and punishment any man who shall give to his employé more than that sum; do you not think that would hold out an additional inducement to volunteer? But who would contend that Congress had any such authority? Manifestly it has not. Nor can I find the constitutional authority to abolish slavery everywhere by act of Congress as a necessity to prosecuting the war.

Then, sir, in my judgment, the only effectual way of ridding the country of slavery, and so that it cannot be resuscitated, is by an amendment of the Constitution forever prohibiting it within the jurisdiction of the United States. This amendment adopted, not only does slavery cease, but it can never be reëstablished by State authority, or in any other way than by again amending the Constitution. Whereas, if slavery should now be abolished by act of Congress or proclamation of the President, assuming that either has the power to do it, there is nothing in the Constitution to prevent any State from reëstablishing it. This change of the Constitution will also relieve us of all difficulty in the restoration to the Union of the rebel States when our brave soldiers shall have reduced them to obedience to the laws.

To secure its passage requires, in the first instance, a vote of two thirds in its favor in each branch of Congress, and its ratification subsequently by three fourths of the States of the Union. Can these majorities be obtained? It is very generally conceded, I believe, by men of all political parties, that slavery is gone; that the value of slavery is destroyed by the rebellion. What objection, then, can there be on the part of any one, in the present state of public feeling in the country, to giving the people an opportunity to pass upon this question? I would appeal to Senators upon the opposite side of the Chamber, and ask them—for I expect some of them to support this measure, and I trust all of them will—what objection they have to submitting this question to the people and letting them pass upon it? Do any of you deny that slavery lies at the bottom of this rebellion? Do you believe that we should have had this terrible war upon us had there been no slavery in the land? I repeat, then, why not afford an opportunity to the people to pass upon this amendment? I trust I do not assume too much when I assume that it will receive the requisite vote of two thirds of each branch of Congress.

Having obtained that, the question then arises, is it probable that it can have the ratification of three fourths of the States? We have now thirty-five States, and bills have passed both branches of Congress and been approved by the President for the creation of two more, Colorado and Nevada, which will make thirty-seven. When these States are admitted it will require the concurring vote of twenty-eight States in order to adopt this amendment.

If Nebraska should be admitted, for the admission of which a bill is now pending, that would make the number of States thirty-eight, and the votes of twenty-nine States would then be requisite to adopt the amendment. But the admission of Nebraska would not probably affect the result, as, if admitted, she would most probably vote for the amendment.

Of the thirty-seven States, twenty-one are free States, including Colorada and Nevada, and I assume that all those States would vote for this constitutional amendment. There are, then, the States of Maryland, West Virginia, Missouri, Arkansas, Tennessee, and Louisiana, all of which have taken initiatory steps for the abolition of slavery within their borders; and I think we might confidently count that they would unite with the free States to pass this amendment. Those six added to the twenty-one free States would make twenty-seven. Then there is the State of Delaware, with hardly slaves enough in it to count, which would be left standing alone with free States all around her. Although she has not yet, so far as I am aware, taken any legislative steps for the abolition of slavery, though the question is agitated among her people, I cannot think she would stand alone in such a locality, resisting a constitutional amendment which would forever give us peace on this question.

I have assumed that all the free States will adopt the amendment. It is now very generally conceded that slavery is not a divine institution. The few in the northern or free States who attempt to uphold it do so on constitutional grounds, denying the authority of the Government to interfere with it; but none of these persons deny or can deny the power of the people to amend the Constitution in the mode prescribed by the instrument itself. If, then, they shall oppose an amendment for the abolition of slavery, it will not be because to abolish it in that form is unconstitutional, but because it is not right, or, if right, not expedient.

I think, then, it is reasonable to suppose that if this proposed amendment passes Congress, it will within a year receive the ratification of the requisite number of States to make it a part of the Constitution. That accomplished, and we are forever freed of this troublesome question. We accomplish then what the statesmen of this country have been struggling to accomplish for years. We take this question entirely away from the politics of the country. We relieve Congress of sectional strifes, and, what is better than all, we restore to a whole race that freedom which is theirs by the gift of God, but which we for generations have wickedly denied them.

I know that the passage of this measure will not end this rebellion. I do not claim that for it. There is but one way to do that; and that is by the power of our brave soldiers. We can never have the Union restored, the authority of the Constitution recognized, and its laws obeyed and respected, until our armies shall overcome and vanquish the rebel armies. We must look to our soldiers, to our patriotic Army, to put down the rebellion. But, sir, when they shall have accomplished that, this measure will secure to us future peace. That is what I claim for it. I trust that within a year, in less time than it will take to make this constitutional amendment effective, our armies will have put to flight the rebel armies. I think it ought long ago to have been done; and I think but for the indecision, the irresolution, the want of plan, and the scattering of our forces, it would have been done long ago. Hundreds of millions of treasure and a hundred thousand lives would have been saved had the power of this Republic been concentrated under one mind and hurled in masses upon the main rebel armies. This is what our patriotic soldiers have wanted, and what I trust is now soon to be done.

But instead of looking back and mourning over the errors of the past, let us remember them only for the lessons they teach for the future. Forgetting the things which are past, let us press forward to the accomplishment of what is before. We have at last placed at the head of our armies a man in whom the country has confidence, a man who has won victories wherever he has been, and I trust that his mind is to be permitted uninterfered with to unite our forces, never before so formidable as to-day, in one or two grand armies and hurl them upon the rebel force. Let him put to flight the main rebel army which has threatened the capital for the last three years, and the small rebel armies will quickly succumb. I look for that result during the coming campaign, and with that result, if we civilians do our duty, we shall have the authority of the Constitution vindicated, constitutional liberty reëstablished, the Union restored, and freedom everywhere proclaimed.

SELECTION  34

Abraham Lincoln's Second Inaugural Address, 1865

In November, 1864, Lincoln was decisively reelected to a second term as President of the United States. During the following months, the war rapidly approached its end. The military struggle entered its final phase. An abortive peace conference aboard a Union transport vessel in Hampton Roads, attended by Lincoln and Alexander H. Stephens, preceded the last campaign. When

Lincoln took his oath of office on March 4, 1865, the end was in sight. His Second Inaugural Address, characteristically brief, was another masterful statement of the character and purpose of the conflict. The dimensions of the revolution that had been achieved with the abolition of slavery were carefully and effectively defined. It was not solely to the people of the North, however, that Lincoln addressed his remarks. The basic humanitarianism which had permeated his management of the war was now extended to the people of the South. His ringing words, so nobly expressed, "with malice toward none; with charity for all," would provide a foundation for the difficult period of restoration he saw ahead. "To bind up the nation's wounds"—this was the task to which Lincoln now dedicated himself.

The text of the Second Inaugural Address is reprinted from Roy P. Basler et al. (eds.), The Collected Works of Abraham Lincoln *(New Brunswick: Rutgers, 1953), 9 volumes, volume 8, pages 332–333.*

A t this second appearing to take the oath of the presidential office, there is less occasion for an extended address than there was at the first. Then a statement, somewhat in detail, of a course to be pursued, seemed fitting and proper. Now, at the expiration of four years, during which public declarations have been constantly called forth on every point and phase of the great contest which still absorbs the attention, and engrosses the energies of the nation, little that is new could be presented. The progress of our arms, upon which all else chiefly depends, is as well known to the public as to myself; and it is, I trust, reasonably satisfactory and encouraging to all. With high hope for the future, no prediction in regard to it is ventured.

On the occasion corresponding to this four years ago, all thoughts were anxiously directed to an impending civil-war. All dreaded it—all sought to avert it. While the inaugural address was being delivered from this place, devoted altogether to *saving* the Union without war, insurgent agents were in the city seeking to *destroy* it without war—seeking to dissolve the Union, and divide effects, by negotiation. Both parties deprecated war; but one of them would *make* war rather than let the nation survive; and the other would *accept* war rather than let it perish. And the war came.

One eighth of the whole population were colored slaves, not distributed generally over the Union, but localized in the Southern part of it. These slaves constituted a peculiar and powerful interest. All knew that this interest was, somehow, the cause of the war. To strengthen, perpetuate, and extend this interest was the object for which the insurgents would rend the Union, even by war; while the government claimed no right to do more than to restrict the territorial enlargement of it. Neither party expected for the war, the magnitude, or the duration, which it has already attained. Neither anticipated that the *cause* of the conflict might cease with, or even before, the conflict itself should cease. Each looked for an easier triumph, and a result less fundamental and astounding. Both read the same Bible, and pray to the same God; and each invokes His aid against the other. It may seem strange that any men should dare to ask a just God's assistance in wringing their bread from the sweat of other men's faces; but let us judge not that we be not judged. The prayers of both could not be answered; that of neither has been answered fully. The Almighty has His own purposes. "Woe unto the world because of offences! for it must needs be that offences come; but woe to that man by whom the offence cometh!" If we shall suppose that American Slavery is one of those offences which, in the providence of God, must needs come, but which, having continued through His appointed time, He now wills to remove, and that He gives to both North and South, this terrible war, as the woe due to those by whom the offence came, shall we discern therein any departure from those divine attributes which the believers in a Living God always ascribe to Him? Fondly do we hope—fervently do we pray—that this mighty scourge of war may speedily pass away. Yet, if God wills that it continue, until all the wealth piled by the bond-man's two hundred and fifty years of unrequited toil shall be sunk, and until every drop of blood drawn with the lash, shall be paid by another drawn with the sword, as was said three thousand years ago, so still it must be said "the judgments of the Lord, are true and righteous altogether."

With malice toward none; with charity for all; with firmness in the right, as God gives us to see the right, let us strive on to finish the work we are in; to bind up the nation's wounds; to care for him who shall have borne the battle, and for his widow, and his orphan—to do all which may achieve and cherish a just, and a lasting peace, among ourselves, and with all nations.

PART ELEVEN

The Danger Within

Abraham Lincoln and Jefferson Davis—the chief executives of the two contending nations—faced many common tasks and problems. Among these was a political opposition that followed a strikingly similar pattern in the United States and in the Confederate States. Lincoln and Davis were both moderate individuals, seeking to follow moderate, middle-of-the-road courses in their administration of the war. But one price each had to pay was opposition from both extremes of the political spectrum, although Davis's opposition was not as clearly delineated as Lincoln's. Each was, in effect, walking a tightrope between opposing views on the nature and character of the war. Neither, in the final analysis, was able to maintain his balance. In the North, Lincoln's compromise with his opposition, however, resulted in a strengthening of the war effort; in the South, Davis's inability to cope with his opposition contributed to the destruction of the Southern nation.

Both Lincoln and Davis had to contend with opponents who reflected radical and revolutionary aims. For Lincoln, this opposition centered in his own party and was concentrated on the effort to establish abolition as a war aim. Northern Radicals sought to introduce a revolutionary purpose into the war, finally achieving success as Lincoln and the national Congress committed the nation to an abolition program. Southern Radical opposition to Davis came from the fire-eaters, the Southern nationalists who likewise considered the conflict to be revolutionary in character. Davis's radical critics took him to task for what they regarded as his reluctance to portray the Southern cause as a true revolution and his apparent hesitation to commit the full energy and resources of the Southern people to the attainment of independence.

Both Presidents likewise faced serious opposition from conservative groups who were convinced that greater dangers lay in the threat of national centralization and the subversion of states' rights than in the military triumph of the enemy. This opposition to Lincoln and Davis assumed a constitutional posture and employed constitutional arguments.

The conservative opposition to Lincoln was focused in the Democratic party. That party faced a serious dilemma during the war, forced to reconcile its opposition to the Republican administration with war-time conditions and circumstances. Some Democrats, called "War Democrats," offered support to the government in the prosecution of the war but opposed the party in power on political grounds, drawing a tenuous (and sometimes untenable) distinction between the government and the administration. Other Democrats, the so-called "Peace Democrats," criticized Lincoln's conduct of the war in almost every respect and urged that the fighting be stopped and the Union restored by peaceful negotiation. Still other Democrats, weary of trying to justify their opposition during the crisis, took the easy way out and joined the Republican party. Some conservative Republicans, disturbed by some of Lincoln's policies, joined the Democrats on certain issues. Party politics was, to say the least, confused in the North during the war. Distinctions between these various groups were not always carefully drawn, and by the later years of the conflict opponents of the administration of whatever ilk were lumped together by Republicans and labeled "Copperheads."

Opposition within the Democratic party to the Lincoln administration was stimulated early in the war by the President's apparent disregard for the civil liberties of Northern citizens. Unaware of the necessity for harsh and sometimes extreme measures during a period of civil insurrection, Democrats registered their opposition to the suspension of habeas corpus, the arbitrary arrests of critics of the war, the suspension of newspapers suspected of printing disloyal statements, the passage of a national conscription law, and finally and most significantly the proclamation by Lincoln of an emancipation policy. Some of the Democratic opposition resulted also from the agrarian dislike of the economic program adopted by the Lincoln administration—protective tariffs and a national centralized banking system, for example. The conservative opposition, with a special strength in the agrarian states of the Northwest, reached its peak in the congressional elections of 1862, when the Republican hold on Congress and the state governments was considerably weakened. In the latter stages of the war, this opposition took the form of a peace movement, as Democrats declared the attempt to coerce the Southern states back into the Union to be an utter failure and urged the conclusion of the fighting through a negotiated settlement with the Confederate States. Many of Lincoln's opponents naively felt that such a settlement would result in the restoration of the Union "as it was." In 1864, such ambiguous sentiments were written into the national platform of the Democratic party. The activities of some of the members of the Copperhead opposition bordered on the treasonable, causing Lincoln such concern that he once expressed his fear of the "fire in the rear."

Davis's conservative opposition came from the states' rights defenders who had played a large role in the formation of the Confederacy but who regarded states' rights as sacred even from Southern encroachment. The opposition came not from a party out of power as in the North but rather from highly placed officials in both the national administration and the state governments. Their criticism of Davis paralleled that of Lincoln in the North. National conscription, the suspension of habeas corpus, and other measures proposed by Davis to centralize the war effort were denounced as unconstitutional, subversive to the rights of sovereign states, and leading to a dangerous and unjustified concentration of power on the national level. Unmindful of the sacrifice necessary to the achievement of Southern independence, Davis's states' rights critics maintained a continuing assault against the national government. A leader of this opposition was the Vice President himself, Georgia's influential Alexander H. Stephens, who once made the amazing statement that he would prefer defeat for the Southern cause to the infringement of states' rights. Stephens was joined by certain Confederate state governors, notably Joseph E. Brown of Georgia and Zebulon Vance of North Carolina. The true contradiction involved in the attempt to establish an independent nation on the basis of a states' rights principle was never fully appreciated by Southern leaders. It proved to be an unworkable principle, especially for a nation that was fighting for its very life.

It is in part a testimony to the quality of Lincoln's leadership that the Northern government, aided by growing economic strength, was able to surmount its political opposition. Davis, however, was no Lincoln. The political disunity, stimulated by the states' rights opposition, proved to be one of the rocks on which the Confederate ship of state eventually foundered.

A Northern Democrat Declares the War a Failure: Clement L. Vallandigham's Speech on "The Great Civil War in America," 1863

Clement Laird Vallandigham (1820–1871) was one of the most outspoken critics of the Lincoln administration during the Civil War. A native of Ohio, Vallandigham was a member of the House of Representatives from 1858 to 1863. He reflected the interests of Middle Western agrarian democracy and took a strong stand against the economic and political program adopted by the Lincoln administration. He struck out boldly against measures for prosecuting the conflict, notably conscription and the infringement of civil liberties, and denounced Lincoln for the conversion of a war for the Union into a war for the abolition of slavery. Vallandigham's speech before the House of Representatives on January 14, 1863, following hard on the Northern defeat at Fredericksburg, was a high point in the conservative (or Copperhead) opposition to Lincoln's government. Not long afterward, he was arrested by General Ambrose E. Burnside, commander of the Department of the Ohio, on a charge of discouraging enlistments, tried by a military commission, and sentenced to imprisonment. President Lincoln, however, commuted his sentence to banishment beyond the Union lines. Vallandigham made his way from the Confederacy to Canada, where he kept up his opposition to the administration. During his exile, he ran unsuccessfully for the governorship of Ohio. By the summer of 1864, he was back in Ohio. Vallandigham supported the peace movement in the North, convinced that the war could be halted and the Union restored through peaceful negotiation with the South. He once summed up his position, declaring, "I am a Democrat—for the Constitution, for law, for the Union, for liberty—this is my only 'crime.'" Many Northerners, however, strongly suspected less patriotic motives for his scathing attacks against the war and against the government. Two fine studies of the Copperhead opposition to Lincoln during the war are Wood Gray, The Hidden Civil War: The Story of the Copperheads *(1942) and Frank Klement,* The Copperheads in the Middle West *(1960). The text of Vallandigham's speech before the House of Representatives (January 14, 1863) is reprinted from* The Record of Hon. C. L. Vallandigham on Abolition, the Union, and the Civil War *(Cincinnati: J. Walter and Co., 1863), pages 173–199.*

. . . It is now two years, sir, since Congress assembled soon after the Presidential election. A sectional anti-slavery party had then just succeeded through the forms of the Constitution. For the first time a President had been chosen upon a platform of avowed hostility to an institution peculiar to nearly one half of the States of the Union, and who had himself proclaimed that there was an irrepressible conflict, because of that institution, between the States; and that the Union could not endure "part slave and part free." Congress met, therefore, in the midst of the profoundest agitation, not here only, but throughout the entire South. Revolution glared upon us. Repeated efforts for conciliation and compromise were attempted, in Congress and out of it. All were rejected by the party just coming into power, except only the promise in the last hours of the session, and that, too, against the consent of a majority of that party both in the Senate and House: that Congress—not the Executive—should never be authorized to abolish or interfere with slavery in the States where it existed. South Carolina seceded; Georgia, Alabama, Florida, Mississippi, Louisiana, and Texas speedily followed. The Confederate Government was established. The other slave States held back. Virginia demanded a peace congress. The commissioners met, and, after some time, agreed upon terms of final adjustment. But neither in the Senate nor the House were they allowed even a respectful consideration. The President elect left his home in February, and journeyed towards this capital, jesting as he came; proclaiming that the crisis was only artificial, and that "nobody was hurt." He entered this city under cover of night and in disguise. On the 4th of March he was inaugurated, surrounded by soldiery; and, swearing to support the Constitution of the United States, announced in the same breath that the platform of his party should be the law unto him. From that moment all hope of peaceable adjustment fled. But for a little while, either with unsteadfast sincerity or in premeditated deceit, the policy of peace was proclaimed, even to the evacuation of Sumpter and the other Federal forts and arsenals in the seceded States. Why that policy was suddenly abandoned, time will fully disclose. But just after the spring elections, and the secret meeting in this city of the Governors of several northern and western States, a fleet carrying a large number of men was sent down ostensibly to provision Fort Sumpter. The authorities of South Carolina eagerly accepted the challenge, and bombarded the fort into surrender, while the fleet fired not a gun, but, just as soon as the flag was struck, bore away and returned to the North. It was Sunday, the 14th of April, 1861; and that day the President, in fatal haste, and without the advice or consent of Congress, issued his proclamation, dated the next day, calling out seventy-five thousand militia for three months, to repossess the forts, places, and property seized from the United States, and commanding the insurgents to disperse in twenty days. Again the gage was taken up by the South, and thus the flames of a civil war, the grandest, bloodiest, and saddest in history, lighted up the whole heavens. Virginia forthwith seceded. North Carolina, Tennessee, and Arkansas, followed; Delaware, Maryland, Kentucky, and Missouri were in a blaze of agitation, and within a week from the proclamation, the line of the Confederate States was transferred from the cotton States to the Potomac, and almost to the Ohio and the Missouri, and their population and fighting men doubled.

In the North and West, too, the storm raged with the fury of a hurricane.

Never in history was anything equal to it. Men, women, and children, native and foreign born, Church and State, clergy and laymen, were all swept along with the current. Distinction of age, sex, station, party, perished in an instant. Thousands bent before the tempest; and here and there only was one found bold enough, foolhardy enough it may have been, to bend not, and him it smote as a consuming fire. The spirit of persecution for opinion's sake, almost extinct in the old world, now, by some mysterious transmigration, appeared incarnate in the new. Social relations were dissolved; friendships broken up; the ties of family and kindred snapped asunder. Stripes and hanging were every where threatened, sometimes executed. Assassination was invoked; slander sharpened his tooth; falsehood crushed truth to the earth; reason fled; madness reigned. Not justice only escaped to the skies, but peace returned to the bosom of God, whence she came. The gospel of love perished; hate sat enthroned, and the sacrifices of blood smoked upon every altar.

But the reign of the mob was inaugurated only to be supplanted by the iron domination of arbitrary power. Constitutional limitation was broken down; *habeas corpus* fell; liberty of the press, of speech, of the person, of the mails, of travel, of one's own house, and of religion; the right to bear arms, due process of law, judicial trial, trial by jury, trial at all; every badge and muniment of freedom in republican government or kingly government—all went down at a blow; and the chief law officer of the crown—I beg pardon, sir, but it is easy now to fall into this courtly language—the Attorney-General, first of all men, proclaimed in the United States the maxim of Roman servility: *Whatever pleases the President, that is law!* Prisoners of State were then first heard of here. Midnight and arbitrary arrests commenced; travel was interdicted; trade embargoed; passports demanded; bastiles were introduced; strange oaths invented; a secret police organized; "piping" began; informers multiplied; spies now first appeared in America. The right to declare war, to raise and support armies, and to provide and maintain a navy, was usurped by the Executive; and in a little more than two months a land and naval force of over three hundred thousand men was in the field or upon the sea. An army of public plunderers followed, and corruption struggled with power in friendly strife for the mastery at home.

On the 4th of July Congress met, not to seek peace; not to rebuke usurpation nor to restrain power; not certainly to deliberate; not even to legislate, but to register and ratify the edicts and acts of the Executive; and in your language, sir, upon the first day of the session, to invoke a universal baptism of fire and blood amid the roar of cannon and the din of battle. Free speech was had only at the risk of a prison; possibly of life. Opposition was silenced by the fierce clamor of "disloyalty." All business not of war was voted out of order. Five hundred thousand men, an immense navy, and two hundred and fifty millions of money were speedily granted. In twenty, at most in sixty days, the rebellion was to be crushed out. To doubt it was treason. Abject submission was demanded. Lay down your arms, sue for peace, surrender your leaders—forfeiture, death—this was the only language heard on this floor. The galleries responded; the corridors echoed; and contractors and placemen and other venal patriots everywhere gnashed upon the friends of peace as they passed by. In five weeks seventy-eight public and private acts and joint resolutions, with declaratory resolutions, in the Senate and House, quite as numerous, all full of slaughter, were hurried through without delay and almost without debate.

Thus was CIVIL WAR inaugurated in America. Can any man today see the end of it? . . .

I did not support the war; and to-day I bless God, that not the smell of so much as one drop of its blood is upon my garments. Sir, I censure no brave man who rushed patriotically into this war; neither will I quarrel with any one, here or elsewhere, who gave to it an honest support. Had their convictions been mine, I, too, would doubtless have done as they did. With my convictions I could not.

But I was a Representative. War existed—by whose act no matter—not mine. The President, the Senate, the House, and the country, all said that there should be war—war for the Union; a union of consent and good-will. Our southern brethren were to be whipped back into love and fellowship at the point of the bayonet. O, monstrous delusion! I can comprehend a war to compel a people to accept a master; to change a form of government; to give up territory; to abolish a domestic institution—in short, a war of conquest and subjugation; but a war for union! Was the Union thus made? Was it ever thus preserved? Sir, history will record that, after nearly six thousand years of folly and wickedness in every form and administration of government—theocratic, democratic, monarchic, oligarchic, despotic and mixed—it was reserved to American statesmanship, in the nineteenth century of the Christian era, to try the grand experiment, on a scale the most costly and gigantic in its proportions, of creating love by force, and developing fraternal affection by war! And history will record, too, on the same page, the utter, disastrous, and most bloody failure of the experiment. . . .

And now, sir, I recur to the state of the Union to-day. What is it? Sir, twenty months have elapsed, but the rebellion is not crushed out; its military power has not been broken; the insurgents have not dispersed. The Union is not restored; nor the Constitution maintained; nor the laws enforced. Twenty, sixty, ninety, three hundred, six hundred days have passed; a thousand millions been expended; and three hundred thousand lives lost or bodies mangled; and to-day the Confederate flag is still near the Potomac and the Ohio, and the Confederate Government stronger, many times, than at the beginning. Not a State has been restored, not any part of any State has voluntarily returned to the Union. And has any thing been wanting that Congress, or the States, or the people in their most generous enthusiasm, their most impassionate patriotism, could bestow? Was it power? And did not the party of the Executive control the entire Federal Government, every State government, every county, every city, town and village in the North and West? Was it patronage? All belonged to it. Was it influence? What more? Did not the school, the college, the church, the press, the secret orders, the municipality, the corporation, railroads, telegraphs, express companies, the voluntary association, all, all yield it to the utmost? Was it unanimity? Never was an Administration so supported in England or America. Five men and half a score of newspapers made up the Opposition. Was it enthusiasm? The enthusiasm was fanatical. There has been nothing like it since the Crusades. Was it confidence? Sir, the faith of the people exceeded that of the patriarch. They gave up Constitution, law, right, liberty, all at your demand for arbitrary power that the rebellion might, as you promised, be crushed out in three months, and the Union restored. Was credit needed? You took control of a country, young, vigorous, and inexhaustible in wealth and resources, and of a Government almost free from public debt, and whose good faith had never been tarnished. Your great national loan bubble failed miserably, as it deserved to fail; but the bankers and merchants of Philadelphia, New York and Boston lent you more than their entire banking capital. And when that failed too, you forced credit by declaring your paper promises to pay, a legal tender for all debts. Was money wanted? You had all the revenues of the United States, diminished indeed, but still in gold. The whole wealth of the country, to the last dollar, lay at your feet. Private individuals, municipal corporations, the State governments, all, in their frenzy, gave you money or means with reckless prodigality. The great eastern cities lent you $150,-000,000. Congress voted, first, $250,000,000, and next $500,000,000 more in loans; and then, first $50,000,000, next $10,000,000, then $90,000,000, and, in July last, $150,000,000 in Treasury notes; and the Secretary has issued also a paper "postage currency," in sums as low as five cents, limited in amount only by his discretion. Nay, more: already since the 4th of July, 1861, this House has appropriated $2,017,864,000, almost every dollar without debate, and without a recorded vote. A thousand millions have been expended since the 15th of April, 1861; and a public debt or liability of $1,500,000,000 already incurred. And to support all this stupendous outlay and indebtedness, a system of taxation, direct and indirect, has been inaugurated, the most onerous and unjust ever imposed upon any but a conquered people.

Money and credit, then, you have had in prodigal profusion. And were men wanted? More than a million rushed to arms! Seventy-five thousand first, (and the country stood aghast at the multitude,) then eighty-three thousand more were demanded; and three hundred and ten thousand responded to the call. The President next asked for four hundred thousand, and Congress, in their generous confidence, gave him five hundred thousand; and, not to be outdone, he took six hundred and thirty-seven thousand. Half of these melted away in their first campaign; and the President demanded three hundred thousand more for the war, and then drafted yet another three hundred thousand for nine months. The fabled hosts of Xerxes have been out-numbered. And yet victory, strangely, follows the standard of the foe. From Great Bethel to Vicksburg, the battle has not been to the strong. Yet every disaster, except the last, has been followed by a call for more troops, and every time, so far, they have been promptly furnished. From the beginning the war has been conducted like a political campaign, and it has been the folly of the party in power that they have assumed, that numbers alone would win the field in a contest not with ballots but with musket and sword. But numbers, you have had almost without number—the largest, best appointed, best armed, fed, and clad host of brave men, well organized and well disciplined, ever marshaled. A Navy, too, not the most formidable perhaps, but the most numerous and gallant, and the costliest in the world, and against a foe, almost without a navy at all. Thus, with twenty millions of people, and every element of strength and force at command—power, patronage, influence, unanimity, enthusiasm, confidence, credit, money, men, an Army and a Navy the largest and the noblest ever set in the field, or afloat upon the sea; with the support, almost servile, of every State, county, and municipality in the North and West, with a Congress swift to do the bidding of the Executive; without opposition anywhere at home; and with an arbitrary power which neither the Czar of Russia, nor the Emperor of Austria dare exercise; yet after nearly two years of more vigorous prosecution of war than ever recorded in history; after more skirmishes, combats and battles than Alexander, Cæsar, or the first Napoleon ever fought in any five years of their military career, you have utterly, signally, disastrously—I will not say ignominiously—failed to subdue ten millions of "rebels," whom you had taught the people of the North and West not only to hate, but to despise. Rebels, did I say? Yes, your fathers were rebels, or your grandfathers. He, who now before me on canvas looks down so sadly upon us, the false, degenerate, and imbecile guardians of the great Republic which he founded, was a rebel. And yet we, cradled ourselves in rebellion, and who have fostered and fraternized with every insurrection in the nineteenth century everywhere throughout the globe, would now, forsooth, make the word "rebel" a reproach. Rebels certainly they are; but all the persistent and stupendous efforts of the most gigantic warfare of modern times have, through your incompetency and folly, availed nothing to crush them out, cut off though they have been, by your blockade, from all the world, and dependent only upon their own courage and resources. And yet, they were to be utterly conquered and subdued in six weeks, or three months! Sir, my judgment was made up, and expressed from the first. I learned it from Chatham: "My lords, you can not conquer America." And you have not conquered the South. You never will. It is not in the nature of things possible; much less under your auspices. But money you have expended without limit, and blood poured out like water. Defeat, debt, taxation, sepulchers, these are your trophies. In vain, the people gave you treasure; and the soldier yielded up his life. "Fight, tax, emancipate, let these," said the gentleman from Maine, [Mr. Pike,] at the last session, "be the trinity of our salvation." Sir, they have become the trinity of your deep damnation. The war for the Union is, in your hands, a most bloody and costly failure. The President confessed it on the 22d of September, solemnly, officially, and under the broad seal of the United States. And he has now repeated the confession. The priests and rabbis of abolition taught him that God would not prosper such a cause. War for the Union was abandoned; war for the negro openly begun, and with stronger battalions than before. With what success? Let the dead at Fredericksburg and Vicksburg answer.

And now, sir, can this war continue? Whence the money to carry it on? Where the men? Can you borrow? From whom? Can you tax more? Will the people bear it? Wait till you have collected what is already levied. How many millions more of "legal tender"—to-day forty-seven per cent. below the par of gold—can you float? Will men enlist now at any price? Ah, sir, it is easier to die at home. I beg pardon; but I trust I am not "discouraging enlistments." If I am, then first arrest Lincoln, Stanton, Halleck, and some of your other generals, and I will retract; yes, I will recant. But can you draft again? Ask New England—New York. Ask Massachusetts. Where are the nine hundred thousand? Ask not Ohio—the Northwest. She thought you in earnest, and gave you all, all—more than you demanded. . . .

But ought this war to continue? I answer, no—not a day, not an hour.

What then? Shall we separate? Again I answer, no, no, no! What then? And now, sir, I come to the grandest and most solemn problem of statesmanship from the beginning of time; and to the God of heaven, illuminer of hearts and minds, I would humbly appeal for some measure, at least, of light and wisdom and strength to explore and reveal the dark but possible future of this land. . . .

And now, sir, I propose to briefly consider the causes which led to disunion and the present civil war; and to inquire whether they are eternal and ineradicable in their nature, and at the same time powerful enough to overcome all the causes and considerations which impel to reunion. . . .

What then, I ask, is the immediate, direct cause of disunion and this civil war? Slavery, it is answered. Sir, that is the philosophy of the rustic in the play—"that a great cause of the night, is lack of the sun." Certainly slavery was in one sense—very obscure, indeed—the cause of the war. Had there been no slavery here, this particular war about slavery would never have been waged. In a like sense, the Holy Sepulcher was the cause of the war of the Crusades, and had Troy or Carthage never existed, there never would have been Trojan or Carthaginian war, and no such personages as Hector and Hannibal; and no Iliad or Æneid would ever have been written. But far better say that the negro is the cause of the war; for had there been no negro here, there would be no war just now. What then? Exterminate him? Who demands it? Colonize him? How? Where? When? At whose cost? Sir, let us have an end of this folly.

But slavery is the cause of the war. Why? Because the South obstinately and wickedly refused to restrict or abolish it at the demand of the philosophers or fanatics and demagogues of the North and West. Then, sir, it was abolition, the purpose to abolish or interfere with and hem in slavery, which caused disunion and war. Slavery is only the *subject,* but Abolition the *cause* of this civil war. It was the persistent and determined agitation in the free States of the question of abolishing slavery in the South, because of the alleged "irrepressible conflict" between the forms of labor in the two sections, or, in the false and mischievous cant of the day, between freedom and slavery, that forced a collision of arms at last. Sir, that conflict was not confined to the Territories. It was expressly proclaimed by its apostles, as between the States also—against the institution of domestic slavery everywhere. But, assuming the platforms of the Republican party as a standard, and stating the case most strongly in favor of that party, it was the refusal of the South to consent that slavery should be excluded from the Territories, that led to the continued agitation, North and South, of that question, and finally to disunion and civil war. Sir, I will not be answered now by the old clamor about "the aggressions of the slave power." That miserable specter, that unreal mockery, has been exorcised and expelled by debt and taxation and blood. If that power did govern this country for the sixty years preceding this terrible revolution, then the sooner this Administration and Government return to the principles and policy of Southern statesmanship, the better for the country; and that, sir, is already, or soon will be, the judgment of the people. But I deny that it was the "slave power" that governed for so many years, and so wisely and well. It was the Democratic party, and its principles and policy, molded and controlled, indeed, largely by Southern statesmen. Neither will I be stopped by that other cry of mingled fanaticism and hypocrisy, about the sin and barbarism of African slavery. Sir, I see more of barbarism and sin, a thousand times, in the continuance of this war, the dissolution of the Union, the breaking up of this Government, and the enslavement of the white race, by debt and taxes and arbitrary power. The day of fanatics and sophists and enthusiasts, thank God, is gone at last; and though the age of chivalry may not, the age of practical statesmanship is about to return. Sir, I accept the language and intent of the Indiana resolution, to the full—"that in considering terms of settlement, we will look only to the welfare, peace, and safety of the white race, without reference to the effect that settlement may have upon the condition of the African." And when we have done this, my word for it, the safety, peace, and welfare of the African will have been best secured. Sir, there is fifty-fold less of anti-slavery sentiment to-day in the West than there was two years ago; and if this war be continued, there will be still less a year hence. The people there begin, at last, to comprehend, that domestic slavery in the South is a question, not of morals, or religion, or humanity, but a form of labor, perfectly compatible with the dignity of free white labor in the same com-munity, and with national vigor, power, and prosperity, and especially with military strength. They have learned, or begin to learn, that the evils of the system affect the master alone, or the community and State in which it exists; and that we of the free States partake of all the material benefits of the institution, unmixed with any part of its mischief. They believe, also, in the subordination of the negro race to the white, where they both exist together, and that the condition of subordination, as established in the South, is far better every way, for the negro, than the hard servitude of poverty, degradation, and crime, to which he is subjected in the free States. All this, sir, may be "pro-slaveryism," if there be such a word. Perhaps it is; but the people of the West begin now to think it wisdom and good sense. We will not establish slavery in our own midst; neither will we abolish it, or interfere with it outside of our own limits. . . .

And now, sir, I come to the great and controlling question within which the whole issue of union or disunion is bound up: Is there "an irrepressible conflict" between the slaveholding and non-slaveholding States? Must "the cotton and rice fields of South Carolina, and the sugar plantations of Louisiana," in the language of Mr. Seward, "be ultimately tilled by free labor, and Charleston and New Orleans become marts for legitimate merchandise alone, or else the rye fields and wheat fields of Massachusetts and New York again be surrendered by their farmers to slave culture and the production of slaves, and Boston and New York become, once more markets for trade in the bodies and souls of men?" If so, then there is an end of all union, and forever. You can not abolish slavery by the sword; still less by proclamations, though the President were to "proclaim" every month. Of what possible avail was his proclamation of September? Did the South submit? Was she even alarmed? And yet, he has now fulmined another "bull against the comet"—*brutum fulmen*—and, threatening ser-vile insurrection with all its horrors, has yet coolly appealed to the judg-ment of mankind, and invoked the blessing of the God of peace and love! But declaring it a military necessity, an essential measure of war to subdue the rebels, yet, with admirable wisdom, he expressly exempts from its operation the only States, and parts of States, in the South, where he has the military power to execute it.

Neither, sir, can you abolish slavery by argument. As well attempt to abolish marriage, or the relation of paternity. The South is resolved to maintain it at every hazard, and by every sacrifice; and if "this Union can not endure, part slave and part free," then it is already and finally dissolved. . . .

But I deny the doctrine. It is full of disunion and civil war. It is disunion itself. Whoever first taught it ought to be dealt with as not only hostile to the Union, but an enemy of the human race. Sir, the fundamental idea of the Constitution is the perfect and eternal compatibility of a union of States "part slave and part free;" else the Constitution never would have been framed, nor the Union founded; and seventy years of successful experiment have approved the wisdom of the plan. In my deliberate judgment, a confederacy made up of slaveholding and non-slaveholding States, is, in the nature of things, the strongest of all popular governments. African slavery has been, and is, eminently conservative. It makes the absolute political equality of the white race everywhere practicable. It dispenses with the English order of nobility, and leaves every white man, North and South, owning slaves or owning none, the equal of every other white man. It has reconciled universal suffrage, throughout the free States, with the stability of government. I speak not now of its material benefits to the North and West, which are many and more obvious. But the South, too, has profited many ways by a union with the non-slaveholding States. Enterprise, industry, self-reliance, perseverance, and the other hardy virtues of a people living in a higher latitude, and without hereditary servants, she has learned or received from the North. Sir, it is easy, I know, to denounce all this, and to revile him who utters it. Be it so. The English is, of all languages, the most copious in words of bitterness and reproach. "Pour on: I will endure."

Then, sir, there is not an "irrepressible conflict" between slave labor and free labor. There is no conflict at all. Both exist together in perfect harmony in the South. The master and the slave, the white laborer and the black, work together in the same field, or the same shop, and without the slightest sense of degradation. They are not equals, either socially or politically. And why, then, can not Ohio, having only free labor, live in harmony with Kentucky, which has both slave and free? Above all, why can not Massachusetts allow the same right of choice to South Carolina, separated as they are a thousand miles, by other States, who would keep the peace, and live in good will? Why this civil war? Whence disunion? Not from slavery—not because the South chooses to have two kinds of labor instead of one—but from *sectionalism,* always and every where a disintegrating principle. Sectional jealousy and hate—these, sir, are the only elements of conflict between these States; and, though powerful, they are yet not at all irrepressible. They exist between families, communities, towns, cities, counties, and States; and if not repressed, would dissolve all society and government. They exist, also, between other sections than the North and South. Sectionalism East, many years ago, saw the South and West united by the ties of geographical position, migration, intermarriage, and interest, and thus strong enough to control the power and policy of the Union. . . .

What then, sir, with so many causes impelling to reunion, keeps us apart to-day? Hate, passion, antagonism, revenge—all heated seven times hotter by war. Sir, these, while they last, are the most powerful of all motives with a people, and with the individual man; but, fortunately, they are the least durable. They hold a divided sway in the same bosoms with the nobler qualities of love, justice, reason, placability; and, except when at their height, are weaker than the sense of interest, and always, in States, at least give way to it at last. No statesman who yields himself up to them can govern wisely or well; and no State whose policy is controlled by them can either prosper or endure. But war is both their offspring and their aliment, and, while it lasts, all other motives are subordinate. The virtues of peace can not flourish, can not even find development in the midst of fighting; and this civil war keeps in motion all the centrifugal forces of the Union, and gives to them increased strength and activity every day. But such, and so many and powerful, in my judgment, are the cementing or centripetal agencies impelling us together, that nothing but perpetual war and strife can keep us always divided. . . .

And now, sir, I will not ask whether the North-west can consent to separation from the South. Never. Nature forbids. We are only a part of the great valley of the Mississippi. There is no line of latitude upon which to separate. Neither party would desire the old line of 36° 30' on both sides of the river; and there is no natural boundary east and west. The nearest to it are the Ohio and Missouri rivers. But that line would leave Cincinnati and St. Louis, as border cities, like Baltimore, to decay, and, extending fifteen hundred miles in length, would become the scene of an eternal border warfare, without example even in the worst of times. Sir, we can not, ought not, will not, separate from the South. And if you of the East who have found this war against the South, and for the negro, gratifying to your hate or profitable to your purse, will continue it till a separation be forced between the slaveholding and your non-slaveholding States, then, believe me, and accept it, as you did not the other solemn warnings of years past, *the day which divides the North from the South, that self-same day decrees eternal divorce between the West and the East.*

Sir, our destiny is fixed. There is not one drop of rain which, descending from the heavens and fertilizing our soil, causes it to yield an abundant harvest, but flows into the Mississippi, and there mingling with the waters of that mighty river, finds its way, at last, to the Gulf of Mexico. And we must and will follow it with travel and trade   not by treaty, but by right— freely, peaceably, and without restriction or tribute, under the same government and flag, to its home in the bosom of that gulf. Sir, we will not remain, after separation from the South, a province or appanage of the East, to bear her burdens and pay her taxes; nor, hemmed in and isolated as we are, and without a sea-coast, could we long remain a distinct confederacy. But wherever we go, married to the South or the East, we bring with us three-fourths of the territories of that valley to the Rocky Moun tains, and it may be to the Pacific—the grandest and most magnificent dowry that bride ever had to bestow. . . .

And let not the States now called Confederate insist upon separation and independence. What did they demand at first? Security against Abolitionism within the Union: protection from the "irrepressible conflict," and the domination of the absolute numerical majority: a change of public opinion, and consequently of political parties in the North and West, so that their local institutions and domestic peace should no longer be endangered. And now, sir, after two years of persistent and most gigantic effort on part of this Administration to compel them to submit, but with utter and signal failure, the people of the free States are now, or are fast becoming, satisfied that the price of the Union is the utter suppression of Abolitionism or anti-slavery as a political element, and the complete subordination of the spirit of fanaticism and intermeddling which gave it birth. In any event, they are ready now, if I have not greatly misread the signs of the times, to return to the old Constitutional and actual basis of fifty years ago: three-fifths rule of representation, speedy rendition of fugitives from labor, equal rights in the Territories, no more slavery agitation anywhere, and transit and temporary sojourn with slaves, without molestation, in the free States. Without all these there could be neither peace nor permanence to a restored union of States "part slave and part free." With it, the South, in addition to all the other great and multiplied benefits of union, would be far more secure in her slave property, her domestic institutions, than under a separate government. Sir, let no man, North or West, tell me that this would perpetuate African slavery. I know it. But so does the Constitution. I repeat, sir, it is the price of the Union. Whoever hates negro slavery more than he loves the Union must demand separation at last. I think that you can never abolish slavery by fighting. Certainly you never can till you have first destroyed the South, and then, in the language, first of Mr. Douglas and afterward of Mr. Seward, converted this Government into an imperial despotism. And, sir, whenever I am forced to a choice between the loss, to my own country and race, of personal and political liberty, with all its blessings, and the involuntary domestic servitude of the negro, I shall not hesitate one moment to choose the latter alternative. The sole question, to-day, is between the Union, with slavery, or final disunion, and, I think, anarchy and despotism. I am for the Union. It was good enough for my fathers. It is good enough for us, and our children after us. . . .

SELECTION

The Vice President of the Confederacy Denounces His Government: Alexander H. Stephens's Speech to the Georgia Legislature, 1864

Conservative, states' rights opposition to the administration of Jefferson Davis was led by no less a figure than the Vice President of the Confederacy, Georgia's Alexander H. Stephens (1812–1883). A former member of Congress (from 1843 to 1859), Stephens had opposed immediate secession in 1861, favoring rather a "reconstruction" of the Union. He was, nonetheless, selected by the Montgomery Convention for the provisional Vice Presidency of the

Confederate States, and elected to a regular full term as Vice President in
November, 1861. To Stephens, the preservation of state sovereignty appeared
more urgent than the establishment of an independent South. He spent little
time tending to his duties as Vice President in Richmond, the Confederate
capital, preferring rather to lead the attack against Davis and the concentration of power on the national level from his home in Georgia. In 1864, the
broadening of the conscription law and the continuation of the suspension of
the writ of habeas corpus, both measures passed by the Confederate Congress,
inspired Stephens to take his opposition to the Davis government before the
Georgia state legislature. Stephens's "Speech on the State of the Confederacy,
March 16, 1864," (the selection that follows) was a long denunciation of the
government's encroachments on the rights of the states and their citizens; the
text is reprinted from Henry Cleveland, Alexander H. Stephens, in Public and
Private, with Letters and Speeches (Philadelphia: National Publishing Co.,
1866), pages 761–786. Like his counterparts in the North, Stephens urged the
settlement of the difficulties between the North and South by peaceful negotiation, and himself participated in several unsuccessful peace movements.
Stephens, however, assumed that any such negotiation would be based on the
independence of the Confederacy. Following the war, he defended his states'
rights position in a compendious work A Constitutional View of the Late War
between the States (1868–1870) in two volumes. Frank L. Owsley has charged
the states' rights opposition with heavy responsibility for the Confederacy's
defeat in his State Rights in the Confederacy (1925). A recent biography of
Stephens is Rudolph von Abele, Alexander H. Stephens, A Biography (1946).

entlemen of the Senate and House of Representatives:

In compliance with your request, or at least with that of a large portion
of your respective bodies, I appear before you tonight to speak of the state
of public affairs. Never, perhaps, before, have I risen to address a public
audience under circumstances of so much responsibility, and never did I
feel more deeply impressed with the weight of it. Questions of the most
momentous importance are pressing upon you for consideration and action.
Upon these I am to address you. Would that my ability, physically, and
in all other respects, were commensurate with the magnitude of the occasion. We are in the midst of dangers and perils. Dangers without and
dangers within. Scylla on the one side and Charybdis on the other. War is
being waged against us by a strong, unscrupulous and vindictive foe; a war
for our subjugation, degradation and extermination. From this quarter
threaten the perils without. Those within arise from questions of policy as to the best means, the wisest and safest, to repel the enemy,
achieve our independence, to maintain and keep secure our rights and
liberties. Upon the decision of these questions, looking to the proper
development of our limited resources, wisely and patriotically, so that
their entire efficiency may be exerted in our deliverance, with at the same
time a watchful vigilance to the safety of the citadel itself, as much depends as upon the skill of our commanders and the valor of our citizen
soldiers in the field. Every thing dear to us as freemen is at stake. An error
in judgment, though springing from the most patriotic motives, whether
in councils of war or councils of state, may be fatal. He, therefore, who

rises under such circumstances to offer words of advice, not only assumes a position of great responsibility, but stands on dangerous ground. Impressed profoundly with such feelings and convictions, I should shrink from the undertaking you have called me to, but for the strong consciousness that where duty leads no one should ever fear to tread. Great as are the dangers that threaten us, perilous as is our situation—and I do not intend to overstate or understate, neither to awaken undue apprehension, or to excite hopes and expectations never to be realized—perilous, therefore, as our situation is, it is far, far from being desperate or hopeless, and I feel no hesitation in saying to you, in all frankness and candor, that if we are true to ourselves, and true to our cause, all may yet be well.

In the progress of the war thus far, it is true there is much to be seen of suffering, of sacrifice and of desolation; much to sicken the heart and cause a blush for civilization and Christianity. Cities have been taken, towns have been sacked, vast amounts of property have been burned, fields have been laid waste, records have been destroyed, churches have been desecrated, women and children have been driven from their homes, unarmed men have been put to death, States have been overrun and whole populations made to groan under the heel of despotism; all these things are seen and felt, but in them nothing is to be seen to cause dismay, much less despair; these deeds of ruin and savage barbarity have been perpetrated only on the outer borders, on the coast, and on the line of the rivers, where by the aid of their ships of war and gunboats the enemy has had the advantage; the great breadth of the interior—the heart of our country—has never yet been reached by them; they have as yet, after a struggle of nearly three years, with unlimited means, at a cost of not less than four thousand millions of dollars (how much more is unknown) and hundreds of thousands of lives, been able only to break the outer shell of the Confederacy. The only signal advantages they have as yet gained have been on the water, or where their land and naval forces were combined. That they should have gained advantages under such circumstances, is not a matter of much surprise. Nations in war, like individual men or animals, show their real power in combat when they stand upon the advantages that nature has given them, and fight on their own ground and in their own element. The lion, though king of the forest, cannot contend successfully with the shark in the water. In no conflict of arms away from gunboats, during the whole war, since the first battle of Manassas to that of Ocean Pond, have our gallant soldiers failed of victory when the numbers on each side were at all equal. . . .

Take courage from the example of your ancestors—disasters caused with them nothing like dismay or despair—they only aroused a spirit of renewed energy and fortitude. The principles they fought for, suffered and endured so much for, are the same for which we are now struggling—State rights, State sovereignty, the great principle set forth in the declaration of independence—the right of every State to govern itself as it pleases. With the same wisdom, prudence, forecast and patriotism; the same or equal statesmanship on the part of our rulers in directing and wielding our resources, our material of war, that controlled public affairs at that time, in the camp and in the cabinet, and with the same spirit animating the breast of the people, devotion to liberty and right, hatred of tyranny and oppression, affection for the cause for the cause's sake; with the same sentiments and feelings on the part of rulers and people in these days as were in those, we might and may be overrun as they were; our interior may be penetrated by superior hostile armies, and our country laid waste as theirs was, but we can never be conquered, as they never could be. The issues of war depend quite as much upon statesmanship as generalship; quite as much upon what is done at the council board, as upon what is done in the field. Much the greater part of all wars, is business—plain practical every-day-life business; there is in it no art or mystery or special knowledge, except good, strong, common sense—this relates to the finances, the quartermaster's and commissary's departments, the ways and means proper—in a word to the resources of a country and its capacities for war. The number of men that can be spared from production, without weakening the aggregate strength—the prospect of supplies, subsistence, arms and munitions of all kinds. It is as necessary that men called out should be armed, clothed, shod and fed, as that they should be put in the field— subsistence is as essential as men. At present we have subsistence sufficient for the year, if it is taken care of and managed with economy. Upon a moderate estimate, one within reasonable bounds, the tithes of wheat and corn for last year were not less, in the States east of the Mississippi, (to say nothing of the other side,) than eighteen million bushels. Kentucky and Tennessee are not included in this estimate. This would bread an army of five hundred thousand men and one hundred thousand horses for twelve months, and leave a considerable margin for waste or loss. This we have without buying or impressing a bushel or pound. Nor need a bushel of it be lost on account of the want of transportation from points at a distance from railroads. At such places it could be fed to animals, put into beef and pork, and thus lessen the amount of these articles of food to be bought. Upon a like estimate the tithe of meat for the last year, will supply the army for at least six months—rendering the purchase of supplies of this article necessary for only half the year—the surplus in the country, over and above the tithes, is ample to meet the deficiency. All that is wanting is men of business capacity, honesty, integrity, economy and industry in the management and control of that department. There need be no fear of the want of subsistence this year, if our officials do their duty. But how it will be next year, if the policy adopted by Congress, at its late session, is carried out, no one can safely venture to say. . . .

It is the beauty of our system of government, that all in authority are responsible to the people. It is, too, always more agreeable to approve than to disapprove what our agents have done. But in grave and important matters, however disagreeable or even painful it may be to express disapproval, yet sometimes the highest duty requires it. No exceptions should be taken to this when it is done in a proper spirit, and with a view solely for the public welfare. In free governments men will differ as to the best means of promoting the public good. Honest differences of opinion should never beget ill feelings, or personal alienations. The expressions of differences of opinion do no harm when truth alone is the object on both sides. Our opinions in all such discussions of public affairs, should be given as from friends to friends, as from brothers to brothers, in a common cause. We are all launched upon the same boat, and must ride the storm or go down together. Disagreements should never arise, except from one cause—a difference in judgment, as to the best means to be adopted, or course to be pursued, for the common safety. . . .

The military act by which conscription is extended so as to embrace all between the ages of seventeen and fifty, and by which the State is to be deprived of so much of its labor, and stripped of the most efficient portion of her enrolled militia, presents a much graver question. This whole system of conscription I have looked upon from the beginning as wrong, radically wrong in principle and in policy. Contrary opinions, however, prevailed. But whatever differences of opinion may have been entertained as to the constitutionality of the previous conscript acts, it seems clear to my mind that but little difference can exist as to the unconstitutionality of this late act. The act provides for the organizing of troops of an anomalous character—partly as militia and partly as a portion of the regular armies. But, in fact, they are to be organized neither as militia or part of the regular army. We have but two kinds of forces, the regular army and the militia—this is neither. The men are to be raised as conscripts for the regular forces, while their officers are to be appointed as if they were militia. If they were intended as militia, they should have been called out, through the governor, in their present organizations—if as regular forces, they cannot be officered as the act provides. It is most clearly unconstitutional. . . .

I come, now, to the last of these acts of Congress. The suspension of the writ of *habeas corpus* in certain cases. This is the most exciting as it is by far the most important question before you. Upon this depends the question, whether the courts shall be permitted to decide upon the constitutionality of the late conscript act, should you submit that question to their decision, and upon it also depend other great essential rights enjoyed by us as freemen. This act upon its face, confers upon the President, secretary of war, and the general commanding in the trans-Mississippi department, (the two latter acting under the control and authority of the President,) the power to arrest and imprison any person who may be simply charged with certain acts, not all of them even crimes under any law; and this is to be done without any oath or affirmation alleging probable cause as to the guilt of the party. This is attempted to be done under that clause of the constitution, which authorizes Congress to suspend the privilege of the writ of *habeas corpus*, in certain cases.

In my judgment this act is not only unwise, impolitic and unconstitutional, but exceedingly dangerous to public liberty. Its unconstitutionality does not rest upon the idea that Congress has not got the power to suspend the privilege of this writ, nor upon the idea that the power to suspend it is an implied one, or that clearly implied powers are weaker as a class and subordinate to others, positively and directly delegated.

I do not understand the executive of this State to put his argument against this act upon any such grounds. He simply states a fact, as it most clearly is, that the power to suspend at all is an implied power. There is no positive, direct power delegated to do it. The power, however, is clear, and clear only by implication. The language of the constitution, that "the privilege of the writ of *habeas corpus* shall not be suspended unless, when in cases of rebellion or invasion, the public safety may require it," clearly expresses the intention that the power may be exercised in the cases stated; but it does so by implication only, just as if a mother should say to her daughter, you shall not go unless you ride. Here the permission and authority to go is clearly given, though by inference and implication only. It is not positively and directly given. This, and this only, I understand the governor to mean when he speaks of the power being an implied one. He raises no question as to the existence of the power, or its validity when rightfully exercised, but he maintains, as I do, that its exercise must be controlled by all other restrictions in the constitution bearing upon its exercise. Two of these are to be found in the words accompanying the delegation. It can never be exercised except in rebellion or invasion. Other restrictions are to be found in other parts of the constitution—in the amendments to the constitution adopted after the ratification of the words as above quoted. These amendments were made, as is expressly declared in the preamble to them, to add "further declaratory and restrictive clauses," to prevent "misconstruction or abuse of the powers" previously delegated. To understand all the restrictions, therefore, thrown around the exercise of this power in the constitution, these additional "restrictive clauses" must be read in conjunction with the original grant, whether that was made positively and directly, or by implication only. These restrictions, among other things, declare, that "no person shall be deprived of life, liberty, or property, without due process of law," and that the right of the people to be secure in their persons, houses, papers and effects, against *unreasonable* searches and *seizures, shall not be violated,* and no warrants shall issue but upon probable cause, supported by oath or affirmation, and particularly describing the place to be searched, and the person or thing to be seized.

All admit that under the clause as it stands in the original grant, with the restrictions there set forth, the power can be rightfully exercised only in cases of rebellion or invasion. With these additional clauses, put in as further restrictions to prevent the abuse of powers previously delegated, how is this clause conferring the power to suspend the privilege of the writ of *habeas corpus,* now to be read? In this way, and in this way only: "The privilege of the writ of *habeas corpus* shall not be suspended, unless when in cases of rebellion or invasion the public safety may require it." And no person "shall be deprived of life, liberty, or property, without due process of law." And further. "The right of the people to be secure in their persons, houses, papers and effects against unreasonable searches and seizures, shall not be violated, and no warrants shall issue but upon probable cause, supported by oath or affirmation, and particularly describing the place to be searched, and the persons or things to be seized."

The attempted exercise of the power to suspend the privilege of the writ of *habeas corpus* in this act, is in utter disregard in the very face and teeth of these restrictions, as much so; as a like attempt in time of profound peace would be in disregard of the restrictions to cases of rebellion and invasion, as the constitution was originally adopted. It attempts to provide for depriving persons "of liberty, without due process of law." It attempts to annul and set at naught the great constitutional "right" of the people, to be secure in their persons against "unreasonable seizures." It attempts to destroy and annihilate the bulwark of personal liberty, secured in our great chart to the humblest as well as the highest, that "no warrants shall issue but upon probable cause, supported by oath or affirmation," and "particularly describing the person to be seized." Nay, more, it attempts to change and transform the distribution of powers in our system of government. It attempts to deprive the judiciary department of its appropriate and legitimate functions, and to confer them upon the President, the secretary of war, and the general officer commanding the trans-Mississippi department, or rather to confer them entirely upon the President, for those subordinates named in the act hold their places at his will, and in arrests under this act are to be governed by his orders. This, by the constitution, never can be done. Ours is not only a government of limited powers, but each department, the legislative, executive and judicial, are separate and distinct. The issuing of warrants, which are nothing but orders for arrests, against civilians or persons in civil life, is a judicial function. The President, under the constitution, has not the power to issue any such. As commander-in-chief of the land and naval forces, and the militia when in actual service, he may order arrests for trials before courts-martial, according to the rules and articles of war. But he is clothed with no such power over those not in the military service and not subject to the rules and articles of war. This act attempts to clothe him with judicial functions, and in a judicial character to do what no judge, under the constitution, can do: issue orders or warrants for arrest, by which persons are to be deprived of their liberty, imprisoned, immured in dungeons, it may be without any oath or affirmation, even as to the probable guilt of the party accused or charged with any of the offences or acts stated. This, under the constitution, in my judgment, cannot be done. Congress can confer no such power upon our chief magistrate. There is no such thing known in this country as political warrants, or *"lettres de cachet."* This act attempts to institute this new order of things so odious to our ancestors, and so inconsistent with constitutional liberty. . . .

Another serious objection to the measure, showing its impolicy, is the effect it will have upon our cause abroad. I have never looked to foreign intervention, or early recognition, and do not now. European governments have no sympathy with either side in this struggle. They are rejoiced to see professed republicans cutting each other's throats, and the failure, as they think, of the great experiment of self-government on this continent. They saw that the North went into despotism immediately on the separation of the South, and their fondest hopes and expectations are that the same destiny awaits us. This has usually been the fate of republics. This is the sentiment of all the governments in Europe. But we have friends there, as you heard last night, in the eloquent remarks of the gentleman [Hon. L. Q. C. LAMAR] who addressed you on our foreign relations, and who has lately returned from those countries. Those friends are anxiously and hopefully watching the issue of the present conflict. In speeches, papers, and reviews they are defending our cause. No argument used by them heretofore has been more effectual than the contrast drawn between the federals and the confederates upon the subject of the writ of *habeas corpus*. Here, notwithstanding our dangers and perils, the military has always been kept subordinate to the civil authorities. Here all the landmarks of English liberty have been preserved and maintained, while at the North scarcely a vestige of them is left. There, instead of courts of justice with open doors, the country is dotted all over with prisons and bastiles. No better argument in behalf of a people struggling for constitutional liberty could have been presented to arouse sympathy in our favor. It showed that we were passing through a fiery furnace for a great cause, and passing through unscathed. It showed that whatever may be the state of things at the North, that at the South at least the great light of the principles of self-government, civil and religious liberty, established on this continent by our ancestors, which was looked to with encouragement and hope by the down-trodden of all nations, was not yet extinguished, but was still burning brightly in the hands of their southern sons, even burning the more brightly from the intensity of the heat of the conflict in which we are engaged. To us, in deed and in truth, is committed the hopes of the world as to the capacity and ability of man for self-government. Let us see to it that these hopes and expectations do not fail. Let us prove ourselves equal to the high mission before us.

One other view only: that relates to the particularly dangerous tendency of this act in the present state of the country, and the policy indicated by Congress. Conscription has been extended to embrace all between seventeen and fifty years of age. It cannot be possible that the intention and object of that measure was really to call and keep in the field all between those ages. The folly and ruinous consequences of such a policy is too apparent. Details are to be made, and must be made, to a large extent. The effect and the object of this measure, therefore, was not to raise armies or procure soldiers, but to put all the population of the country between those ages under military law. Whatever the object was, the effect is to put much the larger portion of the labor of the country, both white and slave, under the complete control of the President. Under this system almost all the useful and necessary occupations of life will be completely under the control of one man. No one between the ages of seventeen and fifty can tan your leather, make your shoes, grind your grain, shoe your horse, lay your plough, make your wagon, repair your harness, superintend your farm, procure your salt, or perform any other of the necessary vocations of life, (except teachers, preachers, and physicians, and a very few others,) without permission from the President. This is certainly an extraordinary and a dangerous power. In this connection take in view this *habeas corpus* suspension act, by which it has been shown the attempt is made to confer upon him the power to order the arrest and imprisonment of any man, woman or child in the confederacy, on the bare charge, unsupported by oath, of any of the acts for which arrests are allowed to be made. Could the whole country be more completely under the power and control of one man, except as to life or limb? Could dictatorial powers be more complete? In this connection consider, also, the strong appeals that have been made for some time past, by leading journals, openly for a dictator. Coming events often cast their shadows before. Could art or ingenuity have devised a shorter or a surer cut to that end, for all practical purposes, than the whole policy adopted by the last Congress, and now before you for consideration? As to the objects, or motives, or patriotism of those who adopted that policy, that is not the question. The presentation of the case as it stands is what your attention is called to. Nor is the probability of the abuse of the power the question. Some, doubtless, think it for the best interests of the country to have a dictator. Such are not unfrequently to be met with whose intelligence, probity, and general good character in private life are not to be questioned, however much their wisdom, judgment, and principles may be deplored. In such times, when considering the facts as they exist, and looking at the policy indicated in all its bearings, the most ill-timed, delusive, and dangerous words that can be uttered are, can you not trust the President? Have you not confidence in him that he will not abuse the powers thus confided in him? To all such questions my answer is, without any reflection or imputation against our present chief magistrate, that the measure of my confidence in him, and all other public officers, is the constitution. To the question of whether I would not or cannot trust him with these high powers not conferred by the constitution, my answer is the same that I gave to one who submitted a plan for a dictatorship to me some months ago: "I am utterly opposed to every thing looking to, or tending toward a dictatorship in this country. Language would fail to give utterance to my inexpressible repugnance at the bare suggestion of such a lamentable catastrophe. There is no man living, and not one of the illustrious dead, whom, if now living, I would so trust."

In any and every view, therefore, I look upon this *habeas corpus* suspension act as unwise, impolitic, unconstitutional, and dangerous to public liberty. . . .

Gentlemen, I have addressed you longer than I expected to be able to do. My strength will not allow me to say more. I do not know that I shall ever address you again, or see you again. Great events have passed since, standing in this place, three years ago, I addressed your predecessors on a similar request, upon the questions then immediately preceding our present troubles. Many who were then with us have since passed away— some in the ordinary course of life, while many of them have fallen upon the battle-field, offering up their lives in the great cause in which we are engaged. Still greater events may be just ahead of us. What fate or fortune awaits you or me, in the contingencies of the times, is unknown to us all. We may meet again, or we may not. But as a parting remembrance, a lasting *memento,* to be engraven on your memories and your hearts, I warn you against that most insidious enemy which approaches with her syren song, "Independence first and liberty afterward." It is a fatal delusion. Liberty is the animating spirit, the soul of our system of government, and like the soul of man, when once lost it is lost forever. There is for it, at least, no redemption, except through blood. Never for a moment permit yourselves to look upon liberty, that constitutional liberty which you inherited as a birthright, as subordinate to independence. The one was resorted to to secure the other. Let them ever be held and cherished as objects co-ordinate, co-existent, co-equal, co-eval, and forever inseparable. Let them stand together "through weal and through woe," and if such be our fate, let them and us all go down together in a common ruin. Without liberty, I would not turn upon my heel for independence. I scorn all independence which does not secure liberty. I warn you also against another fatal delusion, commonly dressed up in the fascinating language of, "If we are to have a master, who would not prefer to have a southern one to a northern one?" Use no such language. Countenance none such. Evil communications are as corrupting in politics as in morals. . . .

I would not turn upon my heel to choose between masters. I was not born to acknowledge a master from either the North or South. I shall never choose between candidates for that office. Shall never degrade the right of suffrage in such an election. I have no wish or desire to live after the degradation of my country, and have no intention to survive its liberties, if life be the necessary sacrifice of their maintenance to the utmost of my ability, to the bitter end. As for myself, give me liberty as secured in the constitution with all its guaranties, amongst which is the sovereignty of Georgia, or give me death. This is my motto while living, and I want no better epitaph when I am dead. . . .

PART TWELVE

Our Fearful Trip Is Done

O n Sunday, April 9, 1865, Robert E. Lee, Commander of the Confederate Army of Northern Virginia, met Ulysses S. Grant, Supreme
Commander of Union forces, in the small village of Appomattox Court
House, Virginia, to discuss terms of surrender. The brief but touching
ceremony marked the virtual end of hostilities in the Civil War. Two weeks
later, General William T. Sherman received the capitulation of Confederate forces in North Carolina; the surrender of units in other parts of the
South followed. By the end of May, all military resistance against the
United States was at an end.

The close of the war came swiftly during the winter and spring months
of 1864–1865. Grant's relentless attacks had driven Lee's army back upon
Richmond and Petersburg the previous summer. By a series of bold and
decisive thrusts, the Union commander forced the evacuation of both cities
on April 2 and sent the Southern army reeling in flight. Sherman's troops
had reached the sea at Savannah late in December, following the dramatic
march through Georgia. Turning north, he pursued Joseph E. Johnston's
retreating army through South and North Carolina. The Confederate
forces were caught in a gigantic pincers, and four long years of bloodshed
and hardship were quickly brought to a close.

The glorious Southern movement for independence and self-determination became a lost cause. The enthusiasm of 1861 turned to despair and
heartbreak in 1865. Why? Historians have been asking this question ever
since that solemn April day at Appomattox Court House. There are no
easy answers, no simple explanations.

The collapse of the Confederacy has been attributed to many causes
and circumstances. Some have been offered as single explanations, others
as but part of a complex set of circumstances. There were the material
factors—the lack of manpower and war matériel, the domestic shortage
of badly needed goods, the financial inadequacy of the government, the
crippling economic instability and chaos, and the failure of the drive for
foreign intervention and aid. There were the contradictions inherent in the

Southern cause itself—seeds of defeat that were planted in the very organization of the Confederate States. The attempt to found a nation on the basis of a states' rights doctrine and the struggle to achieve freedom and self-determination while defending slavery were dilemmas from which the Southern people were unable to extricate themselves. Finally, there were the failures of will—the dismal lack of effective leadership, the internal dissension, and what one Southern writer termed "a general decay of public spirit."

No one of these factors can explain the loss of the Confederate cause by itself, although some explanations seem more fundamental than others. No explanation, of course, can ignore the superiority of the North in numbers, industrial capacity, political organization, leadership, and economic strength; nor should any attempt to discover the causes of Confederate collapse detract from the amazing ability of the North and Northerners to carry their struggle through to victory. But one unmistakable impression left by the study of Confederate history is of the peculiar reluctance of the Southern people to give their cause a full and unflinching support. Although there were countless examples of heroism and sacrifice in the Confederate South, for many Southerners the struggle seemed at best a halfhearted effort to achieve certain dimly understood ends.

The end of four years of bloody strife was greeted with profound feelings of relief in both North and South—relief mixed with triumphant joy in the North and with abject acquiescence and sorrow in the South. But what a frightful toll the war had taken! How staggering its cost! The actual price of the Civil War, in terms of human suffering and its effect on attitudes and emotions for generations to come, is incalculable. The flower of an entire generation of Americans was struck down. Their loss imposed additional burdens on those who survived, burdens of widowhood and orphanage. The number of wounded soldiers and of those who returned to their homes crippled and maimed is simply not known. Added to the frightful human cost of the war is the physical cost: the devastation and destruction, the ruined countryside, the shattered economy, and the millions of dollars that were expended to support the struggle. No one will ever know the real cost of the Civil War, either to the generation that fought it or to those generations that followed.

Part of the war's price was also one of its most tragic consequences. In the first full flush of excitement over the termination of hostilities, the North's wartime leader, the man whose qualities of leadership had enabled the North to fight on even in the moments of deepest despair, fell before the assassin's bullet. Abraham Lincoln was just as surely a casualty of the Civil War as if he had fallen on the battle-field.

The Civil War was a great national trauma. Its results were vast and illimitable. A large servile class had been freed and was being led out into the sunshine of freedom and equality. The Union had been preserved and strengthened, and the great experiment in democracy had been saved. A whole new industrial economy had been boosted. In spite of the cost and the psychic damage done, it would not be difficult to conclude that the United States was better off for having undergone, and survived, the holocaust.

Valedictory for a Nation: Jefferson Davis's Last Address to the Southern People, 1865

On Sunday April 2, 1865, Jefferson Davis was worshipping in his pew at Richmond's St. Paul's Episcopal Church when he received a message from General Lee, bearing news he had long anticipated. Petersburg, Lee wrote, would be evacuated; and with the loss of that city, Richmond too must be evacuated. Preparations had already been made for this final hour. Government archives and specie were loaded on railway cars, officials were summoned. By midnight, the Confederate States government had departed from its capital. Orders were given to burn the remaining government property, including the city's tobacco warehouses. Davis planned to escape to the South, by way of the Richmond and Danville Railroad. He hoped to join the forces of General Joseph E. Johnston facing Sherman in North Carolina and to carry on the stuggle along new interior lines. In Danville, he paused to issue a proclamation to the Southern people in the belief that he might bolster their resistance. His address was one of defiance. The war was not over. The cause for Southern independence, still sacred, could yet be advanced. The situation, however, was hopeless and the words did not ring true. Within a week, Lee had surrendered his army; Johnston was negotiating with General Sherman. Davis's flight continued until May 10, when he was taken prisoner by Union cavalry forces near Irwinsville, Georgia. The Danville address quoted below, is reprinted from James D. Richardson (ed.), A Compilation of the Messages and Papers of the Confederacy *(Nashville, Tenn.: United States Publishing Company, 1906), 2 volumes, volume 1, pages 568–570. Far from signaling a new phase of the struggle, however, it proved to be the Confederacy's valedictory. The short-lived Confederate States of America passed into history, to be cherished henceforth only as a lost cause.*

Many writers during the past century have probed the causes of Southern failure. Among the most recent and useful are Charles H. Wesley, The Collapse of the Confederacy *(1937); Bell I. Wiley,* The Road to Appomattox *(1956); David Donald (ed.),* Why the North Won the Civil War *(1960); and Allan Nevins,* The Statesmanship of the Civil War *(1953), especially chapter 2, "The Southern Dilemma." A convenient collection of selections from the many attempts to explain Southern defeat appears in Henry Steele Commager (ed.),* The Defeat of the Confederacy: A Documentary Survey *(1964).*

Danville, Va., April 4, 1865.

To the People of the Confederate States of America.

The General in Chief of our Army has found it necessary to make such movements of the troops as to uncover the capital and thus involve the withdrawal of the Government from the city of Richmond.

It would be unwise, even were it possible, to conceal the great moral as well as material injury to our cause that must result from the occupation of Richmond by the enemy. It is equally unwise and unworthy of us, as patriots engaged in a most sacred cause, to allow our energies to falter, our spirits to grow faint, or our efforts to become relaxed under reverses, however calamitous. While it has been to us a source of national pride that for four years of unequaled warfare we have been able, in close proximity to the center of the enemy's power, to maintain the seat of our chosen Government free from the pollution of his presence; while the memories of the heroic dead who have freely given their lives to its defense must ever remain enshrined in our hearts; while the preservation of the capital, which is usually regarded as the evidence to mankind of separate national existence, was an object very dear to us, it is also true, and should not be forgotten, that the loss which we have suffered is not without compensation. For many months the largest and finest army of the Confederacy, under the command of a leader whose presence inspires equal confidence in the troops and the people, has been greatly trammeled by the necessity of keeping constant watch over the approaches to the capital, and has thus been forced to forego more than one opportunity for promising enterprise. The hopes and confidence of the enemy have been constantly excited by the belief that their possession of Richmond would be the signal for our submission to their rule, and relieve them from the burden of war, as their failing resources admonish them it must be abandoned if not speedily brought to a successful close. It is for us, my countrymen, to show by our bearing under reverses how wretched has been the self-deception of those who have believed us less able to endure misfortune with fortitude than to encounter danger with courage. We have now entered upon a new phase of a struggle the memory of which is to endure for all ages and to shed an increasing luster upon our country.

Relieved from the necessity of guarding cities and particular points, important but not vital to our defense, with an army free to move from point to point and strike in detail the detachments and garrisons of the enemy, operating on the interior of our own country, where supplies are more accessible, and where the foe will be far removed from his own base and cut off from all succor in case of reverse, nothing is now needed to render our triumph certain but the exhibition of our own unquenchable resolve. Let us but will it, and we are free; and who, in the light of the past, dare doubt your purpose in the future?

Animated by the confidence in your spirit and fortitude, which never yet has failed me, I announce to you, fellow-countrymen, that it is my purpose to maintain your cause with my whole heart and soul; that I will never consent to abandon to the enemy one foot of the soil of any one of the States of the Confederacy; that Virginia, noble State, whose ancient renown has been eclipsed by her still more glorious recent history, whose bosom has been bared to receive the main shock of this war, whose sons and daughters have exhibited heroism so sublime as to render her illustrious in all times to come—that Virginia, with the help of her people, and by the blessing of Providence, shall be held and defended, and no peace ever be made with the infamous invaders of her homes by the sacrifice of any of her rights or territory. If by stress of numbers we should ever be compelled to a temporary withdrawal from her limits, or those of any other border state, again and again will we return, until the baffled and exhausted enemy shall abandon in despair his endless and impossible task of making slaves of a people resolved to be free.

Let us not, then, despond, my countrymen; but, relying on the never-failing mercies and protecting care of our God, let us meet the foe with fresh defiance, with unconquered and unconquerable hearts.

JEFF'N DAVIS.

SELECTION

Robert E. Lee Bids His Army Farewell, April 10, 1865

The scene has been painted so often, in word as well as in picture, that it is familiar to all. It was Palm Sunday, April 9, 1865. In the small gathering in the Wilmer McLean house, Appomattox Court House, sat Robert E. Lee, stiff in his spotless new uniform, and Ulysses S. Grant, mud-spattered and careless in his appearance. The terms of surrender were discussed and signed. As Lee left the house, Grant bared his head and stood silently erect in tribute to a great soldier. The occasion was charged with emotion. The arms of the Army of Northern Virginia were stacked, the battle flags surrendered. Some of the men wept openly, others hurled words of defiance at the enemy they would never fight again. On the following day, General Lee issued his last general order, praising his troops for their steadfastness and bidding farewell to the veterans who remained with him during this darkest, final hour.

Robert E. Lee (1807–1870), more than any other Confederate leader, became the folk hero of the lost cause. He was more nearly the Southern counterpart to Abraham Lincoln than any other son of the South. A proud Virginia aristocrat, Lee was also sensitive, humane and humble. His troops served him with wholehearted devotion, tied by bonds of affection that continued long after the war was over. Lee's military reputation was in stark contrast to that of his last Northern adversary. Some historians have described Lee as one of the last gentleman-soldiers, a leader who little understood or appreciated the brutal, insensitive tactics of modern warfare. He was nonetheless a professional soldier of consummate skill, with a high sense of honor and duty; he was also a man, who once made the statement that "it is a good thing that war is so terrible else we would love it too much."

The monumental, and best, biography of Lee is that of Douglas Southall Freeman, R. E. Lee, A Biography *(1934–1935), four volumes. An appreciation of Lee's postwar career and of his almost legendary role in the South is in Marshall W. Fishwick's* Lee After the War *(1963). The text of Lee's farewell address is reprinted from Clifford Dowdey and Louis H. Manarin (eds.),* The Wartime Papers of R. E. Lee *(Boston: Little, Brown, 1961), pages 934–935, by permission of Little, Brown and Company.*

Headquarters, Army of Northern Virginia,
April 10, 1865.

After four years of arduous service, marked by unsurpassed courage and fortitude, the Army of Northern Virginia has been compelled to yield to overwhelming numbers and resources. I need not tell the survivors of so many hard-fought battles, who have remained steadfast to the last, that I have consented to this result from no distrust of them; but, feeling that valour and devotion could accomplish nothing that could compensate for the loss that would have attended the continuation of the contest, I have determined to avoid the useless sacrifice of those whose past services have endeared them to their countrymen. By the terms of the agreement, officers and men can return to their homes and remain there until exchanged. You will take with you the satisfaction that proceeds from the consciousness of duty faithfully performed; and I earnestly pray that a merciful God will extend to you His blessing and protection. With an increasing admiration of your constancy and devotion to your country, and a grateful remembrance of your kind and generous consideration of myself, I bid you an affectionate farewell.

R. E. LEE, *General.*

SELECTION

A Southern Poet Mourns the Lost Cause: Poems by Father Abram Ryan

Abram J. Ryan (1838–1886) has frequently been called the "poet of the Confederacy." Southern born, he became a Roman Catholic priest, taking his solemn vows in 1856 and later teaching in a seminary in Cape Girardeau, Missouri. In 1862, he joined the Confederate military service as a chaplain. He ministered to the dying and the wounded on the battlefield with a selfless devotion and without regard to his personal safety. Father Ryan developed a deep and emotional attachment to the Confederate cause. When the war was over he, like many Southerners, acquiesced in the result but remained convinced that the cause of Southern independence had been a righteous one. He was unreconstructed until 1878 when Northern relief work during a cholera plague in the South caused him to soften his hostility toward the North. Most of Ryan's poems were written after the war and many of them reflect a sad, nostalgic longing for the lost cause. His poem "The Conquered Banner," written to the measures of a Gregorian hymn, became one of his best known works. "March of the Deathless Dead" and "The Sword of Robert Lee" are tributes to the heroism and sacrifice of Southern soldiers on behalf of the Southern cause. The text of all these poems is reprinted from Father Ryan's Poems *(Mobile, Ala.: John L. Rapier and Company, 1879), pp. 13–15, 18–19, 150–151. All convey Ryan's view of the eternal quality of the Confederate struggle for independence; defeated in battle, it persists in the hearts of Southerners. Ryan's poetry is not as well known as that of other Southern poets: Henry Timrod ("the poet-laureate of the Confederacy"), Paul Hamilton Hayne, and Sidney Lanier, for example, who also devoted their talents to the ennobling of the Confederate cause.*

March of the Deathless Dead

Gather the sacred dust
    Of the warriors tried and true,
Who bore the flag of our People's trust
And fell in a cause, though lost still just
    And died for me and you.

Gather them one and all!
    From the Private to the Chief,
Come they from hovel or princely hall,
They fell for us, and for them should fall
    The tears of a Nation's grief.

Gather the corpses strewn
    O'er many a battle plain;
From many a grave that lies so lone,
Without a name and without a stone,
    Gather the Southern slain.

We care not whence they came,
    Dear in their lifeless clay!
Whether unknown, or known to fame,
Their cause and country still the same—
    They died—and wore the Gray.

Wherever the brave have died,
    They should not rest apart;
Living they struggled side by side—
Why should the hand of Death divide
    A single heart from heart.

Gather their scattered clay,
　　Wherever it may rest;
Just as they marched to the bloody fray;
Just as they fell on the battle day;
　　Bury them breast to breast.

The foeman need not dread
　　This gathering of the brave;
Without sword or flag, and with soundless tread,
We muster once more our deathless dead;
　　Out of each lonely grave.

The foeman need not frown,
　　They all are powerless now—
We gather them here and we lay them down,
And tears and prayers are the only crown
　　We bring to wreathe each brow.

And the dead thus meet the dead,
　　While the living o'er them weep;
And the men by Lee and Stonewall led,
And the hearts that once together bled,
　　Together still shall sleep.

The Sword of Robert Lee

Forth from its scabbard pure and bright,
　　Flashed the sword of Lee!
Far in the front of the deadly fight
High o'er the brave in the cause of Right
Its stainless sheen like a beacon light
　　Led us to Victory.

Out of its scabbard where full long
　　It slumbered peacefully,—
Roused from its rest by the battle's song
Shielding the feeble, smiting the strong
Guarding the right, avenging the wrong
　　Gleamed the sword of Lee.

Forth from its scabbard high in air
　　Beneath Virginia's sky—
And they who saw it gleaming there
And knew who bore it knelt to swear,
That where that sword led, they would dare
　　To follow and to die.

Out of its scabbard!—never hand
　　Waved sword from stain as free,
Nor purer sword led braver band,
Nor braver bled for a brighter land,
Nor brighter land had a Cause so grand,
　　Nor cause a chief like Lee.

Forth from its scabbard! how we prayed,
 That sword might victor be;—
And when our triumph was delayed,
And many a heart grew sore afraid,
We still hoped on while gleamed the blade
 Of noble Robert Lee.

Forth from its scabbard! all in vain
 Bright flashed the sword of Lee;—
'Tis shrouded now in its sheath again,
It sleeps the sleep of our noble slain;
Defeated yet without a stain,
 Proudly and peacefully.

The Conquered Banner

Furl that Banner, for 'tis weary;
Round its staff 'tis drooping dreary;
 Furl it, fold it, it is best;
For there's not a man to wave it,
And there's not a sword to save it,
And there's not one left to lave it
In the blood which heroes gave it;
And its foes now scorn and brave it;
 Furl it, hide it—let it rest!

Take that Banner down! 'tis tattered;
Broken is its staff and shattered;
And the valiant hosts are scattered
 Over whom it floated high.
Oh! 'tis hard for us to fold it;
Hard to think there's none to hold it;
Hard that those who once unrolled it
 Now must furl it with a sigh.

Furl that Banner! furl it sadly!
Once ten thousands hailed it gladly,
And ten thousands wildly, madly,
 Swore it should forever wave;
Swore that foeman's sword should never
Hearts like theirs entwined dissever,
Till that flag should float forever
 O'er their freedom or their grave!

Furl it! for the hands that grasped it
And the hearts that fondly clasped it,
 Cold and dead are lying low;
And that Banner—it is trailing!
While around it sounds are wailing
 Of its people in their woe.

For, though conquered, they adore it!
Love the cold, dead hands that bore it!
Weep for those who fell before it!
Pardon those who trailed and tore it!
But, oh! wildly they deplore it,
    Now who furl and fold it so.

Furl that Banner! True, 'tis gory,
Yet 'tis wreathed around with glory,
And 'twill live in song and story,
    Though its folds are in the dust:
For its fame on brightest pages,
Penned by poets and by sages,
Shall go sounding down the ages—
    Furl its folds though now we must.

Furl that Banner, softly, slowly!
Treat it gently—it is holy—
    For it droops above the dead.
Touch it not—unfold it never,
Let it droop there furled forever,
    For it droops above the dead.

SELECTION

Walt Whitman Laments the Martyred President

Elation and relief in the North at the end of hostilities turned almost immediately to bitter sorrow. Less than a week after Lee's surrender at Appomattox, Abraham Lincoln was assassinated in Ford's Theatre. The death of the President in his moment of glory produced a shock wave that penetrated all parts of the country, South as well as North. The psychological impact of the deed was profound, and to many Northerners the assassination was a crowning act of Southern treachery. Clergymen from their pulpits for weeks to come declared that God had removed the charitable, humane Lincoln to make way for sterner hands which better appreciated the true character of Southern evil. No writer captured the nation's sadness and the real sense of loss so well as Walt Whitman. Whitman's impressions of Lincoln were finely drawn. Lincoln was, Whitman was convinced, "a pretty big President" who had "an almost supernatural tact in keeping the ship afloat at all." He wrote four poems dealing with Lincoln's assassination, three of which were included in his volume of war poetry, Drum-Taps, *and its sequel. In later editions of*

Leaves of Grass, he grouped the four pieces together as "President Lincoln's Burial Hymn." The text of the poems is here reprinted from Walt Whitman, Leaves of Grass (Philadelphia: David McKay, 1884), pages 255–263. "O Captain! My Captain!" is one of Whitman's best-known poems, while many critics have acclaimed "When Lilacs Last in the Dooryard Bloom'd" as one of the finest and most beautiful poems ever written.

A collection of poems dealing with Lincoln's assassination has been published by William W. Betts, Jr. (ed.), Lincoln and the Poets: An Anthology *(1965). For a biography of Whitman, see Henry Seidel Canby,* Walt Whitman *(1943).*

When Lilacs Last in the Dooryard Bloom'd

1

WHEN lilacs last in the dooryard bloom'd,
And the great star early droop'd in the western sky in the night,
I mourn'd, and yet shall mourn with ever-returning spring.

Ever-returning spring, trinity sure to me you bring,
Lilac blooming perennial and drooping star in the west,
And thought of him I love.

2

O powerful western fallen star!
O shades of night—O moody, tearful night!
O great star disappear'd—O the black murk that hides the star!
O cruel hands that hold me powerless—O helpless soul of me!
O harsh surrounding cloud that will not free my soul.

3

In the dooryard fronting an old farm-house near the white-wash'd
    pailings,
Stands the lilac-bush tall-growing with heart-shaped leaves of rich
    green,
With many a pointed blossom rising delicate, with the perfume
    strong I love,
With every leaf a miracle—and from this bush in the dooryard,
With delicate-color'd blossoms and heart-shaped leaves of rich
    green,
A sprig with its flower I break.

4

In the swamp in secluded recesses,
A shy and hidden bird is warbling a song.

Solitary the thrush,
The hermit withdrawn to himself, avoiding the settlements,
Sings by himself a song.

Song of the bleeding throat,
Death's outlet song of life, (for well dear brother I know,
If thou wast not granted to sing thou would'st surely die.)

5

Over the breast of the spring, the land, amid cities,
Amid lanes and through old woods, where lately the violets peep'd
    from the ground, spotting the gray debris,
Amid the grass in the fields each side of the lanes, passing the
    endless grass,
Passing the yellow-spear'd wheat, every grain from its shroud in
    the dark-brown fields uprisen,
Passing the apple-tree blows of white and pink in the orchards,
Carrying a corpse to where it shall rest in the grave,
Night and day journeys a coffin.

6

Coffin that passes through lanes and streets,
Through day and night with the great cloud darkening the land,
With the pomp of the inloop'd flags with the cities draped in black,
With the show of the States themselves as of crape-veil'd women
    standing
With processions long and winding and the flambeaus of the night,
With the countless torches lit, with the silent sea of faces and the
    unbared heads,
With the waiting depot, the arriving coffin, and the sombre faces
With dirges through the night, with the thousand voices rising
    strong and solemn,
With all the mournful voices of the dirges pour'd around the coffin,
The dim-lit churches and the shuddering organs—where amid
    these you journey,
With the tolling tolling bells' perpetual clang,
Here, coffin that slowly passes,
I give you my sprig of lilac.

7

(Nor for you, for one alone,
Blossoms and branches green to coffins all I bring,
For fresh as the morning, thus would I chant a song for you O
    sane and sacred death.

All over bouquets of roses,
O death, I cover you over with roses and early lilies,
But mostly and now the lilac that blooms the first,
Copious I break, I break the sprigs from the bushes,
With loaded arms I come, pouring for you,
For you and the coffins all of you O death.)

8

O western orb sailing the heaven,
Now I know what you must have meant as a month since I
    walk'd,
As I walk'd in silence the transparent shadowy night,
As I saw you had something to tell as you bent to me night after
    night,
As you droop'd from the sky low down as if to my side, (while
    the other stars all look'd on,)
As we wander'd together the solemn night, (for something I know
    not what kept me from sleep,)
As the night advanced, and I saw on the rim of the west how full
    you were of woe,
As I stood on the rising ground in the breeze in the cool trans-
    parent night,
As I watch'd where you pass'd and was lost in the netherward
    black of the night,
As my soul in its trouble dissatisfied sank, as where you sad orb,
Concluded, dropt in the night, and was gone.

9

Sing on there in the swamp,
O singer bashful and tender, I hear your notes, I hear your call,
I hear, I come presently, I understand you,
But a moment I linger, for the lustrous star has detain'd me,
The star my departing comrade holds and detains me.

10

O how shall I warble myself for the dead one there I loved?
And how shall I deck my song for the large sweet soul that has
    gone?
And what shall my perfume be for the grave of him I love?

Sea-winds blown from east and west,
Blown from the Eastern sea and blown from the Western sea, till
    there on the prairies meeting,
These and with these and the breath of my chant,
I'll perfume the grave of him I love.

11

O what shall I hang on the chamber walls?
And what shall the pictures be that I hang on the walls,
To adorn the burial-house of him I love?

Pictures of growing spring and farms and homes,
With the Fourth-month eve at sundown, and the gray smoke lucid
    and bright,
With floods of the yellow gold of the gorgeous, indolent, sinking
    sun, burning, expanding the air,

With the fresh sweet herbage under foot, and the pale green leaves
  of the trees prolific,
In the distance the flowing glaze, the breast of the river, with a
  wind-dapple here and there,
With ranging hills on the banks, with many a line against the sky,
  and shadows,
And the city at hand with dwellings so dense, and stacks of chimneys,
And all the scenes of life and the workshops, and the workmen
  homeward returning.

12

Lo, body and soul—this land,
My own Manhattan with spires, and the sparkling and hurrying
  tides, and the ships,
The varied and ample land, the South and the North in the light,
  Ohio's shores and flashing Missouri,
And ever the far-spreading prairies cover'd with grass and corn.

Lo, the most excellent sun so calm and haughty,
The violet and purple morn with just-felt breezes,
The gentle soft-born measureless light,
The miracle spreading bathing all, the fulfill'd noon,
The coming eve delicious, the welcome night and the stars,
Over my cities shining all, enveloping man and land.

13

Sing on, sing on you gray-brown bird,
Sing from the swamps, the recesses, pour your chant from the
  bushes,
Limitless out of the dusk, out of the cedars and pines.

Sing on dearest brother, warble your reedy song,
Loud human song, with voice of uttermost woe.

O liquid and free and tender!
O wild and loose to my soul—O wondrous singer!
You only I hear—yet the star holds me, (but will soon depart,)
Yet the lilac with mastering odor holds me.

14

Now while I sat in the day and look'd forth,
In the close of the day with its light and the fields of spring, and
  the farmers preparing their crops,
In the large unconscious scenery of my land with its lakes and
  forests,
In the heavenly aerial beauty, (after the perturb'd winds and the
  storms,)
Under the arching heavens of the afternoon swift passing, and the
  voices of children and women,

The many-moving sea-tides, and I saw the ships how they
   sail'd,
And the summer approaching with richness, and the fields all busy
   with labor,
And the infinite separate houses, how they all went on, each with
   its meals and minutia of daily usages,
And the streets how their throbbings throbb'd, and the cities pent
   —lo, then and there,
Falling upon them all and among them all, enveloping me with the
   rest,
Appear'd the cloud, appear'd the long black trail,
And I knew death, its thought, and the sacred knowledge of
   death.

Then with the knowledge of death as walking one side of me,
And the thought of death close-walking the other side of me,
And I in the middle as with companions, and as holding the
   hands of companions,
I fled forth to the hiding receiving night that talks not,
Down to the shores of the water, the path by the swamp in the
   dimness,
To the solemn shadowy cedars and ghostly pines so still.

And the singer so shy to the rest receiv'd me,
The gray-brown bird I know receiv'd us comrades three,
And he sang the carol of death, and a verse for him I love.

From deep secluded recesses,
From the fragrant cedars and the ghostly pines so still,
Came the carol of the bird.

And the charm of the carol rapt me,
As I held as if by their hands my comrades in the night,
And the voice of my spirit tallied the song of the bird.

Come lovely and soothing death,
Undulate round the world, serenely arriving, arriving,
In the day, in the night, to all, to each,
Sooner or later delicate death.

Prais'd be the fathomless universe,
For life and joy, and for objects and knowledge curious,
And for love, sweet love—but praise! praise! praise!
For the sure-enwinding arms of cool-enfolding death.

Dark mother always gliding near with soft feet,
Have none chanted for thee a chant of fullest welcome?
Then I chant it for thee, I glorify thee above all,
I bring thee a song that when thou must indeed come, come unfal-
   teringly.

Approach strong deliveress,
When it is so, when thou hast taken them I joyously sing the dead,
Lost in the loving floating ocean of thee,
Laved in the flood of thy bliss O death.

From me to thee glad serenades,
Dances for thee I propose saluting thee, adornments and feast-
ings for thee,
And the sights of the open landscape and the high-spread sky are
fitting,
And life and the fields, and the huge and thoughtful night.

The night in silence under many a star,
The ocean shore and the husky whispering wave whose voice I
know,
And the soul turning to thee O vast and well-veil'd death,
And the body gratefully nestling close to thee.

Over the tree-tops I float thee a song,
Over the rising and sinking waves, over the myriad fields and the
prairies wide,
Over the dense-pack'd cities all and the teeming wharves and ways,
I float this carol with joy, with joy to thee O death.

15

To the tally of my soul,
Loud and strong kept up the gray-brown bird,
With pure deliberate notes spreading filling the night.

Loud in the pines and cedars dim,
Clear in the freshness moist and the swamp-perfume,
And I with my comrades there in the night.

While my sight that was bound in my eyes unclosed,
As to long panoramas of visions.

And I saw askant the armies,
I saw as in noiseless dreams hundreds of battle-flags,
Borne through the smoke of the battles and pierc'd with missiles
I saw them,
And carried hither and yon through the smoke, and torn and
bloody,
And at last but a few shreds left on the staffs, (and all in silence,)
And the staffs all splinter'd and broken.

I saw battle-corpses, myriads of them,
And the white skeletons of young men, I saw them,
I saw the debris and debris of all the slain soldiers of the war,
But I saw they were not as was thought,

They themselves were fully at rest, they suffer'd not,
The living remain'd and suffer'd, the mother suffer'd,
And the wife and the child and the musing comrade suffer'd,
And the armies that remain'd suffer'd.

16

Passing the visions, passing the night,
Passing, unloosing the hold of my comrades' hands,
Passing the song of the hermit bird and the tallying song of my
    soul,
Victorious song, death's outlet song, yet varying ever-altering song,
As low and wailing, yet clear the notes, rising and falling, flooding
    the night,
Sadly sinking and fainting, as warning and warning, and yet again
    bursting with joy,
Covering the earth and filling the spread of the heaven,
As that powerful psalm in the night I heard from recesses,
Passing, I leave thee lilac with heart-shaped leaves,
I leave thee there in the door-yard, blooming, returning with
    spring.

I cease from my song for thee,
From my gaze on thee in the west, fronting the west, communing
    with thee,
O comrade lustrous with silver face in the night.

Yet each to keep and all, retrievements out of the night,
The song, the wondrous chant of the gray-brown bird,
And the tallying chant, the echo arous'd in my soul,
With the lustrous and drooping star with the countenance full
    of woe,
With the holders holding my hand nearing the call of the bird,
Comrades mine and I in the midst, and their memory ever to
    keep, for the dead I loved so well,
For the sweetest, wisest soul of all my days and lands—and this
    for his dear sake,
Lilac and star and bird twined with the chant of my soul,
There in the fragrant pines and the cedars dusk and dim.

O Captain! My Captain!

O CAPTAIN! my Captain! our fearful trip is done,
The ship has weather'd every rack, the prize we sought is won,
The port is near, the bells I hear, the people all exulting,
While follow eyes the steady keel, the vessel grim and daring;
        But O heart! heart! heart!
            O the bleeding drops of red,
                Where on the deck my Captain lies,
                    Fallen cold and dead.

O Captain! my Captain! rise up and hear the bells;
Rise up—for you the flag is flung—for you the bugle trills,
For you bouquets and ribbon'd wreaths—for you the shores
    a-crowding,
For you they call, the swaying mass, their eager faces turning;
        Here Captain! dear father!
            This arm beneath your head!
                It is some dream that on the deck,
                    You've fallen cold and dead.

My Captain does not answer, his lips are pale and still,
My father does not feel my arm, he has no pulse nor will,
This ship is anchor'd safe and sound, its voyage closed and done,
From fearful trip the victor ship comes in with object won;
        Exult O shores, and ring O bells!
            But I with mournful tread,
                Walk the deck my Captain lies,
                    Fallen cold and dead.

Hush'd Be the Camps To-day

Hush'd be the camps to-day,
And soldiers let us drape our war-worn weapons,
And each with musing soul retire to celebrate,
Our dear commander's death.

No more for him life's stormy conflicts,
Nor victory, nor defeat—no more time's dark events,
Charging like ceaseless clouds across the sky.

But sing poet in our name,
Sing of the love we bore him—because you, dweller in camps,
    know it truly.

As they invault the coffin there,
Sing—as they close the doors of earth upon him—one verse,
For the heavy hearts of soldiers.

This Dust Was Once the Man

This dust was once the man,
Gentle, plain, just and resolute, under whose cautious hand,
Against the foulest crime in history known in any land or age,
Was saved the Union of these States.

PART THIRTEEN

Common Sense and Christian Charity

he war's end was in many ways just a beginning. The American people, North and South, could not return to their prewar attitudes and concerns. The war had changed too much; the emotions engendered by four years of bloody fighting would not be easily overcome. The problem was that most Americans in 1865 were unaware that there could be no return and were unprepared to face up to the challenges which the end of the war brought them.

In the North, there was a vast army to be demobilized. Soldiers wanted to go home and relatives wanted them home without delay. Troops were mustered out of the service with amazing alacrity. The section's burgeoning economic system, boosted by the war itself, was not going to wait. There were fortunes to be made and new frontiers to be conquered. The sooner Americans could return to their former normal pursuits, the better. Southerners were perhaps more aware of the epochal impact of the war upon the nation. The evidence was everywhere around them. They could not return to a normal existence, at least not quickly. They were surrounded by the physical reminders of their defeat: devastation, destruction, and ruin that could not be overlooked. Their section and their lives must be rebuilt, for they had in effect lost a civilization. For the moment, however, the chief concern of the Southern people was in simple survival. The tremendous changes in their way of life that the results of the war would demand were not a matter for serious consideration.

As Americans looked to the future in 1865, they saw little need for change. The nation must return to the old patterns and old relationships as soon as possible with as little disruption as possible. But was such a return practicable, or indeed even possible? Abraham Lincoln gave the cue in his last Cabinet meeting, held on the day he was shot, when he advised, "We must extinguish our resentments if we expect harmony and union." Many Northerners agreed with him. The truest path to restoration and reconstruction lay in the employment, as Herman Melville suggested, of "common sense and Christian charity." Lincoln's successor in the White House, Andrew Johnson, reflected an important segment of Northern opinion when he commented, "I do not want them to come back into this Union a degraded and debased people."

In the South as well there were signs that favored a speedy and harmonious reconciliation of the sections. Edmund Ruffin was not expressing a typical reaction when, after hearing of the Confederacy's defeat, he went out into his garden, wrapped himself in the Stars and Bars, and blew his brains out. Most Southerners accepted defeat. They not only accepted it but also began to feel that they should lose nothing by it. Lincoln's view that the Southern states had in fact never left the Union gained increasing support in the South, in spite of all that had been said to the contrary during the four preceding years. Southerners followed the advice of Robert E. Lee who wrote in August, 1865, "The questions which for years were in dispute having been decided against us, it is the part of wisdom to acquiesce in the result, and of candor to recognize the fact."

But could the accumulated resentments of four years be so easily extinguished? Was it enough for Southerners merely to acquiesce in their defeat? Reconstruction involved a great deal more than the rebuilding of a shattered section or, insofar as it was possible, of a former way of life. The war's business, as one modern historian has reminded us, was not yet finished. It could not so easily be put aside. Questions had to be answered and some hard decisions made. Eleven states of the United States had withdrawn from the Union and had resisted for four years all efforts to draw them back, at a frightful cost to the nation. What of these states now? What was to be their proper role in the nation? How was their restoration to the Union to be accomplished? Could, and even should, they regain their former places as if nothing had happened?

The war had brought freedom to some four million Negro slaves, an event of no little consequence. With one stroke, Southern society had been thrown into turmoil. The fate of the Negro freedman was no longer a Southern problem; it was a national problem. Simply to free the slaves was not enough, although an amazing number of Americans were willing to leave it at that. Something more had to be done to protect the Negro in his new freedom. For whatever reason and however eagerly, the inescapable fact was that the nation had made a commitment to the Negro. Steps must be taken to lead the Negro freedmen along the pathway of social and economic responsibility. How could the nation best fulfill this commitment to freedom for the Negro?

Such questions could not be answered easily. They would require the full energy and devotion of Northerners and Southerners alike. There were indications in 1865, however, that such energy and devotion would not be fully and willingly contributed. Despite the fine intentions of men like Lincoln and Lee, the road ahead would be rocky indeed.

An Ex-Confederate Urges a Spirit of Magnanimity
on the North, 1865

Howell Cobb (1815–1868) was one of the South's leading political figures during the years preceding the Civil War. He represented his native state of Georgia in the House of Representatives on two occasions, from 1843 to 1851 and again from 1855 to 1857, and served as Governor of Georgia from 1851 to 1853. In 1857, President James Buchanan appointed Cobb to his Cabinet as Secretary of the Treasury, a post he held until December, 1860, when he resigned. Cobb was a thorough partisan of Southern rights and supported the secession movement in 1860–1861. Early in 1861, he presided over the Montgomery Convention, taking part in the organization of the Confederate States of America. During the war, he forsook political office for the battlefield, rising to the rank of major general in the Confederate army. In April, 1865, he surrendered to Federal forces at Macon, Georgia. Cobb, like many other prominent Confederates, accepted the defeat of the Southern cause in good faith. He reluctantly acquiesced in the consequences of the war. Slavery, to Cobb, was still the · best system of labor devised for the Negro race; its abandonment, however, was irrevocable. Southerners, he felt, must adapt to the new conditions. In June, 1865, Cobb wrote to Major General James H. Wilson, the Union officer to whom he surrendered, offering his reactions to the problems that faced both North and South at the war's end, and urging the North to pursue a policy of magnanimity and generosity toward the South. (The text of this letter is reprinted from the Andrew Johnson Papers in the Library of Congress).

The desire for a speedy and harmonious reconciliation of the sections expressed by both Northerners and Southerners is described in Paul H. Buck, The Road to Reunion, 1865–1900 (1937). On Cobb, see Horace Montgomery, Howell Cobb's Confederate Career (1959).

Macon 14 June 1865

Brv Maj Genl J. H. Wilson
 comding &c
 Macon Ga

General
 In compliance with my promise, I submit to you in writing, the views and suggestions which I had the honor of presenting in our interview on yesterday. It is due to candor to say, that I was a secessionist, and counselled the people of Georgia to secede. When the adoption of that policy resulted in war, I felt it my duty to share in the privations of the struggle, and accordingly at the commencement of the contest, I entered the army, and declining all civil appointments remained there to its close. I was an earnest supporter of the cause throughout the struggle. Upon the sur-

render of Genl Johnston I regarded the contest at an end, and have since that time conformed my action to that conviction. With that action you are familiar, and I need not therefore speak further of it. In the light of this frank statement, what I have to say should be weighed and considered.

However unpleasant and humiliating it may be, to make the concession, the fact exists, that the contest has ended in the subjugation of the South. The parties stand toward each other in the relative positions of conqueror and conquered; and the question for statesmen to decide, is, the policy, and duty of the respective parties. With the latter the course is plainly marked out alike by the requirements of duty and necessity. They have only to realize the truth, I have already stated, and conform their action to it. To contemplate further resistance would simply be madness. A return to the peaceful and quiet employments of life, obedience to the constitution and laws of the United States, and the faithful discharge of all the duties, and obligations, imposed upon them by the new state of things, constitute their plain and simple duty.

The policy to be adopted by the other party, is not so easily determined, though to my mind it is equally manifest. The hour of triumph, is not necessarily, an hour for calm reflection, or wise judgments. The deep feelings and passions, which for four years, have been kept alive by the exciting scenes of a bitter and bloody warfare, will not calm down, in the first hours of triumph. The impulsive judgment of such an hour may be very properly submitted to the review and criticism of cooler moments.

In the adoption of the policy, which the Government will pursue towards the people of the south, there are two matters, which present themselves for primary and paramount consideration. 1st the present condition of things in the South. 2nd the state of things which it is desirable to produce, and the best mode of doing it.

The war having terminated in the defeat of the south leaves the people necessarily in a depressed condition. The whole country has been more or less devastated. Their physical condition in the loss of property, and the deprivation of the comforts of life; and the means of restoring their former prosperity, is as bad, as their worst enemy could desire. If left to employ all their resources—and use all their means, they could command,—it would require much time to recover from the effects of a devastating war. The abolition of slavery not only deprives them of a large property, but revolutionizes the whole system of agricultural labor; and must necessarily retard the restoration of former prosperity. So completely has this constitution been interwoven with the whole frame work of society, that its abolition involves a revision, and modification of almost every page of the statute books of the States, where it has existed. It is with a people, thus depressed in mind, seriously injured in estate, and surrounded by embarrassing questions of the greatest magnitude that the Government has to deal. With the unquestioned power to mould to a great extent the future destiny of this people it is for the Government to consider, what state of thing it is desirable to produce, and the best mode of doing it. The avowed object of the Government was to restore the Union. The successful termination of the war has effected that result, so far as further resistance on the part of the South is concerned. The people of the South, being prepared to conform to that result, all else for the restoration of the Union, is in the hands of the Government.

Looking to the future interest not only of the southern people, but of the whole country, it is desirable that the bitter animosities, which have been produced, should be softened, as much as possible; and a devastated country restored, as far, and as rapidly as practicable to comparative prosperity. To effect these results requires the exercise of virtues, which the history of the world shows, are not often, if ever found in the hearts of conquerors, magnanimity and generosity. The world is sadly in need of such an example. Let the United States furnish it. There never was a more fitting opportunity. It will never be followed by more satisfactory results.

It is idle to suppose, that such a struggle, as the one, we have just passed through, would not be attended, with the bitterest feeling. Are such feelings to be softened, and kindlier ones restored by acts of harshness? The man who thinks so, has studied human nature in a different school, from the one in which I learned its teachings [.] The prejudices, and passions which have been aroused in this contest; crimsoned in the blood of loved ones, from every portion of the land, will yield only to the mellowing influences of time, and the youngest participant in the struggle, will scarcely live to see the last shadow pass away. It is for those in whose hands, the power is entrusted, to deal with a brave and generous, though conquered people, in such a spirit, as will most certainly and speedily ensure the desired result. The confidence of such a people can be won by kindness and generosity. I leave it for those who counsel a different policy, to foreshadow the effects of a contrary course[.] They may be able to see, how more blood, and more suffering will sooner restore kindlier feelings. I cannot. In the sufferings already endured, and the privations of the present, there appears to me ample atonement, to satisfy the demands of those, who would punish the South for the past. For the security of the future no such policy is required.

Giving to these general principles the form of practical recommendation, I would say that, all prosecutions and penalties should cease, against those, who stand charged alone with the offence of being parties to, and supporters of the Southern cause. If it should be found upon a fair and impartial investigation that any have been guilty of offences outside of the general charge of treason, brought against all participants in the attempted revolution, let such be held responsible, and tried for such offence. The time for the exercise of this form of general amnesty, with which the President is clothed, will arrive, when he is satisfied, that the people of the South have abandoned the contest & have in good faith returned to their allegiance to the United States, and that the peace and quiet of the country have been restored, and the integrity of the Union maintained. I am satisfied that with the people of Georgia, that time has already arrived. In such a policy there would be exhibited a spirit of magnanimity, which would find its reward in the happiest results.

If my voice could be heard in the councils of the Government, I would press with earnestness, upon every question that arose, that policy, which was marked with the greatest magnanimity; and exhibited the greatest generosity. I should seek to restore concord and good feeling by extending it to those, from whom I asked it in return; and by a course of generous confidence to win the willing and cheerful support of those whose loyalty and allegiance when thus won, could be relied upon. No man will doubt, that the man, who is received back into the Union, and feels, that he has been subjected to no severe penalty, and been required to submit to no humiliating test, will make a truer and better citizen, than the one who feels that his citizenship has been obtained by submitting to harsh and degrading terms, which he was compelled to yield to, to secure the rights he has acquired. You wish to restore prosperity to the South; and the South to the union. Rest assured, that you will most certainly effect these objects by a generous and liberal policy. Make the country prosperous by the imposition of the least burthens compatible with the demands of the public interest; and secure the honest loyalty of the people, by extending to them a generous confidence, but do not ask them to win your confidence, by losing their own self respect. The man, whose allegiance is submitted to a test which degrades him in his own estimation, may make you an obedient subject, but will never prove the true and loyal citizen he would be under other circumstances. Deal with the South, as with a brave and generous people—erring if you please—but brave and generous still. Such a course may not satisfy the demands of those, who in the hour of their triumph would see nothing but joy on the one side and humiliation on the other, but in the end, it will be best for the South, best for the North and best for the whole country.

By the abolition of slavery, which either has been or soon will be accomplished, a state of things has been produced, well calculated to excite the most serious apprehensions with the people of the South. I regard the result as unfortunate both for the white and black. The institution of slavery, in my judgment provided the best system of labor that could be devised for the negro race. But that has passed away, and it will tax the ability of the best and wisest statesmen to provide a substitute for it. It is due both to the white population and the negroes that the present state of things, should not remain. You will find that our people are fully prepared to conform to the new state of things; and as a general rule will be disposed to pursue towards the negroes, a course dictated by humanity and kindness. I take it for granted, that the future relations, between the negroes and their former owners, like all other questions of domestic policy, will be under the control and direction of the State Governments. Without going into details, you will readily appreciate the importance of the subject; and from your own observation, will realize the necessity of early action upon it. For the remainder of the present year, there may not be very serious troubles, but there should be a more certain and well defined system for the future, than can be enforced under military regulations which are necessarily vague and indefinite; and do not meet many questions that arise. In this view of the matter, I would urge upon your consideration the importance of the earliest organization of the State Government.

In connection with the subject of slave labor, it is well to consider the difficulties by which the whole agricultural—and indeed any other interest —is surrounded. Whilst there has been no action on the part of the Government to justify it, there is a serious apprehension felt, that a system of taxation is contemplated, which will impose such burthens upon the people, as they cannot meet; and will end in the virtual confiscation of their estates. If the views I have presented, are considered with any favor by the Government, pains should be taken to relieve this apprehension; and let the people know, that only such taxes will be required of them as the necessities of the Government may demand. In the collection of any taxes the fact that there is no money in the hands of the people, and no means of obtaining it at an early day, should be remembered. Time should be given to tax payers to obtain the necessary funds; and thus save the remnants of their former estates.

In giving these views I have only discussed general principles, avoiding as far as possible matters of detail. The application of these principles in good faith, to questions as they arise, will, I am sure, be attended with results, that will cause no regrets, to those who may carry them into practical operation.

I am fully conscious of the fact, that what I have said, is subject to the criticism, of proceeding from an interested party. This is true. I am interested, deeply interested in the question, not so much for myself—for I have no future—but for my family, my friends, my country men,—but we are not the only persons interested in the solution of this great problem which stands in the history of the world, without a precedent or parallel. You General, are interested; and so is any man who feels an interest, in the future not of the South only, but of the whole country. If however the interest I have in the question throws discredit upon what I have said, I may at least claim, that that interest has awakened a deeper reflection; and caused a calmer investigation of the subject. It should not therefore be invoked to blunt the point of the argument or weaken the force of the truths, I have presented.

I am General very respectfully yours &c
IIOWELL COBB

SELECTION

General Grant Reports on "Affairs at the South," 1865

Late in 1865, General Ulysses S. Grant (1822–1885) made a tour of inspection through the Southern states, primarily for military reasons but also to secure information on the attitudes of Southern people toward the national government. In December, he submitted a brief report to President Johnson describing the results of his trip and concluding that the "mass of thinking men" in the South were anxious to return to their former role in the Union. He was, at the same time, mildly critical of the operations of the Freedmen's Bureau in the South and suggested some changes in its organization and administration. Grant was only one of many Northerners who toured the South in the immediate postwar period. Some were newspaper correspondents and writers, others were officials of the government. Not all of their impressions were consistent with Grant's conclusions. Carl Schurz, the prominent German-American Radical Republican who had served in the Union forces during the war, under-

*took an extensive tour of the Southern states in the summer of 1865. His report
to President Johnson was voluminous, detailed, and pessimistic. Many Southerners, he wrote, had not yet accepted the fact of their defeat and lacked a
"hearty attachment to the great republic" (a situation that should hardly have
surprised him). He emphasized continued Southern hostility toward the Negro
and the necessity for protecting the freedman's newly acquired rights. Both
Grant's letter and Schurz's report were submitted by President Johnson to
Congress in January, 1866, and both were published by the Senate. Grant's
letter is reprinted from* Senate Executive Document, *number 2, Thirty-ninth
Congress, first session, pages 106–108. For other accounts of the South and
Southern attitudes immediately after the war see Sidney Andrews,* The South
since the War *(1866); John T. Trowbridge,* The South *(1866); Whitelaw Reid,*
After the War *(1866); and various documents published by the first session
of the Thirty-ninth Congress.*

Headquarters Armies of the United States,
Washington, D.C., December 18, 1865

Sir: In reply to your note of the 16th instant, requesting a report from
me giving such information as I may be possessed of coming within the
scope of the inquiries made by the Senate of the United States in their
resolution of the 12th instant, I have the honor to submit the following:

With your approval, and also that of the honorable Secretary of War, I
left Washington city on the 27th of last month for the purpose of making
a tour of inspection through some of the southern States, or States lately
in rebellion, and to see what changes were necessary to be made in the
disposition of the military forces of the country; how these forces could
be reduced and expenses curtailed, &c.; and to learn, as far as possible, the
feelings and intentions of the citizens of those States towards the general
government.

The State of Virginia being so accessible to Washington city, and information from this quarter, therefore, being readily obtained, I hastened
through the State without conversing or meeting with any of its citizens.
In Raleigh, North Carolina, I spent one day; in Charleston, South Carolina, two days; Savannah and Augusta, Georgia, each one day. Both in
travelling and whilst stopping I saw much and conversed freely with the
citizens of those States as well as with officers of the army who have been
stationed among them. The following are the conclusions come to by me.

I am satisfied that the mass of thinking men of the south accept the
present situation of affairs in good faith. The questions which have heretofore divided the sentiment of the people of the two sections—slavery and
State rights, or the right of a State to secede from the Union—they regard
as having been settled forever by the highest tribunal—arms—that man
can resort to. I was pleased to learn from the leading men whom I met
that they not only accepted the decision arrived at as final, but, now that
the smoke of battle has cleared away and time has been given for reflection, that this decision has been a fortunate one for the whole country,
they receiving like benefits from it with those who opposed them in the
field and in council.

Four years of war, during which law was executed only at the point of the bayonet throughout the States in rebellion, have left the people possibly in a condition not to yield that ready obedience to civil authority the American people have generally been in the habit of yielding. This would render the presence of small garrisons throughout those States necessary until such time as labor returns to its proper channel, and civil authority is fully established. I did not meet any one, either those holding places under the government or citizens of the southern States, who thinks it practicable to withdraw the military from the south at present. The white and the black mutually require the protection of the general government.

There is such universal acquiescence in the authority of the general government throughout the portions of country visited by me, that the mere presence of a military force, without regard to numbers, is sufficient to maintain order. The good of the country, and economy, require that the force kept in the interior, where there are many freedmen, (elsewhere in the southern States than at forts upon the seacoast no force is necessary,) should all be white troops. The reasons for this are obvious without mentioning many of them. The presence of black troops, lately slaves, demoralizes labor, both by their advice and by furnishing in their camps a resort for the freedmen for long distances around. White troops generally excite no opposition, and therefore a small number of them can maintain order in a given district. Colored troops must be kept in bodies sufficient to defend themselves. It is not the thinking men who would use violence towards any class of troops sent among them by the general government, but the ignorant in some places might; and the late slave seems to be imbued with the idea that the property of his late master should, by right, belong to him, or at least should have no protection from the colored soldier. There is danger of collisions being brought on by such causes.

My observations lead me to the conclusion that the citizens of the southern States are anxious to return to self-government, within the Union, as soon as possible; that whilst reconstructing they want and require protection from the government; that they are in earnest in wishing to do what they think is required by the government, not humiliating to them as citizens, and that if such a course were pointed out they would pursue it in good faith. It is to be regretted that there cannot be a greater commingling, at this time, between the citizens of the two sections; and particularly of those intrusted with the law-making power.

I did not give the operations of the Freedmen's Bureau that attention I would have done if more time had been at my disposal. Conversations on the subject, however, with officers connected with the bureau, lead me to think that, in some of the States, its affairs have not been conducted with good judgment or economy, and that the belief, widely spread among the freedmen of the southern States, that the lands of their former owners will, at least in part, be divided among them, has come from the agents of this bureau. This belief is seriously interfering with the willingness of the freedmen to make contracts for the coming year. In some form the Freedmen's Bureau is an absolute necessity until civil law is established and enforced, securing to the freedmen their rights and full protection. At present, however, it is independent of the military establishment of the country, and seems to be operated by the different agents of the bureau according to their individual notions. Everywhere General Howard, the able head of the bureau, made friends by the just and fair instructions and advice he gave; but the complaint in South Carolina was that when he left, things went on as before. Many, perhaps the majority, of the agents of the Freedmen's Bureau advise the freedmen that by their own industry they must expect to live. To this end they endeavor to secure employment for them, and to see that both contracting parties comply with their engagements. In some instances, I am sorry to say, the freedman's mind does not seem to be disabused of the idea that a freedman has the right to live without care or provision for the future. The effect of the belief in division of lands is idleness and accumulation in camps, towns, and cities. In such cases I think it will be found that vice and disease will tend to the extermination or great reduction of the colored race. It cannot be expected that the opinions held by men at the south for years can be changed in a day, and therefore the freedmen require, for a few years, not only laws to protect them, but the fostering care of those who will give them good counsel, and on whom they rely.

The Freedmen's Bureau being separated from the military establishment of the country, requires all the expense of a separate organization. One does not necessarily know what the other is doing, or what orders they are acting under. It seems to me this could be corrected by regarding every officer on duty with troops in the southern States as an agent of the Freedmen's Bureau, and then have all orders from the head of the bureau sent through department commanders. This would create a responsibility that would secure uniformity of action throughout all the south; would insure the orders and instructions from the head of the bureau being carried out, and would relieve from duty and pay a large number of employés of the government.

I have the honor to be, very respectfully, your obedient servant,

U. S. GRANT, Lieutenant General

His Excellency Andrew Johnson
President of the United States

SELECTION

The Need for Forbearance and Moderation: Herman Melville's Supplement to "Battle-Pieces," 1866

Herman Melville (1819–1891) had already, by the time of the Civil War, established his reputation as a first-rate, prolific writer. Between 1846, when he published his first novel, Typee, *and 1857, when his last work of fiction,* The Confidence Man, *appeared, Melville published ten books. Included in the number was the one great work for which he will always be hailed, the finest* novel ever written by an American in the estimation of some critics: Moby Dick, which appeared in 1851. His writing career was therefore virtually over before the outbreak of the Civil War. For almost ten years after 1857, he published nothing. Like Walt Whitman, however, Melville was touched by the war. Although he did not participate in the struggle as Whitman did, he nevertheless thought deeply about it. And, like Whitman, he recorded his thoughts in a volume of poetry. In August, 1866, he published Battle-Pieces and Aspects of the War. Melville's war poems lacked the sensitivity of Whit-man and never achieved much popularity, but they clearly demonstrated the great importance he attached to the Civil War as a crisis in American history. Northern victory, he wrote, was an advance not only for the country but for humanity as well. The interests of the nation, however, demanded a policy of forbearance and moderation toward the South in the difficult postwar years. When Battle-Pieces was published, Melville appended a prose supplement, quoted below, in which he made a moving plea for toleration in Reconstruc-tion. The text of the supplement is reprinted from Battle-Pieces and Aspects of the War (New York: Harper, 1866), pages 259–272. Secession and slavery were "against Destiny" but both were now buried and together North and South once again comprised a nation. Reconstruction, Melville wrote, de-manded "common sense and Christian charity." A recent study of Melville is by Leon Howard, Melville, A Biography (1951) and a convenient selection of Melville's poetry is in Hennig Cohen (ed.), Selected Poems of Herman Melville (1964).

Were I fastidiously anxious for the symmetry of this book, it would close with the notes. But the times are such that patriotism—not free from solicitude—urges a claim overriding all literary scruples.

It is more than a year since the memorable surrender, but events have not yet rounded themselves into completion. Not justly can we complain of this. There has been an upheaval affecting the basis of things; to altered circumstances complicated adaptations are to be made; there are diffi-culties great and novel. But is Reason still waiting for Passion to spend itself? We have sung of the soldiers and sailors, but who shall hymn the politicians?

In view of the infinite desirableness of Re-establishment, and consider-ing that, so far as feeling is concerned, it depends not mainly on the temper in which the South regards the North, but rather conversely; one who never was a blind adherent feels constrained to submit some thoughts, counting on the indulgence of his countrymen.

And, first, it may be said that, if among the feelings and opinions grow-ing immediately out of a great civil convulsion, there are any which time shall modify or do away, they are presumably those of a less temperate and charitable cast.

There seems no reason why patriotism and narrowness should go to-gether, or why intellectual impartiality should be confounded with political trimming, or why serviceable truth should keep cloistered because not partisan. Yet the work of Reconstruction, if admitted to be feasible at all, demands little but common sense and Christian charity. Little but these? These are much.

Some of us are concerned because as yet the South shows no penitence. But what exactly do we mean by this? Since down to the close of the war she never confessed any for braving it, the only penitence now left her is that which springs solely from the sense of discomfiture; and since this evidently would be a contrition hypocritical, it would be unworthy in us to demand it. Certain it is that penitence, in the sense of voluntary humiliation, will never be displayed. Nor does this afford just ground for unreserved condemnation. It is enough, for all practical purposes, if the South have been taught by the terrors of civil war to feel that Secession, like Slavery, is against Destiny; that both now lie buried in one grave; that her fate is linked with ours; and that together we comprise the Nation.

The clouds of heroes who battled for the Union it is needless to eulogise here. But how of the soldiers on the other side? And when of a free community we name the soldiers, we thereby name the people. It was in subserviency to the slave-interest that Secession was plotted; but it was under the plea, plausibly urged, that certain inestimable rights guaranteed by the Constitution were directly menaced that the people of the South were cajoled into revolution. Through the arts of the conspirators and the perversity of fortune, the most sensitive love of liberty was entrapped into the support of a war whose implied end was the erecting in our advanced century of an Anglo-American empire based upon the systematic degradation of man.

Spite this clinging reproach, however, signal military virtues and achievements have conferred upon the Confederate arms historic fame, and upon certain of the commanders a renown extending beyond the sea—a renown which we of the North could not suppress, even if we would. In personal character, also, not a few of the military leaders of the South enforce forbearance; the memory of others the North refrains from disparaging; and some, with more or less of reluctance, she can respect. Posterity, sympathising with our convictions, but removed from our passions, may perhaps go farther here. If George iv. could, out of the graceful instinct of a gentleman, raise an honourable monument in the great fane of Christendom over the remains of the enemy of his dynasty, Charles Edward, the invader of England and victor in the rout at Prestonpans— upon whose head the king's ancestor but one reign removed had set a price—is it probable that the grandchildren of General Grant will pursue with rancour, or slur by sour neglect, the memory of Stonewall Jackson?

But the South herself is not wanting in recent histories and biographies which record the deeds of her chieftains—writings freely published at the North by loyal houses, widely read here, and with a deep though saddened interest. By students of the war such works are hailed as welcome accessories, and tending to the completeness of the record.

Supposing a happy issue out of present perplexities, then, in the generation next to come, Southerners there will be yielding allegiance to the Union, feeling all their interests bound up in it, and yet cherishing unrebuked that kind of feeling for the memory of the soldiers of the fallen Confederacy that Burns, Scott, and the Ettrick Shepherd felt for the memory of the gallant clansmen ruined through their fidelity to the Stuarts—a feeling whose passion was tempered by the poetry imbuing it, and which in no wise affected their loyalty to the Georges, and which, it may be added, indirectly contributed excellent things to literature. But, setting this view aside, dishonourable would it be in the South were she willing to abandon to shame the memory of brave men who with signal personal disinterestedness warred in her behalf, though from motives, as we believe, so deplorably astray.

Patriotism is not baseness, neither is it inhumanity. The mourners who this summer bear flowers to the mounds of the Virginian and Georgian dead are, in their domestic bereavement and proud affection, as sacred in the eye of Heaven as are those who go with similar offerings of tender grief and love into the cemeteries of our Northern martyrs. And yet, in one aspect, how needless to point the contrast.

Cherishing such sentiments, it will hardly occasion surprise that, in looking over the battle-pieces in the foregoing collection, I have been tempted to withdraw or modify some of them, fearful lest in presenting, though but dramatically and by way of a poetic record, the passions and epithets of civil war, I might be contributing to a bitterness which every sensible American must wish at an end. So, too, with the emotion of victory as reproduced on some pages, and particularly toward the close. It should not be construed into an exultation misapplied—an exultation as ungenerous as unwise, and made to minister, however indirectly, to that kind of censoriousness too apt to be produced in certain natures by success after trying reverses. Zeal is not of necessity religion, neither is it always of the same essence with poetry or patriotism.

There were excesses which marked the conflict, most of which are perhaps inseparable from a civil strife so intense and prolonged, and involving warfare in some border countries new and imperfectly civilised. Barbarities also there were, for which the Southern people collectively can hardly be held responsible, though perpetrated by ruffians in their name. But surely other qualities—exalted ones—courage and fortitude matchless, were likewise displayed, and largely; and justly may these be held the characteristic traits, and not the former.

In this view, what Northern writer, however patriotic, but must revolt from acting on paper a part anyway akin to that of the live dog to the dead lion; and yet it is right to rejoice for our triumph, so far as it may justly imply an advance for our whole country and for humanity.

Let it be held no reproach to any one that he pleads for reasonable consideration for our late enemies, now stricken down and unavoidably debarred, for the time, from speaking through authorised agencies for themselves. Nothing has been urged here in the foolish hope of conciliating those men—few in number, we trust—who have resolved never to be reconciled to the Union. On such hearts everything is thrown away except it be religious commiseration, and the sincerest. Yet let them call to mind that unhappy Secessionist, not a military man, who with impious alacrity fired the first shot of the Civil War at Sumter, and a little more than four years afterward fired the last one into his own heart at Richmond.

Noble was the gesture into which patriotic passion surprised the people in a utilitarian time and country; yet the glory of the war falls short of its pathos—a pathos which now at last ought to disarm all animosity.

How many and earnest thoughts still rise, and how hard to repress them. We feel what past years have been, and years, unretarded years, shall come. May we all have moderation; may we all show candour. Though, perhaps, nothing could ultimately have averted the strife, and though to treat of human actions is to deal wholly with second causes, nevertheless, let us not cover up or try to extenuate what, humanly speaking, is the truth—namely, that those unfraternal denunciations, continued through years, and which at last inflamed to deeds that ended in bloodshed, were reciprocal; and that, had the preponderating strength and the prospect of its unlimited increase lain on the other side, on ours might have lain those actions which now in our late opponents we stigmatise under the name of Rebellion. As frankly let us own—what it would be unbecoming to parade were foreigners concerned—that our triumph was won not more by skill and bravery than by superior resources and crushing numbers; that it was a triumph, too, over a people for years politically misled by designing men, and also by some honestly-erring men, who from their position could not have been otherwise than broadly influential; a people who, though, indeed, they sought to perpetuate the curse of slavery, and even extend it, were not the authors of it, but (less fortunate, not less righteous than we) were the fated inheritors; a people who, having a like origin with ourselves, share essentially in whatever worthy qualities we may possess. No one can add to the lasting reproach which hopeless defeat has now cast upon Secession by withholding the recognition of these verities.

Surely we ought to take it to heart that that kind of pacification, based upon principles operating equally all over the land, which lovers of their country yearn for, and which our arms, though signally triumphant, did not bring about, and which law-making, however anxious, or energetic, or repressive, never by itself can achieve, may yet be largely aided by generosity of sentiment public and private. Some revisionary legislation and adaptive is indispensable; but with this should harmoniously work another kind of prudence, not unallied with entire magnanimity. Benevolence and policy—Christianity and Machiavelli—dissuade from penal severities toward the subdued. Abstinence here is as obligatory as considerate care for our unfortunate fellow-men late in bonds, and, if observed, would equally prove to be wise forecast. The great qualities of the South, those attested in the War, we can perilously alienate, or we may make them nationally available at need.

The blacks, in their infant pupilage to freedom, appeal to the sympathies of every humane mind. The paternal guardianship which for the interval Government exercises over them was prompted equally by duty and benevolence. Yet such kindliness should not be allowed to exclude kindliness to communities who stand nearer to us in nature. For the future of the freed slaves we may well be concerned; but the future of the whole country, involving the future of the blacks, urges a paramount claim upon our anxiety. Effective benignity, like the Nile, is not narrow in its bounty, and true policy is always broad. To be sure, it is vain to seek to glide, with moulded words, over the difficulties of the situation. And for them who are neither partisans, nor enthusiasts, nor theorists, nor cynics, there are some doubts not readily to be solved. And there are fears. Why is not the cessation of war now at length attended with the settled calm of peace? Wherefore in a clear sky do we still turn our eyes toward the South, as the Neapolitan, months after the eruption, turns his toward Vesuvius? Do we dread lest the repose may be deceptive? In the recent convulsion has the crater but shifted? Let us revere that sacred uncertainty which for-

ever impends over men and nations. Those of us who always abhorred
slavery as an atheistical iniquity, gladly we join in the exulting chorus of
humanity over its downfall. But we should remember that emancipation
was accomplished not by deliberate legislation; only through agonised
violence could so mighty a result be effected. In our natural solicitude to
confirm the benefit of liberty to the blacks, let us forbear from measures
of dubious constitutional rightfulness toward our white countrymen—
measures of a nature to provoke, among other of the last evils, exterminat-
ing hatred of race toward race. In imagination let us place ourselves in the
unprecedented position of the Southerners—their position as regards the
millions of ignorant manumitted slaves in their midst, for whom some of
us now claim the suffrage. Let us be Christians toward our fellow-whites, as
well as philanthropists toward the blacks, our fellow-men. In all things, and
toward all, we are enjoined to do as we would be done by. Nor should we
forget that benevolent desires, after passing a certain point, cannot undertake their own fulfilment without incurring the risk of evils beyond those
sought to be remedied. Something may well be left to the graduated care
of future legislation, and to heaven. In one point of view the co-existence
of the two races in the South—whether the negro be bond or free—seems
(even as it did to Abraham Lincoln) a grave evil. Emancipation has ridded
the country of the reproach, but not wholly of the calamity. Especially
in the present transition period for both races in the South, more or less of
trouble may not unreasonably be anticipated; but let us not hereafter
be too swift to charge the blame exclusively in any one quarter. With
certain evils men must be more or less patient. Our institutions have a
potent digestion, and may in time convert and assimilate to good all elements thrown in, however originally alien.

But, so far as immediate measures looking toward permanent Re-establishment are concerned, no consideration should tempt us to pervert the
national victory into oppression for the vanquished. Should plausible
promise of eventual good, or a deceptive or spurious sense of duty, lead us
to essay this, count we must on serious consequences, not the least of
which would be divisions among the Northern adherents of the Union.
Assuredly, if any honest Catos there be who thus far have gone with us,
no longer will they do so, but oppose us, and as resolutely as hitherto they
have supported. But this path of thought leads toward those waters of
bitterness from which one can only turn aside and be silent.

But supposing Re-establishment so far advanced that the Southern
seats in Congress are occupied, and by men qualified in accordance with
those cardinal principles of representative government which hitherto have
prevailed in the land—what then? Why, the Congressmen elected by the
people of the South will—represent the people of the South. This may
seem a flat conclusion; but, in view of the last five years, may there not
be latent significance in it? What will be the temper of those Southern
members? and, confronted by them, what will be the mood of our own
representatives? In private life true reconciliation seldom follows a violent
quarrel; but, if subsequent intercourse be unavoidable, nice observances
and mutual are indispensable to the prevention of a new rupture. Amity
itself can only be maintained by reciprocal respect, and true friends are
punctilious equals. On the floor of Congress North and South are to come
together after a passionate duel, in which the South, though proving her

valour, has been made to bite the dust. Upon differences in debate shall acrimonious recriminations be exchanged? shall censorious superiority assumed by one section provoke defiant self-assertion on the other? shall Manassas and Chickamauga be retorted for Chattanooga and Richmond? Under the supposition that the full Congress will be composed of gentlemen, all this is impossible. Yet, if otherwise, it needs no prophet of Israel to foretell the end. The maintenance of Congressional decency in the future will rest mainly with the North. Rightly will more forbearance be required from the North than the South, for the North is victor.

But some there are who may deem these latter thoughts inapplicable, and for this reason: Since the test-oath operatively excludes from Congress all who in any way participated in Secession, therefore none but Southerners wholly in harmony with the North are eligible to seats. This is true for the time being. But the oath is alterable; and in the wonted fluctuations of parties not improbably it will undergo alterations, assuming such a form, perhaps, as not to bar the admission into the National Legislature of men who represent the populations lately in revolt. Such a result would involve no violation of the principles of democratic government. Not readily can one perceive how the political existence of the millions of late Secessionists can permanently be ignored by this Republic. The years of the war tried our devotion to the Union; the time of peace may test the sincerity of our faith in democracy.

In no spirit of opposition, not by way of challenge, is anything here thrown out. These thoughts are sincere ones; they seem natural—inevitable. Here and there they must have suggested themselves to many thoughtful patriots. And, if they be just thoughts, ere long they must have that weight with the public which already they have had with individuals.

For that heroic band—those children of the furnace who, in regions like Texas and Tennessee, maintained their fidelity through terrible trials—we of the North felt for them, and profoundly we honour them. Yet passionate sympathy, with resentments so close as to be almost domestic in their bitterness, would hardly in the present juncture tend to discreet legislation. Were the Unionists and Secessionists but as Guelphs and Ghibellines? If not, then far be it from a great nation now to act in the spirit that animated a triumphant town-faction in the Middle Ages. But crowding thoughts must at last be checked; and, in times like the present, one who desires to be impartially just in the expression of his views, moves as among sword-points presented on every side.

Let us pray that the terrible historic tragedy of our time may not have been enacted without instructing our whole beloved country through terror and pity; and may fulfilment verify in the end those expectations which kindle the bards of Progress and Humanity.

PART FOURTEEN

No Inflexible Plan Can Safely Be Prescribed

The formulation of Reconstruction policy could not, and did not, wait upon the surrender of Southern troops at Appomattox and the destruction of the Confederate government. Actually, thinking about Reconstruction began very early in the conflict. At first, Reconstruction was closely related to Northern war aims, and every statement of the goals of the contest was in fact a statement of Reconstruction policy. The Crittenden resolution of July, 1861, for example, in stating for the first time the war aims of the North, might be considered a first expression of Reconstruction policy: the preservation of the Union and the return of the seceded states to full participation in the government of the United States. As war aims changed and developed, so did the thinking about Reconstruction. The evolution of an abolition policy provided an additional element to postwar planning, implying that the Union as it existed in 1860 would not be preserved but that the war would result in significant social change. With the passage and ratification of the Thirteenth Amendment, it became clear that Reconstruction could not be solely political in character but must involve social and economic considerations as well.

The question of the scope of Reconstruction policy was one of the first to emerge as political figures and government leaders turned their attention to the kind of nation they thought the war should produce. Some felt that Reconstruction should be comprehensive, that it would provide the opportunity for a sweeping social reorganization in the South. Others persisted in viewing Reconstruction in its narrowly political aspects, dealing principally with the status of the seceded states in spite of the obvious changes in the character of the war. The latter view, which was largely Lincoln's, dominated the development of Reconstruction policy during the war itself.

A second question concerned the proper agency through which Reconstruction policy should be established and imposed upon the South. There were, of course, no constitutional directives to provide easy and quick answers. Was the responsibility that of the executive branch of the government or did it rightfully belong to the legislative branch? While the war was being waged, power tended to concentrate in the hands of the President; and that was where authority over Reconstruction first resided.

There was, however, little assurance that the executive branch would be able to continue its direction of Reconstruction once the conflict had ended.

A Reconstruction policy that was specific in details, as contrasted with the general discussion of war aims, became necessary as soon as sections of the Confederacy were occupied by Federal troops. The problem of governing these sections had to be met; there was little time or opportunity for extended discussion or debate of Reconstruction policy in its broader outlines. Initially, then, Reconstruction was an ad hoc *policy, justified as a wartime necessity, and carried out by the President. As a presidential policy, it reflected the limitations of Lincoln's own thinking about the postwar Union. Lincoln's Reconstruction plan was not merely a simple, temporary expedient, however; nor was it intended to be the last word. Rather his program, as it was put into operation during the war, was to serve as a foundation on which additional policies could be laid. What Lincoln intended beyond his stated wartime policy can only be a matter of speculation, since his life was cut short at the very moment when further plans were being made. But it seems clear that he would have continued to regard the political aspect of Reconstruction—the status of the seceded states in the Union—as the most important element in Reconstruction policy so far as the national government was concerned. Lincoln was forced by events to make room for the abolition of slavery in his Reconstruction policy, but his thinking about slavery was strongly influenced by his states' rights position. It is more than likely that the role of abolition in Reconstruction planning would have continued to be affected by this belief in states' rights. Lincoln's plan at best was limited and incomplete but highly flexible; it was this plan, without the flexibility, that Lincoln's successor took over as his own and attempted to carry into fruition.*

The wartime development of Reconstruction policy was not without its critics. Opposition was levelled against the President on both of the serious questions that emerged from the discussions. The scope of Reconstruction, it was thought, must be broadened to encompass in a more meaningful way the problem of slavery and abolition as well as the fate of those Southern whites who supported the "rebellion" against duly constituted government. Secondly, the conviction grew, especially in Congress, that Reconstruction was more clearly the responsibility of the legislative branch than of the executive branch. As long as the war continued, however, the President held the reins of power. Although opposition mounted, it was the presidential plan of Abraham Lincoln that first characterized the Reconstruction policy of the United States. At the war's end, the tables would be turned.

Lincoln Announces His Reconstruction Plans: The Proclamation of Amnesty and Reconstruction, December 8, 1863

Lincoln's first formal statement of Reconstruction policy was submitted to Congress on December 8, 1863, following his annual message. Large areas of the South, particularly in Tennessee, Louisiana, Arkansas, and Virginia, were under Union occupation. Lincoln's plan was designed to speed the restoration of these states to the Union and to establish a formula by which additional states could be restored as the Northern armies advanced. The plan, known as the "ten-per-cent" plan, dealt only with the question of the status of the seceded states and was based on Lincoln's often-stated conviction that these states had in fact never left the Union. Lincoln's plan only indirectly touched the question of slavery. The oath which he prescribed required the faithful support of the President's proclamations concerning slaves—a pledge on Lincoln's part that he would maintain the policy established in his Emancipation Proclamation. All legislation dealing with the former slaves, however, was to be left to each state, in order to modify, as he stated in his annual message, "the confusion and destitution which must, at best, attend all classes by a total revolution of labor throughout whole States." At the same time, Lincoln emphasized the flexibility of his plan. In answer to those who might charge him with acting prematurely and dogmatically, he noted that, "Saying that reconstruction will be accepted if presented in a specified way, it is not said it will never be accepted in any other way." The opportunity for revision and modification of his proposal was left open. Presidential Reconstruction, as outlined by Lincoln, was not in the long run successful. Attacked almost immediately for his proposal, Lincoln found himself forced on several occasions to meet the objections of his critics. Lincoln's "ten-per-cent" plan was a forward-looking, pragmatic, and flexible plan, designed to restore the seceded states to the Union with a minimum of disruption. Even so, it was narrow and limited, and in some respects unrealistic.

The text of Lincoln's proclamation is reprinted from Roy P. Basler et al. (eds.), The Collected Works of Abraham Lincoln (New Brunswick: Rutgers, 1953), 9 volumes, volume 7, pages 53–56. For a discussion of Lincoln's Reconstruction policy, see William B. Hesseltine, Lincoln's Plan of Reconstruction (1900). An earlier work is Charles H. McCarthy, Lincoln's Plan of Reconstruction (1901). See also James G. Randall and Richard N. Current, Lincoln the President: Last Full Measure (1955).

Whereas, in and by the Constitution of the United States, it is provided that the President "shall have power to grant reprieves and pardons for offences against the United States, except in cases of impeachment;" and

Whereas a rebellion now exists whereby the loyal State governments of several States have for a long time been subverted, and many persons have committed and are now guilty of treason against the United States; and

Whereas, with reference to said rebellion and treason, laws have been enacted by Congress declaring forfeitures and confiscation of property and liberation of slaves, all upon terms and conditions therein stated, and also declaring that the President was thereby authorized at any time thereafter, by proclamation, to extend to persons who may have participated in the existing rebellion, in any State or part thereof, pardon and amnesty, with such exceptions and at such times and on such conditions as he may deem expedient for the public welfare; and

Whereas the congressional declaration for limited and conditional pardon accords with well-established judicial exposition of the pardoning power; and

Whereas, with reference to said rebellion, the President of the United States has issued several proclamations, with provisions in regard to the liberation of slaves; and

Whereas it is now desired by some persons heretofore engaged in said rebellion to resume their allegiance to the United States, and to reinaugurate loyal State governments within and for their respective States; therefore,

I, Abraham Lincoln, President of the United States, do proclaim, declare, and make known to all persons who have, directly or by implication, participated in the existing rebellion, except as hereinafter excepted, that a full pardon is hereby granted to them and each of them, with restoration of all rights of property, except as to slaves, and in property cases where rights of third parties shall have intervened, and upon the condition that every such person shall take and subscribe an oath, and thenceforward keep and maintain said oath inviolate; and which oath shall be registered for permanent preservation, and shall be of the tenor and effect following, to wit:

I, ——, do solemnly swear, in presence of Almighty God, that I will henceforth faithfully support, protect and defend the Constitution of the United States, and the union of the States thereunder; and that I will, in like manner, abide by and faithfully support all acts of Congress passed during the existing rebellion with reference to slaves, so long and so far as not repealed, modified or held void by Congress, or by decision of the Supreme Court; and that I will, in like manner, abide by and faithfully support all proclamations of the President made during the existing rebellion having reference to slaves, so long and so far as not modified or declared void by decision of the Supreme Court. So help me God.

The persons excepted from the benefits of the foregoing provisions are all who are, or shall have been, civil or diplomatic officers or agents of the so-called confederate government; all who have left judicial stations under the United States to aid the rebellion; all who are, or shall have been, military or naval officers of said so-called confederate government above the rank of colonel in the army, or of lieutenant in the navy; all who left seats in the United States Congress to aid the rebellion; all who resigned commissions in the army or navy of the United States, and afterwards aided the rebellion; and all who have engaged in any way in treating colored persons or white persons, in charge of such, otherwise than lawfully as prisoners of war, and which persons may have been found in the United States service, as soldiers, seamen, or in any other capacity.

And I do further proclaim, declare, and make known, that whenever, in any of the States of Arkansas, Texas, Louisiana, Mississippi, Tennessee, Alabama, Georgia, Florida, South Carolina, and North Carolina, a number of persons, not less than one-tenth in number of the votes cast in such State at the Presidential election of the year of our Lord one thousand eight hundred and sixty, each having taken the oath aforesaid and not having since violated it, and being a qualified voter by the election law of the State existing immediately before the so-called act of secession, and excluding all others, shall re-establish a State government which shall be republican, and in no wise contravening said oath, such shall be recognized as the true government of the State, and the State shall receive thereunder the benefits of the constitutional provision which declares that "The United States shall guaranty to every State in this union a republican form of government, and shall protect each of them against invasion; and, on application of the legislature, or the executive, (when the legislature cannot be convened,) against domestic violence."

And I do further proclaim, declare, and make known that any provision which may be adopted by such State government in relation to the freed people of such State, which shall recognize and declare their permanent freedom, provide for their education, and which may yet be consistent, as a temporary arrangement, with their present condition as a laboring, landless, and homeless class, will not be objected to by the national Executive. And it is suggested as not improper, that, in constructing a loyal State government in any State, the name of the State, the boundary, the subdivisions, the constitution, and the general code of laws, as before the rebellion, be maintained, subject only to the modifications made necessary by the conditions hereinbefore stated, and such others, if any, not contravening said conditions, and which may be deemed expedient by those framing the new State government.

To avoid misunderstanding, it may be proper to say that this proclamation, so far as it relates to State governments, has no reference to States wherein loyal State governments have all the while been maintained. And for the same reason, it may be proper to further say that whether members sent to Congress from any State shall be admitted to seats, constitutionally rests exclusively with the respective Houses, and not to any extent with the Executive. And still further, that this proclamation is intended to present the people of the States wherein the national authority has been suspended, and loyal State governments have been subverted, a mode in and by which the national authority and loyal State governments may be re-established within said States, or in any of them; and, while the mode presented is the best the Executive can suggest, with his present impressions, it must not be understood that no other possible mode would be acceptable. . . .

SELECTION **45**

Lincoln's Reply to Radical Criticism: The Proclamation concerning Reconstruction, July 8, 1864

Lincoln's "ten-per-cent" plan was assailed almost from the day it was issued. Prominent in the attacks were the Radical members of his own party who countered Lincoln's proposal with one of their own. On July 4, 1864, in the final hours of the congressional session, a bill was passed which reflected the views of Lincoln's opposition. Originally introduced in the House by Maryland's Henry Winter Davis and ushered through the Senate by Benjamin F. Wade of Ohio, the legislation drastically revised Lincoln's plan. Instead of Lincoln's ten per cent, the Radicals insisted that a majority of the white male citizens was necessary to reorganize a state government. The oath prescribed by Lincoln was to be superseded by one of harsher intent. No Southerner who could not swear that he had never voluntarily borne arms against the United States nor given aid or support to persons or governments hostile to the United States could participate in the reorganization of his state. The Wade-Davis Bill, based on the assumption that the seceded states were no longer in the Union, would make it extremely difficult, if not impossible, for a Southern state to be restored to full participation in the national government. Lincoln, opposed to the bill, determined to pocket-veto the legislation. Instead of remaining silent, however, he issued a proclamation stating his refusal to set aside his own "ten-per-cent" plan, but offering the Wade-Davis proposal to the South as an alternative. The bill, of course, did not become law and no Southern state accepted the congressional plan. Lincoln had effectively killed it. If he hoped by this unusual course to conciliate the Radical opposition, he was soon to realize his mistake. On August 5, the two outraged authors of the bill denounced the President's action in a manifesto published in the New York Tribune. *Lincoln was condemned as a usurper and his proclamation as a "studied outrage on the legislative authority of the people." The Wade-Davis manifesto marked a dramatic confrontation between executive and legislature, between the President and Congress, on Reconstruction. No statement more clearly revealed the differences between Lincoln and the Radicals. The "authority of Congress is paramount," wrote the authors of the manifesto. The President should confine himself to his executive duties and "leave political reorganization to Congress."*

The text of Lincoln's proclamation is reprinted from Roy P. Basler et al. (eds.), The Collected Works of Abraham Lincoln *(New Brunswick: Rutgers, 1953), 9 volumes, volume 7, pages 433–434. For Lincoln's relations with the Radicals, see T. Harry Williams,* Lincoln and the Radicals *(1941) and William F. Zornow,* Lincoln and the Party Divided *(1954).*

dramatized. The stalemate persisted. With the end of the war, Reconstruction became a matter of dominant concern to the nation, its discussion now un-trammeled by military considerations. Lincoln and Radicals alike regarded the development of Reconstruction policy with a new conviction of urgency. A showdown between the two contending groups became imminent. Just two days after Lee's surrender at Appomattox, Lincoln spoke to an enthusiastic crowd on the White House grounds. It was to be his last public address. Lincoln devoted his remarks to a defense of his own developing plans for Reconstruction. He emphasized again the need for flexibility in dealing with the defeated Southern states, and indicated that his mind was open to the suggestion of other avenues for the reorganization of the Southern states. He denounced as a "pernicious abstraction" the question whether the Southern states were in the Union or out of it. "Finding themselves safely at home," he commented in an often-quoted passage, "it would be utterly immaterial whether they had ever been abroad." The tone of his speech was in keeping with that of his Second Inaugural Address, delivered only five weeks before. The need was for a policy of moderation and conciliation; only the essential questions should be faced in order to restore the Southern states to their "proper practical relation with the Union." Lincoln concluded his address with the promise that he would soon be making a new announcement relating to the Reconstruction of the South. What this new announcement was to have been can only be a matter of conjecture, for within a few days Lincoln was dead. This last address is reprinted from Roy P. Basler et al. (eds.), The Collected Works of Abraham Lincoln (New Brunswick: Rutgers, 1953), 9 volumes, volume 8 pages 399 406.

We meet this evening, not in sorrow, but in gladness of heart. The evacuation of Petersburg and Richmond, and the surrender of the principal insurgent army, give hope of a righteous and speedy peace whose joyous expression can not be restrained. In the midst of this, however, He, from Whom all blessings flow, must not be forgotten. A call for a national thanksgiving is being prepared, and will be duly promulgated. Nor must those whose harder part gives us the cause of rejoicing, be overlooked. Their honors must not be parcelled out with others. I myself, was near the front, and had the high pleasure of transmitting much of the good news to you; but no part of the honor, for plan or execution, is mine. To Gen. Grant, his skillful officers, and brave men, all belongs. The gallant Navy stood ready, but was not in reach to take active part.

By these recent successes the re-inauguration of the national authority—reconstruction—which has had a large share of thought from the first, is pressed much more closely upon our attention. It is fraught with great difficulty. Unlike the case of a war between independent nations, there is no authorized organ for us to treat with. No one man has authority to give up the rebellion for any other man. We simply must begin with, and mould from, disorganized and discordant elements. Nor is it a small addi-tional embarrassment that we, the loyal people, differ among ourselves as to the mode, manner, and means of reconstruction.

As a general rule, I abstain from reading the reports of attacks upon myself, wishing not to be provoked by that to which I can not properly offer an answer. In spite of this precaution, however, it comes to my knowl-

Whereas, at the late Session, Congress passed a Bill, "To guarantee to certain States, whose Governments have been usurped or overthrown, a republican form of Government," a copy of which is hereunto annexed:

And whereas, the said Bill was presented to the President of the United States, for his approval, less than one hour before the *sine die* adjournment of said Session, and was not signed by him:

And whereas, the said Bill contains, among other things, a plan for restoring the States in rebellion to their proper practical relation in the Union, which plan expresses the sense of Congress upon that subject, and which plan it is now thought fit to lay before the people for their consideration:

Now, therefore, I, Abraham Lincoln, President of the United States, do proclaim, declare, and make known, that, while I am, (as I was in December last, when by proclamation I propounded a plan for restoration) unprepared, by a formal approval of this Bill, to be inflexibly committed to any single plan of restoration; and, while I am also unprepared to declare, that the free-state constitutions and governments, already adopted and installed in Arkansas and Louisiana, shall be set aside and held for nought, thereby repelling and discouraging the loyal citizens who have set up the same, as to further effort; or to declare a constitutional competency in Congress to abolish slavery in States, but am at the same time sincerely hoping and expecting that a constitutional amendment, abolishing slavery throughout the nation, may be adopted, nevertheless, I am fully satisfied with the system for restoration contained in the Bill, as one very proper plan for the loyal people of any State choosing to adopt it; and that I am, and at all times shall be, prepared to give the Executive aid and assistance to any such people, so soon as the military resistance to the United States shall have been suppressed in any such State, and the people thereof shall have sufficiently returned to their obedience to the Constitution and the laws of the United States,—in which cases, military Governors will be appointed, with directions to proceed according to the Bill. . . .

SELECTION

"It May Be My Duty to Make Some New Announcement": Lincoln's Last Public Address, April 11, 1865

The termination of hostilities in April, 1865, brought the discussion of Reconstruction policy into a new phase. Ever since Lincoln's message and proclamation in December, 1863, debate over Reconstruction had continued. The differences between Lincoln and the Radicals in Congress deepened and were edge that I am much censured for some supposed agency in setting up, and seeking to sustain, the new State Government of Louisiana. In this I have done just so much as, and no more than, the public knows. In the Annual Message of Dec. 1863 and accompanying Proclamation, I presented *a* plan of re-construction (as the phrase goes) which, I promised, if adopted by any State, should be acceptable to, and sustained by, the Executive government of the nation. I distinctly stated that this was not the only plan which might possibly be acceptable; and I also distinctly protested that the Executive claimed no right to say when, or whether members should be admitted to seats in Congress from such States. This plan was, in advance, submitted to the then Cabinet, and distinctly approved by every member of it. One of them suggested that I should then, and in that connection, apply the Emancipation Proclamation to the theretofore excepted parts of Virginia and Louisiana; that I should drop the suggestion about apprenticeship for freed-people, and that I should omit the protest against my own power, in regard to the admission of members to Congress; but even he approved every part and parcel of the plan which has since been employed or touched by the action of Louisiana. The new constitution of Louisiana, declaring emancipation for the whole State, practically applies the Proclamation to the part previously excepted. It does not adopt apprenticeship for freed-people; and it is silent, as it could not well be otherwise, about the admission of members to Congress. So that, as it applies to Louisiana, every member of the Cabinet fully approved the plan. The Message went to Congress, and I received many commendations of the plan, written and verbal; and not a single objection to it, from any professed emancipationist, came to my knowledge, until after the news reached Washington that the people of Louisiana had begun to move in accordance with it. From about July 1862, I had corresponded with different persons, supposed to be interested, seeking a reconstruction of a State government for Louisiana. When the Message of 1863, with the plan before mentioned, reached New-Orleans, Gen. Banks wrote me that he was confident the people, with his military co-operation, would reconstruct, substantially on that plan. I wrote him, and some of them to try it; they tried it, and the result is known. Such only has been my agency in getting up the Louisiana government. As to sustaining it, my promise is out, as before stated. But, as bad promises are better broken than kept, I shall treat this as a bad promise, and break it, whenever I shall be convinced that keeping it is adverse to the public interest. But I have not yet been so convinced.

I have been shown a letter on this subject, supposed to be an able one, in which the writer expresses regret that my mind has not seemed to be definitely fixed on the question whether the seceded States, so called, are in the Union or out of it. It would perhaps, add astonishment to his regret, were he to learn that since I have found professed Union men endeavoring to make that question, I have *purposely* forborne any public expression upon it. As appears to me that question has not been, nor yet is, a practically material one, and that any discussion of it, while it thus remains practically immaterial, could have no effect other than the mischievous one of dividing our friends. As yet, whatever it may hereafter become, that question is bad, as the basis of a controversy, and good for nothing at all—a merely pernicious abstraction.

We all agree that the seceded States, so called, are out of their proper practical relation with the Union; and that the sole object of the government, civil and military, in regard to those States is to again get them into that proper practical relation. I believe it is not only possible, but in fact, easier, to do this, without deciding, or even considering, whether these states have even been out of the Union, than with it. Finding themselves safely at home, it would be utterly immaterial whether they had ever been abroad. Let us all join in doing the acts necessary to restoring the proper practical relations between these states and the Union; and each forever after, innocently indulge his own opinion whether, in doing the acts, he brought the States from without, into the Union, or only gave them proper assistance, they never having been out of it.

The amount of constituency, so to speak, on which the new Louisiana government rests, would be more satisfactory to all, if it contained fifty, thirty, or even twenty thousand, instead of only about twelve thousand, as it does. It is also unsatisfactory to some that the elective franchise is not given to the colored man. I would myself prefer that it were now conferred on the very intelligent, and on those who serve our cause as soldiers. Still the question is not whether the Louisiana government, as it stands, is quite all that is desirable. The question is "Will it be wiser to take it as it is, and help to improve it; or to reject, and disperse it?" "Can Louisiana be brought into proper practical relation with the Union *sooner* by *sustaining*, or by *discarding* her new State Government?"

Some twelve thousand voters in the heretofore slave-state of Louisiana have sworn allegiance to the Union, assumed to be the rightful political power of the State, held elections, organized a State government, adopted a free-state constitution, giving the benefit of public schools equally to black and white, and empowering the Legislature to confer the elective franchise upon the colored man. Their Legislature has already voted to ratify the constitutional amendment recently passed by Congress, abolishing slavery throughout the nation. These twelve thousand persons are thus fully committed to the Union, and to perpetual freedom in the state— committed to the very things, and nearly all the things the nation wants— and they ask the nations recognition, and it's assistance to make good their committal. Now, if we reject, and spurn them, we do our utmost to disorganize and disperse them. We in effect say to the white men "You are worthless, or worse—we will neither help you, nor be helped by you." To the blacks we say "This cup of liberty which these, your old masters, hold to your lips, we will dash from you, and leave you to the chances of gathering the spilled and scattered contents in some vague and undefined when, where, and how." If this course, discouraging and paralyzing both white and black, has any tendency to bring Louisiana into proper practical relations with the Union, I have, so far, been unable to perceive it. If, on the contrary, we recognize, and sustain the new government of Louisiana the converse of all this is made true. We encourage the hearts, and nerve the arms of the twelve thousand to adhere to their work, and argue for it, and proselyte for it, and fight for it, and feed it, and grow it, and ripen it to a complete success. The colored man too, in seeing all united for him, is inspired with vigilance, and energy, and daring, to the same end. Grant that he desires the elective franchise, will he not attain it sooner by saving the already advanced steps toward it, than by running backward over them? Concede that the new government of Louisiana is only to what it should be as the egg is to the fowl, we shall sooner have the fowl by hatching the egg than by smashing it? Again, if we reject Louisiana, we also reject one vote in favor of the proposed amendment to the national constitution. To meet this proposition, it has been argued that no more than three fourths of those States which have not attempted secession are necessary to validly ratify the amendment. I do not commit myself against this, further than to say that such a ratification would be questionable, and sure to be persistently questioned; while a ratification by three fourths of all the States would be unquestioned and unquestionable.

I repeat the question. "Can Louisiana be brought into proper practical relation with the Union *sooner* by *sustaining* or by *discarding* her new State Government?

What has been said of Louisiana will apply generally to other States. And yet so great peculiarities pertain to each state; and such important and sudden changes occur in the same state; and, withal, so new and unprecedented is the whole case, that no exclusive, and inflexible plan can safely be prescribed as to details and collaterals. Such exclusive, and inflexible plan, would surely become a new entanglement. Important principles may, and must, be inflexible.

In the present *"situation"* as the phrase goes, it may be my duty to make some new announcement to the people of the South. I am considering, and shall not fail to act, when satisfied that action will be proper.

SELECTION

A New President Takes Over the Reins: Andrew Johnson's First Annual Message to Congress, December 4, 1865

With Lincoln's death, Andrew Johnson (1808–1875) became President of the United States. The task of following Abraham Lincoln in the Presidency would have been difficult for any man; for Johnson the difficulty was compounded. A poor white Southerner from eastern Tennessee, Johnson sprang, like Lincoln, from humble beginnings. He was, in every sense, a self-made man. His political career began at the lowest level (alderman of Greenville, Tennessee), and rose to the height of the Presidency itself. Johnson's vote getting powers were amply demonstrated. A strong Democrat, he took the side of the poor whites in opposition to the Southern aristocracy, and built a career by appealing to the humble folk like himself. He was a member of Congress from 1843 to 1853, Governor of Tennessee from 1853 to 1857, and Senator from 1857 to 1862. During the war he sided with the Union and became one of the leading War Democrats. In 1862, Lincoln appointed him military governor of Tennessee, and in 1864, he was nominated for the Vice

Presidency of the United States. For all his success as a politician, however, Johnson lacked Lincoln's flexibility and political acumen, and had been elected at a time when these traits were sorely needed. As President of the United States he found himself in a difficult and anomalous position. Coming from a former state of the Confederacy, he was almost literally a man without a party. Democrats had disowned him when he accepted nomination on Lincoln's ticket in 1864; Republicans never quite accepted him. When Johnson took the oath of office as President in April, 1865, many Radicals applauded; they thought they recognized him as one of their own. It soon became obvious that Johnson was committed to Lincoln's plan for Reconstruction. With Johnson, however, presidential Reconstruction lost the flexibility Lincoln had insisted upon; instead it became dogmatic and the differences between the executive and Congress hardened all the more. Johnson refused to call Congress into special session following the war, hoping to have the Southern states restored to the Union by the time the regular session opened in December. In his first message to Congress (written, incidentally, by George Bancroft), he reviewed the steps he had taken to achieve Reconstruction and discussed the constitutional aspects of federal-state relations. The text of this message is taken from James D. Richardson (ed.), A Compilation of the Messages and Papers of the Presidents, 1789–1897 *(Washington: Government Printing Office, 1907), 10 volumes, volume 6, pages 353–361. The Radicals were guarded in their reactions to the message, preferring to await further developments before committing themselves. A masterful study of Johnson's Presidency and his role in Reconstruction is Eric L. McKitrick,* Andrew Johnson and Reconstruction *(1960). A provocative series of essays on the politics of Reconstruction, to a large extent revolving about Johnson, is LaWanda Cox and John H. Cox,* Politics, Principle, and Prejudice, 1865–1866: Dilemma of Reconstruction America *(1963).*

Washington, December 4, 1865.

Fellow-Citizens of the Senate and House of Representatives:

To express gratitude to God in the name of the people for the preservation of the United States is my first duty in addressing you. Our thoughts next revert to the death of the late President by an act of parricidal treason. The grief of the nation is still fresh. It finds some solace in the consideration that he lived to enjoy the highest proof of its confidence by entering on the renewed term of the Chief Magistracy to which he had been elected; that he brought the civil war substantially to a close; that his loss was deplored in all parts of the Union, and that foreign nations have rendered justice to his memory. His removal cast upon me a heavier weight of cares than ever devolved upon any one of his predecessors. To fulfill my trust I need the support and confidence of all who are associated with me in the various departments of Government and the support and confidence of the people. There is but one way in which I can hope to gain their necessary aid. It is to state with frankness the principles which guide my conduct, and their application to the present state of affairs, well aware that the efficiency of my labors will in a great measure depend on your and their undivided approbation. . . .

The maintenance of the Union brings with it "the support of the State governments in all their rights," but it is not one of the rights of any State government to renounce its own place in the Union or to nullify the laws of the Union. The largest liberty is to be maintained in the discussion of the acts of the Federal Government, but there is no appeal from its laws except to the various branches of that Government itself, or to the people, who grant to the members of the legislative and of the executive departments no tenure but a limited one, and in that manner always retain the powers of redress.

"The sovereignty of the States" is the language of the Confederacy, and not the language of the Constitution. The latter contains the emphatic words—

> This Constitution and the laws of the United States which shall be made in pursuance thereof, and all treaties made or which shall be made under the authority of the United States, shall be the supreme law of the land, and the judges in every State shall be bound thereby, anything in the constitution or laws of any State to the contrary notwithstanding.

Certainly the Government of the United States is a limited government, and so is every State government a limited government. With us this idea of limitation spreads through every form of administration—general, State, and municipal—and rests on the great distinguishing principle of the recognition of the rights of man. The ancient republics absorbed the individual in the state—prescribed his religion and controlled his activity. The American system rests on the assertion of the equal right of every man to life, liberty, and the pursuit of happiness, to freedom of conscience, to the culture and exercise of all his faculties. As a consequence the State government is limited—as to the General Government in the interest of union, as to the individual citizen in the interest of freedom.

States, with proper limitations of power, are essential to the existence of the Constitution of the United States. At the very commencement, when we assumed a place among the powers of the earth, the Declaration of Independence was adopted by States; so also were the Articles of Confederation; and when "the people of the United States" ordained and established the Constitution it was the assent of the States, one by one, which gave it vitality. In the event, too, of any amendment to the Constitution, the proposition of Congress needs the confirmation of States. Without States one great branch of the legislative government would be wanting. And if we look beyond the letter of the Constitution to the character of our country, its capacity for comprehending within its jurisdiction a vast continental empire is due to the system of States. The best security for the perpetual existence of the States is the "supreme authority" of the Constitution of the United States. The perpetuity of the Constitution brings with it the perpetuity of the States; their mutual relation makes us what we are, and in our political system their connection is indissoluble. The whole can not exist without the parts, nor the parts without the whole. So long as the Constitution of the United States endures, the States will endure. The destruction of the one is the destruction of the other; the preservation of the one is the preservation of the other.

I have thus explained my views of the mutual relations of the Constitution and the States, because they unfold the principles on which I have sought to solve the momentous questions and overcome the appalling difficulties that met me at the very commencement of my Administration. It has been my steadfast object to escape from the sway of momentary passions and to derive a healing policy from the fundamental and unchanging principles of the Constitution.

I found the States suffering from the effects of a civil war. Resistance to the General Government appeared to have exhausted itself. The United States had recovered possession of their forts and arsenals, and their armies were in the occupation of every State which had attempted to secede. Whether the territory within the limits of those States should be held as conquered territory, under military authority emanating from the President as the head of the Army, was the first question that presented itself for decision.

Now military governments, established for an indefinite period, would have offered no security for the early suppression of discontent, would have divided the people into the vanquishers and the vanquished, and would have envenomed hatred rather than have restored affection. Once established, no precise limit to their continuance was conceivable. They would have occasioned an incalculable and exhausting expense. Peaceful emigration to and from that portion of the country is one of the best means that can be thought of for the restoration of harmony, and that emigration would have been prevented; for what emigrant from abroad, what industrious citizen at home, would place himself willingly under military rule? The chief persons who would have followed in the train of the Army would have been dependents on the General Government or men who expected profit from the miseries of their erring fellow-citizens. The powers of patronage and rule which would have been exercised, under the President, over a vast and populous and naturally wealthy region are greater than, unless under extreme necessity, I should be willing to intrust to any one man. They are such as, for myself, I could never, unless on occasions of great emergency, consent to exercise. The willful use of such powers, if continued through a period of years, would have endangered the purity of the general administration and the liberties of the States which remained loyal.

Besides, the policy of military rule over a conquered territory would have implied that the States whose inhabitants may have taken part in the rebellion had by the act of those inhabitants ceased to exist. But the true theory is that all pretended acts of secession were from the beginning null and void. The States can not commit treason nor screen the individual citizens who may have committed treason any more than they can make valid treaties or engage in lawful commerce with any foreign power. The States attempting to secede placed themselves in a condition where their vitality was impaired, but not extinguished; their functions suspended, but not destroyed.

But if any State neglects or refuses to perform its offices there is the more need that the General Government should maintain all its authority and as soon as practicable resume the exercise of all its functions. On this principle I have acted, and have gradually and quietly, and by almost imperceptible steps, sought to restore the rightful energy of the General Government and of the States. To that end provisional governors have been appointed for the States, conventions called, governors elected, legislatures assembled, and Senators and Representatives chosen to the Congress of the United States. At the same time the courts of the United States, as far as could be done, have been reopened, so that the laws of the United States may be enforced through their agency. The blockade has been removed and the custom-houses reestablished in ports of entry, so that the revenue of the United States may be collected. The Post-Office Department renews its ceaseless activity, and the General Government is thereby enabled to communicate promptly with its officers and agents. The courts bring security to persons and property; the opening of the ports invites the restoration of industry and commerce; the post-office renews the facilities of social intercourse and of business. And is it not happy for us all that the restoration of each one of these functions of the General Government brings with it a blessing to the States over which they are extended? Is it not a sure promise of harmony and renewed attachment to the Union that after all that has happened the return of the General Government is known only as a beneficence?

I know very well that this policy is attended with some risk; that for its success it requires at least the acquiescence of the States which it concerns; that it implies an invitation to those States, by renewing their allegiance to the United States, to resume their functions as States of the Union. But it is a risk that must be taken. In the choice of difficulties it is the smallest risk; and to diminish and if possible to remove all danger, I have felt it incumbent on me to assert one other power of the General Government—the power of pardon. As no State can throw a defense over the crime of treason, the power of pardon is exclusively vested in the executive government of the United States. In exercising that power I have taken every precaution to connect it with the clearest recognition of the binding force of the laws of the United States and an unqualified acknowledgment of the great social change of condition in regard to slavery which has grown out of the war.

The next step which I have taken to restore the constitutional relations of the States has been an invitation to them to participate in the high office of amending the Constitution. Every patriot must wish for a general amnesty at the earliest epoch consistent with public safety. For this great end there is need of a concurrence of all opinions and the spirit of mutual conciliation. All parties in the late terrible conflict must work together in harmony. It is not too much to ask, in the name of the whole people, that on the one side the plan of restoration shall proceed in conformity with a willingness to cast the disorders of the past into oblivion, and that on the other the evidence of sincerity in the future maintenance of the Union shall be put beyond any doubt by the ratification of the proposed amendment to the Constitution, which provides for the abolition of slavery forever within the limits of our country. So long as the adoption of this amendment is delayed, so long will doubt and jealousy and uncertainty prevail. This is the measure which will efface the sad memory of the past; this is the measure which will most certainly call population and capital and security to those parts of the Union that need them most. Indeed, it is not too much to ask of the States which are now resuming their places in the family of the Union to give this pledge of perpetual loyalty and peace. Until it is done the past, however much we may desire it, will not be forgotten. The adoption of the amendment reunites us beyond all power of disruption; it heals the wound that is still imperfectly closed; it removes slavery, the element which has so long perplexed and divided the country; it makes of us once more a united people, renewed and strengthened, bound more than ever to mutual affection and support.

The amendment to the Constitution being adopted, it would remain for the States whose powers have been so long in abeyance to resume their places in the two branches of the National Legislature, and thereby complete the work of restoration. Here it is for you, fellow-citizens of the Senate, and for you, fellow-citizens of the House of Representatives, to judge, each of you for yourselves, of the elections, returns, and qualifications of your own members.

The full assertion of the powers of the General Government requires the holding of circuit courts of the United States within the districts where their authority has been interrupted. In the present posture of our public affairs strong objections have been urged to holding those courts in any of the States where the rebellion has existed; and it was ascertained by inquiry that the circuit court of the United States would not be held within the district of Virginia during the autumn or early winter, nor until Congress should have "an opportunity to consider and act on the whole subject." To your deliberations the restoration of this branch of the civil authority of the United States is therefore necessarily referred, with the hope that early provision will be made for the resumption of all its functions. It is manifest that treason, most flagrant in character, has been committed. Persons who are charged with its commission should have fair and impartial trials in the highest civil tribunals of the country, in order that the Constitution and the laws may be fully vindicated, the truth clearly established and affirmed that treason is a crime, that traitors should be punished and the offense made infamous, and, at the same time, that the question may be judicially settled, finally and forever, that no State of its own will has the right to renounce its place in the Union.

The relations of the General Government toward the 4,000,000 inhabitants whom the war has called into freedom have engaged my most serious consideration. On the propriety of attempting to make the freedmen electors by the proclamation of the Executive I took for my counsel the Constitution itself, the interpretations of that instrument by its authors and their contemporaries, and recent legislation by Congress. When, at the first movement toward independence, the Congress of the United States instructed the several States to institute governments of their own, they left each State to decide for itself the conditions for the enjoyment of the elective franchise. During the period of the Confederacy there continued to exist a very great diversity in the qualifications of electors in the several States, and even within a State a distinction of qualifications prevailed with regard to the officers who were to be chosen. The Constitution of the United States recognizes these diversities when it enjoins that in the choice of members of the House of Representatives of the United States "the electors in each State shall have the qualifications requisite for electors of the most numerous branch of the State legislature." After the formation of the Constitution it remained, as before, the uniform usage for each State to enlarge the body of its electors according to its own judgment, and under this system one State after another has proceeded to increase the number of its electors, until now universal suffrage, or something very near it, is the general rule. So fixed was this reservation of power in the habits of the people and so unquestioned has been the interpretation of the Constitution that during the civil war the late President never harbored the purpose—certainly never avowed the purpose—of disregarding it; and in the acts of Congress during that period nothing can be found which, during the continuance of hostilities, much less after their close, would have sanctioned any departure by the Executive from a policy which has so uniformly obtained. Moreover, a concession of the elective franchise to the freedmen by act of the President of the United States must have been extended to all colored men, wherever found, and so must have established a change of suffrage in the Northern, Middle, and Western States, not less than in the Southern and Southwestern. Such an act would have created a new class of voters, and would have been an assumption of power by the President which nothing in the Constitution or laws of the United States would have warranted.

On the other hand, every danger of conflict is avoided when the settlement of the question is referred to the several States. They can, each for itself, decide on the measure, and whether it is to be adopted at once and absolutely or introduced gradually and with conditions. In my judgment the freedmen, if they show patience and manly virtues, will sooner obtain a participation in the elective franchise through the States than through the General Government, even if it had power to intervene. When the tumult of emotions that have been raised by the suddenness of the social change shall have subsided, it may prove that they will receive the kindest usage from some of those on whom they have heretofore most closely depended.

But while I have no doubt that now, after the close of the war, it is not competent for the General Government to extend the elective franchise in the several States, it is equally clear that good faith requires the security of the freedmen in their liberty and their property, their right to labor, and their right to claim the just return of their labor. I can not too strongly urge a dispassionate treatment of this subject, which should be carefully kept aloof from all party strife. We must equally avoid hasty assumptions of any natural impossibility for the two races to live side by side in a state of mutual benefit and good will. The experiment involves us in no inconsistency; let us, then, go on and make that experiment in good faith, and not be too easily disheartened. The country is in need of labor, and the freedmen are in need of employment, culture, and protection. While their right of voluntary migration and expatriation is not to be questioned, I would not advise their forced removal and colonization. Let us rather encourage them to honorable and useful industry, where it may be beneficial to themselves and to the country; and, instead of hasty anticipations of the certainty of failure, let there be nothing wanting to the fair trial of the experiment. The change in their condition is the substitution of labor by contract for the status of slavery. The freedman can not fairly be accused of unwillingness to work so long as a doubt remains about his freedom of choice in his pursuits and the certainty of his recovering his stipulated wages. In this the interests of the employer and the employed coincide. The employer desires in his workmen spirit and alacrity, and these can be permanently secured in no other way. And if the one ought to be able to enforce the contract, so ought the other. The public interest will be best promoted if the several States will provide adequate protection and remedies for the freedmen. Until this is in some way accomplished there is no chance for the advantageous use of their labor, and the blame of ill success will not rest on them.

I know that sincere philanthropy is earnest for the immediate realization of its remotest aims; but time is always an element in reform. It is one of the greatest acts on record to have brought 4,000,000 people into freedom. The career of free industry must be fairly opened to them, and then their future prosperity and condition must, after all, rest mainly on themselves. If they fail, and so perish away, let us be careful that the failure shall not be attributable to any denial of justice. In all that relates to the destiny of the freedmen we need not be too anxious to read the future; many incidents which, from a speculative point of view, might raise alarm will quietly settle themselves. Now that slavery is at an end, or near its end, the greatness of its evil in the point of view of public economy becomes more and more apparent. Slavery was essentially a monopoly of labor, and as such locked the States where it prevailed against the incoming of free industry. Where labor was the property of the capitalist, the white man was excluded from employment, or had but the second best chance of finding it; and the foreign emigrant turned away from the region where his condition would be so precarious. With the destruction of the monopoly free labor will hasten from all parts of the civilized world to assist in developing various and immeasurable resources which have hitherto lain dormant. The eight or nine States nearest the Gulf of Mexico have a soil of exuberant fertility, a climate friendly to long life, and can sustain a denser population than is found as yet in any part of our country. And the future influx of population to them will be mainly from the North or from the most cultivated nations in Europe. From the sufferings that have attended them during our late struggle let us look away to the future, which is sure to be laden for them with greater prosperity than has ever before been known. The removal of the monopoly of slave labor is a pledge that those regions will be peopled by a numerous and enterprising population, which will vie with any in the Union in compactness, inventive genius, wealth, and industry. . . .

SELECTION

"A Harmonious Restoration" Achieved: President Johnson's Special Message to Congress, December 18, 1865

During the months intervening between his assumption of the presidential office and the meeting of Congress in December, 1865, President Johnson had supervised the fulfillment of presidential Reconstruction. In a series of proclamations, he had outlined in specific terms the steps which the Southern states must take to regain their places in the national Union. On May 29, he reiterated Lincoln's proposal for granting amnesty and pardon to the former Confederates, adding additional categories for those for whom general amnesty would not apply, including Southerners whose taxable property exceeded $20,000. In a separate statement, he announced the conditions which the Southern states must satisfy. Provisional governors were to be appointed to each state to direct the formation of new governments. Constitutional conventions would be elected to draft new frames of government, and elections for state officers would follow. The ordinances of secession must be declared illegal, the Confederate debt repudiated, and the Thirteenth Amendment ratified. Once these steps had been taken, Reconstruction would be complete. By the time Congress met, the reorganization outlined by Johnson had been achieved and the senators and representatives from the new states awaited recognition. On December 18, in a special message to Congress, Johnson in effect declared Reconstruction accomplished. The text of this message is reprinted from James D. Richardson (ed.), A Compilation of the Messages and Papers of the Presidents, 1789–1897 (Washington: Government Printing Office, 1907), ten volumes, volume 6, pages 372–373. Congress, however, had other plans. None of the new Johnson governments was recognized, and their elected senators and representatives were denied seats in Congress. The presidential plans for Reconstruction were ignored as Congress appointed a Joint Committee on Reconstruction to assume responsibility for directing the return of the former Confederate States to the Union. The spotlight now shifted to Capitol Hill and the long awaited showdown had arrived.

Washington, December 18, 1865.

To the Senate of the United States:

In reply to the resolution adopted by the Senate on the 12th instant, I have the honor to state that the rebellion waged by a portion of the people against the properly constituted authority of the Government of the United States has been suppressed; that the United States are in possession of every State in which the insurrection existed, and that, as far as it could be done, the courts of the United States have been restored, post-offices reestablished, and steps taken to put into effective operation the revenue laws of the country.

As the result of the measures instituted by the Executive with the view of inducing a resumption of the functions of the States comprehended in the inquiry of the Senate, the people of North Carolina, South Carolina, Georgia, Alabama, Mississippi, Louisiana, Arkansas, and Tennessee have reorganized their respective State governments, and "are yielding obedience to the laws and Government of the United States" with more willingness and greater promptitude than under the circumstances could reasonably have been anticipated. The proposed amendment to the Constitution, providing for the abolition of slavery forever within the limits of the country, has been ratified by each one of those States, with the exception of Mississippi, from which no official information has been received, and in nearly all of them measures have been adopted or are now pending to confer upon freedman the privileges which are essential to their comfort, protection, and security. In Florida and Texas the people are making commendable progress in restoring their State governments, and no doubt is entertained that they will at an early period be in a condition to resume all of their practical relations with the General Government.

In "that portion of the Union lately in rebellion" the aspect of affairs is more promising than, in view of all the circumstances, could well have been expected. The people throughout the entire South evince a laudable desire to renew their allegiance to the Government and to repair the devastations of war by a prompt and cheerful return to peaceful pursuits, and abiding faith is entertained that their actions will conform to their professions, and that in acknowledging the supremacy of the Constitution and laws of the United States their loyalty will be unreservedly given to the Government, whose leniency they can not fail to appreciate and whose fostering care will soon restore them to a condition of prosperity. It is true that in some of the States the demoralizing effects of the war are to be seen in occasional disorders; but these are local in character, not frequent in occurrence, and are rapidly disappearing as the authority of civil law is extended and sustained. Perplexing questions are naturally to be expected from the great and sudden change in the relations between the two races; but systems are gradually developing themselves under which the freedman will receive the protection to which he is justly entitled, and, by means of his labor, make himself a useful and independent member in the community in which he has a home.

From all the information in my possession and from that which I have recently derived from the most reliable authority I am induced to cherish the belief that sectional animosity is surely and rapidly merging itself into a spirit of nationality, and that representation, connected with a properly adjusted system of taxation, will result in a harmonious restoration of the relation of the States to the National Union. . . .

PART FIFTEEN

It Is Time That Congress Should Assert Its Sovereignty

As members of Congress gathered in Washington in December, 1865, for their first regular session following the end of the Civil War, they were determined to assume control over the direction of Reconstruction policy. The political reorganization of states, as Wade and Davis had pointed out in their manifesto, was rightfully a function of the legislative branch, not of the executive. While Congress had been willing to grant the President extraordinary powers during the war, the war was now over. The moment had arrived, as Thaddeus Stevens emphasized, for Congress to assert its sovereignty.

The first step was the repudiation of presidential Reconstruction. Holding the power to judge the qualifications of its own membership, Congress found a ready weapon with which to destroy the efforts of Lincoln and Johnson. When Congress assembled, none of the senators or representatives from the states reorganized under the presidential terms was admitted. Their states were thus declared to be outside the Union and their new governments void. Circumstances in the Southern states themselves contributed to the popularity of Congress' action in the North. Few of the reorganized states had willingly accepted the conditions laid down in the presidential plans. Some states balked at the repudiation of their ordinances of secession and at the ratification of the Thirteenth Amendment, finally taking these actions only after pressure had been exerted from the White House. Mississippi refused to ratify the Thirteenth Amendment, the only Southern state which did refuse. In their elections for state officers, the people of the South turned again to their Confederate leadership in what was viewed in the North as a gesture of defiance. Following their reorganization, many of the states felt it necessary to enact strict and harsh Black Codes, controlling the Negro population in a manner that was reminiscent of slavery. All these actions convinced Northerners that the South had learned little from its defeat and that the presidential plans for Reconstruction were unusually simple and lenient.

Having wrested control over Reconstruction from the hands of the President, Congress proceeded to formulate its own program, dealing with the second of the important questions raised by Reconstruction, that of scope. Unlike Lincoln and Johnson, Congress was not solely concerned with the status of the former Confederate States; nor was it willing to leave further reform to state action. The disastrous results of such a policy had been demonstrated by the passage of the Black Codes. On the day that President Johnson delivered his first annual message to Congress, Senator Charles Sumner of Massachusetts introduced resolutions that reflected the attitude of Congress and of its dominant group, the Radical Republicans. Five conditions were set down for the South: the complete reestablishment of loyalty and allegiance, without any reservations; the enfranchisement of all citizens, without regard to race or color, and the equality of all before the law; the rejection of the Confederate debt; the organization of an educational system for all, regardless of race or color; and the selection of citizens for state and national office whose loyalty was without suspicion. The Southern states had, in Sumner's view, committed suicide and were in fact no longer states. They were subject to the dictates of Congress.

The first Reconstruction Congress sought to implement these goals. In the spring of 1866, a Civil Rights act was passed defining citizenship in a national sense and guaranteeing, through Federal intervention, equal rights before the law for all citizens. When questions were raised regarding the constitutionality of the measure, Congress replied by passing the Fourteenth Amendment to the Constitution, one of the most significant and far-reaching steps taken during Reconstruction. President Johnson was placed on the defensive and began what was to be a long series of presidential vetoes of Reconstruction legislation. The confrontation between executive and Congress that had started with Lincoln's quarrel with the Wade-Davis Bill in 1864 now reached its most serious proportions.

In the congressional elections of 1866, Northern voters sided with Congress against the President, providing the Radical leaders with the mandate they had hoped for. A series of Reconstruction Acts was passed early in 1867, over presidential vetoes, providing the steps by which the Southern states could reorganize and seek readmission into the Union. Military rule was established in the South, to continue until Southerners had satisfied the congressional requirements. Relations between the executive and legislative branches steadily deteriorated until Congress sought to reconstruct the Presidency itself. The unsuccessful attempt by Congress to remove the President through impeachment in 1868 was the last battle in the war between Johnson and the Radicals. The election that year of Ulysses S. Grant removed the final obstacle to congressional Reconstruction.

By the time Grant was elected, however, Reconstruction had moved into its last phase. The reorganization of the Southern states was under way according to congressional standards and requirements. One by one, the states of the Confederacy were readmitted to the Union and their elected senators and representatives were seated in the national legislature.

Historical interpretation of Reconstruction has proved as controversial as Reconstruction itself. The best brief summary of Reconstruction historiography is Bernard Weisberger's article, "The Dark and Bloody Ground of Reconstruction Historiography," Journal of Southern History, *volume 25, November, 1959, pages 427–447. Shortly after the turn of the century, historians expressed a pro-Johnson and anti-Radical view, regarding Reconstruction policy, as devised and administered by Congress, as a "national disgrace." Foremost in reflecting this position were the works of William A. Dunning (e.g., his* Reconstruction, Political and Economic, 1865–1877 *[1907]) and his students who published accounts of Reconstruction in individual Southern states. More recent works which argue this position are Claude G. Bowers,* The Tragic Era: The Revolution after Lincoln *(1929) and E. Merton Coulter,* The South during Reconstruction, 1865–1877 *(1947). Since the late 1930s, however, Reconstruction historiography has taken a different turn, as historians have adopted a more balanced and judicious view. Howard K. Beale's essay, "On Rewriting Reconstruction History,"* American Historical Review, *volume 45, July, 1940, pages 807–827, was one of several important articles suggesting this new trend. The new concern for civil rights in the 1950s and 1960s has stimulated a great deal of new research and publication dealing with Reconstruction, most of it highly critical of Johnson and sympathetic to the Radicals, contradicting the old Dunning position. Two recent syntheses of Reconstruction history are John Hope Franklin,* Reconstruction: After the War *(1961) and Kenneth M. Stampp,* The Era of Reconstruction *(1965). A fine study of a more limited period written by an Englishman is W. R. Brock,* An American Crisis: Congress and Reconstruction, 1865–1867 *(1963).*

A Radical Republican Attacks Presidential Reconstruction:
Thaddeus Stevens, December 18, 1865

One of the leaders in the attack against President Johnson and presidential Reconstruction was Thaddeus Stevens (1792–1868), member of the House of Representatives from Pennsylvania. Stevens served in the House as a Whig from 1849 to 1853 and as a Republican from 1859 until his death in 1868. He was early recognized as a leader of the Radical Republicans, becoming one of the most controversial, and at the same time most intriguing, figures of the Reconstruction period. Stevens combined a bitterly vindictive attitude towards the South with a genuine humanitarianism and sympathy for the Negro freedmen. He was convinced first of all that Congress was the only legitimate agency for carrying out the reorganization of the Southern states. He had opposed Lincoln's Reconstruction policies during the war, and he continued to oppose Johnson with an increasing fervency. Stevens also believed that the leniency of the presidential plans was misplaced. He called out for the punishment of the Southern "traitors." The Southern states, he maintained, were conquered provinces until Congress should see fit to reorganize them. Mixed with these convictions was a strong and inflexible partisanship, a burning desire to guarantee the ascendancy of the Republican party. Yet Stevens was one of the few Radical leaders who saw Reconstruction in its broadest aspects. The task of the nation involved something more than the simple readmission of the errant Southern states. He argued for true equality between Negroes and whites and on one occasion proposed a redistribution of land in the South to the freedman, in order to provide an economic base for Negro freedom. On December 18, 1865, the same day on which Johnson issued his special message, Stevens delivered a speech in the House of Representatives, viciously attacking the President and providing a cue for congressional Reconstruction; the text of this speech is reprinted from the Congressional Globe, *Thirty-ninth Congress, first session, pages 72–75.*

Not only was Stevens controversial in his own time but he has remained so among historians and biographers. A critical biography is that of Richard N. Current, Old Thad Stevens: A Story of Ambition *(1942). Recent, more sympathetic works are Ralph Korngold,* Thaddeus Stevens: A Being Darkly Wise and Rudely Great *(1955) and Fawn M. Brodie,* Thaddeus Stevens: Scourge of the South *(1959).*

A candid examination of the power and proper principles of reconstruction can be offensive to no one, and may possibly be profitable by exciting inquiry. One of the suggestions of the message which we are now considering has special reference to this. Perhaps it is the principle most interesting to the people at this time. The President assumes, what no one doubts, that the late rebel States have lost their constitutional relations to the Union, and are incapable of representation in Congress, except by permission of the Government. It matters but little, with this admission, whether you call them States out of the Union, and now conquered territories, or assert that because the Constitution forbids them to do what they did do, that they are therefore only dead as to all national and political action, and will remain so until the Government shall breathe into them the breath of life anew and permit them to occupy their former position. In other words, that they are not out of the Union, but are only dead carcasses lying within the Union. In either case, it is very plain that it requires the action of Congress to enable them to form a State government and send representatives to Congress. Nobody, I believe, pretends that with their old constitutions and frames of government they can be permitted to claim their old rights under the Constitution. They have torn their constitutional States into atoms, and built on their foundations fabrics of a totally different character. Dead men cannot raise themselves. Dead States cannot restore their own existence "as it was." Whose especial duty is it to do it? In whom does the Constitution place the power? Not in the judicial branch of Government, for it only adjudicates and does not prescribe laws. Not in the Executive, for he only executes and cannot make laws. Not in the Commander-in-Chief of the armies, for he can only hold them under military rule until the sovereign legislative power of the conqueror shall give them law.

There is fortunately no difficulty in solving the question. There are two provisions in the Constitution, under one of which the case must fall. The fourth article says:

New States may be admitted by the Congress into this Union.

In my judgment this is the controlling provision in this case. Unless the law of nations is a dead letter, the late war between two acknowledged belligerents severed their original compacts, and broke all the ties that bound them together. The future condition of the conquered power depends on the will of the conqueror. They must come in as new States or remain as conquered provinces. Congress—the Senate and House of Representatives, with the concurrence of the President—is the only power that can act in the matter. But suppose, as some dreaming theorists imagine, that these States have never been out of the Union, but have only destroyed their State governments so as to be incapable of political action; then the fourth section of the fourth article applies, which says:

The United States shall guaranty to every State in this Union a republican form of government.

Who is the United States? Not the judiciary; not the President; but the sovereign power of the people, exercised through their representatives in Congress, with the concurrence of the Executive. It means the political

Government—the concurrent action of both branches of Congress and the Executive. The separate action of each amounts to nothing, either in admitting new States or guarantying republican governments to lapsed or outlawed States. Whence springs the preposterous idea that either the President, or the Senate, or the House of Representatives, acting separately, can determine the right of States to send members or Senators to the Congress of the Union?

To prove that they are and for four years have been out of the Union for all legal purposes, and being now conquered, subject to the absolute disposal of Congress, I will suggest a few ideas and adduce a few authorities. If the so-called "confederate States of America" were an independent belligerent, and were so acknowledged by the United States and by Europe, or had assumed and maintained an attitude which entitled them to be considered and treated as a belligerent, then, during such time, they were precisely in the condition of a foreign nation with whom we were at war; nor need their independence as a nation be acknowledged by us to produce that effect. . . .

The idea that the States could not and did not make war because the Constitution forbids it, and that this must be treated as a war of individuals, is a very injurious and groundless fallacy. Individuals cannot make war. They may commit murder, but that is no war. Communities, societies, States, make war. . . .

But why appeal to reason to prove that the seceded States made war as States, when the conclusive opinion of the Supreme Court is at hand? . . .

After such clear and repeated decisions it is something worse than ridiculous to hear men of respectable standing attempting to nullify the law of nations, and declare the Supreme Court of the United States in error, because, as the Constitution forbids it, the States could not go out of the Union in fact. A respectable gentleman was lately reciting this argument, when he suddenly stopped and said, "Did you hear of that atrocious murder committed in our town? A rebel deliberately murdered a Government official." The person addressed said, "I think you are mistaken." "How so? I saw it myself." "You are wrong, no murder was or could be committed, for the law forbids it."

The theory that the rebel States, for four years a separate power and without representation in Congress, were all the time here in the Union, is a good deal less ingenious and respectable than the metaphysics of Berkeley, which proved that neither the world nor any human being was in existence. If this theory were simply ridiculous it could be forgiven; but its effect is deeply injurious to the stability of the nation. I cannot doubt that the late confederate States are out of the Union to all intents and purposes for which the conqueror may choose so to consider them.

But on the ground of estoppel, the United States have the clear right to elect to adjudge them out of the Union. They are estopped both by matter of record and matter *in pais*. One of the first resolutions passed by seceded South Carolina in January, 1861, is as follows:

> *Resolved, unanimously,* That the separation of South Carolina from the Federal Union is final, and she has no further interest in the Constitution of the United States; and that the only appropriate negotiations between her and the Federal Government are as to their mutual relations as foreign States.

Similar resolutions appear upon all their State and confederate government records. The speeches of their members of congress, their generals and executive officers, and the answers of their government to our shameful sueings for peace, went upon the defiant ground that no terms would be offered or received except upon the prior acknowledgment of the entire and permanent independence of the confederate States. After this, to deny that we have a right to treat them as a conquered belligerent, severed from the Union in fact, is not argument but mockery. Whether it be our interest to do so is the only question hereafter and more deliberately to be considered.

But suppose these powerful but now subdued belligerents, instead of being out of the Union, are merely destroyed, and are now lying about, a dead corpse, or with animation so suspended as to be incapable of action, and wholly unable to heal themselves by any unaided movements of their own. Then they may fall under the provision of the Constitution which says "the United States shall guaranty to every State in the Union a republican form of government." Under that power can the judiciary, or the President, or the Commander-in-Chief of the Army, or the Senate or House of Representatives, acting separately, restore them to life and re-admit them into the Union? I insist that if each acted separately, though the action of each was identical with all the others, it would amount to nothing. Nothing but the joint action of the two Houses of Congress and the concurrence of the President could do it. If the Senate admitted their Senators, and the House their members, it would have no effect on the future action of Congress. The Fortieth Congress might reject both. Such is the ragged record of Congress for the last four years.

In Luther *vs.* Borden (7 Howard, 1–42) the Supreme Court say:

> Under this article of the Constitution [the one above cited] it rests with Congress to decide what government is the established one in a State. For as the United States guaranty to each State a republican government, Congress must necessarily decide what government is established in the State before it can determine whether it is republican or not.

Congress alone can do it. But Congress does not mean the Senate, or the House of Representatives, and President, all acting severally. Their joint action constitutes Congress. Hence a law of Congress must be passed before any new State can be admitted; or any dead ones revived. Until then no member can be lawfully admitted into either House. Hence it appears with how little knowledge of constitutional law each branch is urged to admit members separately from these destroyed States. The provision that "each House shall be the judge of the elections, returns, and qualifications of its own members," has not the most distant bearing on this question. Congress must create States and declare when they are entitled to be represented. Then each House must judge whether the members presenting themselves from a recognized State possess the requisite qualifications of age, residence, and citizenship; and whether the election and returns are according to law. The Houses, separately, can judge of nothing else. It seems amazing that any man of legal education could give it any larger meaning.

It is obvious from all this that the first duty of Congress is to pass a law declaring the condition of these outside or defunct States, and providing proper civil governments for them. Since the conquest they have been governed by martial law. Military rule is necessarily despotic, and ought not to exist longer than is absolutely necessary. As there are no symptoms that the people of these provinces will be prepared to participate in constitutional government for some years, I know of no arrangement so proper for them as territorial governments. There they can learn the principles of freedom and eat the fruit of foul rebellion. Under such governments, while electing members to the Territorial Legislatures, they will necessarily mingle with those to whom Congress shall extend the right of suffrage. In Territories Congress fixes the qualifications of electors; and I know of no better place nor better occasion for the conquered rebels and the conqueror to practice justice to all men, and accustom themselves to make and to obey equal laws.

As these fallen rebels cannot at their option reënter the heaven which they have disturbed, the garden of Eden which they have deserted, and flaming swords are set at the gates to secure their exclusion, it becomes important to the welfare of the nation to inquire when the doors shall be reopened for their admission.

According to my judgment they ought never to be recognized as capable of acting in the Union, or of being counted as valid States, until the Constitution shall have been so amended as to make it what its framers intended; and so as to secure perpetual ascendency to the party of the Union; and so as to render our republican Government firm and stable forever. The first of those amendments is to change the basis of representation among the States from Federal numbers to actual voters. Now all the colored freemen in the slave States, and three fifths of the slaves, are represented, though none of them have votes. The States have nineteen representatives of colored slaves. If the slaves are now free then they can add, for the other two fifths, thirteen more, making the slave representation thirty-two. I suppose the free blacks in those States will give at least five more, making the representation of non-voting people of color about thirty-seven. The whole number of representatives now from the slave States is seventy. Add the other two fifths and it will be eighty-three.

If the amendment prevails, and those States withhold the right of suffrage from persons of color, it will deduct about thirty-seven, leaving them but forty-six. With the basis unchanged, the eighty-three southern members, with the Democrats that will in the best times be elected from the North, will always give them a majority in Congress and in the Electoral College. They will at the very first election take posession of the White House and the halls of Congress. I need not depict the ruin that would follow. Assumption of the rebel debt or repudiation of the Federal debt would be sure to follow. The oppression of the freedmen; the reamendment of their State constitutions, and the reëstablishment of slavery would be the inevitable result. That they would scorn and disregard their present constitutions, forced upon them in the midst of martial law, would be both natural and just. No one who has any regard for freedom of elections can look upon those governments, forced upon them in duress, with any favor. If they should grant the right of suffrage to persons of color, I think there would always be Union white men enough in the South, aided by the blacks, to divide the representation, and thus continue the

Republican ascendency. If they should refuse to thus alter their election laws it would reduce the representatives of the late slave States to about forty-five and render them powerless for evil.

It is plain that this amendment must be consummated before the defunct States are admitted to be capable of State action, or it never can be.

The proposed amendment to allow Congress to lay a duty on exports is precisely in the same situation. Its importance cannot well be overstated. It is very obvious that for many years the South will not pay much under our internal revenue laws. The only article on which we can raise any considerable amount is cotton. It will be grown largely at once. With ten cents a pound export duty it would be furnished cheaper to foreign markets than they could obtain it from any other part of the world. The late war has shown that. Two million bales exported, at five hundred pounds to the bale, would yield $100,000,000. This seems to be the chief revenue we shall ever derive from the South. Besides, it would be a protection to that amount to our domestic manufactures. Other proposed amendments—to make all laws uniform; to prohibit the assumption of the rebel debt—are of vital importance, and the only thing that can prevent the combined forces of copperheads and secessionists from legislating against the interests of the Union whenever they may obtain an accidental majority.

But this is not all that we ought to do before these inveterate rebels are invited to participate in our legislation. We have turned, or are about to turn, loose four million slaves without a hut to shelter them or a cent in their pockets. The infernal laws of slavery have prevented them from acquiring an education, understanding the commonest laws of contract, or of managing the ordinary business of life. This Congress is bound to provide for them until they can take care of themselves. If we do not furnish them with homesteads, and hedge them around with protective laws; if we leave them to the legislation of their late masters, we had better have left them in bondage. Their condition would be worse than that of our prisoners at Andersonville. If we fail in this great duty now, when we have the power, we shall deserve and receive the execration of history and of all future ages.

Two things are of vital importance.

1. So to establish a principle that none of the rebel States shall be counted in any of the amendments of the Constitution until they are duly admitted into the family of States by the law-making power of their conqueror. For more than six months the amendment of the Constitution abolishing slavery has been ratified by the Legislatures of three fourths of the States that acted on its passage by Congress, and which had Legislatures, or which were States capable of acting, or required to act, on the question.

I take no account of the aggregation of white-washed rebels, who without any legal authority have assembled in the capitals of the late rebel States and simulated legislative bodies. Nor do I regard with any respect the cunning by-play into which they deluded the Secretary of State by frequent telegraphic announcements that "South Carolina has adopted the amendment;" "Alabama has adopted the amendment, being the twenty-seventh State," &c. This was intended to delude the people, and accustom Congress to hear repeated the names of these extinct States as if they were alive; when, in truth, they have now no more existence than the revolted cities of Latium, two thirds of whose people were colonized and their property confiscated, and their right of citizenship withdrawn by conquering and avenging Rome.

2. It is equally important to the stability of this Republic that it should now be solemnly decided what power can revive, recreate, and reinstate these provinces into the family of States, and invest them with the rights of American citizens. It is time that Congress should assert its sovereignty, and assume something of the dignity of a Roman senate. It is fortunate that the President invites Congress to take this manly attitude. After stating with great frankness in his able message his theory, which, however, is found to be impracticable, and which I believe very few now consider tenable, he refers the whole matter to the judgment of Congress. If Congress should fail firmly and wisely to discharge that high duty it is not the fault of the President.

This Congress owes it to its own character to set the seal of reprobation upon a doctrine which is becoming too fashionable, and unless rebuked will be the recognized principle of our Government. Governor Perry and other provisional governors and orators proclaim that "this is the white man's Government." The whole copperhead party, pandering to the lowest prejudices of the ignorant, repeat the cuckoo cry, "This is the white man's Government." Demagogues of all parties, even some high in authority, gravely shout, "This is the white man's Government." What is implied by this? That one race of men are to have the exclusive right forever to rule this nation, and to exercise all acts of sovereignty, while all other races and nations and colors are to be their subjects, and have no voice in making the laws and choosing the rulers by whom they are to be governed. Wherein does this differ from slavery except in degree? Does not this contradict all the distinctive principles of the Declaration of Independence? When the great and good men promulgated that instrument, and pledged their lives and sacred honors to defend it, it was supposed to form an epoch in civil government. Before that time it was held that the right to rule was vested in families, dynasties, or races, not because of superior intelligence or virtue, but because of a divine right to enjoy exclusive privileges.

Our fathers repudiated the whole doctrine of the legal superiority of families or races, and proclaimed the equality of men before the law. Upon that they created a revolution and built the Republic. They were prevented by slavery from perfecting the superstructure whose foundation they had thus broadly laid. For the sake of the Union they consented to wait, but never relinquished the idea of its final completion. The time to which they looked forward with anxiety has come. It is our duty to complete their work. If this Republic is not now made to stand on their great principles, it has no honest foundation, and the Father of all men will still shake it to its center. If we have not yet been sufficiently scourged for our national sin to teach us to do justice to all God's creatures, without distinction of race or color, we must expect the still more heavy vengeance of an offended Father, still increasing his inflictions as he increased the severity of the plagues of Egypt until the tyrant consented to do justice. And when that tyrant repented of his reluctant consent, and attempted to reenslave the people, as our southern tyrants are attempting to do now, he filled the Red sea with broken chariots and drowned horses, and strewed the shores with dead carcasses.

Mr. Chairman, I trust the Republican party will not be alarmed at what I am saying. I do not profess to speak their sentiments, nor must they be held responsible for them. I speak for myself, and take the responsibility, and will settle with my intelligent constituents.

This is not a "white man's Government," in the exclusive sense in which it is used. To say so is political blasphemy, for it violates the fundamental principles of our gospel of liberty. This is man's Government; the Government of all men alike; not that all men will have equal power and sway within it. Accidental circumstances, natural and acquired endowment and ability, will vary their fortunes. But equal rights to all the privileges of the Government is innate in every immortal being, no matter what the shape or color of the tabernacle which it inhabits.

If equal privileges were granted to all, I should not expect any but white men to be elected to office for long ages to come. The prejudice engendered by slavery would not soon permit merit to be preferred to color. But it would still be beneficial to the weaker races. In a country where political divisions will always exist, their power, joined with just white men, would greatly modify, if it did not entirely prevent, the injustice of majorities. Without the right of suffrage in the late slave States, (I do not speak of the free States,) I believe the slaves had far better been left in bondage. I see it stated that very distinguished advocates of the right of suffrage lately declared in this city that they do not expect to obtain it by congressional legislation, but only by administrative action, because, as one gallant gentleman said, the States had not been out of the Union. Then they will never get it. The President is far sounder than they. He sees that administrative action has nothing to do with it. If it ever is to come, it must be constitutional amendments or congressional action in the Territories, and in enabling acts.

How shameful that men of influence should mislead and miseducate the public mind! They proclaim, "This is the white man's Government," and the whole coil of copperheads echo the same sentiment, and upstart, jealous Republicans join the cry. Is it any wonder ignorant foreigners and illiterate natives should learn this doctrine, and be led to despise and maltreat a whole race of their fellow-men?

Sir, this doctrine of a white man's Government is as atrocious as the infamous sentiment that damned the late Chief Justice to everlasting fame; and, I fear, to everlasting fire.

SELECTION

The Fourteenth Amendment to the Constitution, 1866

The Fourteenth Amendment was probably the most significant and far-reaching measure enacted during the Reconstruction period. It had its origins in the qualms many felt concerning the constitutionality of the Civil Rights

Act, passed over the President's veto in April, 1866. In order to quiet these suspicions, the essential features of the Civil Rights Act were incorporated in the Fourteenth Amendment to the Constitution. The amendment was passed by both houses of Congress in June, 1866, and was immediately sent out to the states for their action. Strongly opposed by President Johnson and by the Johnson-organized Southern governments, the amendment failed to receive the required support for ratification. The Radicals promptly made its ratification a condition for reentry into the Union under the terms of the Reconstruction Act of March 2, 1867. By the summer of 1868, the Southern states had reversed their earlier decision and the Fourteenth Amendment was declared duly ratified. Even so, there were many misgivings over the way in which the ratification had been secured. At the time of its passage by Congress, many Republicans felt that ratification of the amendment would constitute the final terms for readmission into the Union; Radical leaders, although desiring harsher terms, did little to disabuse their colleagues of this notion. The state of Tennessee did ratify the amendment and was restored to the Union by a joint congressional resolution. By rejecting the amendment, the other Southern states placed themselves even further at the mercy of the congressional Radicals. In later years, the Fourteenth Amendment became more important as a bulwark of protection for corporations against state regulations than as a means for protecting the civil rights of Negroes. Although some historians have maintained that the framers of the amendment were actually motivated to secure this protection of property against government interference, there is no reliable evidence to support this conclusion. The definitive account of the origins and passage of the Fourteenth Amendment is Joseph B. James, The Framing of the Fourteenth Amendment *(1956). See also Jacobus tenBroek,* The Antislavery Origins of the Fourteenth Amendment *(1951). The text of the Fourteenth Amendment is taken from* U.S. Statutes at Large, *volume 15, page 709.*

Section 1.   All persons born or naturalized in the United States, and subject to the jurisdiction thereof, are citizens of the United States and of the State wherein they reside. No State shall make or enforce any law which shall abridge the privileges or immunities of citizens of the United States; nor shall any State deprive any person of life, liberty, or property, without due process of law, nor deny to any person within its jurisdiction the equal protection of the laws.

Section 2.   Representatives shall be apportioned among the several States according to their respective numbers, counting the whole number of persons in each State, excluding Indians not taxed. But when the right to vote at any election for the choice of electors for President and Vice-President of the United States, Representatives in Congress, the executive and judicial officers of a State, or the members of the legislature thereof, is denied to any of the male inhabitants of such State, being twenty-one years of age, and citizens of the United States, or in any way abridged, except for participation in rebellion or other crime, the basis of representation therein shall be reduced in the proportion which the number of such male citizens shall bear to the whole number of male citizens twenty-one years of age in such State.

Section 3.   No person shall be a Senator or Representative in Congress, or elector of President and Vice-President, or hold any office, civil or military, under the United States, or under any State, who, having previously taken an oath, as a member of Congress, or as an officer of the United States, or as a member of any State legislature, or as an executive or judicial officer of any State, to support the Constitution of the United States, shall have engaged in insurrection or rebellion against the same, or given aid or comfort to the enemies thereof. But Congress may, by a vote of two thirds of each House, remove such disability.

Section 4.   The validity of the public debt of the United States, authorized by law, including debts incurred for payment of pensions and bounties for services in suppressing insurrection or rebellion, shall not be questioned. But neither the United States nor any State shall assume or pay any debt or obligation incurred in aid of insurrection or rebellion against the United States, or any claim for the loss or emancipation of any slave; but all such debts, obligations, and claims shall be held illegal and void.

Section 5.   The Congress shall have power to enforce, by appropriate legislation, the provisions of this article.

SELECTION

The Radical Republicans Present Their Program:
The Reconstruction Acts, 1867–1868

The Radical Republicans, having effectively destroyed presidential Reconstruction through their refusal to seat the senators and representatives from the new Southern governments, and having received a mandate for action in the elections of 1866, set about to implement their own plans for Reconstruction in the second session of the Thirty-ninth Congress. The Radical program took form in a series of acts passed in 1867 and 1868. The first Reconstruction Act, approved on March 2, 1867, was the most important; the rest were supplemental acts designed to speed the reorganization of the Southern states and to clarify the terms of the initial legislation. The first Reconstruction Act declared first of all that no legal state governments existed in the states of the former Confederacy (excluding Tennessee). The ten "rebel" states were then divided into five military districts, each district to be governed by a military commander. Under the direction of the military governors, constitutional conventions were to be elected. The new state constitutions must provide for Negro suffrage and the new state governments must ratify the Fourteenth Amendment. When these conditions were met, Congress would recognize the new states and seat their elected senators and representatives. Until such recognition was achieved, however, the Southern states were to be "subject to the paramount authority of the United States." President Johnson vetoed the first Reconstruction Act, as he did all of the supplemental acts, but the legislation was passed easily and quickly over his objections. Johnson's veto message reflected the objections of the conservative opponents to Radical Reconstruction. He found the terms of Radical Reconstruction to be without constitutional sanction and objected to the authority over the Southern states which Congress had assumed for itself. Fearful that Johnson's constitutional objections might be shared by the Supreme Court (especially in view of the recent decision in the Milligan case) Congress approved a law depriving the Court of jurisdiction over appeals from lower Federal courts where the right of habeas corpus was involved, thus protecting the military rule established in the Reconstruction Acts from review by the highest tribunal. With the reorganization of the Southern states under Radical, congressional auspices, a second period in Reconstruction came to an end.

The text of the acts is reprinted as follows: An Act to provide for the more efficient Government of the Rebel States; An Act supplementary to an Act entitled "An Act to provide for the more efficient Government of the Rebel States," . . . and to facilitate Restoration; An Act supplementary to an Act entitled "An Act to provide for the more efficient Government of the Rebel States," . . . and the Act supplementary thereto . . . ; An Act to amend the Act . . . entitled "An Act supplementary to 'An Act to provide for the more efficient Government of the rebel States,' . . . and to facilitate their Restoration," U.S. Statutes at Large, *volume 14, pages 428–429; volume 15, pages 2–4, 14–16, 41.*

FIRST RECONSTRUCTION ACT, MARCH 2, 1867

Whereas no legal State governments or adequate protection for life or property now exists in the rebel States of Virginia, North Carolina, South Carolina, Georgia, Mississippi, Alabama, Louisiana, Florida, Texas, and Arkansas; and whereas it is necessary that peace and good order should be enforced in said States until loyal and republican State governments can be legally established: Therefore,

Be it enacted by the Senate and House of Representatives of the United States of America in Congress assembled, That said rebel States shall be divided into military districts and made subject to the military authority of the United States as hereinafter prescribed, and for that purpose Virginia shall constitute the first district; North Carolina and South Carolina the second district; Georgia, Alabama, and Florida the third district; Mississippi and Arkansas the fourth district; and Louisiana and Texas the fifth district.

Sec. 2. And be it further enacted, That it shall be the duty of the President to assign to the command of each of said districts an officer of the army, not below the rank of brigadier-general, and to detail a sufficient military force to enable such officer to perform his duties and enforce his authority within the district to which he is assigned.

Sec. 3. And be it further enacted, That it shall be the duty of each officer assigned as aforesaid, to protect all persons in their rights of person and property, to suppress insurrection, disorder, and violence, and to punish, or cause to be punished, all disturbers of the public peace and criminals; and to this end he may allow local civil tribunals to take jurisdiction of and to try offenders, or, when in his judgment it may be necessary for the trial of offenders, he shall have power to organize military commissions or tribunals for that purpose, and all interference under color of State authority with the exercise of military authority under this act, shall be null and void.

Sec. 4. And be it further enacted, That all persons put under military arrest by virtue of this act shall be tried without unnecessary delay, and no cruel or unusual punishment shall be inflicted, and no sentence of any military commission or tribunal hereby authorized, affecting the life or liberty of any person, shall be executed until it is approved by the officer in command of the district, and the laws and regulations for the government of the army shall not be affected by this act, except in so far as they conflict with its provisions: *Provided,* That no sentence of death under the provisions of this act shall be carried into effect without the approval of the President.

Sec. 5. And be it further enacted, That when the people of any one of said rebel States shall have formed a constitution of government in conformity with the Constitution of the United States in all respects, framed by a convention of delegates elected by the male citizens of said State, twenty-one years old and upward, of whatever race, color, or previous condition, who have been resident in said State for one year previous to the day of such election, except such as may be disfranchised for participation in the rebellion or for felony at common law, and when such constitution shall provide that the elective franchise shall be enjoyed by all such persons as have the qualifications herein stated for electors of delegates, and when such constitution shall be ratified by a majority of the persons voting on the question of ratification who are qualified as electors for delegates, and when such constitution shall have been submitted to Congress for examination and approval, and Congress shall have approved the same, and when said State, by a vote of its legislature elected under said constitution, shall have adopted the amendment to the Constitution of the United States, proposed by the Thirty-ninth Congress, and known as article fourteen, and when said article shall have become a part of the Constitution of the United States, said State shall be declared entitled to representation in Congress, and senators and representatives shall be admitted therefrom on their taking the oath prescribed by law, and then and thereafter the preceding sections of this act shall be inoperative in said State: *Provided,* That no person excluded from the privilege of holding office by said proposed amendment to the Constitution of the United States, shall be eligible to election as a member of the convention to frame a constitution for any of said rebel States, nor shall any such person vote for members of such convention.

Sec. 6. And be it further enacted, That, until the people of said rebel States shall be by law admitted to representation in the Congress of the United States, any civil governments which may exist therein shall be deemed provisional only, and in all respects subject to the paramount authority of the United States at any time to abolish, modify, control, or supersede the same; and in all elections to any office under such provisional governments all persons shall be entitled to vote, and none others, who are entitled to vote, under the provisions of the fifth section of this act; and no person shall be eligible to any office under any such provisional governments who would be disqualified from holding office under the provisions of the third *article* of said constitutional amendment.

SECOND RECONSTRUCTION ACT, MARCH 23, 1867

Be it enacted by the Senate and House of Representatives of the United States of America in Congress assembled, That before the first day of September, eighteen hundred and sixty-seven, the commanding general in each district defined by an act entitled "An act to provide for the more efficient government of the rebel States," passed March second, eighteen hundred and sixty-seven, shall cause a registration to be made of the male citizens of the United States, twenty-one years of age and upwards, resident in each county or parish in the State or States included in his district, which registration shall include only those persons who are qualified to vote for delegates by the act aforesaid, and who shall have taken and subscribed the following oath or affirmation: "I, _____, do solemnly swear (or affirm), in the presence of Almighty God, that I am a citizen of the State of _____; that I have resided in said State for _____ months next preceding this day, and now reside in the county of _____, or the parish of _____, in said State (as the case may be); that I am twenty-one years old; that I have not been disfranchised for participation in any rebellion or civil war against the United States, nor for felony committed against the laws of any State or of the United States; that I have never been a member of any State legislature, nor held any executive or judicial office in any State and afterwards engaged in insurrection or rebellion against the United States, or given aid or comfort to the enemies thereof; that I have never taken an oath as a member of Congress of the United States, or as an officer of the United States, or as a member of any State legislature, or as an executive or judicial officer of any State, to support the Constitution of the United States, and afterwards engaged in insurrection or rebellion against the United States, or given aid or comfort to the enemies thereof; that I will faithfully support the Constitution and obey the laws of the United States, and will, to the best of my ability, encourage others so to do, so help me God"; which oath or affirmation may be administered by any registering officer.

Sec. 2.   And be it further enacted, That after the completion of the registration hereby provided for in any State, at such time and places therein as the commanding general shall appoint and direct, of which at least thirty days' public notice shall be given, an election shall be held of delegates to a convention for the purpose of establishing a constitution and civil government for such State loyal to the Union, said convention in each State, except Virginia, to consist of the same number of members as the most numerous branch of the State legislature of such State in the year eighteen hundred and sixty, to be apportioned among the several districts, counties, or parishes of such State by the commanding general, giving to each representation in the ratio of voters registered as aforesaid as nearly as may be. The convention in Virginia shall consist of the same number of members as represented the territory now constituting Virginia in the most numerous branch of the legislature of said State in the year eighteen hundred and sixty, to be apportioned as aforesaid.

Sec. 3. And be it further enacted, That at said election the registered voters of each State shall vote for or against a convention to form a constitution therefor under this act. Those voting in favor of such a convention shall have written or printed on the ballots by which they vote for delegates, as aforesaid, the words "For a convention," and those voting against such a convention shall have written or printed on such ballots the words "Against a convention." The persons appointed to superintend said election, and to make return of the votes given thereat, as herein provided, shall count and make return of the votes given for and against a convention; and the commanding general to whom the same shall have been returned shall ascertain and declare the total vote in each State for and against a convention. If a majority of the votes given on that question shall be for a convention, then such convention shall be held as hereinafter provided; but if a majority of said votes shall be against a convention, then no such convention shall be held under this act: *Provided,* That such convention shall not be held unless a majority of all such registered voters shall have voted on the question of holding such convention.

Sec. 4. And be it further enacted, That the commanding general of each district shall appoint as many boards of registration as may be necessary, consisting of three loyal officers or persons, to make and complete the registration, superintend the election, and make return to him of the votes, list of voters, and of the persons elected as delegates by a plurality of the votes cast at said election; and upon receiving said returns he shall open the same, ascertain the persons elected as delegates, according to the returns of the officers who conducted said election, and make proclamation thereof; and if a majority of the votes given on that question shall be for a convention, the commanding general, within sixty days from the date of election, shall notify the delegates to assemble in convention, at a time and place to be mentioned in the notification, and said convention, when organized, shall proceed to frame a constitution and civil government according to the provisions of this act, and the act to which it is supplementary; and when the same shall have been so framed, said constitution shall be submitted by the convention for ratification to the persons registered under the provisions of this act at an election to be conducted by the officers or persons appointed or to be appointed by the commanding general, as hereinbefore provided, and to be held after the expiration of thirty days from the date of notice thereof, to be given by said convention; and the returns thereof shall be made to the commanding general of the district.

Sec. 5. And be it further enacted, That if, according to said returns, the constitution shall be ratified by a majority of the votes of the registered electors qualified as herein specified, cast at said election, at least one half of all the registered voters voting upon the question of such ratification, the president of the convention shall transmit a copy of the same, duly certified, to the President of the United States, who shall forthwith transmit the same to Congress, if then in session, and if not in session, then immediately upon its next assembling; and if it shall moreover appear to Congress that the election was one at which all the registered and qualified electors in the State had an opportunity to vote freely and without restraint, fear, or the influence of fraud, and if the Congress shall be satisfied that such constitution meets the approval of a majority of all the qualified electors in the State, and if the said constitution shall be declared by Congress to be in conformity with the provisions of the act to which this is supplementary, and the other provisions of said act shall have been complied with, and the said constitution shall be approved by Congress, the State shall be declared entitled to representation, and senators and representatives shall be admitted therefrom as therein provided.

Sec. 6. And be it further enacted, That all elections in the States mentioned in the said "Act to provide for the more efficient government of the rebel States," shall, during the operation of said act, be by ballot; and all officers making the said registration of voters and conducting said elections shall, before entering upon the discharge of their duties, take and subscribe the oath prescribed by the act approved July second, eighteen hundred and sixty-two, entitled "An act to prescribe an oath of office": *Provided,* That if any person shall knowingly and falsely take and subscribe any oath in this act prescribed, such person so offending and being thereof duly convicted shall be subject to the pains, penalties, and disabilities which by law are provided for the punishment of the crime of wilful and corrupt perjury.

Sec. 7. And be it further enacted, That all expenses incurred by the several commanding generals, or by virtue of any orders issued, or appointments made, by them, under or by virtue of this act, shall be paid out of any moneys in the treasury not otherwise appropriated.

Sec. 8. And be it further enacted, That the convention for each State shall prescribe the fees, salary, and compensation to be paid to all delegates and other officers and agents herein authorized or necessary to carry into effect the purposes of this act not herein otherwise provided for, and shall provide for the levy and collection of such taxes on the property in such State as may be necessary to pay the same.

Sec. 9. And be it further enacted, That the word "article," in the sixth section of the act to which this is supplementary, shall be construed to mean "section."

THIRD RECONSTRUCTION ACT, JULY 19, 1867

Be it enacted by the Senate and House of Representatives of the United States of America in Congress assembled, That it is hereby declared to have been the true intent and meaning of the act of the second day of

March, one thousand eight hundred and sixty-seven, entitled "An act to provide for the more efficient government of the rebel States," and of the act supplementary thereto, passed on the twenty-third day of March, in the year one thousand eight hundred and sixty-seven, that the governments then existing in the rebel States of Virginia, North Carolina, South Carolina, Georgia, Mississippi, Alabama, Louisiana, Florida, Texas, and Arkansas were not legal State governments; and that thereafter said governments, if continued, were to be continued subject in all respects to the military commanders of the respective districts, and to the paramount authority of Congress.

Sec. 2. And be it further enacted, That the commander of any district named in said act shall have power, subject to the disapproval of the General of the army of the United States, and to have effect till disapproved, whenever in the opinion of such commander the proper administration of said act shall require it, to suspend or remove from office, or from the performance of official duties and the exercise of official powers, any officer or person holding or exercising, or professing to hold or exercise, any civil or military office or duty in such district under any power, election, appointment or authority derived from, or granted by, or claimed under, any so-called State or the government thereof, or any municipal or other division thereof, and upon such suspension or removal such commander, subject to the disapproval of the General as aforesaid, shall have power to provide from time to time for the performance of the said duties of such officer or person so suspended or removed, by the detail of some competent officer or soldier of the army, or by the appointment of some other person, to perform the same, and to fill vacancies occasioned by death, resignation, or otherwise.

Sec. 3. And be it further enacted, That the General of the army of the United States shall be invested with all the powers of suspension, removal, appointment, and detail granted in the preceding section to district commanders.

Sec. 4. And be it further enacted, That the acts of the officers of the army already done in removing in said districts persons exercising the functions of civil officers, and appointing others in their stead, are hereby confirmed: *Provided,* That any person heretofore or hereafter appointed by any district commander to exercise the functions of any civil office, may be removed either by the military officer in command of the district, or by the General of the army. And it shall be the duty of such commander to remove from office as aforesaid all persons who are disloyal to the government of the United States, or who use their official influence in any manner to hinder, delay, prevent, or obstruct the due and proper administration of this act and the acts to which it is supplementary.

Sec. 5. And be it further enacted, That the boards of registration provided for in the act entitled "An act supplementary to an act entitled 'An act to provide for the more efficient government of the rebel States,' passed March two, eighteen hundred and sixty-seven, and to facilitate restoration," passed March twenty-three, eighteen hundred and sixty-seven, shall have power, and it shall be their duty before allowing the registration of any person, to ascertain, upon such facts or information as they can obtain, whether such person is entitled to be registered under said act, and the oath required by said act shall not be conclusive on such question, and no person shall be registered unless such board shall decide that he is entitled thereto; and such board shall also have power to examine, under oath, (to be administered by any member of such board,) any one touching the qualification of any person claiming registration; but in every case of refusal by the board to register an applicant, and in every case of striking his name from the list as hereinafter provided, the board shall make a note or memorandum, which shall be returned with the registration list to the commanding general of the district, setting forth the grounds of such refusal or such striking from the list: *Provided,* That no person shall be disqualified as member of any board of registration by reason of race or color.

Sec. 6. And be it further enacted, That the true intent and meaning of the oath prescribed in said supplementary act is, (among other things,) that no person who has been a member of the legislature of any State, or who has held any executive or judicial office in any State, whether he has taken an oath to support the Constitution of the United States or not, and whether he was holding such office at the commencement of the rebellion, or had held it before, and who has afterwards engaged in insurrection or rebellion against the United States, or given aid or comfort to the enemies thereof, is entitled to be registered or to vote; and the words "executive or judicial office in any State" in said oath mentioned shall be construed to include all civil offices created by law for the administration of any general law of a State, or for the administration of justice.

Sec. 7. And be it further enacted, That the time for completing the original registration provided for in said act may, in the discretion of the commander of any district be extended to the first day of October, eighteen hundred and sixty-seven; and the boards of registration shall have power, and it shall be their duty, commencing fourteen days prior to any election under said act, and upon reasonable public notice of the time and place thereof, to revise, for a period of five days, the registration lists, and upon being satisfied that any person not entitled thereto has been registered, to strike the name of such person from the list, and such person shall not be allowed to vote. And such board shall also, during the same period, add to such registry the names of all persons who at that time possess the qualifications required by said act who have not been already registered; and no person shall, at any time, be entitled to be registered or to vote by reason of any executive pardon or amnesty for any act or thing which, without such pardon or amnesty, would disqualify him from registration or voting.

Sec. 8. And be it further enacted, That section four of said last-named act shall be construed to authorize the commanding general named therein, whenever he shall deem it needful, to remove any member of a board of registration and to appoint another in his stead, and to fill any vacancy in such board.

Sec. 9.   And be it further enacted, That all members of said boards of registration and all persons hereafter elected or appointed to office in said military districts, under any so-called State or municipal authority, or by detail or appointment of the district commanders, shall be required to take and to subscribe the oath of office prescribed by law for officers of the United States.

Sec. 10.   And be it further enacted, That no district commander or member of the board of registration, or any of the officers or appointees acting under them, shall be bound in his action by any opinion of any civil officer of the United States.

Sec. 11.   And be it further enacted, That all the provisions of this act and of the acts to which this is supplementary shall be construed liberally, to the end that all the intents thereof may be fully and perfectly carried out.

FOURTH RECONSTRUCTION ACT, MARCH 11, 1868

Be it enacted by the Senate and House of Representatives of the United States of America in Congress assembled, That hereafter any election authorized by the act passed March twenty-three, eighteen hundred and sixty-seven, entitled "An act supplementary to 'An act to provide for the more efficient government of the rebel States,' passed March *two,* [second,] eighteen hundred and sixty-seven, and to facilitate their restoration," shall be decided by a majority of the votes actually cast; and at the election in which the question of the adoption or rejection of any constitution is submitted, any person duly registered in the State may vote in the election district where he offers to vote when he has resided therein for ten days next preceding such election, upon presentation of his certificate of registration, his affidavit, or other satisfactory evidence, under such regulations as the district commanders may prescribe.

Sec. 2.   And be it further enacted, That the constitutional convention of any of the States mentioned in the acts to which this is amendatory may provide that at the time of voting upon the ratification of the constitution the registered voters may vote also for members of the House of Representatives of the United States, and for all elective officers provided for by the said constitution; and the same election officers who shall make the return of the votes cast on the ratification or rejection of the constitution, shall enumerate and certify the votes cast for members of Congress.

SELECTION **52**

The Election of 1868: "Moral Significance of the Republican Triumph"

With the passage of the Reconstruction Acts and the gradual reorganization of the Southern states under the dictates of Congress, the achievement of Radical Reconstruction was well-nigh complete. The only remaining obstacle to Republican plans was the President himself. The attempt to impeach Andrew Johnson failed but it little mattered. Within less than a year following his trial, his term of office had expired and he was replaced by a new President who was more congenial to Radical aspirations. The election of 1868 was a final step in entrenching the Republican party in the national government and so completing Radical congressional Reconstruction. The Democrats did not nominate Andrew Johnson for the Presidency, but they did not do much better. After many ballots and considerable wrangling, Horatio Seymour, wartime Governor of New York, was nominated. In an impressive demonstration of unanimity, the Republicans nominated Ulysses S. Grant on the first ballot. Thus the military hero of the Civil War was pitted against a wartime governor who had opposed Lincoln and was suspected of Copperhead leanings. Although the choice between the two might seem obvious, Seymour ran a fairly close race in the popular vote, receiving only three hundred thousand votes less than Grant. Grant's majority in the electoral college, however, was clear and decisive. For the Republicans one sobering aspect of the contest was the realization that without the support of Negro voters in the reconstructed Southern states, Grant would have received fewer popular votes than Seymour. Their next step was indicated by the election results. Early in 1869, the Fifteenth Amendment, providing for Negro suffrage, was passed and early in the following year it became a part of the Constitution. The victory of the Republicans in 1868 was hailed as the final "crowning victory of the War of the Rebellion, and its real close." Republican writers and spokesmen found a "moral significance" in the election results. The story of the election is told in Charles H. Coleman, The Election of 1868 *(1933). The text of the passage that follows is quoted from* Atlantic Monthly, *volume 23, January, 1869, pages 124–128.*

The victory which the Republican party gained in the November election, after the most fiercely contested struggle recorded in our political history, is the crowning victory of the War of the Rebellion, and its real close. A war such as raged in this country between April, 1861, and April, 1865, is ended, not when the defeated party ceases to fight, but when it ceases to hope. The sentiments and principles which led to the

Rebellion were overturned, not in 1865, but in 1868. After the exhaustion of physical power, which compelled the Rebels to lay down their arms, came the moral struggle which has resulted in compelling them to surrender their ideas. If these ideas had been on a level with the civilization of the age, or in advance of it; if the "Lost Cause" had been the cause of humanity and freedom, of reason and justice, of good morals and good sense,—such a catastrophe would be viewed by every right-minded man as a great calamity. But the Rebellion was essentially a revolt of tyrants for the privilege to oppress, and of bullies for the right to domineer. Its interpretation of the Constitution was an ingenious reversal of the purposes for which the Constitution was declared to be made, and its doctrine of State Rights was a mere cover for a comprehensive conspiracy against the rights of man. The success of such a "cause" could not have benefited even its defenders, for the worst government for the permanent welfare even of the governing classes is that in which the intelligent systematically prey upon the ignorant, and the strong mercilessly trample on the weak. In a large view, the South is better off to-day for the military defeat which dissipated its wild dream of insolent domination, and for the political defeat which destroyed the last hopes of its reviving passions.

Those who are accustomed to recognize a providence in the direction of human affairs may find in the course and conduct equally of this military and political struggle the strongest confirmation of their faith. The great things that have been done appear to have been done through us, rather than by us. During the war, it seemed as if no mistakes could hinder us from gaining victories, no reverses obstruct our steady advance, no conservative prudence prevent us from being the audacious champions of radical ideas. The march of events swept forward government and people on its own path, converting the distrusted abstraction of yesterday into the "military necessity" of to-day and the constitutional provision of to-morrow. President, Congress, parties, all felt the propulsion of a force more intelligent than individual sagacity, and mightier than associated opinion. So strong was the stress on the minds of Republicans, that the charge of inconsistency, made by such politicians as had succeeded in secluding themselves from the heroic impulse of the time, not only fell pointless, but was welcomed as an indication that the men conducting the war were intelligent enough to read aright its grim facts as they successively started into view. The result proved that the very absence of what is called "a leading mind" indicated the presence of a Mind compared with which Cæsars and Napoleons are as little as Soubises and Macks.

What was true of the military is true of the political contest. After the armed Rebellion was crushed by arms, and the meaner rebellion of intrigue, bluster, and miscellaneous assassination began, both parties had reason to be surprised at the issue. The Rebels found that their profoundest calculations, their most unscrupulous plottings, their most vigorous action, only led them to a more ruinous defeat. Their opponents had almost equal reason for wonder, for the plan of reconstruction, which they eventually passed and repeatedly sustained by more than two thirds of both Houses of Congress, would not have commanded a majority in either House at the time the problem of reconstruction was first presented. Whether we refer this unexpected and unpremeditated result to Providence, to the nature of things, or to the logic of events, it still shows that our forecast did little more than "make mouths at the invisible event." The country was not so much ruled as overruled.

The form which reconstruction eventually took was, however, the form which from the first reason would have decided to be the best. It offended strong prejudices and roused bitter animosities; but it was necessary to insure the safety and honor of the nation, and it was fitted to the peculiar facts and principles of the case. The question to be decided referred primarily to suffrage. The Republicans were at first inclined to think it should be conferred on the educated alone. How would this principle have applied to the Rebel States? Those who could read and write in those States were the originators of the Rebellion, and remained, after its military overthrow, in a state of sullen discontent with the government by which they had been subdued. To give them the suffrage, and deny it to the great body of the blacks and the poor whites, would be to put the Rebel States into the hands of the enemies of the United States. This condition of things would be little improved by allowing all whites to vote, and only such blacks as should happen to possess educational qualifications. The class on whose loyalty the government could depend would be practically sacrificed to the classes whose loyalty the government had the best reason to distrust. It is true that the blacks were, as a general thing, ignorant; but they at least possessed the instinct of self-preservation, and they were placed in such a position that the instinct of self-preservation would inevitably lead them to take the side of orderly government. Their interests, hopes, and passions, their very right to own themselves, were all bound up in the success of the national cause, to which the interests, hopes, and passions of the so-called educated classes were opposed. Besides, it might be said that education implies the recognition of sentiments of humanity, ideas of freedom, duties of beneficence, which are on a level with the civilization of the age; and the blacks were better educated in this sense than the great majority of their former masters, who had notoriously perverted natural feeling, right reason, and true religion in their vain effort to defend an indefensible institution. Southern education, for many years before the Rebellion broke out, had been an education in self-will, and its most shining results were men distinguished for the vehemence of manner and sharpness of intellect with which they defended paradoxes that affronted common sense, and assailed truths too tediously true to admit of serious debate. They were reasoning beings without being reasonable ones. Now, the blacks could not help being more in sympathy with the sentiments and ideas of the age than such men as these, for their simple, selfish instincts identified them with advanced opinions. And education, if not made the condition of suffrage, would be its result. If made its condition, the negroes would hold no political power, and common schools for all classes are only established by those legislative assemblies in which all classes are represented. At first, therefore, they would vote right, because they would vote as their instincts taught them; and by the time that their instincts might not be the measure of their true interests, they would be educated.

In the first step made towards reconstruction, that called "the President's Plan," no heed was paid to these considerations. The negroes were practically delivered over to the tender mercies of their former masters, and the political power of the Rebel States was put into Rebel hands. Profligate as this scheme really was, it had sufficient plausibility to deceive many honest minds, and at one period there was imminent danger of its adoption. The reaction consequent on a long conflict, the desire of the people for a speedy settlement of the questions growing out of the war, the natural indisposition of the Republican leaders to quarrel with the President, the fear to face resolutely the question of negro suffrage, the seeming apathy or paralysis of the great body of Republican voters,—all seemed to point to a settlement which would be a surrender, and by which the supporters of the war would be swindled out of its fair and legitimate results. Fortunately, however, the great enemy of the President's plan was the President. His vulgarity undid the work which his cunning had planned. The force which impelled the Republican party to overturn Mr. Johnson's policy was derived from Mr. Johnson himself. It is needless here to recapitulate the mistakes by which he succeeded in concentrating Northern opinion, and making his opponents irresistible. The Republicans owe to him a debt of gratitude they can never pay, for the peculiar manner in which he schemed to split them into factions made them a unit. The small, intelligent, and unscrupulous clique of politicians known as "the President's friends" sorrowfully admit that Mr. Johnson's policy was a magnificent political game, which must have succeeded had it not been for the bad playing of Mr. Johnson. If the executive department of the government lost the respect of all parties during his administration, it was due to the fact that the President confounded the office with his personality. Nobody could respect the officer, and yet the officer persistently identified himself with the office.

After Mr. Johnson had broken with Congress, he became a President in search of a party. He sought it everywhere, and particularly at the South. At the North he could get politicians enough, but he could get no representative politicians,—no politicians who had "a following." At the South he obtained the support of the great body of the Rebels, but they were without any political power. They could speak for him, mob for him, kill negroes for him, but they could not vote for him. Believing, however, in the certainty of his eventual success, they repudiated, with a great display of indignant eloquence, the first "Congressional Plan" of reconstruction, which merely contemplated the identification of their political interests with the enfranchisement of the colored race, and denied them the privilege of counting, in the basis of representation, four millions of people to whom they refused political rights. Certainly no conquerors ever before proposed such mild terms to the vanquished, and yet the terms were rejected with a fury of contempt such as would have misbecome a triumphant faction, mad with the elation both of military and political success. The ludicrous insolence of this course ruined the last prospect these men had of rebuilding Southern society on its old foundations. The plan of reconstruction which has recently triumphed at the polls was the necessary result of their folly and arrogance. The reorganization of the Southern States on the comprehensive principle of equality of rights became possible only through the madness of its adversaries. Congress and the people repeatedly hesitated, but in every moment of hesitation they were pushed forward by some new instance of Mr. Johnson's brutality of speech, or by some fresh examples of Southern proclivity to murder.

As it regards the right of the government of the United States to dictate conditions of reconstruction, it must be remembered that the difference between the President's Plan and the Congressional Plan was not, in this respect, a difference in principle; and that the position held by the Democratic party—that the Rebellion was a rebellion of individuals, and not of States—equally condemns both. This position, however, can only be maintained by the denial of the most obvious facts. The enormous sacrifices of blood and treasure in putting down the Rebellion were made necessary by the circumstance that it was a rebellion of States. Had it been merely an insurrection of individuals, it would have been an insurrection against State governments as well as against the government of the United States. We had, both before the war and during its continuance, examples of such insurrections. The Whiskey Insurrection in Pennsylvania, and Shays's Rebellion in Massachusetts, were risings of individuals against the laws; but nobody believes that Pennsylvania and Massachusetts lost any State rights by those disturbances. In Kentucky and Missouri, during the recent war, there was a tenfold more terrible rebellion of individuals against the United States government, but nobody pretends that Missouri and Kentucky forfeited any State rights by this crime of their individual citizens. In all these cases, the governments of the States remained in loyal hands. But the peculiarity of our war against the Confederate States consisted in the fact that all the State governments were *voted* by the people into Rebel hands. The result was, that the supreme powers of taxation and conscription, placing every man and every dollar at the service of the Confederate States, were lodged in a revolutionary government, and the cost of suppressing the Rebellion was increased at least fourfold by this fact. After losing two hundred and fifty thousand men, and two billions and a half of dollars,—more than would have been necessary to crush a rebellion of individual insurgents,—we are told that the States never rebelled; that the loyal but bodiless souls of these communities still existed, whilst certain Rebel "individuals" exercised their supreme powers; and that, the moment these Rebel individuals succumbed, the bodiless souls instantly became embodied and continued loyal in the Rebel individuals aforesaid! Out of Bedlam no such argument was ever propounded before.

In truth, there was no possibility that the Rebel States could "resume their practical relations" with the United States except by the intervention of the United States in their internal affairs. Though the plan of reconstruction eventually adopted is called the "Congressional Plan," it was really the plan of the government of the country. In our system, a mere majority of Congress is impotent, provided the President, however "accidental" he may be, however mean, base, false, and traitorous he may be, nullifies its legislation by his vetoes; but Congress becomes constitutionally the governing power in the nation, when its policy is supported by two thirds of the Representatives of the people in the House, and two thirds of the Representatives of the States in the Senate. President Johnson has pushed to the extreme the powers granted to the executive by the Constitution, and if he has failed in carrying his policy it has been through no encroachments of the legislature on his constitutional rights. Passed over his vetoes, he was bound to consider the reconstruction laws as the acts of the government. It is notorious that he has systematically attempted to nullify the operation of the laws which, by the Constitution, it was his simple duty to execute.

It was almost inevitable, however, that, in the measures by which Congress attempted to make Mr. Johnson perform his duties, it should commit errors of that kind which tell against the popularity of a party, if not against its patriotism and intelligence. In spite of executive opposition Congress had succeeded in getting new State governments organized at the South, and the representatives of the legal people of those States were in the Senate and House of Representatives. Mr. Johnson and the Democratic party pronounced these reconstructed State governments to be utterly without validity, though their Representatives formed part of the Congress of the United States, and though Congress has by the Constitution the exclusive right of judging of the qualifications of its own members, and, by the decision of the Supreme Court, has the exclusive right of judging of the validity of State governments. Whatever popularity, therefore, the Republicans may have lost by their reconstruction policy, it was more than offset by the blunder made by their opponents in proposing the overthrow of that policy by revolutionary measures. Elections are commonly decided by the votes of a class of independent citizens, who belong strictly to neither of the two parties; and the course pursued by the Democrats pushed this class for the time into the Republican ranks. The intellect of the Democratic party is concentrated, to a great degree, in its Copperhead members; and these had become so embittered and vindictive by the turn events had taken, that their malignity prevented their ability from having fair play. They assailed the Republicans for not giving peace and prosperity to the nation, and then laid down a programme which proposed to reach peace and prosperity through political and financial anarchy. They selected unpopular candidates, and then placed them on a platform of which revolution and repudiation were the chief planks. Perhaps even with these drawbacks they might have cajoled a sufficient number of voters to succeed in the election, had it not been for the frank brutality of their Southern allies. To carry the North their reliance was on fraud, but the Southern politicians were determined to carry their section by terror and assassination, and no plausible speech could be made by a Northern Democrat the effect of which was not nullified by some Southern burst of eloquence, breathing nothing but proscription and war. The Democratic party was therefore not only defeated, but disgraced. To succeed as it succeeded in New York and New Jersey, in Louisiana and Georgia, did not prevent its fall, but did prevent its falling with honor. To the infamy of bad ends it added the additional infamy of bad means; and it comes out of an overwhelming general reverse with the mortifying consciousness that its few special victories have been purchased at the expense of its public character. The only way it can recover its *prestige* is by discarding, not only its leaders, but the passions and ideas its leaders represent.

The moral significance of the struggle which has just closed is thus found in the fact that the good cause was best served by its bitterest enemies. A bad institution, like slavery, generates a bad type of character in its supporters, and urges them blindly on to the adoption of measures which, intended for its defence, result in its ruin. The immense achievement of emancipating four millions of slaves, and placing them on an equality of civil and political rights with their former masters, is due primarily to such men as Calhoun and McDuffie, Davis and Toombs, Vallandigham, Pendleton, Belmont, Johnson, and Seymour. The prejudice in the United States against the colored race was strong enough to overcome everything but their championship of it. These persons taught the nation that its safety depended on its being just. The most careless glance over the chief incidents in the long contest shows that all the enemies of human freedom needed for success was a little moderation and good sense, but moderation and good sense are fortunately not the characteristics of men engaged in doing the Devil's work for the Devil's pay. "The Lord reigns,"—a simple proposition, but one which politicians find it hard to accept, and which they often waste immense energies in the impotent attempt to overturn.

PART SIXTEEN

We Want Peace and Good Order at the South

With the passage of the Reconstruction Acts of 1867 and 1868, Reconstruction entered a third and final stage. The presidential plans which had served as a basis for national policy in the former states of the Confederacy during the war and until late in 1865 had been set aside. Congressional Reconstruction had followed, as Congress established its leadership and legislated its own plans for the reorganization of the Southern states. As the plans of the congressional Radicals were carried out, beginning in 1868, the burden of Reconstruction passed to the Southern states themselves. One by one, the state governments (excluding that of Tennessee) were reshaped under Radical Republican auspices and readmitted into the Union. Before the end of 1868, six Southern states (Arkansas, North Carolina, South Carolina, Louisiana, Alabama, and Florida) had regained their former places in the Union. Within two years, the remaining four (Mississippi, Georgia, Virginia, and Texas) had returned.

These new states depended upon the support of three groups, members of which provided the political leadership: the scalawags—native Southerners (many of them Unionists during the war) who threw in their lot with the Radical Republicans and who could qualify for political activity under the terms of the Reconstruction Acts; the carpetbaggers—men from the North who moved South to take part in Reconstruction for a variety of reasons, both selfish and idealistic; and the Negroes—the ex-slaves who now enjoyed the franchise and full political rights for the first time. Large numbers of Southern whites had been disfranchised by Radical legislation and were thus barred from participation in the new governments. Standing behind these groups was a variety of Northern agencies, private and public (notably the Freedmen's Bureau and the United States Army), whose assistance was crucial to the maintenance of the Radical governments.

This third phase of Reconstruction, that is, Reconstruction by the Southern states themselves, has traditionally been labelled "Black Reconstruction," presumably because of the Negro leadership in many of the states.

It has often been portrayed as a dismal period of corruption and irresponsibility in government. One recent Southern historian reflected this point of view when he described this stage of Reconstruction as a "blackout of honest government." Recent studies have shown that such an appraisal is extreme and unduly pessimistic. The new state constitutions, providing for Negro suffrage, were often copied from Northern state constitutions. As a result, many reforms which had been incorporated in Northern state governments many years before made their first inroads in the South. New public school systems were established, the reorganization of the structure of state and local government was attempted, such measures as the abolition of imprisonment for debt were enacted, and the social and economic life of the South was rebuilt.

There was, to be sure, an abundance of corruption and inefficiency in the administration of the Radical Southern state governments. The leadership was, on the whole, inexperienced. Gargantuan rebuilding problems faced the states, problems the leaders were poorly equipped to solve. State debts mounted, and there were many examples of outright waste and extravagance. To emphasize the more sordid aspects of the story, as many historians have done, however, is to ignore the many bright features that characterized Radical Reconstruction in the South. Viewed in the context of the two Grant administrations, a period not noted for governmental honesty and efficiency, the experiences of the Southern states do not seem unusual at all.

Although conditions varied from state to state, the Radical Republican régimes in the South were generally short-lived. The governments were weakened by both internal and external difficulties. The corruption and mismanagement that prevailed tended to discredit the new states in the eyes of the North and aroused opposition even among some Northern Radicals. Bitter internal rivalries between competing power groups in some of the states—often pitting scalawag against carpetbagger—provided an element of instability that proved difficult to overcome. Organized intimidation and terroristic activities, undertaken by such groups as the Ku Klux Klan and aimed at preventing the Negro from exercising his franchise, deprived the Radical governments of much-needed support. Finally, the recovery of the franchise by Southern whites through various means, including the passage by Congress in 1872 of an Amnesty Act, resulted in the growth of formidable opposition. As the strength of the Republican party in the North began to wane in the early 1870s, and as the number of Army troops in the South steadily diminished, the reconstructed Southern governments became less able to withstand opposition. By 1875, seven of the ten Southern states had reverted to conservative white control. The movement was completed in 1877 when the last troops were withdrawn from the South and the last three Radical Republican governments fell.

Although their existence was brief, the Radical Republican governments had made a sincere effort to repair the damage, both physical and psychic, which the war had left. Steps were taken to protect the Negro in his freedom and to lead him along the road to political and economic maturity. The hated Black Codes were repealed and civil rights legislation was enacted. For all their shortcomings, the leaders of the reconstructed states had tried to bring "peace and good order" to the South. One of the tragedies of Reconstruction is that when the conservative whites regained control over their governments, they reacted with equal bitterness against the good as well as the bad which the Radical Republicans had brought to their states.

A Former Confederate General Describes Conditions in Georgia: John B. Gordon, 1871

Alarmed by reports of the widespread intimidation of Negro voters in the newly reconstructed Radical Southern states, Congress enacted a series of force acts in 1870 and 1871. These acts sought to protect the Negroes in their right to the franchise by extending the jurisdiction of Federal courts over any interference in the free exercise of the ballot; by providing for the appointment of election supervisors by the Federal courts; and by declaring that the unlawful activities of such armed combinations as the Ku Klux Klan constituted a rebellion against the government of the United States and would be punished as such. The third enforcement act, passed on April 20, 1871, and known as the Ku Klux Act, was accompanied by the establishment of a new investigating committee to "inquire into the condition of the late insurrectionary states." This committee summoned witnesses and held hearings during 1871 and 1872, finally publishing its report in thirteen large volumes. The report, described by one historian as "one of the most extensive that a congressional committee had ever made," provided a valuable and complete picture of life and conditions in the South during Black Reconstruction. One of the witnesses who testified before the committee was John B. Gordon (1832–1904), formerly a major general in the Confederate Army, and a native of Georgia. Gordon, settling down to a legal career in Atlanta after the war, became active in Democratic party politics. He served as United States Senator from Georgia on two occasions, 1873–1880 and 1891–1897, and was Governor of Georgia from 1886 to 1890. Gordon's testimony, reprinted from Senate Reports, *number 41, part 6, Forty-second Congress, second session, pages 304–319 passim, revealed the attitude of Southern white conservatives toward the course of Radical Reconstruction. On the Ku Klux Klan, see Stanley F. Horn,* Invisible Empire: The Story of the Ku Klux Klan, 1866–1871 *(1939). There are many state studies of Reconstruction, most of them following the argument of William A. Dunning. For contemporary accounts of Southern conditions during Black Reconstruction see Robert Somers,* The Southern States since the War *(1871); Charles Nordhoff,* The Cotton States in the Spring and Summer of 1875 *(1876); and Edward King,* The Great South *(1875).*

. . . If it is worth anything to the committee I will give a statement as to the condition of affairs on the coast. Directly after the war I went with my family to Brunswick to engage in the lumber business. On my arrival there I found the place occupied, as were a number of places along the coast, by negro troops. In that portion of Georgia, all along the belt of sea-coast, for probably a hundred miles from the coast and up nearly to the middle portion of the State, the negroes, as a rule, largely outnumber the whites in every county. . . . When I reached Brunswick I found there was a very bad state of feeling between those negro troops and the citizens. I paid very little attention to the matter, but in walking the streets at times I found that these troops were insulting toward those whom they had heard were in the army. In passing by them in the street you would hear such remarks as this: "There is a damned rebel." Meeting you on the sidewalk they would, without being absolutely violent, get you off the sidewalk; they would refuse to divide it with you. These things attracted my attention. . . .

Such things of course created a good deal of feeling in the little town of Brunswick, which is now called a city; and especially did they excite the population very much, because of the immense number of negroes in the immediate vicinity of Brunswick on the islands around. The negro population generally became very obnoxious. They obtruded themselves everywhere they could. There was not only apprehension but decided alarm among the people, so much so that I was asked, not only by the people of that town, but of Darien, Georgia, and along the coast where these negroes were, to go to Savannah immediately and apply to General Brenham to have the negro troops removed. On my arrival, I found General Grant was just starting to Brunswick on his tour through the South. I applied to him, and submitted affidavits, as well as told him what I had personally seen. After hearing the testimony, he said to me, "Well, I think there is no danger of bloodshed." I replied that our people were doing all they could; they were forbearing any violence; they were suffering the indignities offered them rather than create a difficulty; but that while we were observing our parole, and were determined to keep the peace and abide by the laws, things had come to such a pass that they might soon be beyond endurance, and that very certainly there would be bloodshed unless these negro troops were removed; I doubted whether even that would check the hostile demonstrations of the negro population, although I thought it would go very far toward it. On further consideration, General Grant did order General Brenham to remove the negro troops from that point. . . .

Question. As to those negroes along the black belt, . . . with what sort of intelligence do they seem to exercise the right of suffrage? How are they controlled and managed?

Answer. Well, sir, they had just begun voting when I left there; they were at that time, and are still, so far as my knowledge of the State extends—I know it is true of a large portion of the State—controlled almost entirely by the League organizations. The negroes were introduced very early into what they called the Union Leagues; and they were controlled by those Leagues. They seemed to be under the impression that by voting they were to acquire some sort of property, and were influenced mainly

by ideas of that sort, which had been instilled into them by these people
who had gone there among them. I, however, know less about the particular
influence brought to bear now, in that part of the State, with regard to
voting, than in any other part, because I have been in that portion of the
State less since they have been voting. When I left there they had just
commenced voting. But they were then, as they are now generally throughout the State, under the control of men who have gone in our midst since
the war—men who, I am sorry to say, are, as a general rule, without any
character at home, so far as we have been able to learn; men who, as a
rule, were not in the army; for I want to say very distinctly that our people
have not entertained animosity and bitterness toward the troops, the men
who were in the army; our feelings are directed toward these camp-follow-
ers and men who have come in our midst since the war—men without
character and without intelligence, except a certain sort of shrewdness by
which they have been enabled to impose themselves upon the negro and
acquire gain, some of them very much gain, out of the pittances they were
able to get out of the negro one way and another. Some of them have
gotten into office from counties where they never were but once or twice
during the whole canvass. . . .

Question.   What do you know of any combinations in Georgia, known
as Ku-Klux, or by any other name, who have been violating law?

Answer.   I do not know anything about any Ku-Klux organization, as
the papers talk about it. I have never heard of anything of that sort except
in the papers and by general report; but I do know that an organization
did exist in Georgia at one time. . . . The organization was simply this—
nothing more and nothing less: it was an organization, a brotherhood of
the property-holders, the peaceable, law-abiding citizens of the State, for
self-protection. The instinct of self-protection prompted that organization;
the sense of insecurity and danger, particularly in those neighborhoods
where the negro population largely predominated. The reasons which led
to this organization were three or four. The first and main reason was the
organization of the Union League, as they called it, about which we knew
nothing more than this: that the negroes would desert the plantations,
and go off at night in large numbers; and on being asked where they had
been, would reply, sometimes, "We have been to the muster;" sometimes,
"We have been to the lodge;" sometimes, "We have been to the meeting."
These things were observed for a great length of time. We knew that the
"carpet-baggers," as the people of Georgia called these men who came
from a distance and had no interest at all with us; who were unknown to
us entirely; who from all we could learn about them did not have any very
exalted position at their homes—these men were organizing the colored
people. We knew that beyond all question. We knew of certain instances
where great crime had been committed; where overseers had been driven
from plantations, and the negroes had asserted their right to hold the
property for their own benefit. Apprehension took possession of the entire
public mind of the State. Men were in many instances afraid to go away
from their homes and leave their wives and children, for fear of outrage.
Rapes were already being committed in the country. There was this general organization of the black race on the one hand, and an entire dis-

organization of the white race on the other hand. We were afraid to have
a public organization; because we supposed it would be construed at once,
by the authorities at Washington, as an organization antagonistic to the
Government of the United States. It was therefore necessary, in order to
protect our families from outrage and preserve our own lives, to have
something that we could regard as a brotherhood—a combination of the
best men of the country, to act purely in self-defense, to repel the attack in
case we should be attacked by these people. That was the whole object
of this organization. I never heard of any disguises connected with it;
we had none, very certainly. This organization, I think, extended nearly
all over the State. It was, as I say, an organization purely for self-defense.
It had no more politics in it than the organization of the Masons. I never
heard the idea of politics suggested in connection with it. . . .

Question. Do you know what the debt of the State is now?

Answer. No, sir; nobody knows what it is. We know that it has probably been trebled by our present State administration.

Mr. Blair. If I were in the place of the people of Georgia, I would let
those who made the debt pay it.

Answer. I am very willing to say here and elsewhere that the feeling of
the people of Georgia is very distinctly this. that but for the odium and
possible damage which would be brought upon the credit of the State, not
one dollar of those bonds would be paid; there is no sort of question about
that; but the people, I think, will pay the debt rather than damage the
credit of the State. I know that the general feeling at the North is that
our people are hostile toward the Government of the United States. Upon
that point I wish to testify, and hence I have introduced it; I want to state
what I know upon that subject. Commanding as I did, Jackson's corps of
the confederate army, for some time before the surrender, and at the time
of the surrender one wing of that army, I know very well that if the
programme which our people saw set on foot at Appomattox Court-House
had been carried out—if our people had been met in the spirit which we
believe existed there among the officers and soldiers, from General Grant
down—we would have had no disturbance in the South, and we would long
since have had a very different state of things in this country. I believe
that as firmly as I believe in my own existence. I know it was generally
felt that there was shown toward the officers and men who surrendered at
Appomattox Court-House a degree of courtesy and even deference which
was surprising and gratifying, and which produced at the time a very fine
effect. I want to say, moreover, that the alienation of our people from the
Government—an alienation which, resulting from the war, continued to
some extent immediately after the war—has been increased since that time,
by the course which our people believe has been wrongfully pursued
toward them. Whether right or wrong, it is the impression of the southern
mind—it is the conviction of my own mind, in which I am perfectly sincere
and honest—that we have not been met in the proper spirit. We, in
Georgia, do not believe that we have been allowed proper credit for our
honesty of purpose. We believe that if our people had been trusted, as
we thought we ought to have been trusted—if we had been treated in the

spirit which, as we thought, was manifested on the Federal side at Appomattox Court-House—a spirit which implied that there had been a conflict of theories, an honest difference of opinion as to our rights under the General Government—a difference upon which the South had adopted one construction, and the North another, both parties having vindicated their sincerity upon the field in a contest, which, now that it had been fought out, was to be forgotten—if this had been the spirit in which we had been treated, the alienation would have been cured. There is no question about that.

But to say to our people, "You are unworthy to vote; you cannot hold office; we are unwilling to trust you; you are not honest men; your former slaves are better fitted to administer the laws than you are"—this sort of dealing with us has emphatically alienated our people. The burning of Atlanta and all the devastation through Georgia never created a tithe of the animosity that has been created by this sort of treatment of our people. Not that we wanted offices; that is not the point at all, though our people feel that it is an outrage to say that the best men in our midst shall not hold office. The feeling is that you have denied that we are worthy of trust; that we are men of honor; that we will abide by our plighted faith. We feel a sense of wrong as honorable men. We do not think we have done anything in the dark. We think that when we tried to go out, we did it boldly, fairly and squarely, staking our lives upon the issue. We thought we were right. I am one who thought so at the time; I thought I had a perfect right to do as I did. I am not going into that question except to say that our people were conscientious in what they did. They were conscientious when they took the obligation at Appomattox and elsewhere at the time of surrender. They felt that as honest men they ought to be trusted, and that there ought to have been an end of the thing. We had fought the contest out; we had been defeated; and we thought that ought to be the last of it. That was the way we felt at the South. By the course that has been pursued toward us since the surrender we have been disappointed, and the feeling of alienation among our people has in this way been increased more than by any other one fact. In addition to that we in Georgia think that some of the most grievous outrages have been inflicted upon our people by the military authorities sustained by the Government. . . .

Question. What class of the citizens of Georgia are affected by the disabilities imposed by the fourteenth amendment?

Answer. The very best men in our State. It is very hard to find a first-class man who is not affected by them. There are some few (I include myself among the good people of Georgia) who are not affected by those disabilities. I never held an office before the war, and I believe General Wright never did. But I believe that we are among the very few. There are very few men in the State, who have any sort of prominence, who were not affected by the fourteenth amendment, imposing disabilities. I never was a candidate for any office in my life, until the last election.

Question. Does not the disability provision exclude from office the great mass of the intelligence of the State?

Answer. It embraces all the leading, educated gentlemen of our State. A very large majority of the intellect of Georgia is disfranchised.

Question. Is it, or is it not, a matter of complaint and discontent to the entire people of the State, that they should thus be deprived of the services of their best men?

Answer. O, yes, sir. They feel it to be a very great wrong. It comes very nearly home to us in our State legislation. We want our good men in the legislature, and we cannot get them there. Our legislatures are notoriously weak on account of the disfranchisement of our best men. Our legislators are probably as good as the young men of any country could be; but their youth and inexperience deprives them of that efficiency which older and more experienced men would have. The fact that we cannot put our good men in the legislature, creates a vast deal of dissatisfaction. The disfranchisement of our best and most intelligent citizens is one of the prime sources of dissatisfaction in our State. As I said a while ago, the feeling of alienation toward the Government has been vastly increased by this disfranchisement. We feel that it is a great wrong upon us, not only in the light in which I spoke of it a while ago, but in depriving the State of the services of those men in making and administering the laws. . . .

SELECTION

A Negro Senator Defends "Black Reconstruction": Blanche K. Bruce, 1876

Blanche K. Bruce (1841–1898) was born and raised a slave in Virginia. At the beginning of the Civil War, he fled to Missouri where he secured a position teaching Negroes in Hannibal. He later attended Oberlin College. Bruce returned to the South in 1869, where he became a planter in Mississippi. His political career began soon afterward. He held a variety of elective positions, including those of tax collector, sheriff, and county superintendent of schools, before he was elected to the United States Senate in 1875 as a Republican. Bruce served in the Senate until the expiration of his term in 1881. Through-out his career, Bruce demonstrated ability as a political figure and won praise from many influential Mississippi whites as well as from Negroes. On March 31, 1876, Bruce delivered a speech before the Senate on the disputed Mississippi election of 1875. In that year, Mississippi Democrats resolved to overturn the Radical Republican state government by whatever means necessary. The intimidation, terror, and force employed by Mississippians to prevent Negroes from voting reached new heights of organization and became known as the "Mississippi Plan," to be copied in other states. The efforts were

*met with success. Thousands of Negroes stayed away from the polls on
election day, and the Democrats were swept into office. Radical Reconstruction
came to an end in Mississippi in 1875.*

Bruce's speech is reprinted from the Congressional Record, *Forty-fourth
Congress, first session, pages 2101–2104. For details of the election, see Vernon
L. Wharton,* The Negro in Mississippi, 1865–1890 *(1947). There is no adequate
general account of the Negro in Reconstruction.*

. . . The conduct of the late election in Mississippi affected not merely the
fortunes of partisans—as the same were necessarily involved in the defeat
or success of the respective parties to the contest—but put in question and
jeopardy the sacred rights of the citizen; and the investigation contemplated in the pending resolution has for its object not the determination
of the question whether the offices shall be held and the public affairs of
that State be administered by democrats or republicans, but the higher
and more important end, the protection in all their purity and significance
of the political rights of the people and the free institutions of the country. . . .

The demand of the substitute of the Senator from Michigan proceeds
upon the allegation that fraud and intimidation were practiced by the
opposition in the late State election, so as not only to deprive many citizens of their political rights, but so far as practically to have defeated a
fair expression of the will of a majority of the legal voters of the State of
Mississippi, resulting in placing in power many men who do not represent
the popular will.

The truth of the allegations relative to fraud and violence is strongly
suggested by the very success claimed by the democracy. In 1873 the
republicans carried the State by 20,000 majority; in November last the
opposition claimed to have carried it by 30,000; thus a democratic gain of
more than 50,000. Now, by what miraculous or extraordinary interposition
was this brought about? I can conceive that a large State like New York,
where free speech and free press operate upon intelligent masses—a State
full of railroads, telegraphs, and newspapers—on the occasion of a great
national contest, might furnish an illustration of such a thorough and
general change in the political views of the people; but such a change of
front is unnatural and highly improbable in a State like my own, with
few railroads, and a widely scattered and sparse population. Under the
most active and friendly canvass the voting masses could not have been so
rapidly and thoroughly reached as to have rendered this result probable.

There was nothing in the character of the issues nor in the method of
the canvass that would produce such an overwhelming revolution in the
sentiments of the colored voters of the State as is implied in this pretended
democratic success. The republicans—nineteen-twentieths of whom are
colored—were not brought, through the press or public discussions, in contact with democratic influences to such an extent as would operate a
change in their political convictions, and there was nothing in democratic
sentiments nor in the proscriptive and violent temper of their leaders to
justify such a change of political relations. . . .

The evidence in hand and accessible will show beyond peradventure that in many parts of the State corrupt and violent influences were brought to bear upon the registrars of voters, thus materially affecting the character of the voting or poll lists; upon the inspectors of election, prejudicially and unfairly thereby changing the number of votes cast; and, finally, threats and violence were practiced directly upon the masses of voters in such measure and strength as to produce grave apprehensions for their personal safety, and as to deter them from the exercise of their political franchises.

Lawless outbreaks have not been confined to any particular section of the country, but have prevailed in nearly every State at some period in its history. But the violence complained of and exhibited in Mississippi and other Southern States, pending a political canvass, is exceptional and peculiar. It is not the blow that the beggared miner strikes that he may give bread to his children, nor the stroke of the bondsman that he may win liberty for himself, nor the mad turbulence of the ignorant masses when their passions have been stirred by the appeals of the demagogue; but it is an attack by an aggressive, intelligent, white political organization upon inoffensive, law-abiding fellow-citizens; a violent method for political supremacy, that seeks not the protection of the rights of the aggressors, but the destruction of the rights of the party assailed. Violence so unprovoked, inspired by such motives, and looking to such ends, is a spectacle not only discreditable to the country, but dangerous to the integrity of our free institutions.

I beg Senators to believe that I refer to this painful and reproachful condition of affairs in my own State not in resentment, but with sentiments of profound regret and humiliation.

If honorable Senators ask why such flagrant wrongs were allowed to go unpunished by a republican State government, and unresented by a race claiming 20,000 majority of the voters, the answer is at hand. The civil officers of the State were unequal to meet and suppress the murderous violence that frequently broke out in different parts of the State, and the State executive found himself thrown for support upon a militia partially organized and poorly armed. When he attempted to perfect and call out this force and to use the very small appropriation that had been made for their equipment, he was met by the courts with an injunction against the use of the money, and by the proscriptive element of the opposition with such fierce outcry and show of counter-force, that he became convinced a civil strife, a war of races, would be precipitated unless he staid his hand. As a last resort, the protection provided in the national Constitution for a State threatened with domestic violence was sought; but the national Executive—from perhaps a scrupulous desire to avoid the appearance of interference by the Federal authority with the internal affairs of that State—declined to accede to the request made for Federal troops.

It will not accord with the laws of nature or history to brand the colored people as a race of cowards. On more than one historic field, beginning in 1776 and coming down to this centennial year of the Republic, they have attested in blood their courage as well as love of liberty. I ask Senators to believe that no consideration of fear or personal danger has kept us quiet and forbearing under the provocations and wrongs that have so sorely tried our souls. But feeling kindly toward our white fellow-citizens, appreciating the good purposes and offices of the better classes, and, above all, abhorring a war of races, we determined to wait until such time as an appeal to the good sense and justice of the American people could be made.

A notable feature of the outrages alleged is that they have referred almost exclusively to the colored citizens of the State. Why is the colored voter to be proscribed? Why direct the attack upon him? While the methods of violence, resorted to for political purposes in the South, are foreign to the genius of our institutions as applied to citizens generally—and so much is conceded by even the opposition—yet they seem to think we are an exceptional class and citizens, rather by sufferance than right; and when pressed to account for their bitterness and proscription toward us they, with more or less boldness, allege incompetent and bad government as their justification before the public opinion of the country. Now, I declare that neither political incapacity nor venality are qualities of the masses of colored citizens. The emancipation of the colored race during the late civil strife was an expression alike of the magnanimity and needs of the nation; and the subsequent and early subtraction of millions of industrial values from the resources of the insurrectionary States and the presence of many thousand additional brave hearts and strong hands around the flag of the country vindicated the justice and wisdom of the measure.

The close of the war found four millions of freedmen, without homes or property, charged with the duty of self-support and with the oversight of their personal freedom, yet without civil and political rights! The problem presented by this condition of things was one of the gravest that has ever been submitted to the American people. Shall these liberated millions of a separate race, while retaining personal liberty, be deprived of political rights? The practical sense of the American people definitely settled this delicate and difficult question, and the demand for a more pronounced loyal element in the work of reconstruction in the lately rebellious States furnished an opportunity for the recognition of the political rights of the race, both in the interest of justice and good government.

The history of my race since enfranchisement, considered in connection with the difficulties that have environed us, will exhibit hopeful progress and attest that we have been neither ungrateful for the civil and political privileges received nor wanting in appreciation of the correspondingly weighty obligations imposed upon us. . . .

Again, we began our political career under the disadvantages of the inexperience in public affairs that generations of enforced bondage had entailed upon our race. We suffered also from the vicious leadership of some of the men whom our necessities forced us temporarily to accept. Consider further that the States of the South, where we were supposed to control by our majorities, were in an impoverished and semi-revolutionary condition—society demoralized, the industries of the country prostrated, the people sore, morbid, and sometimes turbulent, and no healthy controlling public opinion either existent or possible—consider all these conditions, and it will be seen that we began our political novitiate and formed the organic and statutory laws under great embarrassments.

Despite the difficulties and drawbacks suggested, the constitutions formed under colored majorities, whatever their defects may be, were improvements on the instruments they were designed to supersede; and the statutes framed, though necessarily defective because of the crude and varying social and industrial conditions upon which they were based, were more in harmony with the spirit of the age and the genius of our free institutions than the obsolete laws that they supplanted. Nor is there just or any sufficient grounds upon which to charge an oppressive administration of the laws. . . .

We want peace and good order at the South; but it can only come by the fullest recognition of the rights of all classes. The opposition must concede the necessity of change, not only in the temper but in the philosophy of their party organization and management. The sober American judgment must obtain in the South as elsewhere in the Republic, that the only distinctions upon which parties can be safely organized and in harmony with our institutions are differences of opinions relative to principles and policy of government, and that differences of religion, nationality, or race can neither with safety nor propriety be permitted for a moment to enter into the party contests of the day. The unanimity with which the colored voters act with a party is not referable to any race prejudice on their part. On the contrary, they invite the political co-operation of their white brethren, and vote as a unit because proscribed as such. They deprecate the establishment of the color line by the opposition, not only because the act is unwise and wrong in principle, but because it isolates them from the white men of the South, and forces them, in sheer self-protection and against their inclination, to act seemingly upon the basis of a race prejudice that they neither respect nor entertain. As a class they are free from prejudices, and have no uncharitable suspicions against their white fellow-citizens, whether native born or settlers from the Northern States. They not only recognize the equality of citizenship and the right of every man to hold, without proscription, any position of honor and trust to which the confidence of the people may elevate him; but owing nothing to race, birth, or surroundings, they, above all other classes in the community, are interested to see prejudices drop out of both politics and the business of the country, and success in life proceed only upon the integrity and merit of the man who seeks it. They are also appreciative—feeling and exhibiting the liveliest gratitude for counsel and help in their new career, whether they come from the men of the North or of the South. But withal, as they progress in intelligence and appreciation of the dignity of their prerogatives as citizens, they, as an evidence of growth, begin to realize the significance of the proverb, "When thou doest well for thyself, men shall praise thee;" and are disposed to exact the same protection and concession of rights that are conferred upon other citizens by the Constitution, and that, too, without the humiliation involved in the enforced abandonment of their political convictions.

We simply demand the practical recognition of the rights given us in the Constitution and laws, and ask from our white fellow-citizens only the consideration and fairness that we so willingly extend to them. Let them generally realize and concede that citizenship imports to us what it does to them, no more and no less, and impress the colored people that a party defeat does not imperil their political franchise. Let them cease their attempts to coerce our political cooperation, and invite and secure it by a policy so fair and just as to commend itself to our judgment, and resort to no motive or measure to control us that self-respect would preclude their applying to themselves. When we can entertain opinions and select party affiliations without proscription, and cast our ballots as other citizens and without jeopardy to person or privilege, we can safely afford to be governed by the considerations that ordinarily determine the political action of American citizens. But we must be guaranteed in the unproscribed exercise of our honest convictions and be absolutely, from within or without, protected in the use of our ballot before we can either wisely or safely divide our vote. In union, not division, is strength, so long as White League proscription renders division of our vote impracticable by making a difference of opinion opprobrious and an antagonism in politics a crime. On the other hand, if we should, from considerations of fear, yield to the shot-gun policy of our opponents, the White League might win a temporary success, but the ultimate result would be disastrous to both races, for they would first become aggressively turbulent, and we, as a class, would become servile, unreliable, and worthless.

It has been suggested, as the popular sentiment of the country, that the colored citizens must no longer expect special legislation for their benefit, nor exceptional interference by the National Government for their protection. If this is true, if such is the judgment relative to our demands and needs, I venture to offset the suggestion, so far as it may be used as reason for a denial of the protection we seek, by the statement of another and more prevalent popular conviction. Back of this, and underlying the foundations of the Republic itself, there lies deep in the breasts of the patriotic millions of the country the conviction that the laws must be enforced, and life, liberty, and property must, alike to all and for all, be protected. But I allege that we do not seek special action in our behalf, except to meet special danger, and only then such as all classes of citizens are entitled to receive under the Constitution. We do not ask the enactment of new laws, but only the enforcement of those that already exist.

The vicious and exceptional political action had by the White League in Mississippi has been repeated in other contests and in other States of the South, and the colored voters have been subjected therein to outrages upon their rights similar to those perpetrated in my own State at the recent election. Because violence has become so general a quality in the political canvasses of the South and my people the common sufferers in each instance, I have considered this subject more in detail than would, under other circumstances, have been either appropriate or necessary. As the proscription and violence toward the colored voters are special and almost exclusive, and seem to proceed upon the assumption that there is something exceptionally offensive and unworthy in them, I have felt, as the only representative of my race in the Senate of the United States, that I was placed, in some sort, upon the defensive, and I have consequently endeavored to show how aggravated and inexcusable were the wrongs worked upon us, and have sought to vindicate our title to both the respect and goodwill of the just people of the nation. The gravity of the issues involved has demanded great plainness of speech from me. But I have endeavored to present my views to the Senate with the moderation and deference inspired by the recollection that both my race and myself were once bondsmen, and are to-day debtors largely to the love and justice of a great people for the enjoyment of our personal and political liberty. While my antecedents and surroundings suggest modesty, there are some considerations that justify frankness, and even boldness of speech.

Mr. President, I represent, in an important sense, the interest of nearly a million of voters, constituting a new, hopeful, permanent, and influential political element, and large enough to affect in critical periods the fortunes of this great Republic; and the public safety and common weal alike demand that the integrity of this element should be preserved and its character improved. They number more than a million of producers, who, since their emancipation and outside of their contributions to the production of sugar, rice, tobacco, cereals, and the mechanical industries of the country, have furnished nearly forty million bales of cotton, which, at the ruling prices of the world's market, have yielded $2,000,000,000, a sum nearly equal to the national debt; producers who, at the accepted ratio that an able-bodied laborer earns, on an average $800 per year, annually bring to the aggregate of the nation's great bulk of values more than $800,000,000.

I have confidence, not only in my country and her institutions, but in the endurance, capacity, and destiny of my people. We will, as opportunity offers and ability serves, seek our places, sometimes in the field of letters, arts, sciences, and the professions. More frequently mechanical pursuits will attract and elicit our efforts; more still of my people will find employment and livelihood as the cultivators of the soil. The bulk of this people— by surroundings, habits, adaptation, and choice—will continue to find their homes in the South, and constitute the masses of its yeomanry. We will there probably, of our own volition and more abundantly than in the past, produce the great staples that will contribute to the basis of foreign exchange, aid in giving the nation a balance of trade, and minister to the wants and comfort and build up the prosperity of the whole land. Whatever our ultimate position in the composite civilization of the Republic and whatever varying fortunes attend our career, we will not forget our instincts for freedom nor our love of country. Guided and guarded by a beneficent Providence, and living under the genial influence of liberal institutions, we have no apprehensions that we shall fail from the land from attrition with other races, or ignobly disappear from either the politics or industries of the country.

Mr. President, allow me here to say that, although many of us are uneducated in the schools, we are informed and advised as to our duties to the Government, our State, and ourselves. Without class prejudice or animosities, with obedience to authority as the lesson and love of peace and order as the passion of our lives, with scrupulous respect for the rights of others, and with the hopefulness of political youth, we are determined that the great Government that gave us liberty, and rendered its gift valuable by giving us the ballot, shall not find us wanting in a sufficient response to any demand that humanity or patriotism may make upon us; and we ask such action as will not only protect us in the enjoyment of our constitutional rights, but will preserve the integrity of our republican institutions. . . .

SEVENTEEN

A Reunion of the Great American Nationality

Radical Reconstruction came to an end in 1877. The last Army troops were withdrawn from the South, and the last three Southern Radical state governments fell quickly to conservative white control. The end came as the result of a final sectional compromise between North and South—the Compromise of 1877. Southern Democrats agreed to acquiesce in the inauguration of Republican President Rutherford B. Hayes (whose election had been hotly disputed) in return for certain concessions, including the removal of troops from the South, the distribution of patronage to Southerners, and the voting of funds for Southern internal improvements.

Although the Compromise of 1877 terminated Reconstruction, Northern interest in the restoration of the South had begun to wane several years before. The enthusiasm for Reconstruction which had characterized the early postwar years had burned itself out. Northern ears became less and less receptive to the calls of the Radicals for a strict and vindictive policy against the "rebel" states, new issues appeared, notably economic ones, to distract Northern attention away from the South. The strength of the Republican party in the national government began to decline as the Democratic party recovered some of its prewar status. The Republican party itself was split over Reconstruction and the corruption of the Grant administrations; many leading Republicans drifted into the Democratic fold. Northerners were weary of supporting the Southern Radical governments in which they had little faith and virtually welcomed the return of conservative white power in the South as the return of stable government. All these signs pointed to the abandonment of Reconstruction.

The tragedy was that the abandonment of Reconstruction also meant the abandonment of the Southern Negro. The job which had begun during and immediately after the war was left unfinished. Nothing can minimize the tremendous achievements of the Civil War and Reconstruction in the area of Negro rights. The Thirteenth, Fourteenth, and Fifteenth Amendments to the Constitution stand as enduring monuments to freedom and *equality. The civil rights legislation of the Reconstruction period provided valuable groundwork for later advances. However, something more was needed to make Reconstruction a success. The commitment established by the legislation had to be fulfilled beyond the statute books. This Northerners were apparently unwilling to do. As a result, the business of the war remained unfinished and the fulfillment of the commitment was deferred for almost a century.*

By the mid-1870s most Americans were hoping more for a rapid reunion and reconciliation of the nation than for the completion of their obligations to the Southern Negroes. The controversy over slavery, the four years of bloody fighting, the postwar tensions and bitterness had all interrupted the progress of the nation toward its glorious destiny. It was time to return to the optimism and hope for America's future that had characterized the 1840s. The occasion to celebrate this return was offered in 1876—the centennial of American independence. What better time to put an end to the disruption of Reconstruction, to lay aside the bitter memories of civil conflict, to achieve "a reunion of the great American nationality"?

"What the Centennial Ought to Accomplish"

An editorial in Scribner's Monthly *the year before the centennial observation,
volume 10, August, 1875, pages 509–510, gave voice to what Paul H. Buck has
called the "emotional yearning for peace." The centennial of the nation's
birth, the author pointed out, should be more than simply a celebration of
events a century in the past; its leading object should be the "reunion of the
two sections of the country in the old fellowship."*

*The story of the Compromise of 1877 and the end of Reconstruction is told
in C. Vann Woodward,* Reunion and Reaction *(1951). For the impulse toward
reconciliation and reunion, see Paul H. Buck,* The Road to Reunion, 1865–1900
(1937).

We are to have grand doings next year. There is to be an Exposition.
There are to be speeches, and songs, and processions, and elaborate ceremonies and general rejoicings. Cannon are to be fired, flags are
to be floated, and the eagle is expected to scream while he dips the tip of
either pinion in the Atlantic and the Pacific, and sprinkles the land with
a new baptism of freedom. The national oratory will exhaust the figures of
speech in patriotic glorification, while the effete civilizations of the Old
World, and the despots of the East, tottering upon their tumbling thrones,
will rub their eyes and sleepily inquire, "What's the row?" The Centennial is expected to celebrate in a fitting way—somewhat dimly apprehended, it is true—the birth of a nation.

Well, the object is a good one. When the old colonies declared themselves free, they took a grand step in the march of progress; but now, before
we begin our celebration of this event, would it not be well for us to inquire whether we have a nation? In a large number of the States of this
country there exists not only a belief that the United States do not constitute a nation, but a theory of State rights which forbids that they ever
shall become one. We hear about the perturbed condition of the Southern
mind. We hear it said that multitudes there are just as disloyal as they
were during the civil war. This, we believe, we are justified in denying.
Before the war they had a theory of State rights. They fought to establish
that theory, and they now speak of the result as "the lost cause." They
are not actively in rebellion, and they do not propose to be. They do not
hope for the re-establishment of slavery. They fought bravely and well
to establish their theory, but the majority was against them; and if the
result of the war emphasized any fact, it was that *en masse* the people
of the United States constitute a nation—indivisible in constituents, in
interest, in destiny. The result of the war was without significance, if it
did not mean that the United States constitute a nation which cannot be
divided; which will not permit itself to be divided; which is integral,
indissoluble, indestructible. We do not care what theories of State rights
are entertained outside of this. State rights, in all the States, should be

jealously guarded, and, by all legitimate means, defended. New York should be as jealous of her State prerogatives as South Carolina or Louisiana; but this theory which makes of the Union a rope of sand, and of the States a collection of petty nationalities that can at liberty drop the bands which hold them together, is forever exploded. It has been tested at the point of the bayonet. It went down in blood, and went down for all time. Its adherents may mourn over the fact, as we can never cease to mourn over the events which accompanied it, over the sad, incalculable cost to them and to those who opposed them. The great point with them is to recognize the fact that, for richer for poorer, in sickness and health, until death do us part, these United States constitute a nation; that we are to live, grow, prosper, and suffer together, united by bands that cannot be sundered.

Unless this fact is fully recognized throughout the Union, our Centennial will be but a hollow mockery. If we are to celebrate anything worth celebrating, it is the birth of a nation. If we are to celebrate anything worth celebrating, it should be by the whole heart and united voice of the nation. If we can make the Centennial an occasion for emphasizing the great lesson of the war, and universally assenting to the results of the war, it will, indeed, be worth all the money expended upon and the time devoted to it. If around the old Altars of Liberty we cannot rejoin our hands in brotherly affection and national loyalty, let us spike the cannon that will only proclaim our weakness, put our flags at half-mast, smother our eagles, eat our ashes, and wait for our American aloe to give us a better blossoming.

A few weeks ago, Mr. Jefferson Davis, the ex-President of the Confederacy, was reported to have exhorted an audience to which he was speaking to be as loyal to the old flag of the Union now as they were during the Mexican War. If the South could know what music there was in these words to Northern ears—how grateful we were to their old chief for them—it would appreciate the strength of our longing for a complete restoration of the national feeling that existed when Northern and Southern blood mingled in common sacrifice on Mexican soil. This national feeling, this national pride, this brotherly sympathy *must be restored;* and accursed be any Northern or Southern man, whether in power or out of power, whether politician, theorizer, carpet-bagger, president-maker or plunderer, who puts obstacles in the way of such a restoration. Men of the South, we want you. Men of the South, we long for the restoration of your peace and your prosperity. We would see your cities thriving, your homes happy, your plantations teeming with plenteous harvests, your schools overflowing, your wisest statesmen leading you, and all causes and all memories of discord wiped out forever. You do not believe this? Then you do not know the heart of the North. Have you cause of complaint against the politicians? Alas! so have we. Help us, as loving and loyal American citizens, to make our politicians better. Only remember and believe that there is nothing that the North wants so much to-day, as your recognition of the fact that the old relations between you and us are forever restored—that your hope, your pride, your policy, and your destiny are one with ours. Our children will grow up to despise our childishness, if we cannot do away with our personal hates so far, that in the cause of an established nationality we may join hands under the old flag.

To bring about this reunion of the two sections of the country in the old fellowship, should be the leading object of the approaching Centennial. A celebration of the national birth, begun, carried on, and finished by a section, would be a mockery and a shame. The nations of the world might well point at it the finger of scorn. The money expended upon it were better sunk in the sea, or devoted to repairing the waste places of the war. Men of the South, it is for you to say whether your magnanimity is equal to your valor—whether you are as reasonable as you are brave, and whether, like your old chief, you accept that definite and irreversible result of the war which makes you and yours forever members of the great American nation with us. Let us see to it, North and South, that the Centennial heals all the old wounds, reconciles all the old differences, and furnishes the occasion for such a reunion of the great American nationality, as shall make our celebration an expression of fraternal good-will among all sections and all States, and a corner-stone over which shall be reared a new temple to national freedom, concord, peace, and prosperity.